The Licensing Acts 1833–1995

AUSTRALIA

The Law Book Company
Brisbane • Sydney • Melbourne • Perth

CANADA

Carswell
Ottowa • Toronto • Calgary • Montreal • Vancouver

Agents

Steimatzky's Agency Ltd., Tel Aviv;
N.M. Tripathi (Private) Ltd., Bombay;
Eastern Law House (Private) Ltd., Calcutta;
M.P.P. House, Bangalore;
Universal Book Traders, Delhi;
Aditya Books, Delhi;
Macmillan Shuppan KK, Tokyo;
Pakistan Law House, Karachi, Lahore.

The Licensing Acts 1833–1995

Constance Cassidy

Barrister-at-Law

Dublin
Round Hall Sweet & Maxwell
1996

Published in 1996 by
Round Hall Sweet & Maxwell,
Brehon House, 4 Upper Ormond Quay,
Dublin 7.

Typeset by
Gough Typesetting Services,
Dublin.
Printed by Redwood Books,
Trowbridge, Wiltshire.

Reprinted 1996

ISBN 1-899738-11-8

A catalogue record for this book
is available from the British Library.

This book is dedicated
to the memory of

my father
John B.Cassidy, S.C.,
the former Judge of the Western Circuit

and my mother
Eleanor Foreman Cassidy.

FOREWORD

The licensing laws of Ireland are numerous and complex. In this learned book Ms Cassidy has brought together the laws from 1635 to date. The subject is technical yet the book, in a precise style, takes us through the intricate weave of legislation and case law to a clear determination. Fascinating nuggets of information can be obtained; thus we read that in 1994 12 sweet retailers off-licences were granted, and that "sweets" means any liquor made from fruit and sugar, or from fruit and sugar mixed with any other material which has undergone a process of fermentation in the manufacture thereof and that they include British wines, made wines, mead and metheglin.

This is a book which will delight legal practitioners. The law is set out clearly and immediately related to practical matters. Thus the chapters on the duties of a solicitor, planning permission and the tax clearance certificate address issues which are of importance and benefit to professionals advising in the area, whilst the inclusion of precedents makes the volume a comprehensive practitioners' guide.

However, this is not just a guide for practitioners. In her analysis of the law, Constance Cassidy has set out for all of us interested in the topic the foundation stones on which the current law rests.

It is a great pleasure to read this book and to see the author continuing a family tradition in legal expertise on the licensing laws. Her father, the late Judge John Cassidy, was the eminent expert in this field in his generation. He would have been very proud to read this magnum opus for this volume is an important textbook on Irish law. I have no doubt that we are seeing only the first edition of a text which will become the standard reference.

Susan G. Denham
The Supreme Court

July 1996

PREFACE

A wise man once said that to justify one's existence one should plant a tree, rear a son and write a book. As my apple tree and my son are flourishing, I now offer my last hostage to fortune.

It is not unusual for a lawyer to write a book about the law. It is inevitable, given my background, that the subject of this book should be licensing law. I have childhood memories of my grandfather, a former chairman of the Licensed Grocers and Vintners Association, reminiscing about conditions in the trade in Dublin city in the early years of the century. On my father's library shelves, O'Connor's *Justice of the Peace* and Shillman's *Licensing Laws of Ireland* stood cheek by jowl with *The Pickwick Papers* and *Huckleberry Finn*. Often his papers flowed over from his desk onto the dining table and we sometimes had to dine standing up. As a law student I carried my father's books and papers about the Law Library and listened to his submissions in court. My father was my mentor; he taught me all I know about the law but not, alas, all that he knew. He should have written this book.

The licensing code is a strange and esoteric field. It includes statutes promulgated from the reign of Charles I, regulating among other things the licensing of bogs and the treatment of servants in alehouses. This work gives the history of the code, the present statutory framework and a guide to practice and procedure. That the code urgently needs consolidation goes without saying, but that is another day's work.

A workman is only as good as his tools: books are the tools of the lawyer's trade. I offer this volume to my fellow practitioners and hope that it will prove a useful aid. I cannot claim that it is the result of long years of erudition or of practice. It merely comprises observations from the decade I have spent practising law. In fact I may say, like Topsy, "I 'spect it grow'd".

I here record my indebtedness to my late mother, Eleanor Foreman Cassidy, for her invaluable and inestimable assistance in the initial stages of this work and to our amanuensis, Helen Cassidy.

I am grateful to the following for their research: Nick Kelly, Finbarr McElligott and Caroline Costello and my devils Michael Greene, Maura McNally and Patrick O'Callaghan. I am also grateful to Maeve Hayes for her contribution, to John Clerkin and Morgan Sharpe of the Ordnance Survey office, and to Anthony Manahan.

I thank the staff of Round Hall Sweet and Maxwell, in particular my editor, Michael Diviney for his patience and direction; Catherine Ware for her expert, speedy and efficient typing and Julitta Clancy for an exemplary index.

I owe a special debt of gratitude to Pamela Cassidy and Isobel Cassidy for their critical advice and review.

My especial thanks to Caoive Collins and Simon McDonald for their diligence and thoroughness in reading the entire text at proof stages and for making valuable suggestions which I have gratefully adopted.

Finally, my warmest gratitude to my husband, Edward Walsh who inspired this work and to our children Elanor, Harry and Kate.

Constance Cassidy
Morristown Lattin

July 1996

TABLE OF CONTENTS

PART IV: THE COURTS: LICENSING JURISDICTION

PART V: RIGHTS AND OBLIGATIONS ENFORCEMENT

PART VI: PRACTICAL ISSUES

APPENDICES

TABLE OF CASES

Para.

Para.

Para.

Para.

Para.

Para.

Para.

TABLE OF STATUTES

Para.

Para.

Para.

Para.

Para.

Para.

Para.

Para.

Para.

Para.

Para.

Para.

Para.

Para.

Para.

Para.

Para.

Para.

Para.

Para.

TABLE OF STATUTORY INSTRUMENTS

Para.

Part I

GENERAL PRINCIPLES

CHAPTER 1

HISTORY

Introduction

Although the collective citation of the statutes comprising the licensing code is the "Licensing Acts 1833 to 1995", the first licensing statute which affected Ireland was passed in 1635.[1] The concern of the English Parliament throughout the centuries was to restrain the "regrettable excess in drinking" of the Irish populace.[2] The preamble to the 1635 Act states: **1–1**

> "Forasmuch as it is found by daily experience, that many mischiefes and inconveniences doe arise from the excessive number of ale-houses, from the erection of them in woods, bogges, and other unfit places, and many of them not in towne-ships, but dispersedly, and in dangerous places, and kept by unknown persons not under-taken for, whereby many times they become resceptacles for rebels and other malefactors and harbours for gamesters and other idle, disordered, and unprofitable livers, and that those that keep those ale-houses for the most part are not fitted or furnished to lodge or entertaine travellers in any decent manner: For the redresse of these inconveniencies, and many other mischiefes dayly observed to grow by the course now, held and to reduce those needlesse multitudes of ale-houses to a fewer number, to more fit persons, and to more convenient places".

This Act provided that no person was to keep an ale-house or tippling house or to sell ale or beer by retail unless licensed by commissioners appointed from time to time for each county from among the justices of the peace, along with other persons to be selected by the Lord Deputy. Licences were to be granted annually by at least two commissioners to persons of good character, for a proper number of houses in convenient places and were to endure for a year and no longer.

---

[1] 10 & 11 Cha. 1, c. 5. An Act for Keepers of Ale-Houses to be bound by Recognizance. Repealed by 14 & 15 Cha. 2, c. 18, s.9(I).

[2] *Final Report of Royal Commission on Liquor Licensing Laws, 1897-99*, Vol. 35 (Royal Commission on Liquor Licensing Laws, 1899) p.35.

1–2 Subsequent statutes laid down the licence duty payable on licensed premises and the hours of closing. In 1695 it was enacted that all licensed premises were to be closed during the hours of Divine Service on Sundays.[3]

An Act for regulating the issuing of licences (1791) provided that no person was to hold a spirit licence unless he also held an ale licenc; a certificate of good character from the justices was also required.[4] This Act recited that "the use of spiritous liquors prevails to an immoderate excess to the great injury of the health, industry, and morals of the people". A limitation on the grant of licences was introduced by the Spirit Licences Act 1798[5] whereby the justices, before signing the certificates of good character, were to determine the number of houses to be licensed, having due regard to the morals and sobriety of the people. Until the enactment of the Licensing (Ireland) Act 1833, the powers of the justices to refuse or annul licences were absolute.

1–3 The Commission of Inquiry into the Operation of the Laws relating to the Sale and Supply of Intoxicating Liquor 1957, appointed by the Minister for Justice on July 4, 1956, found that there existed some 70 pieces of licensing legislation dating back to the eighteenth century. Since then nine further statutes have come into force which are included in the above citation. In addition to this, several Finance Acts have contained provisions which affect the licensing code.

1–4 The courts have consistently lamented the failure of the legislature to codify the Licensing Acts. In *R. (Byrne) v. Dublin Justices* Andrews J. stated:

> "I may add, that so long ago as 1833, the Licensing Laws got into a condition analagous to that in which they are at present, and an Act was then passed codifying the various Acts. I think it would be eminently desirable that what was done in 1833 should be again done in 1904."[6]

The purpose of the Licensing (Ireland) Act 1833 was to codify the existing law as:

> ". . . the Laws for regulating the Conduct of Persons licensed to sell Wine, Spirits, Beer, Ale, and Cider by Retail in *Ireland*, to be drank or consumed on the Premises, have become very numerous and complicated, and it would greatly tend to the public Benefit to amend and simplify the same, and for that Purpose to collect into One Act the several Regulations and Provisions thereof."[7]

This foundation statute provides, *inter alia*, for the grant and renewal of

---

[3] 7 Will. 3, c. 17. An Act for the Observance of the Lord's Day. Repealed in part by the Statute Law Revision (Ireland) Acts 1878–1879.

[4] 31 Geo. 3, c. 13. An Act for regulating the issuing of licences for the sale of spiritous liquors by retail, and for remedying the abuses which have arisen from the immoderate use of such liquors. Repealed by the Statute Law Revision (Ireland) Act 1879.

[5] 38 Geo. 3, c. 73.

[6] (1904) 37 I.L.T.R. 250 at 251.

[7] 3 & 4 Will. 4, c. 68.

licences, the procedure and venue for such applications and for objections thereto. The authority of the justices was limited; they were given power to refuse new licences on three grounds: unsuitability of the applicant, or of premises, or on the basis of the number of previously licensed houses in the neighbourhood. Transfers were regulated by the same provisions as new licences, but renewals were to be granted directly by the Excise on production of a certificate signed by six householders to the good and peaceable conduct of the house during the past year.

Grant of a New Licence

Until the enactment of the Courts of Justice Act 1924, magistrates were empowered to grant certificates entitling an applicant to receive a new on-licence. Since then, a certificate leading to the grant of a new publican's licence is granted only by a Circuit Court judge.[8] However, the jurisdiction formerly enjoyed by magistrates in issuing certificates relating to the grant of off-licences now resides in the District Court.[9] 1–5

Prior to the enactment of the Licensing (Ireland) Act 1902 any person was entitled to apply for a new excise licence to sell beer, cider or spirits for consumption on the premises. The applicant had to comply with stringent procedural requirements and his application could be refused by a magistrate for failure to comply with such requirements or on foot of a successful objection. However, no restriction as to the number of licences which could be granted applied and it was not necessary for an applicant to show that his premises would, in effect, take over from a business in the area which had become defunct.

Likewise, the Beerhouses (Ireland) Act 1864 provided for the grant and transfer of beer retailers' off-licences and regulated the procedural requirements relating to objections. In the case of these licences and spirit retailers' off-licences (both of which are commonly referred to as an "off-licence"), no restriction whatever was imposed on the number of licences that could be granted, nor did an applicant have to prove that there was a need for such a licence or that he was replacing a facility which was no longer available. The Beer Retailers' and Spirit Grocers' Retail Licences (Ireland) Act 1900 regulates the grant of certificates for spirit retailers' on-licences and contains no prohibitions on the number of such licences which can be granted.

The Sale of Intoxicating Liquors (Licences) (Ireland) Bill 1902 led to the enactment of the Licensing (Ireland) Act 1902, and was known as "Clancy's 1–6

---

[8] Courts of Justice Act 1924, s.50, repealed by the Courts (Supplemental Provisions) Act 1961, s.3, and see also s.24 of the 1961 Act.

[9] See the Courts of Justice Act 1924, s.77(C).

Act", having being introduced and piloted through Parliament by John J. Clancy, M.P. and barrister. The Bill was debated for four years and received huge support in both Houses of Parliament. The Earl of Mayo noted that "the wholesale granting of licences in Ireland has become a positive scandal",[10] adding that the Bill was "only a small Bill – a small step, but a step in the right direction".[11] Earl Grey supported the Bill stating: "I think the fact that a Bill containing matters so doubly contentious as that of Ireland and liquor should come to us in so peaceful a garb, is matter for congratulation".[12]

The Licensing (Ireland) Act 1902 was the first to restrict the number of new licences which could be granted. Bernard Shillman notes:

> "Up to the year 1902, the right of any person to apply to the licensing authorities for the grant to him of a licence for the sale of intoxicating liquor in Ireland was a common law right. That right was absolute and the licensing authorities were bound to hear the applicant for the particular form of licence sought."[13]

Mr Shillman considered the number of licences being granted as a "reckless multiplication" and a "mischief".[14] In essence, the 1902 Act prohibited the grant of any further licences, save in certain exceptional circumstances expressly provided for. Further statutory exceptions were subsequently enacted.

Section 2 of the 1902 Act provides, *inter alia*:

> "2. From and after the passing of this Act no licence shall be granted for the sale of intoxicating liquors, whether for consumption on or off the premises, except . . .".

1–7 In *R. (O'Leary) v. Kerry Justices*, O'Brien L.C.J. described section 2 of the Licensing (Ireland) Act 1902 as being "of a most severe and peremptory character".[15] In *R. (Collins) v. Donegal Justices* he noted that this section:

> ". . . in so many words forbade the issue of new licences – that is to say, the scope and object of the Act was to restrict and suspend for a time limited by the Act the sale of intoxicating liquor. Now, the public house was the great source of supply of drink to the public, though a spirit grocer's may be fraught with special danger to the limited class of women who are addicted to drink, and who might avail themselves to a more or less secret way of getting drink."[16]

In *Re Application of Power Supermarkets Ltd*, Walsh J. explained the objective of the 1902 Act as being:

---

[10] Sale of Intoxicating Liquors (Licences) (Ireland) Bill [second reading], Vol. 109, 4th series, p. 1244.
[11] *Ibid.*, p. 1245.
[12] *Ibid.*, p. 1246.
[13] *The Licensing Laws of Ireland* (Dublin, 1941) p. 1.
[14] *Ibid.*
[15] (1903) 3 N.I.J.R. 251 at 251.
[16] [1903] 2 I.R. 533 at 535.

"... for the purpose of preventing the granting of further licences save within the grounds permitted by that Act. The object of the Act was to safeguard the public interest by preventing a proliferation of licensed premises ...".[17]

The Licensing (Ireland) Act 1902 came into force on July 31, 1902, and remained in force until December 31, 1907. It was renewed annually until 1924 by the Expiring Laws Continuance Acts. Section 14 of the Intoxicating Liquor (General) Act 1924 made it permanently operative "until the Oireachtas otherwise determines". The 1902 Act remains in force as at the date of publication. **1–8**

In 1925, the Liquor Commission was established to ascertain whether the number of licensed premises in the country was in excess of requirements, and if so, to suggest methods to reduce the excess. In that year the number of licensed premises, including public houses and hotels, stood at 13,427. This, in the opinion of the Commission, was excessive, and their recommendations resulted in the enactment of the Intoxicating Liquor Act 1927 whereby redundant licences could be abolished in return for compensation.

This scheme was operated for only one year and during that year 299 licences were abolished. By 1956 the number of licensed premises had been reduced to 11,953, but, in the opinion of the 1957 Liquor Commission this was still "in excess of reasonable requirements". That Commission made recommendations which resulted in the enactment of the Intoxicating Liquor Act 1960. Certain provisions contained in that Act reduced further the number of licensed premises: for example, section 13 of the 1960 Act provided for the grant of a new licence in a rural area, but only where an applicant had obtained the consent to the extinguishment of two licences of the same character situated anywhere in the State. Section 23 of the 1960 Act restricted the operation of section 2(1) of the Licensing (Ireland) Act 1902, providing that an application to revive a lapsed licence can only be brought within five years of the date of the lapse of the licence.

Renewal of Licence

Section 1 of the Licensing (Ireland) Act 1833 authorised the proper officer of excise to grant licences to persons who held licences in the preceding year upon production of a certificate of good character and as to the peaceable and orderly manner in which the applicant's premises was conducted in the previous year, such certificate to be signed by six householders of the parish. **1–9**

Section 11 of the Spirits (Ireland) Act 1854 required an applicant to produce a justice's certificate as to his good character and as to the peaceable and orderly manner in which his house had been conducted in the previous year. Under

[17] [1988] I.R. 206 at 210.

section 4 of the Courts (No. 2) Act 1986 it is not now necessary, where renewal of a licence is sought in respect of premises which have been licensed in the previous year, to produce a certificate of the District Court to an officer of the Revenue Commissioners empowered to grant the renewal of such licence, unless objections have been lodged.[18] Section 242 of the Finance Act 1992 prohibits the renewal of a licence unless an applicant has produced a tax clearance certificate.

Class of Licence

1–10 Schedule 1 to the Finance (1909–10) Act 1910 lists the classes of licence for the sale of intoxicating liquor. In all, the 1910 Act enumerates 25 classes of licence of which only one, the refreshment house licence, has been abolished.[19]

Hotel Licence

1–11 The Licensing (Ireland) Act 1902 created a completely new form of publican's licence, restrictive in nature, which is commonly known as a hotel licence. The licence which may be granted for a hotel pursuant to section 2(2) of the 1902 Act is a publican's licence and is subject to the provisions applicable to publican's licences. However, to qualify for such a licence an applicant must comply with the statutory definition contained in section 2(2) of that Act, as amended by section 21 of the Intoxicating Liquor Act 1960. The hotel must contain 10 apartments (or 20 if situate in a county borough or the Dublin Metropolitan District) set apart and used exclusively for the sleeping accommodation of travellers, and must not have a public bar for the sale of intoxicating liquors.

In view of the recommendations made by the 1957 Commission and the "complaints" from the ordinary licensed trade that there was little or no difference between some of these "dispense bar arrangements" and "public bars", section 19 of the Intoxicating Liquor Act 1960 removed the prohibition on having a public bar in a hotel where a full seven-day publican's on-licence attaching to a premises elsewhere in the State was offered for surrender or extinguishment to the court. This amendment had the result of further reducing the number of on-licences, in keeping with the stated objectives of the 1902 Act.

---

[18] Courts (No. 2) Act 1986, s.4(5) lists the circumstances where a certificate of the court is required at the renewal stage.
[19] Finance Act 1989, s.50.

Special Restaurant Licence

The Intoxicating Liquor Act 1988 created the special restaurant licence which does not depend for its grant on the extinguishment of another licence. Prior to its enactment, a restaurateur required either a wine retailer's on-licence or a full publican's on-licence together with a restaurant certificate to serve intoxicating liquor with food after permitted hours. If the licensee had a wine retailer's on-licence and not a publican's licence he was only entitled to sell wine on the premises. The advantage of having a special restaurant licence is that the holder is entitled to sell all types of intoxicating liquor on his premises. He is not, however, entitled to have a bar on the premises nor can he obtain special exemption orders. **1–12**

Clubs

The Registration of Clubs (Ireland) Act 1904 was enacted to put a stop to "bogus clubs where drink could be sold at all hours irrespective of those which applied to public houses generally".[20] It had the support of the licensed victuallers and those in favour of temperance reform "who recognised that our indulgence in strong drink had been, and still was, a great distress of which Ireland was the victim".[21] **1–13**

The 1904 Act was passed to regulate the conduct of clubs and provided that clubs were only entitled to supply excisable liquor where a certificate of registration was obtained and where the club had a constitution which complied with the Act. This was to ensure that the club was genuine and legitimate and was not established merely for the supply of excisable liquor. During the Commons debate one member noted that "the real mischief against which the Bill was aimed was shebeening, which should be put down with the strongest possible hand".[22]

More recent legislation has provided that the number of members in a registered club must be at least 150 and has prohibited the advertising of functions to be held in a club.[23] It is now possible for any person to object to the renewal of a certificate of registration.[24]

Theatres

The licensing of theatres is regulated by section 7 of the Excise Act 1835 which provides for the licensing of: **1–14**

---

[20] *Hansard*, H.C. 4th series, Vol. 134, 1904, p. 648.
[21] *Ibid.*
[22] *Ibid.*, p. 656.
[23] Intoxicating Liquor Act 1988, ss.45, 46.
[24] Registration of Clubs (Ireland) Act 1904, s.3, as amended by the Intoxicating Liquor Act 1988, s.44.

1. theatres established under royal patent;
2. theatres licensed by the Lord Chamberlain or by justices; and
3. places of public entertainment licensed by the Lord Chamberlain or by justices.

Until recently, the only theatre licences which were granted in Dublin were in respect of theatres which had been granted patents under the Dublin Theatres Act 1786. In *Point Exhibition Co. Ltd v. The Revenue Commissioners,*[25] the applicant company sought an order directing the Commissioners of Customs and Excise to issue a theatre licence in respect of the Point Depot, on the grounds that it was a place of public entertainment licensed by justices. The application was granted on the grounds that the premises in question was a place of public entertainment as provided for in section 7 of the 1835 Act.

Since the *Point* decision, theatre licences have issued to a number of premises in Dublin which are licensed for public music and singing.

Fire Services Act 1981

1–15 On February 14, 1979, a licensed premises in Artane, Dublin, known as the Stardust, caught fire with the tragic loss of 48 young lives. This resulted in the enactment of the Fire Services Act 1981 which provides that applicants for the grant or renewal of certain licences are obliged to notify the fire authority in the functional area within which their premises are situate of such application. Registered clubs are also caught by this requirement; the secretary of a club applying for a grant or renewal of a certificate of registration is obliged to notify the fire officer of his intention so to do. It is common practice for the courts to require proof that there is no objection from the fire officer before the appropriate certificate will issue. An applicant for the grant or renewal of an off-licence is not obliged to notify the fire officer.

Recent Developments

1–16 The Courts (No. 2) Act 1986 restored the discretion of the District Court and on appeal, the Circuit Court, to endorse a recordable offence. This discretion is only appropriate to offences which relate to prohibited hours.

The Intoxicating Liquor Act 1988 extended "drinking-up time" from 10 minutes after closing time to half an hour after closing time. That Act increased the power of the Garda Síochána in relation to offences committed under the Licensing Acts, particularly with regard to underage persons. The Act also sought to prevent the sale of any intoxicating liquor in an off-licence premises

[25] [1993] 2 I.R. 551.

by self-service method and to restrict such sale to behind an intoxicating liquor counter.[26] This particular provision is not in force as the Minister has not yet executed the required statutory instrument.

The Intoxicating Liquor Act 1995 was passed to allow shops and supermarkets which are licensed to sell intoxicating liquor by retail and other licensed premises to remain open on Christmas Eve and December 23 in any year that either day falls on a Sunday as if that day were a weekday.

Conclusion

Although the general prohibition against the granting of new licences has not been removed, the current trend is to consider the "legitimate commercial aspirations" of publicans.[27] In his address to the Dáil at the second stage of the Intoxicating Liquor Bill 1988, the Minister for Justice said that the consumption of intoxicating liquor in "a moderate and responsible way" should be accepted as a normal aspect of social and business life. He was satisfied that "the great majority of people who take a drink do so in a mature and responsible way and it is quite reasonable to liberalise the licensing laws to the extent necessary to meet their legitimate requirements".[28] **1–17**

The licensing laws in this country are numerous, complex, and in need of codification. Fitzgerald L.J. in 1877 stated: **1–18**

> "The provisions of the numerous statutes which regulate licences for the sale of intoxicating liquors in Ireland are so complex, uncertain, and contradictory, that it is difficult to carry them into effect, or to reach the meaning and intention of the legislature."[29]

At the date of writing, the Oireachtas is actively considering, yet again, the codification of all licensing legislation.

The general intention of the legislature in this century has been to decrease the number of licensed outlets: statistics show that there were 21,326 public houses in the year 1838 and now, more than 150 years later, the number has decreased to nearly one third of that figure. According to the Licensed Vintners' Association, as at the date of publication, approximately 8,000 licences exist, 800 of which are in Dublin. The Finance Act 1992, requiring the production of a tax clearance certificate as a condition of the renewal of various types of licence, has probably done more than any single piece of legislation in the entire licensing code to reduce the number of licences in existence. The mischief which Parliament has always been so eager to control, *i.e.* an excessive number of licences, has clearly been remedied.

---

[26] Intoxicating Liquor Act 1988, s.47.

[27] Intoxicating Liquor Bill 1988, *Dáil Reports*, 2nd stage, p. 1993.

[28] *Ibid.*, p. 1994.

[29] *Dowling v. O'Loughlin* [1877–78] I.R. 11 C.L. 488 at 495.

Chapter 2

CHARACTERISTICS OF A LICENCE

Introduction

2–1 A licence to sell intoxicating liquor possesses certain distinct characteristics. It is an authority to a particular person to carry on the trade authorised by the licence in certain specified premises.[1] It cannot be transferred by the holder from one premises to another. Palles C.B. in *Murphy v. Crean* noted:

> "There is not in the whole licensing code any provision for the transfer of a licence from one house to another house."[2]

Thus, if an applicant wishes to license premises, he must apply for a new licence and bring himself within one of the jurisdictional exceptions to the terms of the Licensing (Ireland) Act 1902.[3] As a corollary, the licence and the premises in which the intoxicating liquor is to be sold, must be held together. An agreement to sell a licence is illegal, although it is possible for a publican to enter into an agreement for the extinguishment of a licence.[4]

Further, a licence cannot be granted subject to an undertaking unless the licence is a conditional or restricted licence, for which the legislature has specifically made provision.

A question often arises as to the precise area which is covered by a licence. The law in this area is confusing and complex.

The making of any internal communication between a licensed premises and an area of public entertainment or resort can result in the commission of an offence leading to the forfeiture of a licence.

---

[1] *Murphy v. Crean* [1915] 1 I.R. 111 at 142 and 143

[2] *Ibid.* at 142.

[3] As discussed below, in chapter 6, "Public House Licence", at paras. 6–10 *et seq.*

[4] *Macklin v. Greacen* [1983] I.R. 61 (Sup. Ct.).

Licensed Premises

2–2 A licence is an authority to a named person to carry on trade in a "specified house".[5] The licence authorises the holder to "carry on the trade or business mentioned in such licence in . . . one separate and distinct set of premises, such premises being all adjoining or contiguous to each other, and situate in one place, and held together for the same trade or business".[6] One licence can cover a number of buildings, although O'Higgins J. in *Application of McElvaney*[7] refused to "regard two buildings comparatively widely separated by other buildings and by open space as one distinct whole capable of being licensed as one unit".[8]

The practice, however, is to interpret the expression "adjoining or contiguous" in a liberal way and to grant a licence in respect of a number of buildings which although they are close to each other, are not attached.[9] The expression "set of premises" as contained in section 10 of the Excise Licences Act 1825 can be contrasted with the expression "premises" and contemplates a number of buildings.

The buildings must form part of a cohesive unit in pursuance of the one business. For example, it is unlikely that a hotel licence will be granted in respect of a number of buildings where one of the buildings functions solely as a public house.

2–3 It is clear that for the purposes of the licensing code, the terms "premises" and "licensed premises" do not necessarily coincide and that each has a different significance. The importance of this distinction cannot be over emphasised: a licence to sell at a named house does not authorise a licensed person to sell in the yard and offices at the rear. A "licensed premises" is a "premises in respect of which a licence . . . has been granted and is in force".'[10] This definition can be contrasted with that of "premises" as contained in section 77 of the Licensing Act 1872 which defines premises to include "house or place as defined by section 12 of the Spirits (Ireland) Act 1854, *i.e.* "any other place whatsoever of, belonging, or in any manner appertaining to such house or place".

In *Application of Denis Guiney* it appeared to Judge Davitt to be:

> "clear on the authorities that when a licence is granted for a house or building it attaches to the structure and not merely to the site, and will continue to exist and will be renewed only so long as there is no substantial change in the identity of the structure".[11]

---

[5] *Murphy v. Crean*, above n.1, *per* Palles C.B.
[6] Excise Licences Act 1825, s.10.
[7] Unreported, High Court, O'Higgins J., April 2, 1974.
[8] *Ibid.* at p. 3.
[9] See *Application of Waterhouse* [1955–56] 21–22 Ir. Jur. Rep. 59 and *Re Gold Coast Golf and Leisure Ltd,* unreported, Carlow Circuit Court, Sheridan J., October 3, 1995.
[10] Licensing Act 1872, s.77.
[11] (1941) 75 I.L.T.R. 110 at 112.

In *Murnane v. Adams*[12] the owner of the premises opened a bar at the end of his yard and sold intoxicating liquor there. It was held that the licence authorised him to sell intoxicating liquor in a particular house situated at a particular address and that the sale of intoxicating liquor in a bar at the end of his yard was illegal and not covered by the licence.

Madden J. stated:

> "The policy of the licensing laws requires that the sale of intoxicating liquors should be strictly confined to the place mentioned in the licence."[13]

2–4 In *R. (Beirne) v. Liston*,[14] the court held that a yard, which was used for agricultural purposes and which did not originally form part of the licensed premises, formed part of the licensed premises for the purposes of a conviction for allowing consumption of intoxicating liquor during prohibited hours. In that case, however, it would appear that the court did not appreciate the distinction which was drawn between that area which is licensed for the purposes of the sale of intoxicating liquor and that area upon which the police are entitled lawfully to enter.

Section 12 of the Spirits (Ireland) Act 1854 does not confer any right to sell intoxicating liquor in outhouses or yards: it merely extends the right of entry to the police to those areas.

This section authorises the police to enter upon yards, outhouses, sheds, and other places belonging to a licensed premises for the purposes of detecting an offence against the licensing code. Section 23 of the Licensing Act (Ireland) 1874 gives power to the police to at "all times enter on any licensed premises", for the purpose of detecting offences under the licensing code. So, the sale of intoxicating liquor is confined to the place expressly mentioned in the licence and identified by a map lodged in court.

Beer Garden

2–5 Where an applicant seeks to license premises which includes a yard which may be used as a "beer garden", the practice is for the Garda Síochána to insist upon that yard being licensed. Certainly, the decision of the court in *R. (Beirne) v. Liston*,[15] although questionable, clearly acknowledges the concept of using an uncovered area or a yard as a licensed premises for the purposes of allowing the consumption of intoxicating liquor thereon. The practice where the licensee wishes to use part of the rear of his premises as a beer garden is to include this area within the red line on the licensing map. However, if the licensee wishes to extend his public house into his yard by adding a few rooms, even if that yard had been included within the red line on the licensing map, he must apply to

---

[12] [1910] 2 I.R. 175.
[13] *Ibid.* at 184.
[14] (1910) 44 I.L.T.R. 82.
[15] *Ibid.*

the court for a certificate entitling him to receive a new licence in respect of the existing licensed area and the proposed building.

In *Murnane v. Adams* Madden J. noted that the place which was licensed for the sale of intoxicating liquor must be defined by the terms of the licence and observed: 2–6

> "The licence may be so granted as to include a yard or garden attached to a public house."[16]

However, this must be specified in the licence and the court must be satisfied that the premises which is to be licensed is suitable to sell intoxicating liquors. O'Brien L.C.J. stated:

> "The dominating factor in the case is the licence — the character — the precise extent of the licence. . . . Now, that licence specifies in the very clearest terms where the liquor is to be sold, that is to say, in the original permanent public-house, as distinguished from the temporary bar."[17]

Madden J. continued:

> "Where the licence is granted in sufficiently wide terms to include premises attached to a dwelling house, the entire of the premises are licensed, and constitute the 'place' within the meaning of the third section of the Act of 1872 and liquor may be lawfully sold on any part of the licensed premises."[18]

Internal Communication[19]

Any person who makes or uses or allows to be made or used any internal communication between a licensed premises and an unlicensed premises which is used for public entertainment or resort or as a refreshment house, has committed an offence and is liable to a penalty.[20] 2–7

A similar offence exists in respect of a spirit retailer's off-licence.[21] The offence is to permit an internal and not an external communication from the licensed premises itself to another, unlicensed, premises. There is no requirement to fence off a yard at the back of a public house from a neighbouring premises, although the court might be disposed to insist on this on the grounds of the general unsuitability of the premises and the difficulty of exercising sufficient police control. The Court of Appeal in England has held that section 9 of the Licensing Act 1872 does not apply to an internal communication existing at the time of the grant of the licence. So, the grant of a licence for a

[16] Above, n.12, at 183.
[17] *Ibid.* at 181 and 182.
[18] *Ibid.* at 183 and 184.
[19] See also below, chap. 26, "Forfeiture", at para. 26–13.
[20] Licensing Act 1872, s.9. See also chap. 26, "Forfeiture", at para. 26–13
[21] *Ibid.*, s.85.

pub or supermarket in a shopping centre cannot form the basis of a prosecution under section 9. In *Commissioners of Customs and Excise v. Griffith*, Scrutton J. stated:

> "The words 'make or allow to be made' clearly refer to a communication made since the date of the licence."[22]

Structural Separation

2–8 A licensed premises must be structurally separate from an unlicensed area which is used for public entertainment or resort. The structural separation must be permanent: a locked door or a wire network frame which is removable does not constitute a structural separation of a permanent kind.[23]

In *Beirne v. Duffy (No. 1)*[24] it was held that the separation between a bar and a billiard room (which was unlicensed) was not a structural separation. In that case, the billiard room contained a glass partition through which an order for a drink could be given and received. This could result in the delivery of the drink ordered by taking the drink from the bar to the billiard room through a yard. Mrs Duffy was prosecuted a year later under section 2 of the Intoxicating Liquors (Ireland) Act 1906 (which is now repealed) for having failed to close her licensed premises as required by statute, since she kept the billiard room open after hours.[25] Although she had blocked up the partition between the bar and the billiard room, they were adjacent to each other. Both opened out onto a licensed yard. It was held that there was internal communication. Palles C.B. stated:

> "In the present case the dividing line passes through the yard, and in it there are two gaps where there is no structural separation, *viz.*, the door between the billiard room and the yard, and the door between the yard and the other part of the premises, i.e. that containing the bar. These two gaps are internal, *i.e.* within the licensed premises."[26]

Cherry L.C.J. dissented, his view being that the true test of structural separation was:

> "Is there or is there not any internal communication between the different parts of the building?"[27]

---

[22] [1924] 1 K.B. 735 at 748.
[23] *R. (Richardson) v. Sweeney* (1908) 42 I.L.T.R. 174; *Toppin v. Coleman* [1910] 2 I.R. 200.
[24] [1914] 2 I.R. 68.
[25] *Beirne v. Duffy (No. 2)* [1915] 2 I.R. 251.
[26] *Ibid.* at 258.
[27] *Ibid.* at 260.

Property in a Licence

There is no property in a licence, or goodwill, apart from the ownership of the premises to which the licence attaches. In *Kelly v. Montague* FitzGibbon L.J. stated: 2–9

> "Though the good-will of a man's business is, generally speaking, part of his personal estate, these English cases show that if the business is so attached to certain premises that it cannot be carried on at any other place, nor by any person who is not entitled to possession of the premises, its value goes with them, and it cannot be separately valued, or included as money's worth in the property of any person other than the owner of the premises."[28]

In that case, the Court of Appeal disapproved of the headnote to *Brennan v. Dorney*.[29] Barry L.J. stated:

> "I confined myself, in *Brennan v. Dorney*, to deciding the broad point in the case, and I laid it down as directly as the English language could express, that a licence is not property at all. But the reporter has converted that proposition into its present form in the marginal note, or perhaps he passed me over, or takes no notice of me at all."[30]

A licence attached to a premises is inalienable; an agreement for the sale of the licence is unenforceable and specific performance of the agreement cannot be given by the court. So held the Supreme Court in *Macklin and McDonald v. Greacen & Co. Ltd, Patton and McElvaney*.[31] In that case, the first defendant agreed to sell a seven-day licence attached to a public house to the plaintiff. The premises to which the licence attached was owned by the first defendant and the licence was held by Robert Greacen Patton as nominee of the first defendant. The premises had been virtually demolished by a bomb the previous year and no trading had since been carried on, although a renewal had been obtained from the District Court at the licensing sessions after the premises were destroyed and at the following annual licensing sessions. The solicitors for the first defendant purported to make time of the essence when the sale to the plaintiff was not timely completed. Thereafter, the second defendant entered into an agreement with Robert Greacen Patton as nominee of the first defendant for the sale of the licence to him. The plaintiff obtained an ad interim injunction from the High Court restraining the first defendant and nominee from completing the sale to the second defendant and instituted a claim for specific performance of the agreement. In dismissing the plaintiff's claim, Griffin J. noted: 2–10

[28] [1892–93] 29 L.R.Ir. 429 at 442 and 443.
[29] [1888–89] 21 L.R.Ir. 353.
[30] *Kelly v. Montague*, above, n.28, at 446.
[31] Above, n.4.

> "For almost one hundred years it has been accepted that a licence to sell intoxicating liquor is inalienable and must be attached to premises. The law on the matter has been stated succinctly in O'Connor's *Irish Justice of the Peace* 2nd edition, Vol. 2 at page 688 as follows: 'The doctor cannot sell his degree, because it is attached to himself; on the other hand, the holder of a licence cannot sell the licence to any other person, unless such other person also buys the premises. The licence *per se* is inalienable. It must always, so long as it exists at all, remain attached to premises . . .'."[32]

Where the holder of a licence wishes to dispose of it for consideration, he may consent to the extinguishment of that licence upon the grant of another licence after a successful application under the licensing code. As a matter of law, his licence will become extinguished, but only upon the grant of the new licence.

Mortgage of a Licensed Premises

2–11 A licensed premises, being a valuable asset, may be offered as security in respect of an advance or loan made by a financial institution. A loan in the normal course would be secured by a deed of mortgage. The mortgage should refer to the premises and to the licence attaching thereto. It is usual for the mortgage deed to include covenants on the part of the borrower obliging him to conduct the subject premises in a good, peaceable and orderly manner. In addition, the borrower is now obliged to secure a tax clearance certificate in order to renew the licence at the end of each licensing year.

Equitable Mortgage

2–12 In the absence of a reference to the licence, an issue may arise as to whether a mortgage extends to and includes the actual licence attaching to the premises. This issue was the subject of some controversy, which was in part due to a misleading interpretation of the decision of Chatterton V.-C. in *Brennan v. Dorney*.[33] The principle that the licence attached to the premises was specifically endorsed and accepted by Chatterton V.-C. in his judgment. His views were indeed accepted in the Court of Appeal but his decision was reversed, having regard to the specific facts of the case.

In the course of his decision, Chatterton V.-C., having reviewed the statutes, came to the following conclusions:

> "First, that no right to the benefit of a publican's licence can exist apart from the ownership and possession of the licensed premises; secondly, that the

[32] *Ibid.* at 66.
[33] Above, n.29.

possession of the licence itself by a person not entitled to such ownership or possession confers no right to either transfer or renewal of the licence; thirdly, that the rightful possession of the licensed premises carries with it the right to the transfer or renewal, subject to the statutory requirements applicable to such cases; fourthly, that such right cannot be defeated by the wrongful withholding of the actual licence from the person entitled in respect of possession or ownership; and that the statutory requirement of endorsement of the transfer on the licence can be complied with by endorsement on a certified copy of the licence or perhaps dispensed with in such cases by holding this provision to be directory only."[34]

In the later decision of *Kelly v. Montague*,[35] Ashbourne L.J. held that there was no property in the licence apart from the ownership of the premises to which the licence was attached. As the licence attaches only to the premises and is not severable, a mortgage of the premises captures the licence, even in the absence of a specific reference to the licence. **2–13**

This was accepted by Miller J. in *Re O'Brien (a Bankrupt)*.[36] That case concerned an equitable mortgage on a licensed premises granted to a firm of brewers to secure money lent and porter as supplied. Several changes had occurred in the composition of the firm. The business and the debts were on each occasion assigned, the deeds deposited by way of equitable mortgage were transferred to the new partners and trading was carried on under the name of the original firm. Porter was continuously supplied to the mortgagor on the security and payments were made by him on account.

The mortgagor was adjucated a bankrupt. The assignees in bankruptcy of the mortgagee licensee claimed to be entitled to such proportion of the proceeds of sale as related to the licence. Miller J. held that the benefit of the equitable mortgage passed to the persons for the time being constituting the firm and extended to goods supplied by them as well as to goods supplied by the original members of the firm. Thus, the equitable mortgage of the licensed public house created by the deposit of the title deeds conferred upon the mortgagees the right to the licence as against the assignees in bankruptcy of the licensed owner of the public house.

The issue would now appear to be beyond argument in the light of the decision of Hamilton J. in *Re Brendan J. Sherry-Brennan (a Bankrupt)*.[37] There the bankrupt was the owner of premises known as "The Pike Inn". A mortgage dated January 22, 1974, and registered on February 20, 1974, was secured against the premises in favour of Equity Securities Ltd. A charge in favour of the Bank of Ireland was created by an indenture dated September 24, 1974, and **2–14**

[34] *Ibid.* at 361.
[35] Above, n.28.
[36] [1883–84] 1 L.R. Ir. 213.
[37] [1979] I.L.R.M. 113.

registered on October 7, 1974. A charge in favour of a Mr B. O'Cleirigh was granted on October 14, 1974, and registered on January 13, 1975. A judgment mortgage in favour of A.I.B. had been registered on April 10, 1975. The premises were sold for the sum of £42,000. The Official Assignee in Bankruptcy claimed to be entitled to retain the value of the excise licence annexed to the premises out of the proceeds of the sale for the benefit of the unsecured creditor, arguing that the licence was not captured by the mortgage of January 22, 1974, nor the charges dated September 24, 1974, and October 14, 1974, nor indeed by the judgment mortgage registered on April 10, 1975. None of the instruments made reference to the excise licence attached to the lands and premises of the bankrupt.

Hamilton J. reviewed the authorities and concluded that:

> "As the licence cannot be regarded as property capable of separation from the licensed premises I am satisfied that the licence is subject to the same charges and incumbrances as the property and hold that it is incapable of passing to the Official Assignee in priority to incumbrances registered against the property to which it is attached."[38]

Judgment Mortgage

2–15 The position of a judgment mortgagee is different. It has been held that a judgment mortgage created under the Judgment Mortgage (Ireland) Act 1850 in respect of premises in the possession of a judgment debtor to which a publican's licence is attached does not operate to assign the licence nor to bind the debtor to endorse or hand over the licence to a purchaser on a sale by the court.[39]

However, all is not lost for a judgment mortgagee. An application to revive the licence can be made by the purchaser on proof that the premises were licensed within five years preceding the date of the service of the notice of application on the District Court or the county registrar, as the case may be.[40] Where the mortgagee is a body corporate, the objects clause in the memorandum of association should, as a matter of prudence, extend to permit the holding of a licence or the conduct of the licensed trade by the body corporate.

Licence Granted Subject to Undertaking

2–16 A licence is *per se* unconditional. Unless a statutory provision authorises the grant of a conditional or restricted licence, the court may not impose conditions. The power to insert a condition in a restricted licence, namely an early closing

---

[38] *Ibid.* at 117.
[39] *O'Brien v. Irish Industrial Benefit Building Society* [1941] I.R. 1.
[40] The application is made under the Licensing (Ireland) Act 1902, s.2(1).

licence or a six-day licence, is vested in the court by statute.[41] The licence commonly referred to as a "hotel licence" and which was created by section 2(2) of the Licensing (Ireland) Act 1902 is a publican's licence but continues to be a protection to the holder only where the conditions pursuant to which the licence was granted are maintained.[42] A special restaurant licence, though it is a retailer's on-licence for the purposes of the Finance (1909–10) Act 1910, is a licence granted subject to the condition that it shall not contain a bar. These restrictions and conditions are imposed by statute and not the courts.

The grant of a licence subject to conditions "is not a grant according to law".[43] It is not unusual for licence holders to agree certain terms with objectors or to give an undertaking to the court: a breach of this undertaking or the agreement does not invalidate the licence but it can be brought to the attention of the next annual licensing District Court and can constitute evidence of the character of the applicant publican. In *R. (Bourke) v. Dublin Justices*, Palles C.B. commented on the practice of giving undertakings and described them as "irregular": in that case, he held that one of two undertakings given by the applicant:

> "was void *ab initio*; that in point of law it was non-existent; and that the legal rights of the applicant must be determined as if it had not been entered into at all".[44]

There, an undertaking was given not to use a bar to serve persons other than hotel guests after a given period of time. On that basis, the objectors withdrew their objection. It was held that the breach of this undertaking was evidence to sustain the decision of the court that the applicant was not of good character within the meaning of the licensing code.

In *Re Application of Power Supermarkets Ltd*,[45] McWilliam J. noted the difficulty of enforcing a condition confining the sale of intoxicating liquor for consumption on the premises to a bar at the rear of the supermarket premises where the principal purpose of the grant of the licence was for sales off the premises.

[41] Intoxicating Liquor Act 1927, ss.8 and 9, and the Courts (No. 2) Act 1986, s.4.
[42] *Quinn v. Bourke* [1906] 2 I.R. 94; *State (Quirke) v. Tipperary Justices* (1931) 65 I.L.T.R. 157.
[43] *R. v. Beesly* [1912] 3 K.B. 583.
[44] [1903] 2 I.R. 429 at 437.
[45] [1981] I.L.R.M. 270 at 273.

CHAPTER 3

THE LICENSEE

Introduction

3–1 A licence is an authority to a named person to carry on trade in a specified house.[1] No person can carry on a licensed business or sell or supply intoxicating liquor and derive a profit therefrom other than the person whose name is on the licence,[2] his servants or agents. Ridley J. in *Peckover v. Defries* stated:

> ". . . the Legislature intended that the sale of liquors are to take place through the licensed person, not necessarily by himself, but if not by himself then through somebody who is his agent or his servant".[3]

This calls into question the legality of franchise or management agreements whereby a publican enters into an agreement with a so-called manager to carry on business on the publican's premises, from which the manager would derive a profit.

In *Edwards v. Edwards*[4] a retiring publican agreed with his daughter-in-law, to whom he wished to transfer his business, that she should carry on the business, pay the rent and other outgoings and pay for goods supplied and take all the profits. It was agreed that the licence should remain in his name until the next annual licensing sessions. If, at the end of the year, she considered herself to be able to work the business successfully, the agreement was that the licence should then be transferred to her. In holding that the contract did not contravene the Licensing Acts, Holmes L.J. stated:

> "There was nothing in the agreement to alter the position of the plaintiff as a licensed publican, liable, as such, for the rent of the house, and responsible for its proper management."[5]

---

[1] *per* Palles C.B. in *Murphy v. Crean* [1915] 1 I.R. 111 at 142 and 143.

[2] The grant of an ad interim transfer authorises the person whose name is endorsed on the back of the licence until the next annual licensing sessions.

[3] (1906) 21 Cox 323 at 329.

[4] (1905) 39 I.L.T.R. 73.

[5] *Ibid.* at 74.

Although the daughter-in-law did not have possession of the premises, she was carrying on business under the licence and deriving profit from it: it could not, therefore, be said that she was acting as agent or manager for the licensee.

It is doubtful whether the courts would now permit a person other than the licensee or his servant or agent to operate the business authorised by the licence. As Palles C.B. stated in *R. (Cottingham) v. Cork Justices:* 3–2

> "... the licensee was not bound to carry on the trade by himself personally. He might lawfully carry it on ... not by himself, but by his manager."[6]

A doorman who is not authorised by the licensee to sell intoxicating liquor and who does so without the knowledge of the licensee is not considered to be acting as agent of the licensee.[7]

Although, throughout this chapter, a person trading under the licence is referred to as the "licensee", a distinction must be drawn between the expression "licensee" and "the holder of the licence". Both persons are authorised to trade and both can be convicted of offences under the licensing code. The licensee, however, is the person "to whom the excise, pursuant to a certificate of the court, had issued a licence".[8] The person to whom an ad interim transfer has been granted, though he is not the licensee, is the "holder of the licence" for the purpose of carrying on the business. He is also liable for offences committed in respect of the licence.[9]

Qualifications of Licensee

To be entitled to trade under a licence, the applicant must possess certain qualifications. 3–3

(a) Possession of Premises

One of the cardinal principles of licensing law is that the licensee must hold the lowest estate and interest in the premises.[10] A considerable amount of case law has arisen concerning the validity of an order permitting the renewal of a licence where the licence has issued to a person who does not hold such estate; a question also arises whether the assignment by a publican of his interest to some other person who has not applied for an authority to trade invalidates the licence.

---

[6] [1906] 2 I.R. 415 at 421.
[7] *O'Halloran v. Taylor* (1926) 60 I.L.T.R. 6.
[8] *Fitzpatrick v. McCormack* [1986] I.R. 380, *per* Finlay C.J. at 391.
[9] For a detailed discussion as to the distinction between on the one hand, the licensee and on the other hand, "the holder of a licence", see below, chap. 18, "Transfer".
[10] *R. (Murphy) v. Cork Justices* [1895] 2 I.R. 104.

In *R. (Cox) v. Recorder of Dublin*, Fitzgibbon L.J. stated:

> "I hold it an essential condition to the grant of a licence that the person to be licensed should be *de facto* and *de jure*, upon receiving his licence, entitled to the possession of the premises, and ready to carry on the business there, then, and thenceforward . . .".[11]

Holmes J. in *R. (Murphy) v. Cork Justices*, stated:

> ". . . the holder of a licence must have such an estate or interest in the licensed premises as entitles him to occupy them"[12],

and referred to the principles enunciated by Chatterton V.-C. in *Brennan v. Dorney,*[13] *viz.* that no right to the benefit of a publican's licence can exist separate and apart from the ownership and possession of the licensed premises and that the right of possession of the licensed premises carries with it the right of transfer or renewal, subject to the relevant statutory requirements.

3–4 Neither a licence nor a caretaker's agreement confers sufficient estate or interest in a licensed premises for the purpose of satisfying the above principles. The estate or interest must be such that the holder thereof is entitled to evict persons from the premises for trespass. A licence, in contrast to a lease, merely permits the licensee to be upon the premises; his presence thereon would otherwise be unlawful. A licensee has no estate or interest entitling him to remain on the premises. A caretaker's agreement confers no interest upon the caretaker: he is merely entitled to enter into possession on behalf of the true owner. The essence of a lease, in contrast, is that the tenant is given the right to exclusive possession, *i.e.* the right to exclude all other persons from the premises.[14]

Although this principle has always been accepted as central to this area of licensing law, Holmes J. in *R. (Murphy) v. Cork Justices* acknowledged that there is nothing in the licensing statutes or in the general law

> "for holding that the certificate of the Justices involves a declaration that the grantee of the licence has a possessory interest in the licensed premises".[15]

Thus, although it is unlikely that such a certificate will issue without proof of possession as described above, the issue of a licence where such possession does not exist does not apparently invalidate the licence. So held McWilliam J. in *The State (Reddy) v. District Justice Johnson,*[16] where he was satisfied that the District Court Judge had acted within his jurisdiction in issuing a certificate

[11] [1885–86] 16 L.R.Ir. 424 at 438.
[12] Above, n.10, at 113.
[13] [1888–89] 21 L.R.Ir. 353.
[14] *Megarry & Wade* (19th ed.) p. 633.
[15] Above n.10, at 115.
[16] Unreported, High Court, McWilliam J., July 31, 1980.

entitling the applicant to apply for a renewal of the licence, even though the applicant had no estate or interest in the premises.

In *Application of Catherine Allen*,[17] a licence was renewed in the name of Gerard Allen for 10 years although his mother held the lowest estate and interest in the premises during that period. In the High Court, McWilliam J. held that the District Court had no jurisdiction to renew a licence for Gerard Allen at any time after he had transferred his interest in the premises to his mother and thus the certificate of transfer could not now be granted to her.[18] 3–5

Since the enactment of the Courts (No. 2) Act 1986 the renewal of a licence, in most cases, is not now dependent upon a certificate of the court. Thus, there is no longer, in such cases "involved in the granting of the licence a decision by a competent tribunal that the person to whom it is given is qualified to receive it".[19] The question remains whether the issue of a licence by the excise authorities to a person who does not hold sufficient estate or interest in the premises as required by the licensing code, is invalid. 3–6

If the estate or interest entitling the licensee to possession terminates during the currency of the licence, the publican is not entitled to carry on the business. McWilliam J., in the *Reddy* case, noted:

> "It seems to me to follow that if the estate or interest which entitles the publican to possession were to terminate either by assignment or otherwise, during the currency of the annual licence, and if he were allowed to remain in the licensed house as permissive occupant, he would not be entitled to carry on the business."[20]

The licence will, however, remain valid until the date of expiry but becomes inoperable unless and until some other person acquires authority to trade thereunder. McWilliam J., in the *Reddy* case stated:

> "The licence would still be valid and available for the protection of the assignee on his complying with the statutory conditions but would cease to have any other operation."[21]

(b) Residence of Applicant

Most of the statutes providing for the grant of a certificate leading to the grant or renewal of a licence require that such a certificate be granted by the judge or judges presiding in the district in which the applicant resides. In *R. (Gilbey)* 3–7

---

[17] Unreported, High Court, McWilliam J., No. 60SS, 1981.
[18] See the discussion of these cases in chapter 16, "Jurisdiction", paras. 16–25 to 16–30.
[19] Holmes J. in *R. (Murphy) v. Cork Justices*, above, n.10, at 114.
[20] *The State (Reddy) v. District Justice Johnson*, above, n.16, at p. 9.
[21] *Ibid.*

v. Fermanagh Justices,[22] Sir Walter Gilbey was refused a certificate in respect of premises in Enniskillen because he resided in London. In a case which is referred to in the *Irish Law Times*,[23] the applicant for a licence, who owned a hotel premises in Dun Laoghaire, resided in Great Britain. It was argued before Judge McCarthy in the Dublin Circuit Court that it was undesirable that a person who resided outside the jurisdiction be allowed, through a nominee, to acquire the ownership of a licensed premises in this country. Judge McCarthy stated that he could find no authority to deprive a person residing outside the jurisdiction of the right to own licensed premises in this country and arrange for his licensed nominee to manage such premises.

Given the principle of non-discrimination against nationals of E.U. Member States embodied in the Treaty of Rome there is no reason why nationals of other E.U. Member States cannot hold a licence in Ireland. In order to ensure that proper control is exercised over the licensed premises, it is, however, suggested that a nominee be appointed.

The requirement as to residence in the district within which the judge or judges presides does not appear to apply now either to the grant of a new licence or to renewal. Section 24 of the Courts (Supplemental Provisions) Act 1961. provides that the judge having jurisdiction in respect of the grant of a new on-licence is the judge of the circuit in which the premises in question are situate. Where a certificate of the District Court is required, prior to the renewal of a licence, a certificate of the District Court for the District Court area within which the premises concerned are situate must be produced.

(c) Householder

3–8 Section 13 of the Licensing (Ireland) Act 1833 requires that the applicant be a householder: a "householder" is a person owning or renting a house. This provision reinforces the notion that the licensee must be in possession of the premises.

(d) Residence on the Premises

3–9 In *R. (Kinsella and Kavanagh) v. Wicklow Justices*, Fitzgerald J. stated:

> ". . . non-residence does not necessarily amount to unfitness; but it would appear that it might be an element in making out a case of unfitness — for instance, if the applicant resided at a remote distance from the premises for which he sought a licence, and where he should be personally present to fulfil the requirements of the law, and attend to his interests and those of the customers."[24]

---

[22] [1897] 2 I.R. 559.
[23] (1952) 86 I.L.T. & S.J. 168.
[24] (1877) 11 I.L.T.R. 32 at 34.

This must be viewed in the context of the practice of many modern publicans to live in premises other than their licensed premises. It has been held that in circumstances where a publican does not live over his licensed premises and does not intend to supervise his business it can:

> "require coercive authority to compel me to hold that under these circumstances the magistrates were bound to decide that he was 'fit' ".[25]

However, to require an applicant to give an undertaking that he will live and sleep on the premises every night has been held to be unreasonable.[26] The test which the courts are likely to use is that the applicant, wherever he lives, is clearly involved in the management, supervision and control of the business.

Obligations of Licensee

(a) Obligation to Trade

A licensee runs the risk of attracting an objection to the peaceable and orderly manner in which he conducts his business if he does not carry on trading during the licensing year. There is a wealth of authority to the effect that if the licensed trade is abandoned during the year then the licensee is not entitled to the renewal of his licence.[27] In *R. (Lambe) v. Armagh Justices*, Holmes J. stated: 3–10

> "the licensing code assumes that licences to be granted under it are to be used, and not to be allowed to lie dormant".[28]

Further, the court will not countenance an application to revive a licence where the avowed intention is to part with it for money or money's worth.[29] Token trading is not permitted and a licensee must, upon the grant of his licence, be "ready to carry on the business there, then, and thenceforward".[30]

(b) Obligation to Serve Customers

According to O'Connor in *The Irish Justice of the Peace*: 3–11

> "There is no foundation for the current popular belief that a publican is under any legal obligation to serve any customer, even if such customer be sober and orderly."[31]

In his view, a licensed person was entitled to refuse to serve any customer at any time and to require any person to leave and to use such force as was

---

[25] *R. (Leslie) v. Monaghan Justices* (1901) 35 I.L.T.R. 35 at 37, *per* Palles C.B.
[26] *R. (Perry) v. Tyrone Justices* (1904) 38 I.L.T.R. 26, *per* Andrews J.
[27] See below, chap. 21, "Objections", paras. 21–32 to 21–35.
[28] [1897] 2 I.R. 57 at 68.
[29] *Re Application of Philip Ryan* [1964] 30 Ir. Jur. Rep. 41.
[30] *R. (Cox) v. Recorder of Dublin*, above, n.11, at 438, *per* Fitzgibbon J.
[31] (2nd ed., 1915), Vol. II, p. 759.

reasonably necessary for the purpose of ejecting him.[32] O'Connor points out, however, that a "capricious refusal" to serve customers could be made a cause of objection to the renewal of a publican's licence in circumstances whereby the refusal could be said to be "in pursuance of a boycotting conspiracy to which the publican is a party".[33]

In *R. (Delaney) v. Queen's County Justices*,[34] the publican refused to supply drink to persons who were boycotted and demanded excessive charges from others. It was held on a motion for certiorari that these facts constituted evidence to support the justice's refusal of the annual certificate. A publican will, however, normally take the view that serving unpopular persons with intoxicating liquor will probably deprive him of other custom. At the time of writing the legislature is in the process of enacting equal status legislation to make it unlawful to refuse facilities on the ground of unlawful discrimination. An erosion of the publican's right to refuse is inconsistent with his statutory obligation to conduct his business in a peaceable and orderly manner.

It is open, for example, for a judge to refuse to issue a certificate as to the good character and peaceable and orderly manner in which a licensed premises has been conducted where there is evidence that women are not served on the premises or portion thereof.

Persons Eligible to Apply for Licence

Individual or Individuals

3–12 Section 5 of the Licensing (Ireland) Act 1833 envisages a "licensed person" as one or more individuals.

STATUTORY PROVISION

Section 5 of the Licensing (Ireland) Act 1833 provides for the form of certificate to be given to the person or persons entitled thereto, by the clerk of the court (District Court clerk)

> ". . . upon each Application being disposed of by the Justices attending at such Sessions, it shall be lawful for the Clerk of the Peace or his Deputy, and he is hereby required, to give or cause to be given to the Person entitled thereto, a Certificate in the Form following:
>
> "AB, Clerk of the Peace of ...., To certify that CD is [or CD and EF are] duly entitled to receive a licence for the Sale of Beer, Cider or Spirits...by Retail at .... in the Parish of........... in this County........Dated this .... Day of............
>
> AB, Clerk of the Peace for ...."

---

[32] O'Connor quotes the cases of *Sealey v. Tandy* [1902] 1 K.B. 296 and *R. (Lambe) v. Armagh Justices*, above, n.28, as authorities for this proposition.

[33] O'Connor, *op. cit.*, above, n.31, Vol. II, p. 759.

[34] [1887] 20 L.R.Ir. 167.

Thus, a number of persons who possess the necessary qualifications, may hold a licence.

Individual as Nominee for an Individual

The concept of an individual holding a licence as a nominee for another is recognised by section 79 of the Finance Act 1993 which amends the definition of "beneficial holder" of a licence contained in section 242 of the Finance Act 1992. While there is no reported case on the subject, it would seem unjust that, for example, a widow who did not wish to carry on a licensed business but who wished to retain possession of the premises should not be entitled to appoint a manager or relative as a nominee.[35] **3–13**

Partnership

Section 242 of the Finance Act 1992 acknowledges the entitlement of a partnership to hold a licence. **3–14**

Company

Section 11(c) of the Interpretation Act 1937 provides that unless the contrary intention appears, the word "person" can be construed to include a body corporate. Although section 5 of the Licensing Ireland Act 1833 does not refer to a body corporate, it is now well established that a company can hold a licence, despite the reservations expressed by James O'Connor in *The Licensing Laws of Ireland*: **3–15**

> "The provisions of the Licensing Code go to show that a licence cannot be granted to a limited company, but the application may be made in the name of the secretary or other servant or nominee."[36]

Kenny J. in *The State (Hennessy) and Chariot Inns Ltd v. Commons* stated that:

> "There is a myth — widely accepted by members of the District Court bench and by branches of the legal profession — that a company incorporated under the Companies Acts cannot be granted a licence to sell intoxicating drink and that, when it seeks to be licensed in respect of premises or when it acquires licensed premises, the licence must be granted to its nominee. The basis of this myth is a passage at p. 86 of O'Connor's *Licensing Laws of Ireland* which was published in 1904; but a Divisional Court of the King's Bench in Ireland decided two years after the date of publication that a company could be granted a licence: *R. (Cottingham) v. Cork Justices*.[37] An examination of the relevant sections in

---

[35] See *Brown v. Watson* (1903) 37 I.L.T.R. 246 at 250.
[36] O'Connor, *The Licensing Laws of Ireland* (1904) p. 86.
[37] See above, n.6.

the Licensing Acts convinces me that the court was right and that the passage in O'Connor was wrong".[38]

The Judge continued:

"The illusion that a company cannot be licensed under the Licensing Acts springs from a belief that a company cannot have a character and hence is not a person. The word "person" may have been inappropriate in 1833 to include a joint stock company without corporate personality, but it certainly includes the modern company with corporate personality. The latter can sue and be sued: it can be prosecuted in the District Court and can be indicted: injunctions may be granted against it and its property may be sequestrated. For tax purposes it may be resident in a country and it, as distinct from its directors and shareholders, may have a reputation and so a character".[39]

He referred to the judgment of Palles C.B. in the *Cottingham* case where he stated:

"I cannot see why a public Company cannot have a character . . . 'Character', as used in the section, means 'reputation'. Reputation is acquired by conduct. The conduct of the authorised agents of a Company is *its* conduct. Why should not that conduct give rise to a reputation as to its character, good, bad, or indifferent? . . . But this reputation is not that of an individual. It is, or may be, something different from the reputation of each."[40]

In that case Johnson J. examined the character of a company:

"I think if the house is conducted in a disorderly way, if convictions are had for breaches of the Licensing Acts, if improper characters are allowed to resort there for improper purposes, or public feeling is outraged by lewd or improper acts knowingly permitted, this 'Company' would, through their agent or manager, whom they put in charge of, or whose omissions or acts they are liable for, have an evil reputation and a bad character; but if, on the contrary, the house is conducted in an orderly and decent manner, the provisions of the Licensing Acts observed, and, perhaps I may venture to add, reasonably good and wholesome beer supplied, the local and public reputation of this Company, through their agent or manager whom this Company placed in charge and for whom they are responsible, would be good, and this Company would be, as the Justices have certified them to be, of good character."[41]

Nominee of Company

3–16 Despite the reasoning in *The State (Hennessy) and Chariot Inns Ltd v. Commons* (see above), companies continue to indulge in the widespread practice of

[38] [1976] I.R. 238 at 251.
[39] *Ibid.*
[40] *R. (Cottingham) v. Cork Justices*, above, n.6, at 422 and 423.
[41] *Ibid.* at 427.

appointing nominees. Usually, the nominee is an individual, although there is no reason to assume that a company could not be a nominee of another company.

This practice has been recognised by the legislature in section 28 of the Intoxicating Liquor Act 1960 which provides for the transfer of a licence held by a nominee of a body corporate to such other person as the body corporate may nominate. However, the courts have expressed their dissatisfaction at the practice, leading as it does to confusion as to which person should be liable for breaches of the licensing code. In *McMahon v. Murtagh Properties Ltd* Barrington J. indicated his concern, noting:

> "it is probably too late now, to hold that the practice of companies holding licences through nominees is wrong".[42]

Noting that section 28 of the 1960 Act acknowledges this practice, Barrington J. asserted that the practice of companies holding their licences through nominees "has no basis in sound logic"[43] and would give rise to difficulties in administering the licensing code. He pointed out that although a nominee could be referred to as the holder it must be remembered that the limited liability company was the real holder of the licence: he stated that the nominee was "in effect, no more than a peg on which the company finds it convenient to hang its licence".[44] He held that the summons issued as against the company as holder of the licence was properly issued and directed the District Court judge to enter continuances.

The question which then arises is, who is the holder of the licence: the company or the nominee. In *McMahon v. Murtagh Properties Ltd* Barrington J. noted that a nominee has no beneficial interest in the licence and he is obliged to comply with all lawful directions of the body corporate in relation to the licence. He stated:

> "While the Statute acknowledges that he holds the licence, he holds it only for the body corporate which is the beneficial and, indeed, the real holder of the licence, just as it is the real holder of the premises in which the business is carried on".[45]

It is the company itself which is required to satisfy the court that it possesses the sufficient interest and estate in the premises, not the nominee.

Carroll J. in *Desmond v. Kennedy*,[46] distinguished the *Murtagh Properties* case (see above). She was satisfied that the *Murtagh Properties* decision was not authority for the proposition that a nominee, provided he does no more than 3–17

---

[42] [1982] I.L.R.M. 342 at 346.
[43] *Ibid.* at 348.
[44] *Ibid.* at 345.
[45] *Ibid.* at 346.
[46] Unreported, High Court, Carroll J., November 4, 1983, and recorded judgment in [1984] I.L.R.M. 564.

hold a licence, cannot commit an offence under the Licensing Acts. In *Desmond v. Kennedy*, the nominee was charged on foot of the usual six-point summons. The evidence revealed that neither the nominee nor the company was aware that intoxicating liquor had been served or consumed on the premises after hours. The defence submitted that, having regard to the *Murtagh Properties* decision, the company was the proper person to be charged with the offences, not the nominee. The defence also argued that as the defendant was not the manager in control of the business and was not present when the alleged offence took place, he had not committed any offence arising from the unauthorised acts by other persons of which he, the nominee, had no knowledge.

Noting that in this case the defendant was charged with breaches of the Licensing Acts "as a person duly licensed to sell intoxicating liquor by retail", Carroll J. stated:

> "In my opinion, it cannot seriously be argued that the nominee of a limited company who has been appointed by it to hold the licence and to whom the licence has actually been granted is not 'the holder of a licence', even though he is not beneficially the owner of the licence or the licensed premises."[47]

She continued:

> "There is nothing to prevent a prosecution being brought against a nominee as the actual holder of the licence as an alternative to suing the limited company as beneficial owner thereof."[48]

The pivotal consideration in Carroll J.'s judgment was her concern that where a person agrees to be nominee he "impliedly undertakes responsibility under the Licensing Acts to see that the business is run in accordance with the law".[49]

Carroll J.'s approach in *Desmond v. Kennedy*, finding the nominee responsible as the holder of the licence, illustrates the concern expressed by Barrington J. in the *Murtagh Properties* decision. The fact that the nominee in *Desmond v. Kennedy* had delegated the management of the licensed business to a full-time manager and had taken no active part in the business, did not absolve him from being liable for offences committed while he was nominee.

3–18 The Supreme Court in *D.P.P. v. Roberts*[50] endorsed Barrington J.'s view in *Murtagh Properties*. Here the defendant was the nominee of a limited liability company but had ceased thereafter to have any part in the running of the business. Some time subsequently, she was convicted of three offences of selling intoxicating liquor during prohibited hours and of permitting intoxicating liquor to be consumed on the premises during prohibited hours, which resulted in the forfeiture of the licence.

---

[47] *Ibid.* at p. 8.
[48] *Ibid.*
[49] *Ibid.* at p. 10.
[50] [1987] I.R. 268.

It was argued on behalf of the defendant that although she held the licence as nominee of R. Ltd, as the company remained the real holder of the licence she could not incur liability unless she took an active part in the running of the premises. She could not, it was submitted, be convicted of an offence in the absence of *mens rea*. The Supreme Court held that as the nominee in this case had no "hand, act or part in the running of the premises", she could not be convicted as holder of the licence. Finlay C.J. accepted the arguments of "Mr Cassidy (as he then was)"[51] and accepted that as the offences were criminal offences, the defendant could not, in the absence of *mens rea* be convicted of such offences.

Finlay C.J. expressed his dissatisfaction with the practice of a body corporate holding a licence through a nominee and stated:

> "it seems to me there is a duty on the relevant authorities, having ascertained the facts as best they can, to raise the question of the responsibility of the nominee and his or her capacity to be answerable to the court, and the court would, in my view, be quite entitled, upon it being established to its satisfaction, that a nominee had not got an active role in the affairs of the licensed premises themselves, to refuse to renew a licence in that nominee's name."[52]

McCarthy J. in agreeing with Finlay C.J.'s conclusions observed:

> "But, it is said, once she agreed to be the nominee, she is liable; it would be invidious if it were otherwise. It is, indeed, invidious but that quality springs not from Mrs. Roberts but from those responsible for scrutinising applications for renewal at annual licensing sessions."[53]

Finlay C.J. stated that the legislature should address the issue as to whether licences should be confined to the body corporate itself or, if a nominee were to be appointed, that such nomination should be subject to certain qualifications including the extent of the participation which the nominee would have in the running of the licensed premises and the nominee's responsibility for the commission of offences in the licensed premises.

The more correct view is that the holder of the licence is the body corporate: the practice of appointing a nominee is inelegant and gives rise to confusion.

Persons who are not Entitled to Trade under a Licence

There are certain persons who are disqualified by law from holding a licence. **3–19**

[51] John Cassidy argued the case for Mrs Roberts but was appointed to the Circuit Court bench before judgment was delivered.
[52] *D.P.P. v. Roberts*, above, n.50, at 274.
[53] *Ibid.* at 282.

STATUTORY PROVISION

A licence cannot be granted to a person who is disqualified by law from holding a licence. Section 90 of the Licensing Act 1872 provides as follows:

> "In Ireland no licence or excise licence, as respectively defined in the preceding provisions of this Act in relation to Ireland, shall be granted under the Intoxicating Liquor Licensing Acts to any person or in respect of any premises declared by or in pursuance of any of the Intoxicating Liquor Licensing Acts or this Act to be disqualified persons or disqualified premises during the continuance of such disqualification. Any licence or excise licence held by any person so disqualified or attached to premises so disqualified shall be void."

Disqualified Persons

3–20 The following persons are disqualified from holding an intoxicating liquor licence:

1. a pawnbroker[54];
2. a moneylender[55];
3. a distiller, rectifier, compounder of spirits, bailiff, gaoler, police officer, sheriff's officer, or any person not being a householder[56];
4. a process server[57];
5. the holder of a licence who is convicted of an offence under sections 22, 23 or 24 of the Illicit Distillation (Ireland) Act 1831, is "for ever" disqualified from holding a licence for the sale of intoxicating liquor by retail.[58] Sections 22, 23 and 24 of the 1831 Act impose penalties for concealing, possessing or selling illicitly distilled spirits and a conviction results in the forfeiture of the licence;
6. a licensee who is convicted of permitting his premises to be a brothel shall be "disqualified for ever" from holding any licence for the sale of intoxicating liquor.[59] A conviction results in the forfeiture of the licence;

---

[54] Pawnbrokers' Act 1964, s.10.

[55] Moneylenders' Act 1933, s.6.

[56] Licensing (Ireland) Act 1833, s.13, provides:

> "No Distiller, nor Rectifier or compounder of Spirits, Bailiff, Gaoler, Turnkey, Constable, Sheriff, Sub-Sheriff, Sheriff's Officer, Peace Officer, or Keeper of any Turnpike Gate, nor any Person not being a Householder, shall be capable of receiving or holding a licence to sell Beer, Cider, or Spirits by Retail, to be drank or consumed on the Premises."

[57] Licensing (Ireland) Act 1833, s.2, provides:

> "No person appointed to serve Civil Bill process shall be capable, while he holds such office, of receiving or holding a licence to sell beer, cider, wine, or spirits by retail."

[58] Intoxicating Liquor (General) Act 1924, s.27(3).

[59] Licensing Act 1872, s.15.

7. although there is no statutory provision requiring that the holder of a licence be over the age of 18 years, the provisions contained in section 20 of the Excise Management Act 1827 providing that no entry of licensed premises can be made in the name of a person who is under 21 years of age would appear to apply. In *Rose v. Frogley*[60] it was held that a person under the age of 21 years was not disqualified from trading under a licence. However, O'Connor in *Irish Justice of the Peace*[61] noted that "the attention of the court in this case was not called to the Excise Management Act, 1827, section 20".

8. In *Re Brett*, the Recorder of Belfast expressed strong reservations as to whether a solicitor could properly carry on the trade of a licensed publican. He stated:

> "It seems to me a very improper position for any solicitor to place himself in, of applying for a licence, which means that he undertakes to conduct and manage a public house."[62]

[60] (1893) 17 Cox 685.
[61] O'Connor, *op. cit.* above, n.31, Vol. II, p. 747.
[62] (1899) 33 I.LT.R. 14 at 14.

Part II

LICENCES

Chapter 4

LICENCES TO SELL INTOXICATING LIQUOR BY RETAIL

Introduction

This chapter sets forth the categories and classifications of licences to sell intoxicating liquor to the public by retail from various premises. The Finance (1909–10) Act 1910 lists the various liquor licences, the excise duty payable in respect of each of them at that time and their duration. Since then, other licences for the sale of intoxicating liquors in certain places and which require the production of a certificate of the court or a Minister for their issue have been created by the legislature. The granting of certain licences by the Revenue Commissioners is, however, not conditional upon the production of either a court certificate or a certificate from a Minister. The statutory requirements pertaining to the grant or renewal of retail licences are grouped under the following categories: **4–1**

1. licences which are granted upon production of a certificate of the court;
2. licences which are granted without production of a certificate of the court or a Minister;
3. licences which are granted upon production of a certificate of a Minister.

A. Licences Granted upon Production of a Certificate of the Court

4–2 The grant and renewal of some licences does not depend upon the production of a tax clearance certificate. The practitioner is advised to consult the current Finance Act to confirm that the position as stated in this work has not changed. The excise duty on some licences is calculated with reference to the annual turnover of the premises. Section 66 of the Finance Act 1996 provides that turnover from the sales of meals shall not be taken into account as turnover for the purposes of calculating duty in respect of a spirit retailer's on-licence.

1. Public House

4–3 **Licence** This is also known as a spirit retailer's on-licence. It authorises the sale at any one time to one person for consumption on or off the premises of any liquor. Schedule 1 of the Finance (1909–10) Act 1910 specifies that such liquor may be sold in the following quantities:

1. sales of spirits, wine or sweets: any quantity not exceeding two gallons or not exceeding one dozen reputed quart bottles;
2. sales of beer or cider: any quantity not exceeding four and a half gallons, or not exceeding two dozen reputed quart bottles, but not in any larger quantity.

4–4 **Expiry** The licence expires on September 30 of each year. Where an application for a tax clearance certificate is made before June 1 (being not less than four months prior to the commencement date of the licence for the following year), and the certificate has not yet been issued or refused or it has been refused and the applicant has appealed against such refusal in accordance with section 242(6) of the Finance Act 1992, then the licence continues in force beyond its expiry date, pending either the issue or refusal of the certificate or, in the case of an appeal, the final determination of that appeal.

Where the tax clearance certificate issues thereafter, the licence expires upon the grant of a new licence. Where the certificate is refused or the applicant's appeal against the refusal is unsuccessful, the licence expires not later than seven days after such refusal or the determination of the appeal.

4–5 **Excise Duty**[1] The excise duty payable on the licence is provided for in section 155 of the Finance Act 1992. Where the annual turnover is not yet established,

[1] A registration fee of £0.12 is also payable in respect of all licences.

the duty is equal to the sum paid when the premises was last licensed, subject to a minimum rate of £200; where a licence is granted in respect of premises not previously licensed, a rate of duty of £200 is payable. Section 155(2)(b)(iii) measures the appropriate rate of excise duty in accordance with the level of the annual turnover of the licensed premises. The table referred to specifies the rates of excise duty in accordance with the level of annual turnover as follows:

Where the level of annual turnover is under £150,000, the excise duty is £200. However, where the level exceeds:

1. £150,000, but is less than £300,000 the excise duty is £400;
2. £300,000, but is less than £500,000 the excise duty is £900;
3. £500,000, but is less than £750,000, the excise duty is £1,400;
4. £750,000 but is less than £1,000,000, the excise duty is £2,000;
5. £1,000,000 or more, the excise duty is £3,000.

Tax Clearance Certificate A spirit retailer's on-licence shall not be granted or renewed by the Collector of Customs and Excise unless a tax clearance certificate in relation to that licence has been issued in accordance with section 242 of the Finance Act 1992.[2] 4–6

Court Certificate: Grant The grant of the licence by the Collector of Customs and Excise is conditional upon the production of a certificate of the Circuit Court.[3]

Court Certificate: Renewal Where renewal of the licence is sought, it is not necessary to produce a certificate of the District Court to an officer of the Revenue Commissioners empowered to grant a renewal of the licence except in certain circumstances.[4]

Type of Premises This licence attaches to a public house.

2. Hotel

Licence There are several types of licence which can attach to premises purporting to be hotels.[5] These are as follows: 4–7

---

[2] Finance (1909–10) Act 1910, s.49, as amended by the Finance Act 1992, s.156.
[3] Licensing (Ireland) Act 1833 and the Courts (Supplemental Provisions) Act 1961.
[4] See the Courts (No. 2) Act 1986, s.4, where these circumstances are enumerated.
[5] See below, chap. 8, "Hotels".

1. a publican's licence[6];
2. a licence issued pursuant to the provisions of section 2(2) of the Licensing (Ireland) Act 1902 which for the purposes of the Finance (1909–10) Act 1910 is deemed to be a spirit retailer's on-licence or publican's licence;
3. a licence in respect of which effect was given to section 42(1) of the Tourist Traffic Act 1952.

4–8 **Expiry** The licence expires on September 30 of each year. Where an application for a tax clearance certificate is made before June 1 (being not less than four months prior to the commencement date of the licence for the following year) and the certificate has not yet been issued or refused or it has been refused but the applicant has appealed against such refusal in accordance with section 242(6) of the Finance Act 1992, then the licence continues in force beyond its expiry date, pending either the issue or refusal of the certificate or, in the case of an appeal, the final determination of that appeal.

Where the tax clearance certificate issues thereafter, the licence expires upon the grant of a new licence. Where the certificate is refused or the applicant's appeal against the refusal is unsuccessful, the licence expires not later than seven days after such refusal or the determination of the appeal.

4–9 **Excise Duty** The excise duty payable on the licence is provided for in section 155 of the Finance Act 1992. Where the annual turnover is not yet established, the duty is equal to the sum paid when the premises was last licensed, subject to a minimum rate of £200; where a licence is granted in respect of premises not previously licensed, a rate of duty of £200 is payable. Section 155(2)(b)(iii) measures the appropriate rate of excise duty in accordance with the level of the annual turnover of the licensed premises. The table referred to specifies the rates of excise duty in accordance with the level of annual turnover as follows:

Where the level of annual turnover is under £150,000, the excise duty is £200. However, where the level exceeds:

1. £150,000, but is less than £300,000 the excise duty is £400;
2. £300,000, but is less than £500,000 the excise duty is £900;
3. £500,000, but is less than £750,000, the excise duty is £1,400;
4. £750,000 but is less than £1,000,000, the excise duty is £2,000;
5. £1,000,000 or more, the excise duty is £3,000.

4–10 **Tax Clearance Certificate** The licence shall not be granted or renewed by the Collector of Customs and Excise unless a tax clearance certificate in relation

[6] See above, para. 4–3.

to that licence has been issued in accordance with section 242 of the Finance Act 1992.[7]

Court Certificate: Grant The grant of the licence by the Collector of Customs and Excise is conditional upon the production of a certificate of the Circuit Court.

Court Certificate: Renewal Where a renewal of the licence is sought, it is not necessary to produce a certificate of the District Court to an officer of the Revenue Commissioners empowered to grant a renewal of the licence except in certain circumstances.[8]

Other Conditions Although a certificate of the court is not required for the renewal of a licence granted under the provisions of section 2(2) of the Licensing (Ireland) Act 1902, the licence shall not be renewed without production to the Revenue Commissioners of a certificate that the hotel in respect of which the licence was granted registered in the register of hotels kept by Bord Fáilte Éireann.[9] **4–11**

This, however, only applies to licences granted after the passing of the Intoxicating Liquor Act 1960, by virtue of section 2(2) of the 1902 Act. Licences issued pursuant to the provisions of section 42(1) of the Tourist Traffic Act 1952 cannot be renewed without production to the Revenue Commissioners of a certificate that the hotel in respect of which the licence was granted is registered in the register of hotels kept by Bord Fáilte.

In applying for a renewal of a hotel licence, an applicant should notify the Revenue Commissioners that the licence is one in respect of which effect was given to section 42(1) of the Tourist Traffic Act 1952, or which was granted under section 2(2) of the 1902 Act after the Intoxicating Liquor Act 1960 was passed.

3. Restaurant

Licence The special restaurant licence was created by the Intoxicating Liquor Act 1988. It is granted by the Revenue Commissioners to a person in respect of a restaurant of which he is the owner and occupier. It authorises: **4–12**

1. the supply of intoxicating liquor for consumption on those premises; and
2. the consumption of intoxicating liquor on those premises;

if, in each case, the intoxicating liquor is:

---

[7] Finance (1909–10) Act 1910, s.49, as amended by the Finance Act 1992, s.156.
[8] See Courts (No. 2) Act 1986, s.4.
[9] *Ibid.*, s.4(9).

(i) ordered by or on behalf of the person for whom a substantial meal has been ordered;

(ii) supplied in either the waiting area or the dining area of the restaurant;

(iii) consumed in the waiting area of the restaurant before the meal by the person for whom the meal has been ordered, or consumed by that person in the dining area of the restaurant either during the meal or any time not later than thirty minutes after the meal has ended; and

(iv) paid for at the same time as the meal is paid for,

providing always that suitable beverages other than intoxicating liquor (including drinking water) are also available for consumption.

A special restaurant licence is deemed, for the purposes of the Finance (1909–10) Act 1910, to be a retailer's on-licence.[10]

4–13 **Expiry** The licence expires on September 30 of each year. Where an application for a tax clearance certificate is made before June 1 (being not less than four months prior to the commencement date of the licence for the following year) and the certificate has not yet been issued or refused or it has been refused but the applicant has appealed against such refusal in accordance with section 242(6) of the Finance Act 1992, then the licence continues in force beyond its expiry date pending either the issue or refusal of the certificate or, in the case of an appeal, the final determination of that appeal.

Where the tax clearance certificate issues thereafter, the licence expires upon the grant of a new licence. Where the certificate is refused or the applicant's appeal against the refusal is unsuccessful, the licence expires not later than seven days after such refusal or the determination of the appeal.

4–14 **Excise Duty** A fee of £3,000 is payable to the Revenue Commissioners on the initial grant of the special restaurant licence.[11] The rate of excise duty on renewal is £200.[12]

Tax Clearance Certificate A tax clearance certificate must be produced to the Revenue Commissioners before a special restaurant licence will be granted or renewed.[13]

Court Certificate: Grant The grant of the licence by the Revenue Commissioners is conditional upon the production of a certificate of the Circuit Court (and the specified fee and a tax clearance certificate).[14]

---

[10] Intoxicating Liquor Act 1988, s.7(2).
[11] *Ibid.*, s.9(1)(b).
[12] Finance Act 1992, s.155(2)(b).
[13] Finance (1909–10) Act 1910, s.49, as amended by the Finance Act 1992, s.156.
[14] Intoxicating Liquor Act 1988, s.9(1)(a).

Court Certificate: Renewal A court certificate need not be produced at renewal stage unless an objection to the renewal has been duly made.

Other Conditions A special restaurant licence is not renewable without the production to the Revenue Commissioners of a Bord Fáilte certificate within the meaning of the Intoxicating Liquor Act 1988.[15] When applying for the renewal of a special restaurant licence, the applicant is obliged to inform the Revenue Commissioners that the licence is a special restaurant licence granted under the Intoxicating Liquor Act 1988. 4–15

Type of Premises The type of premises to which the special restaurant licence attaches is a premises structurally adapted and used for the purposes of supplying substantial meals to the public for consumption on the premises. Other business carried on therein must be ancillary and subsidiary to the provision of such meals. The premises must not contain a bar. 4–16

4. Holiday Camp Premises

Licence This licence was created by Part VI of the Tourist Traffic Act 1952 and provides for the grant of an on-licence in respect of a holiday camp premises, or a part or parts thereof, and which has proper residential accommodation for at least 250 guests at any one time. The rateable valuation of the premises must not be less than £200, and the buildings thereon must be wholly or mainly of a permanent character. A holiday camp must be registered for the time being in the register of holiday camps kept by Bord Fáilte. 4–17

The holder of the licence is entitled to supply intoxicating liquor to any person on the licensed premises at the time specified in section 13 of the Intoxicating Liquor Act 1927, as in the case of hotels and restaurants. The holder is also entitled to apply for special exemption orders.[16] He is not obliged to separate structurally the premises to which his licence attaches from areas in which non-licensed business is conducted.

Expiry The licence expires on September 30 of each year. Where an application for a tax clearance certificate is made before June 1 (being not less than four months prior to the commencement date of the licence for the following year) and it has not yet been issued or refused or it has been refused and the applicant has appealed against such refusal in accordance with section 242(6) of the Finance Act 1992, then the licence continues in force beyond its expiry date pending either the issue or refusal of the certificate or, in the case of an appeal, the final determination of that appeal. 4–18

---

[15] Courts (No. 2) Act 1986, s.4(9A).
[16] Tourist Traffic Act 1952, s.52.

Where the tax clearance certificate issues thereafter, the licence expires upon the grant of a licence. Where the certificate is refused or the applicant's appeal against the refusal is unsuccessful, the licence expires not later than seven days after such refusal or the determination of the appeal.[17]

4–19 **Excise Duty** The excise duty payable on the grant and renewal of a licence is provided for in section 155(2)(b)(ii) of the Finance Act 1992 and is £200.

Tax Clearance Certificate A spirit retailer's on-licence shall not be granted by the Collector of Customs and Excise unless a tax clearance certificate in relation to that licence has been issued in accordance with section 242 of the Finance Act 1992.[18]

4–20 **Court Certificate: Grant** The applicant must apply to the Circuit Court for a certificate declaring him to be duly entitled to receive an on-licence in respect of the premises.[19]

Court Certificate: Renewal A court certificate is not required to renew the licence unless an objection has been lodged.[20] Where an unsuccessful objection has been made to the renewal of the licence, the certificate of the court should be as to:

1. the good character of the licensee;
2. the peaceable and orderly manner in which the licensed premises were conducted in the year ending on the expiry of the licence;
3. the orderly manner in which the holiday camp in which the premises are situate was conducted in the year ending on the expiry of the licence.[21]

Type of Premises There are at present two holiday camp premises in this country, namely Trabolgan and Mosney.[22] Bord Fáilte requirements for registration are extremely stringent which is probably why there are not more such premises in the country.

---

[17] Finance Act 1993, s.77, provides that a licence in respect of any holiday camp premises or a part or part thereof shall be deemed, for the purposes of the Finance (1909–10) Act 1910, to be a spirit retailer's on-licence.
[18] Finance Act 1992, s.156, which amends the Finance (1909–10) Act 1910, s.49, and the Finance Act 1993, s.77.
[19] Tourist Traffic Act 1952, s.44.
[20] Courts (No. 2) Act 1986, s.4.
[21] *Ibid.*, s.4(7).
[22] Only one holiday camp licence was issued in the licensing year 1994–1995.

5. Railway Refreshment Room

Licence A licence attaching to a railway refreshment room is a full publican's licence and in that regard the holder is entitled to sell to all persons, during permitted hours, for consumption on and off the premises. Section 14 of the Intoxicating Liquor Act 1927 provides that intoxicating liquor can be sold at any time at a railway station to persons "who have travelled or hold tickets entitling them to travel on those trains for a distance of not less than ten miles to or from such railway station". The provisions relating to prohibited hours do not apply in respect of those particular persons. 4–21

Furthermore, section 5 of the Intoxicating Liquor Act 1962 inserted a new section, namely section 14(aa) of the Intoxicating Liquor Act 1927 which provides for the sale "at any time" at a railway station "being a station to which persons who have recently travelled or are about to travel by ship resort for refreshment" of intoxicating liquor to passengers who have recently travelled or hold tickets entitling them "and are about to travel by ship for a distance of not less than fifty miles".

This licence is an on-licence for the sale of intoxicating liquor in railway refreshment rooms. The restriction against the grant of licences for the sale of intoxicating liquor for consumption on or off the premises contained in the Licensing (Ireland) Act 1902 does not apply to the grant of a licence for railway refreshment rooms.

Expiry The licence expires on September 30 of each year. Where an application for a tax clearance certificate is made before June 1 (being not less than four months prior to the commencement date of the licence for the following year), and the certificate has not yet been issued or refused or it has been refused but the applicant has appealed against such refusal in accordance with section 242(6) of the Finance Act 1992, then the licence continues in force beyond its expiry date, pending either the issue or refusal of the certificate or, in the case of an appeal, the final determination of that appeal. 4–22

Where the tax clearance certificate issues thereafter, the licence expires upon the grant of a new licence. Where the certificate is refused or the applicant's appeal against the refusal is unsuccessful, the licence expires not later than seven days after such refusal or the determination of the appeal.

Excise Duty The excise duty payable on the licence is provided for in section 155 of the Finance Act 1992. Where the annual turnover is not yet established, the duty is equal to the sum paid when the premises was last licensed, subject to a minimum rate of £200; where a licence is granted in respect of premises not previously licensed, a rate of duty of £200 is payable. Section 155(2)(b)(iii) measures the appropriate rate of excise duty in accordance with the level of the annual turnover of the licensed premises. The table referred to specifies the rates of excise duty in accordance with the level of annual turnover as follows: 4–23

Where the level of annual turnover is under £150,000, the excise duty is £200. However, where the level exceeds:

1. £150,000, but is less than £300,000 the excise duty is £400;
2. £300,000, but is less than £500,000 the excise duty is £900;
3. £500,000, but is less than £750,000, the excise duty is £1,400;
4. £750,000 but is less than £1,000,000, the excise duty is £2,000;
5. £1,000,000 or more, the excise duty is £3,000.

4–24 **Tax Clearance Certificate** A licence shall not be granted by the Collector of Customs and Excise unless a tax clearance certificate in relation to that licence has been issued in accordance with section 242 of the Finance Act 1992.[23]

Court Certificate: Grant The established mode is to apply to the Circuit Court for a certificate entitling the applicant to receive a licence in respect of a railway refreshment room.[24]

Court Certificate: Renewal It is not necessary to apply to the annual licensing District Court for a certificate to renew the licence unless an objection has been lodged.

Type of Premises Four railway refreshment room licences have been issued by the Revenue Commissioners for the licensing year 1994–1995.

6. Beer Retailer's On-Licence

4–25 **Licence** This licence authorises the sale for consumption either on or off the premises of beer and cider in retail quantities, *i.e.* the sale at any one time to any one person of up to four and a half gallons, or up to two dozen reputed quart bottles. It is also known as a "beerhouse licence". This licence is rarely applied for now as the spirit retailer's on-licence, also known as the publican's licence, authorises the sale of any liquor. A person who at any one time holds a six-day beerhouse licence and a seven-day beerhouse licence may apply to the District Court for an order transferring the seven-day licence to the premises to which the six-day licence attaches and the six-day licence cannot be renewed thereafter.[25] The application will be granted on proof that the applicant has obtained the consent of the holder of the seven-day licence to the transfer.[26]

[23] Finance (1909–10) Act 1910, s.49, as amended by the Finance Act 1992, s.156.

[24] It is accepted that the Licensing (Ireland) Act 1833, which applies to licences to sell beer, cider or spirits to be consumed in the house where sold, applies to a railway refreshment room.

[25] Intoxicating Liquor Act 1943, s.31(2).

[26] Intoxicating Liquor Act 1960, s.26.

Expiry The licence expires on September 30 of each year.

Excise Duty The licence attracts an excise duty of £200.[27]

Tax Clearance Certificate No tax clearance certificate is required for the grant or renewal of a beer retailer's on-licence.

Court Certificate: Grant A certificate of the Circuit Court is required for the grant of such licence.[28]

Court Certificate: Renewal It is not necessary to produce a certificate of the annual licensing District Court in order to renew the licence, unless an objection has been lodged to the renewal.[29]

Type of Premises These licences attach to public houses: only seven were issued for the licensing year 1993–1994.[30]

7. Cider Retailer's On-Licence

A cider retailer's on-licence authorises the sale of cider, in retail quantities, for consumption either on or off the premises to any one person of any quantity up to four and a half gallons, or not exceeding two dozen reputed quart bottles.[31] No more than seven cider retailer's on-licences were issued for the licensing year 1993–1994.[32] 4–26

Expiry The licence expires on September 30 of each year.

Excise Duty The excise duty payable on the licence is £200.[33]

Tax Clearance Certificate A tax clearance certificate is not required.

Court Certificate: Grant A certificate of the Circuit Court is required for the grant of this licence.[34]

---

[27] Finance Act 1992, Sched. 6, Pt. I

[28] Excise Licences Act 1825, s.13 and Licensing (Ireland) Act 1833, s.2. Note also that the Intoxicating Liquor Act 1943, s.31(1), provided for the conversion of these licences into full publican's licences by virtue of the transfer of an ordinary publican's licence to such premises. This has now been repealed by the Intoxicating Liquor Act 1960, s.3.

[29] Courts (No. 2) Act 1986, s.4.

[30] Statistical Report of the Revenue Commissioners 1994.

[31] Finance (1909–10) Act 1910, Sched. 1.

[32] Statistical Report of the Revenue Commissioners 1994.

[33] Finance Act 1992, s.154.

[34] Excise Licences Act 1825, s.13, and the Licensing Act (Ireland) Act 1833, s.2.

Court Certificate: Renewal It is not necessary to produce a certificate of the annual licensing District Court in order to renew this licence except where an objection has been lodged.[35]

8. Beer Retailer's Off-Licence

4–27 **Licence** This licence authorises the sale of beer and cider for consumption off the premises to any one person of any quantity up to four and a half gallons, or up to two reputed quart bottles.[36] This licence is commonly referred to as an off-licence and is one of the three types of licence which may attach to supermarket premises.

Expiry The licence expires on September 30 of each year.

Excise Duty The excise duty payable on the licence is £200.[37]

4–28 **Tax Clearance Certificate** The holder of a beer retailer's off-licence is not *per se* obliged to apply for a tax clearance certificate for the purposes of the grant or renewal of such licence. However, as most supermarkets also hold a wine retailer's off-licence and a spirit retailer's off-licence and the grant of the latter requires the production of a tax clearance certificate, a tax clearance certificate is usually obtained.

Court Certificate: Grant When applying for such licence, a certificate must be obtained from the District Court as to the good character of the applicant, the suitability of the premises and the fact that the premises are rated at £15 or more, if situate in a city or town with a population exceeding 10,000. If the premises are situate elsewhere, the rateable valuation must be £8 or more. The court must also certify that the premises has been in the exclusive occupation of the applicant for the three months prior to the date of the certificate.[38]

Court Certificate: Renewal A court certificate is not necessary unless an objection has been lodged.[39] However, an applicant for renewal must produce a statutory declaration that the conditions in section 2 of the Beer Licences Regulation (Ireland) Act 1877 concerning the rateable valuation of the premises

---

[35] Courts (No. 2) Act 1986, s.4.
[36] Finance (1909–10) Act 1910, Sched. 1, Scale 7.
[37] Finance Act 1992, s.154.
[38] Beerhouses (Ireland) Act 1864, s.3; Licensing Act (Ireland) 1874, ss.8, 37; Beer Licences Regulation (Ireland) Act 1877, s.2; Beer Retailers' and Spirit Grocers' Retail Licences (Ireland) Act 1900.
[39] Courts (No. 2) Act 1986, s.4

have been met and that the premises have been in the exclusive occupation of the licence holder for at least three months preceding the date of the application for renewal.[40]

Type of Premises This licence is one of three licences commonly attached to a supermarket premises, the other two being the spirit retailer's off-licence and the wine retailer's off-licence.

9. Spirit Retailer's Off-Licence

Licence This licence (previously known as the spirit grocer's licence) authorises the sale, for consumption off the premises, of spirits to any one person, in any quantity up to two gallons, or up to one dozen reputed quart bottles, but not in open vessels.[41] **4–29**

Expiry The licence expires on September 30 of each year. Where an application for a tax clearance certificate is made before June 1 (being not less than four months prior to the commencement date of the licence for the following year) and the certificate has not yet been issued or refused or it has been refused but the applicant has appealed against such refusal in accordance with section 242(6) of the Finance Act 1992, then the licence continues in force beyond its expiry date, pending either the issue or refusal of the certificate or, in the case of an appeal, the final determination of that appeal.

Where the tax clearance certificate issues thereafter, the licence expires upon the grant of a new licence. Where the certificate is refused or the applicant's appeal against the refusal is unsuccessful, the licence expires not later than seven days after such refusal or the determination of the appeal.

Excise Duty The excise duty payable on the licence is £200 per year.[42]

Tax Clearance Certificate The licence will not be granted by the Revenue Commissioners unless a tax clearance certificate in relation to the licence has been issued in accordance with section 242 of the Finance Act 1992.[43] **4–30**

Court Certificate: Grant An application must be made to the District Court for a certificate as to the good character of the applicant and suitability of the premises.[44]

---

[40] *Ibid.*
[41] Finance (1909–10) Act 1910, Sched. 1.
[42] Finance Act 1992, s.154.
[43] *Ibid.*, s.156, which amends the Finance (1909–10) Act 1910, s.49.
[44] Licensing Act 1872, s.82; Licensing Act (Ireland) 1874, s.9.

Court Certificate: Renewal Since the entry into force of the Courts (No. 2) Act 1986 it has not been necessary to apply to the annual licensing District Court for a certificate, unless an objection has been lodged.[45]

Type of Premises This licence usually attaches to a supermarket or a premises which sells intoxicating liquor for consumption off the premises. It is held together with a beer retailer's off-licence and a wine retailer's off-licence.

10. Cider Retailer's Off-Licence

4–31 **Licence** This licence authorises the sale of cider for consumption off the premises to any one person of any quantity up to four and a half gallons or up to two dozen reputed quart bottles.[46]

The grant of a cider retailer's off-licence is now restricted by the provisions of subsection (2) of section 28 of the Intoxicating Liquor Act 1962 which provides as follows:

> "The Revenue Commissioners shall not grant, whether by way of new licence or of transfer or renewal of an existing licence, a cider retailer's off-licence, in respect of any premises other than premises in respect of which a spirit retailer's off-licence or a wholesale dealer's licence for the sale of spirits, beer or wine is in force."

This licence is now very rare. The holder of a beer retailer's off-licence is entitled to sell cider and beer by retail without taking out a cider retailer's off-licence.[47]

Expiry The licence expires on September 30 of each year.

Excise Duty The excise duty payable on the licence is £200.[48]

4–32 **Tax Clearance Certificate** A tax clearance certificate is not required for the grant or renewal of this licence.

Court Certificate: Grant A certificate from the District Court is required for the grant of this licence.[49]

Court Certificate: Renewal It is not necessary to produce a certificate of the annual licensing District Court in order to renew this licence except where an objection has been lodged.

---

45 Courts (No. 2) Act 1986, s.4.
46 Finance (1909–10) Act 1910, Sched. 1.
47 *Ibid.*
48 Finance Act 1992, s.154.
49 See O'Connor, *The Irish Justice of the Peace* (2nd ed., 1915) Vol. II.

Type of Premises This licence is granted by the Revenue Commissioners to a person who is:

1. the holder of a spirit retailer's off-licence; or
2. the holder of a wholesale dealer's licence for the sale of spirits, beer or wine.

The licence is granted only in respect of premises to which a spirit retailer's off-licence or a wholesale dealer's licence for the sale of spirits, beer or wine attaches and is in force.[50]

B. Licences Granted without Production of a Certificate of the Court or the Minister

1. Theatre

Licence This licence entitles the holder to sell or expose for sale by retail intoxicating liquor in the theatre to which the licence attaches during the period beginning half an hour before the commencement of a performance in the theatre and ending half an hour after the termination of such performance. It authorises the sale of intoxicating liquor to employees in the theatre and to persons who have engaged or paid for seats in the theatre for the performance taking place, or which took place during the permitted time or either of the permitted times then current.[51] Twenty-three of these licences have been issued by the Revenue Commissioners for the licensing year 1994–1995. 4–33

Expiry The licence expires on September 30 of each year. Where an application for a tax clearance certificate has been made before June 1 (being not less than four months prior to the commencement date of the licence for the following year) and the certificate has not yet been issued or refused or it has been refused but the applicant has appealed against such refusal in accordance with section 242(6) of the Finance Act 1992, then the licence continues in force beyond its expiry date, pending either the issue or refusal of the certificate or, in the case of an appeal, the final determination of that appeal. 4–34

Where the tax clearance certificate issues thereafter, the licence expires upon the grant of a new licence. Where the certificate is refused or the applicant's appeal against the refusal is unsuccessful, the licence expires not later than seven days after such refusal or the determination of the appeal.

Excise Duty The excise duty payable on a theatre licence is £200.[52] 4–35

[50] Intoxicating Liquor Act 1960, s.34, and Intoxicating Liquor Act 1962, s.28(2).
[51] Intoxicating Liquor Act 1927, s.21.
[52] Finance Act 1992, s.155(2)(b)(ii).

Tax Clearance Certificate A tax clearance certificate must be produced to the Revenue Commissioners before the licence will be granted or renewed.[53]

Court Certificate It is not necessary to obtain a certificate of the court that the applicant is entitled to receive a theatre licence, nor is a court certificate necessary at renewal stage. However, since *Point Exhibition Company Ltd v. The Revenue Commissioners,*[54] theatres which have not obtained a patent from the Department of An Taoiseach have applied to the District Court for a music and singing licence. Accordingly, a theatre licence can issue in respect of the premises on the basis that it is a place of public entertainment for the purposes of section 7 of the Excise Act 1835.

2. Wine Retailer's Off-Licence

4–36 **Licence** This licence, which is one of the three licences normally attaching to a supermarket premises, authorises the retail sale of wine for consumption off the premises, at any one time, to any one person of any quantity up to two gallons, or up to one dozen reputed quart bottles.

The Revenue Commissioners can grant a wine retailer's off-licence, whether by way of a new licence, or transfer or renewal of an existing licence, to a chemist and druggist, a pharmaceutical chemist or registered druggist, or a person who is for the time being the holder of a spirit retailer's off-licence or a beer retailer's off-licence then in force. The licence may be granted only in respect of premises where a business of the kind described above[55] is being carried on or in respect of which a spirit retailer's off-licence or a beer retailer's off-licence is in force. Thus, the grant of this licence is restricted to persons who already hold the above off-licences and to persons who carry on business as chemists and druggists.

Expiry The licence expires on September 30 of each year.

Excise Duty The excise duty payable on this licence is £200.[56]

4–37 **Tax Clearance Certificate** An applicant for a wine retailer's off-licence need not obtain a tax clearance certificate as a precondition to the grant of a licence.

Court Certificate: Grant and Renewal The application is directed to the Revenue Commissioners and no court certificate is necessary.

[53] Finance (1909–10) Act 1910, s.49, as amended by the Finance Act 1992, s.156.
[54] [1993] 2 I.R. 551.
[55] Intoxicating Liquor Act 1927, s.61, and the Intoxicating Liquor Act 1962, s.28(1).
[56] Finance Act 1992, s.154.

3. Wine Retailer's On-Licence

Licence This licence authorises the retail sale, for consumption on and off the premises, of wine to any one person in any quantity up to two gallons or up to one dozen reputed quart bottles. 4–38

Section 50 of the Finance Act 1989 abolished the refreshment house licence. However, the grant of a wine retailer's on-licence licence is confined to a person who owns a refreshment house. Refreshment house is defined in section 50 as:

> "all houses, rooms, shops or buildings kept open for public refreshment, resort and entertainment at any time between the hours of 10 o'clock and 7 o'clock of the following morning, not being licensed for the sale of beer, cider, wine or spirits respectively, shall be deemed to be refreshment houses within this Act".

The holder of the licence is entitled to sell fine wine, sherry and any fermented liquor containing less than 23 per cent vol. of proof spirit.[57]

Expiry The licence expires on September 30 each year. Where an application for a tax clearance certificate is made according to statute and a tax clearance certificate has not yet been issued or refused, or a tax clearance certificate has been refused and the applicant has appealed against such refusal, then the licence continues in force beyond its expiry date. Where the tax clearance certificate issues thereafter, the licence expires upon the grant of the new licence. Where it is refused or the appeal is unsuccessful, the licence expires seven days later. 4–39

Excise duty The excise duty payable on this licence is £200.[58]

Tax Clearance Certificate The applicant must produce a tax clearance certificate for the grant and renewal of the licence.

Licence: Grant Section 13 of the Refreshment Houses (Ireland) Act 1860 sets forth the procedure which must be followed and the details which must be provided to the Commissioners of Inland Revenue by a prospective applicant. The applicant must specify the following: 4–40

1. his true christian name, surname and place of abode;
2. description and situation of the house for which the licence is required;
3. net annual value of such house.

The Commissioners then forward a copy of the relevant form to the superintendent of the Garda Síochána within whose area the premises are situate and

---

[57] Imposition of Duties (No. 244) (Excise Duties on Spirits, Beer and Hydrocarbon Oils) Order 1979 (S.I. No. 415 of 1979), art. 16, Sched. 2.
[58] Finance Act 1992, s.154.

to the District Court clerk. The Commissioners notify the Garda Síochána and the District Court clerk of the fact that a licence will be granted pursuant to such requisition on or immediately after a date to be specified in the notice, unless a notice of objection is lodged. This notice of objection must be signed by a District Court judge.

The licence must be granted if no notice of objection thereto has been lodged within the 30-day period prescribed. As in the case of an on-licence, if the District Court judge refuses to allow the licence to be issued, he must declare the grounds of such refusal. Where the judge has refused to allow the licence to issue, the applicant for the licence can appeal to the Circuit Court. Section 15 of the Refreshment Houses (Ireland) Act 1860 Act provides that there must be 15 days between the making of the order of refusal and the hearing of the appeal. The Circuit Court judge is not entitled to accept any ground of objection other than those stated in the District Court judge's order of refusal. If the appeal succeeds the Supervisor of Excise "shall grant such licence to the appellant on the production . . . of a certificate from the Clerk of the Peace . . . that the order of refusal had been reversed".[59]

Thus, it is only when an objection has been lodged to the grant of this licence that the District Court is involved. When a notice of objection has been lodged, the applicant for the licence is summoned to a sitting of the District Court to show cause against the objection. Otherwise, the licence is renewed as described above and is not necessary to produce a certificate of the court.

4–41 **Licence: Renewal** A wine retailer's on-licence is renewed without a court certificate, unless objections are lodged in the form as required by the Courts (No. 2) Act 1986. Section 50 of the Intoxicating Liquor Act 1988 amended the definition of "licence" contained in section 4 of the Courts (No. 2) Act 1986. Section 4 of the 1986 Act as amended provides:

> " 'licence' means a licence for the sale of intoxicating liquor for the grant of which the production of a certificate of the District Court or the Circuit Court is required and includes a licence granted under section 13 of the Refreshment Houses (Ireland) Act, 1860".

Type of Premises The wine retailer's on-licence attaches to restaurants and night clubs. A person who holds a wine retailer's on-licence is entitled to apply to the District Court at any time for a restaurant certificate. The restaurant certificate entitles him to apply for special exemption orders, if he can prove that the occasion to which the special exemption order relates is a special event, or if the premises to which the application relates has the benefit of a public dancing licence.

Many night-clubs first obtain a wine retailers' on-licence by fulfilling the criteria above and then apply to the District Court for a full restaurant certificate.

---

[59] Refreshment Houses (Ireland) Act 1860, s.16.

4. Greyhound Racetrack[60]

Licence The holder of a greyhound racetrack licence may apply to the Revenue Commissioners for a licence to sell intoxicating liquor at the racetrack. Section 18 of the Intoxicating Liquor Act 1962, as amended by section 49 of the Intoxicating Liquor Act 1988, provides for the grant of the licence. The licence authorises the sale of intoxicating liquor at the track on the occasion of: 4–42

1. a greyhound race meeting;
2. a greyhound sale;
3. greyhound trials,

during a period:

(i) beginning 30 minutes before the commencement of the race meeting, sale, or trials, as the case may be; and

(ii) ending, in the case of a race meeting, 30 minutes after the time at which the last race of the meeting starts and, in the case of a sale or trials, at the conclusion of the sale or trials, as the case may be.

Expiry The licence expires on September 30 of each year but is deemed to continue in force if an application for a tax clearance certificate is duly made. 4–43

Excise Duty The annual excise duty payable on this licence is £200.[61]

Tax Clearance Certificate This licence is classified as a spirit retailer's on-licence as specified in the First Schedule to the Finance (1909–10) Act 1910, so a tax clearance certificate is required for the grant and renewal of the licence.[62]

5. Railway Restaurant Car

Licence This licence authorises the retail sale of any intoxicating liquor to railway passengers in a railway car. The licence is taken out by the railway company or other person owning the car.[63] Forty-seven of these licences have been issued by the Revenue Commissioners for the licensing year 1994–1995. 4–44

Expiry The licence expires on September 30 of each year.

---

[60] Thirteen greyhound racetrack licences were issued by the Revenue Commissioners for the licensing year 1994–1995.

[61] Finance Act 1992, s.155, as amended by s.78 of the Finance Act 1993.

[62] Finance Act 1993, s.77(1).

[63] Finance (1909–10) Act 1910, Sched. 1.

Excise Duty The excise duty payable on this licence is £200.[64]

Tax Clearance Certificate It is not necessary to apply for a tax clearance certificate for the grant or renewal of this licence.

6. Passenger Vessel

4–45 **Licence** This licence authorises the retail sale of intoxicating liquor to passengers on a vessel of any description employed for the carriage and conveyance of passengers which goes from any place in the State to any other place in the State, or goes from and returns to the same place in the State on the same day.[65] Twenty-three annual passenger vessel licences were issued by the Revenue Commissioners in the licensing year 1994–1995.

There are two types of licence. The first is the annual licence which may be taken out by the master or other person belonging to the vessel nominated by the owner of the vessel. Secondly, a day licence which is in force for one day only, may be taken out by the master or other person belonging to the boat nominated by the owner of the boat. The licence is granted to the master of the vessel (the captain) and where he ceases to be captain, the licence may be transferred to any person who is for the time being captain. Where the vessel is sold or leased to some other person, the licence may be transferred to another vessel owned by the owner. Where a sale or lease of a licensed vessel takes place, an application by the new owner for a licence should be made as the original licence ceases to have effect, once the transfer has taken place. The licence authorises the sale of intoxicating liquor at any time to persons on the ship. Section 72 of the Licensing Act 1872 provides that the provisions in that Act which relate to offences under the Licensing Acts and related penalties, shall not apply in relation to the sale of intoxicating liquor in packet boats. The unrestricted sale and supply of intoxicating liquor to passengers during whatever hours the passengers are on the vessel is permitted.[66]

Excise Duty The excise duty payable on the annual licence is £200; the excise duty on the day licence is £40.

Expiry The licence expires on September 30 of each year.

Tax Clearance Certificate An applicant for the grant or renewal of a passenger vessel licence need not obtain a tax clearance certificate as a condition for the grant or renewal of the licence.

---

[64] Finance Act 1992, Sched. 6.
[65] Finance (1909–10) Act 1910, s.52.
[66] Intoxicating Liquor Act 1927, s.14.

7. National Concert Hall

Introduction

In the early 1980s, when the National Concert Hall was established in Earlsfort Terrace, an application was made to the Circuit Court for a theatre licence pursuant to the provisions of the Excise Act 1835. This application was successful but the Garda Síochána appealed the decision of the then President of the Circuit Court, Mr Justice Neilan, to the High Court. The appeal did not proceed, as an Act to make provision for the grant of a licence authorising the sale of intoxicating liquor in the National Concert Hall, Dublin, was passed on September 13, 1983. This Act is known as the Intoxicating Liquor (National Concert Hall) Act 1983. **4–46**

Licence Section 2(1) of the 1983 Act provides that the Revenue Commissioners, on application to them by the National Concert Hall Company, shall grant to the Company or a person nominated by it, a licence for the sale of intoxicating liquor at the National Concert Hall. The licence operates to authorise the sale of intoxicating liquor at the National Concert Hall for consumption in the National Concert Hall by persons attending or taking part in the function, and the persons employed in the National Concert Hall during the period beginning half an hour before the commencement of a function and ending one hour after its conclusion. The expression "function" is defined in section 1 of the Act as: **4–47**

> "a concert or conference at the Concert Hall to which persons are admitted upon payment or by invitation and, where a function extends over more than one day, that part of the function held on any day shall be deemed, for the purposes of this Act, to be a separate function".

These are the only times during which intoxicating liquor may be served on the premises. Furthermore, the licence only authorises the sale of intoxicating liquor during such time as the National Concert Hall is occupied by the Company. The licence, therefore, is particular to the Company. The person/entity entitled to operate the premises, pursuant to the licence, is the Company or a person nominated by the Company.

The licence is operable during such time as the National Concert Hall is occupied by the Company and the Company is prohibited from leasing or granting an estate in the premises to another party.

The provisions relating to prohibited hours which are contained in the licensing code do not apply to the National Concert Hall. Furthermore, although an offence can be committed pursuant to the provisions of section 2(3) of the 1983 Act, such offence is not recordable on the licence and no provision has been made for forfeiture of the licence. The sale of intoxicating liquor otherwise than in accordance with the section is an offence, the penalty for which is a fine not exceeding £500.

Expiry The licence operates from the date of its grant and need not be renewed.

Excise Duty No excise duty is payable on this licence.

Tax Clearance Certificate A tax clearance certificate is not required.

8. Passenger Aircraft

4–48 **Licence** Section 29 of the Intoxicating Liquor Act 1943 provides that the Revenue Commissioners shall grant to any air transport concern a licence for the sale of intoxicating liquor to passengers on an aircraft owned or hired by that concern for consumption whilst the aircraft is in flight. The licence operates only in respect of such aircraft owned or hired by the air transport concern as specified on the licence.

The sale of intoxicating liquor to passengers in the aircraft for consumption therein, while the aircraft is in flight, is authorised by the licence.[67]

Expiry The licence expires on September 30 of each year.

Excise Duty The excise duty payable on this licence is £200.[68]

Tax Clearance Certificate A tax clearance certificate is not required for the grant or renewal of such a licence.

9. Military Canteen

4–49 **Licence** Section 314 of the Defence Act 1954 provides for the grant of an excise licence under the Licensing Acts for a person holding a canteen under the authority of the Minister for Defence. The provisions contained in the Intoxicating Liquor Act 1927 relating to prohibited hours do not apply to the military canteen.[69] The licence permits the sale of intoxicating liquor to a civilian.[70]

Expiry There is no statutory provision requiring the renewal of this licence, but in practice it expires on September 30 of each year.

Excise Duty There is no excise duty payable on this licence.

---

[67] Intoxicating Liquor Act 1943, s.29(3).
[68] Finance Act 1992, s.154.
[69] Intoxicating Liquor Act 1927, s.23(b).
[70] *Dickeson v. Mayes* [1910] 1 K.B. 452.

Tax Clearance Certificate The licence is not a spirit retailer's on-licence for the purposes of the Finance (1909–10) Act 1910. Thus, no tax clearance certificate is required.

10. Authorised Racecourse

Licence By virtue of Part IX of the Irish Horseracing Industry Act 1994 the Revenue Commissioners are empowered to grant to the executive of an authorised racecourse, or a person nominated by the executive body, a licence for the sale of intoxicating liquor at that racecourse for consumption at the racecourse. **4–50**

The licence authorises the sale of intoxicating liquor for consumption at the racecourse to persons attending the race-fixture. Sales are authorised during the period beginning from the time that the race-going public are permitted admission by the executive of the authorised racecourse concerned to a race-fixture (but not before 10.30 a.m.) and ending one hour after the conclusion of the last race of the fixture. This is the only period during which intoxicating liquor may be sold at the racecourse.

A licence can only be granted in respect of an authorised racecourse, and once a racecourse ceases to be an authorised racecourse, the licence automatically ceases to have effect.[71] An authorised racecourse means a racecourse, including the precincts thereof which is authorised by the Irish Horseracing Authority under section 59 of the Irish Horseracing Industry Act 1994.[72] It is a matter for the Authority to consider whether to grant such authorisation. The Authority will grant the authorisation where it considers a racecourse:

> "able to provide appropriate facilities and services to carry on horseracing at race-meetings, and accommodate persons associated with horseracing (including members of the public watching horseracing)".[73]

An authorisation expires five years from the date of its grant or renewal. The holder of the licence cannot apply for general exemption orders or special exemption orders, nor can convictions be recorded on the licence, nor do the provisions relating to prohibited hours in the Licensing Acts apply to any authorised racecourse in respect of which a licence has been granted under section 65 of the 1994 Act.[74]

A member of the Garda Síochána, may, if he is of the opinion that there are reasonable grounds for supposing that the holder of a licence is not complying with the provisions of section 65, or where a complaint has been made to him, enter into and search a racecourse without a warrant.

---

[71] Irish Horseracing Industry Act 1994, s.65(4).
[72] Racing Board and Racecourses Act 1945 introduced the concept of authorised racecourses.
[73] Irish Horseracing Industry Act 1994, s.59.
[74] *Ibid.*, s.66.

Offences under the 1994 Act are not endorsable offences for the purposes of the Intoxicating Liquor Act 1927, Part III.[75]

4–51 **Excise Duty** The excise duty payable on the grant and renewal of the licence is £200.[76]

Expiry The licence granted remains in force for the period specified in the licence.[77] In fact, the licence issued by the Revenue Commissioners commences on October 1 each year and expires on September 30 of the following year. Where an application for a tax clearance certificate has been duly made, the licence continues in force during the period specified in section 49(1A) of the Finance (1909–10) Act 1910 as amended by section 115 of the Finance Act 1995.

Tax Clearance Certificate A tax clearance certificate is required for the grant and renewal of the licence.[78]

Type of Premises Twenty-one licences have issued to racecourses for the licensing year 1994–1995.

11. Sweet Retailer's On-Licence

4–52 **Licence** A sweet retailer's on-licence authorises the retail sale for consumption, either on or off the premises, of sweets to any one person at any one time in any quantity up to two gallons, or up to one dozen reputed quart bottles.[79] "Sweets" means any liquor made from fruit and sugar, or from fruit and sugar mixed with any other material, and which has undergone a process of fermentation in the manufacture thereof, and includes British wines, made wines, mead and metheglin.[80] No sweet retailer's on-licence was issued for the licensing year ending 1994.[81]

Expiry This licence expires on September 30 of each year.

Excise Duty The excise duty payable on this licence is £200.[82]

Tax Clearance Certificate A tax clearance certificate is not required.

---

75 *Ibid.*
76 Finance Act 1995, s.111.
77 Irish Horseracing Industry Act 1994, s.65(2).
78 Finance Act 1993, s.77(1)(e).
79 Finance (1909–10) Act 1910, Sched. 1
80 *Ibid.*, s.52.
81 Statistical Report of the Revenue Commissioners 1994.
82 Finance Act 1992, s.154.

12. Sweet Retailer's Off-Licence

Licence This licence authorises the retail sale of "sweets" for consumption off the premises, to any one person, at any one time, in any quantity up to two gallons, or up to one dozen reputed quart bottles. Only 12 such licences were issued for the licensing year ending 1994.[83] **4–53**

Expiry This licence expires on September 30 of each year.

Excise Duty The excise duty payable on this licence is £200.[84]

Tax Clearance Certificate A tax clearance certificate is not required.

C. Licences Granted upon Production of a Certificate of the Minister

Introduction

Section 77 of the Finance Act 1993 provides, *inter alia*, that a licence in respect of an aerodrome premises, a bog and Áras Mhic Dhiarmada shall be deemed to be a spirit retailer's on-licence for the purposes of the Finance (1909–10) Act 1910. The effect of this is that the applicant for the grant or renewal of such licence is obliged to apply for a tax clearance certificate. The approval of the Minister for Transport, Energy and Communications is required in respect of each of the following licences.[85] **4–54**

1. Aerodrome Premises

Minister's Certificate: Grant Part IV of the Intoxicating Liquor Act 1943 provided for the grant of an on-licence for an aerodrome premises approved by the Minister. Where the Minister is satisfied that an on-licence should be granted for the entire or a part of an aerodrome premises, he may, by virtue of section 25(1) of the Intoxicating Liquor Act 1943, issue to a person "who appears to him to be a fit and proper person to hold such on-licence" a certificate **4–55**

---

[83] See above, n.81.

[84] Finance Act 1992, s.154.

[85] Communications (Transfer of Departmental Administration and Ministerial Functions) (No. 2) Order 1987 (S.I. No. 92 of 1987); Tourism Transport and Communications (Alteration of Name of Department and Title of Minister) Order 1993 (S.I. No. 17 of 1993); Tourism and Trade (Transfer of Departmental Administration and Ministerial Functions) Order 1993 (S.I. No. 422 of 1993).

certifying that the aerodrome in which the aerodrome premises is situate is an approved aerodrome premises and that he approves of the grant by the Revenue Commissioners of an on-licence in respect of that premises to that person. By virtue of section 25(3) the Minister may also issue a certificate "certifying that the aerodrome in which the premises thereby licensed are situate continues to be an approved aerodrome and that the Minister approves of the renewal of such on-licence to the said holder thereof in respect of the said premises". The Minister can issue a certificate in respect of the whole or a part of an aerodrome premises so it is possible for all or part of the buildings in an aerodrome premises to be licensed.

Renewal The licence is renewed upon production of a certificate of the Minister certifying that the aerodrome continues to be an approved aerodrome and that the Minister approves of the renewal.[86]

4–56 **Minister's Certificate: Transfer** The Minister is also entitled either by virtue of the death of the licence holder or "for any other reason" to issue to a person who appears to him to be a fit and proper person to hold such on-licence, a certificate that the Minister approves of the transfer of the licence to him. The Revenue Commissioners, under section 26(2) of the 1943 Act, may then transfer the licence to such person. The necessity of applying for an ad interim transfer and the consequent certificate of transfer appears to be avoided by section 26 of the 1943 Act: the Revenue Commissioners are entitled at any time during the licensing year to issue a new licence to an approved person.

4–57 **Minister's Certificate: Variation of Premises** Section 26(3) authorises the Minister to issue a certificate permitting the Revenue Commissioners to amend the on-licence to which the certificate relates. The Minister may issue any one of the following certificates:

1. a certificate approving the extension of the on-licence to a specified part of the aerodrome premises where the existing licence already applies to another part of the premises;
2. a certificate approving the exclusion from the premises to which the on-licence applies of a specified part of those premises;
3. a certificate approving the transfer of the said on-licence from the premises to which it applies to another part of the same premises.

All transactions involving the grant, renewal, transfer and alteration of the premises to which the licence attaches must receive the approval of the Minister before the Revenue Commissioners can issue a licence.

[86] Intoxicating Liquor Act 1943, s.25(3). Twenty-one of these licences have been issued by the Revenue Commissioners for the licensing year 1994–1995.

Licence Section 27 of the 1943 Act provides for the circumstances in which it is lawful to sell intoxicating liquor in a licensed aerodrome. Section 27(a) and (b) set forth the categories of persons entitled to consume intoxicating liquor on a licensed aerodrome "at any time" as follows. 4–58

1. Persons who have arrived at the aerodrome in which the licensed premises are situate as passengers in an aircraft engaged in an authorised air transport service and who have, immediately before their arrival, travelled in that aircraft for a distance of not less than 50 miles measured by the ordinary flying route of such aircraft to the aerodrome.
2. Persons who intend to travel from the aerodrome as passengers in an aircraft engaged in an authorised air transport service and who hold tickets entitling them to travel from the aerodrome on aircraft for a distance of not less than 50 miles, measured by the ordinary flying route of the aircraft from the aerodrome.

Otherwise, normal permitted hours apply.

Exemptions Unlicensed business (*i.e.* business which does not require a licence) may be carried on at any time on a licensed aerodrome premises.[87] 4–59

In relation to licensed business the holder of the licence is treated in the same way as the holder of an on-licence for a hotel or restaurant premises. Intoxicating liquor can be served up to 12.30 a.m. on weekdays, and on Sundays between 2 p.m. and 3 p.m., and on Christmas Day between 1 p.m. and 3 p.m. and between 7 p.m. and 10 p.m. where the intoxicating liquor is ordered, consumed, and paid for in conjunction with a meal.[88] The holder is also entitled to apply for special exemption orders.[89]

Excise Duty The excise duty payable on grant and renewal of the licence is £200.[90] 4–60

Expiry The licence expires on September 30 of each year. Where an application for a tax clearance certificate has been duly made, the licence continues in force during the period specified in section 49(1A) of the Finance Act (1909–10) Act 1910, as amended by section 115 of the Finance Act 1995.

Tax Clearance Certificate A licence shall not be granted by the Commissioners of Customs and Excise unless a tax clearance certificate in relation to that licence has been issued in accordance with section 242 of the Finance Act 1992.[91]

---

[87] Intoxicating Liquor Act 1943, s.28(1).
[88] *Ibid.*, s.28(3).
[89] *Ibid.*, s.28(2).
[90] Finance Act 1993, s.78.
[91] *Ibid.*, s.77.

2. Bog Premises

4–61 **Minister's Certificate: Grant** The Intoxicating Liquor Act 1946 provided for the licensing of premises in certain bogs. The Minister for Transport, Energy and Communications who issues the certificate approving of the grant and renewal of licences for premises in bogs. Section 2(1) of the 1946 Act provides for the issue of a certificate to a person "who appears to him to be a fit and proper person to hold such on-licence". The Minister has to be satisfied that "an on-licence should be granted in respect of the whole or a particular part of any particular bog premises". The distinction is drawn between "bog premises" and "licensed bog premises". A bog premises means all the buildings for the time being erected in the bog, irrespective of the purpose for which such premises are used. The expression "licensed bog premises" means those premises in a bog in respect of which a licence is granted or renewed. It is possible for a licence to issue in respect of one, some or all buildings in the bog. Again, as in the case of an aerodrome licence, the Minister must issue a certificate in respect of the grant and the renewal of the bog licence.

Renewal The Revenue Commissioners will renew the licence on presentation of a certificate that the Minister approves the renewal.[92]

4–62 **Minister's Certificate: Transfer** The Minister can issue a certificate to "a fit and proper person" to hold a bog licence where the original holder of the licence has died "or for any other reason". Section 3 of the 1946 Act empowers the Revenue Commissioners to transfer the licence on presentation of the certificate from the Minister approving the transfer. This transfer can be made at any time and there is no provision for an ad interim transfer or a certificate of transfer. The Minister has discretion to issue a certificate in respect of the grant, renewal and transfer of bog licences.

4–63 **Minister's Certificate: Variation of Premises** The Minister is also entitled "for any reason" to issue a certificate approving a variation in the place to which the licence attaches. He can issue any one of the following certificates:

1. a certificate approving an extension of the licence to a specified part of the bog premises where the existing licence already applies to another part of the premises;

2. a certificate approving the exclusion from the premises to which the licence applies of a specified part of those premises;

3. a certificate approving the transfer of the said licence from the premises to which it applies to another part of the same bog premises.

The provisions in the 1927 Act relating to prohibited hours apply.

---

[92] Intoxicating Liquor Act 1946, s.2(3).

Excise Duty The excise duty payable on grant and renewal of the licence is £200.[93] 4–64

Expiry The licence expires on September 30 of each year. Where an application for a tax clearance certificate has been duly made, the licence will continue in force during the period specified in section 49(1A) of the Finance (1909–10) Act 1910 as amended by section 115 of the Finance Act 1995.

Tax Clearance Certificate A licence shall not be granted or renewed by the Commissioners of Customs and Excise unless a tax clearance certificate in relation to that licence has been issued in accordance with section 242 of the Finance Act 1992.[94]

3. Bus Station in Áras Mhic Dhiarmada at Store Street, Dublin

Minister's Certificate: Grant The Intoxicating Liquor Act 1953 provides 4–65
for the licensing of the bus station in Store Street for the sale of intoxicating liquor. The Minister has discretion "if he thinks proper that an on-licence should be granted" to issue to Bus Éireann[95] a certificate approving the grant of an on-licence in respect of any particular part of the station. The licence is issued to the Board of Bus Éireann.

Minister's Certificate: Renewal The Revenue Commissioners may renew the licence on presentation of a certificate of the Minister approving the renewal.[96]

Minister's Certificate: Variation of Premises The Minister may issue a 4–66
certificate approving an alteration of the area covered by the licence, "whether the licence should be extended or transferred to another part of the bus station or should cease to apply to any part of the station".[97]

Licence The provisions contained in the Intoxicating Liquor Act 1927 relating to prohibited hours apply.

Exemptions Unlicensed business (*i.e.* business which does not require a licence) may be carried on at any time.[98] The Board can apply for special

---

[93] Finance Act 1993, s.78.
[94] *Ibid.*, s.77.
[95] Transport (Reorganisation of Corás Iompair Éireann) Act 1986 (Vesting Day) Order 1987 (S.I. No. 25 of 1987).
[96] Intoxicating Liquor Act 1953, s.3.
[97] *Ibid.*, s.4.
[98] *Ibid.*, s. 5(1).

exemption orders.[99] Intoxicating liquor may be served up to 12.30 a.m. on weekdays, and on Sunday between 2 p.m. and 3 p.m., and on Christmas day between 1 p.m. and 3 p.m., and between 7 p.m. and 10 p.m. where the drink is ordered, consumed and paid for in conjunction with a meal.[100]

The legislature did not deem it appropriate to extend permitted hours for the service or supply of intoxicating liquor to persons who intend to travel or persons who had already travelled as in the case of aerodrome premises.

4–67 **Excise Duty** Unlike the case of a licensed aerodrome, the legislature did not provide that the excise duty payable be set at a particular figure. The provisions contained in section 155(2)(b)(iii) of the Finance Act 1992 which compute the amount of excise duty in accordance with the level of annual turnover apply.

Expiry The licence expires on September 30 of each year. Where an application for a tax clearance certificate has been duly made, the licence will continue in force during the period specified in section 49(1A) of the Finance (1909–10) Act 1910 as amended by section 115 of the Finance Act 1995.

Tax Clearance Certificate

A licence shall not be granted by the Collectors of Customs and Excise unless the relevant tax clearance certificate in relation to that licence has been issued in accordance with section 242 of the Finance Act 1992.[101]

---

[99] *Ibid.*, s.5(2).
[100] *Ibid.*
[101] Finance Act 1993, s.77.

Chapter 5

LICENCES TO DEAL IN AND MANUFACTURE INTOXICATING LIQUOR

Introduction

The Finance (1909–10) Act 1910 lists the various types of wholesale dealers' licences and licences to manufacture intoxicating liquor. With one exception, it is not necessary to obtain a certificate of the court for the grant of a wholesale dealer's licence or a licence to manufacture intoxicating liquor.[1] The dates of expiry of wholesale dealer's licences differ from those applicable to licences to sell intoxicating liquor by retail. Where a premises has the benefit of both a wholesale dealer's licence and a retailer's off-licence for the sale of any liquor, the retailer's licence must expire on the same day as that on which the wholesale dealer's licence expires.[2] No wholesale dealer's licence can be granted without the production of a tax clearance certificate.[3] The holder of a manufacturer's licence is not obliged to produce a tax clearance certificate. **5–1**

The practitioner is advised to consult the most recent Finance Act for the time being to confirm that the position stated in this work has not changed. The wholesale dealer is entitled to sell in wholesale quantities at any hour unless his premises also has the benefit of a retailer's off-licence in which case the provisions relating to prohibited hours contained in Part II of the Intoxicating Liquor Act 1927 apply.[4]

---

[1] The exception is the wholesale beer dealer's licence.
[2] Finance (1909–10) Act 1910, s.49(1).
[3] *Ibid.*, s.49, as amended by the Finance Act 1993, s.79.
[4] Intoxicating Liquor Act 1927, s.23(c) and *Findlater v. Brennan* (1933) 67 I.L.T.R. 40.

A. Wholesale Dealers' Licences

1. Wholesale Beer Dealer

5–2 **Licence** A wholesale beer dealer's licence authorises the sale at any one time to any one person of beer or cider in any quantity not less than four and a half gallons, or not less than two dozen reputed quart bottles, but not in any lesser quantities. The holder of a wholesale beer dealer's licence may take out a cider retailer's off-licence in respect of the premises licensed for wholesale dealing, on payment of an excise duty of £200.[5]

Expiry This licence expires on June 30 of each year.[6] When an application for a tax clearance certificate has been made not less than four months prior to the commencement date of the licence for the following year, and the certificate has not yet been issued or refused, or it has been refused and the applicant has appealed against such refusal in accordance with section 242(6) of the Finance Act 1992, the licence continues in force beyond its expiry date, pending either the issue or refusal of the certificate, or in the case of an appeal, the final determination of that appeal. Thus, the application for the tax clearance certificate should be made on or before February 28 (or 29).

Where a tax clearance certificate is timely issued, *i.e.* before June 30, the existing licence expires upon the grant of a new licence. Where the tax clearance certificate is refused or the applicant's appeal against the refusal of a tax clearance certificate is unsuccessful, the licence expires not later than seven days after such refusal or the determination of the appeal.

Excise Duty[7] The excise duty payable on the licence is £200 as provided for in section 154 of the Finance Act 1992, Schedule 6.

Tax Clearance Certificate A wholesale beer dealer's licence shall not be granted by the Collector of Customs and Excise unless a tax clearance certificate in relation to that licence has been issued in accordance with section 242 of the Finance Act 1992.[8]

5–3 **Court Certificate: Grant** The grant of the licence by the Revenue Commissioners is conditional upon the production of a certificate of the District Court as to the good character of the applicant and the suitability of the premises, that they are rated, if in a city or town of a population exceeding 10,000, at £15 or

[5] Intoxicating Liquor Act 1960, s.34; Intoxicating Liquor Act 1962, s.28, and Finance Act 1992, Sched. 6.
[6] Finance (1909–10) Act 1910, s.49.
[7] A registration fee of £0.12 is also payable in respect of all licences.
[8] Finance (1909–10) Act 1910, s.49, as amended by the Finance Act 1993, s.79.

upwards, if elsewhere at £8 or upwards and that they have been in the exclusive occupation of the applicant for three months prior to the certificate.[9]

An application for a certificate leading to the grant of a wholesale beer dealer's licence may be made to the District Court at any time. The Licensing (Ireland) Act 1902 does not apply to beer dealers so the applicant does not have to proffer an existing licence for extinguishment.[10]

Court Certificate: Transfer The Revenue Commissioners may issue the licence in the name of a person other than the previous holder where a certificate of transfer has been granted by the District Court. The certificate must certify as to the good character of the applicant and the rateable valuation of the premises. If the transfer arose otherwise than on the death or removal of the person in occupation immediately prior to the transfer, it must certify as to the exclusive occupation of the applicant.[11]

Court Certificate: Renewal It is not necessary to produce a certificate of the District Court to an officer of the Revenue Commissioners empowered to grant a renewal of the licence except in the circumstances detailed in section 4(5) of the Courts (No. 2) Act 1986. However, an applicant for renewal must produce statutory declarations to the Revenue Commissioners stating the rateable valuation of the premises and confirming that the premises have been in his exclusive occupation for at least three months preceding the date of application for renewal.[12] 5–4

Type of Premises A wholesale beer dealer's licence is one of the licences obtained by a trading concern such as Musgraves or other wholesale dealers. It is usually obtained in conjunction with a wholesale spirit dealer's licence and a wholesale wine dealer's licence.

General The District Court has jurisdiction to grant the certificates required to obtain and renew these licences.[13] The fire officer is not a notice party to the application. There is authority to the effect that the premises must actually be valued at the time of the application; a provisional valuation may not be sufficient.[14] However, it appears that the court may pronounce itself satisfied that the rateable valuation of the premises will not be less than the statutory figure.[15]

---

[9] Licensing Act (Ireland) 1874, s.8 and the Beerhouses (Ireland) Act 1864, s.3.
[10] Licensing (Ireland) Act 1902, s.8.
[11] Licensing Act (Ireland) 1874, s.8.
[12] Courts (No. 2) Act 1986, s.4(10).
[13] Courts of Justice Act 1924, s.77(C), as applied by s.48 of the Courts (Supplemental Provisions) Act 1961.
[14] *R. (Morris) v. Derry Justices* (1901) 1 N.I.J.R. 66.
[15] *Re Application of Thomas Kiernan* [1965] 31 Ir. Jur. Rep. 4 and the Intoxicating Liquor Act 1960, s.33(2).

The provisions contained in the Intoxicating Liquor Act 1927 regarding trading hours do not apply in respect of wholesale dealers' licences.[16] The dealer therefore may sell the intoxicating liquor authorised by the licence at any time. However, where a premises has the benefit of both a wholesale dealer's licence and a licence to sell intoxicating liquor by retail, the provisions relating to prohibited hours which govern retail licences apply to both wholesale and retail sales.[17]

2. Wholesale Spirit Dealer

5–5 **Licence** A wholesale spirit dealer's licence authorises the sale at any one time to any one person of spirits in any quantity not less than two gallons, or not less than one dozen reputed quart bottles but not in any lesser quantities. The holder of a wholesale spirit dealer's licence may take out a cider retailer's off-licence in respect of the premises licensed for wholesale dealing on payment of an excise duty of £200.[18]

Expiry The licence expires on June 30 each year.[19] When an application for a tax clearance certificate has been made not less than four months prior to the commencement date of the licence for the following year, and the certificate has not yet been issued or refused, or it has been refused and the applicant has appealed against such refusal in accordance with section 242(6) of the Finance Act 1992, the licence continues in force beyond its expiry date pending either the issue or refusal of the certificate, or in the case of an appeal, the final determination of that appeal. Thus, the application for the certificate should be made on or before February 28 (or 29).

Where a tax clearance certificate is timely issued, *i.e.* before June 30, the existing licence expires upon the grant of a new licence (or June 30, if later). Where the tax clearance certificate is refused or the applicant's appeal against the refusal of a tax clearance certificate is unsuccessful, the licence expires not later than seven days after such refusal or the determination of the appeal.

5–6 **Excise Duty** The excise duty payable on the licence is £200, as provided for in section 154 of the Finance Act 1992, Schedule 6.

Tax Clearance Certificate A wholesale spirit dealer's licence shall not be granted by the Collector of Customs and Excise unless a tax clearance certifi-

[16] Intoxicating Liquor Act 1927, s.23.
[17] *Findlater v. Brennan*, above, n.4.
[18] Intoxicating Liquor Act 1960, s.34; Intoxicating Liquor Act 1962, s.28; and Finance Act 1992, Sched. 6.
[19] Finance (1909–10) Act 1910, s.49.

cate in relation to that licence has been issued in accordance with section 242 of the Finance Act 1992.[20]

Court Certificate: Grant or Renewal A certificate of the court is not required for the grant or renewal of this licence.

Type of Premises This licence attaches to a premises which sells, *inter alia*, intoxicating liquor in wholesale quantities.

3. Wholesale Wine Dealer

Licence A wholesale wine dealer's licence authorises the sale at any one time to any one person of wine in any quantity not less than two gallons, or not less than one dozen reputed quart bottles; but not in any lesser quantities. The holder of a wholesale wine dealer's licence may take out a cider retailer's off-licence in respect of the premises licensed for wholesale dealing on payment of an excise duty of £200.[21] A person who holds a wholesale wine dealer's licence is also entitled to deal wholesale in sweets without taking out any further wholesale dealer's licence.[22] **5–7**

Expiry The licence expires on June 30 each year.[23] When an application for a tax clearance certificate has been made not less than four months prior to the commencement date of the licence for the following year, and the certificate has not yet been issued or refused, or it has been refused and the applicant has appealed against such refusal in accordance with section 242(6) of the Finance Act 1992, the licence continues in force beyond its latest expiry date pending either the issue or refusal of the certificate, or in the case of an appeal, the final determination of that appeal. Thus, the application for a certificate should be made on or before February 28 (or 29).

Where a tax clearance certificate issues thereafter, the existing licence expires upon the grant of a new licence. Where the tax clearance certificate is refused or the applicant's appeal against the refusal of a tax clearance certificate is unsuccessful, the licence expires not later than seven days after such refusal or the determination of the appeal.

Excise Duty The excise duty payable on the licence is £200 as provided for in section 154 of the Finance Act 1992, Sixth Schedule. **5–8**

---

20 *Ibid.*, s.49 as amended by the Finance Act 1993, s.79.

21 Intoxicating Liquor Act 1960, s.34; Intoxicating Liquor Act 1962, s.28; and Finance Act 1992, Sched. 6.

22 Finance (1909–10) Act 1910, Sched. 1.

23 *Ibid.*, s.49.

Tax Clearance Certificate A wholesale wine dealer's licence shall not be granted by the Collector of Customs and Excise unless a tax clearance certificate in relation to that licence has been issued in accordance with section 242 of the Finance Act 1992.[24]

Court Certificate: Grant or Renewal A certificate of the court is not required for the grant or renewal of this licence.

Type of Premises This licence attaches to a premises which sells, *inter alia*, intoxicating liquor in wholesale quantities.

4. Wholesale Sweet Dealer

5–9 **Licence** A wholesale sweet dealer's licence authorises the sale at any one time to any one person of sweets in any quantity not less than two gallons, or not less than one dozen reputed quart bottles, but not in any lesser quantities. The expression "sweets" means any liquor which is made from fruit and sugar, or from fruit and sugar mixed with any other material, and which has undergone a process of fermentation in the manufacture thereof, and includes British wines, made wines, mead, and metheglin.[25]

The holder of a wholesale wine dealer's licence need not apply for a wholesale sweet dealer's licence as he is automatically entitled to sell sweets by virtue of his licence. This automatic entitlement does not extend to holders of wholesale spirit dealer's licences and wholesale beer dealer's licences. The holder of the wholesale sweet dealer's licence is not entitled to take out a cider retailer's off-licence as in the case of a wholesale dealer for the sale of spirits, beer, or wine. The provisions relating to prohibited hours which are contained in Part II of the Intoxicating Liquor Act 1927 do not apply in respect of a premises to which a wholesale sweet dealer's licence is attached, so the product can be sold in wholesale quantities at any time.[26]

Expiry The licence expires on June 30 of each year.[27] When an application for a tax clearance certificate has been made not less than four months prior to the commencement date of the licence for the following year and the certificate has not yet been issued or refused, or it has been refused and the applicant has appealed against such refusal in accordance with section 242(6) of the Finance Act 1992, the licence continues in force beyond its expiry date pending either the issue or refusal of the certificate, or in the case of an appeal, the final determination of that appeal. Thus, the application for the tax clearance certificate should be made on or before February 28 (or 29).

---

[24] Finance (1909–10) Act 1910, s.49, as amended by the Finance Act 1993, s.79.
[25] Finance (1909–10) Act 1910, s.51.
[26] Intoxicating Liquor Act 1927, s.23(c).
[27] Finance (1909–10) Act 1910, s.49.

Where a tax clearance certificate issues thereafter, the existing licence expires upon the grant of a new licence. Where the tax clearance certificate is refused or the applicant's appeal against the refusal of a tax clearance certificate is unsuccessful, the licence expires not later than seven days after such refusal or the determination of the appeal.

Excise duty The excise duty payable on the licence is £200 as provided for in section 154 of the Finance Act 1992, Schedule 6.

Tax Clearance Certificate A wholesale sweet dealer's licence shall not be granted by the Collector of Customs and Excise unless a tax clearance certificate in relation to that licence has been issued in accordance with section 242 of the Finance Act 1992.[28] **5–10**

Court Certificate: Grant and Renewal A certificate of the court is not required for the grant or refusal of this licence.

Type of Premises This licence attaches to a premises which sells, *inter alia*, intoxicating liquor in wholesale quantities.

B. Manufacturers' Licences

General

A manufacturer's licence authorises the manufacture of the liquor to which it refers and dealing wholesale in that liquor. **5–11**

The manufacture of intoxicating liquor without taking out the appropriate licence attracts a penalty of £500 in respect of each offence and results in the forfeiture of all spirits, vessels, utensils and materials used for distilling or brewing.[29] Contravention of the terms of the licence or selling otherwise than as authorised by the licence attracts a penalty of £50 in respect of each offence, where the offence is not an offence for which any specific penalty is imposed by any acts relating to excise duties or licences.[30]

Accordingly, the holder of a manufacturer's licence need not take out a wholesale dealer's licence in respect of wholesale dealing in the liquor at the premises where it was manufactured. This is where that liquor is supplied wholesale to the purchaser direct from the premises where it is manufactured.[31]

---

[28] *Ibid.*, s.49, as amended by the Finance Act 1993, s.79.
[29] *Ibid.*, s.50.
[30] *Ibid.*, s.50, as amended by the Finance Act 1963, s.104(3), and the Finance Act 1983, s.69.
[31] *Ibid.*, Sched. 1.

1. Spirit Distiller

5–12 **Licence** A distiller and rectifier or compounder of spirits may not hold a licence to sell beer, cider or spirits by retail to be consumed on the premises.[32] There is no limit to the amount of spirits which a manufacturer is entitled to distil. Any fermented liquor containing a proportion greater than 23 per cent vol. spirit is deemed to be spirits.[33] Three distillers' licences were issued in the licensing year ending September 1994.[34]

Expiry The licence expires on September 30 of each year.[35]

Excise Duty The excise duty payable on the licence is £200 as provided for in section 154 of the Finance Act 1992, Sixth Schedule.

Tax Clearance Certificate A tax clearance certificate is not required for the grant and renewal of the licence.

Court Certificate: Grant and Renewal A certificate of the court is not required for the grant or renewal of this licence.

2. Rectifier or Compounder of Spirits

5–13 **Licence** A rectifier or compounder of spirits may not hold a licence to sell beer, cider or spirits by retail to be consumed on the premises (a publican's licence).[36] Nineteen of these licences were issued in the licensing year ending September 1994.[37]

Expiry The licence expires on September 30 of each year.[38]

Excise Duty The excise duty payable on the licence is £200 as provided for in section 154 of the Finance Act 1992, Sixth Schedule.

Tax Clearance Certificate A tax clearance certificate is not required.

Court Certificate: Grant and Renewal A certificate of the court is not required for the grant or renewal of this licence.

---

[32] Licensing (Ireland) Act 1833, s.13.
[33] Refreshment Houses (Ireland) Act 1850, s.23, as substituted by S.I. No. 415 of 1979, art. 16, Sched. 2. See above, para. 4–38.
[34] Statistical Report of the Revenue Commissioners 1994.
[35] Finance (1909–10) Act 1910, s.49.
[36] Licensing (Ireland) Act 1833, s.13.
[37] Statistical Report of the Revenue Commissioners 1994.
[38] Finance (1909–10) Act 1910, s.49.

3. Brewer of Beer Not for Sale

Licence This licence is taken out by a private brewer who does not sell beer. The beer must be brewed by the brewer solely for his own domestic use. Where a private brewer brews beer and offers it for sale or sells it to any person, he is guilty of an offence and is liable on summary conviction to an excise penalty of £1,000. Any beer in respect of which the offence was committed and any vessels, utensils and materials for brewing in the possession of a private brewer of beer in respect of which the offence was committed shall be liable to forfeiture.[39] This licence does not authorise wholesale dealing in beer.[40] 5–14

Expiry The licence expires on September 30 of each year.[41]

Excise Duty No excise duty is payable on the licence.[42]

Tax Clearance Certificate A tax clearance certificate is not required for the grant and renewal of this licence.

Court Certificate: Grant and Renewal A certificate of the court is not required for the grant and renewal of this licence.[43]

4. Brewer of Beer for Sale

Licence Beer includes ale, porter, spruce beer, black beer, any other type of beer and any liquor which is made or sold as a description of beer or as a substitute for beer and which on analysis of a sample thereof at any time is found to contain more than two per cent proof spirit.[44] 5–15

Expiry The licence expires on September 30 of each year.[45]

Excise Duty The excise duty payable on the licence is £200 as provided for in section 154 of the Finance Act 1992, Sixth Schedule.

Tax Clearance Certificate A tax clearance certificate is not required for the grant and renewal of this licence.

---

[39] Finance Act 1989, s.51.
[40] Finance (1909–10) Act 1910, Sched. 1.
[41] *Ibid.*, s.49.
[42] Finance Act 1989, s.51.
[43] *R. (Cottingham) v. Cork Justices* [1906] 2 I.R. 415.
[44] Finance (1909–10) Act, s.49.
[45] *Ibid.*

Court Certificate: Grant and Renewal A certificate of the court is not required for the grant or renewal of this licence.

5. Maker of Cider or Perry for Sale

5–16 **Licence** Four of these licences issued for the year ending September 1994.

Expiry The licence expires on September 30 each year.[46]

Excise Duty The excise duty payable on the licence is £200.[47]

Tax Clearance Certificate A tax clearance certificate is not required for the grant and renewal of this licence.

Court Certificate: Grant and Renewal A certificate of the court is not required for the grant or renewal of this licence.

6. Maker of Sweets for Sale

Licence Three of these licences were issued for the licensing year ending September 1994.[48]

5–17 **Expiry** The licence expires on September 30 each year.[49]

Excise Duty The excise duty payable on this licence is £200 as provided for in section 154 of the Finance Act 1992, Schedule 6.

Tax Clearance Certificate A tax clearance certificate is not required for the grant and renewal of this licence.

Court Certificate: Grant and Renewal A certificate of the court is not required for the grant and renewal of this licence.

---

[46] Finance Act 1940, s.10(3).
[47] Finance Act 1992, s.154.
[48] Statistical Report of Revenue Commissioners 1994.
[49] Finance (1909–10) Act 1910, s.49.

Part III

LICENSED PREMISES, CLUBS AND PLACES OF PUBLIC ENTERTAINMENT

CHAPTER 6

PUBLIC HOUSE LICENCE

INTRODUCTION

The most common liquor licence is the publican's licence (ordinary). A publican's licence entitles the holder to sell intoxicating liquor for consumption on and off the premises to which the licence attaches. It will not be granted in respect of any premises where it is intended to sell intoxicating liquor for consumption off the premises only. The licence, which is also known as a spirit 6–1 retailer's on-licence, authorises the sale at one time to any one person of any liquor, in the following quantities:

(a) in the case of spirits, wine or sweets, any quantity not exceeding two gallons, or not exceeding one dozen reputed quart bottles; and

(b) in the case of beer or cider, any quantity not exceeding four and a half gallons, or not exceeding two dozen reputed quart bottles.[1]

The licence entitles the holder thereof and his employees, but no other person, to sell intoxicating liquor as authorised by the licence on the premises to which the licence relates. The licence expires on September 30 each year.

Restriction on Grant

6–2 Before 1833 there was no restriction on the grant by the Collector of Customs and Excise of a publican's licence. The requirement to produce a certificate of the Justices to officers of Customs and Excise before a licence could issue was introduced by the Licensing (Ireland) Act 1833.[2] It was accepted that once a "regular application" was made, to which no objection was taken, the court could not refuse to issue the certificate. Andrews J. stated in *R. (Perry) v. Tyrone Justices*:

> "In order to give jurisdiction to prohibit the issue of the licence, there must be an objection such as the Act [of 1833] refers to by someone . . .".[3]

If an objection was made, the court was obliged to enquire into the "sufficiency and validity" of such objection.[4]

This absence of statutory restriction upon the exercise of the court's licensing jurisdiction resulted in the grant of vast numbers of licences for a period of almost 70 years. The legislature considered that this gave rise to a public nuisance and the Licensing (Ireland) Act 1902 was enacted to correct the situation. The main purpose of this Act was to limit the grant of new retail licences.

Section 2 of the Licensing (Ireland) Act 1902 provides, *inter alia*:

> "From and after the passing of this Act, no licence shall be granted for the sale of intoxicating liquors, whether for consumption on or off the premises . . .".

The measure was initially intended to be a temporary one, and the statute as enacted had a life of only five years. This was extended from time to time

[1] Finance (1909–10) Act 1910, Sched. 1 (provisions applicable to retailers' licences).
[2] Licensing (Ireland) Act 1833, s.6.
[3] (1904) 38 I.L.T.R. 26.
[4] Licensing (Ireland) Act 1833, s.4.

until, ultimately, section 14 of the Intoxicating Liquor (General) Act 1924 provided that the 1902 Act,

> "shall continue in force until the Oireachteas otherwise determines".

To date the Act has not been repealed by the Oireachteas.

Policy of 1902 Act: No New Licences

The general policy of the 1902 Act has been outlined in various cases. In *Application of Patrick Belton*, the policy was explained by Judge Davitt: 6–3

> "The Act. . . provided for the redistribution of the licences to meet such an expansion without any absolute increase in the total number of licensed premises. Such, briefly and roughly, is the underlying policy of the Act as I see it."[5]

Walsh J. referred to the 1902 Act in *Re Application of Power Supermarkets Ltd*:

> "The object of the Act [of 1902] was to safeguard the public interest by preventing a proliferation of licensed premises."[6]

Exceptions in 1902 Act

The 1902 Act sets out certain exceptions to the wholesale prohibition on the grant of new licences. For example, section 4 of the 1902 Act provides for the grant of a new licence in a city or town where a minimum increase in population has occurred and where a licence or licences within a city or town is/are available for extinguishment; section 2(2) of the 1902 Act provides for the grant of a hotel licence for a premises which comes within the statutory definition contained therein.[7] 6–4

Subsequent Statutory Exceptions

Legislation subsequent to the 1902 Act has provided for additional circumstances in which a licensing court can entertain an application for a certificate leading to the grant of a new licence. The Intoxicating Liquor Act 1943 made provision for the licensing of new premises in substitution for premises destroyed by fire and for the licensing of more convenient premises in a rural area. 6–5

---

[5] (1939) 73 I.L.T.R. 34 at 35-36.
[6] [1988] I.R. 206 at 210.
[7] For a list of circumstances in which a new licence can be granted, see below, Appendix D.

The Intoxicating Liquor Act 1960 provided for the licensing of premises situated in a rural area, and for premises situate in the immediate vicinity of a premises which was licensed at the time it was demolished.

Application for New Publican's Licence

6–6 To qualify for the grant of a new publican's licence, an applicant must bring himself within one of the statutory exceptions contained in the 1902 Act or in subsequent legislation. Each application involves the extinguishment of one or more licences or proof that the premises concerned were licensed during the previous five years.[8]

Extinguishment of Licence or Licences

6–7 The creation of a new licence in respect of a previously unlicensed premises requires the extinguishment of an existing licence or licences, with a view to substituting a more suitable licensed premises for an existing public house for the convenience of the public. The existing licence is extinguished upon the grant of the new licence. An intending applicant does not purchase the existing licence: he may, however, enter into an agreement with the existing licensee whereby the licensee consents to the extinguishment of his existing licence. Griffin J. in *Macklin v. Greacen*[9] accepted that such agreements were enforceable. He stated, however:

> "... the holder of a licence cannot sell the licence to any other person, unless such other person also buys the premises. The licence *per se* is inalienable. It must always, so long as it exists at all, remain attached to the premises."[10]

There has been a tendency to transfer licences from decaying parts of a city to more fashionable areas, such as in the Temple Bar area of Dublin. Licences attaching to premises in the vicinity of fashionable drinking areas which may become available for extinguishment are becoming increasingly valuable. However, licences in country areas where an applicant need not satisfy the "immediate vicinity" test may be obtained at a fraction of the cost.

---

[8] Note that an application for a hotel licence without a public bar and an application for a special restaurant licence do not require the extinguishment of a licence.

[9] [1982] I.L.R.M. 182.

[10] *Ibid.* at 185.

Checklist

The circumstances in which a new licence may be granted are dealt with in this chapter. Where a solicitor is advising an intending applicant he should consider, *inter alia*, the following matters: 6–8

1. that the application falls within one of the statutory exceptions detailed below;
2. that an appropriate licence (or licences) is/are available for extinguishment in accordance with the exception relating thereto;
3. that such licence (or licences) are valid and subsisting at the time required pursuant to the appropriate statutory exception, *e.g.* at the time the old premises were demolished or on the date on which the application is made;
4. that the licence available for extinguishment is not a hotel licence granted pursuant to section 2 (2) of the Licensing (Ireland) Act 1902, or a greyhound racetrack licence or a special restaurant licence.[11]

The duties of a solicitor acting for a licensee are outlined below in chapter 29.

NEW LICENCES

A new publican's licence is issued by the Collector of Customs and Excise for the district or area within which the premises sought to be licensed are situate. The licence is issued upon production to the Collector of Customs and Excise of a certificate signed by the county registrar for the county within which the premises are situate, together with a tax clearance certificate and the appropriate excise duty. The Licensing (Ireland) Act 1833, as amended, requires a person seeking a new licence to apply to the court for an order directing the issue of a certificate. The form of certificate should show on its face the jurisdictional exception invoked. 6–9

In *R. (McClinchy) v. Greer*, Palles C.B. considered the certificate:

> "I think it is well worthy of consideration, where such a vast amount of property depended upon these licences, that it should be considered whether, having regard to the ordinary rule applicable to documents of this description issued by inferior tribunals, with the necessity of showing jurisdiction upon their face, the Act of 1902 did not necessitate certain alteration in their form, either by describing the premises as premises which were licensed within the dates mentioned in the Act or otherwise by bringing them within the exceptions in the Act."[12]

[11] Intoxicating Liquor Act 1962, s.20, as amended by the Intoxicating Liquor Act 1988, s.23.
[12] (1903) 37 I.L.T.R. 156 at 157.

The form of certificate which the county registrar signs is stipulated in section 5 of the 1833 Act.

CIRCUMSTANCES IN WHICH NEW LICENCE GRANTED

6–10 A new publican's licence (ordinary) may be sought by an applicant where he can prove to the court that he comes within an exception to the general prohibitory terms contained in the Licensing (Ireland) Act 1902. These exceptions are divided into the following categories and (with a number of exceptions detailed below) all involve the extinguishment of an existing licence or licences or the replacement of a previously licensed premies:

A. Premises Licensed within the Previous Five Years.

B. Premises Situate in a City or Town.

C. Premises Situate in the Immediate Vicinity of Another Premises.

D. Premises Situate in a Rural Area.

E. Premises already Licensed, but Different Licence Sought.

F. Licensed Premises Acquired by Local Authority.

A. Premises Licensed within Previous Five Years

Introduction

6–11 1. The first exception contained in section 2(1) of the Licensing (Ireland) Act 1902, as amended by section 23 of the Intoxicating Liquor Act 1960, provides for the grant of a new licence in the following circumstances:

(a) where the licensee seeks to reduce the area of his licensed premises;

(b) where an applicant requires to revive a lapsed licence.

2. The second exception is set out in section 6 of the Licensing (Ireland) Act 1902 as amended by section 24 of the Intoxicating Liquor Act 1960, which provides for the grant of a new licence for premises adjoining existing licensed premises or premises which were licensed within the past five years.

1. Reduction in Area of Licensed Premises; Revival of a Lapsed Licence

STATUTORY PROVISION

Section 2(1) of the Licensing (Ireland) Act 1902 as amended by section 23 of the Intoxicating Liquor Act 1960, provides: 6–12

> "2. From and after the passing of this Act *no licence shall be granted* for the sale of intoxicating liquors, whether for consumption on or off the premises, except—
>
> (1) For premises (not being premises which were licensed by virtue of paragraph (2) of this section) which were licensed at any time during the period of five years immediately before the day on which notice of an application for the grant of a certificate entitling the holder to receive a licence in respect of the premises is given, pursuant to rules of court, to the appropriate County Registrar or to the appropriate District Court Clerk, as the case may be. . . ".[13]

Limited scope

Section 2(1) of the 1902 Act does not apply in the following circumstances: 6–13

1. to licences created by section 2(2) of the 1902 Act, namely hotel licences;
2. to a premises to which a seven-day licence, which has been extinguished by order of the court pursuant to section 19 of the Intoxicating Liquor Act 1960, attached[14];
3. where a licence is extinguished on the grant of a licence for substituted premises, an application pursuant to section 2(1) of the 1902 Act cannot be made in respect of the extinguished licence. In other words, it is not possible to revive a licence for premises where the licence which previously attached thereto was tendered for extinguishment for the purposes of the grant of another licence[15];
4. where a licence becomes forfeit as a result of convictions for recordable offences.[16]

---

[13] [Emphasis added].

[14] Intoxicating Liquor Act 1960, s.19(2)(c) and (4).

[15] Intoxicating Liquor Act 1943, s.21(2)(e) and s.22(2)(e); Intoxicating Liquor Act 1953, s.7(3)(e); Intoxicating Liquor Act 1960, s.13(2)(e), s.14(2)(e) and s.27(3)(b).

[16] Section 28(2) of the Intoxicating Liquor Act 1927 provides that where a licence is forfeited under this section, no new licence shall at any time thereafter be granted in respect of the premises or any part of the premises to which the licence was attached.

Rateable Valuation

6–14 Section 5 of the Licensing (Ireland) Act 1902, which stipulates a minimum valuation, does not apply to an application made pursuant to the provisions of section 2(1) of the 1902 Act.

STATUTORY CONSEQUENCES

6–15 **New Licence: Endorsements Not Carried Forward** Judge Sheridan in *D.P.P. v. Farrell*,[17] dealt with the status of a new licence where offences were recorded on the old licence. He noted that certain sections of the licensing code preserve, at least in part, endorsements attaching to a prior licence upon the granting of a new licence. Referring to those sections he stated:

> "It therefore cannot be said that the Legislature, in any way, were not conscious of the need, in certain instances, to impose the restrictions of endorsements in varying degrees on new licences …".[18]

That case concerned, *inter alia*, the construction of the provision relating to the grant of a new licence contained in section 6 of the 1902 Act. The judge noted that section 6 was not amended to preserve endorsements existing in respect of a previous licence upon the grant of a new licence. Similarly, the legislature has not seen fit to import such a restriction upon the grant of a new licence under section 2(1) of the 1902 Act. Thus, where a new licence is granted pursuant to section 2(1) of the 1902 Act, endorsements on the old licence are not carried forward.

Judge Sheridan's decision in the *Farrell* case was endorsed by Finlay C.J. in *Doyle v. Hearne (No. 2)*:

> "I would accept the true consequence, in effect, of a licence of extended premises granted pursuant to the provisions of section 6 of the Act of 1902, is to create a like new licence, freed from any previous endorsements as was decided by the present learned Circuit Court Judge in *Director of Public Prosecutions v. Farrell*."[19]

6–16 **New Licence: Equal or Lesser Character to Old Licence** The general principle is that an applicant cannot obtain a licence which is greater than the licence which is to be tendered for extinguishment. For example, a seven-day licence cannot be granted where the licence tendered for extinguishment is a six-day licence[20] nor can a seven-day licence be granted where the licence

[17] (1980) 114 I.L.T.R. 106.
[18] *Ibid.* at 109.
[19] [1988] I.R. 317 at 325.
[20] *The State (Tuomey) v. Circuit Court Judge of the Midland Circuit* [1932] I.R. 95; *R. (Henderson) v. Louth Justices* (1911) 2 I.R. 312.

tendered is a spirit grocer's licence.[21] Since the decision of the Supreme Court in *O'Rourke and Flanagan v. Grittar*,[22] it has been accepted that an application might be made pursuant to section 2(1) of the 1902 Act for a new off-licence where the premises had the benefit of an on-licence within the past five years. In his judgment Blayney J. stated:

> "[I]t is possible also that an applicant for a new off-licence in the place of an existing on-licence might come within the exception to the prohibition in section 2 of the Act of 1902 against the granting of new licences".[23]

He continued:

> "[I]t would appear very likely that the holder of such a licence would be able to acquire a new off-licence on the ground that his premises came within the exception in 1902, that is, that they are premises which are now licensed".

Nonetheless, although this was by way of *obiter dicta* in the *Grittar* decision it is authority for the proposition that an applicant, in invoking section 2(1) could apply for a licence of a different (although less comprehensive) character such as an off-licence, upon proof that his premises were licensed within the past five years (albeit with an on-licence). It remains the case that a greater licence cannot be sought where a lesser licence is offered for extinguishment, as was the case in *R. (Collins) v. Donegal Justices*, where O'Brien L.C.J. in rejecting the application stated:

> "… the word 'licence' is to be read distributively, and that the rule of construction *reddendo singula singulis* is to be applied—i.e. that on each application for a licence regard must be had to the character of the licence already attached to the premises. You must not give to the applicant a licence more comprehensive in character and quality than that he previously had. The *status quo* was to be preserved, not extended."[24]

This aspect is dealt with in more detail below, chapter 15, "Changes in the Character, Scope and Attributes of a Licence".

(a) Reduction in Area of Licensed Premises

Premises It may upon occasion be desirable to restrict the area licensed to that portion of the premises actually used or intended to be used for the supply and sale of intoxicating liquor. A licensee may find that a portion of his licensed premises which he does not require for the supply and sale of intoxicating liquor has other commercial potential but, because it forms part of, or intercommunicates with the area open to the public it cannot be so used due to the provisions 6–17

[21] *R. (Collins) v. Donegal Justices* (1902) 36 I.L.T.R. 184, 229.
[22] [1995] 1 I.R. 541.
[23] *Ibid.* at 567.
[24] Above, n.21, at 229.

governing prohibited hours and the provisions relating to the times when persons may legitimately be permitted to be upon the licensed premises.

It therefore becomes necessary to effect what is called a "delicensing" of that portion of the premises which are to be used for some purpose other than the licensed trade. The portion to be "delicensed" should be structurally separate from that portion of the premises used for the licensed trade and an application should be made to the court for a new licence in respect of the portion to be used in the future for licensing business.

6–18 A licence granted for a house or building, attaches to the structure and not to the site. In *Re Denis Guiney, Applicant*, Judge Davitt stated:

> ". . . when a licence is granted for a house or building, it attaches to the structure and not merely to the site, and will continue to exist and will be renewed only so long as there is no substantial change in the identity of the structure. It is true that licensed premises can be taken down and rebuilt without causing the loss of the licence or the right to renewal, but only where the original structure is restored and such rebuilding is effected without any substantial alterations."[25]

There, Denis Guiney applied pursuant to section 2(1) of the 1902 Act for a certificate entitling him to obtain a new publican's licence for part of the premises known as Clery & Co. Ltd, 18–25 Lower O'Connell Street, and 1–3 Sackville Place, Dublin. Judge Davitt was satisfied that the application could not succeed as it related only to a small part of the existing licensed premises together with large areas which had never been licensed.[26] He continued:

> "In deciding the question whether I have jurisdiction to grant this application I have to ask myself one question: Were the premises the subject of the application licensed on 31st July, 1902? The answer is clearly and certainly that they were not. They did not exist in 1902. They did not come into being until twenty years later. The old Imperial Hotel whose licence affords the sole basis for this application disappeared forever in the smoke and flame of the conflagration of 1916 and all the arguments of eminent counsel cannot operate effectually to recreate it, even notionally."[27]

Judge Davitt's decision does not, however, prevent an applicant from applying to reduce the area of his licenced premises: such an applicant has no difficulty in proving that his premises were licensed within the appropriate period. "Licensed premises" as defined by the Licensing Act of 1872, means "premises in respect of which a licence as defined has been granted and is in force".

---

[25] (1941) 75 I.L.T.R. 110 at 112.

[26] Section 20 of the Intoxicating Liquor Act 1943, provided for the grant of a new licence in respect of certain restaurant premises. The section continued in force until December 31, 1944, and was enacted to allow Clery's restaurant to obtain a certificate entitling the applicant to an on-licence.

[27] *Re Denis Guiney, Applicant*, above, n.25, at 113.

In *R. (Beirne) v. Limerick Justices*[28] it was held that an application may be made pursuant to section 2(1) of the 1902 Act to license a portion of the originally licensed premises. Here the applicant sought to license part of a premises which had been licensed at the time of the passing of the Licensing (Ireland) Act 1902. At the date of the passing of that Act, an ordinary publican's licence was in existence for house No. 1 and the upper portion of the adjoining house, No. 2. The licence lapsed in October 1903 and an application for a new licence in respect of house No. 1 alone was made in 1911. The question before the Appeal Court, presided over by Palles L.C.B., was whether the 1902 Act took away the jurisdiction to grant a licence in respect of portion of the originally licensed premises, from the magistrates. The court held that "premises which are now licensed" included every portion of such licensed premises, therefore a licence might properly be granted in respect of part of the previously licensed premises. **6–19**

Section 2(1) cannot be invoked to create more than one licensed premises by sub-dividing the physical area of a premises to which a licence attaches, as this would be contrary to the object of the 1902 Act. **6–20**

In *R. (Croghan) v. Mayo Justices*[29] an application for two new licences in lieu of one original licence was refused. Wright J. stated:

> "The dropping of a licence which was in force in 1902, may occur from a variety of causes and the Act which aims at preventing an increase in the number of licensed houses, allowed, in such cases, an application for a new licence, subject to all the objections which can be urged against such an application; but it seems to me, not merely from the general policy of the Act and of the Licensing Code but also from the language of the section that a new licence for premises, licensed when the Act was passed, means a new licence for the same premises, which means the same premises substantially, and does not mean that the original premises may be indefinitely subdivided and a new licence granted for each subdivision. To do so would be to use the Act for the purpose of creating a number of small 'shebeens'."[30]

In the *Croghan* case the licensee, Mrs Judge, held a publican's licence in respect of a public house which comprised two adjoining houses. She surrendered her tenancy in one of the houses to the landlord and obtained a renewal of her licence in respect of the second house. The landlord of the first house then applied for a new licence but his application was refused. **6–21**

In *Re Moses Hunter's Licence*[31] Mr Hunter, in order to reduce the cost of his excise licence, had two portions of his licensed premises separately rated: the shop at £130 and his residential portion at £35. He then applied to have the

[28] (1911) 45 I.L.T.R. 215.
[29] [1907] 2 I.R. 474.
[30] *Ibid.* at 479 and 480.
[31] (1910) 44 I.L.T.R. 220.

shop portion licensed. The Recorder of Belfast granted the application: the licensed business was carried on wholly or substantially in the portion for which the new licence was required which was completely separate from the remainder of the premises and was otherwise suitable to be licensed.

In his judgment, the Recorder of Belfast stated:

> "The premises for which a licence is here asked are not substantially the same premises as hitherto licensed, though they are the portion of the premises used for trading purposes. ... Having regard ... to the fact that the intention of the Licensing Act, 1902, was to prevent an increase in the number of licensed premises, I have come to the conclusion that it is in my power to grant this licence."[32]

The submission made by the solicitor for the applicant was as follows:

> "Unless the licensing authority can deal with the whole licensed premises, or any part thereof, s. 2(1) has no meaning since it is clearly disjunctive, dealing with premises licensed at the passing of the Act or at any time since January 1, 1902. Enlargements are provided for by section 6 and the only orders to be asked for in reference to premises 'now licensed' must be curtailments."[33]

(b) Revival of Lapsed Licence

6–22 **Time Limit** Prior to the enactment of the Intoxicating Liquor Act 1960, the owner of a premises which was licensed at the date of the passing of the 1902 Act (July 31, 1902) or was licensed during the period between January 1, 1902 and that date, could apply to the court for a new licence in respect of the premises formerly licensed; the grant of such licence was not prohibited by the 1902 Act. So, even where a licence had lapsed for over half a century, there was still jurisdiction to "revive" it, or more correctly, to seek a new licence in respect of the formerly licensed premises.

This gave rise to abuses, particularly during the licensing boom in the 1950s when a practice grew up of relicensing premises or reviving licences when the intention of the applicant for the revival or new licence was simply to sell it for extinguishment to another applicant for a new licence. As a result of this, the 1957 Commission of Inquiry into the Operation of the Law relating to the Sale and Supply of Intoxicating Liquor recommended "a curtailment of the power to revive licences". It recommended that where the period of lapse exceeds five years, a licence should not be capable of being revived, adding:

> "In allowing the period of five years we have in mind the possibility of a person being compelled through force of financial circumstances to abandon temporarily the operation of his licence".[34]

---

[32] *Ibid.* at 221.

[33] *Ibid.*

[34] See para. 41, Reports of the 1957 Commission of Inquiry into the Operation of the Law relating to the Sale and Supply of Intoxicating Liquor.

Section 23 of the 1960 Act provides that an applicant must prove that the premises in respect of which he seeks to revive the licence has been licensed within five years immediately preceding the application for the grant of a new licence in respect of the formerly licensed premises. This provision had the desired effect.

Equity to Revive The primary purpose of the exception in section 2(1) of the 1902 Act was to preserve existing interests. These applications are subject to statutory objections on the merits, set out in section 4 of the Licensing (Ireland) Act 1833 as amended and extended, as indeed are all applications for new publican's licences. 6–23

However in the case of lapsed licences the High Court has held that where premises were licensed at the relevant time and the lapse was not due to breach of the licensing law, a right in equity to a new licence exists. In *Application of Catherine Bonner*[35] the applicant sought a new licence under section 2(1) of the 1902 Act. No objection was made either to the applicant or to the premises. Objection was taken on the grounds of sufficiency of existing licensed facilities and of declining population. Maguire J. held that the onus was on the objector to sustain his objection. In this case, there was evidence before the court that a licence was in existence in 1902 and continuously thereafter in respect of the same premises. Moreover, the premises had been rebuilt on substantially the same site and licensed until 1941. As the lapse of the licence was not due to a breach of the licensing laws, an equity of revival arose in favour of the applicant.

Policy The right to a licence saved by section 2(1) of the 1902 Act, according to Gibson J. in *R. (Collins) v. Donegal Justices*, attaches: 6–24

> "not to the licence-holder, but to the premises. The intention was probably not so much to protect the property of existing owners as to safeguard the interests of a locality, which by the lapse of a licence might have been deprived of the means of satisfying its legitimate requirements".[36]

Madden J. pronounced himself satisfied that the exception implicitly recognised, *viz.* that an owner of premises licensed by virtue of the section has

> "a claim for consideration, if for any reason he should during the statutory period find himself excluded from the provisions of the law with regard to renewal and transfer, and should be compelled to appear before the licensing authority as an applicant for a new licence".[37]

In general, therefore, there is a recognition by the courts that an applicant in such a case has a proprietorial right, even if this is said to be for the benefit of the public.

---

[35] (1947) 81 I.L.T.R. 143.
[36] See above, n.21: [1903] 2 I.R. 533 at 536.
[37] *Ibid.* at 539.

6–25 **Applicant Must Trade** The practice of reviving a lapsed licence for the purpose of extinguishing it for monetary consideration has been severely censored by the Superior Courts. A licence to sell intoxicating liquor is granted to a person who intends to carry on the licensed trade in a suitable premises identified in the licence. There is no separate property in a licence and the courts have indicated that they will not tolerate what has been called "trafficking in licences".

In *Application of Philip Ryan*,[38] the applicant applied to the Circuit Court for a certificate to enable him to obtain a licence in respect of certain premises which were licensed on the date of the passing of the 1902 Act and thereafter until 1909, when the licence was allowed to lapse. The premises were sold to the applicant who carried on a tobacconist and confectionary business and lived overhead with his family. He admitted that he had no intention of using the premises for the sale of intoxicating liquor and that he had entered into an agreement to extinguish the licence for monetary reward, if permitted by the court. The Circuit Court judge granted the application. However, an objector appealed this decision to the High Court which allowed the appeal. In the course of his judgment in the *Ryan* case, Murnaghan J. stated:

> "The respondent has informed me frankly that he has no intention of using these premises for the sale of intoxicating liquor and that he has agreed to extinguish for a monetary reward such licence as may be granted to him. I have already stated in the course of the argument that it offends my idea of the proper function of the Court to be asked to grant a licence which is to be extinguished immediately."[39]

He continued:

> "In my view no Court should be put into the position of being asked to make such an order as was made by the Circuit Court and such an order does nothing to enhance the reputation of the Courts generally."[40]

It is clear, therefore that a licence cannot be revived for the purposes of its "sale". Since the coming into force of the Finance Act 1992, a substantial number of publicans have been unable to renew their publicans' licences as they have failed to obtain a tax clearance certificate. When this happens, the licence will lapse and a bank or building society may enter into possession of the premises in its capacity as mortgagee and either make an application itself (if so permitted by its constitutive documents) or through a nominee or another publican to revive the licence. The intention of the mortgagee in this situation is to dispose of the premises as distinct from merely the licence in early course, once the licence has been obtained. This practice can be distinguished from the trading in licences disapproved of by the courts as the mortgagee's objective is usually to sell the licensed premises to a purchaser who will continue the trade.

---

[38] [1964] 30 Ir. Jur. Rep. 41.
[39] *Ibid.* at 42.
[40] *Ibid.* at 43.

Evidence of Licence In order to succeed in an application under section 2(1) of the 1902 Act, an applicant is required to adduce evidence that the premises were licensed within the appropriate period, *i.e.* within five years prior to the date of the service of the notice of application on the county registrar. The usual practice is to require the attendance in court of the District Court clerk who keeps the register of licences provided for in section 16 of the Licensing Act (Ireland) 1874 to adduce evidence of when the premises were last licensed.[41] 6–26

Section 36 of the 1874 Act provides that any copy or certificate of any licence which purports to be signed and certified as a true copy or certificate by an officer of the Inland Revenue "shall for every purpose be conclusive evidence of such licence or excise licence". Where there is any doubt whether a licence issued in respect of a particular year, a Customs and Excise official can be required to attend the court to give evidence as to whether a licence issued in respect of that year.

Where it appears from the District Court licensing register that an order entitling an applicant to receive a publican's licence has been made, this is not necessarily sufficient to satisfy the requirements of section 2(1) of the 1902 Act. In *The State (Attorney General) v. Judge Durcan*[42] the applicant applied to the Circuit Court for the issue of a certificate declaring him to be entitled to receive a new licence for the sale of intoxicating liquors in certain premises owned by him but which were not then licensed. He relied upon his application being within the terms of section 2(1) as amended and adduced evidence to establish that his premises had been licensed within the relevant period of time. This evidence was accepted by the Circuit Court judge as establishing that the premises had been licensed within that period and the judge made an order declaring the applicant to be entitled to the certificate. The excise authorities, however, refused to grant the licence on the grounds that the premises mentioned in the certificate had not been licensed within the relevant period of time; a certificate had issued within the period authorising the grant of a licence but the licence had not been taken up. Davitt P. held in the High Court that a conditional order of certiorari to quash the order of Judge Durcan should be discharged because even if he had erred in holding that the premises had been licensed within the relevant period, such error was made by him in the course of his exercise of the unrestricted jurisdiction conferred by the provisions of section 24(2) of the Courts (Supplemental Provisions) Act 1961 and accordingly could not be questioned on certiorari.

---

[41] The Licensing Act (Ireland) 1874, s.35 provides that every entry in any register of licences of any licence, certificate or endorsement "shall for every purpose be evidence of such licence . . . certificate . . . and conviction".

[42] [1964] I.R. 279.

6–27 In *Connolly v. The Collector of Customs and Excise*[43] the applicant had neglected to renew his licence for almost six years. The court refused to direct the defendants to issue a licence in respect of year one of that period, even though the applicant had paid and the respondents had accepted the appropriate excise duty for that year and a certificate of the court entitling the applicant to receive a licence in respect of that year had been granted. The court held that as the applicant had not held a licence during the year preceding his application for renewal, his licence could not be renewed. Accordingly, the applicant was not in a position to prove that he was licensed within the past five years.

2. Premises Adjoining Licensed Premises

Purpose of Exception

6–28 Section 6 of the 1902 Act, as amended by section 24 of the Intoxicating Liquor Act 1960, contemplates the development by structural alteration or by taking in additional premises, of premises which are already licensed or which have been licensed within the past five years. Section 6 was enacted by way of a special exception to the general restriction on the grant of new licences contained in section 2 of the 1902 Act and it applied where the alteration or expansion was such as to "render the said licensed premises more suitable for the business carried on therein".[44]

Section 24 of the Intoxicating Liquor Act 1960 limits the time during which premises were to be licensed for the purposes of the application, to a period of five years prior to the date on which the notice of application is served on the County Registrar. Before this, an applicant had to prove that adjoining premises were attached to the premises which were originally licensed, and that such premises were licensed at the date of the 1902 Act.

In *The State (O'Malley) v. Circuit Court Judge of Dublin*[45] where application was made for the grant of a new licence in respect of premises comprising Nos. 8, 9, 10 and 11 Upper Ormond Quay, the Circuit Court judge held that he did not have jurisdiction to grant the application as No. 11 was not attached to or adjoining premises which were licensed at the date of the passing of the 1902 Act. Only No. 8 had been licensed for the sale of intoxicating liquor at that date.

The Supreme Court, reversing the High Court, held that the Circuit Court judge had jurisdiction to grant the application. It was not necessary, in the opinion of Kennedy C.J., that the same licence should be subsisting at the date of the application for the new licence as was subsisting in 1902, but it was necessary that some of the premises should have been licensed in 1902.

---

[43] [1988–93] 4 I.T.R. 419.
[44] See the Licensing (Ireland) Act 1902, s.6.
[45] (1934) 68 I.L.T.R. 79 at 81, *per* Kennedy C.J.

The five-year time limit introduced by section 24 of the Intoxicating Liquor Act 1960 is a recognition by the legislature that several section 6 applications may be brought and that there is no necessity to prove that the extension attaches to the original licensed structure. Further, section 6 applications can be brought in respect of premises licensed long after 1902.

STATUTORY PROVISION

Section 6 of the Licensing (Ireland) Act 1902, as amended by section 24 of the Intoxicating Liquor Act 1960, provides: 6–29

> "Nothing in this Act shall operate to prevent the granting of new licences, where the licensing authority thinks fit, to premises attached to or adjoining premises licensed for the sale of intoxicating liquors at any time during the period of five years immediately before the day on which notice of an application for the grant of a certificate entitling the holder thereof to receive any such new licence is given, pursuant to rules of court, to the appropriate County Registrar or to the appropriate District Court Clerk, as the case may be; provided always, that such new licence as last herein-before mentioned shall only be granted in order to render the said licensed premises more suitable for the business carried on therein."

Rateable Valuation

There is no requirement in the licensing code that an application pursuant to section 6 of the 1902 Act must fall within the provisions relating to the valuation of a licensed premises contained in section 5 of that Act. 6–30

Extension to be Unlicensed at Date of Application

O'Flaherty J. in *Re Application of Oshawa Limited* expresses the view that in a section 6 application two elements must be present: 6–31

> "*viz.* a licensed premises and an existing, adjoining, unlicensed premises. The section does not appear to contemplate the grant of a new licence in respect of the amalgamation of two existing licensed premises. The whole tenor of the section envisages licensed premises being amalgamated with what had up until then been unlicensed premises."[46]

He pointed out that the reference in section 6 to "the said licensed premises" would be meaningless if both premises were licensed. McCarthy J. however, reserved for the future the question as to whether section 6 is necessarily limited to cases where the premises attached to or adjoining licensed premises at the relevant time are themselves unlicensed.

---

[46] [1992] 2 I.R. 425 at 435.

STATUTORY CONSEQUENCES

New Licence

6–32 1. A licence granted under section 6 of the Licensing (Ireland) Act 1902 should be a licence of the same character and not more comprehensive in quality and character than the licence attaching to the existing premises adjoining the extension. In *R. (Collins) v. Donegal Justices*, Lord O'Brien L.C.J. said, *inter alia*:

> "I think that the exception or enabling power in the 6th section extended only to the licensing of new premises in a manner identical with the way in which the original premises, which the new premises were intended to improve, were licensed".[47]

6–33 2. Judge Sheridan dealt expressly with new licences granted under section 6 of the 1902 Act in his judgment in *D.P.P. v. Farrell* where he stated:

> "There is nothing in section 6 to circumscribe in any way the issue of the new licence or make it conditional upon a transfer of existing endorsements or conditions....I have, therefore, come to the conclusion that any endorsements prior to the date of the second Order under section 6 of the 1902 Act in 1977 disappeared."[48]

Any endorsements which existed in respect of the original licence, therefore, disappear upon the grant of a new licence under section 6.

Attached to or Adjoining

6–34 The question often arises as to whether an extension must physically touch the existing licensed premises. The expression "attached to" implies actual contiguity. The interpretation of the expression "adjoining" is more difficult.

In *R. (McClinchy) v. Greer*,[49] the applicant applied for a new licence under section 6 of the 1902 Act in respect of premises in Buncrana. The "attached to or adjoining" premises were separated from the licensed premises by three intervening houses. Palles C.B. was quite satisfied that in these circumstances the licensing authority had no power to grant a new licence pursuant to section 6.

In determining whether or not two premises adjoin one another for the purposes of falling within section 6, the test appears to be whether the application would result in the grant of a licence for one premises, or two separate and distinct premises or units.

---

[47] Above, n.36, at 536. The same case is also reported at (1902) 36 I.L.T.R. 229 where O'Brien L.C.J. is quoted as saying "I think that the exception or enabling power under section 6 extends only to the licensing of new premises in a manner identical with the manner of the licence attached to the old premises."

[48] Above, n.17, at 109.

[49] Above, n.12.

In *Re McElvaney*,[50] O'Higgins J. stated that:

> "the section envisages two buildings attached to one another or so close to one another as to be described aptly as adjoining ... it would seem to me to be impossible to regard two buildings comparatively widely separated by other buildings and by open space as one distinct whole, capable of being licensed as one unit".[51]

In that case, both buildings were separated by other buildings and by two gardens. O'Higgins J. held that the application did not fall within the provisions of section 6.

This interpretation of section 6 is reinforced by reference to section 10 of the Excise Licences Act 1825 which provides for the grant of a licence in respect of "one separate and distinct *set of* premises, such premises being all adjoining or contiguous to each other, and situate in one place, and held together for the same trade or business". The expression "adjoining" is again used here; it is clear that a licence cannot be granted in respect of different drinking outlets. However, two buildings can constitute a set of premises, provided each building serves a common purpose, being the business referred to in the licence.

New Licence

The section does not authorise the grant of a further licence for the adjoining premises in addition to the licence attaching to the existing premises. A new licence is granted for premises comprising the existing licensed area together with the adjoining premises. The existing licence becomes extinguished upon the grant of the new licence for the composite premises. In *The State (O'Malley) v. Circuit Court Judge of Dublin,*[52] it was held that a licence granted under section 6 of the Licensing (Ireland) Act 1902 should take the form of a new licence in respect of the whole premises, comprising the old and the new. In this case, Fitzgibbon J. was satisfied that the proper interpretation of the section was that it authorised the issue of a new licence in respect of both the old and the new premises regarded as a whole. He stated that this was clear from the requirement that the new premises should be such as to render the old more suitable for the business carried on therein.[53] 6–35

Thus, where a licence is granted under section 6 of the 1902 Act, it is a new licence and not an extension of the existing licence. In *Re Centennial Properties Ltd*,[54] it was established that the grant of a licence under section 6 constituted a new licence "first granted" from the time the licence issues to the licence 6–36

[50] Unreported, High Court, O'Higgins J., April 2, 1974.
[51] *Ibid.* at p. 3.
[52] Above, n.45.
[53] *Ibid.* at 81.
[54] Unreported, High Court, Finlay P., December 20, 1983.

holder following the issue by the court of the requisite certificate. The licence, therefore, was not a graft on the original licence. In that case, a publican objected to the application on the ground, *inter alia*, that the proposed premises was within one mile of his premises[55] (the Jobstown Inn) which had been licensed from about 1860 and remained licensed up to 1982. However, in 1982, a substantial extension was constructed to the premises and a licence under section 6 of the 1902 Act was granted. Finlay P. stated:

> "I am satisfied that creates an anomaly and does not appear to be consistent with the provisions of section 6 of the 1902 Act which apparently encourages the bringing of an application under that section so as to improve the premises for the purpose of the licensed trade, but it is not within my function nor should I by judicial decision in the interpreting of the statute seek to remove anomalies unless the statute would justify me in so doing."[56]

Existing Licence

6–37 The applicant does not have to prove in a section 6 application that the premises are licensed at the date of the application: the section merely requires proof that the premises were licensed at any time during the five-year period immediately before the day on which notice of an application for the grant of a certificate was given to the county registrar.

Proviso

6–38 The proviso to section 6 of the 1902 Act precludes the grant of a new licence by the court except for the purpose of rendering the licensed premises more suitable for the business carried on therein. In *Re Brannigan and the Licensing (Ireland) Act 1902*,[57] Haugh J. held that an increase in the amount of trade of a licensed public house, the effect of which is to render the existing accommodation inadequate, will not *per se* entitle the licensee to an extension of the licensed premises. This is notwithstanding that the provision of additional accommodation would render the existing premises more suitable for the business carried on therein. Haugh J. accepted the submission that the provision of better sanitary accommodation, cellarage, bottling and storage space would render the existing premises more suitable for the business carried on. He did not accept the applicant's argument that owing to an increase in custom, he should add extra drinking space to avoid overcrowding at peak times. He stated:

> "This argument I cannot accept. I might just as well give the applicant a new

[55] The application was made pursuant to section 13 of the Intoxicating Liquor Act 1960. This affects the right of publicans in a rural area who have expanded their premises to object to the grant of a new publican's licence for a premises situate within one mile of their established pubs.
[56] *Re Centennial Properties Ltd*, above, n.54, at p. 3.
[57] [1947] 13 Ir. Jur. Rep. 1.

> licence for premises across the street... I am not going to provide added drinking space . . .".[58]

In *Re Moylan*[59] an application was made under section 6 to increase the licensed area to include an adjoining building to be used for storage purposes and the housing of boiler equipment for central heating. The Circuit Court was not satisfied that the premises as so extended was "suitable" within the meaning of section 6. In the appeal to the High Court, Dixon J. stated:

> "There is a possibility that the extended portion of the applicant's premises may be used for drinking purposes, for once a licence is granted it permits drinking on all parts of the premises, and it is my view that the entire premises, as extended, are unsuitable for drinking purposes."[60]

He was, however, prepared to grant the new licence on an undertaking from the applicant to the court and to the police authorities that the user be confined to storage and the installation of boiler equipment. The Court was satisfied that the extension on the basis of the proposed user was suitable but would not have granted the application if the extension were to be used for drinking purposes.

This section is very frequently invoked. It has been the experience of the courts that the evidence adduced by applicants under this section is similar to the facts found by Haugh J. in *Brannigan* (above) and that little or no additional evidence is adduced. The vast majority of these applications have been allowed. Having regard to the wording of the section, this approach is correct as the court in each case may act within the discretion given it by the section.

In *R. (Blackburne) v. Down Justices*,[61] Palles C.B. considered whether there was any evidence that the licensed premises was more suitable for the business carried on therein. He stated:

> "... the new building in which it is intended that the new business should be carried on, does not include any substantial part of the former premises. The part common to both sets of premises, is infinitesimal. The proviso of section 6 is that any such new licence shall only be granted in order to render "the said licensed premises", which means the premises formerly licensed, more suitable for the business carried on therein. "Therein" means in the formerly licensed premises. Here it is not intended to carry on the business in the formerly licensed premises, or in any substantial part of them. The intention is to carry it on in premises which, with an infinitesimal exception, are wholly different."[62]

The court will have regard to the user of the existing licensed area in deciding whether the section can be invoked to license adjoining premises whose intended user is a restaurant, function room, dance hall, or for off-sales. If it is 6–39

---

[58] *Ibid.* at 2.
[59] [1947] 13 Ir. Jur. Rep. 3.
[60] *Ibid.* at 4.
[61] (1904) 38 I.L.T.R. 67.
[62] *Ibid.* at 68 and 69.

proposed to introduce a completely new element to the existing licensed business, it may well be that the proviso is not satisfied. The view could be taken that if the existing premises were restricted to bar or bar and lounge facilities and the sale of intoxicating liquor only, an extension for the purpose of creating or accommodating a new business or businesses does not render the existing "licensed premises" more suitable for the business carried on therein".

Palles C.B. in *R. (Blackburne) v. Down Justices* (above) referring to "the business carried on therein" was of the view that this refers to business already carried on and not business which is to be carried on in the future.[63] The court therefore in assessing whether or not an application comes within the proviso, should deal with the business as it presently stands and not an expected increase or development in the business.

In *R. (Kennedy) v. Antrim Justices*,[64] Palles C.B. also concluded that the words "to render the said licensed premises more suitable for the business carried on therein" mean the premises formerly licensed.

B. Premises Situate in a City or Town

Introduction

6–40 Section 4 of the Licensing (Ireland) Act 1902 provides for the licensing of premises which are situate in a city or a town, once the increase in population as defined by section 8 of the 1902 Act has occurred, in accordance with the conditions laid down in the section, as amended.

STATUTORY PROVISION

Section 4 of the Licensing (Ireland) Act 1902, as amended by section 19 of the Intoxicating Liquor Act 1962, provides:

> "Where, owing to increase in population, there is a growth or extension of any city or town, and the licensing authority are satisfied that the restrictions in this Act on the granting of licences may be relaxed, they may grant a licence to any applicant, notwithstanding that the same would be otherwise forbidden by this Act; provided that such licence shall be granted only for premises situate in the parish in which such increase in population has taken place, and in substitution for an existing licence or licences held in respect of premises situate within the city or town, as the case may be, comprising the whole or any part of the parish or for premises situate in a parish in which the increase aforesaid has not taken place if the premises are situate in the city or town and either—

---

[63] Although FitzGibbon and Walker JJ. expressed the view that "therein" referred to the premises to which the new licence must be granted.

[64] (1903) 37 I.L.T.R. 130 at 131.

(a) the city or town is within the parish and there is an increase in population in the area comprising the city or town, or
(b) a part only of the city or town is within the parish and there is an increase in population in the area comprising such part,

and the licence is in substitution for an existing licence or licences held in respect of premises situate in the city or town aforesaid in the parish aforesaid."[65]

Scope of Section

This exception provides for three different sets of circumstances: 6–41

1. Where the application concerns premises situate in a parish in which the required increase in population has taken place and the licence being tendered for extinguishment is an existing licence held in respect of premises situate within the same city or town.

   This provision is the original section 4 before it was extended by section 19 of the Intoxicating Liquor Act 1962. It can only be invoked where it can be proved that the appropriate increase in population has taken place in the parish within which the premises are situate. However, the licence to be offered for extinguishment need not be attached to premises situate within the same parish: it is sufficient if the licence offered is an existing licence held in respect of premises situate within the city or town. It is not sufficient if the existing licence attaches to premises situate within the same parish but outside the city or town boundaries. The statute clearly requires that the licence to be tendered is attached to premises situate within the referenced city or town which comprises the entire or a portion of the parish.

2. Where the premises are situate in a parish in which such increase in population has not taken place and the city or town is within the parish.

   In such a case the following must be satisfied:

   (i) there must be an increase in population in the area comprising the city or town within which the parish is situate;

   (ii) the licence tendered for extinguishment must be an existing licence held in respect of premises situate in the city or town aforesaid and also the parish aforesaid.

[65] In *Jennings v. Kelly* [1940] A.C. 206 it was held that it is sufficient for an applicant for the grant of a licence under section 4 to prove that there had been an increase of not less than 25 per cent in the population in the particular ward of the city or town in which the premises for which the licence is sought are situate; he is not required to prove such increase as regards the city or town as a whole.

In this case, the applicant does not have to prove that an increase in population takes place in the parish within which his premises are situate. Having proved that his premises are situate in the city or town and that the city or town is within the parish within which his premises are situate, he must satisfy the court that the appropriate increase in population in the area of the parish which comprises the city or town has occurred. This amendment was passed to remedy the situation where a substantial parish included a rural area as well as the city or town area and the increase in population only occurred in the city or town area. The drawback to invoking this portion of the jurisdiction is that the licence being offered for extinguishment must not only come from premises situate in the city or town but also from the parish within which the premises in question are situate.

3. Where the premises are situate in a parish in which the increase in population has not taken place and a part only of the city or town is within the parish within which the premises are situate. In this case, an applicant must prove the following:

   (i) there is the required increase in population in the area comprising the part of the city or town which is within the parish;

   (ii) the licence tendered for extinguishment must be an existing licence held in respect of premises situate in the city or town and also the parish.

   Where the appropriate increase in population has not taken place in the parish within which the premises in question are situate and a part only of the city or town is within the parish, the applicant will have to prove to the court that the required increase in population has taken place within that part of the city or town which is within such parish. Similarly, the licence to be extinguished must be attached to a premises situate in both the city or town and the parish.

JURISDICTIONAL REQUIREMENTS

6–42 Proof of the following matters are necessary to found the jurisdiction of the court:

1. Increase in Population

   The expression "increase in population" is defined in section 8 of the Licensing (Ireland) 1902 Act as "an increase of not less than 25 per cent of the population according to the last census". Section 14(2) of the Intoxicating Liquor (General) Act 1924 construes the expression as an "increase of the population according to the last census of not less than 25 per cent over the population according to the census taken in the year 1901". In *R. (Gamble) v. Westmeath Justices*,[66] it was held that as the population of

[66] (1912) 46 I.L.T.R. 76.

Mullingar in 1901 had not been proved, the court had no basis upon which to determine whether there had been an increase of 25 per cent in the population of Mullingar since the census of 1901. Proper evidence could not be supplemented by local knowledge. O'Brien L.C.J. stated that there was no basis of fact which furnished evidence of an increase of 25 per cent in the population since 1901: "it was mere speculation". On this ground the order of the justices granting the licence was quashed.

The legislature intervened in the form of section 30 of the Intoxicating Liquor Act 1962 which provided that where an application was made to a court under the 1902 Act, documents compiled by the Central Statistics Office are evidence, until the contrary is proven, of matters relating to population statistics. Section 30(1) defined "last census" as referred to in section 8 of the 1902 Act as "the last census of population taken under the Statistics Acts 1926 and 1946 from which statistics of population other than statistics which purport to be provisional only, published by the Stationery Office, have been derived". Section 30(2)(c) of the Intoxicating Liquor Act 1962 provides for certification by the Central Statistics Office of statistics contained in the most recent census and the section provides that the certificate shall be evidence of such statistics.

Section 30(2)(c) of the Intoxicating Liquor Act 1962 provides:

> "a certificate purporting to be signed by the Director, or other person for the time being in charge, of the Central Statistics Office and containing statistics of population and purporting to certify that the statistics are derived from the last census and, either that no later census has been taken or that statistics of population derived from a later census will not be published during the two months immediately following the date on which the certificate is given, shall, without proof of the signature of the person purporting to sign the certificate or that he was the Director, or for the time being in charge, of the Central Statistics Office, be evidence, until the contrary is proved, of the matters relating to statistics contained in the certificate and of the matters certified in and by the certificate".

A similar provision is contained in paragraph (d) which provides for certification in a similar form of statistics derived from the census taken in the year 1901. The Central Statistics Office will issue:

(i) a certificate as to the census figures in the year 1901; and

(ii) a certificate containing statistics as to the population of the relevant parish according to the most recent census. This certificate will also state that no later census has been taken.

The certificate issued pursuant to section 30(2)(c) is valid for a period of two months only from the date of issue.

6–43 2. City or Town

Where he brings himself within any of the circumstances provided for in section 4 the applicant must prove that his premises are situate within a city or town for the purposes of section 4. In *Re McCann*[67] it was held that the words "city" or "town" means "the corporate or quasi corporate entity established by law as a community for municipal or legal administration." The popular interpretation of the words as a mere assembly of houses and buildings was rejected by the court. Section 8 of the 1902 Act provides that expressions not expressly defined therein "shall have respectively the same meaning as in the Licensing (Ireland) Acts 1833 to 1900". The word "town" is defined by section 37 of the Licensing Act (Ireland) 1874 and includes the following:

> "Any parliamentary or municipal borough;
>
> Any town having commissioners under [the Lighting of Towns (Ireland) Act 1828];
>
> Any town having municipal commissioners [under the Municipal Corporations (Ireland) Act 1840];
>
> Any town having town commissioners or commissioners under the Towns Improvement Act 1854, or under any Local and Personal Act."

The whole system of local administration of towns and cities became more streamlined under the Local Government (Ireland) Act 1898. It provided that districts controlled by urban sanitary authorities were to become urban districts, except for Dublin, Cork, Limerick and Waterford which were constituted county boroughs. Under the Local Government (Reorganisation) Act 1985, Galway city was elevated to county borough status. The Local Government Act 1994 declassified Dun Laoghaire as a borough and it has since been incorporated into the administrative area of Dun Laoghaire Rathdown County Council. Other urban districts, *i.e.* Clonmel, Drogheda, Kilkenny, Sligo and Wexford, which had ancient charters, were to be known as municipal boroughs. To date, 32 towns have been given legally defined boundaries under the Towns Improvement (Ireland) Act 1854 although under the Local Government Act 1994, some towns have lost this status.[68] All these boundaries are subject to alteration for local development and administration reasons. These changes are published on the ordnance survey maps as soon as the new revisions take place.

[67] [1953] I.R. 118.
[68] Local Government Act 1994, s.62.

County Boroughs Cork, Dublin, Galway, Limerick, Waterford 6–44

Municipal Boroughs Clonmel, Drogheda, Kilkenny, Sligo, Wexford

Towns with Commissioners set up under the Towns Improvement (Ireland) Act 1854 Ardee, Balbriggan, Ballybay, Ballyshannon, Bandon, Bantry, Belturbet, Boyle, Cootehill, Droichead Nua (Newbridge), Edenderry, Gorey, Granard, Greystones, Kilkee, Leixlip, Lismore, Loughrea, Mountmellick, Muine Beag (Bagenalstown), Mullingar, Passage West, Portlaoise, Shannon, Tramore, Tuam.[69]

Urban District Councils Section 22 of the Local Government (Ireland) Act 1898 provided that the existing "urban sanitary authorities" should thenceforth be called "Urban District Councils" and those areas having these bodies are: 6–45

> Arklow, Athlone, Athy, Ballina, Ballinasloe, Birr, Bray, Buncrana, Bundoran, Carlow, Carrickmacross, Carrick-on-Suir, Cashel, Castlebar, Castleblayney, Cavan, Ceanannus Mor (Kells), Clonakilty, Clones, Cobh, Dundalk, Dungarvan, Ennis, Enniscorthy, Fermoy, Killarney, Kilrush, Kinsale, Letterkenny, Listowel, Longford, Macroom, Mallow, Midleton, Monaghan, Naas, Navan, Nenagh, New Ross, Skibereen, Templemore, Thurles, Tipperary, Tralee, Trim, Tullamore, Westport, Wicklow and Youghal.

County Borough of Dublin In *Re McCann*,[70] it was held that the County Borough of Dublin constituted a city within the meaning of section 4. In this case, it was held that the word "town" contained in section 4 of the 1902 Act was to be construed in accordance with the definition of town as provided by section 37 of the Licensing Act (Ireland) 1874, and that the interpretation of the word "city" should be equally strict. O'Byrne J. stated: 6–46

> "In determining whether I should apply the definition clause, I consider that I should ask myself whether there is anything in section 4 which clearly indicates that the word "town" is not used in the special sense in which it is to be construed in the code. After careful consideration I can find no such indication."[71]

He continued:

> "[T]he question whether premises were situate in the city or town in question depended upon whether they were within or without the legal boundaries of such city or town."[72]

In that case, as the licence which it was proposed to surrender was held in respect of premises which were situate outside the municipal boundaries of

[69] Local Government Act 1994, s.62, provides that the 1854 Act does not apply to the towns of Callan, Fethard, Newcastle West, Rathkeale, Roscommon and Tullow.
[70] Above, n.67.
[71] *Ibid.* at 123.
[72] *Ibid.*

the city of Dublin, it was held that such licence was not an "existing licence" as contemplated in section 4.

6–47 *Dublin Metropolitan District* The County Borough of Dublin is deemed for the purposes of the licensing code to include the whole of the Dublin Metropolitan District and such Borough and District is deemed, for the purposes of the Acts, to be a city.[73]

In *The State (Wyer) v. O'Sullivan*, the majority of the Supreme Court were of the view, affirming Davitt P., that the words "city or town" in section 4 of the 1902 Act must be read as including the "notional County Borough in which the Dublin Metropolitan Area is deemed to be".[74] Murnaghan J., who dissented, refused to sanction the grant of a licence for a premises in Stillorgan which were situate in a parish which was partly in the Borough of Dun Laoghaire and partly in the County of Dublin, where the licence being offered for extinguishment attached to a premises situate in Harold's Cross which was situate in the County Borough of Dublin. The entire of the parish within which the premises at Harold's Cross were situate was within the boundaries of the County Borough of Dublin and no part thereof was within the County of Dublin or in the Borough of Dun Laoghaire. However, both areas were situated within the Dublin Metropolitan area, and the Dublin Metropolitan area, pursuant to section 1(2) of the Intoxicating Liquor Act 1927, is, for the purposes of the application of the 1927 Act deemed to be the County Borough of Dublin. Murnaghan J. was not satisfied that the Dublin Metropolitan area constituted a city or town within the ambit of section 4 of the 1902 Act. He noted that the words "County Borough" were used in the 1902 Act.

Section 35 of the Intoxicating Liquor Act 1962 removed any doubt as to the interpretation of "city" by providing as follows:

> "35(1) References in the Licensing Acts to the Dublin Metropolitan Area shall be deemed to be references to the Dublin Metropolitan District.
>
> (2) The county borough of Dublin shall be deemed, for the purposes of the Licensing Acts, to include the whole of the Dublin Metropolitan District, and such borough and District shall be deemed, for the purposes of those Acts, to be a city."

So, the County Borough of Dublin, as well as the Dublin Metropolitan Distict, is a city. The boundary of the Dublin Metropolitan District has been extended over the years, but for the purposes of the licensing code, the boundary referred to is the boundary as it was in 1945.[75]

---

[73] Intoxicating Liquor Act 1962, s.35(2).
[74] [1953] I.R. 109 at 117, *per* Lavery J.
[75] Intoxicating Liquor Act 1981, s.1.

3. Civil Parish

It is important to identify the parish correctly, as an applicant must be able to prove that the increase in population occurred in a parish, or that the city or town is within the parish, or that a part only of the city or town is within the parish. Proof from the Ordnance Survey Office is adduced as to the parish within which the premises are situate and where necessary, within which the premises to which the licence being offered for extinguishment are situate. The Ordnance Survey Office always refers to the civil parish: the ecclesiastical parish is an informal entity, not having its origins in statute. 6–48

4. Rateable Valuation 6–49

In the case of an application under section 4 of the 1902 Act, an applicant must prove that the rateable valuation of the premises is not less than:

£30 in the city of Dublin;

£20 in the cities of Cork, Limerick, Waterford;

£15 in the city of Kilkenny and the town of Galway;

£12 in any other town of over 10,000 inhabitants as ascertained by the most recent census; and

£10 in all other places.

The prescribed rateable valuations have not changed since the enactment of section 5 of the 1902 Act. Section 33(2) of the Intoxicating Liquor Act 1960 provided that in construing section 5 of the 1902 Act "rateable valuation" is deemed to include a provisional valuation issued by the Commissioner of Valuation. In *Re Application of Thomas Kiernan*[76] it was held that proof of valuation at declaratory stage was not necessary where it was evident that section 5 would be complied with on completion of the premises. Prior to the enactment of this provision, a certificate of rateable valuation was required before a certificate for a new licence could be granted; a provisional valuation did not satisfy the requirements of the section.[77]

5. Licence to be Extinguished 6–50

Licence or Licences The licence or licences to be extinguished must be an existing licence or licences. The court may require the extinguishment of more than one licence in an application for the grant of a publican's licence. The author has no experience of such a requirement being imposed by the court. The universal practice is that the extinguishment of one licence is sufficient to meet the statutory requirement. In 1957 the Commission of

[76] [1965] 31 Ir. Jur. Rep. 4
[77] *R. (Harrington) v. Roscommon Justices* [1913] 2 I.R. 332.

Inquiry into the Operation of the Laws relating to the Sale and Supply of Intoxicating Liquor recommended that the statutory provision be "amended" to require the extinguishment of two licences. This recommendation was never given legislative effect.

6–51 *Location* In all the circumstances contemplated by section 4 as set forth at the beginning of this chapter, it seems clear that the licence to be extinguished must be situate within the city or town itself. Section 19 of the Intoxicating Liquor Act 1962 introduced the requirement that the licence be situate in the city or town and also in the parish within which the premises are situate, in certain circumstances.

6–52 *Existing* The licence or licences to be tendered for extinguishment must be current at the date of the hearing of the application. The Superior Courts have not conclusively determined that the "existing" licence must be a trading licence, *i.e.* that it attaches to premises in which trading was being carried on at the time it is offered for extinguishment. In *Southside Taverns Ltd (nominee: Kevin Molloy)*,[78] Judge Sheehy noted that the objectors to the application had submitted, *inter alia*:

> "... that the said licence was not an "existing licence" but had lapsed, or had been rendered invalid by reason of the failure of the Savings Bank to trade in the premises".

The licence was held by Tolima Investments Ltd through their nominee, Edmund Ryan, who had entered into an agreement with the applicant for the extinguishment of the licence. The owner of the premises to which the licence attached was the Trustee Savings Bank which did not at any time carry on trade in the licensed premises and did not intend to do so. The bank did not apply for an ad interim transfer of the licence. Judge Sheehy held that as the licence holder had no title, estate or interest in the licensed premises and the licence attached thereto, he was satisfied in the light of this and "also in particular the undisputed fact that no trade had been carried on in the said premises since 24th February, 1982", that the licence was not an existing licence for the purposes of section 4. He referred to the decision of Carroll J. in *The State (Pheasantry Ltd) v. District Justice Donnelly* where she had noted in the course of her judgment:

> "... the Intoxicating Liquor Act 1960, ... permits the sale of licences for the purposes of extinguishment. But the person selling had to continue trading so that when the application was made to extinguish it, it was a valid and subsisting licence".[79]

---

[78] Unreported, Circuit Court, Judge Sheehy, July 12, 1982.
[79] [1982] I.L.R.M. 512 at 515.

In contrast, Butler J., in *Re Irish Cinemas Ltd*,[80] where the application was under section 14 of the Intoxicating Liquor Act 1960, rejected the objector's submission that the original premises were not validly licensed at the time they were demolished, because no business had been carried on in the premises during the year prior to the granting of the last renewal of the licence. He stated: 6–53

> "However, there is now and was at the relevant date a licence in existence granted on foot of a certificate issued by a court of competent jurisdiction. This Court is bound to accept that licence as having been properly granted and as being valid and subsisting unless and until the order of that court is quashed on certiorari."[81]

In *Re Tivoli Cinemas Ltd*[82] Lynch J. held that despite the fact that the licence tendered for extinguishment attached to premises in which trade had not been carried on from June 1989 to September 1989, the licensee had been entitled to renew his licence in September 1989. He held that an objection that the licence was not valid or subsisting at the relevant time failed.

In *Application of Bresc Inns*,[83] Judge Smith rejected the objector's argument that the licence which was offered for extinguishment was not an existing licence for the purposes of section 4. The premises to which the licence attached had not traded for a period of three to four years previously; it comprised a solicitor's office and hairdressing salon.

C. Premises Situate in the Immediate Vicinity of Another Premises

Introduction

There are three exceptions to the 1902 Act which are discussed under this heading. A further exception involving the concept of immediate vicinity which is contained in section 21 of the Intoxicating Liquor Act 1943, which provides for the grant of a new licence in a rural area, is not dealt with under this heading, but is discussed below at paragraph 6–100. It should be noted that the exceptions categorised under this heading can be invoked in respect of a premises located in a rural area. The categories of exception are as follows: 6–54

[80] (1972) 106 I.L.T.R. 17
[81] *Ibid.* at 21.
[82] [1992] 1 I.R. 412
[83] Unreported, Circuit Court, Judge Smith, February 25, 1994.

1. grant of new licence for a suitable premises in the vicinity of premises in respect of which a licence has just been extinguished or surrendered by virtue of an expiring lease (see below paragraphs 6–65 *et seq.*);
2. grant of new licence in respect of premises substituted for destroyed premises (see below paragraphs 6–75 *et seq.*);
3. grant of new licence in respect of premises substituted for demolished premises (see below paragraphs 6–85 *et seq.*);

Immediate Vicinity

6–55 The concept of immediate vicinity in relation to the grant of new licences was introduced by the Licensing (Ireland) Act 1902. Section 3 of the 1902 Act requires that the substituted premises must be in the immediate vicinity of the original premises to which the surrendered licence was attached. Section 22 of the Intoxicating Liquor Act 1943 requires that the substituted premises be in the immediate vicinity of the demolished premises.

Section 14 of the Intoxicating Liquor Act 1960 in contrast, requires that the substituted premises be located on the site of the original premises, or, if they are not located on the site of the original premises, that they be located either partly on that site, or in the immediate vicinity of that site. An application under section 3 of the 1902 Act and section 22(1) of the 1943 Act cannot succeed where the substituted premises are on the same site as the original premises. A premises which is mainly built on the ground occupied by the previously licenced premises cannot be said to be in the immediate vicinity of the previously licensed premises.[84]

6–56 The expression "immediate vicinity" has not been defined by statute. However, there are a number of cases which have dealt with the expression; each case depends upon its own facts. The interpretation of the expression by the courts differs depending on whether the premises are situate in a rural area or in a city or a town. It is a matter for the applicant to prove whether the premises are situate in a city or town or in a rural area.

Judge Moonan, in *Re Application of Campbell and Gallagher*, was satisfied that the expression "immediate vicinity" was incapable of rigid definition:

> "[the] application [of "immediate vicinity"] must depend upon the facts and circumstances of each particular case; and upon the personal views of each individual judge upon the evidence adduced".[85]

[84] *Re The Dunleath Arms* [1902] 36 I.L.T.R. 184.
[85] (1944) 78 I.L.T.R. 121 at 122.

In *Application of Leo Ward*,[86] Ó Dálaigh C.J. sought to define the expression by having recourse to the *Shorter Oxford Dictionary* (second edition). He was satisfied that the legislature was deliberately avoiding a precise definition by its use of the word "vicinity". He noted that the qualification of vicinity by its adjective of "immediate" effected a limitation and that the expression applied to premises situate in the city, town and country and added:

> "In its policy of encouraging the abandonment and demolition of old and unsuitable licensed premises the Oireachtas did not wish to lay down any very precise test of propinquity and considered that this was a matter that could in each case be decided by the Courts, with the safeguard that licensing of the new premises should not be unreasonably detrimental to other licensed premises in the neighbourhood of the new premises."[87]

Relevant Considerations

From a review of the case law which deals with the question of immediate vicinity, the following factors have been taken into account by the courts. **6–57**

(i) Distance between original premises and new premises The test which the courts appear to use is whether a distance is of "no account".[88] As the phrase applies in respect of premises situate in a city, town or rural area, however, the distance between two premises in a rural area can be considerably greater than that between premises which are situate in a city or town. **6–58**

1. City or Town

   In the *Ward* case (above), the distance in question was approximately 312 yards and Ó Dálaigh C.J. was satisfied that this constituted "immediate vicinity". The Chief Justice also indicated that in determining the test of propinquity, regard should be had to the policy of abandoning old and unsuitable premises. In *Application of James Walls,*[89] an application to license 19a Upper O'Connell Street and to offer the licence which previously attached to the Cosmo Bar at the corner of Hawkins Street and Townsend Street, some 733 yards distant for extinguishment was refused. A further application to license 19a Upper O'Connell Street was successful where the licence offered in substitution attached to premises situate at 42 Parnell Street, 420 yards away.[90] An application to license Jonathan's,

[86] [1966] I.R. 413.
[87] *Ibid.* at 425.
[88] *Ibid.*
[89] (1969) 103 I.L.T.R. 113.
[90] Referred to by O'Hanlon J. in *Application of Brendan McGrath*, unreported, High Court, August 4, 1987, at p. 4.

situate in Grafton Street and to offer the old Cosmo Bar licence for extinguishment, where the distance involved was 720 yards, was unsuccessful.[91] Butler J. in *Re Irish Cinemas Ltd*[92] followed the decision of the Supreme Court in the *Ward* case where he held that a distance of 300 yards came within the expression "immediate vicinity".

A distance of 645 yards was rejected by O'Hanlon J. in *Application of Brendan McGrath*[93] although he accepted that a distance of 421 yards came within the expression.

Lynch J. in *Re Tivoli Cinema Ltd*[94] was satisfied that a distance of 510 yards by road, being within "easy walking distance" and within the same shopping or business and social area was sufficient to satisfy the requirement of "immediate vicinity".

A distance of 472 yards was held to be sufficient in *Perfect Pies Ltd v. Redmond Doran* where Lynch J. stated:

> "These distances can easily be walked in four to five minutes, and are therefore of little account, to adapt the wording used in the case of *In re Leo Ward.* ... Moreover, these distances are within the range which the courts have declared as being within the immediate vicinity in a number of previously decided cases."[95]

6–59 2. Rural Area

The distance in question in *Re Wright and the Intoxicating Liquor Act, 1943*[96] was two and a quarter miles but both premises were in the same District Court area, electoral division and parish. In *Re Application of Campbell and Gallagher*,[97] Mrs Campbell sought to use a licence on Rutland Island for the purposes of applying for a full seven-day publican's licence in Burtonport, a distance of half a mile, *i.e.* half a mile of the Atlantic. Judge Moonan was satisfied that the intention of the legislature was that the two premises "must be in the same social and economic entity and must cater for much the same community or class". He did not regard the separation of the premises by water as being a barrier: "In this area of small islands . . . archipelagoes, narrow straits of water, so far from being barriers, are in fact the natural highways of the inhabitants."[98]

---

[91] *Application of Power Supermarkets Ltd* (1969) 103 I.L.T.R. 137.
[92] Above, n.80.
[93] Above, n.90.
[94] Above, n.82.
[95] [1993] I.L.R.M. 737 at 739.
[96] [1947] 13 Ir. Jur. Rep. 56.
[97] Above, n.85.
[98] *Ibid.* at 122.

(ii) Same Trading Area

1. City or Town 6–60

In *Application of James Walls*, McLoughlin J. was not satisfied that the new premises were in the immediate vicinity of the original premises. He stated:

> "If a visitor standing outside 19, O'Connell Street which is beside the Gresham Hotel were to enquire of an average well-informed Dublin person as to the whereabouts of the Cosmo Bar, he would, I think, be told 'you are in the wrong part of the city'—'it is in a different neighbourhood altogether—go south', 'cross the bridge and continue to the end of D'Olier Street'."[99]

The application to license Jonathan's in Grafton Street and use the old Cosmo Bar licence situate at the corner of Hawkins Street and Townsend Street was refused on the basis that the premises were situated in completely different trading areas of the city.[100]

Butler J. granted a licence for the Savoy Cinema in Limerick where the licence offered for extinguishment was that attached to the old Imperial Hotel and both premises were "within the business and commercial centre of Limerick".[101]

In granting a licence for 33 Upper O'Connell Street, where the licence being offered was attached to the Hamlet Lounge at the corner of Summer Hill and Middle Gardiner Street, O'Hanlon J. stated:

> "I reach this conclusion not without some difficulty, and it appears to me that in doing so I am pushing the interpretation of 'immediate vicinity' to the limit or very close to the limit, to which it can go in relation to an urban area without doing violence to the language of the section."[102]

In *Application of Charton Investments*,[103] O'Hanlon J. refused a licence for Giordani's situate at Nos. 40 and 41 Grafton Street where the old premises were situated at 56 Lower Kevin Street (the Good Times Bar) a distance of 634 yards. He noted that the distance involved, a journey 6–61

> "up the remainder of Grafton Street ... along the west side of St Stephen's Green for the full length of that side, a right hand turn into Cuffe Street, and having again traversed the full length of Cuffe Street, one comes upon the site of the old licensed premises, the Good Times Bar, at the corner of Lower Kevin Street and Redmond's Hill at the point where the intersection with Wexford Street is located".

---

[99] Above, n.89, at 116.
[100] *Application of Power Supermarkets Ltd*, above, n.91.
[101] *Re Irish Cinemas Ltd*, above, n.80, at 21.
[102] *Application of Brendan McGrath*, above, n.90, at p. 5.
[103] Unreported, High Court, O'Hanlon J., August 4, 1987.

He referred to the evidence given and "my own knowledge of the area" and stated:

> "I would regard the two locations as being completely different in character, the transition having taken place from the fashionable centre of Dublin in Upper Grafton Street, to the rather decayed and down-graded area surrounding the intersection of the four streets already mentioned."[104]

Having regard to the distance involved and the "marked difference in the two trading areas" he was not satisfied that the premises were in the immediate vicinity of each other.

In *Re Tivoli Cinema Ltd*[105] Lynch J. noted that the two premises were in the same south inner city area within easy walking distance of each other, were within the same civil parish and the same Roman Catholic parish; that they were within the same historic liberty of St Sepulchre and that they were in the same shopping or business and social area.

6–62 In the *Perfect Pies* case[106] Lynch J. was satisfied that Bartley Dunnes beside Mercer's Hospital was in the same social and economic area as 40, Dawson Street. Historically, the two premises were in the same ward and parish but since the 1920's this had changed. He noted that the difference in wards was a factor to be taken into account but was only a factor. Although both premises were in different planning zones according to the Dublin Corporation plans, Lynch J. was of the view that this resulted mainly from the necessity to ensure the preservation of the facade of Mercer's Hospital. Having assessed all the evidence, Lynch J. concluded that both premises were within the Grafton Street trading and social area. He stated:

> "The fact that the Stephen Street area has become run down and is in need of redevelopment and indeed appears to be on the verge of redevelopment judging by planning applications to Dublin Corporation relating to it, does not prevent it from being in the Grafton Street area. Cities and areas within cities need to be redeveloped from time to time as former prime buildings become decayed and obsolete and the fact of designation for the purposes of the Urban Renewal Act 1986, seems to me to be largely irrelevant."[107]

6–63 2. Rural Area

Trading area is taken into consideration in assessing whether two premises are in the immediate vicinity for the purposes of an application for a licence in a rural area. However, 'contiguity', in rural cases, is not to be measured merely by yards, "but perhaps even by miles": In *Re Application of Campbell and Gallagher* Judge Moonan was satisfied that where both places can

---

104 *Ibid.* at p. 3.
105 Above, n.82, at 419.
106 Above, n.95.
107 *Ibid.* at 740.

be part and parcel of the "same social and economic entity", special conditions and circumstances must be taken into account when interpreting the expression "immediate vicinity".[108]

The special circumstances exist when the two premises can be said to constitute one "communal and social centre for the rural portion of the parish surrounding it."[109] In *Re Campbell and Gallagher* Judge Moonan said:

> "I am of opinion that the intention is that the two premises must be in the same social and economic entity and must cater for much the same community or class".[110]

(iii) Measurement Measurement in all cases is taken by reference to the public thoroughfare. Lynch J. in the *Perfect Pies*[111] case refers to the shortest walking route from the site of the former Bartley Dunnes to the front door and the rear door of the proposed new premises in Dawson Street. He also refers to the distance "as the crow flies".[112] The measurement which the court uses is the distance as measured by foot. Section 22(a) of the Intoxicating Liquor 1962 Act introduces the concept of shortest "public" thoroughfare and this method of measuring distance has always been used in immediate vicinity cases. **6–64**

1. Expiring Lease

Introduction

Section 3 of the Licensing (Ireland) Act 1902 provides for the grant of a new licence in the immediate vicinity of a premises to which a licence, which falls either by extinguishment or surrender on the expiration of the lease of the premises, was attached. **6–65**

STATUTORY PROVISION

Section 3 of the Licensing (Ireland) Act 1902, as amended by section 23 of the Intoxicating Liquor Act 1943, provides:

> "Where, by reason of the expiration of a lease, a licence for the sale of intoxicating liquors for consumption on or off the premises comprised in the lease is extinguished or surrendered, the licensing authority may, notwithstand-

[108] Above, n.85, at 122.
[109] *Re Wright*, above, n.96.
[110] Above, n.85, at 122.
[111] Above, n.95.
[112] *Ibid.* at 739.

ing anything in this Act grant a licence for a suitable premises in the immediate vicinity of the premises to which the licence so extinguished or surrendered was attached."

JURISDICTIONAL REQUIREMENTS

6–66 Proof of the following matters are necessary to found the jurisdiction of the court.

1. Who May Apply

The courts have expressed the view that section 3 of the 1902 Act was not intended to confer any personal privilege or benefit upon a publican whose lease had expired. As Holmes L.J. states in *R. (Rigg) v. Tipperary Justices*:

> "This enactment was designed to meet the convenience of the public, and any person in the occupation of neighbouring premises might avail himself of its provisions for the purpose of applying for a licence."[113]

The right to apply for a licence under section 3 is not personal to the tenant and can be exercised by any member of the public who can prove that his premises are "suitable" and in the "immediate vicinity".

Madden J. noted in *R. (Supple) v. Clare Justices* that the section was not concerned with the protection of any quasi-proprietorial interests which might have attached to the old licence and that the owner of the premises was protected by section 2(1) stating:

> "As regards the former tenant of the premises, he is in no better position than any other member of the public applying as the owner of a suitable house in the immediate vicinity."[114]

In the *Supple* case, the tenancy was terminated by a notice to quit and the landlord obtained a new licence pursuant to section 2(1) of the 1902 Act. The tenant subsequently applied under section 3 for a new licence in respect of premises in the immediate vicinity. However, the Court of Appeal held that as there was already in existence a new licence for the original premises, the state of affairs necessary to ground an application under section 3 did not exist, as the new licence which was granted in respect of the old premises constituted a "graft or continuation of the former licence so as to prevent it being regarded as permanently extinguished at the date of the second application".[115]

[113] (1907) 41 I.L.T.R. 152 at 155.
[114] [1907] 2 I.R. 299 at 305.
[115] *Ibid.* at 306.

Furthermore, the old case law demonstrates that a landlord's right to revive the licence where his tenant's lease has expired, is a "prior right".[116] In *R. (Rigg) v. Tipperary Justices*, Gibson J. was satisfied that the right conferred by section 2 was prior in time and quality to the right given by section 3, "which is not original, but substitutional".[117]

In *Application of James Murray*,[118] the former tenant of a public house surrendered his interest in that premises and an application was made by a neighbouring publican under section 3 for a new seven-day licence for premises in respect of which he already held a six-day early closing licence. The tenant objected and gave evidence that he wished that his son would at some future date "get a seven-day licence". **6–67**

Judge Binchy was satisfied that once the applicant was entitled by law to the licence sought, the only discretion which the court could exercise to refuse the application was by sustaining an objection on one of the usual grounds. He referred to the policy of section 3 as being for the benefit of the public by protecting their existing drinking facilities and held that the jurisdiction conferred by section 3 is not confined to the grant of the new licence to the former tenant: the new licence could be granted to a person who had no interest in the extinguished licence.

Andrews L.C.J. in *R. (Mulhern) v. Recorder of Londonderry*[119] endorsed the "unbroken chain of opinion" expressed by the Law Lords in the *Wright*,[120] *Supple* and *Rigg* cases (see above) that section 3 was not passed merely for the benefit of the former tenant in respect of the extinguished licence, but in the interest and for the benefit of the public. In *Mulhern*, it was held that it is not necessary that an applicant should have been the tenant or licensee of the premises to which the extinguished licence was attached. It can be seen, therefore, that the consent of the tenant who was the previous holder of the licence to the making of the application is not required.

2. Expiry of Lease **6–68**

The applicant must establish that the lease has expired. The manner of expiry does not appear to be relevant. However, the expiry of the lease must result in the extinguishment or surrender of the licence. This section applies where a yearly tenancy is terminated by a notice to quit.[121]

It has been held in the Northern Irish courts that premises have not ceased to be available for the business carried on in them by reason of the

[116] Above, n.113, at 153, *per* O'Brien L.C.J.
[117] *Ibid.* at 154.
[118] (1956) 91 I.L.T.R. 4.
[119] (1938) 72 I.L.T.R. 149 at 151.
[120] *R. (Wright) v. Cork Justices* [1906] 2 I.R. 349.
[121] *Ibid.*

termination of a tenancy where the tenancy was determined by service of a notice to quit by a tenant on his landlord, as the cessation of availability contemplated by the Second Schedule to the Licensing Act (Northern Ireland) 1971 was one brought about by an act or event outside the control of the licensee.[122]

Section 3 of the 1902 Act applies where a tenant surrenders his interest in the licensed premises. In *Application of James Murray*,[123] Judge Binchy was satisfied and counsel for the objector conceded that the lease had expired within the meaning of the section. It is submitted that the section would also apply where a lease was terminated by forfeiture and re-entry by the lessor pursuant to the provisions of the lease.

The expiration of a lease signifies that the "lease" ceases to continue pursuant to the contract of the parties, "with the legal incidents and consequences flowing from such expiration or cessor of the lease".[124] Palles C.B. has stated that the expiration of a lease "includes any ending of the estate by virtue of the contract".[125]

6–69 3. Extinguishment or Surrender of a Licence

The applicant must prove that his licence became extinguished or surrendered by reason of the expiration of a lease. Certainly, the licence becomes inoperable as regards the tenant once the lease expires as he has no estate in the licensed premises and has no right to be present thereon.[126] However, the fact that the licence is inoperable is not sufficient: it would be advisable therefore to ensure that the licence has been surrendered either to the District Court clerk or the Collector of Customs and Excise upon the expiry of the lease. The surrender of a licence involves an active giving up of the document to the licensing authority which, according to the Supreme Court in *Re Application of Oshawa Ltd*[127] is divided between the courts and the administration. The court investigates any objections, the suitability of the proposed licensee and the premises and ensures compliance with the law; the clerk or registrar issues the certificate; once a certificate issues, the Revenue Commissioners then grant the appropriate licence.

6–70 In referring to the "extinguishment" of a licence on the expiry of a lease, the precise intent of the legislature is unclear. In the *Oshawa* case (above), the Supreme Court held that upon the grant of a new licence pursuant to section 6 of the 1902 Act, the old licence becomes extinguished by "operation of law". Section 3 is framed in such a way, however, that the actual

---

[122] *McKeown Vintners Ltd v. Agnew & Co. Ltd* (1983) N.I. 18.
[123] Above, n.118.
[124] Above, n.120, at 356, *per* Johnson J.
[125] *Ibid.* at 354.
[126] *State (Reddy) v. Johnson*, unreported, High Court, McWilliam J., July 31, 1980.
[127] Above, n.46.

extinguishment of the licence takes place in advance of the application for the new licence. Case law supports the notion that the extinguishment can occur immediately upon the termination of the tenant's interest where there is no surrender of the licence.

In *R. (Wright) v. Cork Justices*, Palles C.B. defined extinguishment as follows:

> "If, however, the circumstances were such that the person who acquired possession of the premises upon, and by reason of, the expiration of the lease did not become transferee of the licence . . . the licence became extinguished upon the licensed person quitting, and in that case (as well as in the case of the licensed person surrendering the licence) the Justices had jurisdiction to grant a new licence for 'suitable premises in the immediate vicinity of the' formerly licensed premises."[128]

Madden J. in *R. (Supple) v. Clare Justices*[129] held that the old licence was extinguished on the termination of the lease by the eviction of the tenant at the moment of its expiration.

4. Suitable Premises **6–71**

Section 3 requires only that the substituted premises be "suitable", not more suitable: it does not require that the new premises be similar in size or character to the substituted premises. The court could, however, take the view that "suitable" in the context of ensuring that the drinking public would not be inconvenienced requires that the substituted premises should serve the same section of the public as had enjoyed the hospitality of the previously licensed premises. If it were the intention of the applicant, for example, to construct a public house which would appeal to a completely different clientele, then it may be open to the court to refuse the application.

STATUTORY CONSEQUENCES

1. Existing Licensed Premises **6–72**

It has been held that a licence can be granted pursuant to section 3 of the 1902 Act in respect of existing licensed premises. In *R. (Mulhern) v. Recorder of Londonderry*,[130] a full seven-day publican's licence was granted under section 3 for premises in the immediate vicinity which had an early closing licence, although no reference was made to this in the judgment of Andrews L.C.J.

---

[128] Above, n.120, at 353–354.
[129] Above, n.114.
[130] Above, n.119.

Judge Binchy in *Application of James Murray*,[131] rejected the submission of counsel for the objector that the granting of a seven-day licence in respect of premises to which a six-day licence was already attached, pursuant to section 3, would afford no adequate substituted facilities to the drinking public. The objector's argument was that as only one licence can be granted in lieu of an extinguished licence, the effect of granting that application would be to ensure that in an area where there were two public houses, in the future there would only be one. The judge dealt succinctly with this point:

> "I consider that it would be wrong to refuse the applicant on the ground that he already has a six-day licence attached to the premises in respect of which the seven-day licence is sought."[132]

This view may be at odds with the views of O'Flaherty J. in the *Oshawa* case, where he held that section 6 of the 1902 Act does not contemplate the grant of a new licence in respect of the amalgamation of two existing licensed premises.[133]

6–73 2. Status of New Licence

As section 3 of the 1902 Act does not make the grant of a new licence conditional upon a transfer of endorsements which existed upon the surrendered or extinguished licence, it would appear on the authority of *D.P.P. v. Farrell*[134] that the new licence, when granted, must be free of endorsements.

Policy of the Exception

6–74 One of the clearest statements of the policy of the licensing code was expressed by Palles C.B. in *R. (Wright) v. Cork Justices* where he explained the object of section 3:

> "Now, the object of this provision being one for the benefit of the public, to prevent inconvenience to it by the permanent closing of a public house, presumably required, without a substitute being provided, the words should *prima facie* be construed so as to make the remedy co-extensive with the mischief."[135]

The mischief referred to was the creation of an abundance of public houses: this was to be balanced where an applicant could bring himself within the exception provided for in section 3. In *R. (Supple) v. Clare Justices*, Wright J. concurred with the views expressed by Palles C.B. where he stated:

---

131 Above, n.118.
132 *Ibid.* at 7.
133 *Re Application of Oshawa Ltd*, above, n.46, at 435.
134 Above, n.17.
135 Above, n.120, at 354.

> "But it will be seen that the language of the section is general, and has no reference to the interest, or privilege, or whatever it may be called, of the evicted lessee. Any one of the public may apply when the conditions of that section are found to exist; and I fully adopt the view of the Lord Chief Baron that the section was for the benefit of the public, and to prevent inconvenience to the locality."[136]

In the *Supple* case, Madden J. was not disposed to adopt a construction of section 3 which conflicted with the manifest intention of the section "that is, that the new licence should be in substitution for a former licence which has ceased to exist".[137] The suggestion that it was possible both to revive the old licence and grant a licence for alternative premises in the immediate vicinity was dismissed.

> "This result is certainly contrary to the whole policy and object of the Act and is, I think, not justified by the words of the section, which, in my judgment, apply to the case, not of a licence temporarily suppressed or withdrawn from a house, but to the case of a house from being a licensed house, becoming, and continuing up to the time of the application to Quarter Sessions, in this case April, 1906, to be unlicensed."[138]

2. Destroyed Premises

Introduction

Section 22 of the Intoxicating Liquor Act 1943 confers jurisdiction upon the court to grant a new licence for premises situate in the immediate vicinity of licensed premises which were burnt down or were otherwise destroyed or rendered uninhabitable by fire or other unavoidable cause or accident. 6–75

Further, where an applicant reconstructs the destroyed premises or builds new premises on the site of the original premises or on a site substantially the same, he may apply to the court for a new licence in respect of the reconstructed premises, but only where the court has already granted a new licence for premises situate in the immediate vicinity of the destroyed premises. On the grant of this licence, the licence attaching to the premises in the immediate vicinity is extinguished.

Section 22 of the 1943 Act is contrasted with and must be distinguished from section 14 of the Intoxicating Liquor Act 1960 which deals with demolished premises; section 14 is concerned with a situation where a deliberate intention has been formed to demolish premises or where premises have been deliberately demolished. Section 22 of the Intoxicating Liquor Act 1943 is concerned only with the accidental destruction of a premises.

---

136 Above, n.114, at 307.
137 *Ibid.* at 306.
138 *Ibid.* at 308, *per* Wright J.

One can conceive of circumstances in which the two jurisdictions might overlap but it is clear that the legislature intended to deal with quite different circumstances. Section 22 is somewhat unsatisfactory and perhaps in need of amendment or substitution. It seems to have been enacted in contemplation of a situation where a licensee, whose licensed premises have burnt down or have been accidentally destroyed, may be accommodated in another premises, pending the reconstruction or rehabilitation of the original premises. The jurisdiction to grant a new licence in respect of the premises which had been destroyed and were then reconstructed only arises where a licensee has already applied to the court for a new licence in respect of premises situate in the immediate vicinity of the destroyed premises. The section does not permit an applicant to apply to the court for a new licence in respect of premises which were destroyed, where no application had been made in the intervening period for a licence for substituted premises.

Section 22 can be divided into two parts or stages:

(a) the grant of a new licence in respect of the substituted premises;

(b) where the applicant seeks to relicense the reconstructed premises, having already obtained a licence in respect of the substituted premises.

(a) Substituted Premises

STATUTORY PROVISION

6–76 Section 22(1) and (2) of the Intoxicating Liquor Act 1943, as amended by section 26 of the Intoxicating Liquor Act 1960, and section 22(2) of the Intoxicating Liquor Act 1943, provide:

> "(1) Where a person (in this section referred to as the applicant) duly gives notice of his intention to apply for a licence in respect of premises (in this section referred to as the substituted premises) to which no licence is attached and, at the proceedings in the Circuit Court in relation to such application, the applicant shows to the satisfaction of the Court[139]—
>
> (a) that premises (in this section referred to as the original premises) in the immediate vicinity of the substituted premises were burnt down, or otherwise destroyed, or rendered uninhabitable by fire or other unavoidable cause or accident not more than two years before the date on which the said notice by the applicant was served on the county registrar, and
> (b) that a licence was attached to the original premises when they were so burnt down or otherwise destroyed or rendered uninhabitable, and
> (c) that at the time of the said hearing before the Circuit Court the applicant is in lawful occupation of the original premises or of the site and remains

[139] An applicant can also apply for an off-licence: see s.25 of the Intoxicating Liquor Act 1960.

thereof or that he has procured the consent of the lawful occupier of such premises or site and remains thereof to the making of an application, and if the licence referred to in paragraph (b) of this subsection is then subsisting, to the extinguishing thereof if and when a licence is granted pursuant to this section, and

(d) that no certificate under section 5 of the Act of 1833 has already been given by virtue of this section by reference to the original premises having been so burnt down or otherwise destroyed or rendered uninhabitable, and

(e) that no trade or business had been carried on in the original premises since they were so burnt down or otherwise destroyed or rendered uninhabitable

the Court shall, notwithstanding anything contained in the Act of 1902, cause such certificate as is mentioned in section 5 of the Act of 1833 to be given to the applicant declaring him to be duly entitled to receive a licence in respect of the substituted premises, unless the Court, in consequence of an objection made under section 4 of the Act of 1833, prohibits under that section the issuing of such licence on one or more of the following grounds, that is to say, the character, misconduct or unfitness of the applicant or the unfitness or inconvenience of the substituted premises.

(2) Where, in a case to which the foregoing sub-section of this section applies, the certificate referred to in that sub-section is given to the applicant, the following provisions shall apply and have effect, that is to say:—

(a) the licence (in this sub-section referred to as the new licence) to which the applicant is declared by the said certificate to be entitled and which is granted to him in pursuance of that certificate shall be a licence of the same character in all respects (including conditions inserted therein) as the licence (in this sub-section referred to as the old licence) which was attached to the original premises when they were burnt down or otherwise destroyed or rendered uninhabitable;

(b) nothing contained in the Act of 1902 shall operate to prevent the grant of a new licence to the applicant;

(c) upon the grant of the new licence, the old licence (if then subsisting) shall be extinguished;

(d) every (if any) conviction which was recorded on the old licence under section 25 of the Act of 1927 and either (as the case may be) would, but for the expiry of that licence, have continued to be so recorded thereon at the time of the grant of a new licence or continues to be so recorded on the old licence immediately before it is extinguished shall be deemed to be recorded on the new licence under the said section and to have been so recorded on the date on which it was recorded on the old licence;

(e) if paragraph (1) of section 2 of the Act of 1902 applies in respect of the original premises, those premises shall, upon the grant of the new licence, cease to be premises to which the said paragraph applies, and the Act of 1902 shall (subject to the provisions of the next following sub-section of this section) thenceforward have effect accordingly in relation to the original premises."

JURISDICTIONAL REQUIREMENTS

6–77 Proof of the following matters are necessary to found the jurisdiction of the court.

1. Who May Apply

   (i) The holder of the licence which attached to the premises at the time they were destroyed.

   (ii) The purchaser or lessee of the destroyed premises or the site and remains thereof.

   (iii) Any person who entered into an agreement with either of the above for the making of the application for the substituted licence and the extinguishment (if still subsisting) of the existing licence.

6–78 2. Extent of Destruction

The applicant must prove that the premises were burnt down or otherwise destroyed or rendered uninhabitable by fire or other unavoidable cause or accident. It is sufficient to prove to the court that as a result of the accident, it is not possible to carry on the licensed business therein. Unlike an application under section 14 of the 1960 Act (which relates to demolished premises), it is not necessary to prove that the premises were completely destroyed or razed to the ground.

3. Time Limit

Evidence must be adduced that the fire or accident or unavoidable cause occurred within two years of the service of the notice of application for a new licence upon the county registrar. Failure to notify the county registrar within this period deprives an applicant of the chance of applying for a new licence for the substituted premises and ultimately the chance to relicense the original premises.

6–79 4. Immediate Vicinity

An applicant will have to prove that the substituted premises are situate in the immediate vicinity of the original premises.

5. Original Premises Licensed

Proof must be adduced that a licence was attached to the destroyed premises at the time when they were so burnt down or otherwise destroyed or rendered uninhabitable. A difficulty could arise if the accident occurs while the applicant is in the course of applying for the renewal of his publican's licence. On the authority of *D.P.P. (O'Halloran) v. Cronin,*[140]

---

[140] Unreported, High Court, Geoghegan J., February 10, 1995.

the premises are not licensed until the date on which a licence issues in respect thereof.[141]

6. Occupation

An applicant must prove either of the following:

(i) that he is in lawful occupation of the destroyed premises or of the site and its remains. A contract to purchase the destroyed premises would not be sufficient: it is submitted that an applicant must prove that he holds the lowest estate and interest in the original premises or the site upon which it existed. The section, therefore, contemplates that an application for the licence for the substituted premises can only be made by the person who owns the premises at the time of its destruction, or by the purchaser or lessee; or

(ii) that he has procured the consent of the lawful occupier of the premises or site and remains to the making of the application to license substituted premises. The legislature, therefore, is protecting the interests of the former licence holder by ensuring that a situation does not arise whereby a third party who had no interest whatever in the original premises can apply for a licence without entering into an agreement (presumably for consideration) with the previous licensee.

7. Previous Court Certificate **6–80**

The applicant must also prove that no certificate entitling an applicant to receive a licence has already been granted by the court by virtue of the original premises having been destroyed. So, it must be shown that the licensee did not transfer the original premises or site and remains to any other person, nor gave his consent to the making of an application for a licence for substituted premises nor entered into an agreement to consent to the extinguishment of such licence, if then subsisting.

8. Nature of Licence to be Extinguished

An application will not be granted if the licence which is tendered for extinguishment is what is commonly known as a hotel licence, *i.e.* a licence granted by virtue of section 2(2) of the 1902 Act, or a greyhound race track licence granted under section 18 of the Intoxicating Liquor Act 1962 or a special restaurant licence.[142]

9. Trade in Original Premises **6–81**

An applicant must prove that no business has been carried on in the premises since they were destroyed. A publican will therefore deprive

---

141 Although if he has applied for a tax clearance certificate in accordance with the Finance Act 1992 as amended by the Finance Act 1995, then his licence may be deemed to continue in force.

142 Intoxicating Liquor Act 1962, s.20, as amended by the Intoxicating Liquor Act 1988, s.23.

himself of the right to invoke the jurisdiction if he carries on trade in a part of the premises which survives the accident or conflagration.

STATUTORY CONSEQUENCES

6–82 1. New licence

Same Character The licence for the substituted premises must be of the same character in all respects as the licence which attached to the destroyed premises. Therefore, a seven-day publican's on-licence cannot be granted in respect of the substituted premises where the licence which originally attached to the destroyed premises was a six-day licence or an early closing licence. In the same way, a seven-day publican's on-licence cannot be granted where the licences which attached to the previous premises were off-licences. As the licence which is to be granted in respect of the substituted premises must be of the same character in all respects, it is not possible to obtain an off-licence in respect of the substituted premises where an on-licence attached to the original premises, even though the on-licence is a licence "more comprehensive in character and quality" than the previous licence.[143]

Hamilton C.J. in *O'Rourke and Flanagan v. Grittar* stated:

> "An 'on-licence' is of completely different character to an 'off-licence'; it permits the sale of intoxicating liquors for consumption on and off the premises whereas the "off-licence" only permits the sale of intoxicating liquors for consumption off the premises. This is a fundamental difference between the characters of both licences".[144]

Endorsements Carried Forward Section 22(2)(d) of the Intoxicating Liquor Act 1943 provides that convictions recorded on the original licence are to be carried forward onto the new licence. However, the Intoxicating Liquor Act 1960, section 26(3)(b), provides that where a new licence is granted for the substituted premises that any convictions which were recorded on the original licence shall not be carried forward, unless such conviction/convictions which were recorded on the original licence became so recorded when the applicant for the substituted licence was the holder of the original licence. This relates to convictions for offences to which Part III of the Intoxicating Liquor Act 1927 applies.

6–83 2. Old licence: Extinguishment on Grant of New Licence

If the licence which attached to the destroyed premises is still subsisting, that licence shall be extinguished upon the grant of the new licence. Section 22(2)(c) is an acknowledgement by the legislature that even where a

---

143 *R. (Collins) v. Donegal Justices*, above, n.36, at 535–536, *per* O'Brien L.C.J.
144 Above, n.22, at 563.

premises is destroyed to the extent that trade cannot be carried on therein, this does not result in the automatic falling of the licence at the time of the destruction of the premises. Palles C.B. has expressed the view that a licence can continue in force although the licensed premises have been taken down with a view to their being rebuilt,[145] but only if the trade of publican was carried on during a substantial part of the year covered by the licence. If an objection is made to the renewal of such a licence after the premises to which it attached have been destroyed, it is submitted that renewal could not be effected, as no premises exist in respect of which a licence could be granted.

3. Original Premises

Where a successful application is made for a licence for substituted premises, it is not possible to revive the licence in respect of the original premises, unless such application is made under section 22(3) of the Intoxicating Liquor Act 1943, *i.e.* for the grant of a new licence for the destroyed premises where the licence for the substituted premises was previously granted.

(b) Reconstructed Premises (or New Premises Erected on the Site of the Original Premises or on a Site Substantially the Same)

Introduction

This is the second stage of the jurisdiction referred to above, at paragraphs 6–75 *et seq*. This application can only be made where the court has already made an order entitling an applicant to receive a licence in respect of substituted premises, where the original premises in its immediate vicinity were destroyed within the meaning of section 22(1) of the 1943 Act. 6–84

It is not possible to apply for a new licence in respect of destroyed premises, where an application for a substitute licence for premises in the immediate vicinity has not been granted. Section 22(1) therefore imposes upon a publican whose premises have been destroyed by an accident, the substantial cost of having to purchase or take a lease on a premises in the immediate vicinity and to make an application to the Circuit Court for a certificate in respect of the substituted premises. This application also involves dealing with planning authorities and the fire authorities, which can involve considerable expense. It is submitted that a licensee should be in a position, if his premises were destroyed by accident, to apply to the court to relicense that premises or a building built on the same site, without the necessity of having to apply for a substitute licence in respect of other premises. Some publicans demolish the entire premises after they have been destroyed in order to bring themselves

[145] See *R. (Blackburne) v. Down Justices*, above, n.61.

within the meaning of section 14 of the Intoxicating Liquor Act 1960. In this way they are spared the necessity of having to acquire a substitute premises before reconstructing their original premises.

Section 22(3) applications are not often made because of the conditions imposed by statute which must be complied with before an application can proceed. It has happened that parts of a building which have survived a conflagration or other cause of accident have been demolished and the premises have been described as a demolished premises in the course of a section 14 application. More commonly, reliance has been placed upon the dictum of Judge Davitt in the *Guiney* case:

> "It is true that licensed premises can be taken down and rebuilt without causing the loss of the licence or the right to renewal, but only where the original structure is restored and such rebuilding is effected without any substantial alterations. If the new premises are substantially different from the old the licence and the right to its renewal is gone and under the law prior to 1902 the owner would be faced with the necessity of applying for a new licence."[146]

A more cautious approach, however, is advised. If a licence holder wishes to rebuild the original structure without substantial alteration, he should apply for a declaratory order and bring himself within the exception provided for in section 14 of the Intoxicating Liquor Act 1960. Alternatively, if he can prove that he comes within the circumstances envisaged by Judge Davitt in the *Guiney* case, he may apply to restore the building under section 2(1) of the Licensing (Ireland) Act 1902.

STATUTORY PROVISION

6–85 Section 22(3) of the Intoxicating Liquor Act 1943:

> "Where, in a case to which the foregoing sub-sections of this section apply, the original premises are reconstructed or new premises are erected on the site of the original premises (or on a site substantially the same as that site) and, at any time thereafter while a licence is attached to the substituted premises, the holder of that licence duly gives notice of his intention to apply for a licence in respect of the premises so reconstructed or newly erected, the Court shall cause such certificate as is mentioned in section 5 of the Act of 1833 to be given to the said holder declaring him to be duly entitled to receive a licence in respect of the said reconstructed or newly erected premises, and the Court, in consequence of an objection made under section 4 of the Act of 1833, prohibits under that section the issuing of such licence to the said holder on one or more of the following grounds, that is to say, the character, misconduct, or unfitness of the said holder or the unfitness or inconvenience of the said reconstructed or newly erected premises, and, if the Court causes such certificate to be given to the said holder, the provisions contained in sub-section (2) of this section shall apply and have effect with the necessary modifications and, in particular, with the

[146] *Re Denis Guiney, Applicant*, above, n.25, at 112.

modifications that the expression "the new licence" shall mean the licence to which such certificate relates and the expression "the old licence" shall mean the said licence then attached to the substituted premises."

JURISDICTIONAL REQUIREMENTS

Proof of the following matters is necessary to found the jurisdiction of the court: 6–86

1. Who May Apply

   The only person entitled to apply for a licence under section 22(3) of the 1943 Act is the holder of the licence attaching to the substituted premises. The statute envisaged a situation whereby the licensee of the original premises, which have subsequently been reconstructed, wishes to recommence trading in the original premises and would have no use for the substituted premises.

2. Location of Premises

   This application relates to the original premises and an applicant must prove one of the following:

   (i) reconstruction of the original premises. This is where the premises have been damaged, rather than destroyed;

   (ii) erection of new premises on the site of the original premises. Where premises have been destroyed, the applicant is confined to rebuilding on the original site;

   (iii) erection of new premises on a site substantially the same as the site of the original premises. An applicant is permitted to build on an area not comprising the entire of the original site, once the site upon which the premises is to be built is substantially the same as the site upon which the original premises were built. Therefore, it appears that some portion of the premises can be built outside the original site once this does not result in a substantial change to the site occupied by the original premises.

3. Licence

   Evidence must be adduced that at the time of service of the notice of application on the county registrar, a licence attached to the substituted premises. The statute does not require proof that a licence actually attaches to the substituted premises at the time of the application.

4. Evidence that Licence granted for Substituted Premises

   This application cannot succeed unless proof is adduced that a licence has been granted in respect of substituted premises.

5. Time Limit

The application to license the reconstructed premises may be made at any time after the original premises are reconstructed or the new premises are built. There is no limitation imposed by the statute as to the time during which the premises must be reconstructed or as to when the application must be brought.

STATUTORY CONSEQUENCES

6–87 The statutory consequences following the grant of a new licence in respect of the original premises as reconstructed or rebuilt are similar to those which apply in respect of a new licence for substituted premises.

OBJECTIONS

6–88 The grounds of objection which are open to those persons who are entitled to object to such an application are dealt with in detail below, in chapter 21, "Objections". It should be noted, however, that the statute specifically excludes the sufficiency of licensed premises in the neighbourhood as a ground of objection which may be entertained by the court.

3. Demolished Premises

Introduction

6–89 The matters which must be proved by an applicant for a licence pursuant to section 14 of the Intoxicating Liquor Act 1960 are set forth clearly in the judgment of Finlay C.J. in *Jaggers Restaurant Ltd v. Ahearne.*[147] The main difference between section 14 of the 1960 Act and section 22 of the 1943 Act is that where a premises is deliberately demolished under section 14, there is no requirement to apply for a licence in respect of a premises in the immediate vicinity of such demolished premises for the interim period pending rebuilding, nor is the application for the new licence confined to the holder of the existing licence which is required in the case of an application pursuant to section 22(3) of the 1943 Act. In a section 14 application, the new premises can be located on the site of the original premises or partly on the site or in the immediate vicinity of that site. If the premises are not located on the site of the original premises, then the applicant must further prove that the new location is unlikely *per se* to have a materially adverse affect on the business carried on in any licensed premises in the neighbourhood.

---

[147] [1988] I.R. 308.

Demolition of a premises can be a protracted business and it is always advisable that photographic evidence be adduced to prove the commencement, the interim period, and the conclusion of such demolition.

STATUTORY PROVISION

Section 14 of the Intoxicating Liquor Act 1960 provides: 6–90

"(1) Where a person (in this section referred to as the applicant), duly gives notice of his intention to apply for a licence in respect of premises (in this section referred to as the new premises) to which no licence is attached and at the proceedings in the Court in relation to such application, the applicant shows to the satisfaction of the Court—

(a) that premises (in this section referred to as the original premises) were demolished not more than two years before the date on which the said notice by the applicant was served on the County Registrar or District Court Clerk, as the case may be, and

(b) that a licence was attached to the original premises when they were so demolished, and

(c) that at the time of the said hearing before the Court the new premises are lawfully occupied by the applicant and—
  (i) that they are located on the site of the original premises, or
  (ii) if they are not so located, that they are located either, partly on that site or in the immediate vicinity and that the location of the new premises where they are rather than on the site of the original premises is unlikely of itself to have a materially adverse effect on the business carried on in any licensed premises in the neighbourhood, and

(d) that at the time of the said hearing before the Court the applicant is in lawful occupation of the site and any remains of the original premises or that he has procured the consent of the lawful occupier of such site and remains to the making of the application, and if the licence referred to in paragraph (b) of this subsection is then subsisting, to the extinguishing thereof if and when a licence is granted pursuant to this section, and

(e) that the new premises are more suitable than the original premises for the business of selling intoxicating liquor,

the Court shall, notwithstanding anything contained in the Act of 1902, cause such certificate as is mentioned in section 5 of the Licensing (Ireland) Act, 1833, to be given to the applicant declaring him to be duly entitled to receive a licence in respect of the new premises, unless the Court, in consequence of an objection made under section 4 of that Act, prohibits under that section the issuing of such licence on one or more of the following grounds, that is to say, the character, misconduct, or unfitness of the applicant or the unfitness of the new premises.

(2) Where, in a case to which the foregoing sub-section of this section applies, the certificate referred to in that sub-section is given to the applicant, the following provisions shall apply and have effect, that is to say:—

(a) the licence (in this subsection referred to as the new licence) to which the applicant is declared by the said certificate to be entitled and which is granted to him in pursuance of that certificate shall be a licence of the same character in all respects (including conditions inserted therein) as the licence (in this sub-section referred to as the old licence) which was attached to the original premises when they were so demolished;

(b) nothing in the Act of 1902 shall operate to prevent the grant of the new licence to the applicant;

(c) upon the grant of the new licence, the old licence (if then subsisting) shall be extinguished;

(d) any conviction which became recorded on the old licence under section 25 of the Act of 1927 at a time (if any) when the applicant was the holder of the licence and which, either is still recorded thereon or would, but for the expiry of that licence, be still recorded thereon at the time of the grant of the new licence by the Revenue Commissioners shall be deemed to be recorded on the new licence under that section and to have been so recorded on the date when it became recorded on the old licence;

(e) upon the grant of the new licence, the original premises shall, for the purposes of the Act of 1902, be deemed never to have been licensed.

(3) Where, before the demolition of the original premises, an application in relation to the new premises or (if the new premises have not been constructed) the proposed new premises is made to the Court under section 15 of this Act, the original premises shall be deemed, for the purposes of that section, but not otherwise, to have been demolished, but an application under section 17 of this Act in respect of the new premises shall not be granted unless the Court (being otherwise satisfied, having regard to the provisions of that section, to grant the application) is satisfied that the original premises have been demolished."

JURISDICTIONAL REQUIREMENTS

6–91 An applicant under section 14 of the 1960 Act must satisfy the court of certain matters in respect of both the old (demolished) premises and the new premises which are the subject of the application.

1. Who May Apply

(a) The lawful occupier of the site and any remains of the original premises.

(b) An applicant who has procured the consent of the lawful occupier of the site and where the licence which attached to the original premises is still subsisting, the consent of the lawful occupier to the extinguishing of that licence, if and when a licence is granted pursuant to section 14. Again, this protects the interests of the holder of the licence attaching to the original premises or his assigns. Thus, a neighbouring publican cannot invoke section 14 without proving that he has come to an agreement with the original licensee.

2. Old Premises

Demolition The applicant must prove that the original premises were demolished. The expression "demolished" is not defined by the statute although section 14(1)(d) seems to envisage a situation other than complete demolition as it refers to the site "and any remains of the original premises". Ó Dálaigh C.J. in *Application of Leo Ward* in assessing whether a premises were demolished for the purposes of section 14 stated:

> "Where 'the original site' is made use of, it follows that the premises in respect of which the application is made will be a new premises, that is to say, it is not the old premises or any part of the old premises. The indications are that 'the site' is capable, when cleared of the remains of the original premises, of being used for a new building. The original premises, it is contemplated, have been destroyed to that extent."[148]

Ó Dálaigh C.J. was satisfied that the original premises in the *Ward* case were not demolished within the meaning of the section. He noted that the four walls and the roof were intact and that the demolition which had been carried out was a "large internal demolition or gutting". He referred to a dictionary definition of the verb "demolish" and found that the premises were not "destroyed, pulled down, pulled to pieces, reduced to ruin". He drew a distinction between the expression "reconstruct" and "demolition". It could perhaps be argued that where extensive demolition has taken place and the intention is to apply for a licence for a new premises, that the building of a completely new premises does not involve a reconstruction even where a portion of the pre-existing foundation or building remains.

Licence Attached It is necessary to prove that a licence attached to the original premises at the time they were demolished. It is of the utmost importance to ensure that, prior to any demolition work, the publican holds an existing licence in respect of the premises. It is not sufficient that he can prove that he obtained a publican's licence some days after the final act of demolition has taken place.

Occupation The applicant must also prove either:

(i) that he is in lawful occupation of the site and any remains of the original premises; or

(ii) that he has procured the consent of the lawful occupier to the making of the application.

3. New Premises 6–92

Unlicensed The new premises must be unlicensed. Section 22 of the Intoxicating Liquor Act 1943 provides that the applicant must prove that the premises in respect of which he seeks a licence are unlicensed. This

[148] Above, n.86, at 421.

contrasts with the exceptions provided for in the 1902 Act which do not make this express stipulation. O'Flaherty J. in *Re Application of Oshawa Ltd*[149] pronounced that the extension in a section 6 application must be unlicensed. It should be noted that McCarthy J. reserved for future consideration the question of whether section 6 was necessarily limited to cases where premises attached to or adjoining premises which are licensed for the sale of intoxicating liquor at the relevant time are themselves unlicensed.

More Suitable The applicant must prove that the new premises are more suitable than the original premises for the business of selling intoxicating liquor. Evidence must be adduced that the facilities available in the new premises will be superior to those available in the original premises. There is nothing to say that the new premises cannot be larger or more luxurious than the original premises; this is a matter which will be taken into account by the Court in determining whether or not the shift in location of the premises would have a materially adverse effect on the business carried on by licensed premises in the neighbourhood.

Location of Premises The applicant must prove one of the following:

(i) that the new premises are located on the site of the original premises. He need not prove that the premises are constructed within the structure of the original licensed premises once they are located within its site;

(ii) that the premises are located partly on the site of the original premises. This may result in an applicant building a more substantial premises than that which was located on the original site;

(iii) that the new premises are located in the immediate vicinity of the site upon which the original premises was located.

4. Time Limit

Proof of demolition not more than two years before the date of service of the notice of application on the county registrar is required. Failure to meet this statutory time limit will result in the refusal of the application.

6–93 5. Material Adverse Effect

If an application for a new licence is made and the applicant cannot prove that the new premises are located on the site of the original premises, he must adduce evidence that the location of the new premises is unlikely *per se* to have a materially adverse effect on the business carried on in any licensed premises in the neighbourhood. McLoughlin J. considers the expression in *Application of James Walls*:

> "If new premises are constructed on the same site with up-to-date and attractive

---

[149] Above, n.46.

> facilites, the business carried on in other licensed premises in the neighbourhood might be adversely affected, but that factor would not be relevant and no difficulty arises. If there is any shift, even if the new construction is still partly on this old site and partly on a new site, the adverse effect on other licensed business has to be considered."[150]

If a new public house is built on the same site as the original demolished premises, the court is not entitled to take into account the prospective adverse effect such new premises might have on other licensed premises in the neighbourhood.

In *Re Irish Cinemas Ltd* Butler J. dealt with the onus of proof which an applicant under section 14 had to discharge:

> "It will be seen that here the applicant is required to establish a negative, and a negative with regard to conditions which do not exist at the time of the application and in relation to the business carried on in other premises of which, in the ordinary way, he can have no first hand knowledge. It follows, in my view, that all the applicant can be required to do is to establish prima facie by evidence of existing conditions or of what has happened and/or by competent opinion as to what is likely to happen, that the granting of the licence to him will not have the materially adverse effect mentioned in the section."[151]

The applicant, therefore, establishes his prima facie case that the shift in location is unlikely to affect adversely the neighbouring businesses to a material extent. The onus of proof then shifts to the objector who must "himself adduce affirmative evidence, from experience of his own trade and its figures or otherwise, to show that the new licence in the new location would have this materially adverse effect".[152]

In *Perfect Pies Ltd v. Redmond Doran*,[153] Lynch J. was satisfied that the applicant had established a sufficient case, on the basis of the evidence he offered, to shift the onus onto the objectors to prove that the location of the new premises would *per se* have a materially adverse effect on the business carried on by one or more of them. He considered the question of "material adverse effect" in the light of the present economy of the State and stated: 6–94

> "At the present time, the economy of this State along with many other states is in recession and as a result businesses, including the businesses of the objectors, may be more easily adversely affected than in better times. … I think however that for the purposes of judging whether the location of the new premises at No. 40, Dawson Street will of itself be likely to have a materially adverse effect on any of the objectors, I should assume normal economic conditions, neither boom times nor recession nor exceptionally high interest rates."[154]

---

150 Above, n.89, at 115.
151 Above, n.80, at 20.
152 *Ibid.*
153 Above, n.95.
154 *Ibid.* at 742.

This was a novel approach: *i.e.* not taking into account factors which obtain at the time of the application in order to assess whether the effect is adverse, and materially so.

6–95 In *Re Thank God It's Friday Ltd,*[155] Barr J. interpreted the expression "material adverse effect" as that which is "likely to be adversely affected to a significant extent". He was satisfied that the proviso specifically recognised and protected the rights of other licensees in the neighbourhood of the proposed new premises.

O'Hanlon J. in considering the question of material adverse effect in *Application of Brendan McGrath* was satisfied that in dealing with the question the Court should have regard

> "not merely to the stated intentions of the applicant as to the manner in which he proposes to carry on his business and utilise the premises, if licensed, but also to the potential for the future in the hands of the applicant or of any assignee, to whom he might see fit to dispose of the premises".[156]

He indicated that the court was entitled to take into account the possibility that the premises could be expanded in the future. O'Hanlon J. also took account in that case of the fact that the premises in question could attract customers who would be unlikely to patronise other licensed premises in the neighbourhood.

The President of the Circuit Court (overruled on the substantive issue by Butler J. in the High Court on appeal) in the *Irish Cinemas*[157] case, contrasted the expression "materially adverse effect" with the words "unreasonably detrimental" contained in section 13 of the Intoxicating Liquor Act 1960. He ruled that "materially" meant something of "some substance and not merely trivial", but that it was not necessary "that it should be a grave or crippling effect". He considered that section 13 implied a higher degree of detriment than section 14.

6. Consent to Extinguishment

The applicant must prove that if the licence which attached to the original premises still subsists, he has procured the consent of the lawful occupier of the site and remains of the original premises to its extinguishment.

7. Nature of Licence to be Extinguished

An application pursuant to section 14 shall not be granted if the licence which is tendered for extinguishment is what is commonly known as a hotel

---

[155] [1990] I.L.R.M. 228.
[156] Above, n.90, at p. 6.
[157] *Re Irish Cinemas Ltd*, above, n.80.

licence, *i.e.* a licence which is granted by virtue of section 2(2) of the 1902 Act, or a greyhound race-track licence or a special restaurant licence.[158]

STATUTORY CONSEQUENCES

1. New Licence Similar to Old Licence 6–96

The licence to be granted must be of the same character in all respects, including conditions inserted therein, as the old licence. Thus, it is not possible to obtain an on-licence instead of an off-licence, nor an off-licence instead of an on-licence, nor a full licence in substitution for a restricted licence and vice versa.

2. Extinguishment of Old Licence

If the licence which attached to the original premises still subsists, then the old licence becomes extinguished as a matter of law upon the granting of the new licence. In this regard, it is not necessary for the court to make an order extinguishing the licence as it becomes extinguished by operation of law.

3. Endorsements Carried Forward to New Licence

As with an application under section 22 of the Intoxicating Liquor Act 1943, if a conviction is recorded on the old licence which the applicant held and is either still recorded or would, but for the expiry of the licence, be so recorded at the time of the grant of the new licence, that conviction will be recorded on the new licence. This relates to convictions for offences to which Part III of the Intoxicating Liquor Act 1927 applies. Where the applicant did not hold the licence at the time the convictions became recorded, the endorsements are not recorded on the new licence.

4. Old Premises

Where the new licence is granted under section 14, the licence which originally attached to the demolished premises can never be revived pursuant to section 2(1) of the Licensing (Ireland) Act 1902.

OBJECTIONS

Objections are dealt with in chapter 21. It should be noted that the court is not entitled to consider the number of previously licensed houses in the neighbourhood in an application under section 14 of the 1960 Act. In *Jaggers Restaurant Ltd v. Ahearne*[159] the Chief Justice held that an objection to a section 14 application was not co-extensive with the three grounds of objection 6–97

[158] Intoxicating Liquor Act 1962, s.20, as amended by Intoxicating Liquor Act 1988, s.23.
[159] Above, n.147.

provided for in section 4 of the 1833 Act "but is confined to two grounds, namely, the character, misconduct or unfitness of the applicant or the unfitness of the new premises".[160]

DECLARATORY ORDER

6–98 Section 14(3) provides that an application for a declaratory order in respect of the new premises can be made prior to the demolition of the original premises. This order approves the plans of the new premises. The requirement to demolish the original premises can be satisfied at certificate stage, *i.e.* on an application pursuant to section 17 of the Intoxicating Liquor Act 1960.

D. Premises Situate in Rural Area

Introduction

6–99 Two exceptions to the general prohibitory terms contained in the 1902 Act are dealt with here. The first is contained in section 21 of the Intoxicating Liquor Act 1943 which provides for the grant of a licence for more convenient premises in a rural area upon the extinguishment of a licence of the same character situate in the same District Court licensing area. The licence to be offered for extinguishment must also be in the immediate vicinity of the new premises. The second is the exception contained in section 13 of the Intoxicating Liquor Act 1960 which provides for the grant of a new licence, upon the extinguishment of two licences of the same character. These licences can be attached to premises situate anywhere in the State. The premises which are the subject of the application must not be situate within one mile of another licensed premises.

1. More Convenient Premises in a Rural Area

6–100 This exception is appropriate where a licence of the same character and which is in the immediate vicinity of the premises the subject of the application is available for extinguishment.

STATUTORY PROVISION

Section 21 of the Intoxicating Liquor Act 1943, as amended by section 33(1)(b) of the Intoxicating Liquor Act 1960, provides:

---

[160] *Ibid.* at 315.

"(1) Where a person (in this section referred to as the applicant) duly gives notice of his intention to apply for a licence in respect of premises (in this section referred to as the new premises) to which no licence is attached and, at the proceedings in the Circuit Court in relation to such application, the applicant shows to the satisfaction of the Court—

(a) that the applicant is the holder of a licence attached to premises (in this section referred to as the existing premises) situate in the immediate vicinity of the new premises, and
(b) that the new premises and the existing premises are both situate in the same District Court area prescribed by law for the purposes of the transaction of licensing business, and
(c) that neither the new premises nor the existing premises is situate in a county or other borough, an urban district, or a town, and
(d) that the rateable valuation of the new premises is not less than the rateable valuation of the existing premises, and
(e) that the new premises is more suitable than the existing premises for the business of selling intoxicating liquor,

the Court shall, notwithstanding anything contained in the Act of 1902, cause such certificate as is mentioned in section 5 of the Act of 1833 to be given to the applicant declaring him to be duly entitled to receive a licence in respect of the new premises, unless the Court, in its absolute discretion, prohibits the issuing of such licence either on the ground of the unfitness or inconvenience of the new premises or on the ground that the existence of a licence in respect of the new premises would be unreasonably detrimental to the business then carried on in some licensed premises in the neighbourhood of the new premises.

(2) Where, in a case to which the foregoing sub-section of this section applies, the certificate referred to in that sub-section is given to the applicant, the following provisions shall apply and have effect, that is to say:—

(a) the licence (in this sub-section referred to as the new licence) to which the applicant is declared by the said certificate to be entitled and which is granted to him in pursuance of that certificate shall be a licence of the same character in all respects (including conditions inserted therein) as the licence (in this sub-section referred to as the old licence) attached to the existing premises;
(b) nothing contained in the Act of 1902 shall operate to prevent the grant of the new licence to the applicant;
(c) upon the grant of the new licence, the old licence shall be extinguished;
(d) every (if any) conviction which is recorded on the old licence under section 25 of the Act of 1927 at the time of the grant of the new licence shall be deemed to be recorded on the new licence under the said section and to have been so recorded on the date on which it was recorded on the old licence;
(e) if paragraph (1) of section 2 of the Act of 1902 applies in respect of the existing premises, those premises shall, upon the old licence being extinguished in pursuance of this sub-section, cease to be premises to which the said paragraph applies, and the Act of 1902 shall thenceforward have effect accordingly in relation to the existing premises.

JURISDICTIONAL REQUIREMENTS

6–101 Proof of the following matters are necessary to found the jurisdiction of the court.

1. Who May Apply

The applicant must prove that either:

(i) he is the holder of a licence which attaches to premises in the immediate vicinity of the new premises; or

(ii) he has procured the consent of the holder to the extinguishing thereof.

2. Location

Immediate Vicinity The existing premises must be in the immediate vicinity of the new premises. As discussed above, at paragraph 6–55, the expression "immediate vicinity" in a rural area is given a broader meaning than where premises are situated in a city or town.

District Court Licensing Area An applicant is required to prove that the new premises and the existing premises are both situate in the same District Court licensing area. Proof of the boundaries of the District Court licensing area can be adduced by calling the appropriate District Court clerk to give evidence.

Rural Area The exception cannot be availed of unless it is shown that both premises are situate in an area which is not a county borough, or other borough, or an urban district or a town. The practice is to require the Ordnance Survey to certify that this is the case and to require the attendance of an appointed officer in court to adduce such evidence. As the definition of "town" for licensing purposes is a town with town commissioners[161] section 21 applies in the case of a small country town or a village.

6–102 3. Rateable Valuation

The rateable valuation of the new premises must not be less than that of the existing premises. In fact, the valuation of the new premises normally exceeds that of the existing premises. The rateable valuation is deemed to include a provisional valuation issued by the Commissioner of Valuation.[162]

6–103 4. New Premises

Unlicensed Premises The premises in respect of which the application is made cannot be licensed. This jurisdictional section cannot be invoked

---

[161] Licensing Act (Ireland) 1874, s.37, and see paras. 6–56 *et seq.*

[162] Intoxicating Liquor Act 1960, s.33.

where an applicant wishes to apply for a licence which differs from that which already attaches to his premises.

Suitable Premises The new premises must be more suitable than the existing premises for the business of selling intoxicating liquor. This requirement is also imposed in respect of applications under section 14 of the Intoxicating Liquor Act 1960. Evidence must be adduced of the suitability of both the existing premises and the new premises to enable the court to assess whether the facilities provided in the new premises are superior to those of the existing premises. Factors such as improved car parking, lavatory accommodation, more comfortable accommodation for patrons, etc., will be taken into account by a court in assessing suitability.

5. Licence to be Extinguished

   (i) The licence to be extinguished must be of the same character as that which is being sought.

   (ii) The licence cannot be a hotel licence (that is, a licence granted by virtue of section 2(2) of the 1902 Act) or a greyhound racetrack licence or a special restaurant licence.[163]

Discretion of Court

Character There are only two matters which the court is entitled to consider in determining whether or not to permit or prohibit the issuing of a licence under section 21 of the Intoxicating Liquor Act 1943 as amended. The first is the unfitness or inconvenience of the new premises and the second is that the existence of a licence in respect of the new premises would be unreasonably detrimental to the business then carried on in some licensed premises in the neighbourhood of the new premises. The court, although it has an "absolute discretion" appears to be entitled to prohibit the grant of a licence on those two grounds alone. A curious consequence of this is that a court is not entitled to prohibit the issue of the licence where it is dissatisfied with the applicant's bona fides or his character, conduct or fitness. The question of an applicant's character is so fundamental to the consideration of an application for the grant of a new licence that it would be strange indeed if the court could not take it into account in determining an application. Finlay C.J. in *Jaggers Restaurant Ltd v. Ahearne*[164] held that the grounds for objection under section 14 of the Intoxicating Liquor Act 1960 were not coextensive with the grounds for objection under section 4 of the 1833 Act. The grounds of objection available under section 4 in a section 14 application are, however, specifically confined in that section as in section 21 of the Intoxicating Liquor Act 1943. 6–104

[163] Intoxicating Liquor Act 1962, s.20, as amended by Intoxicating Liquor Act 1988, s.23.
[164] Above, n.147.

Section 21 of the 1943 Act can be contrasted with section 13 of the 1960 Act which, although it does not refer to the 1833 Act, includes the character, misconduct, or unfitness of the applicant as a ground of objection to be considered by the court. It is interesting to note that it is not open to a court to refuse on any ground, an application under section 17 of the Intoxicating Liquor Act 1960 for a certificate on the basis that a declaratory order was granted where section 21 of the 1943 Act is the jurisdictional section invoked. The court, therefore, would appear to be expressly precluded from considering an objection on the grounds of the character, misconduct or unfitness of the applicant.[165]

6–105 *Unfitness or Inconvenience of New Premises* In *R. (Marshall) v. Tyrone Justices,* Palles C.B., in considering an application for a spirit grocer's licence, stated that "the character of suitability is not the neighbourhood but the premises".[166] However, Teevan J. in *In Re Application of Thomas Flynn,*[167] noted that the subject might be wider for public house licences as opposed to spirit grocers' licences. He held that such an objection is not confined to unfitness or inconvenience of the structure:

> "I think it proper that a Court, invested with some, if restricted, discretion in the matter of certifying premises suitable for licensing, should take into consideration whether the operation of the licence is likely to be seriously detrimental to the quiet enjoyment of adjoining property."[168]

He expressed the view that a court was entitled, in determining the question of the unfitness or inconvenience of the new premises, to have regard to environmental matters. In that case, he was satisfied that the proposed public house and projected trade would be a considerable nuisance to the adjoining residents.

A court may take into account whether or not car parking facilities are provided for the patrons. In the *Flynn* case, Teevan J. stated: "I have already found that from every point of view the car park is an essential appurtenance to the public house."[169] This statement, however, must be interpreted by reference to the requirements of the appropriate planning authority in relation to the provision of car parking facilities. In practice, the Planning Authority does not require that publicans provide car parking facilities for their patrons in the centre of Dublin city. Teevan J. stated:

> "In modern conditions and in the case of new premises, it is a factor which may, and in some cases should, be taken into consideration in assessing fitness and convenience of premises."[170]

---

165 Intoxicating Liquor Act 1960, s.17, as substituted by Intoxicating Liquor Act 1962, s.32.
166 [1895] 2 I.R. 174.
167 [1963] I.R. 301.
168 *Ibid.* at 315.
169 *Ibid.* at 316.
170 *Ibid.* at 317.

In *Re Thomas O'Brien, Applicant*[171] Budd J. upheld an objection based on the unfitness or inconvenience of premises on the grounds that the proposed site would endanger public safety.

Finlay P. in *Re Centennial Properties Ltd*[172] construed the words "unfitness" and "inconvenience" disjunctively. He held that "unfitness" dealt with the premises themselves and "inconvenience" was to be construed as meaning and including the location of the premises. He came to the conclusion that the location of a licensed premises at the particular site was inconvenient within the meaning of the subsection. The factors which he took into account were that the proposed premises would be situated in close proximity to a large open space devoted to leisure and sport, covering about 50 acres; that they would be immediately beside a significant shopping centre and that it would be close to a housing estate containing young married people starting to rear families and children both of primary school age and in their early teens.[173]

Unreasonably Detrimental The applicant does not assume the onus of proving that the grant of a licence in respect of the new premises would not be unreasonably detrimental to the business carried on in licensed premises in the neighbourhood. This is in contrast to the provisions contained in section 14 of the Intoxicating Liquor Act 1960 which require an applicant to adduce evidence that the shift in location of the premises is, of itself, unlikely to have a materially adverse effect on the business carried on in any licensed premises in the neighbourhood. However, as the court is entitled have regard to "unreasonable detriment" in determining whether or not to sanction or prohibit the issue of the licence, it is wiser for an applicant to adduce prima facie evidence that the grant of a licence to the new premises would not be unreasonably detrimental to businesses in the neighbourhood. The statute contemplates a situation where the grant of a licence could be somewhat detrimental to some existing businesses: what the court must consider, however, is whether the extent to which existing businesses are detrimentally affected is unreasonable. The expression "unreasonably detrimental" also occurs in section 13 of the Intoxicating Liquor Act 1960. Therefore, publicans objecting in rural areas as opposed to urban areas have a much higher onus of proof to discharge, as they must satisfy the court that: **6–106**

1. the grant of the new licence would, (not could), affect them;
2. the effect would be detrimental to their business;
3. this detriment would be unreasonable.

171 (1974) 108 I.L.T.R. 141.
172 Above, n.54.
173 *Ibid.* at pp. 4 and 5.

What constitutes an "unreasonable detriment" is a "difficult question".[174] Finlay J. in the *Centennial* case, thought that the onus of proof on the objectors imposed by the statute, was a "heavy onus".[175] In that case, he was satisfied that it would be detrimental, "... but I am not satisfied it would be unreasonably detrimental". The President of the Circuit Court was of the view that the expression "unreasonably detrimental" indicated a higher degree of injurious effect than "materially adverse effect".[176] Budd J. in *Re Thomas O'Brien, Applicant*[177] was not prepared to sustain an objection that the grant of the new licence would be unreasonably detrimental to businesses already carried on in the neighbourhood. He was satisfied that the applicant would not compete "unduly" or "successfully" with certain premises in the neighbourhood nor would other premises be likely to be "unreasonably affected".

STATUTORY CONSEQUENCES

6–107 1. New Licence

(i) The new licence is of the same character in all respects, including any conditions which may be inserted, as the old licence.

(ii) Only convictions which were recorded on the old licence at a time when the applicant was the holder thereof are carried forward onto the new licence.[178] This means that if convictions are recorded on a licence and the licensee successfully applies for a transfer of the licence to a new premises, the convictions follow him. If, however, somebody other than the current licensee applies to the court for a new licence, the convictions do not follow and the new licensee receives a clean licence with no recorded convictions.

2. Old Licence

(i) Upon the grant of the new licence, the old licence shall be extinguished.

(ii) The premises to which the old licence attached cannot be licensed again on the basis that they were licensed within the previous five years.

---

174 *Re Application of Thomas Flynn*, above, n.167, *per* Teevan J.
175 Above, n.54, at p. 7.
176 *Re Irish Cinemas Ltd*, above, n.80.
177 Above, n.171.
178 Intoxicating Liquor Act 1960, s.26(3)(b).

2. Premises in Rural Area in Substitution for Two Existing Licences

Introduction

The Licensing (Ireland) Act 1902 made no provision for the grant of a new licence where there was development in a country or rural area with a consequential increase in population. Many new licences were granted in peripheral areas around the big towns and cities in the State where the statutory increase in population could be proved but, subject to the exceptions discussed below at paragraphs 6-100 *et seq.* the grant of a new publican's licence in a rural area was forbidden. Section 13 of the Intoxicating Liquor Act 1960 provides for the grant of a new licence in a rural area or, more correctly, a new licence in respect of premises not situate "in a County or other Borough, an urban district or a town". The expression "rural area", although in common use, has no legal definition in the Licensing Acts. It is used in contradistinction to the expression "city" or "town". **6–108**

This statutory exception was much availed of immediately following its enactment on July 4, 1960. It became so frequently used that the legislature considered that its application should be restricted to give reasonable protection to existing interests. This restriction was effected by section 20 of the Intoxicating Liquor Act 1962, which imposed a requirement that the premises sought to be licensed be situate more than one mile from a premises in respect of which there is in force a publican's or other on-licence first granted before the passing of the 1960 Act .

STATUTORY PROVISION

Section 13 of the Intoxicating Liquor Act 1960 provides: **6–109**

> "(1) Where a person (in this section referred to as the applicant) duly gives notice of his intention to apply for a licence in respect of premises (in this section referred to as the new premises) to which no licence is attached and, at the proceedings in the Court in relation to such application, the applicant shows to the satisfaction of the court that—
>
> (a) in respect of each of two premises (in this section referred to as the existing premises) a licence is in force and in respect of each licence either—
> (i) the applicant is the holder thereof, or
> (ii) if he is not the holder thereof he has procured the consent of the holder thereof to the extinguishing of the licence if and when a licence in respect of the new premises is granted to the applicant pursuant to this section,
>
> (b) the licences (in this section referred to as the old licences) attached to the existing premises are of the same character,
>
> (c) the rateable valuation of the new premises is not less than ten pounds, and
>
> (d) the new premises are not situate in a county or other borough, an urban district or a town,

the Court shall, notwithstanding anything contained in the Act of 1902, cause a certificate to be given to the applicant entitling him to receive a licence in respect of the new premises, unless the Court in its absolute discretion prohibits the issuing of the licence—

(I) on the ground of the character, misconduct or unfitness of the applicant, the unfitness or inconvenience of the new premises or the number of previously licensed premises in the neighbourhood, or

(II) on the ground that the existence of a licence for the new premises would be unreasonably detrimental to the business then carried on in some premises licensed for the sale by retail of intoxicating liquor in the neighbourhood.

(2) (a) The licence granted in pursuance of this section shall be of the same character and be subject to the same conditions as the licences attached to the existing premises.

(b) Nothing in the Act of 1902 shall prevent the grant of the new licence.

(c) Upon the grant of the new licence, the licences attached to the existing premises (in this section referred to as the old licences) shall be extinguished.

(d) Any conviction which became recorded on either of the old licences under section 25 of the Act of 1927 at a time (if any) when the applicant was the holder of the licence and which is still recorded thereon at the time of the grant of the new licence by the Revenue Commissioners shall be deemed to be recorded on the new licence under that section and to have been so recorded on the date when it became recorded on the old licence, provided that if more than two convictions are so recorded on the old licences, only the latest two shall be deemed to be recorded on the new licence.

(e) Upon the grant of the new licence, the existing premises shall, for the purposes of the Act of 1902, be deemed never to have been licensed."

JURISDICTIONAL REQUIREMENTS

6–110 1. Who May Apply

(i) The holder of both of the existing licences; or

(ii) the person who has procured the consent of the holder or holders of both of the existing licences to their extinguishment for the purpose of his application for the grant of a licence in respect of the new premises.

2. Licences to be Extinguished

(i) This is the only provision in the licensing code which specifically requires the extinguishment of more than one licence. Section 4 refers to "licence or licences" but in a section 4 application, it is the practice of the courts to require the extinguishment of only one licence.

(ii) Existing licences: the licences which attach to each of the premises which are to be tendered for extinguishment must be "in force" at the proceedings in the court in relation to such application. Section 17 of the Intoxicating Liquor Act 1960 envisages a situation where existing licences can be tendered at the declaratory stage and proof of their currency at certificate stage is not essential.

(iii) The licences to be extinguished can be attached to premises situate anywhere in the State. Section 13 does not impose any restriction as to the location from where the licence must come.

(iv) The old licences must be of the same character as that being sought. They must also be of the same character as each other.

(v) The licences to be extinguished cannot be hotel licences granted by virtue of section 2(2) of the Licensing (Ireland) Act 1902 or a greyhound licence or a special restaurant licence.[179]

3. New Premises 6–111

(i) The new premises must be unlicensed.

(ii) Their rateable valuation must not be less than £10. This rateable valuation can be a provisional valuation.[180]

4. The Mile Rule 6–112

Section 20 of the Intoxicating Liquor Act 1962 introduced a restriction to the jurisdiction of the court to grant a new licence pursuant to section 13 of the 1960 Act. This restriction, in effect, requires the applicant to prove that the subject premises are situate not less than one mile from the premises in respect of which a licence currently in force was first granted on or before July 4, 1960, such licence being of the same character as the licence applied for.

The consequence of this, as will be seen, is that publicans who upgraded or expanded their premises since the coming into effect of the Intoxicating Liquor Act 1960 (July 4, 1960) lost the jurisdictional protection afforded by section 20.

STATUTORY PROVISION

Section 20(2) of the Intoxicating Liquor Act 1962 provides: 6–113

"(a) An application to the Circuit Court under section 13 of the Act of 1960 shall not be allowed in respect of premises situate less than one mile measured by the shortest public thoroughfare from premises in respect of which there is in force a licence that was first granted on or before the 4th day of July,

[179] Intoxicating Liquor Act 1962, s.20, as amended by Intoxicating Liquor Act 1988, s.23.
[180] Intoxicating Liquor Act 1960, s.33.

1960, and is of the same character as the licence that would fall to be granted if the application were allowed.

(b) For the purposes of this subsection all on-licences shall be deemed to be licences of the same character."

6–114 (a) Measurement

The measurement as required by statute is by "the shortest public thoroughfare". This expression was considered in *Re Application of Thomas Flynn*.[181] Teevan J. held that the court must be satisfied that the distance between the two terminals mentioned in section 20(2) of the 1962 Act has been measured along the shortest line of public thoroughfare. He stated:

> "Plainly, the statute has one measurement and one alone in contemplation. For such purpose as here intended, there can be one measurement only and that is achieved by two directives. The measurement is to be taken *from* and not *to* the previously licensed house: and it is to be by the *shortest* public thoroughfare."[182]

The measurement must be along the "shortest line of public thoroughfare between the two premises". The judge found it unnecessary in establishing the measurement, to consider whether the nearest point of the building itself or the nearest point of the premises in the more general sense (*i.e.* including the car park) should be taken as the relevant measuring point, as regardless of the point used, the measurement still fell at less than one statute mile.[183]

6–115 (b) Public Thoroughfare

In *Application of Mormur Ltd*,[184] the superintendent of the Garda Síochána objected to the application on the ground that the new premises would be located less than one mile, measured by the shortest public thoroughfare, from an existing public house. McMahon J. found that the distance between the new premises and the existing public house by public road was a few yards more than a mile, but that in addition to using the public road there were two other ways of arriving at the new premises from the existing premises. The issue before the court was whether either of these ways was a public thoroughfare. The first way was by departing from the public road and taking a short cut across a supermarket car park. The Judge was satisfied that persons passing over the car park to the new premises would not be using a public thoroughfare. McMahon J. stated:

> "I am satisfied that the car park is not a thoroughfare. It is not possible to pass through the car park to any other place. A throroughfare must be a passage or way through."[185]

---

[181] Above, n.167.
[182] *Ibid.* at 311.
[183] *Ibid.* at p. 312.
[184] Unreported, High Court, McMahon J., February 1, 1984.
[185] *Ibid.* at p. 3.

He referred to the *Concise English Oxford Dictionary* definition of thoroughfare, being: "a road or street or path open at both ends especially one through which much traffic passes". The other way, which measured a few yards short of a mile, involved leaving the public thoroughfare and taking a short cut through a new housing estate and over a pathway and over part of the car park. The judge noted that the pathway was part of the supermarket property and was provided for by the supermarket for pedestrian access to the car park and thence to the supermarket. McMahon J. stated:

> "It is not a thoroughfare because it is part of the supermarket property and does not provide a way to any other place. ... There was no evidence of public user of this path and I doubt if such user as may have occurred by the residents was sufficient to justify calling it a thoroughfare."[186]

3. Other Premises: On-Licence **6–116**

All premises which are situate within a radius of one mile of the new premises as required by section 20(2)(a) of the 1962 Act and which have the benefit of an on-licence granted on or prior to July 4, 1960 must be taken into account by the court when considering the application. On-licences include restricted licences, hotel licences, greyhound race track licences, holiday camp premises and publicans' licences, as these are licences for the sale of intoxicating liquor for consumption either on or off the premises for the grant of which the production of a certificate of the District Court or the Circuit Court, as the case may be, is required.[187]

An application for an off-licence pursuant to section 13 of the Intoxicating Liquor Act 1960 is not caught by this requirement. Also, the existence of an off-licensed premises situate within a mile of a premises which is the subject of the application does not constitute a bar to the jurisdiction of the court to grant an on-licence.

Licence First Granted on or Before July 4, 1960 The mile rule only causes a difficulty for an applicant where the premises already licensed within the mile were licensed prior to July 4, 1960. In the *Centennial*[188] case, a publican objected to the grant of a declaratory order on the grounds that his premises were situated within a mile of the proposed premises. The evidence established that the objector had expanded his premises in 1982 and consequently had obtained an order pursuant to section 6 of the Licensing (Ireland) Act 1902. Finlay P. held that the grant of a new licence pursuant to section 6 constituted a new licence first granted after July 4, **6–117**

---

[186] *Application of Mormur Ltd*, above, n.184, at pp. 4 and 5.

[187] The reference to the District Court also relates to an application under s.27 of the Intoxicating Liquor Act 1960. Note: a special restaurant licence will not be taken into account as this type of licence introduced by the Intoxicating Liquor Act 1988, *i.e.* after July 4, 1960.

[188] *Re Centennial Properties Ltd*, above, n.54.

1960 and that the objector's premises could not be taken into account for the purposes of section 20 of the 1962 Act.

In both that case and in the case of *Doyle v. Hearne (No. 2)*, Finlay J. accepted that this created an anomaly and stated:

> "... it is difficult to conceive, without some imaginative speculation, of the exact reason why the legislature should have been prompted to protect in an absolute fashion certain licensees and to leave freed from absolute protection other licensees even though they still receive the discretionary protection under section 13 of the Act of 1960."[189]

In that case, a restricted licence was converted to a full licence on August 3, 1961. The Supreme Court held that this constituted the grant of a new licence and that accordingly, section 20 of the Intoxicating Liquor Act 1962 did not apply.

STATUTORY CONSEQUENCES

6–118 1. Same Character

The licence granted upon a successful application must be of the same character and subject to the same conditions as each of the licences attaching to the old premises. Blayney J. in *O'Rourke and Flanagan v. Grittar* interpreted section 13(2)(a) of the Intoxicating Liquor Act 1960 as follows:

> "The clear effect of the statute, accordingly, is that if an applicant wishes to apply under the section for an on-licence, he must be in a position to extinguish two on-licences, and if he wishes to apply for an off-licence, he must be in a position to extinguish two off-licences."[190]

He continued:

> "... since it cannot be disputed that an on-licence and an off-licence are licences of a different character, an off-licence cannot be granted on the extinction of two on-licences."[191]

The reference in the subsection to "the same conditions" is a reference to restricted licences (six-day licences or early closing licences). Section 20(2)(b) of the Intoxicating Liquor Act 1962 provides that all on-licences are deemed to be licences of the same character.

6–119 2. Old Licences

Once the new licence has been granted, the old licences become extinguished. An order of the court directing their extinguishment in a section

---

[189] Above, n.19, at 324.
[190] Above, n.22, at 565.
[191] *Ibid.* at 566.

13 application is of no effect as the extinguishment of a licence is effected by operation of law and takes effect on the grant of the new licence.

3. Endorsements

   If a conviction or convictions was/were recorded on either of the licences, those convictions shall only be carried forward onto the new licence if the endorsements occurred when the applicant was the holder of the licence or licences upon which such convictions were recorded. However, only the latest two convictions in respect of the licence or licences will be carried forward onto the new licence. If someone other than the holder of the original licences applies to the court for a new licence pursuant to section 13, the convictions do not follow.

4. Revival of Old Licence

   It is not possible to revive the licence or licences in respect of the premises to which the licence or licences formerly attached, once a new licence is granted, on the grounds that the premises were licensed within the past five years.

OBJECTIONS

The grounds of objection set forth in section 13 of the Intoxicating Liquor Act 1960 are similar to those provided for in section 4 of the Licensing (Ireland) Act 1833, with one additional ground. The grounds of objection under section 13 are as follows: **6–120**

1. the character, misconduct or unfitness of the applicant;
2. the unfitness or inconvenience of the new premises;
3. the number of previously licensed premises in the neighbourhood;
4. that the existence of a licence for the new premises would be unreasonably detrimental to the business then carried on in some premises licensed for the sale by retail of intoxicating liquor in the neighbourhood.

The first three grounds are co-extensive with those set forth at section 4 of the 1833 Act and are discussed in greater detail in chapter 27, "Objections". The final ground concerning unreasonable detriment is discussed in detail above, at paragraph 6–106.

E. Premises already Licensed but Different Licence Sought

6–121 Section 27 of the Intoxicating Liquor Act 1960 provided for yet another exception to the general prohibitory terms contained in the 1902 Act against the grant of a new on-licence. It provides for an application to the District Court for the grant of a new on-licence where a restricted licence is already in existence.[192] As provided for in section 24 of the Courts (Supplemental Provisions) Act 1961, the Circuit Court has jurisdiction in the case of all on-licences.

However, section 27 of the Intoxicating Liquor Act 1960 provides for the one and only exception to this. An application for a new publican's on-licence where a restricted licence is in existence is made to the District Court. Section 27(4) of the 1960 Act, as amended by section 33 of the Intoxicating Liquor Act 1962, provided for the grant of a full licence where a person previously held a restricted licence, upon the payment of £200 to the Revenue Commissioners, once the application for the new licence was made within three years after the passing of the Intoxicating Liquor Act 1960. Quite a number of new publicans' licences were granted pursuant to this subsection within that three-year period.

The statutory requirements are dealt with in detail at chapter 15, "Changes in Character, Scope and Attributes of a Licence", paragraphs 15–2 to 15–10.

F. Licensed Premises Acquired by Local Authority

Introduction

6–122 This jurisdiction was introduced to provide for a situation where licensed premises have been or are about to be compulsorily acquired by a local authority and the local authority approves another location as a site for licensed premises in substitition for the former premises. There is no requirement that the new premises be in the immediate vicinity of the old or demolished premises. This jurisdictional exception is rarely invoked although the author is aware that at least two such applications have been made in Dublin within the last 10 years. Section 7 of the Intoxicating Liquor Act 1953 provides for the grant of a certificate entitling an applicant to receive a licence in respect of premises on an approved site. Section 8 provides for the grant of a declaration as to fitness and convenience of proposed premises to be constructed on an approved site. An applicant in either case must prove that he is the holder of a certificate issued by the local authority pursuant to section 6 of the Intoxicating Liquor Act 1953.

---

[192] An early closing licence or a six-day licence.

Local Authority Certificate

STATUTORY PROVISION

Section 6 of the Intoxicating Liquor Act 1953 provides: **6–123**

"(1) A local authority may, if they think fit, issue to any person a certificate declaring that—

(a) after the passing of this Act particular licensed premises have been or are to be demolished by or by direction of the authority in exercise of any of their functions, and
(b) a particular site acquired by them is approved by them as a site for licensed premises in substitution for the former premises.

(2) The local authority shall not issue a certificate to any person other than the person (or nominee of the person) who holds the lowest estate or tenancy in the premises or, where the premises have been acquired by the local authority, held it immediately before such acquisition unless that person has been offered and has not accepted a certificate.

(3) Where the lowest estate or tenancy is subject to a condition (whether in respect of intoxicating liquor generally or any class of intoxicating liquor) that the holder of such estate or tenancy shall sell only such liquor purchased from or through the immediate lessor, then, for the purposes of subsection (2), the immediate lessor shall be deemed to be the person who holds (or held) the lowest estate or tenancy."

(a) Content of Certificate

The certificate must deal with both the licensed premises and the new site. **6–124**

Licensed Premises The certificate must state that the licensed premises have been or are to be demolished by the local authority, or by direction of the local authority in exercise of any of its functions. This is where the local authority has acquired the premises by virtue of a compulsory purchase order for the purposes of demolition. Demolition would be construed in accordance with Ó Dálaigh C.J.'s directions in *Application of Leo Ward*[193] as "destroyed, pulled down, pulled to pieces, reduced to ruin".

New Premises The site in respect of which it is proposed to make the application must have been acquired by the local authority. Not only must the local authority approve the location as a site for licensed premises, but the certificate must indicate that the new site is approved in substitution for the former premises.

[193] Above, n.86, at 421.

(b) Issue of Certificate

6–125 The certificate issues to one of the following:

1. The person who holds the lowest estate or tenancy in the premises. This refers to the licence holder who himself must hold such an estate. This person can be a freehold owner or the lessee. The intention is to protect the interest of the licensee where his business must cease as a result of the local authority's actions;
2. the nominee of the holder of the lowest estate or tenancy in the premises. The intention here is that if the previous holder of the licence is not inclined to continue carrying on the business or wishes to appoint another person to so do, he may in effect assign his right to another person (for consideration if he so wishes);
3. the immediate lessor, where the tenancy in the licensed premises is subject to a condition that the lessee shall sell only such intoxicating liquor purchased from the immediate lessor;
4. where a certificate has been offered to any of the above persons and has been refused, the local authority is entitled to issue a certificate to any other person.

(c) Cancellation of Certificate

6–126 The local authority may cancel this certificate and may issue a similar certificate relating to a different site.[194]

However, if either an application for a declaratory order or a certificate leading to the grant of a licence has already been granted, the certificate cannot be cancelled.[195]

Application for Court Certificate

STATUTORY PROVISION

6–127 Section 7 of the Intoxicating Liquor Act 1953, which deals with the grant of the certificate entitling an applicant to receive a licence in respect of premises on the approved site, provides:

---

194 Intoxicating Liquor Act 1960, s.41(1).
195 *Ibid.*, s.41(2).

"(1) Where the holder of a certificate under section 6, having duly given notice of his intention, applies to the Court for a certificate entitling him to receive a licence in respect of premises on the approved site the Court shall, notwithstanding anything contained in the Act of 1902, cause such certificate to be given to him unless the Court, in its absolute discretion, prohibits the issuing of the licence—

(a) on the ground of the character, misconduct or unfitness of the applicant or the unfitness or inconvenience of the premises, or
(b) subject to sub-section (2), on the ground that the existence of a licence for the premises would be unreasonably detrimental to the business then carried on in some licensed premises in the neighbourhood.

(2) The ground of objection mentioned in paragraph (b) of sub-section (1) shall not be considered if—

(a) the premises are erected on the site of the previously licensed premises, or
(b) the local authority certify that that site is not available as a site for licensed premises and it appears to the Court that the location of the premises where they are rather than on the former site is unlikely of itself to have a materially adverse effect on the business carried on in the neighbouring premises.

(3) (a) The licence granted in pursuance of this section shall be of the same character and be subject to the same conditions as the licence attached to the former premises.
(b) Nothing in the Act of 1902 shall prevent the grant of the new licence.
(c) Upon the grant of the new licence the former licence (if it has not already lapsed) shall be extinguished.
(d) Any conviction recorded on the former licence under section 25 of the Act of 1927 at the time of the grant of the new licence shall, if the licensee was the holder of the former licence, be deemed to be recorded on the new licence under that section and to have been so recorded on the date when it was recorded on the former licence.
(e) If the former premises were premises to which paragraph (1) of section 2 of the Act of 1902 applied, that paragraph shall, upon the grant of the new licence, cease to apply to them and shall be deemed to apply to the new premises.
(f) If the former premises were premises to which section 6 of the Act of 1902 applied, the new premises shall be deemed to be premises to which this section applies."

JURISDICTIONAL REQUIREMENTS

1. Who May Apply **6–128**

The only person who may apply for a court certificate is the holder of a certificate of the local authority granted pursuant to section 6 of the 1953 Act.

2. Site

(i) The application must be made in respect of the particular site acquired by the local authority. The applicant must prove that he has entered into an agreement with the local authority whereby he, as tenant, holds the lowest estate and interest in such site.

(ii) The expression "site" is defined by the *Concise English Oxford Dictionary* as "the ground chosen or used for a town or building". This appears to contemplate a situation where a local authority could approve an existing building acquired by them as a site for licensed premises.

3. Unusual Features

Once the local authority certificate has been obtained and an application made to the court, the court will grant the application except where successful objection is made on the grounds set forth in section 6 of the 1953 Act. The applicant need not prove that the original premises were licensed or demolished. This appears to be covered by the certificate.

There is no time limit stipulated in the statute as to when an application can be made pursuant to section 6. The only proof required is that the licensed premises were demolished after the passing of the Intoxicating Liquor Act 1953.

A further unusual feature is that there is no requirement that the substituted premises be within the immediate vicinity of the existing licensed premises or premises which have been demolished by the local authority. It seems possible, therefore, that an application could be made by the holder of a section 6 certificate in respect of premises within the bailiwick of a local authority which are situate at a considerable distance from the original premises. Both premises must be within the area of one local authority administration.

OBJECTIONS

6–129 The grounds for objection differ from those available in other licensing applications. See chapter 21, "Objections", at paragraph 21–22.

STATUTORY CONSEQUENCES

6–130 1. New Licence

(i) The new licence must be of the same character as the old licence.

(ii) Any convictions which were recorded on the old licence are carried forward to the new licence, but only if the convictions were sustained and recorded where the applicant was the holder of the old licence.

2. Old Licence

   (i) When the new licence is granted, the old licence becomes extinguished.

   (ii) The licence which attached to the old premises cannot be revived pursuant to section 2(1) of the Licensing (Ireland) Act 1902.

Section 8 of the Intoxicating Liquor Act 1953 provides for the grant of a declaration as to the fitness and convenience of the proposed premises where an applicant holds a section 6 certificate. This application and procedure is dealt with below, in chapter 20, "Declaratory Jurisdiction", at paragraphs 20–34 to 20–41. **6–131**

CHAPTER 7

OFF-LICENCES

Introduction

7–1 Frequent reference is made to an "off-licence" in contrast to an on-licence, *i.e.* a publican's licence. The on-licence issued to a publican by the Collector of Customs and Excise is one document. The off-licence, however, normally comprises three separate documents representing three distinct licences:

1. a beer retailer's off-licence;
2. a spirit retailer's off-licence;
3. a wine retailer's off-licence.

It is unusual for an application to be made for a cider retailer's off-licence as the beer retailer's off-licence automatically entitles the holder to sell cider by retail for consumption off the premises, or for a sweet retailer's licence, as the wine retailer's off-licence automatically entitles the holder to sell sweets by retail for consumption off the premises.

A retailer's off-licence authorises the sale at any one time to any one person of liquor for consumption off the premises, in the following quantities, namely:

(a) in the case of spirits, wine, or sweets, in any quantity not exceeding two gallons or up to one dozen reputed quart bottles but not in any larger quantities; and

(b) in the case of beer or cider, in any quantity up to four and a half gallons or up to two dozen reputed quart bottles; but not in any larger quantities.[1]

Although the First Schedule to the Finance (1909–10) Act 1910 lists the cider retailer's off-licence as a separate licence, very few are issued as the holder of a beer retailer's off-licence is entitled to sell by retail both cider and beer.[2]

In order to apply for a spirit retailer's off-licence or a beer retailer's off-licence, the applicant must first obtain a certificate of the court. **7–2**

He must show to the court that he comes within one of the jurisdictional exceptions to the general prohibitory terms of the Licensing (Ireland) Act 1902 and be in a position to tender for extinguishment a licence or licences, in substitution for the grant of the new licence or licences. An application for a certificate leading to the grant of a spirit retailer's off-licence and a beer retailer's off-licence is made to the District Court.[3]

The provisions which relate to the ad interim transfer of a licence[4] apply to the spirit retailer's off-licence, the beer retailer's off-licence and the cider retailer's off-licence.[5]

Where the holder of off-licences which were granted on foot of certificates of the District Court applies for the renewal of those licences, the provisions of the Courts (No. 2) Act 1986 apply. Unless objections have been lodged, application is made directly to the Revenue Commissioners for a renewal of those licences. The application for the wine retailer's off-licence is made directly to the Revenue Commissioners. No court certificate is necessary.[6]

All off-licences expire on September 30 of each year.[7] However, where the holder of a wholesale dealer's licence also holds a retailer's off-licence for the sale of the same liquor, the retailer's off-licence must expire on the same day as that on which the wholesale dealer's licence expires.[8] **7–3**

VENUE

Applications for certificates leading to the grant of a beer retailer's off-licence are regulated by the Beerhouses (Ireland) Act 1864, the Beer Licences Regulation (Ireland) Act 1877 and the Beer Retailers' and Spirit Grocers' Retail **7–4**

---

[1] Finance (1909–10) Act 1910, Sched. 1.
[2] *Ibid.*
[3] Beer Retailers' and Spirit Grocers' Retail Licences (Ireland) Act 1900, s.1, as applied by the Courts of Justice Act 1924, s.77(C), and the Courts (Supplemental Provisions) Act 1961, s.48.
[4] Public Houses (Ireland) Act 1855, s.1.
[5] Intoxicating Liquor Act 1960, s.29.
[6] Intoxicating Liquor Act 1962, s.28.
[7] Finance (1909–10) Act 1910, s.49.
[8] *Ibid.*, s.49(2).

Licences (Ireland) Act 1900.[9] Section 2 of the 1900 Act, which has not been repealed, provides that certificates for any such licences shall, notwithstanding anything in any Act, be granted at annual licensing sessions and not at any other time. The provision was reflected in rule 93 of the District Court Rules 1948 which, however, has since been amended by substitution by rule 11 of the District Court Rules 1955[10] which states that the application may be made to the District Court at any time. Rule 11 provides as follows:

> "An application for the grant of a certificate for a licence to sell spirits or beer in retail quantities for consumption off the premises or an application for the grant of a certificate for a wholesale beer dealer's licence may be made at any sitting of the District Court for the court area in which the premises for which the licence is required are situated."

PROCEDURE

The procedure which governs applications for the beer and the spirit retailer's off-licences is dealt with in detail below, in chapter 17, "Practice and Procedure", at paragraphs 17–31 to 17–39. It should be noted that the applicant must specify details of licences held by him in the preceding two years in his notice of application.[11]

A. Off-Licences for which Court Certificate is required

1. Beer Retailer's Off-Licence

7–5 Section 3 of the Beerhouses (Ireland) Act 1864 prohibited the grant by the Collectors of Customs and Excise of a beer retailer's off-licence without the production of a certificate of the court.

STATUTORY PROVISION

Section 3 of the Beerhouses (Ireland) Act 1864, as amended by section 9 of the Courts (No. 2) Act 1986, provides:

> ". . . save as hereinafter mentioned, it shall not be lawful for any Officer of Excise in Ireland to grant a Licence or Transfer of a Licence for the Sale of Beer by Retail, to be drunk or consumed elsewhere than on the Premises where sold, to any Person applying for such Licence or Transfer of a Licence, without such

[9] Licensing Act 1872, s.82.
[10] S.I. No. 83 of 1955.
[11] District Court Rules 1948, r. 94(2) (S.I. No. 431 of 1947).

> Person producing a Certificate signed by Two or more Justices of the Peace presiding at the Petty Sessions of the District in which such Person resides, or if in the Dublin Metropolitan Police District by a Divisional Justice of the District in which such Person resides, to the good character of such Person, and the Suitability of the Premises for the Purpose of such Sale, and where the Application shall be for the Transfer of an existing Licence without a similar Certificate to the good Character of the Person to whom such Transfer is proposed to be made, and to the peaceable and orderly Manner in which such House had been conducted in the past Year."

The certificate required for the grant of a licence, therefore, differs from that required where the application is for the transfer of a licence.

Rateable Valuation

Section 2 of the Beer Licences Regulation (Ireland) Act 1877 provides that the court, upon an application for the grant or transfer of a beer retailer's off-licence, should also certify to a certain minimum valuation in respect of the premises. **7–6**

STATUTORY PROVISION

Section 2 of the Beer Licences Regulation (Ireland) Act 1877, as amended by section 9 of the Courts (No. 2) Act 1986, provides, *inter alia*:

> ". . . it shall not be lawful for any officer of excise in Ireland to grant a licence or transfer of a licence for the sale of beer, ale, or porter to be drunk or consumed elsewhere than on the premises where sold, to any person whomsoever, in respect of any premises, unless upon the production of a certificate that such premises, with premises belonging thereto and occupied therewith, if any, are rated for the relief of the poor for the sum of £8 or upwards, or in respect of any premises situate in any city or town, as defined by "The Licensing Act (Ireland), 1874", containing a population exceeding 10,000, according to the then last parliamentary census, unless upon the production of a certificate that such premises, with the premises belonging thereto and occupied therewith, if any, are rated for the relief of the poor in the sum of £15 or upwards".

In *R. (Morris) v. Derry Justices*[12] it was held that where a certificate of valuation is required, a valuation in respect of the premises must be in existence at the time that the application is made, and a provisional valuation is not sufficient. This ruling caused a delay in the licensing of many new premises constructed for the sale of intoxicating liquor off the premises.

It is arguable that this requirement does not apply where the application is brought pursuant to an exception to the prohibitory terms of the Licensing

[12] (1901) 1 N.I.J.R. 66.

(Ireland) Act 1902 which requires proof of a minimum valuation under section 5 of that Act.

7–7 Section 33 of the Intoxicating Liquor Act 1960 provides, *inter alia*, that a rateable valuation, in construing section 5 of the 1902 Act, as amended, shall be deemed to include a provisional valuation issued by the Commissioners of Valuation. Thus, a provisional valuation will be sufficient where the applicant invokes a jurisdiction whereby he is obliged to satisfy section 5 of the 1902 Act. Furthermore, proof of rateable valuation at declaratory stage, whether or not section 5 of the 1902 Act applies, is not necessary where the plans show that the proposed buildings "when built, would attract a valuation exceeding the very modest minimum valuation required".[13]

Exclusive Occupation

7–8 Section 2 of the Beer Licences Regulation (Ireland) Act 1877 provides that an applicant for the grant of a licence must produce a certificate that the premises have been in his exclusive occupation for at least three months preceding the date of the court certificate.

The requirement of exclusive occupation does not, however, apply in the case of a transfer of a licence where the previous holder of the licence died or was removed prior to the granting of the transfer.

STATUTORY PROVISION

7–9 Section 3 of the Beer Retailers' and Spirit Grocers' Retail Licences (Ireland) Act 1900 provides as follows:

> "The provision requiring the production of a certificate as to the exclusive occupation of rated premises for a period of three months contained in section 2 of the Beer Licences Regulation (Ireland) Act, 1877, shall not apply to the case of a transfer of a licence being granted on the death or removal of the person in occupation of the rated premises immediately prior to the granting of such transfer."

The certificate which the court issues on the application for the grant of a beer retailer's off-licence differs from the certificates which issue in the case of its transfer or renewal. The contents of the certificates required for the grant, renewal and transfer are detailed below.

Certificate of the Court: Grant

7–10 1. Good character of the applicant.

[13] *Application of Thomas Kiernan* [1965] 31 Ir. Jur. Rep. 4 at 14, *per* Lavery J.

2. Suitability of the premises for the purpose of the sale of beer by retail for consumption off the premises.

3. (a) Where the premises are situate in a city or town which contains a population exceeding 10,000 persons, that the premises are rated at £15 or upwards; or

   (b) where the premises are situate elsewhere, that the premises are rated at £8 or upwards.

4. That the premises have been in the exclusive occupation of the applicant for a period of three months preceding the date of the certificate.

Certificate of the Court: Transfer

1. Good character of the applicant. 7–11

2. That the premises were conducted in a peaceable and orderly manner in the past year.

3. (a) Where the premises are situate in a city or town with a population exceeding 10,000 persons, that the premises are rated at £15 or upwards; or

   (b) where the premises are situate elsewhere, that the premises are rated at £8 or upwards.

4. Where the application for the certificate of transfer is made immediately after the removal or death of the previous licence holder, the requirement as to exclusive occupation of the premises for three months prior to the granting of the certificate of transfer does not apply. In all other cases, however, this requirement still holds.

Certificate of the Court: Renewal

1. Good character of the applicant. 7–12

2. That the premises were conducted in a peaceable and orderly manner in the past year.

3. Appropriate rateable valuation.

4. That the premises have been in the exclusive occupation of the applicant for a period of three months preceding the date of the certificate.

Where objections to the renewal of the licence are lodged in accordance with section 4 of the Courts (No. 2) Act 1986, then the certificate of the court is required. If no objections to the renewal are lodged, the applicant obtains a renewal of the licence from the Revenue Commissioners. He is not obliged to notify the fire authority. His licence will not be renewed unless he produces a statutory declaration that the conditions in section 2 of the 1877 Act concerning the rateable valuation and exclusive occupation have been met.[14]

2. Spirit Retailer's Off-Licence

7–13 The spirit retailer's off-licence was created by the Finance (1909–10) Act 1910 and replaces the old spirit grocer's licence which was created in 1791. In *R. (McKenney) v. Antrim Justices* Holmes L.J. noted that Bateman's Excise Laws stated that the reason for the creation of the spirit grocer's licence was to enable persons purchasing spirits in small quantities to procure them without having to resort to a public house "and thus, I presume, to promote the cause of temperance".[15] The spirit retailer's off-licence is usually sought in conjunction with the beer retailer's off-licence and the licence will not be granted without a certificate of the court.[16] An applicant for the transfer of such a licence is also required to obtain a court certificate. The contents of the certificates for the grant, renewal and transfer are discussed below:

Certificate of the Court: Grant and Transfer[17]

7–14
1. Good character of the applicant.
2. Where an applicant has within the preceding two years held a spirit retailer's off-licence or a beer retailer's off-licence for the same premises which has expired, the certificate must also deal with the peaceable and orderly manner in which the premises were conducted during the year preceding the expiration of the licence.

Certificate of the Court: Renewal

7–15
1. Good character of the applicant.
2. Peaceable and orderly manner in which the premises was conducted during the year preceding the expiration of the licence.

There is no requirement in the case of a spirit retailer's off-licence to obtain a certificate as to the rateable valuation or exclusive occupation of the premises by the applicant.

[14] Courts (No. 2) Act 1986, s.4(10).
[15] [1901] 2 I.R. 133 at 178 and 179.
[16] Licensing Act 1872, s.82.
[17] *Ibid.*, and Licensing Act (Ireland) 1874, s.9.

Renewal of Spirit Retailer's Off-Licence Unless objections are lodged in accordance with section 4 of the Courts (No. 2) Act 1986 the applicant obtains a renewal of the licence from the Revenue Commissioners. 7–16

3. Cider Retailer's Off-Licence

A cider retailer's off-licence authorises the sale of cider in retail quantities for consumption off the premises. The jurisdiction to grant this licence arises under section 49 of the Finance (1909–10) Act 1910. James O'Connor in *The Irish Justice of the Peace*,[18] states that a certificate of justices of petty sessions is required for the grant of a cider retailer's off-licence. 7–17

A beer retailer's off-licence entitles the holder to sell cider as well as beer,[19] so he is not obliged to apply for a cider retailer's off-licence. It is unusual for the holder of a spirit retailer's off-licence not to hold a beer retailer's off-licence also. However, in the unlikely event that he does not, it is necessary for him to apply for a cider retailer's off-licence if he wishes to sell cider.[20] A cider retailer's off-licence can only be granted in respect of premises to which either a spirit retailer's off-licence or a wholesale dealer's licence for the sale of spirits, wine or beer attaches.[21]

B. Off-Licences for which no Court Certificate is required

1. Wine Retailer's Off-Licence

This licence, which is one of the three licences which usually attaches to a supermarket premises (the other two licences being the spirit retailer's off-licence and the beer retailer's off-licence), authorises the sale of wine by retail for consumption off the premises in the quantities mentioned at paragraph 7–1 above. "Wine" means wine imported into Ireland[22] and sherry is classified as a foreign wine.[23] A person who holds a wine retailer's licence may also sell sweets by retail without taking out any further licence. 7–18

The grant of this licence is authorised by section 49 of the Finance (1909–10) Act 1910, and no court certificate is required. Only a chemist or the holder of a current beer retailer's off-licence or a current spirit retailer's off-licence may obtain a wine retailer's off-licence.

---

[18] (2nd ed., 1915) Vol. II, p. 652.
[19] Finance (1909–10) Act 1910, Sched. 1.
[20] Twenty-one cider retailer's off-licences were issued in 1994.
[21] Intoxicating Liquor Act 1962, s.28(2).
[22] Finance (1909–10) Act 1910, s.52.
[23] *Richards v. Banks* (1887) 52 J.P. 23.

A retailer's off-licence is void if it is granted to the holder of a retailer's on-licence, where the off-licence authorises the sale of liquor which is not authorised by the on-licence. This provision is contained in Schedule I to the Finance (1909–10) Act 1910, but its provisions have little relevance to modern times as most on-licences authorise the sale of beer, wine and spirits, and all on-licences except the special restaurant licence authorise the sale for consumption on and off the premises.

Licensee

7–19 The grant of a wine retailer's off-licence is restricted to certain persons.

STATUTORY PROVISION

Section 61(1) of the Intoxicating Liquor Act 1927 provides:

> "(1) Notwithstanding anything to the contrary contained in any other Act, the Revenue Commissioners shall not grant, whether by way of new licence or of transfer or renewal of an existing licence, a wine retailer's off-licence to any person other than a person who is carrying on the business of chemist and druggist, pharmaceutical chemist, or registered druggist, or a person who is for the time being the holder of a spirit retailer's off-licence or a beer retailer's off-licence then in force."

The sale of wine by retail for consumption off the premises is confined, therefore, to the holder of the off-licences mentioned in the statute or persons carrying on the business of chemists.

2. Sweet Retailer's Off-Licence

7–20 As the holder of a wine retailer's off-licence may also sell sweets without taking out a sweet retailer's off-licence, very few sweet retailer's off-licences are issued.[24] "Sweets" in this context means:

> ". . . any liquor which is made from fruit and sugar, or from fruit and sugar mixed with any other material, and which has undergone a process of fermentation in the manufacture thereof, and which includes British wines, made wines, mead and metheglin."[25]

The grant of the licence is authorised by the Finance (1909–10) Act 1910 and it authorises the sale at any one time to any one person of sweets in any quantity up to two gallons or one dozen reputed quart bottles, but not in any larger quantitites, for consumption off the premises only.

[24] Twelve were issued by the Revenue Commissioners in 1994.
[25] Finance (1909–10) Act 1910, s.52.

Restriction on Grant of Off-Licences

Section 2 of the Licensing (Ireland) Act 1902 provided, *inter alia*, that no licence should be granted for the sale of intoxicating liquor "whether for consumption on or off the premises" except in certain circumstances. The exceptions to the general prohibitory terms of the 1902 Act are contained in that Act and further exceptions were enacted in subsequent statutes. These exceptions are dealt with in detail in chapter 6, "Public House Licence". The restriction imposed by the 1902 Act applies to off-licences also, but only those in respect of which a court certificate is required.[26] **7–21**

Every applicant for a retailer's off-licence which requires a certificate of the court must bring himself within one of the exceptions to the Licensing (Ireland) Act 1902. Each of the exceptions involves the eventual extinguishment of a licence or licences or proof that the premises was licensed within the past five years. Some of the exceptions require that such licence or licences must be of the same character as the licence being granted. For a detailed explanation of how to "convert" an on-licence into an off-licence, the reader is referred to chapter 15, "Changes in the Character, Scope and Attributes of a Licence".

Circumstances in which New Off-Licences can be granted

An applicant may apply for a new off-licence where he can prove to the court that he comes within an exception to section 2 of the Licensing (Ireland) Act 1902. These exceptions are divided into the following categories: **7–22**

(a) Premises which were licensed within the previous five years

(b) Premises which are situate in a city or town

(c) Premises which are situate in the immediate vicinity of another premises

(d) Premises which are situate in a rural area

(e) Licensed premises which were acquired by the Local Authority

(f) Grant of new off-licence in lieu of renewal of on-licence in County Borough.

(a) Premises Licensed within Previous Five Years

There are two exceptions under this category: **7–23**

1. The first concerns the situation where the licensee wishes either to reduce the area of his licensed premises or to revive a licence which has lapsed.

[26] Licensing (Ireland) Act 1902, s.8.

This exception is contained in section 2(1) of the Licensing (Ireland) Act 1902. Where an applicant for an off-licence invokes section 2(1), the licences which will be extinguished upon the grant of the new off-licences or the licences which previously existed in respect of the premises will in most circumstances be off-licences. However, Blayney J. in *O'Rourke and Flanagan v. Grittar*[27] indicated that it was possible that an applicant for a new off-licence in the place of an existing on-licence might come within the exception to the prohibition against the granting of new licences in section 2 of the 1902 Act. It is conceivable, therefore, that an applicant for an off-licence who invokes section 2(1) of the 1902 Act who can show that his premises benefitted from an on-licence within the previous five years can establish that he is entitled to the certificate sought.

2. The second exception is contained in section 6 of the Licensing (Ireland) Act 1902 which provides for the licensing of premises attached to and adjoining the existing off-licensed premises. An applicant for an off-licence who invokes section 6 of the 1902 Act must prove to the court that his premises were licensed within the past five years. The proviso to section 6 of the 1902 Act permits the granting of the licence in respect of the existing licensed area and the extension only for the purpose of rendering the licensed premises more suitable for the business carried on therein. So, an application to convert a licence from an on-licence to an off-licence could not succeed under section 6 as this stipulation would not be satisfied.

(b) Premises situate in a City or Town

7–24 Section 4 of the Licensing (Ireland) Act 1902 provides for the grant of a new licence in a city or a town in substitution for another licence or licences attaching to a premises situate within the city or town. An applicant for an off-licence must prove that he falls within this jurisdictional exception, but in order to succeed in an application for a new off-licence, he need not tender a licence of the same character for extinguishment as the one which he seeks. In other words, if he is applying for a beer retailer's off-licence and a spirit retailer's off-licence, he need not acquire an existing beer retailer's off-licence and an existing spirit retailer's off-licence. It is sufficient if he produces an existing on-licence.[28]

---

[27] [1996] I.R. 541.
[28] *Re Application of Power Supermarkets* [1988] I.R. 206 (the "Killarney case").

(c) Premises situate in Immediate Vicinity of Another Premises

(i) Expiring Lease An applicant for an off-licence can invoke section 3 of the Licensing (Ireland) Act 1902 which provides for the grant of a licence for a premises in the immediate vicinity of a premises to which there was attached a licence which was surrendered or became extinguished by virtue of the expiration of a lease. This section was amended by section 23 of the Intoxicating Liquor Act 1943 which inserted the words "or off" after the words contained in section 3, "for consumption on". The applicant must prove that he comes within the terms of section 3: there is no specific requirement that the licence which is surrendered or becomes extinguished by virtue of the expiration of the lease should be a licence of the same character as that being sought. Therefore, where the extinguished/surrendered licence is an on-licence, this is sufficient for the purposes of satisfying the statute, where the application is for a certificate entitling the applicant to an off-licence. 7–25

(ii) Grant of New Licence in respect of Premises Substituted for Destroyed Premises Section 22 of the Intoxicating Liquor Act 1943 as amended by section 26 of the Intoxicating Liquor Act 1960 applies to both off-licences and on-licences. Section 25 of the Intoxicating Liquor Act 1960 extended the ambit of section 22 to include an application to the District Court for a certificate entitling the applicant to the grant of an off-licence. The licence to be granted in the immediate vicinity of the destroyed premises must be of the same character as that licence which attached to the destroyed premises. Therefore, an applicant cannot seek an off-licence in the immediate vicinity of the destroyed premises where the destroyed premises had the benefit of an on-licence. Where the licence which attached to the destroyed premises was an off-licence, however, an off-licence can be obtained in respect of the substituted premises and the original destroyed premises can be relicensed with an off-licence. 7–26

(iii) Grant of a New Licence in respect of Premises Substituted for Demolished Premises An application can be made under section 14 of the Intoxicating Liquor Act 1960 for a certificate entitling the applicant to receive off-licences where he can bring himself within the jurisdictional requirements stipulated therein. The licence to be granted pursuant to section 14 must, however, be of the same character as the licence which attached to the premises prior to demolition. Therefore, if the applicant is seeking a new off-licence, the licence which attached to the original premises at the time prior to demolition must have been an off-licence. He cannot seek a new off-licence where the licence which attached to the premises prior to their demolition was an on-licence. 7–27

(d) Premises situate in a Rural Area

7–28 Both exceptions contained under this heading require that where an applicant is seeking a certificate entitling him to receive an off-licence, then the licence or licences which is or are tendered for extinguishment must also be off-licences.

7–29 **(i) Grant of New Licence in respect of More Convenient Premises in a Rural Area** Section 21 of the Intoxicating Liquor Act 1943 provides for the grant of a new on-licence where the appropriate certificate has been obtained. Section 25 of the Intoxicating Liquor Act 1960 expanded the ambit of section 21 to include an application for an off-licence. The new licence must be a licence of the same character in all respects as the licence attached to the existing premises. Therefore, it is not possible to apply for an off-licence under this section where the licence being tendered for extinguishment is an on-licence.

7–30 **(ii) Section 13 of the Intoxicating Liquor Act 1960** This provides for the grant of a new licence in a rural area in substitution for two existing licences. Section 13 does not refer to the District Court and the Circuit Court: it merely refers to "the Court". The section can, however, be invoked in respect of an application for the grant of any licence for which the certificate of the court is required, including an off-licence.[29] An application for a new off-licence under this section requires that the licences which are offered for extinguishment be of the same character as the licences being sought. Thus, if the applicant is seeking a certificate entitling him to a spirit retailer's off-licence and a beer retailer's off-licence, he must be in a position to offer two distinct spirit retailer's off-licences and two distinct beer retailer's off-licences for extinguishment from anywhere in the State.

In *O'Rourke and Flanagan v. Grittar*[30] the Supreme Court (O'Flaherty J. dissenting) held that as the statute specifically required that the licence to be granted must be of the same character and be subject to the same conditions as the licences attaching to the existing premises, it was not sufficient to proffer two on-licences for extinguishment for the purposes of obtaining a new off-licence (namely a spirit retailer's off-licence and a beer retailer's off-licence).

7–31 **The Mile Rule** The mile rule does not apply in respect of off-licences. Section 20(2) of the Intoxicating Liquor Act 1962 provides that an application for an on-licence shall not be allowed in respect of premises situate less than one mile measured by the shortest public thoroughfare, from premises in respect of which a licence granted on or before July 4, 1960, is in force, and which is of the same character as the licence that would be granted if the application were

[29] Intoxicating Liquor Act 1960, s.2.
[30] Above, n.27.

allowed. For the purposes of section 20(2), all on-licences are deemed to be licences of the same character. This section refers only to on-licences. Thus, an application for an off-licence under section 13 of the 1960 Act would not fail if a premises to which either an on-licence or an off-licence is attached is situate within one mile of the premises which is the subject of the off-licence application.

(e) Licensed Premises Acquired by Local Authority

Section 7 of the Intoxicating Liquor Act 1953, provides for the grant of a certificate entitling an applicant to a new licence in respect of premises substituted for licensed premises demolished by the local authority. As with an application under section 13 of the Intoxicating Liquor Act 1960 an application under section 7 of the Intoxicating Liquor Act 1953 does not specify the court to which an application for a certificate entitling an applicant to a licence is to be made, nor does it restrict the type of licence which is to be granted pursuant to the section. However, section 1 of the Intoxicating Liquor Act 1953 provides that "the court" in relation to proceedings in respect of an on-licence means the Circuit Court and in relation to proceedings in respect of an off-licence, it means the District Court. Section 7 can be invoked to obtain an off-licence. **7–32**

However, if an applicant is seeking an off-licence, the licences which attached to the original premises prior to their demolition must have been an off-licence, as section 7(3)(a) of the 1953 Act requires that the licence granted under the section should be of the same character and subject to the same conditions as the licence attaching to the demolished premises.

(f) Grant of New Off-licence in lieu of Renewal of On-licence in County Borough

Section 62 of the Intoxicating Liquor Act 1927, as amended by section 18 of the Intoxicating Liquor Act 1943 and by section 9 of the Courts (No. 2) Act 1986, provides for the grant of a new off-licence in substitution for the renewal of an on-licence. The applicant must prove to the court that the sale of intoxicating liquor for consumption on the premises is not the principal business carried on in the premises to which the on-licence is attached. The circumstances in which this off-licence can be granted are dealt with in more detail in chapter 15, "Changes in Character, Scope and Attributes of a Licence" at paragraphs 15–11 *et seq.* The provision may be availed of only in county boroughs.[31] **7–33**

[31] Dublin, Cork, Limerick, Waterford and Galway.

Discretion of Court

7–34 In *R. (Marshall) v. Tyrone Justices* the Court of Appeal, in considering the question of suitability of the premises, held that it was not entitled to take into account the suitability of the neighbourhood or locality. Palles C.B. stated:

> "The structure and site of the house are matters of moment. The governing provision is that spirits sold shall not be consumed on the premises; fittings of the shop or place in which the sale is transacted should be such as to render public and open to the view of all persons entering the part of the shop in which the sale takes place, and to render it impossible, or at least unlikely, that illicit drinking should be secretly carried on therein."[32]

He rejected the argument that "unsuitability of the premises" in section 9 of the Licensing Act (Ireland) 1874 was the same as "unfitness or inconvenience of the house or place" in section 4 of the Licensing Act (Ireland) 1833. This case was decided before the coming into force of the Beer Retailers' and Spirit Grocers' Retail Licences (Ireland) Act 1900, section 1 of which provides:

> "Notwithstanding anything in any Act, the licensing justices shall be at liberty, in their free and unqualified discretion, either to refuse a certificate . . . on any grounds appearing to them sufficient, or to grant the same to such persons as they, in the execution of their statutory powers, and in the exercise of their discretion deem fit and proper . . .".

Section 1 entitles the court to hear objections and evidence tendered by any resident or owner of the property in the parish. In *Re Application of Power Supermarkets Ltd* Walsh J. stated:

> "The discretion given to the learned Circuit Court judge by s. 1 of the Act of 1900 does not give him an absolute or an unqualified or an arbitrary power to grant or refuse a licence. The discretion must be exercised in accordance with the objectives of the licensing code".[33]

It is likely that the courts today would hold that the suitability of an off-licenced premises from the point of view of its location is a matter to which the court is entitled to have regard.

Conclusion

7–35 The sale of intoxicating liquor in premises to which off-licences attach has become prevalent over the last 20 years. The licensed supermarket has replaced the pub/grocery as the place to which today's shopper resorts. Attempts have

[32] (1894) 28 I.L.T.R. 133 at 134.
[33] Above, n.28, at 210.

been made to create off-licences in place of on-licences, some of which have been successful.[34] The legislature has sought to restrict under-age persons being on, or being employed on, licensed premises and has created various new offences which apply to the holder of an off-licence/licences.[35]

The legislative concern in preventing the sale of intoxicating liquor before permitted hours is reflected in section 7 of the Intoxicating Liquor Act 1988 which prohibits the sale of any intoxicating liquor by self-service methods. Section 47(6) stipulated that section 7 was to come into operation "on such day as the Minister may appoint by order". At the time of writing, section 47 is not in operation. Wine continues to be sold from gondolas in supermarkets, although most, if not all, supermarkets serve beer and spirits from behind an intoxicating liquor counter.

---

[34] *Ibid.*

[35] Intoxicating Liquor Act 1988, s.36.

CHAPTER 8

HOTELS

Introduction

8–1 Hotels operate under a variety of licences. Some of the older hotels for example, the Shelbourne Hotel and the Gresham Hotel, have the benefit of ordinary publicans' licences. Such licences were in many cases obtained before the coming into force of the Licensing (Ireland) Act 1902. Section 2(2) of the 1902 Act created a new type of publican's licence commonly referred to as a "hotel licence", which depends for its grant and renewal upon compliance with the requirements contained in that statute (and in further legislation detailed below).

The third category of licence which can attach to a hotel premises is that which was granted pursuant to Part VI of the Tourist Traffic Act 1952, which provided for the licensing of a hotel following the grant of a declaratory order pursuant to section 41 of the 1952 Act. This particular jurisdiction, which was rarely invoked, required proof that receipts from the sale of intoxicating liquor did not exceed one third of the total receipts from the business of the premises as a precondition to renewal. The statutory provisions relating to the grant of a declaratory order and a certificate in respect of such premises have been repealed, although a number of these types of licences still exist.[1]

Before the Licensing (Ireland) Act 1902 came into force, attempts were made by the courts to limit the scope of publicans' licences, where they were granted in respect of hotels, by imposing undertakings that the bar on the

---

[1] Intoxicating Liquor Act 1960, s.3.

premises be opened and used for hotel purposes only. In *R. (Bourke) v. Dublin Justices*,[2] Palles C.B. referred to the practice of accepting and acting on such undertakings as "irregular". He stated:

> "... the learned Recorder can now legally grant an hotel licence, the legal effect of which will be that, and no more than that, which the old publican's licence would have had, had it been capable in law of being controlled by an undertaking such as that which we have here."[3]

Palles C.B. noted the effect of section 2(2) of the 1902 Act:

> "... a licence can now be granted by the sole operation of which Mr Bourke would be legally bound to limit his trade in the manner contemplated by the undertaking."[4]

Section 2(2) of the Licensing (Ireland) Act 1902 created an exception to the prohibition against granting new licences if the licence was sought in respect of premises which fell within the definition of "hotel" contained therein: such hotel had to contain a specified number of bedrooms and could not have a bar. **8–2**

In 1960, the legislature intervened and the Intoxicating Liquor Act 1960 provided for a method whereby the holder of a hotel licence could apply to the court for an order extinguishing a licence, the statutory consequence being that he was then entitled to have public bar facilities on his hotel premises. Licences to sell intoxicating liquor in hotel premises differ in the scope and to the extent detailed below.

Form of Licence

Despite the fact that the publican's licence and the hotel licence are subject to different conditions under the licensing code, the form of licence which is issued by the Revenue Commissioners to the hotelier, whether he has obtained an order under section 2(2) of the 1902 Act, or an order directing the issue of a certificate entitling him to receive a publican's licence, is identical. The reason for this is that a licence obtained on foot of either of these certificates is a publican's licence; although the licences granted pursuant to the provisions of section 2(2) of the 1902 Act or renewed under the Tourist Traffic Act 1952 are restricted publicans' licences, their continued validity being dependant upon compliance with various statutory requirements. Following legal advice, the Revenue Commissioners placed a note at the foot of all licences issued to publicans and hoteliers which reads: **8–3**

> "This form of licence is used for both:

---

[2] [1903] 2 I.R. 429.
[3] *Ibid.* at 439.
[4] *Ibid.*

(1) public houses, and
(2) certain hotels licensed under paragraph 2 of section 2 of the Licensing (Ireland) Act 1902.

These hotel licences are subject to certain restrictions which do not apply to public houses."

As the same licence issues to all hoteliers, confusion can be caused, particularly where the purchase of a licensed premises is being negotiated. The District Court licensing register should always be inspected to ascertain the nature of the licence which attaches to the premises.[5]

Licensing Exemptions for Hotels

8–4 Where a hotel falls within the definition of "hotel" in section 1 of the Intoxicating Liquor Act 1927, the licensee may take advantage of certain benefits. Section 1 of the Intoxicating Liquor Act 1927 defines "hotel" as a:

> "licensed premises structurally adapted for use and bona fide used as a hotel or a hotel and restaurant and having not less than ten apartments set apart and exclusively used for the sleeping accommodation of travellers".

So, irrespective of whether the licence is an ordinary publican's licence or the conditional licence granted pursuant to section 2(2) of the 1902 Act, or the licence granted pursuant to the Tourist Traffic Act 1952, once the premises satisfy the statutory description above, the licensee is entitled to avail of the following exemptions contained in the licensing code.

(a) Special Exemption Orders

8–5 The licensee may apply for special exemption orders which permit trading, subject to certain conditions, during hours normally prohibited by the licensing code as discussed below in chapter 23, "Exemption Orders and Occasional Licences".[6]

(b) Mixed Trading

8–6 It is not an offence to carry on business other than the sale of intoxicating liquor in hotel premises. Section 3(3) of the Intoxicating Liquor Act 1927 provides that the prohibition against carrying on non-licensed business in a licensed premises during prohibited hours does not apply to "any hotel".[7]

---

[5] See below, chap. 29, "Duties of a Solicitor".
[6] Intoxicating Liquor Act 1927, s.5, as amended by the Intoxicating Liquor Act 1988, s.29.
[7] Whether it holds a publican's licence or the more restricted "hotel" licence.

(c) Extended Hours with Meals

Intoxicating liquor may be served with meals in the premises up until 12.30 a.m. on the following day. A hotelier can serve intoxicating liquor with meals to any person on a Sunday between the hours of 2 p.m. and 3 p.m. but not from 3 p.m. until 4 p.m. There is no provision for an extension of the normal permitted hours on a Sunday evening even when meals are served (unless it falls on December 23 or 24, in which case the Sunday is treated as a weekday), and the licensee must therefore abide by the normal permitted hours on a Sunday evening. The licensee can serve intoxicating liquor with meals to any person on Christmas day between the hours of 1 p.m. and 3 p.m. or the hours of 7 p.m. and 10 p.m.[8] **8–7**

(d) Lodger

As in the case of the holder of a publican's licence for premises which are not a hotel, a hotelier is entitled to sell intoxicating liquor at any hour on his licensed premises to a person then lodging in such premises. The only exception to this is that on Christmas Day, Good Friday and St Patrick's Day, no intoxicating liquor can be sold to any such person except and with the consumption of a meal to be consumed by such person in the premises.[9] **8–8**

Statutory Obligation of Hotelier

A premises which holds itself out as a hotel is obliged to be registered in the register of hotels kept by Bord Fáilte Éireann and the proprietor of the hotel must be registered as such. It matters not whether the licence is the conditional licence created by the 1902 Act or whether the licence is a full publican's licence. **8–9**

STATUTORY PROVISION

Section 33 of the Tourist Traffic Act 1939, as amended by the Tourist Traffic Act 1983, section 3, provides:

> "(1) It shall not be lawful for the proprietor of any premises to describe or hold out or permit any person to describe or hold out such premises as an hotel unless such premises are registered in the register of hotels and such proprietor is registered in that register as the registered proprietor of such premises.
>
> (2) Any person who acts in contravention of this section shall be guilty of an offence under this section and shall be liable on summary conviction thereof to a fine not exceeding £500 together with, in the case of a continuing offence, a

---

[8] Intoxicating Liquor Act 1927, s.13, as inserted by the Intoxicating Liquor Act 1988, s.28.
[9] Intoxicating Liquor Act 1927, s.14(e).

further fine (not exceeding £300 in all), not exceeding £20 for every day during which the offence is continued."

Where a vendor represents a property to be a hotel but fails to prove current registration with Bord Fáilte, this will amount to an "actionable misdescription".[10]

Carney J. in an *ex tempore* judgment in *Mann v. O'Keeffe*[11] held that the plaintiff was entitled to a declaration that her contract had been validly rescinded, and to the return of her deposit where the property in question had been represented as a hotel although it was not registered with Bord Fáilte.

Differences between Publican's Licence and "Hotel" Licence

8–10 Although the holder of a publican's licence can be a hotelier for the purposes of the licensing code, there are differences between a publican's licence ordinary and a hotel licence, whether it is the conditional licence granted under section 2(2) of the 1902 Act or the Tourist Traffic Act 1952. These differences can be summarised as follows:

1. A hotel licence cannot be tendered for extinguishment on an application for the grant of a publican's on-licence.[12]
2. A hotel licence cannot be tendered for extinguishment on an application for an order permitting the holder of a hotel licence to have public bar facilities in his hotel.[13]
3. An applicant who seeks renewal of a hotel licence must prove that his premises are registered with Bord Fáilte, where the licence was granted pursuant to the provisions of Part VI of the Tourist Traffic Act 1952 or where he obtained a hotel licence under section 2(2) of the Licensing (Ireland) Act 1902 after July 4, 1960.[14]

Types of Licences for Hotels

1. Publican's Licence

8–11 A number of hotels, often those licensed prior to 1902, are premises to which a publican's licence attaches. These premises are entitled to all the exemptions mentioned at paragraphs 8–5 to 8–8.

---

[10] *Pierse v. Allen*, unreported, High Court, Murphy J., June 9, 1993; *Professional Negligence Law Reports* (1993) p. 486.
[11] Unreported, Circuit Court Appeal, Tullamore High Court, Carney J., March 29, 1995.
[12] Intoxicating Liquor Act 1962, s.20.
[13] Intoxicating Liquor Act 1960, s.19.
[14] Courts (No. 2) Act 1986, s.4(9).

2. Hotel Licence: Tourist Traffic Act 1952

A hotel licence cannot now be granted under Part VI of the Tourist Traffic Act 1952.[15] The Revenue Commissioners still issue licences in respect of hotel premises where they were licensed prior to the date of the repeal of Part VI, Chapter II of the Tourist Traffic Act 1952. 8–12

A licence for a hotel in respect of which effect was given to section 42(1) of the 1952 Act is not renewable on expiry without the production to the Revenue Commissioners of a Bord Fáilte certificate.[16]

Application for Renewal

An applicant who applies to renew a licence granted under section 42(1) of the Tourist Traffic Act 1952, must prove that the premises are registered with Bord Fáilte. The requirement to prove that the excise duty payable under the Finance (1909–10) Act 1910 on the current licence, was subject to reduced duty under section 45 of that Act no longer applies. 8–13

The additional requirement to produce a certificate from the Revenue Commissioners confirming that receipts from the sale of intoxicating liquor in the preceding year for the purposes of section 45 of the Finance (1909–10) Act 1910 were less than one third of total receipts in that year from business of all descriptions carried on by the licence holder in the premises was imposed by section 42 of the Tourist Traffic Act 1952 (since repealed) and is not carried forward by the Courts (No. 2) Act 1986.[17]

There is no statutory bar to the offering for extinguishment of a licence granted under the 1952 Act upon an application for the grant of a publican's licence. Section 20 of the Intoxicating Liquor Act 1962, as amended by section 23 of the Intoxicating Liquor Act 1988, forbids the grant of a new licence pursuant to various statutory provisions, where the licence tendered for extinguishment in substitution is any of the following: a greyhound race track licence, a special restaurant licence, or a hotel licence granted under section 2(2) of the Licensing (Ireland) Act 1902.

3. Hotel Licence: Licensing (Ireland) Act 1902, Section 2(2)

The licence granted under section 2(2) of the Licensing (Ireland) Act 1902 is in the same form as the publican's licence. This is because it is a publican's licence with all its characteristics and attributes. It is, however, a conditional or restricted publican's licence. It is not defined by statute as a "hotel licence"; for 8–14

[15] Intoxicating Liquor Act 1960, s.3.
[16] Courts (No. 2) Act 1986, s.4(9).
[17] Intoxicating Liquor Act 1960, s.3.

the purposes of the Finance (1909–10) Act 1910, it is however deemed to be a retailer's on-licence. This is in contrast to the special restaurant licence which is defined by statute.[18]

So, the expression "hotel licence" has no legal connotation: Judge Shannon stated "there is no such thing known to the law as a hotel licence".[19] There is jurisdiction to grant a publican's licence in respect of a premises which comes within the definition of hotel contained in section 2(2) of the Licensing (Ireland) Act 1902. The applicant for the licence must satisfy the court that the premises sought to be licensed fulfil the requirements contained in section 2(2) of the 1902 Act as amended. Further the premises must continue to answer to and correspond with this definition, otherwise the licence becomes inoperable, cannot be renewed and although valid on its face, is no protection to the licence holder. A hotel licence which was granted after the enactment of the Intoxicating Liquor Act 1960, by virtue of section 2(2) of the 1902 Act, is not renewable on expiry without the production to the Revenue Commissioners of a Bord Fáilte certificate.[20]

STATUTORY PROVISION

8–15 Section 2(2) of the Licensing (Ireland) Act 1902, as amended by section 21 of the Intoxicating Liquor Act 1960, provides:

> "From and after the passing of this Act, no licence shall be granted for the sale of intoxicating liquors, whether for consumption on or off the premises, except—
>
> …
>
> (2) For an hotel, which expression shall refer to a house containing at least ten, or if situate in a County Borough (which expression shall be deemed, for the purposes of this section, to include the Dublin Metropolitan District), twenty apartments set apart and used exclusively for the sleeping accommodation of travellers, and having no public bar for the sale of intoxicating liquors".

Conditional licence

8–16 Where the conditions specified at section 2(2) cease to exist, the licence ceases to be a protection to the holder. In *Quinn v. Bourke*, Madden J. dealt with the nature of the licence:

> "I think that the licence, on the face of it, imports that the licensed house is an hotel which is not only *ab initio* structurally in accordance with the Act but continues to be used in accordance with it. If the ten apartments cease to be used

[18] Intoxicating Liquor Act 1988, ss.6, 7(1).
[19] *The State (Walsh) v. Judge Shannon* (1936) 70 I.L.T.R. 149 at 150.
[20] Courts (No. 2) Act 1986, s.4(9).

exclusively for the sleeping accommodation of travellers or, if an innocent structure which passed muster when the licence was granted were by user converted into a bar for the sale of intoxicating liquors, I am of opinion that the licence would cease to be a protection to the holder."[21]

In this case the defendant was charged with selling intoxicating liquor at a public bar on premises to which a hotel licence was attached (the Phoenix Park Hotel), in contravention of the terms of her licence. Much of the case was concerned with the definition of "public bar". The case was remitted to the magistrate to determine whether, on the facts, the arrangement of the premises constitued a public bar.

At the time of the application for the court certificate the premises must answer the description of hotel; they must also continue to answer the definition of a hotel during the currency of the licensing year.

In *The State (Quirke) v. Circuit Court Judge of Co. Tipperary*,[22] evidence was given that a bar counter had been erected on premises to which a hotel licence had attached and that there was not sufficient sleeping accommodation for travellers. An objection to the renewal of the licence was made by the local superintendent. The judge of the District Court concluded that he should not renew the licence. The applicant sought to make absolute a conditional order of certiorari and mandamus directed to the District Court judge on the basis that his order did not sufficiently set forth the grounds for refusing the application to renew. The District Court order stated: **8–17**

> "Application to have renewal certificate signed refused on the grounds of character of applicant and the manner in which the house has been conducted during the past year. A licence had been granted in 1922 and during the previous year there was a bar on the premises and the statutory number of bedrooms had not been set aside for travellers."[23]

Sullivan P. rejected the contention that the order was irregular in form and invalid as it stated that the certificate was refused on the ground of the character of the applicant. Sullivan P. stated:

> ". . . if a person holding a hotel licence reduces the number of rooms below that required by the Act or maintains a public bar on his premises, these are matters which touch his character as a licensed trader."[24]

The general principle is that the conditions under which the licence was granted must continue to be observed and if the licensee is in breach of the terms or conditions of the licence, he is not entitled to continue to trade thereunder.

---

[21] [1906] 2 I.R. 94 at 102.
[22] (1931) 65 I.L.T.R. 157.
[23] *Ibid.* at 158.
[24] *Ibid.* at 159.

House

8–18 The expression "house" in the subsection has been interpreted by the courts to include houses or separate unconnected, but adjacent, structures. In *Application of Waterhouse*[25] Judge O'Briain granted a hotel licence under section 2(2) of the 1902 Act in respect of premises consisting of two structurally unconnected buildings and separated by a lawn. Neither building, standing alone, contained bedrooms, but the two buildings viewed as one contained more than 10 bedrooms. Judge O'Briain stated: "I am entitled to read 'house' in the section as 'houses'."[26]

A hotel licence was granted for the Kildare Hotel and Country Club (the "K" club), a substantial hotel premises consisting of a main building comprising bedrooms, dining areas, restaurant and kitchen facilities, and another building which was a golf pavilion and a restaurant. Both premises were situated 400 yards apart, but the Circuit Court and the High Court on appeal (McKenzie J.) accepted the applicant's contention that it was not necessary that all of the premises be under the same roof. In Athy Circuit Court on May 11, 1995, Judge Smith, accepting and applying this principle, granted a licence for Kilkea Castle in respect of existing licensed premises and a golf pavilion situated some 200 yards away from the main premises.[27]

Both the "K" Club and Kilkea Castle rely heavily on business from tourists and golfers and the provision of a golf pavilion in each case was seen as very much part of the essential business of each hotel.

However, if the premises consist of more than one building, the applicant must prove that the buildings are "held together for the same trade or business".[28] A hotelier cannot carry on a hotel business in one building and a public house business in another.

Sleeping Accommodation

8–19 On an application for a certificate entitling an applicant to receive a hotel licence, proof of user of the appropriate number of bedrooms is required. In *R. (Sale) v. Fermanagh Justices*,[29] Palles C.B. noted that section 2 of the 1902 Act prohibited the grant of a licence for the sale of intoxicating liquors except "for an hotel, which expression shall refer to a house containing at least 10 apartments set apart and used exclusively for the sleeping accommodation of travellers . . .". At the time of the application, the premises contained 10 rooms which were intended and suitable for use as bedrooms, but none of them were

---

[25] [1955–56] Ir. Jur. Rep. 59.
[26] *Ibid.* at 60.
[27] *Kilkea Castle, Jim Cassidy, Applicant*, unreported, Athy Circuit Court, Judge Smith, May 11, 1995. *Kildare Hotel and Country Club, Application of*, unreported, High Court, April 4, 1990.
[28] Excise Licences Act 1825, s.10.
[29] (1906) 40 I.L.T.R. 75.

furnished. Palles C.B. although of the view that the words "set apart and used" did refer to an "actual user for sleeping accommodation", indicated that he was prepared, if the rooms were furnished as bedrooms, to grant the licence. He stated, *obiter*:

> "I would, however, go this length—if the rooms are furnished as bedrooms, so that the licensee upon obtaining his licence would be able then and there to carry on the premises as an hotel, I think he would be sufficiently within the exception."[30]

In *Application of Mulvihill*,[31] it was proved that nine of the bedrooms in the reconstructed hotel had been part of the old guest house and had been used previously for the accommodation of travellers. The additional 10 bedrooms were furnished and ready to receive travellers, but no travellers had ever used them. Judge O'Briain adopted the reasoning of Palles C.B.in the *Sale* case and held that if the rooms were furnished as bedrooms so that the licensee upon obtaining his licence would be able then and there to operate the premises as a hotel, the court should grant the application.

Thus an applicant for a certificate leading to the grant of a new hotel licence need not open his premises prior to the application to the court; so he does not have to prove an existing user of the bedrooms. It is sufficient if he can prove that they are furnished as bedrooms and are ready and available for such use.

Public Bar

A person who obtains a hotel licence under section 2(2) of the 1902 Act is not entitled, unless he makes a contemporaneous or subsequent application pursuant to section 19 of the Intoxicating Liquor Act 1960, to have a public bar on his premises. **8–20**

In *R. (Bourke) v. Dublin Justices*, Palles C.B. stated:

> "I am of opinion that a sale under an hotel licence under this Act of Edward VII. will not authorise a sale at a bar erected contrary to its provisions, and that such a sale can be prosecuted for as a sale by an unlicensed person."[32]

In *Quinn v. Bourke* he adopted the definition of a public bar contained in *Murray's Dictionary* as follows:

> "A barrier or counter, from which drink (or food) is served out to customers in an inn, hotel or tavern; and hence in a coffee house, at a railway station, etc.; also the space behind the barrier, and sometimes the whole apartment containing it."[33]

---

[30] *Ibid.* at 76.
[31] [1960] 26 Ir. Jur. Rep. 17.
[32] (1903) 3 N.I.J.R. 130 at 133. See above, n.2.
[33] Above, n.21, at 97.

Sale of Intoxicating Liquor to the General Public

8–21 There is nothing to prohibit the sale of intoxicating liquor to the general public in a hotel premises licensed under section 2(2) of the 1902 Act.

Palles C.B. in *Quinn v. Bourke* refers to *R. (Bourke) v. Dublin Justices* and states:

> "It, however, by no means follows from what I said, nor did I intend to suggest, that the effect of the Act was that in an hotel having a licence under that Act, intoxicating drink could not be sold to the public, if the sale were not at, or in, a public bar."[34]

He continued:

> "How can the prohibition against supplying the public with drink in one particular way justify a legal tribunal, such as we are, in taking it upon itself to say that that amounts to a prohibition against supplying the public in any way. If the Court were to so decide, its decision would work a prohibition different from, and greater than, that imposed by the Act of Parliament. The decision would work a total exclusion of the public, whilst the restriction in the Act was against that particular mode of getting drink which is involved in being supplied at or from a public bar."[35]

Kenny J. in the same case concluded that the condition against having a public bar on the premises did not mean that the sale of liquor was confined to mere travellers or lodgers in the hotel. The court held that there was some evidence that there was a "public bar" within the meaning of section 2(2) of the 1902 Act on the defendant's premises. For that reason, the case was remitted to the magistrate for rehearing to determine whether there was a public bar on the premises in accordance with the interpretation of "public bar" given by the King's Bench. There is no note at the foot of the judgment of the magistrate's ultimate decision as to whether the arrangement of the premises as set forth in a plan included in the report did constitute a public bar.

8–22 Lavery J. in *Doyle v. Foley*,[36] expressed himself dissatisfied with the decision in *Quinn v. Bourke* but accepted that the general public could be served with intoxicating liquor. He stated:

> "So far as it establishes that under a "hotel licence" liquor may be supplied to persons other than travellers or lodgers it has been accepted and recognised as law by statute and Court decisions for over fifty years and this is not now in dispute. In passing, I think that the Court engaged itself too much with the meaning of the word "bar" considered as a structure and too little with the word "public" in construing the condition that there should be no public bar. The purpose of the Act was to restrict public drinking accommodation and the

---

[34] *Ibid.* at 97.
[35] *Ibid.* at 99 and 100.
[36] Unreported, Supreme Court, June 3, 1965.

exception was made to provide a proper accommodation for travellers and lodgers."[37]

Discretion of the Court

In deciding whether to grant a hotel licence, the Court must be satisfied that the premises in question is a hotel. It is a question of fact as to whether or not they are a hotel. Murnaghan J. in *Re Duffy* stated: 8–23

> "It is difficult to lay down any hard or fast rule to govern all cases as to the minimum standard, and this fact was recognised by the legislature which felt it necessary to specify a minimum in the case of the number of bedrooms. This requirement has, I am afraid, tended to encourage applicants to think that if they comply with it they must get a licence. This is not so. No premises can be licensed until a competent Court is satisfied that it is a hotel and that it complies with the provisions of paragraph 2 of section 2 of the 1902 Act".[38]

Murnaghan J. expressed the view that a hotel must have accommodation for the preparation and the storage of food of all kinds and other perishable commodities and a place in which to serve the food to the customers when prepared. He noted that one room should be set aside as a dining room which, in his view, would be "a *sine qua non* for any hotel".

Hotel business: ancillary

A question may arise as to whether premises can properly be described as a hotel where the sale of intoxicating liquor to the public is not subsidiary to the hotel business proper but constitutes the hotelier's main business. Since the introduction by the legislature of a hotelier's right to have a public bar on his premises, despite the prohibition in section 2(2) of the 1902 Act, many hoteliers have obtained an order pursuant to section 19 of the Intoxicating Liquor Act 1960 entitling them to have public bar facilities on their premises. 8–24

In some cases the business from the public bar is greater than the hotel business. The Supreme Court has held that this is a matter which is to be considered by a court in the context of an objection to the unfitness or inconvenience of the premises. In *Doyle v. Foley*,[39] Murnaghan J. stated a case to the Supreme Court as to whether premises were a hotel within the meaning of section 2(2) of the Licensing (Ireland) Act 1902. He found the following facts:

1. that an essential part of the business which the applicant intended to be carried on in the proposed premises was a "lounge bar trade";

---

[37] *Ibid.* at p. 4.
[38] Unreported, High Court, Murnaghan J., January 15, 1959.
[39] Above, n.36.

2. that the lounge bar trade would not be subsidiary to the business to be conducted in the rest of the premises and that the probabilities were that the hotel business proper would be of secondary importance to the lounge bar trade.

In giving judgment, Lavery J. stated:

> "It does not appear to have been intended to define the word "hotel". The intention, in my opinion, was to restrict the exception to the general rule that no licences should be granted to a particular kind of hotel. It was supposed that everyone would know what a hotel was but that only those hotels with at least ten rooms for guests and no public bar and a certain valuation should be eligible for the grant of a licence."[40]

Walsh J. stated that the findings of fact of Murnaghan J. (see above),

> "simply indicate the relative importance or value of the different parts of the business, the whole of what may lawfully be carried on by the applicant in the proposed premises should a licence be granted. They do not affect the jurisdiction to grant the declaration sought."[41]

Lavery J. agreed and held that the court had jurisdiction to grant a declaration that the premises would be fit and convenient to be licensed as a hotel. His judgment contained an important proviso, however. Although he accepted that the Supreme Court had no further function with regard to the case stated, he added that the judge, as licensing authority, is obliged to consider the grounds of objection under section 4 of the Licensing (Ireland) Act 1833. He stated:

> "The unfitness or inconvenience of the premises for the carrying on of a licensed trade in premises which may only be licensed as a hotel has to be considered and it is this which has prompted the learned Judge to invite the opinion of this Court on the question of jurisdiction. The nature and size of the proposed lounge bar would seem to be proper for consideration on this admissible ground of objection. The number of existing licensed premises in the neighbourhood has also to be considered. Is there a need for further facilities for the sale of intoxicating liquor under the conditions proposed?"[42]

Ó Dálaigh C.J. agreed with the conclusions of Lavery and Walsh JJ.

The conclusion therefore was that the court had jurisdiction to grant the application. The case was remitted to Murnaghan J. Counsel for the objector[43] referred Murnaghan J. to the notes taken by the judge during the hearing of the case and asked him to address himself to the unfitness and inconvenience of the premises. In an unreported and *ex tempore* judgment, Murnaghan J. refused the application for a declaratory order on the grounds of the unfitness of the premises.

---

[40] *Ibid.* at p. 4.
[41] *Ibid.* at p. 2.
[42] *Ibid.* at p. 6.
[43] John B. Cassidy.

Accordingly, if the premises sought to be licensed can be brought within the statutory definition, no question of jurisdiction to license then arises. The application should be considered on the merits, due regard being had to any evidence which would support or ground the statutory objections to the grant of a new on-licence, particularly those set out in section 4 of the Licensing (Ireland) Act 1833.

Rateable Valuation

An applicant for a certificate under section 2(2) of the 1902 Act must prove that the rateable valuation is not less than the figures set forth in section 5 of the Licensing (Ireland) Act 1902, as amended by section 33 of the Intoxicating Liquor Act 1960, which are: 8–25

£30 in the city of Dublin;

£20 in the cities of Cork, Limerick and Waterford;

£15 in the cities of Kilkenny and Galway;

£12 in any other town of over 10,000 inhabitants at the last census; and

£10 in all other places.

As in other applications for on-licences, the term "rateable valuation" includes the provisional valuation issued by the Commissioner of Valuation.[44]

Removal of Prohibition against Public Bar

Section 2(2) of the 1902 Act expressly prohibits a premises to which a hotel licence attaches from having a public bar. The 1957 Commission of Inquiry referred to complaints from the ordinary licensed trade that there was "little or no difference between some of these dispense bar arrangements and public bars". It is also noted "on the other hand the case was made to us by hoteliers ... that the dispense bar was a cause of annoyance to customers who liked to see their drinks poured out".[45] The Commission recommended that the prohibition on having a public bar on the premises be removed on application to the court and that this should be conditional on the surrender of an existing public house licence. It proposed further that the law should be amended to abolish the prohibition on having a public bar and to provide for the surrender of an existing licence in respect of "new" hotel licences. Section 19 of the Intoxicating Liquor Act 1960 provides for the removal of the prohibition contained in section 2(2) of the 1902 Act against having public bar facilities on a premises, on condition that the applicant secure a publican's on-licence for extinguishment. 8–26

---

44 Intoxicating Liquor Act 1960, s.33.

45 Reports of the Commission of Inquiry into the Operation of the Laws Relating to the Sale and Supply of Intoxicating Liquor 1957, pp. 16 and 17.

It is important to note, however, that section 19 is not a licensing provision. It does not convert a hotel licence into an unrestricted publican's licence ordinary. The licence is a hotel licence: it continues to retain all the characteristics inherent in a licence granted under section 2(2) of the 1902 Act, save that the prohibition on having a public bar on the premises is removed.

Application for Public Bar Facilities in Hotel

8–27 **(i) Section 19 Order in Respect of Existing Premises** Section 19(1) and (2) of the Intoxicating Liquor Act 1960 deal with the removal of the prohibition on having a public bar on existing hotel premises.

STATUTORY PROVISION

Section 19(1) and (2) of the Intoxicating Liquor Act 1960 provide:

> "(1) Where a person who holds a licence in respect of a hotel which was granted by virtue of paragraph 2 of section 2 of the 1902 Act shows to the satisfaction of the District Court, on application thereto at any sitting thereof for the Court area in which the hotel is situate, that, in respect of an ordinary seven-day licence (not being a licence granted by virtue of section 2(2) of the 1902 Act), either:
>
> (a) he is the holder thereof; or
> (b) he has procured the consent of the holder to the extinguishing thereof,
>
> the Court may order that the ordinary seven day licence be extinguished.
>
> (2) When an order under subsection (1) of this section is made:
>
> (a) it shall be lawful, notwithstanding anything contained in the Act of 1902, to have in the hotel a public bar for the sale of intoxicating liquor,
> (b) the ordinary seven-day licence shall be extinguished, and
> (c) if the premises to which the ordinary seven-day licence was attached immediately before the making of the order were premises to which section 2(1) of the Act of 1902 applied, that paragraph shall cease to apply to them."

JURISDICTIONAL REQUIREMENTS

8–28 The provisions of section 19(1) and (2) of the 1960 Act apply where the applicant already holds a licence in respect of a hotel which was granted under section 2(2) of the 1902 Act. The application is made *ex parte* and the court must grant the application once the applicant has fulfilled the statutory conditions.

1. Venue

The application can be made at any sitting of the District Court and the order made by the court is that the ordinary seven-day licence tendered by the applicant be extinguished.

2. Licence

The licence to be extinguished must be an ordinary seven-day licence and cannot be an early closing licence or a six-day licence.[46] It must not be a hotel licence, *i.e.* a licence granted pursuant to the provisions of section 2(2) of the 1902 Act.[47] The licence must be an existing licence at the time of the making of the application. The applicant need not prove that he is the holder of the licence but where he is not the holder he must prove that he has obtained the consent of the holder of the licence. If a section 19 order is appealed, the licence tendered for extinguishment in the Court of Appeal stage must be the same as that which was offered in the District Court.[48]

3. Court Order

The order which the court makes in a section 19 application is an order extinguishing a licence. This is the only statutory provision in the licensing code which empowers a court to direct the extinguishment of a licence. In all other circumstances, a licence becomes extinguished by operation of law or where it has lapsed due to failure to renew.

Discretion of the Court The question of whether section 19 of the 1960 Act conferred a discretion on the court was considered by the Supreme Court in *Application of Thomas J. Dunne*.[49] In that case it was held that where the statutory expression "may order" confers on the court jurisdiction to make an order, subject to the fulfilment by the applicant of certain statutory conditions, the statutory expression should be construed as imposing an obligation on the court to make the order once it is satisfied that those conditions have been fulfilled by the applicant. **8–29**

Walsh J. stated:

> "Section 19 quite clearly exists for the benefit of persons holding hotel licences. If such holders comply with the requirements of the section they can obtain the right to have a public bar. The section provides the matters upon which the court must be satisfied before such right can arise. The section does not make any provision for the consideration of any other matters by the court in question upon such an application, or for the consideration of the views of any other person or persons upon the application … Having regard to the general policy of the Acts and the requirements of obtaining new licences, it is remarkable that in this section the Oireachtas has made no provision whatever for the giving of notice of the hearing of objections. This, in my view, is a very strong indication that the extinguishment of the licence in applications under section 19 of the

---

[46] Intoxicating Liquor Act 1960, s.19(1).
[47] *Ibid.*
[48] *Application of Thomas J. Dunne* [1968] I.R. 105.
[49] *Ibid.*

Act of 1960 was not intended to be a matter of discretion. This was also emphasised by the fact that such an application could be made at any sitting of the District Court."[50]

Once the jurisdictional requirements are satisfied, the court cannot exercise any discretion; the applicant is entitled as of right to obtain his section 19 order. Walsh J. continued:

> "In my view, when one has regard to the context in which the use of the word 'may' appears in section 19, and when one has regard to the object of the section and to the fact that the persons to benefit from the section are clearly identified, to the absence of requirement as to notice, to the absence of any reference to objections and to the informality of the procedure, one cannot but conclude that the correct construction of the section is that, upon the giving of the proofs required by the section in the particular case, there is no discretion in the Court to decline to make the order sought, namely, that the ordinary seven-day licence in question be extinguished."[51]

Walsh J. also stated:

> "The provisions of the Act of 1960 do not legislate for any grounds of objection which might be put forward on any such application and indeed it would be difficult to do so when the statute does not make any provision for any objectors."[52]

STATUTORY CONSEQUENCES

8–30 The application is not an application for the right to have a public bar: it is an application to extinguish a licence. The statutory consequences are as follows:

1. the licence which has been tendered for extinguishment is extinguished;
2. the premises to which the existing licence attached cannot be relicensed pursuant to section 2(1) of the 1902 Act, namely by proof that the premises were licensed within the past five years;
3. it is lawful to have a public bar in the hotel for the sale of intoxicating liquor. The right of a hotelier to have a number of public bars on his premises has not been judicially determined. It is however notorious that hotels have successfully applied to the court under section 19 of the 1960 Act not alone have a public bar but sometimes several areas in the hotel premises containing a counter or being operated as a public bar. To justify this position, the section must be construed to mean that the expression "public bar" in the singular, includes the plural, or that the expression "it shall be lawful" means

[50] *Application of Thomas J. Dunne*, above, n.48, at 117.
[51] *Ibid.* at 118.
[52] *Ibid.*, above, n.48, at 115.

it is not unlawful to have a public bar anywhere on the premises. Furthermore, the provisions of the 1902 Act excluding a house which has a public bar from the definition of a hotel have no application at all to a hotel licence where the section 19 jurisdiction has been availed of.

(ii) Section 19 Order in Conjunction with Application for New Hotel Licence Section 19(3) and (4) provide for the removal of the prohibition contained in section 2(2) of the 1902 Act, on the extinguishment of a seven-day publican's licence. 8–31

STATUTORY PROVISION

Section 19(3) and (4) of the Intoxicating Liquor Act 1960 provide:

"(3)Where—

(a) a certificate entitling the holder thereof to receive a licence in respect of a hotel has been granted by virtue of paragraph 2 of section 2 of the Act of 1902, and

(b) on the hearing of the application for the grant of the certificate the holder—

(i) has indicated to the Court that he wishes to have in the hotel a public bar for the sale of intoxicating liquor and has shown, to the satisfaction of the Court, in relation to an ordinary seven-day licence (not being a licence granted by virtue of paragraph 2 of section 2 of the Act of 1902) either—

I. that he is the holder thereof, or

II. that he has procured the consent of the holder thereof to the extinguishing of the licence if and when a licence in respect of the hotel is granted, or

(ii) has shown to the satisfaction of the Court that an order has previously been made under this section in relation to the hotel,

then, the court may by order direct that, upon the grant of the licence in respect of the hotel, the ordinary seven-day licence be extinguished.

(4) When an order under subsection (3) of this section is made, then, upon the grant of the licence in respect of the hotel—

(a) it shall be lawful, notwithstanding anything contained in the Act of 1902 to have in the hotel a public bar for the sale of intoxicating liquor,

(b) the ordinary seven-day licence shall be extinguished, and

(c) if the premises to which the ordinary seven-day licence was attached immediately before the making of the order, were premises to which paragraph 1 of section 2 of the Act of 1902 applied that paragraph shall cease to apply to them."

JURISDICTIONAL REQUIREMENTS

8–32 1. Venue

As the section 19 application is brought in conjunction with an application for a certificate entitling the applicant to receive a new hotel licence, application is made to the Circuit Court.

2. Licence

The licence tendered for extinguishment must be an existing ordinary seven-day licence, but not a hotel licence granted by virtue of section 2(2) of the 1902 Act. The applicant must show that he holds that licence or, if he is not the holder of the licence, that he has obtained the consent of the holder of the licence to its extinguishment.

3. Previous Section 19 Order

If at the time of making his application the applicant can prove to the court that a previous section 19 order has been made in respect of the premises, he is not obliged to tender a seven-day on-licence for extinguishment. Section 19(3)(b)(ii) envisages a situation where an applicant applies for a new hotel licence for a hotel which has been substantially altered by extension or even reduced in size. It then becomes necessary to apply for a new licence in respect of the new, different hotel. The applicant, however, is not required to tender another existing publican's licence for extinguishment. Section 19(3) is also invoked in a situation where a hotel licence has lapsed and the applicant is seeking a new hotel licence. The courts, in such circumstances, have been content to accept proof that a licence was previously extinguished in respect of the premises and that a previous section 19 order was made, rather than requiring the extinguishment of a further licence.[53]

8–33 4. Order of the Court

In practice, an applicant making a fresh application for a new hotel licence in conjunction with a section 19 application is not required to prove during the course of his section 19 application that the court has granted the order entitling him to receive a hotel licence. Both applications are normally taken contemporaneously and the court will grant the section 2(2) order and the section 19 order at the same time.

8–34 **Discretion of the Court** Where a section 19 application is made in conjunction with an application for a certificate leading to the grant of a new hotel licence, the objector is normally on notice of both applications as the applicant must publish the application for the hotel licence. Walsh J. has stated:

---

[53] See Intoxicating Liquor Act 1960, s.19(3), and below, para. 8–39.

> "I do not think that that confers any right upon the objector to be heard upon the question of whether or not an order should be made by the court extinguishing the seven-day licence. In my view his only right is to be heard in the application for the hotel licence under the Act of 1902."[54]

So an objector cannot object to an application under section 19(3): his objection is confined to the application in respect of the hotel licence simpliciter. However, on the basis of *Doyle v. Foley*[55] where objections pursuant to section 4 of the Licensing (Ireland) Act 1833 are made, the court, in deciding whether or not to grant the application, may assess the size of the public bar facilities on a hotel premises or a proposed hotel premises when determining their suitability. Such facilities are taken into account when considering objections to suitability.

Hotels licensed before July 4, 1960

Section 19(5) of the Intoxicating Liquor Act 1960 defines "hotel" as **8–35**

> "a house containing at least ten, or, if situate in a County Borough (which expression shall be deemed for the purposes of this section to include the Dublin Metropolitan District), 20 apartments set apart and used exclusively for the sleeping accommodation of travellers and having no public bar for the sale of intoxicating liquor".

Ten bedroomed hotels which were licensed before July 4, 1960, and which are situated in county boroughs are excluded from the benefit of section 19 because they do not come within the statutory definition.

Renewal

The "hotel licence" on the face of it, imports that the licensed house is a hotel **8–36** "which is not only *ab initio* structurally in accordance with the Act but continues to be used in accordance with it".[56] Where the 10 or 20 bedrooms cease to be used exclusively for the sleeping accommodation of travellers, or where there is a public bar in the hotel and no section 19 order has been obtained, the licence ceases to be a protection to the holder. An objection to the renewal of a hotel licence can be made where the conditions pursuant to which the licence was granted have been breached.[57]

A hotel licence cannot be renewed without the production to the Revenue Commissioners of a Bord Fáilte certificate, where the licence was granted under

[54] *Application of Thomas J. Dunne*, above, n.48, at 115 and 116.
[55] Above, n.36.
[56] *Quinn v. Bourke*, above, n.21, *per* Madden J. at 102.
[57] *State (Quirke) v. Circuit Court Judge of Tipperary*, above, n.22.

section 42(1) of the Tourist Traffic Act 1952, or section 2(2) of the 1902 Act after July 4, 1960.[58]

The 1957 Commission of Inquiry recommended that the "licensing provisions in the 1902 Act be repealed or that the provisions of the 1952 Act will apply to the grant of all new hotel licences". This recommendation resulted in the change in the definition of hotel to include the requirement that a hotel situate in a County Borough must have at least 20 bedrooms.[59]

Every hotel licensed by virtue of the Tourist Traffic Act 1952 must be registered with Bord Fáilte or its licence cannot be renewed. The licensee of a hotel which was licensed under section 2(2) of the 1902 Act prior to July 4, 1960 need not produce a Bord Fáilte certificate as a condition of renewal as the requirement relates only to premises which were licensed after that date. So, although all hotels should be registered with Bord Fáilte,[60] the unlawful description of a premises as a hotel does not disentitle the licensee to its renewal unless the hotel licence was granted after July 4, 1960.

Lapse

8–37 Where a hotel licence was granted under section 2(2) of the 1902 Act prior to the passing of the 1960 Act and has been allowed to lapse, an application must be made to the Circuit Court for a new licence. The consequences for the applicant are as follows:

1. Where the premises to which the lapsed licence attached are situate in a county borough but were licensed before the coming into force of section 21 of the Intoxicating Liquor Act 1960 (which increased the bedroom requirement in county boroughs to 20), the applicant who applies to revive his licence is not obliged to prove that he has 20 bedrooms for travellers provided he can satisfy the court that:

   (a) his premises contain more than nine and less than 20 apartments set apart and used exclusively for the sleeping accommodation of travellers;

   (b) there is no public bar on the premises;

   (c) the premises are situate in a county borough;

   (d) the former licence was granted under section 2(2) of the 1902 Act;

   (e) the licence has expired and has not since been renewed; and

   (f) the day on which the former licence expired is not more than five years before the day on which notice of the application is given to the county registrar.[61]

---

[58] Courts (No. 2) Act 1986, s.4(9).
[59] Intoxicating Liquor Act 1960, s.21.
[60] Tourist Traffic Act 1939, s.33, as amended by the Tourist Traffic Act 1983, s.3.
[61] Intoxicating Liquor Act 1960, s.21(2).

The holder of the licence attaching to such hotel is not permitted to apply for public bar facilities on its premises. A premises whose licence has been revived under section 21 does not answer the statutory definition of hotel contained in section 19 of the Intoxicating Liquor Act 1960.

2. Where a hotel licence was granted prior to the 1960 Act, but the licence has since lapsed, the applicant is obliged to apply for a certificate entitling him to receive a new hotel licence. However, this new licence will now fall within the provisions of section 4(9) of the Courts (No. 2) Act 1986. Thus, where there is a failure to prove registration with Bord Fáilte to the Revenue Commissioners at renewal stage, a new licence cannot issue. In *Re Application Declan Bannerton*,[62] the Circuit Court, on March 29, 1960, made an order entitling one Daniel Scannell to receive a hotel licence under section 2(2) of the Licensing (Ireland) Act 1902. The licence was renewed annually until September 1975, but a transfer made in that year was not confirmed nor was the licence renewed at the annual licensing sessions in September 1976. On July 28, 1978, the Circuit Court made an Order entitling one Owen Gannon to receive a hotel licence in respect of the premises. In 1982 the Garda Síochána objected to the renewal of the applicant's licence on the grounds that the premises, which had not been registered with Bord Fáilte since 1975, had ceased to be a hotel. The District Court judge stated a case to the High Court as to whether he was precluded from issuing the certificate of renewal. **8–38**

Barron J. in the High Court noted that section 20 of the 1960 Act (repealed by the Courts (No. 2) Act 1986) did not refer to premises, but to a licence: it was immaterial, therefore, that the existence of the premises preceded the passing of the 1960 Act as the licence under which the premises were now licensed was granted since the passing of that Act. He noted:

> "In the present case, the vitiating element is one which continues from year to year. The orders which were made in error and which have not been quashed on certiorari nor reversed on appeal are in effect declarations that the hotel was registered at the date of the making of each order in the register of hotels kept by Bord Fáilte Éireann."[63]

The judge was satisfied that an application for a certificate for renewal, where the licence was granted after the coming into effect of the Intoxicating Liquor Act 1960, must be accompanied by proof that the hotel is registered in the register of hotels kept by Bord Fáilte. Although the orders of renewal had not been impeached, the licensee was still required to prove registration with Bord Fáilte.

The decision was upheld by the Supreme Court. Finlay C.J. noted that proof of registration was not necessary when the premises were first licensed in

[62] [1986] I.R. 758 (Sup. Ct.).
[63] *Ibid.* at 762.

March 1960.[64] The judge stated that the scheme of the legislation was to require the Bord Fáilte certificate at renewal stage and not at the stage of the application for the certificate leading to the grant of the new licence. Referring to the judgment of Barron J. Finlay C.J. stated:

> . . . a consideration of the register of licences kept by the District Court Clerk for the area would have indicated that having been licensed for the first time in 1960, quite clearly, pursuant to subsection (2) of section 2 of the Act of 1902, that licence, for no apparent reason, had been allowed to lapse and an application for a new licence had been made in 1978. A consideration of the certificate issued in respect of that licence which should have been one of the ordinary enquires made by a purchaser of these premises intending to carry them on as a licensed hotel would have indicated at least a suspicion or presumption that in reality that licence was granted under the same sections as that granted in March of 1960. It seems to me therefore, that the applicant had good reason on proper advice to at least suspect that it would probably be necessary, if the true facts became known to the licensing sessions, for him to register this hotel pursuant to the provisions for registering hotels with Bord Fáilte, if he wished to continue renewing the licence of it. In these circumstances, and having regard to the very clear statutory provisions applicable, I am not satisfied that it would be proper or possible to exempt the applicant from the consequences of section 20."[65]

The stringent requirements introduced by the Finance Act 1992 requiring an applicant for renewal to produce a tax clearance certificate have made it difficult, if not impossible, for some hotel proprietors to renew their licences, requiring them to make applications to the Circuit Court for new certificates. So, where a hotel was licensed prior to July 4, 1960 but the licence has lapsed since that date, and a new licence has been granted, the holder is obliged before his licence can be renewed, to have his premises registered with Bord Fáilte. Some hoteliers have found this quite impossible to do: bringing a hotel premises up to Bord Fáilte standard can involve considerable expense.

8–39 3. Where a hotel licence lapses and the licensee has previously obtained a section 19 order, the question arises as to whether the effect of the section 19 order continues, although the licence has lapsed. Section 19(3)(b)(ii) applies, in the author's view, in a situation where a hotelier is applying for an order for a new hotel licence where his premises have been altered, whether by expansion or otherwise and where the hotel licence in respect of the premises remains current up until the time of the application for the certificate. It is, however, unlikely that a court would require a hotelier, whose licence has lapsed (due to financial difficulties or otherwise), to extinguish another licence in order to obtain public bar facilities on the premises, where a section 19 order was made prior to the lapse of the licence.

---

[64] *Re Application of Declan Bannerton*, above, n.62.
[65] *Ibid.* at 475.

In *Breen v. Keane*[66] Judge Sheridan noted that where a hotel licence is not renewed, the applicant applies in the ordinary way for a new hotel licence. He stated:

> "Mr Cassidy on behalf of the applicant dealt with this matter and stated that even if this be the case, it is by no means certain, in law, that the right to have a public bar in the premises would be carried over and this would result in great expense to his clients."[67]

Judge Sheridan did not address this point and there is no decided case on the matter. It is interesting to note, however, that the order of the court in a section 19(3) application, is that "upon the grant of the licence in respect of the hotel, the ordinary seven-day licence be extinguished" even where an applicant has shown to the satisfaction of the court that a section 19 order has previously been made in relation to the premises.

Expansion

Where a hotelier requires to extend the area to which the licence attaches, he applies for a new hotel licence under section 2(2) of the 1902 Act in respect of a new or different "house". Where he has already obtained a section 19 order in respect of the hotel, he must make an application under section 19(3). This is because the court when making the section 19 order, makes it in respect of a different premises: the section 19 order which existed up to the date of the Circuit Court application related to the old premises. The applicant must satisfy the court that the premises are a hotel for the purposes of section 2(2) of the Licensing (Ireland) Act 1902, as amended by section 21 of the Intoxicating Liquor Act 1960 and the premises must, therefore, *inter alia*, contain the requisite number of bedrooms. **8–40**

A difficulty arises where the holder of a hotel licence in extending his premises, applies for a new licence under section 6 of the 1902 Act, rather than section 2(2) of the 1902 Act. He may do this in an effort to escape the requirement imposed by section 4(9) of the Courts (No. 2) Act 1986 of obtaining a Bord Fáilte certificate as a condition of the renewal of this licence.

He may then advance the argument that his licence is not one granted by virtue of section 2(2) of the 1902 Act and he is not thereby caught by the requirement to produce a certificate from Bord Fáilte before he can obtain the renewal of his licence.

It is unlikely that the legislature, when introducing the concept of "hotel licence" into the licensing code, intended section 6 of the 1902 Act to apply where the hotel premises were to be expanded. The section does not however **8–41**

[66] [1981] I.L.R.M. 279 (Cir. Ct.).
[67] *Ibid.* at 281.

expressly exclude such an application. Where section 6 is invoked it is questionable whether the previous section 19 order applies in respect of the altered area.

Where a premises is first licensed by virtue of section 2(2) of the 1902 Act, and an applicant subsequently obtains a section 6 order in respect of the premises, it is arguable that he can tender this licence for extinguishment on an application for a full publican's licence, notwithstanding section 20 of the Intoxicating Liquor Act 1962, which provides:

> "(1) An application to the Circuit Court under section 4 of the Act of 1902, section 21 or 22 of the Act of 1943 or section 13, 14 or 27 of the Act of 1960 (which sections relate to the grant of new licences in certain circumstances upon the extinguishment of existing licences) shall not be allowed if the licence, or either of the licences, as the case may be, that would fall to be extinguished if the application were allowed and a licence were granted in pursuance of the section under which the application is made is a licence granted by virtue of paragraph 2 of section 2 of the Act of 1902, or under section 18 of this Act or a special restaurant licence granted by virtue of the Intoxicating Liquor Act 1988."

The grant of a licence under section 6 of the 1902 Act is not and cannot be "a licence granted by virtue of paragraph 2 of section 2 of the 1902 Act"; it would seem to make nonsense of section 20 if a hotelier whose premises were first licensed under the exception introduced by section 2(2) of the 1902 Act could ultimately tender for extinguishment this conditional licence, just because he had obtained an order pursuant to section 6 of the 1902 Act.

CHAPTER 9

RESTAURANTS

Introduction

The special restaurant licence was introduced into the licensing code by the Intoxicating Liquor Act 1988. Prior to this, the only means by which a restaurateur could serve intoxicating liquor and food on his premises was to obtain a restaurant certificate, in conjunction with either a wine retailer's on-licence or a publican's licence pursuant to section 12 of the Intoxicating Liquor Act 1927. It is not necessary for a restaurateur to apply for a licence in order to serve food on his premises: however, if he wishes to sell intoxicating liquor and food and keep his premises open after permitted hours, he must apply for a special restaurant licence or a restaurant certificate, as the case may be. **9–1**

The rights and obligations conferred upon the holder of a special restaurant licence differ from those which apply in respect of a premises to which a full restaurant certificate or a limited restaurant certificate attaches.

The special restaurant licence permits the supply of intoxicating liquor with a substantial meal during the hours set out in the legislation. It is deemed to be an on-licence.

In contrast, the restaurant certificate certifies that a premises to which an on-licence (including a wine retailer's on-licence) is attached is a restaurant for the purposes of the Intoxicating Liquor Act 1927. The holder of a special restaurant licence and the licensee of a premises to which a restaurant certificate attaches are obliged to display the licence or certificate, as the case may be, prominently on the premises to which the licence or certificate relates.[1]

1. SPECIAL RESTAURANT LICENCE

The jurisdiction providing for the grant of a special restaurant licence is
9–2 contained in Part II of the Intoxicating Liquor Act 1988.[2] Such licence is, for the purposes of the Finance (1909–10) Act 1910, a retailer's on-licence, notwithstanding the fact that it does not authorise the sale of intoxicating liquor for consumption off the premises.[3] The holder of a special restaurant licence is entitled to sell spirits, wine, sweets, beer, cider on the premises, in the quantities specified in Schedule 1 to the Finance (1909–10) Act 1910.

The special restaurant licence is granted by the Revenue Commissioners, on the production, *inter alia*, of a certificate of the Circuit Court, which is granted under section 8 of the Intoxicating Liquor Act 1988.

An applicant for the grant and renewal of a special restaurant licence must notify the fire authority. This is not required in the case of an application for a restaurant certificate.

Policy

The special restaurant licence was introduced despite the prohibition contained
9–3 in the Licensing (Ireland) Act 1902 against the grant of further licences. Its grant does not depend upon the extinguishment of one or more licences and there is no statutory limit on the number of new licences which may be granted. The grant of a special restaurant licence depends upon the production of a Bord Fáilte certificate and the payment of a specified fee to the Revenue Commissioners. The present fee payable to the Revenue Commissioners is £3,000. In his address to the Dáil at the second stage of the Intoxicating Liquor Bill 1988, the Minister for Justice stated:

> "In deciding on the amount of the fee, the Government bore in mind the

---

[1] Intoxicating Liquor Act 1988, s.17(1), and Intoxicating Liquor Act 1927, s.12(5).

[2] This came into force on July 1, 1988, by virtue of the Intoxicating Liquor Act 1988 (Commencement of Part II) (Special Restaurant Licences) Order 1988 (S.I. No. 146 of 1988).

[3] Intoxicating Liquor Act 1988, s.7(2).

> considerable commercial value of any licence which permits the sale of a full range of alcoholic drinks. It was necessary, in order to help prevent a proliferation of these licences, to settle on a figure which was more than just nominal. At the same time, it was considered that the fee should be less than what is believed to be the going rate for new pub licences obtainable from the 'in pocket' or non-trading stock of such licences."[4]

The applicant must also produce a tax clearance certificate and pay the appropriate excise duty.

Scope

The special restaurant licence authorises the following: 9–4

1. the supply of intoxicating liquor for consumption on the licensed restaurant premises; and
2. the consumption of intoxicating liquor on those premises.

Such supply and consumption may only take place where the intoxicating liquor is:

1. ordered by or on behalf of a person for whom a substantial meal has been ordered; or
2. supplied in either the waiting area or the dining area of the restaurant; or
3. consumed in the waiting area of the restaurant prior to a meal by the person for whom the meal has been ordered, or is consumed by that person in the dining area of the restaurant either during the meal or at any time not later than 30 minutes after the meal has ended; and
4. paid for at the same time as the meal is paid for.

The holder of the licence is obliged to ensure that "suitable beverages" other than intoxicating liquor (including drinking water) are also available for consumption.[5] A person who does not intend to eat a substantial meal on the premises cannot, therefore, be served with intoxicating liquor. The service of intoxicating liquor is not restricted to the dining area: a person waiting to be seated is entitled to consume intoxicating liquor before the meal. The consumption of intoxicating liquor by a person who finished a meal more than 30 minutes previously, is not permitted.

[4] Intoxicating Liquor Bill 1988, *Dáil Reports*, 2nd stage, p. 1997.
[5] Intoxicating Liquor Act 1988, s.7(1).

Prohibited Hours

9–5 The hours during which the holder of a special restaurant licence may supply intoxicating liquor are dealt with below, in chapter 22, at paragraphs 22–38 *et seq*. The sale, supply and consumption of intoxicating liquor on a premises to which a special restaurant licence attaches is not permitted during the following times:

1. on a weekday, before 12.30 p.m., and after 12.30 a.m.; and
2. on a Sunday, before 12.30 p.m., between 3 and 6 p.m., and after 11 p.m.

There are also special provisions relating to Christmas Day and Good Friday and Sundays which falls on December 23 and 24.

Mixed Trading

9–6 The proprietor of a premises to which a special restaurant licence attaches is entitled to open such premises at any time for non-licensed business.[6]

Special Exemption Order

9–7 A special exemption order entitles the holder of an on-licence, in certain circumstances, to permit persons to be on his licensed premises and consume intoxicating liquor during hours normally prohibited by the licensing code. Section 22 of the Intoxicating Liquor Act 1988 prohibits the grant of a special exemption order in respect of a premises to which a special restaurant licence attaches. There are no circumstances whereby the holder of a special restaurant licence may supply intoxicating liquor other than in accordance with the times specified in Part II of the Intoxicating Liquor Act 1988. There is no reason why the holder of a special restaurant licence cannot have functions or weddings on his premises but these must be held during permitted hours and the main purpose of the functions must be the supply of a substantial meal to the public and not, for example, dancing.

Difference between Special Restaurant Licence and Publican's Licence

9–8 Although the special restaurant licence is deemed to be a retailer's on-licence, for the purposes of the Finance (1909–10) Act 1910 there are four marked differences between it and the publican's licence.

---

[6] *Ibid.*, s.14(2).

(i) Bar

The holder of a special restaurant licence is expressly prohibited from having a bar on the premises.[7] A "bar" is 9–9

> "any open bar or any part of a licensed premises exclusively or mainly used for the sale and consumption of intoxicating liquor and shall include any counter or barrier across which drink is or can be served to the public".[8]

This statutory definition incorporates the definition of "public bar" in section 12A of the Intoxicating Liquor Act 1927 (which relates to the grant of limited restaurant certificates) and the judicial interpretation of "public bar" pronounced by Palles C.B. in *Quinn v. Bourke*[9] adopting the definition given in *Murray's Dictionary*. The intention was to give as wide a definition as possible to ensure that no area in a restaurant could be used solely for the sale of intoxicating liquor to members of the public. A contravention of this provision is an offence to which Part III of the Intoxicating Liquor Act 1927 applies and is, therefore, an endorsable offence. A District Court judge and a Circuit Court judge on appeal have no discretion: the conviction must be recorded unless it is a first conviction. A number of convictions for this offence can lead to the forfeiture of the licence.[10]

(ii) Occasional Licence

The holder of a special restaurant licence is not entitled to apply for an occasional licence: this is confined to the holder of a publican's licence.[11] 9–10

(iii) Extinguishment of Special Restaurant Licence

In an application for a publican's licence or an off-licence it is not possible to tender for extinguishment a special restaurant licence or licences for extinguishment.[12] 9–11

(iv) Declaratory Procedure

An applicant for a special restaurant licence is not entitled to apply for a declaration as to the fitness and convenience of his proposed premises for use as a restaurant.[13] It is curious that the legislature did not see fit to give the protection afforded by the declaratory procedure to a person proposing to apply 9–12

---

[7] Intoxicating Liquor Act 1988, s.16.
[8] *Ibid.*, s.2(1).
[9] [1906] 2 I.R. 94 at 97.
[10] Intoxicating Liquor Act 1927, s.28(1).
[11] Intoxicating Liquor Act 1988, s.21.
[12] Intoxicating Liquor Act 1962, s.20, as amended by Intoxicating Liquor Act 1988, s.23.
[13] Intoxicating Liquor Act 1988, s.19.

for a special restaurant licence. It may be that the view was taken that an applicant for a special restaurant licence was not at such financial risk as an applicant for a publican's licence, as an objection to the grant of the special restaurant licence cannot be made on the ground of the sufficiency of licensed premises in the neighbourhood. Nor does the applicant incur the expense of obtaining one or more licences for extinguishment. The applicant is not automatically assured of success in his court application even where he has equipped his restaurant in accordance with Bord Fáilte requirements and with the Special Restaurant Licence (Standards) Regulations of 1988.[14]

Application to Court

9–13 A person who wishes to apply for a special restaurant licence must first obtain a certificate of the Circuit Court entitling him to receive a special restaurant licence in respect of his restaurant premises on payment of £3,000

STATUTORY PROVISION

9–14 Section 8(1) of the Intoxicating Liquor Act 1988 provides:

> "Where a person (in this section referred to as the applicant) duly gives notice of his intention to apply for a special restaurant licence in respect of a restaurant of which the applicant is the owner and occupier and, at the proceedings in the Circuit Court in relation to such application, the applicant shows to the satisfaction of that Court that there is in force a Bord Fáilte Certificate in respect of the restaurant, that Court shall cause a certificate to be given to the applicant entitling him to receive, on payment to the Revenue Commissioners of the fee specified in *section 9* of this Act, a special restaurant licence in respect of the restaurant unless that Court, in consequence of an objection under section 4 of the Licensing (Ireland) Act, 1833, prohibits under that section the issue of the licence on the grounds of the character, misconduct or unfitness of the applicant or of the unfitness or inconvenience of the premises."

JURISDICTIONAL REQUIREMENTS

9–15 1. Venue

The application for the certificate is made to the Circuit Court.

2. Notice

Notice of the applicant's intention to apply for the special restaurant licence must be "duly" given, *i.e.* in accordance with the statutory requirements which apply to on-licences. Publication of the notice of application,

---

[14] S.I. No. 147 of 1988.

therefore, is required together with the service of notification of intention to apply for the licence on the appropriate statutory notice parties.

3. Bord Fáilte Certificate

Upon application by the owner and occupier of the restaurant and subject to compliance with the conditions detailed in the Special Restaurant Licence (Standards) Regulations 1988, Bord Fáilte grants a certificate signed by an officer of the Board stating that it is satisfied that the restaurant complies with the Regulations. These Regulations detail the standards for restaurants required by Bord Fáilte and, *inter alia*, provide that the overall capacity of the total dining area of the restaurant must not exceed 250 diners,[15] that meals must be ordered from and served at tables by waiting staff, that the facilities, equipment and fittings in the restaurant comply with the requirements of the Food Hygiene Regulations, that a minimum number and type of sanitary fittings is prescribed by regulation 9(4) and that the floor area of the waiting area does not exceed 20 per cent of the floor area of the dining area of the restaurant.

The Bord Fáilte certificate signed in accordance with section 8(2) of the 1988 Act is sufficient evidence, in an application to the Circuit Court for a certificate leading to the grant of a licence, of the matters contained in the certificate, until the contrary is shown.[16]

4. Owner and Occupier **9–16**

A mere franchise or permission to use the premises for restaurant purposes is not sufficient to entitle the holder of such franchise or licence to apply to the court for a special restaurant licence. This is important in considering the application of the law where a right to use part of a licensed premises as a restaurant or dance hall is granted to a restaurateur or discotheque operator. The legality of such practice may be called into question independently of any provision in the 1988 Act. Moreover, Part II of the 1988 Act establishes beyond any doubt or question that only the legal owner and occupier of the premises sought to be licensed is entitled to that licence: the "estate or interest" in the premises must be sufficient to satisfy section 6 of the 1988 Act.

5. "Restaurant"

Restaurant means any premises which are structurally adapted and used for the purpose of supplying substantial meals to the public for consumption on the premises and in which other business carried on is ancillary and subsidiary to the provision of such meals.[17] It was thought at one time that

---

[15] *Ibid.*, reg. 7(3).
[16] Intoxicating Liquor Act 1988, s.8(3).
[17] *Ibid.*, s.6.

the word "used" occurring in licensing statutes could be construed as "ready for user". The statutory expression "used" was considered in the case *R. (Sale) v. Fermanagh Justices.*[18] The court decided that the words "set apart and used" referred to "actual user" for sleeping accommodation. It held, however, that the expression could also include a situation where, at the time of the application for a licence for a hotel, the appropriate number of rooms were furnished as bedrooms, although there was no proof that they had been used as such for the accommodation of travellers. In this context, it seems clear that there must be actual use, as the definition of restaurant imports an existing user. Also, it is a condition precedent to the exercise of the jurisdiction of the court that the applicant produce a Bord Fáilte certificate certifying that the premises comply with the Special Restaurant Licence (Standards) Regulations 1988. These Regulations clearly contemplate and provide for a situation where there is an established restaurant business at the time of the application.

Court Certificate

9–17 Following compliance with statutory requirements as to notice and publication and where the applicant has shown that he is the owner and occupier of the restaurant, for which a Bord Fáilte certificate is in force, the court must grant the certificate entitling him to the special restaurant licence, unless it refuses to do so on foot of one or other of the grounds of objection specified in the statute. The court is not entitled, therefore, to inquire into whether or not Bord Fáilte should have granted its certificate, nor can it exercise any discretion on the basis of the general policy of the licensing code against the proliferation of licensed premises as to whether the certificate should issue once the necessary proofs have been adduced in evidence before the court. This can be contrasted with section 4 of the Licensing (Ireland) Act 1902, which confers upon the court a discretion to grant the application where it is "satisfied that the restrictions in this Act on the granting of licences may be relaxed".

Discretion of the Court

9–18 Once the applicant satisfies the jurisdictional proofs and where an objection has not been made or successfully maintained, the court "shall" grant the application. Two statutory grounds of objection are open to a competent objector, namely the character, misconduct or unfitness of the applicant or the unfitness or inconvenience of the premises.[19] The statutory ground of objection contained in section 4 of the 1833 Act, based on the number of licensed premises in the neighbourhood, is not available and cannot be used as a ground of objection to

[18] (1906) 40 I.L.T.R. 75.

[19] See below, chap. 21, "Objections", at paras. 21–83 *et seq.*, dealing with the legal principles applicable to competent objectors and each particular ground of objection.

the grant of a special restaurant licence. Even if Bord Fáilte is satisfied that the restaurant complies with the regulations made by the Minister for Tourism and Transport (now the Minister for Tourism and Trade), the court may still refuse the application where an objection is successful.

Grant

Section 9 of the Intoxicating Liquor Act 1988 provides for the grant of the special restaurant licence by the Revenue Commissioners following production by the owner and occupier of the restaurant of the certificate of the Circuit Court the fee of £3,000. A tax clearance certificate in accordance with section 242 of the Finance Act 1992 must also be produced. 9–19

Bord Fáilte

Where an applicant wishes to apply for a renewal of his special restaurant licence, he should apply to Bord Fáilte between May 1 and June 30 in that year for the renewal of the Bord Fáilte certificate in respect of the period commencing immediately after the expiration of the Bord Fáilte certificate then held by him.[20] 9–20

Where Bord Fáilte grants the application for the certificate, it is obliged to notify the applicant within 21 days of such decision and upon payment of the requisite fee it should issue the certificate. Where the Bord Fáilte certificate is refused, Bord Fáilte should inform the applicant by notice in writing of its refusal, and of its reasons "as soon as may be".

The Board is entitled to cancel a Bord Fáilte certificate where the restaurant no longer complies with the standards specified in the Regulations.[21] If the Board takes this view, it is obliged to notify the certificate holder and require him to take certain steps within a specified period in order to bring the restaurant into compliance with the standards required. The holder of the certificate must be informed that if the requirements in the notice are not complied with, the certificate will be cancelled. If the certificate holder does not comply with a requirement in the notice, the Board "shall" cancel the certificate. Notification of cancellation of the certificate must be given to the holder of the special restaurant licence, the District Court clerk for the District Court area in which the premises are situated, the Revenue Commissioners and the superintendent of the Garda Síochána for the Garda district within which the premises are situate.[22]

[20] Special Restaurant Licence (Standards) Regulations 1988, above, n.14, reg. 15.
[21] Intoxicating Liquor Act 1988, s.13.
[22] *Ibid.*, s.13(3).

Renewal

9–21 As in the case of other on-licences, an application for renewal of a special restaurant licence is made to the Revenue Commissioners; a District Court certificate as to the peaceable and orderly trading of the premises and as to the good character of the applicant is not required unless an objection is lodged in accordance with the Courts (No. 2) Act 1986. The applicant must, however, produce a Bord Fáilte certificate to the Revenue Commissioners, as well as his tax clearance certificate and the appropriate excise duty before a new special restaurant licence will issue in respect of the premises.[23]

Lapse

9–22 A difficulty arises where a special restaurant licence lapses, where for example, the holder is not in a position to obtain tax clearance in sufficient time to renew his special restaurant licence. If his special restaurant licence lapses, application must be made to the Circuit Court for a new special restaurant licence. The application will have to be made pursuant to the provisions of section 8 of the 1988 Act. The applicant must satisfy the court that he has obtained the Bord Fáilte certificate and that the other criteria detailed at paragraph 9–21 above have been complied with. He may have to pay a further fee of £3,000 specified in section 9(1)(b) of the 1988 Act. However, he may submit to the Revenue Commissioners that his application to the Circuit Court is merely to revive the pre-existing special restaurant licence.

The Revenue Commissioners have been known to waive the requirement for a further fee of £3,000 in circumstances where the original licence lapsed.

Alteration of Restaurant

9–23 Where the holder of an on-licence wishes to reduce or enlarge the area of his premises, application must be made to the Circuit Court for a new licence in respect of the altered area.[24]

Where the holder of a special restaurant licence wishes to expand or reduce the size of his premises he is obliged to apply for a new licence. It is again questionable as to whether the application should be brought under section 6 of the Licensing (Ireland) Act 1902 or under section 2(1) of the Act of 1902, or whether the application should be for a new special restaurant licence pursuant to section 8 of the Intoxicating Liquor Act 1988. It is unlikely that the legislature intended that an applicant should pay the fee specified in section 9 of the 1988 Act where he seeks merely to expand or reduce the area of the restaurant. The

---

[23] Courts (No. 2) Act 1986, s.4, as amended by the Intoxicating Liquor Act 1988, s.18.
[24] *Re Denis Guiney, Applicant* (1941) 75 I.L.T.R. 110.

Minister for Justice in his address to the Dáil on April 26, 1988, referred to the fee of £3,000 "for the initial grant of the special restaurant licence". In practice, the Revenue Commissioners rarely insist on the payment of a second fee: however, this lacuna in the legislation should be rectified.

2. RESTAURANT CERTIFICATE

Introduction

A restaurant certificate does not authorise or permit the sale of intoxicating liquor on the premises to which it relates – such certificate is granted in respect of a premises to which a publican's licence or a wine retailer's on-licence attaches and confers upon the licence-holder certain advantages not enjoyed by publicans whose premises are not a restaurant for the purposes of the Intoxicating Liquor Act 1927, such as the right to serve intoxicating liquor with food after normal closing times, and the right to apply for special exemption orders. A restaurant certificate which relates to the entire of such premises is generally referred to as a full restaurant certificate; a restaurant certificate which issues in respect of a portion of a premises is known as a limited restaurant certificate. 9–24

A. Full Restaurant Certificate

The restaurant certificate which is granted pursuant to section 12(1) and section 12(1A) of the Intoxicating Liquor Act 1927, is generally referred to as a "full restaurant certificate". This expression is used in contradistinction to the expression "limited restaurant certificate" introduced by section 9 of the Intoxicating Liquor Act 1960 as section 12A of the Intoxicating Liquor Act 1927. 9–25

The statutory jurisdiction contained in section 12 of the Intoxicating Liquor Act 1927 authorises the court to certify that a premises, or portion thereof, is a restaurant. Section 12(1) authorises the grant of a full restaurant certificate in respect of premises to which there is attached a publican's licence. Section 12(1A) provides for the grant of a restaurant certificate to the holder of a wine retailer's on-licence. It is important to note that the grant of a restaurant certificate to the holder of a wine retailer's on-licence does not permit the sale of any intoxicating liquors other than wine.

Exemptions

9–26 1. The holder of an on-licence in respect of premises which are a restaurant for the purposes of the Intoxicating Liquor Act 1927 is entitled to supply intoxicating liquor, in conjunction with a meal, to persons on the premises up until 12.30 a.m. on the following day. He does not commit an offence by permitting the consumption of alcohol on his premises up to an hour and a half after normal closing hours if he falls within the proviso in section 13 of the Intoxicating Liquor Act 1927.[25] On a Sunday, he can serve alcohol in conjunction with food between 2 p.m. and 3 p.m. whereupon he must close for an hour. The permitted hours applicable to a restaurant premises are dealt with in chapter 22, "Trading Hours".

2. The holder of an on-licence for a restaurant premises is entitled to apply for special exemption orders pursuant to section 5 of the Intoxicating Liquor Act 1927, as amended by section 29 of the Intoxicating Liquor Act 1988. He may seek an order exempting him from normal prohibited hours on the occasion of a special event, a private function, or on the occasion of a dance which is held in a ballroom licensed under the Public Dance Halls Act 1935.

3. A premises to which an on-licence attaches and which is a restaurant, is entitled to open and carry out non-licensed business at times during which a licensed premises must be closed.[26] However, although non-licensed business can be carried on, the sale of intoxicating liquor during unauthorised hours is not permitted. So, a pub to which a full restaurant certificate attaches can open early or late for the purposes of the restaurant business but the sale of intoxicating liquor must be confined to hours which are permitted by the law.

Revocation

9–27 An application pursuant to section 12(4) of the Intoxicating Liquor Act 1927 may be made at any time to a judge of the District Court for an order revoking a restaurant certificate by the officer in charge of the Garda Síochána for the licensing area. The court must be satisfied, on hearing the officer and the holder of the restaurant certificate, that the premises have ceased to be structurally adapted for use as a restaurant or have ceased to be bona fide or mainly used as a restaurant, before it grants an order revoking the restaurant certificate.

---

[25] As amended by the Intoxicating Liquor Act 1988, s.28 and the Intoxicating Liquor Act 1995, s.4.

[26] Intoxicating Liquor Act 1927, s.3(3).

Duration

Every restaurant certificate, unless earlier revoked, remains in force until the next annual licensing District Court for the licensing area within which the premises to which it attaches is situate.[27] 9–28

Type of premises

A full restaurant certificate attaches to a premises which has the benefit of a publican's on-licence or a wine retailer's on-licence. 9–29

A(i). Grant of Restaurant Certificate for Public House

Section 12(1) and (1B) of the Intoxicating Liquor Act 1927 provide for an application for a full restaurant certificate by the holder of a publican's licence. 9–30

STATUTORY PROVISION

> "1. Where on the occasion of any application for a certificate for a new on-licence or a certificate for the transfer or renewal of an on-licence, the applicant requests the Court to certify that the premises in respect of which the certificate is sought are a restaurant for the purposes of this Act, the Court, if satisfied after hearing the officer in charge of the Garda Síochána for the licensing area that such premises are structurally adapted for use and bona fide and mainly used as a restaurant, refreshment house or other place for supplying substantial meals to the public, shall grant to such applicant a certificate (in this section referred to as a restaurant certificate) certifying that the premises are a restaurant for the purposes of this Act."
>
> . . .
>
> "(1B) Where, following application pursuant to section 4 of the Courts (No. 2) Act, 1986, to an officer of the Revenue Commissioners for the renewal of an on-licence without the production of a certificate of the District Court, the applicant applies to the Court to certify that the premises in respect of which the renewal of the on-licence is sought are a restaurant for the purposes of this Act, the provisions of subsection (1) of this section shall apply and have effect as if that application to the Court were an application, in accordance with that subsection, for a restaurant certificate."[28]

[27] Intoxicating Liquor Act 1927, s.12(3).
[28] As inserted by the Intoxicating Liquor Act 1988, s.48.

On-Licence

9–31 There is nothing to prevent the holder of a restricted on-licence, namely a six-day licence or an early closing licence, from applying for a restaurant certificate. Indeed, the legislature contemplates that the holder of a six-day licence can hold a restaurant certificate. Section 13 of the Intoxicating Liquor Act 1927, as amended by section 28 of the Intoxicating Liquor Act 1988 and section 4 of the Intoxicating Liquor Act 1995, provides that the holder of an on-licence in respect of hotel or restaurant premises is exempted from the provisions related to prohibited hours, on any Sunday, between the hours of 2 and 3 p.m., "unless his licence is a six-day licence". There is no statutory restriction limiting the time during which the holder of an early closing licence can exercise the exemption conferred upon holders of on-licences by section 13 of the 1927 Act: in other words, the holder of an early closing licence is entitled to serve intoxicating liquor with meals within the same periods as the holder of a seven-day publican's licence.

JURISDICTIONAL REQUIREMENTS

9–32 1. Venue

Application for a full restaurant certificate must be made in conjunction with the grant, renewal or transfer of an on-licence. An application for a full restaurant certificate may only be brought in connection with one of the applications set forth at section 12(1) and (1B) of the Intoxicating Liquor Act 1927. In contrast, an application for a limited restaurant certificate can be made to the District Court at any time.

Circuit Court An application for a full restaurant certificate may be brought in conjunction with an application for a certificate leading to the grant of a new on-licence. This application is made to the Circuit Court as provided for in section 24 of the Courts (Supplemental Provisions) Act 1961.

Annual Licensing District Court An application for a certificate of transfer of an on-licence is made to the annual licensing District Court.[29] An application for a restaurant certificate in respect of premises not previously certified as a restaurant, or an application for a restaurant certificate in respect of premises which were, up to the date of the annual licensing sessions, certified as a restaurant, can be brought in conjunction with the application for the certificate of transfer.

An application for a restaurant certificate can be made "following" the making of an application for renewal to the Revenue Commissioners. The application for the restaurant certificate cannot be made in isolation but must

[29] Licensing Act (Ireland) 1874, s.12, and the District Court Rules 1948, r.100.

be made in conjunction with or as part of the chain of events in an application for renewal of a publican's licence. The application should therefore be made at the annual licensing District Court or at an adjourned sitting thereof, and not during the licensing year.

2. Premises 9–33

A restaurant means "licensed premises" certified under the Intoxicating Liquor Act 1927 to be a restaurant for the purposes of the Intoxicating Liquor Act 1927: an applicant for a certificate for a new licence does not have to prove that the premises are licensed when applying for the restaurant certificate. A restaurant certificate, however, only issues in respect of a "licensed premises".

A restaurant certificate attaches to a particular premises. If the premises change in character, *i.e.* if they are enlarged or made smaller, then where an applicant is seeking a new licence, he should also make an application for a new restaurant certificate in respect of the new area to which the licence will attach. Thus, in a section 6 application, an applicant will seek an order that the entire of the premises, including the extended area, is a restaurant for the purposes of the Intoxicating Liquor Act 1927 and the same applies in a "de-licensing" application.

3. Evidence from the Garda Síochána 9–34

Where the court is satisfied, upon hearing the officer in charge of the Garda Síochána, that the premises are a restaurant for the purposes of the Intoxicating Liquor Act 1927, it will grant the restaurant certificate. The statutory requirement to hear the officer in charge of the Garda Síochána is mandatory. In *The State (Doyle) v. Carr,*[30] Henchy J. was satisfied that rule 97 of the District Court Rules 1948 which derive from statute, was mandatory as opposed to merely directory. The *Doyle* case concerned the power of a judge of the District Court to transfer temporarily a licence and the words in question were "if he shall think proper so to do after examination on oath of the necessary parties". There was no sworn testimony by the applicant and the court had to consider the question as to whether such non-compliance with the rule invalidated the order made. Henchy J. stated:

> "But in a case such as this, where there is no public notification of the intended application, where opposition to the application could come only from the Garda Síochána, where the entitlement of the applicant to transfer may be established by second best evidence, I consider that the scope and purpose of the statutory requirement of a *viva voce* examination on oath show that it is a peremptory rather than a directory provision and that, even if it were held to be merely directory, it could not be said that a total disregard of such a direction is tantamount to a substantial compliance with it. While it is clear that the District

[30] [1970] I.R. 87.

> Justice had jurisdiction to enter on a hearing of the application, I consider that he exceeded jurisdiction when he proceeded to make the order without first hearing sworn testimony."[31]

9–35 A District Court judge is obliged to hear the officer in charge of the Garda Síochána. A statement to the court by a Garda superintendent as follows: "I am not formally objecting. I am leaving it to the Court",[32] may not be sufficient to satisfy the section. In *Application of Patrick Walsh* it was held that the mere fact that the Garda Síochána do not object to the application does not oblige a court to grant the application "with no more than the absence of objection by the officer in charge of the Garda Síochána for the licensing area".[33] Even if the superintendent objects or is not satisfied that the premises are a restaurant, it is open to the court to find that the premises are a restaurant: the court is, however, obliged to acquaint itself with the views of the Garda superintendent.

Restaurant

9–36 The premises must comply with the following requirements.

(a) That they are structurally adapted for use as a restaurant, refreshment house or other place for the supplying of substantial meals to the public

In assessing whether a premises is structurally adapted for use as a restaurant, a court will have regard to the kitchen facilities, compliance with the Food Hygiene Regulations, storage facilities for food, facilities for the staff, the facilities offered in the premises for dining, whether these are contained in a room designated "restaurant" *per se* or in other areas of the licensed premises such as the bar and lounge. McWilliam J. in *Application of Michael Glennon*,[34] noted that the premises in question contained on its ground floor a substantial counter, a small dance floor and a dining room. On the first floor, there was a room containing seven snooker tables and a bar. Although the question which the Judge considered was the effect which was to be given to the word "mainly", he referred to the structural layout of the premises and stated:

> "It must be very rare indeed for the holder of an on-licence not to have a bar on the premises and I reject the suggestion that the presence of a bar in any way restricts the right of the applicant to obtain a certificate unless the part allotted to the bar is out of all proportion to the part allotted to the restaurant, which is not the case here."[35]

---

[31] *Ibid.* at 92.
[32] *Application of Patrick Walsh*, unreported, High Court, Gannon J., November 30, 1981.
[33] *Ibid.* at p. 17.
[34] Unreported, High Court, McWilliam J., November 13, 1984.
[35] *Ibid.* at p. 4.

He noted that there was a large snooker room with another bar, but gave a "liberal interpretation" to section 12 of the 1927 Act and upheld the granting of the restaurant certificate.

(b) That they are Bona Fide Used as a Restaurant

The applicant's evidence as to his use of the premises will be assessed by the court in determining whether the premises are bona fide used as such. **9–37**

(c) That they are Mainly Used as a Restaurant

This expression refers to use of the restaurant by those persons referred to in section 13 of the Intoxicating Liquor Act 1927, who order, consume and pay for intoxicating liquor in conjunction with the consumption of a meal. In *Re John O'Connor* Judge O'Briain notes that the phrase "mainly used as a restaurant" must refer to its use by those people referred to in section 13: **9–38**

> "That is, persons who come in, order a meal and a drink in the restaurant and pay for them at the same time. This involves that the Court must exclude hotel guests and segregate them from "casuals", as normally such persons would not pay for meals at the time they are served."[36]

So, residents or guests of a guest house who do not pay for their meals as they receive them are excluded and only persons who pay for food at the same time as they receive it are taken into account by the court in determining the application.

In *Whelan v. Tobin*,[37] counsel on behalf of the superintendent successfully urged that the finding of fact by the District Court that the applicant did not carry on a restaurant business at the time of the making of his application was fatal to the success of his application. The expression "*bona fide* and mainly used as a restaurant" necessarily involves proof of an established user of the premises mainly as a restaurant at the time the application comes before the court. In that case, Finlay P. was satisfied that the only possible construction of section 12A of the 1927 Act, as amended, was that at the time of the making of the application to the District Court judge for a certificate: **9–39**

> "... it is a precondition to the exercise by him of his jurisdiction that the applicant should prove to his satisfaction that the portion of the premises in respect of which the certificate is sought was then *bona fide* and mainly used as a restaurant for supplying substantial meals to the public".[38]

---

[36] [1952] 18 Ir. Jur. Rep. 51 at 52.
[37] [1976–77] I.L.R.M. 199.
[38] *Ibid.* at 202.

Citing also the decision reached in *Re John O'Connor*[39] that an actual user at the time of the application is a necessary ingredient, Finlay P. was not satisfied that proof of an intention in the future to use a premises as a restaurant is sufficient. So, actual use of the premises mainly as a restaurant at the time the application is made, is essential. The President concluded that it would be inconsistent with the declaratory procedure applicable to restaurant certificates to hold that section 12 conferred a jurisdiction upon the District Court to grant a certificate upon "mere proof of an intention in the future to trade".[40]

In assessing whether a premises is mainly used as a restaurant, the courts tends to interpret the expression "mainly" in a liberal sense. In the *Glennon*[41] case McWilliam J. noted that a large part of the premises consisted of bars and the upper floor comprised a snooker room in which there were no restaurant facilities. He stated:

> "If I were to apply the section literally I would have to hold that the entire of the premises included in the on-licence is not mainly used as a restaurant".[42]

The judge, however, took into consideration the evidence that the snooker room was only open from 5 p.m. until closing hours and that the restaurant was open all day. He concluded:

> "Under the circumstances I think I should give a liberal interpretation to [section 12]".[43]

9–40 Over the past 10 years, publicans all over the country have expanded their business to cater for office workers requiring meals at lunch time and also late night diners. Excessive lunchtime drinking is rare, and the sales from food during the lunch time period will possibly exceed the sales from drink during the same period. However, despite their best efforts, it is unlikely that most publicans can prove that the turnover from the restaurant part of the business exceeds that of the bar and lounge. In view of the interpretation given by McWilliam J. to section 12, a requirement to prove that at least 50 per cent of the turnover from the premises comprises food and that less than 50 per cent comprises intoxicating liquor, appears unduly restrictive. As a restaurant business includes the service of beverages such as spirits, beer and wine, an applicant should be entitled to rely upon evidence of the sale of food and intoxicating liquor served in conjunction with such food in support of his contention that the premises are mainly a restaurant.

---

[39] Above, n.36.
[40] *Whelan v. Tobin*, above, n.37, at 203.
[41] Above, n.34.
[42] *Ibid.* at p. 4.
[43] *Ibid.*

To the public

Food served at private functions or in circumstances where exemption orders are granted cannot be taken into account by the court in assessing whether a premises is a restaurant for the purposes of the Intoxicating Liquor Act 1927. In *Application of Patrick Walsh*, Gannon J. stated that: 9–41

> "Upon an application for a renewal of an off-licence with a certificate under section 12 of the 1927 Act, the applicant must be able to show, if so required, that apart from lawfully exempted occasions or events he has used his premises bona fide and mainly for supplying substantial meals to the public."[44]

Gannon J. rejected the argument of counsel for the applicant that a service may be offered to the public in cases where the public at large may not be able to avail of it even if those who can and do avail of such a service are members of the public stating:

> "In my view a service is not given to the public if those permitted to avail of the service are chosen not as members of the public but as persons having some special qualification prescribed by the person giving the service. Undoubtedly a service may be a service to the public when subject to a condition which may be freely accepted or rejected by any member of the public, such as payment of an admission charge or the price for the service."[45]

This reasoning led Gannon J. to the conclusion that the supply of substantial meals at private functions could not be taken into account by the court in assessing whether or not a premises were a restaurant for the purposes of the 1927 Act. The judge also held that the supply of substantial meals in circumstances provided for by exemption orders could not be taken into account, although this includes dances which are open to the public.

An applicant must therefore prove that his premises are available to the public as a restaurant within permitted hours in order for the court to find that the premises are bona fide mainly used for the supply of substantial meals to the public. In the *Walsh* case Gannon J. stated :

> "A Court might take the view that there are special circumstances of the location and pattern of public resort thereto which might justify the licensee as a matter of prudence to not keep his premises continuously open during all permitted hours for supplying substantial meals to the public. On the other hand the court might take the view, taking all the circumstances into consideration, that members of the public resorting to the premises have insufficient opportunity to avail of the services of substantial meals and consequently the premises is not bona fide or mainly used as a restaurant."[46]

The court must therefore look at the user of the premises during the normal permitted hours.

---

[44] Above, n.32, at p. 14.
[45] *Ibid.* at p.13.
[46] *Ibid.* at p.16.

Renewal

9–42 **Annual Licensing District Court** Following an application to the Revenue Commissioners for the renewal of a publican's on-licence, the applicant should apply to the annual licensing District Court for a restaurant certificate in respect of the premises. Section 48 of the Intoxicating Liquor Act 1988, amends section 12 of the 1927 Act by the insertion of the new subsection 12(1B). It provides that following the application for renewal, the applicant then applies to the court for a restaurant certificate in respect of the premises which is entertained by the court pursuant to section 12(1) of the 1927 Act.

Declaratory Jurisdiction

9–43 In contrast to an application for a special restaurant licence, an applicant may apply for a declaratory order requesting the court to certify that premises are a restaurant for the purposes of the Intoxicating Liquor Act 1927. This is dealt with in chapter 20, "Declaratory Jurisdiction", at paragraph 20–56 *et seq.*

A(ii). Grant of Restaurant Certificate in Conjunction with Wine Retailer's On-Licence

9–44 Section 8 of the Intoxicating Liquor Act 1943 provides for the grant of a full restaurant certificate to the holder of a wine retailer's on-licence. A wine retailer's on-licence is granted by the Revenue Commissioners and does not require a certificate of the court. The provisions relating to the grant of wine retailers' on-licence are dealt with at chapter 4: once an applicant can satisfy the Revenue Commissioners that his premises are a refreshment house and that certain requirements regarding, *inter alia*, the location of his premises and its rateable valuation have been met, a wine retailer's on-licence may issue after approximately one month. Those matters which the court must take into account in assessing whether premises to which a wine retailer's on-licence attach constitute a restaurant for the purposes of the Intoxicating Liquor Act 1927 apply with equal force as if the application were for a certificate for the grant or transfer of an on-licence or an application to court following an application to the Revenue Commissioners for the renewal of an on-licence. The premises must be structurally adapted for use and be used mainly as a restaurant. The officer in charge of the Garda Síochána for the licensing area within which the premises are situate must indicate his attitude to the court in relation to such application. Once the premises is certified as a restaurant, the exemptions conferred by the licensing code on premises which have the benefit of a full restaurant certificate, apply.

STATUTORY PROVISION

Section 12(1A) of the Intoxicating Liquor Act 1927, as amended by section 8 of the Intoxicating Liquor Act 1943, provides: **9–45**

> "A person who is the holder of a wine retailer's on-licence within the meaning of the Finance (1909–10) Act, 1910, may, at any sitting of the justice of the District Court, apply to the Court to certify that the premises to which such licence is attached are a restaurant for the purposes of this Act and the Court, if satisfied after hearing the officer in charge of the Garda Síochána for the licensing area that such premises are structurally adapted for use and *bona fide* and mainly used as a restaurant, refreshment house or other place for supplying substantial meals to the public, shall grant to such a person a certificate (in this section also referred to as a restaurant certificate) certifying that such premises are a restaurant for the purposes of this Act."

JURISDICTIONAL REQUIREMENTS

1. Venue

   This application may be made at any sitting of the District Court for the licensing area within which the premises are situate. This should be contrasted with the provisions governing the grant of a restaurant certificate to a person who is applying for the grant, transfer or renewal of a publican's on-licence. **9–46**

2. Applicant

   The applicant must prove that he is the holder of an existing wine retailer's on-licence. This contrasts with the provisions relating to the application for the grant of a restaurant certificate brought in conjunction with an application for the grant or renewal of a publican's licence. In that case the applicant is not required to prove that he is the holder of an existing on-licence.

B. Limited Restaurant Certificate

Section 9 of the Intoxicating Liquor Act 1960 introduced the limited restaurant certificate. This operates to certify that a portion of a premises, specified in the application, is a restaurant but only for the purposes of permitting persons to be on or consume intoxicating liquor on that portion of the premises during hours specified under section 13 of the Intoxicating Liquor Act 1927. The portion of the premises to which a limited restaurant certificate attaches cannot contain a public bar. The holder of the certificate is obliged to display the certificate prominently in the portion of the premises to which such certificate relates. **9–47**

Exemptions

9–48 1. Where a limited restaurant certificate is in force, the holder of the licence can avail of the exemption afforded by section 13 of the Intoxicating Liquor Act 1927, as amended by section 28 of the Intoxicating Liquor Act 1988 and section 4 of the Intoxicating Liquor Act 1995 and serve intoxicating liquor in conjunction with meals during the times specified in that section.

2. No offence is committed by a person who is "found on" the portion of the premises to which the restaurant certificate attaches during that extended time: however, if such person is "found" in the public bar in the licensed premises to which the limited restaurant certificate attaches, an offence is committed.[47]

Revocation

9–49 An application can be made by the officer of the Garda Síochána for the licensing area at any time to a judge of the District Court for the revocation of a limited restaurant certificate. The court shall accede to this application after it has heard the officer and the holder of the limited restaurant certificate, but only if it is satisfied that the portion of the premises to which the certificate relates has ceased to be structurally adapted for the use as a restaurant or to be bona fide or mainly used as a restaurant, refreshment house or other place for supplying substantial meals to the public, or that it includes a public bar, or part of a room in another part of which there is a public bar, or that there is no public access to it otherwise than through a public bar.[48]

Duration

9–50 Every limited restaurant certificate remains in force until the next annual licensing District Court for the licensing area within which the premises are situate, unless sooner revoked.[49]

Grant of Limited Restaurant Certificate

STATUTORY PROVISION

9–51 Section 12A(1) of the Intoxicating Liquor Act 1927, as inserted by the Intoxicating Liquor Act 1960, section 9, provides:

---

[47] Intoxicating Liquor Act 1927, s.12A(6).
[48] *Ibid.*, s.12A(4).
[49] *Ibid.*, s.12A(3).

"Where on application to a Justice of the District Court in relation to premises to which an on-licence is attached or on the occasion of an application for a new on-licence, the applicant requests the Court to certify that any portion of the premises to which the application relates is a restaurant for the purposes of section 13 of this Act, the Court, if satisfied, in relation to that portion of the premises, after hearing the officer in charge of the Garda Síochána for the licensing area that—

(a) it is structurally adapted for use and *bona fide* and mainly used as a restaurant, refreshment house or other place for supplying substantial meals to the public, and
(b) it does not include a public bar or part of a room in another part of which there is a public bar, and
(c) there is public access to it otherwise than through a public bar,

shall grant to the applicant a certificate (in this section referred to as a limited restaurant certificate) certifying that that portion of the premises is a restaurant for the purposes of section 13 of this Act."

JURISDICTIONAL REQUIREMENTS

1. Venue **9–52**

District Court An application can be made at any time to a judge of the District Court for a limited restaurant certificate in respect of a premises to which an on-licence is attached. There is no requirement to apply at the annual licensing District Court nor does the statute specifically require that the application be brought in conjunction with the transfer or renewal of an on-licence. However, proof is required that an on-licence attaches to the premises if the application is to be made to the District Court. It is probable that the holder of a wine retailer's on-licence may apply for a limited restaurant certificate: the section is loosely drafted and it is not inconceivable that such application may be made.

Circuit Court Where an applicant seeks a new on-licence, an application for a limited restaurant certificate may be made in conjunction with this application.

2. Premises **9–53**

The court must be satisfied of the following:

(a) That a specified portion of the premises to which the application relates is structurally adapted for use and bona fide and mainly used as a restaurant, refreshment house or other place for the supply of substantial meals. As in the case of a full restaurant certificate, that particular portion the subject-matter of the application, must, at the time of the grant, be mainly so used and an intention to use same in the future is not sufficient.

(b) That the portion to which the application relates does not include a public bar, nor must it consist of part of a room in another part of which there is a public bar. Public bar is defined by section 12A(7) as including "any place exclusively or mainly used for the sale and consumption of intoxicating liquor". The intention here is that members of the public who are not dining in the restaurant or availing of the restaurant facilities should not be deemed to be exempt from the provisions relating to prohibited hours. In *Whelan v. Tobin*,[50] evidence was adduced that there existed in the portion of the premises in respect of which the certificate was sought a counter which was clearly a bar, even though there also existed a method of closing it down by shutters. Finlay P. rejected the respondent's contention that the use of shutters complied with the section. He found that section 12A dealt not with any particular user of a public bar at any particular time but with the structural layout of the premises in respect of which a limited restaurant certificate was sought. He stated:

> "It seems to me again to do violence to the plain meaning of that sub-clause to say that in a particular room or hall as arises in this case where there is a large public bar which, I must assume on the evidence found by the District Justice, to be open and operating during the permitted hours for an ordinary publican's on-licence but which again it is presumably intended to close with a shutter at the end of that time and during the extra permitted hours for a restaurant licence is a premises which does not include a public bar."[51]

(c) The applicant must prove that there is public access to the portion of the premises to which the limited restaurant certificate is sought otherwise than through a public bar. Where access to that portion of the premises, the subject matter of the application, is only through a public bar, the limited restaurant certificate cannot be granted.

---

[50] Above, n.37.
[51] *Ibid.* at 204.

Chapter 10

PUBLIC DANCING LICENCES

Introduction

Until 1935 public dancing was regulated by Part IV of the Public Health Acts Amendment Act 1890. The Public Dance Halls Act 1935[1] repealed the 1890 Act in so far as it related to public dancing, and introduced a more rigorous statutory scheme in its stead.[2] At that time, it was recognised by the legislature that: **10–1**

> "additional control and supervision of dance halls is required where public dancing is organised for profit in places which are quite unsuitable for the purpose. The object of this Bill is to provide that all halls used for public dancing shall be inspected by the Garda Síochána and licensed by the District Court".[3]

Many dance halls were considered by the authorities at the time to be so unsuitable that it was deemed necessary to legislate for their supervision by the courts and the Garda Síochána. The provisions contained in the 1935 Act apply throughout the State and not, as is the case of the provisions relating to the music and singing licence, merely to those areas where the urban authority has adopted Part IV of the Public Health Acts Amendment Act 1890.

---

[1] This Act came into force on February 19, 1935.

[2] Public Dance Halls Act 1935, s.14(1) provides:

> "Immediately upon the passing of this Act, s.51 of the Public Health Acts Amendment Act, 1890, shall cease to apply or have effect in relation to public dancing within the meaning of this Act."

[3] *Dáil Debates* 1934, Vol. XX, para. 12.5.1; see also *Seanad Debates* 1934, Cols. 791–792, addresses of the Minister for Justice, Mr Ruttledge.

STATUTORY PROVISION

10–2 Section 2(1) of the Public Dance Halls Act 1935 provides:

> "Subject to the provisions of this Act, any person may apply to the Justice of the District Court exercising jurisdiction in any licensing area for a licence (in this Act referred to as a public dancing licence) to use a particular place, whether licensed or not licensed for the sale of intoxicating liquor, situate in such licensing area for public dancing, and such Justice may, if he so thinks proper, grant such licence to such person."

Place

10–3 The word "place" is defined by section 1 of the 1935 Act to mean:

> "a building (including part of a building), yard, garden, or other enclosed place, whether roofed or not roofed, and whether the enclosure and the roofing (if any) are permanent or temporary".

This definition contemplates the grant of a public dancing licence for any outdoor area provided that it is enclosed. It does not have to be roofed, and both the enclosure and the roofing can be temporary. Thus, a licence is not required for a public dance at a crossroads.

In *Application of Joseph Chamberlain*[4] the applicant sought to licence an entire field in which a marquee was to be erected. The court accepted that the field was very securely fenced and could not be entered except at one point where there was a gate which was to be used as the entrance gate to the dances and at which the admission fee would be collected and the tickets issued. Judge Binchy stated:

> "Having regard to these conditions, I am satisfied that this field is an "enclosed place" contemplated by the Act."[5]

Since a "place" can include part of a building, it is possible to obtain a licence in respect of different areas in one building. For example, if a licensee intends to hold two or three different functions which include dancing on his premises, he may apply for a licence in respect of each area. A single public dancing licence can be obtained in respect of an entire building which contains a number of rooms used for public dancing, but each room must be clearly defined on the map before the court, and the licence must specify each room.

---

[4] [1958] 24 Ir. Jur. Rep. 39.
[5] *Ibid.* at 40.

Public Dancing

The expression "public dancing" is defined by section 1 of the Public Dance Halls Act 1935 and means: 10–4

> "dancing which is open to the public and in which persons present are entitled to participate actively."

It is instructive to look at the legislative history behind this expression as the definition is not always easy to apply. Originally, the Bill defined "public dancing" as "dancing in which members of the public actively participate". These were the terms used when the original Bill was initially passed by the Dáil. At the second stage of the Bill in the Seanad, Senator Cummins raised a point of concern with the Minister:

> "[It] would be possible to . . . exclude from the operation of the Bill private balls in private houses. Would the Minister consider if a dance held in a private house for which subscriptions were required, would come within the operation of this measure? On the other hand, does he consider a dance, for which an admission fee is charged, is a public dance within the meaning of this definition?"[6]

The Minister for Justice, Mr Ruttledge, agreed to consider an amendment to this definition and the words "which is open to the public" were added.[7]

In consequence, a private dance in a dwelling house is not subject to the provisions of the Act. Mr Ruttledge stated during the second reading of the Bill in the Seanad:

> "It is not intended to deal with the class of dances that the Senator has in mind, because it is set out in the Bill that there must actually be over the door of the dance hall a notice setting out that the place has been licensed for the purposes of public dancing. That indicated, it is not the intention to bring within the measure people who hold private dances."[8]

Special functions which are organised in hotels and conference centres, such as twenty-first birthday parties and weddings, do not easily come within the definition of "open to the public". There is little doubt, however, that members of the public participate in such activities and the spirit of the Act appears to require that places in which such events occur must be licensed under the 1935 Act. 10–5

The expression "public" was considered by Gannon J. in *Application of Patrick Walsh*.[9] In that case, John Cassidy, S.C., for the applicant, argued that a service may be provided to the public in cases where although the public at

[6] *Seanad Debates* 1934, Cols. 792–793 (Second stage).
[7] *Seanad Debates* 1934, Cols. 922–923 (Fourth and Fifth stages).
[8] *Ibid.*
[9] Unreported, High Court, Gannon J., November 30, 1981.

large may not be able to avail of the service, those who can and do are members of the public. Gannon J. said that he would accept that this was so if the choice to avail or not of the service was left to the public, but that if eligibilty of persons to do so is prescribed by the provider of the service without the statutory authority of an exemption, he would not accept that proposition. He stated:

> "I would not accept that a user of the premises confined to a section of the public such as members of a group or organisation would be a service to the public. In my view, a service is not given to the public if those permitted to avail of the service are chosen not as members of the public but as persons having some special qualification prescribed by the person giving the service. Undoubtedly a service may be a service to the public when subject to a condition which may be freely accepted or rejected by any member of the public, such as payment of an admission charge or the price for the service. But if the condition be a qualification prescribed by the person giving the service which may not be freely accepted or rejected by any or every member of the public, such as the membership of a named organisation, that service is not in my view a service to the public".[10]

In *Application of Barrett*[11] Gannon J. held that an occasional licence cannot be granted in respect of a wedding as the persons for whose benefit the licence is granted is not "the public at large".

Clubs

10–6 A difficulty can arise where a private members' club holds a dance. Can the private members be said to be members of the public for the purposes of the Public Dance Halls Act 1935? In *Re Grocers' Assistants' Association Club*,[12] it was held that a certificate of registration should not be granted in respect of a premises on which public dances were held. In view of the decision in the *Walsh*[13] case it is unlikely that dancing which takes place on the premises of a registered club can be said to be dancing "which is open to the public". Clubs are not permitted to publish any advertisment drawing attention to any function to be held on their premises.[14] Where members of the public are to participate in the event, it is the practice to apply for a public dancing licence.

Ancillary

10–7 In *Fayne v. Mason*[15] the owner of a restaurant submitted that he was not obliged to have a public dancing licence in respect of his restaurant premises, where patrons were required to order a meal before being allowed to dance. The facts

---

[10] *Ibid.* at p.13.
[11] Unreported, Gannon J., High Court, May 8, 1984.
[12] (1936) 70 I.L.T.R. 284.
[13] Above, n.9.
[14] Intoxicating Liquor Act 1988, s.45.
[15] (1959) 93 I.L.T.R. 105.

were that anyone who ordered a meal would be allowed to dance without any extra charge being made; anyone who came to the restaurant but did not order a meal would not be allowed to dance. Davitt P. held that there could be no doubt that the restaurant was a "place" within the meaning of section 1 of the 1935 Act and stated:

> "Now "public dancing" is defined as meaning "dancing which is open to the public and in which persons present are entitled to participate actively"; active participation being made essential to distinguish it from what I may call exhibition dancing. There is nothing in the Act which says that dancing which is ancillary to the service of a meal in a restaurant of which the main purpose is the service of meals and which is open to the public is not to be considered public dancing."[16]

Licence

There are two types of public dancing licence: the annual public dancing licence and the temporary public dancing licence.

1. Annual Public Dancing Licence

This licence expires at the conclusion of the annual licensing court of the following year.[17] Section 6(2) of the 1935 Act provides for the continuation in force of the licence "until the conclusion of the annual licensing District Court held in the same licensing area next after the annual licensing District Court or other sitting at which said licence was granted". The licence authorises the licensee thereunder but no other person to use the place specified in the licence for public dancing as long as the licence continues in force. There is no requirement that the premises in respect of which the application is made be licensed for the sale of intoxicating liquor.[18] The application must be made at the annual licensing District Court unless it relates to a place for which no such licence is in existence at the time of the application.[19] **10–8**

Until the coming into force of the Public Dance Halls Act 1935 confusion existed as to which court had jurisdiction to deal with applications for public dancing licences. It was held in *Re Bailey*[20] that the Circuit Court was the appropriate court. Section 2 of the Act 1935 Act resolved the matter by conferring jurisdiction upon the District Court.

It is a condition precedent to the application that notice of the applicant's

[16] *Ibid.* at 107.
[17] Public Dance Halls Act 1935, s.6.
[18] *Ibid.*, s.2(1).
[19] *Ibid.*, s.2(4).
[20] [1933] I.R. 722.

intention to apply is inserted in a newspaper circulating in the district in which the place to which the application relates is situate, at least one month before the hearing.[21] The applicant is also obliged to notify the superintendent of the Garda Síochána within whose district the place is situate, the local authority within whose functional area the place is situate and the fire authority within whose functional area the place is situate.[22]

2. Temporary Public Dancing Licence

10–9 An application for a public dancing licence for a defined period not exceeding one month can be made at any time to a judge of the District Court.[23] There is no requirement to publish this application, but 48 hours' notice of the application should be given to the superintendent of the Garda Síochána. The fire officer must also receive notice of the application.[24]

Discretion of the Court

10–10 A judge of the District Court granting a public dancing licence may insert whatever conditions and restrictions he may think proper and in particular conditions limiting the days on which and the hours during which the place may be used for public dancing. In the course of the application, the court is entitled to hear any member of the Garda Síochána and any person interested in the application for the purposes of supporting or opposing the application.

However, it is not permissible to grant what is in effect a reviewable licence by the imposition of conditions. In *Sheehan v. Reilly*[25] a public dancing licence and a music and singing licence were granted by the District Court judge but such licences were reviewable on the following terms:

> "Granted with liberty to T. Dalton, Solicitor for Objectors, to have matter re-entered in Court list on forty-eight hours' notice to the Licensee and Gardaí."

Barron J. held, in making an order of certiorari by way of judical review, that as neither order contained any condition the breach of which gave the District Court judge jurisdiction to revoke either licence, he was not entitled to revoke the licences upon the matters being re-entered and further evidence being adduced. Barron J. stated:

> "The Respondent was not entitled, in effect, to grant a reviewable licence."[26]

[21] Public Dance Halls Act 1935, s.3(1).
[22] *Ibid.*, s.3(2)(b); Fire Services Act 1981, s.24.
[23] Public Dance Halls Act 1935, s.2(4).
[24] *Ibid.*, s.3(2)(a); Fire Services Act 1981, s.24.
[25] [1992] 1 I.R. 368.
[26] *Ibid.* at 374.

In considering the application the District Court judge must take into account the matters set forth at section 2(2) of the Public Dance Halls Act 1935. It is now established practice for a District Court judge to insert a condition into the licence requiring that the holder arrange that public liability insurance of the premises be effected. In determining the application, he is not confined to considering only those matters which are listed in section 2(2) of the 1935 Act. These are as follows: 10–11

> "In considering an application under this section for a public dancing licence, a Justice of the District Court shall, in addition to any other matter which may appear to him to be relevant, have regard to the following matters, that is to say—
>
> (a) the character and the financial and other circumstances of the applicant for such licence;
> (b) the suitability of the place to which such application relates;
> (c) the facilities for public dancing existing in the neighbourhood of such place at the time of such application;
> (d) the accommodation for the parking of vehicles in the neighbourhood of such place;
> (e) the probable age of the persons who would be likely to make use of such place for public dancing;
> (f) whether the situation of such place is or is not such as to render difficult the supervision by the Garda Síochána of the management of and proceedings in such place;
> (g) the hours during which the applicant proposes that public dancing should be permitted in such place."

In *Application of Michael Quinn*,[27] the Supreme Court held that a District Court judge is obliged to have regard to "any other matter which may appear to him to be relevant", in addition to those matters set forth at section 2(2) of the 1935 Act. Henchy J. stated: 10–12

> "In the present case, not alone is the District Justice (or on appeal, the Circuit Court Judge) entitled to have regard to 'any other matter which may appear to him to be relevant' but he is bound to do so; and the generality of the expression 'any other matter which may appear to him to be relevant' is not in any way narrowed by the fact that he is required to have regard 'in addition' to the specific matters set out in paragraphs (a) to (g). So long as the discretion is exercised in good faith, the decision as to what considerations are relevant would appear to be unchallengable subject to two qualifications. First, the District Justice (or the Circuit Court Judge) may not take into consideration a matter which would put his decision *ultra vires* the Act and, secondly, he may not exercise his discretion in such a way as to infringe a constitutionally guaranteed right. The former is necessary because, wide though the legislature has framed the discretion of the court, it cannot have intended that it be exercised so as to exceed the ambit of

[27] [1974] I.R. 19.

> the Act as delineated by the long title and a reading of the Act as a whole. The latter arises because the Act, having been enacted before the coming into operation of the present Constitution, is carried over only to the extent that it is not inconsistent with the Constitution: see Article 50. Apart from those two necessary limitations, a decision to have regard to any particular matter on the ground that it is relevant, if made in good faith, cannot be challenged."[28]

Griffin J. stated:

> "In my opinion, the conduct of patrons of the dance hall going to and coming from the dance and also during the hours when the dance is being held, in a residential area . . . is a relevant matter to which the District Justice, or the Circuit Court Judge, may have regard notwithstanding the fact that such conduct is a matter over which the licensee of the dance hall has no control".[29]

An application for a public dancing licence can be refused on the grounds that the place to which the application relates is unsuitable for public dancing.[30]

Duration

10–13 Every public dancing licence granted comes into force immediately upon the grant thereof and continues in force until the conclusion of the annual licensing District Court, unless sooner revoked or surrendered.[31] Where objections are lodged, the licence continues in force until the court has adjudicated upon those objections. There is no need to apply for a temporary licence during that period.

Surrender

10–14 The licensee may at any time surrender the licence by notifying the District Court clerk.[32]

Revocation

10–15 An application by a person for a public dancing licence in respect of a premises which is already licensed can be made with the consent of the existing licensee and the grant of this licence operates as a revocation of the existing licence.[33]

---

[28] *Ibid.* at 22 and 23.
[29] *Ibid.* at 31 and 32.
[30] *Application of Harold Crean* (1945) 79 I.L.T.R. 183.
[31] Public Dance Halls Act 1935, s.6(2).
[32] *Ibid.*, s.7.
[33] *Ibid.*, s.8(2).

Transfer

A public dancing licence is not transferable from the licensee thereunder to another person.[34] The appropriate course is to make an application under section 8(2) of the 1935 Act for a new licence with the consent of the existing licensee. **10–16**

Death of Licensee

Where the licensee dies whilst the licence is in force, a personal representative is deemed for all purposes to be the licensee and has all the rights, powers and duties of the licensee in respect of the licence, until the occurrence of whichever of the following events take place first: the expiration, revocation or surrender of the licence or the expiration of three months from the death of the licensee.[35] **10–17**

Appeal

An appeal lies to the Circuit Court in the following cases: **10–18**

1. by the applicant for a public dancing licence from an order of the District Court refusing to grant the application;
2. by the applicant for a public dancing licence from so much of the District Court order granting the licence as requires an insertion in the licence of particular conditions or restrictions;
3. by a person who appeared at and was heard in opposition to an application for a public dancing licence, from an order or any particular part of an order of the District Court granting the licence.[36]

This jurisdiction is exercised by the judge of the Circuit Court having jurisdiction in the circuit where the court house in which the order appealed from was made is situate.[37] In *Murphy v. Heavey*[38] the licensee of a dancing hall who had obtained his public dancing licence at the previous annual licensing sessions, applied to the District Court for an extension of hours for dancing in respect of a particular night. This application was refused by the District Court judge. Judge Shannon in the Circuit Court affirmed the decision of the District Court and agreed with submissions made by the State Solicitor that no appeal

[34] *Ibid.*, s.8(1).
[35] *Ibid.*, s.5(2).
[36] *Ibid.*, s.9(1).
[37] *Ibid.*, s.9(2).
[38] (1936) 70 I.L.T.R. 109.

lies from a decision of the District Court refusing an extension of time. The State Solicitor pointed out that the Public Dance Halls Act 1935 contained no provision whereby the District Court judge could grant a licence for any period other than that originally granted, whilst the original licence was in existence.

Obligation of Licensee

10–19 The licensee is obliged, so long as the licence is in force, to place in a conspicuous position at or near the principal entrance to the licensed place, a notice "in easily legible letters" as follows:

> "LICENSED UNDER ACT OF THE OIREACHTAS FOR PUBLIC DANCING"[39]

This applies both to the holder of an annual public dancing licence and a temporary public dancing licence.

Incidental Music

10–20 Section 14(3) of the Public Dance Halls Act 1935 provides:

> "Where a public entertainment consists mainly of public dancing as defined by this Act, but includes, as a subsidiary or incidental part thereof, exhibition dancing by special performers, dancing competitions, vocal or instrumental music (in addition to the music provided for the said public dancing) or any other similar entertainment, such public entertainment shall be public dancing to which this Act applies and shall not be a public entertainment to which the said section 51 of the Public Health Acts Amendment Act, 1890, applies."

Thus, if the entertainment which is incidental to the public dance comprises:

1. exhibition dancing by special performers; or
2. dancing competitions; or
3. vocal or instrumental music (in addition to the music provided for the said public dancing); or
4. any similar entertainment;

this incidental entertainment does not require a separate music and singing licence under the 1890 Act. Although section 14 of the 1935 Act does not stipulate that the music which accompanies the public dancing (such as disco

---

[39] Public Dance Halls Act 1935, s.12(1).

music) is exempt, the better view is that such accompanying music is an integral part of public dancing and as such does not require the additional licence under the 1890 Act.

Exemptions

The provisions of the Public Dance Halls Act 1935 do not apply in relation to public dancing carried on in any recreation room which is managed or conducted under the authority of the Commissioner of the Garda Síochána.[40] 10–21

[40] *Ibid.*, s.15.

CHAPTER 11

LICENCES FOR SINGING, MUSIC OR OTHER PUBLIC ENTERTAINMENT OF THE LIKE KIND

Introduction

11–1 The playing of music and singing and public entertainment in places which are licensed for the sale of intoxicating liquor and places which are not so licensed, is regulated by the Public Health Acts Amendment Act 1890. This legislation ceased to have effect in relation to public dancing from February 19, 1935.[1]

Part IV of the 1890 Act applies only to places situate in a district where an urban authority has adopted the appropriate provisions. Accordingly, it is not necessary to apply for a music and singing licence in an area where the urban authority has not adopted Part IV of the Public Health Acts Amendment Act 1890. Authorities which have adopted Part IV of the Act include the County Boroughs of Dublin, Cork, Limerick, Waterford and Dun Laoghaire/Rathdown. The areas to which the Act relates are the urban areas over which the Corporations have control, the extent of which can be ascertained by a perusal of the appropriate maps in the office of the relevant authority. Section 3 of the Public Health Acts Amendment Act 1890 provides for the adoption of Part IV of that Act, which relates to music and dancing, by urban authorities. Part IV of the 1890 Act deals with the licensing of places for "public . . . music, or other public entertainment of the like kind" where Part IV has been adopted by an urban authority.

[1] Public Dance Halls Act 1935, s.14(1).

STATUTORY PROVISION

Section 51 of the Public Health Acts Amendment Act 1890 provides: **11–2**

> "For the regulation of places ordinarily used for public . . . music, or other public entertainment of the like kind, the following provisions shall have effect (namely):
>
> (1) After the expiration of six months from the adoption of this part of this Act, a house, room, garden, or other place, whether licensed or not for the sale of wine, spirits, beer, or other fermented or distilled liquors, shall not be kept or used for public...singing, music or other public entertainment of the like kind without a licence for the purpose or purposes for which the same respectively is to be used first obtained from the licensing justices of the licensing district in which the house, room, garden, or place is situate, and for the registration thereof a fee of five shillings shall be paid by the person applying therefor."

Places

It is possible to obtain a music and singing licence for a house, room, garden, or other place. If a number of rooms in a premises are used for any of the purposes mentioned in the 1890 Act, it is important to ensure that the licence refers to each room. The premises/place does not have to be licensed for the sale of intoxicating liquor. **11–3**

Ordinarily Used

The phrase is not statutorily defined. The definition of "ordinary" provided by the *Concise Oxford Dictionary* (1991 edition), is: "regular, normal, customary, usual (in the ordinary course of events)". So, it appears that occasional use of a licensed or unlicensed premises for music or singing or other public entertainment does not come within the ambit of section 51. The frequency with which the place is used for music, singing, or entertainment is obviously an important factor. Where the event is a one-off occasion, then it is unlikely that the 1890 Act is intended to apply. However, the statutory intent is that places of public entertainment be regulated. So, where there is no regular usage of the premises for this entertainment, it is possible to apply for a temporary music and singing licence for a period not exceeding 14 days. **11–4**

Public

Where the entertainment provided is open to the public, then a music and singing licence must be obtained. However, as in the case of the public dancing **11–5** licence, it is questionable whether it is necessary for a registered club providing music and singing to apply for a licence under the 1890 Act. Where members of the public participate in the entertainment then a music and singing licence is necessary. There is a strong argument to be made that a music and singing licence is not necessary where a place is a private members' club and not ordinarily used for public music or entertainment. Where members of the public attend and participate in the entertainment, a music and singing licence is generally sought.

Public Entertainment of the Like Kind

11–6 "Public entertainment of the like kind" is not defined in the 1890 Act but Geoghegan J. in *Point Exhibition Company Ltd v. The Revenue Commissioners*[2] described the Point Depot premises in Dublin as a place of public entertainment, being "a building in which there was such a variety of activities, such as pop concerts and exhibitions".[3] The definition of the expression "other public entertainment of the like kind" must be read in conjunction with the previous expression "public dancing, singing, music". While public dancing has been deleted from this section, the expression "other public entertainment of the like kind" is read in conjunction with "singing and music". The *ejusdem generis* principle applies to exclude forms of entertainment which do not fall within the category of music and literary readings, such as sketches and plays, etc.

A question which commonly arises is whether or not piped music in supermarkets, hotels or licensed premises falls within the ambit of the 1890 Act. In the author's view, piped music is not the entertainment contemplated by the 1890 Act. The intention of the statute is that the main focus of the gathering is the entertainment itself. The Public Health Acts Amendment Act 1890 provides for a situation where a number of people are gathered together and are actively, rather than passively, entertained. Piped music is passive entertainment used to create a certain ambience or background to another activity.

In *Bangor Borough Council v. Goldstein*,[4] it was held by the Court of Appeal for Northern Ireland that the use of a juke box in an amusement hall involved public music for which a licence was required under the relevant Northern Ireland provisions. In some circumstances, it is a matter of fact and degree as to whether or not a licence is required, and whether juke box music is merely background music.

---

[2] [1993] 2 I.R. 551.
[3] *Ibid.* at 557.
[4] [1958] N.I. 189.

Incidental Music

STATUTORY PROVISION

The Public Dance Halls Act 1935, section 14(1) and (3), provides: 11–7

> "(1) Immediately upon the passing of this Act, section 51 of the Public Health Acts Amendment Act, 1890, shall cease to apply or have effect in relation to public dancing within the meaning of this Act.
>
> . . . .
>
> (3) Where a public entertainment consists mainly of public dancing as defined by this Act, but includes, as a subsidiary, or incidental part thereof, exhibition dancing by special performers, dancing competitions, vocal or instrumental music (in addition to the music provided for the said public dancing), or any other similar entertainment, such public entertainment shall be public dancing to which this Act applies and shall not be a public entertainment to which the said section 51 of the Public Health Acts Amendment Act, 1890, applies."

The Public Dance Halls Act 1935 does not define the expression "public dancing" as including accompanying music. Thus, the issue as to whether disco music is entertainment which requires a music and singing licence is unclear. One view is that disco music does not come within the definition of section 14(3) of the 1935 Act and therefore a licence under the 1890 Act must be sought. This imposes two layers of regualtion on an entertainment consisting of a disco dance. It is unlikely that this was the intention of the legislature. The better view is that the music element in such entertainment is necessarily incidental to and included in the scheme of regulation laid down by the 1935 Act.

Licence

A licence for music, singing or public entertainment of the like kind may take three forms: 11–8

1. annual licence;
2. licence for less than one year;
3. licence for less than 14 days.

The annual licence is the most common form. The licence for less than a year operates to license public entertainment up to the annual licensing sessions at which stage an annual licence may be applied for. The licence for less than 14 days operates to licence a particular type of temporary public entertainment. In essence, there is one type of licence which authorises public entertainment for different periods.

An application for an annual licence and an application for a licence for less than one year must be notified to the District Court clerk and the superintendent of the Garda Síochána at least 14 days prior to the date of the hearing. The application should be made at the annual licensing sessions or at any adjournment thereof, or at any special session convened at 14 days' notice.[5] The court can grant a licence for a period not exceeding 14 days despite the fact that no notices have been given.[6]

An applicant who seeks the renewal of an existing licence which is held by him in respect of the same premises is not obliged to notify the Garda Síochána or the District Court clerk, but must notify the fire officer.[7] References to "licensing justices" contained in the 1890 Act are to be construed as references to the District Court.[8] Jurisdiction in these applications is exercised by the judge of the District Court for the time being assigned to the district where the house, room, garden, or other place in respect of which the licence is sought, is situate.

Discretion of the Court

11–9 In considering an application for a music and singing licence the District Court judge must have regard to the matters listed at section 2(2) of the Public Dance Halls Act 1935, "in addition to any other matter which may appear to him to be relevant".[9] Any member of the Garda Síochána and any interested person may appear and be heard in opposition to the application and may adduce evidence in support of such opposition.[10] The matters listed in section 2(2) of the 1935 Act are:

(a) the character and the financial and other circumstances of the applicant for such licence;

(b) the suitability of the place to which the application relates;

(c) the facilities for public music, or singing, or other public entertainment, as the case may be, existing in the neighbourhood of such place at the time of such application;

(d) the accommodation for the parking of vehicles in the neighbourhood of such place;

(e) the probable age of the persons who would be likely to make use of such place for public music, or singing, or other public entertainment of the like kind, as the case may be;

(f) whether the situation is or is not such as to render difficult the supervision by the Garda Síochána of the management of and proceedings in such place;

---

[5] Public Health Acts Amendment Act 1890, s.51(2).
[6] *Ibid.*, s.51(11).
[7] *Ibid.*, s.51(10), and the Fire Services Act 1981, s.24.
[8] Courts (Supplemental Provisions) Act 1961, s.33(2)(b).
[9] *Ibid.*, s.33(2)(b).
[10] Public Dance Halls Act 1935, s.2(3), as applied by the Courts (Supplemental Provisions) Act 1961, s.33(2)(d).

(g) the hours during which the applicant proposes that music, or singing, or public entertainment of the like kind, as the case may be, should be permitted in such place.

In *Application of Michael Quinn*,[11] the Supreme Court held that evidence of misconduct on the part of persons intending to attend public dances at a dance hall (even where they did not in fact gain admission), and on the part of persons who had attended such dances and were on their way home, could be regarded by a District Court judge or a judge on appeal as a relevant matter within the meaning of the words "other matter which may appear to him to be relevant". Henchy J. stated: **11–10**

> "In the present case, not alone is the District Justice (or on appeal, the Circuit Court Judge) entitled to have regard to "any other matter which may appear to him to be relevant" but he is bound to do so; and the generality of the expression "any other matter which may appear to him to be relevant" is not in any way narrowed by the fact that he is required to have regard "in addition" to the specific matters set out in paragraphs (a) to (g)".[12]

However, the court is not entitled to grant a reviewable licence. In *Sheehan v. Reilly*,[13] a public music and singing licence was granted subject to the following conditions, the first four of which are inserted in a public music and singing licence as a matter of course: **11–11**

> "1. The licence shall continue in force and effect until the date of the next annual licensing District Court for the said Court area unless the same shall have been previously revoked as provided by the Acts.
>
> 2. There shall be affixed and kept up in some conspicuous place on the door or entrance of the said premises an inscription in large capital letters in the words following:—
>
> LICENSED IN PURSUANCE OF AN ACT OF THE OIREACHTAS FOR PUBLIC MUSIC AND SINGING.
>
> 3. The said place shall not be open for any of the said purposes except during the following hours, and that is the hours during which the premises may lawfully be open for the sale of intoxicating liquor.
>
> 4. The grant of the licence shall be subject to compliance with the conditions of the fire officer of which a copy is attached hereto.
>
> 5. Granted with liberty to T. Dalton, Solicitor for Objectors, to have the matter re-entered in the Court list on forty-eight hours notice to the Licensee and Gardaí."

[11] [1974] I.R. 19.
[12] *Ibid.* at 22.
[13] [1992] 1 I.R. 368.

Subsequently the matter was re-entered before the District Court and an order was made by the respondent revoking the music and singing licence as and from that date. Leave to apply for an order of certiorari by way of application for an order of judical review was granted on the grounds that the respondent did not have jurisdiction to revoke the said licence, save in the circumstances expressly provided for in the Public Health Acts Amendment Act 1890, and in particular section 51 of that Act.

Section 51(9) of the 1890 Act provides that in the case of a breach or disregard of a term or condition of the licence, such licence may be revoked by the District Court. The apppellant contended that the respondent had jurisdiction to revoke the licence only for breach of a condition and that no conditions in the licence had been broken. The applicant further submitted that conditions of a licence, breach of which could lead to revocation, must be such that the licensee knows as a matter of certainty what he has to do or not to do. In the High Court, Barron J. was of the view that having granted the licence, the respondent District Court judge was *functus officio*. The matter could come before him again upon a prosecution as provided for in the Public Health Acts Amendment Act 1890, which would have given him jurisdiction, if successful, to revoke the licence. Barron J. stated:

> "Whatever might have been the intention of the respondent, neither order contains any condition the breach of which gave the respondent jurisdiction to revoke either licence. The liberty given by the orders to the solicitor for the objectors to re-enter the matter cannot be construed as a condition, the breach of which would entitle the respondent to revoke the licences which he had granted."[14]

Duration

11–12 Section 51(2) provides that "every licence shall be in force for one year, or for such shorter period as the justices on the grant of the licence shall determine, unless the same shall have been previously revoked as hereinafter provided".

The licence issued by the Dublin Metropolitan District Court has, as a condition, that the licence shall continue in force and effect until the next annual licensing District Court, unless it has been previously revoked. Thus, if the licence is granted in June, as a matter of practice, it continues in force and effect until the next annual licensing District Court.

It is not clear whether the licence continues in effect after the September annual licensing sessions if the application for renewal is not determined on the actual date when these applications are taken. It is arguable that the licence continues in force and effect until the determination of the application

[14] *Sheehan v. Reilly*, above, n.13, at 373–374.

for renewal at the adjourned sitting of the annual licensing District Court, where that court is adjourned pursuant to rule 99 of the District Court Rules 1948.[15] In contrast to section 6 of the Public Dance Halls Act 1935, however, the 1890 Act does not use the expression "the conclusion of the annual licensing District Court". Accordingly, a prudent applicant will seek a temporary music and singing licence, returnable for the actual annual licensing District Court, and ensure that such licence is in force up to and including the adjourned date.

Revocation

The District Court may revoke the licence for a breach or disregard of any of its terms or conditions.[16] **11–13**

Transfer

Unlike the public dancing licence, a licence granted under the 1890 Act can be transferred, from time to time, on 14 days' notice to the District Court clerk and the superintendent of the Garda Síochána, to such person as the court thinks fit.[17] **11–14**

Appeal

An appeal lies to the Circuit Court in the following circumstances: **11–15**

1. by the applicant for a licence under the 1890 Act from an order of the District Court refusing to grant the application;
2. by the applicant for a licence under the 1890 Act from so much of an order of the District Court granting such licence as requires an insertion in the licence of particular conditions or restrictions;
3. by a person who appeared at and was heard in opposition to an application for a licence under the 1890 Act, from an order or any particular part of an order of the District Court granting such licence.[18]

---

[15] S.I. No. 431 of 1947.
[16] Public Health Acts Amendment Act 1890, s.51(9).
[17] *Ibid.*, s.51(3).
[18] Public Dance Halls Act 1935, s.9, as applied by the Courts (Supplemental Provisions) Act 1961, s.33(2)(d).

Obligations of Licensee

11–16 The holder of a licence must put up a notice in large capital letters in a conspicuous place "LICENSED IN PURSUANCE OF AN ACT OF THE OIREACHTAS FOR PUBLIC MUSIC AND SINGING". The affixing and keeping up of such a notice is made a condition of every licence.[19]

Conclusion

11–17 The grant of a music and singing licence is confined to areas in the bailiwick of urban authorities. To ascertain whether such a licence is required, a study of the map delimiting the functional area of the appropriate authority is necessary. Accordingly, each individual proprietor should carry out a search on this map and make enquiry of his local authority. Music and singing and other forms of public entertainment of the like kind can be performed in rural areas without a licence.

[19] Public Health Acts Amendment Act 1890, s.51(6).

CHAPTER 12

THEATRE LICENCE

Under the licensing code, separate and distinct provisions govern the sale and supply of intoxicating liquor in theatres. The Intoxicating Liquor Act 1927, section 1, defines a "theatre" as: **12–1**

> "a theatre or place of public entertainment licensed for the sale of intoxicating liquor under section 7 of the Excise Act, 1835."

Theatre Licence

A theatre licence is a licence for the sale of intoxicating liquor granted under section 7 of the Excise Act 1835 in respect of a theatre.[1] It is a retailer's on-licence but the sale of intoxicating liquor for consumption off the theatre premises is not specifically authorised by statute. A theatre licence authorises the sale of intoxicating liquor, during permitted times, to theatre employees or persons who have engaged or paid for seats in the theatre for the performance taking place or which took place during the permitted time or either of the permitted times then current.[2] It is not lawful to sell or expose for sale by retail intoxicating liquor in a theatre of which any part is accessible to persons other than permitted persons.[3] The only time during which intoxicating liquor can be sold is during the period beginning half an hour before the commencement of a performance in the theatre and ending half an hour after the termination of such a performance.[4] **12–2**

The admission of persons other than those stipulated by the statute after 9.30 p.m. is unlawful.[5] Persons who can be admitted after 9.30 p.m. are employees

[1] Intoxicating Liquor Act 1927, s.1.
[2] *Ibid.*, s.21.
[3] *Ibid.*
[4] *Ibid.*
[5] *Ibid.*, s.20.

of the theatre, or persons who have business with employees, or a person who has previously engaged or paid for a seat in the theatre for the performance or entertainment then in progress or about to commence.

The provisions of the licensing code relating to prohibited hours contained in the Intoxicating Liquor Act 1927 do not apply to theatres.[6] A theatre, accordingly, is entitled to put on a show at any time of the day or night and the sale of intoxicating liquor is restricted as outlined above. Non-licensed business may take place at any time in a theatre.[7]

There is no prohibition against permitting internal communication between a theatre and any unlicensed premises used for public entertainment or resort or as a refreshment house, as section 9 of the Licensing Act 1872 does not apply to theatres.[8] Offences against public order, many of which are contained in sections 12 to 18 of the Licensing Act 1872, do not apply to a theatre.[9]

Form of Licence

12–3 The form of licence issued differs from the ordinary publican's licence. The words "or off" are deleted from the expression "retail for consumption on or off" on the front of the pre-printed licence. A note at the bottom of the document reads "see overleaf". The following is written on the back of the document:

> "This licence, issued pursuant to section 7 of the Excise Act, 1835, is granted subject to the condition in section 20 and section 21 of the Intoxicating Liquor Act, 1927, that intoxicating liquor is not sold under the licence except while the premises are open and being used, to persons *bona fide* using the premises as a theatre."

Grant of Licence

STATUTORY PROVISION

12–4 Section 7 of the Excise Act 1835 provides for the grant of a theatre licence states:

> ". . . it shall be lawful for the Commissioners and Officers of Excise, and they are hereby authorised and empowered, to grant Retail Licences to any Person to sell Beer, Spirits and Wine in any Theatre established under a Royal Patent or in any Theatre or other Place of Public Entertainment licensed by the Lord

6 *Ibid.*, s.21(1).
7 *Ibid.*, s.3(3).
8 Licensing Act 1872, s.72(4): note also that a theatre is not a licensed premises as a certificate of the court is not required for the grant of a theatre licence.
9 *Ibid.*

> Chamberlain or by Justices of the Peace, without the Production by the Person applying for such Licence or Licences of any Certificate or Authority of such person to keep a common Inn, Alehouse or Victualling House; anything in this Act or Acts to the contrary notwithstanding."

A certificate of the court entitling an applicant to receive a licence is not required. However, a premises must come within one of the categories in section 7 of the 1835 Act in order to qualify for a theatre licence.

Premises which Qualify as a Theatre

(a) Theatre established under a Royal Patent

Under an Act of the old Irish Parliament entitled "an Act for regulating the Stage in the City and County of Dublin",[10] passed in 1786 and adopted into Irish law by the Adaptation of Enactments Act 1931,[11] the operation of theatres was limited to the recipients of letters patent from the heirs and successors of the King of England. The penalty imposed for the establishment of a premises as a theatre "under any colour or pretence whatsoever, save and except such theatre as shall be so established or kept by letters patent as aforesaid", was the forfeiture of the sum of £300 for every such offence. **12–5**

STATUTORY PROVISION

Section 1 of the Act of 1786 provides:

> "Whereas the establishing [of] a well regulated theatre in the city of Dublin being the residence of the chief governor or governors of Ireland, will be productive of publick advantage, and tend to improve the morals of the people: be it therefore enacted by the King's most excellent Majesty, by and with the advice and consent of the lords spiritual and temporal, and commons in this present Parliament assembled, and by the authority of the same,
>
> That it shall and may be lawful to and for the Governor General of the Irish Free State acting on the advice of the Executive Council of the Irish Free State to grant under the great Seal of Saorstát Éireann for such term not exceeding twenty-one years, and under such restrictions, conditions, and limitations as to him shall seem meet, from time to time, and when and as often as he shall think fit, one or more letters patent, to one or more person or persons for establishing and keeping one or more well-regulated theatre or theatres, playhouse, or playhouses in the city of Dublin, and in the liberties, suburbs, and county thereof, and in the county of Dublin."

Since the Act, four theatres have been established: the Gaiety, the Abbey,

[10] 26 Geo. 3, c. 57.
[11] 26 Geo. 3, c. 57 (Irish) Adaptation Order, 1931 (S.R. & O. No. 69 of 1931).

the Olympia and the Gate. The letters patent, which are now granted by the Department of An Taoiseach, cannot exceed a term of twenty-one years.[12] The theatre must apply for a new patent prior to the expiry of this term. The most recent letters patent issued were granted to the Gate Theatre in the 1950s. Since then, no new letters patent have been granted.

12–6 In *Re Tivoli Cinema Ltd*,[13] Lynch J. considered whether the 1786 Act survived the coming into force of the Constitution. Having decided the appeal on the substantive facts and law relating to the grant of intoxicating liquor licences he stated:

> It is settled law that in the absence of exceptional circumstances a court should not pronounce on the validity of a law where the case can be decided on other grounds . . . ".[14]

In *Point Exhibition Company Ltd v. The Revenue Commissioners*,[15] Geoghegan J. was of the view that the 1786 Act was intended to apply only to theatres in the narrow sense of the word. He referred to section 2 of the 1786 Act which provided that:

> ". . . no person or persons shall, for hire, gain, or any kind of reward whatsoever or howsoever, act, represent, or perform, or cause to be acted, represented, or perfomed, any interlude, opera, tragedy, comedy, prelude, burletta, play, farce, pantomime, or any part or parts therein, on any stage, or in any theatre, house, booth, tent, or other place within the said city of Dublin, or the liberties or suburbs, or county thereof, or within the county of Dublin, under any colour or pretence whatsoever, save and except in such theatre or playhouse as shall be so established or kept by letters patent as aforesaid, under the penalty of forfeiting the sum of £300 sterling for every such offence . . . ".

He was satisfied that this Act was intended to apply to "a place where on a regular and reasonably continuous basis, plays, operas and pantomimes are performed" and that the expression "theatre" in the Excise Act 1835 had a similar connotation. Having regard to the range of diverse entertainments carried on in the Point Depot premises, he held that this premises was not a theatre within the meaning of the 1786 Act or the 1835 Act.

(b) Place of Public Entertainment licensed by Justices of the Peace

12–7 In *Point Exhibition Company Ltd v. The Revenue Commissioners*[16] Geoghegan J. held that section 7 of the Excise Act 1835 did not confer a new jurisdiction

---

[12] An Act for regulating the Stage in the City and County of Dublin 1786, Preamble and section 1, above, n.10.
[13] [1992] 1 I.R. 412.
[14] *Ibid.* at 424.
[15] [1993] 2 I.R. 551
[16] *Ibid.*

on justices of the peace to license theatres and he rejected the argument that the reference to "licensed by Justices of the Peace" in section 7 of the 1835 Act referred to a licence given under some other statutory provision already existing in 1835.

He was satisfied that music and singing licences granted in respect of places of public entertainment were licences covered by section 7 of the Excise Act 1835. He held that the Point Depot premises was a place of public entertainment, having as it did:

> "such a variety of activities, such as pop concerts and exhibitions, not even contemplated at that time . . . is more naturally and certainly in 1835 would have been more naturally, described as an 'other place of public entertainment' ".[17]

Thus, a music and singing licence granted under section 51 of the Public Health Acts (Amendment) Act 1890 by a District Court judge in respect of a place of public entertainment constitutes a licence granted by the District Court within the meaning of section 7 of the Excise Act 1835.[18]

Place of Public Entertainment

In the *Point* case, Geoghegan J. made it clear that the case turned upon the court's finding that the premises were essentially a "place of public entertainment". He declined to express an opinion as to whether a "theatre" within the meaning of section 7 of the 1835 Act which was situate in Dublin and was not established by letters patent, but which had a music and singing licence granted under section 51 of the Public Health Acts (Amendment) Act 1890, was automatically a place of public entertainment within the meaning of section 7 of the 1835 Act. Nor would he express a view as to whether a premises in respect of which a music and singing licence had been granted was automatically a place of public entertainment for the purposes of section 7. He was doubtful as to whether a premises licensed under the Public Dance Halls Act 1935 could be a place of public entertainment within the meaning of section 7 of 1835 Act. 12–8

Geoghegan J. refused to follow *Morrison v. Commissioners of Customs*[19] where the Northern Ireland High Court held in a mandamus application that justices of the peace had power to grant a theatre licence to perform plays, etc. under an implied authority contained in section 7 of the 1835 Act. He stated:

> "In my view, by the plain language of section 7 of the Act of 1835, it is not conferring a new jurisdiction on justices of the peace and this is particularly obvious from the juxtaposition of the Lord Chamberlain with Justices of the

[17] *Ibid.* at 557 and 558.
[18] *Ibid.*
[19] [1927] N.I. 115.

> Peace in the section. I suspect that the justices' licence referred to in *Morrison's* case was in reality a licence under the Public Health Acts (Amendment) Act, 1890."[20]

Since the *Point* decision, a substantial number of applications have been made to the Revenue Commissioners for a licence pursuant to section 7 of the Excise Act 1835, on the basis that the premises comes within the definition of "places of public entertainment" in that statute. As at the date of writing, the Revenue Commissioners have issued 18 licences under section 7 in the Dublin area.

National Concert Hall

12–9 An attempt was made to license the National Concert Hall pursuant to the provisions of section 7 of the Excise Act 1835 by way of application to the Circuit Court for a certificate. The initial application was successful but was appealed by the Chief State Solicitor. The Intoxicating Liquor (National Concert Hall) Act 1983 was passed to resolve the matter. The licence granted under the 1983 Act authorises the sale of intoxicating liquor at the National Concert Hall for consumption in the National Concert Hall to persons attending or taking part in the function, during the period beginning half an hour before the commencement of a function and ending one hour after its completion. It also includes people employed at the National Concert Hall. Section 1 of the 1983 Act defines "function" as being:

> "a concert or conference at the Concert Hall to which persons are admitted upon payment or by invitation and, where a function extends over more than one day, the part of the function held on any date shall be deemed, for the purposes of this Act, to be a separate function".

The provisions relating to prohibited hours contained in the licensing code do not apply to the National Concert Hall. Further, although an offence can be committed pursuant to the provisions of section 2(3) of the 1983 Act, such an offence is not endorsable and no provision has been made for forfeiture of the licence.

Conclusion

12–10 Until the successful attempt by the Point Exhibition Company for an order directing the Revenue Commissioners to issue a licence pursuant to the provisions of section 7 of the Excise Act 1835, owners of theatres which were not

---

[20] *Point Exhibition Company Ltd v. The Revenue Commissioners*, above, n.15, at 558.

patented theatres were obliged to take out wine retailers' on-licences: some even attempted to obtain publicans' licences in respect of their premises. In September 1990, Tivoli Cinema Ltd, the proprietor of the Tivoli theatre in Francis Street, Dublin applied to the Circuit Court in Dublin for a full seven-day publican's on-licence in respect of the entire of the theatre premises. The application was granted in the Circuit Court but, on appeal to the High Court, Lynch J. held that the premises were not suitable to be licensed as a public house. He stated as follows:

> "There is no contest as to the suitability of the premises for a theatre licence with the restrictions appropriate to such a licence: see sections 20 and 21 of the Intoxicating Liquor Act, 1927. What is sought by the applicant, however, is a full ordinary seven day publican's licence in lieu of such licence now extinguished in relation to No. 7 Dean Street. The bar on the mezzanine floor of the Tivoli Theatre is only 810 square feet in area and capable of accommodating no more than 170-180 people. There is approximately another 8,000 square feet excluding the stairs etc. where drink might be consumed by up to 800 people if this licence is granted and planning permission for such extended use were obtained. Mr Byrne is undoubtedly a committed theatre enthusiast and not interested in running a mere public house, but Mr Byrne may not always be the person in charge of these premises. He himself indicated a desire to use the premises during the day time for business conferences and lunches and other like functions, but even if so used, how can intoxicating liquor be consumed other than in the small bar area without contravening the planning code? A theatre licence would not allow the use of the bar at all except during theatrical performances and for half an hour before and half an hour after such performances, but the ordinary seven day publican's licence would allow the sale of drink throughout the whole of the day and during the same hours as any public house."[21]

The Revenue Commissioners will not, as a matter of course, issue a licence where a premises has a music and singing licence. The practice is that the Arts Council is consulted, the premises are inspected and if the Revenue Commissioners are satisfied that the premises is a place of public entertainment, then the licence will issue.

---

[21] *Re Tivoli Cinema Ltd*, above, n.13, at 421.

CHAPTER 13

CLUBS

Introduction

13–1 Prior to 1904, no certificate or authorisation was necessary to sell intoxicating liquor in a club. It was considered that the sale of liquor in a club was merely a manner of distributing the joint property of the members, and that no licence was therefore required. In *Graff v. Evans*,[1] the manager of a club who supplied intoxicating liquor to a member for consumption off the premises was charged with selling by retail intoxicating liquors without being duly licensed. On a case stated by the magistrate, Huddleston B. stated:

> "If the conviction was right it must follow that sales of liquor in every club are illegal without a licence. I think those who have framed the legislation … never considered or intended clubs to come within the Licensing Acts."[2]

The court held that the transaction did not constitute a sale. Field J. stated:

> "The question here is, did Graff, the manager, who supplied the liquors to Foster, effect a "sale" by retail? I think not. I think Foster was an owner of the property together with the other members of the club. Any member was entitled to obtain the goods on payment of the price. A sale involves the element of a bargain. There was no bargain here, nor any contract with Graff with respect to the goods. Foster was acting upon his rights as a member of the club, not by reason of any

---

[1] [1881–82] 8 Q.B.D. 373.
[2] *Ibid.* at 379.

new contract, but under his old contract of association by which he subscribed a sum to the funds of the club, and became entitled to have ale and whisky supplied to him as a member at a certain price."[3]

It has been held that a "club" must be a bona fide private members' club and the property in the "excisable articles" must vest in the members of the club and no other person.[4] The so-called sale of intoxicating liquor must be to a member either for consumption by himself or by a visitor, and the visitor cannot himself purchase intoxicating liquor. In *Stevens v. Wood*[5] a member, using a visitor's money, purchased two pints of ale for the visitor and his friend. The respondent member was convicted of selling intoxicating liquor to a stranger without a licence. Hawkins J. stated:

> "After all, it is quite clearly a sale of beer to Ball, and although it is quite true that the actual purchase of the beer for him was made through the mouth of another person, and the actual money that was paid by the hand of another person, nobody, honestly looking at this transaction, with a view to arrive at a conclusion as to what the real transaction was, could hesitate.
>
> Ball was introduced to the club, he was introduced to the respondent for the purpose of enabling him to buy a pint of beer, respondent helped him as far as he could by ordering the beer and taking his money. I cannot for the life of me conceive how you can say that is other than a sale."[6]

Registration of Clubs (Ireland) Act 1904

The Registration of Clubs Acts 1904 to 1995 provide for the grant and renewal of a certificate of registration for a bona fide club. The Registration of Clubs (Ireland) Act 1904 distinguishes a registered club from a licensed premises: the registration of a club under the Act "shall not constitute the club licensed premises or authorise any sale of excisable liquors therein which would otherwise be illegal".[7] Practitioners frequently refer to "club licences": there is, in fact, no such thing. A club does not receive a licence in the same way as a public house or a hotel premises, but rather a certificate of registration under the hand and signature of the registrar of clubs in the statutory form set out in Schedule 2 to the 1904 Act.[8] 13–2

[3] *Graff v. Evans*, above, n.1, at 378.
[4] *Lynam v. O'Reilly* [1898] 2 I.R. 48.
[5] (1890) 54 J.P. 742.
[6] *Ibid.* at 743.
[7] Registration of Clubs (Ireland) Act 1904, s.1(2).
[8] This is the form of certificate signed by the District Court clerk as registrar of clubs:

> "I ...., Registrar of Clubs, hereby certify that the club, of .... is registered under the Registration of Clubs (Ireland) Act 1904. This certificate remains in force until the .... day of .... 19 ......; application for its renewal must be made no later than the .... day of .... 19 ....
> Given under my hand this .... day of .... 19 "
> Registrar of Clubs

In *Butlins Mosney Holiday Camp*, Fawsitt J. stated:

> "At the outset, I would like to dispel the rather widely held impression that applications of the kind with which I am now concerned are applications for licences or for certificates for licences for the consumption of alcoholic liquors on and off club premises. These applications are not applications for licences or for certificates for licences for the sale or consumption of alcoholic liquors on or off club premises: they are applications for the registration of applicant clubs in the Register of Clubs now kept by every District Court Clerk pursuant to the provisions of the Registration of Clubs (Ireland) Act, 1904, and the relevant provisions of the Intoxicating Liquor (General) Act, 1924 … and the Intoxicating Liquor Act, 1927."[9]

Section 7 of the Registration of Clubs (Ireland) Act 1904 made it an offence to sell excisable liquors to a member or other person on the premises of an unregistered club. If a club is duly registered, the provisions of section 7 of the 1904 Act do not apply to it nor to its members or employees.

Registered Club

13–3 To be eligible for the grant of a certificate of registration, a club must be a bona fide members' club. Members of the committee, and persons employed in the club may not have any personal interest in the sale of intoxicating liquor in the club, or in the profits arising from the sale of intoxicating liquor. Furthermore, the club must not be a "proprietary" club. In *Butlins Mosney Holiday Camp*,[10] Judge Fawsitt refused to grant a certificate of registration, one of the reasons being that the club was not a bona fide members' club. "This club has, in my view, many of the characteristics of a proprietary club."[11] He found as a fact that the club was neither owner nor tenant of any premises and had a licence only to use and occupy three separate buildings which were part of the estate of a limited company; it did not have an exclusive licence to use and occupy all the buildings or any one or more of those buildings. The Judge noted that the buildings would never be assets in the hands of the trustees of the club for the benefit of its members or creditors and that the club's so-called possession of all buildings by the club was such that it could not maintain an action for trespass.

13–4 In *Baird v. Wells*,[12] Stirling J. distinguished a club "of the ordinary kind" and a proprietary club. In that case, the plaintiff claimed an injunction to restrain the defendants who were the proprietor and secretary of the committee of the Pelican Club from interfering with his use and enjoyment of the club as a

---

[9] (1948) 82 I.L.T.R. 93 at 95.
[10] *Ibid.*
[11] *Ibid.* at 99.
[12] [1890] 44 Ch. D. 661.

member thereof. The committee had previously acquitted the plaintiff on the charge of hiring "roughs" who were present at a fight in Bruges and had resolved that his language, although unbecoming to a gentleman and a member of the club, was not such which would have required his resignation or expulsion. The Marquis of Queensbury (a man not unknown for his own pugilistic demeanour) objected to this conclusion and the plaintiff was requested to resign his membership. The plaintiff's application was refused: Stirling J. referred[13] to an excerpt from Sir George Jessel's judgment in *Rigby v. Connol*:

> "... the plaintiff, if he can succeed at all, must succeed on the ground that some right of property to which he is entitled has been taken away from him. That this is the foundation of the interference of the Courts as regards clubs I think is quite clear."[14]

Stirling J. then defined the "ordinary" club:

> "In all the cases of this nature, in which up to the present time an injunction has been granted, the club has been one of the ordinary kind, i.e., it has been possessed of property (such as a freehold or a leasehold house, furniture, books, pictures and money at a bank), which was vested in trustees upon trust to permit the members for the time being to have the personal use and enjoyment of the club-house and effects in and about it. But the interest of the members is not confined to that purely personal right. The members might, if they all agreed, put an end to the club; and in that case they would be entitled, after the debts and liabilities of the club were satisfied, to have the assets divided among them."[15]

The Judge distinguished such a club from the Pelican Club against which the plaintiff was seeking an injunction and he stated as follows:

> "In the present case, the club, as such, has no property. The club-house and furniture belong to the defendant ... and by him the subscriptions are taken. He is not a trustee, but the owner, of the property. If the club were dissolved at any moment, there would be nothing whatever to divide among the members."[16]

It was held therefore, that as the plaintiff was a member of a proprietary club, he had no right of property for the protection of which the court should interfere by way of injunction.

In *National Sporting Club Ltd v. Cope* Channell J. distinguished "purely members' clubs" and "proprietary clubs". 13–5

> ". . . to take the case of what is known as a proprietary club, an individual or one or two individuals joining together (it does not matter which) in popular

[13] *Ibid.* at 667.
[14] [1880] 14 Ch. D. 482 at 487 and 488.
[15] *Baird v. Wells*, above, n.12, at 675.
[16] *Ibid.*

language "run" the club, provide everything that is provided, but only to members of the club. The proprietor does not allow everybody to come into the place, to sit in the rooms, to read the newspapers, or to have his meals, or to have his liquors as a hotel proprietor would do. … Nevertheless the proprietor manages the whole thing; the property in it is his both in law and in fact; the members have no share in that property at all."[17]

Channell J. rejected the suggestion that the sale among members in a proprietary club is a mere distribution and a mere mode of enjoying property in which they have a common interest. In his view,

> "the sale to members of intoxicating liquors in an ordinary proprietary club – that is, in a club where the proprietor gets the profits of the transaction, and is carrying on the business – is a sale by retail within the Licensing Acts."[18]

He noted that the profits in a members' club go towards the general purposes of the club and would therefore be distributed amongst the members as a mode of enjoying common property.

13–6 The leading case as to what constitutes a bona fide subscription club is *Graff v. Evans* where the manager of a "bona fide" members' club was charged with selling by retail intoxicating liquors to a member without being licensed. Field J. stated:

> "I think the true construction of the rules is that the members were the joint owners of the general property in all the goods of the club, and that the trustees were their agents with respect to the general property in the goods, although they had other agents with respect to special properties in some of the goods."[19]

As the member who was supplied with the intoxicating liquor was, together with all the other members of the club, the owner of the property, he was entitled to obtain the goods on payment of the price. Huddleston B. stated:

> "It seems to me clear that Foster [the member] had a property or at least an interest in the goods which were transferred to him. … Foster on payment got from the barman who served him the interest of the 1099 members who thereby transferred their interest to him."[20]

Sale by Club Manager of Intoxicating Liquor

13–7 A club is entitled to employ a manager but it cannot place the control of the club in the hands of the manager on the basis that he receives a profit from the sale of intoxicating liquor on the premises as remuneration for his services. In

---

[17] (1900) 82 L.T. 352 at 355.
[18] *Ibid.*
[19] Above, n.1, at 378.
[20] *Ibid.* at 379.

Lynam v. O'Reilly,[21] a club was carried on by the manager "at his own risk". Evidence was produced that the manager had complained that the club was not supporting itself, and that he had been "grumbling and growling" because it was not paying and he was asked to keep it on at his own risk. The manager received the entrance fees and subscriptions for membership, and the profits. In a case stated arising from a prosecution against him for the sale by retail of intoxicating liquor without a licence it was held that the evidence did not sustain a finding that this was a bona fide club, in which the members had any common property or interest in the excisable articles supplied to them. O'Brien L.C.J. considered whether the club was a bona fide members' club:

> "This in my opinion, depends upon the question whether the property in the excisable articles in the establishment was in the members of the so-called club or in the defendant O'Reilly. This is the test plainly adopted in the leading case of *Graff v. Evans* 8 Q.B.D. 373. ... It is in my opinion obvious, under the circumstances of the case ... and to the controlling action of the defendant O'Reilly ... that the property in the excisable articles was in O'Reilly exclusively. He therefore sold by retail excisable articles without a licence and has rendered himself liable to the penalties prescribed by law."[22]

Club as Incorporated Body

The retail sale of intoxicating liquor by a company having a separate legal entity to that of the members of the club to those club members is not a distribution of the common property of the members amongst themselves and constitutes a sale for which a licence is required. In *National Sporting Club Ltd v. Cope* Channell J. stated: 13–8

> "Now, the present case is not a case in which the members of the club have been incorporated into a simple corporation consisting solely and entirely of the members of the club. If that were the case the argument might be—as indeed it is—a strong one that it is within the principle of members' clubs".[23]

The judge noted that the shareholders in the company included persons other than club members. He continued:

> "However, there are some outside shareholders, and there being some [who] have got a legal entity (the corporation) which is not either in law or in fact identical with the members of the club. It is to this outside body that the property of the club belongs, and if the members of the club in buying any of that property, by taking a glass of whisky or whatever it is, are distributing some common property, they are distributing not their own common property but the common property of a different body—the shareholders of the company."[24]

[21] Above, n.4.
[22] *Ibid.* at 55 and 56.
[23] Above, n.17, at 355–356.
[24] *Ibid.* at 356.

The court held that the company was the proprietary body which made a profit from the club.

13–9 If the body corporate acts as agent or trustee for the members and the shareholders in the body corporate comprise club members exclusively, the supply of liquor to a member is a release of the interest of the other members in such liquor. In *Trebanog Working Men's Club and Institute Ltd v. Macdonald*, Hewart C.J. stated:

> "... it is difficult to draw any legal distinction between the various legal entities which may be entrusted with the duty of holding the property on behalf of the members, be it an individual, or a body of trustees, or a company formed for the purpose, so long as the real interest in the liquor remains, as in this case it clearly does, in the members of the club.... What is essential is that the holding of the property by the agent or trustee must be a holding for and on behalf of, and not a holding antagonistic to, the members of the club."[25]

In *Application by Parnell G.A.A. Club Ltd*,[26] an objection to the renewal of a certificate of registration was taken on the ground that the club, being a limited company, was a separate entity from the members, and therefore, the supply of excisable liquor was not under the control of the members nor of a committee appointed by the members. McWilliam J. distinguished the *National Sporting Club* case noting that in that case the company was limited by shares, not by guarantee, and its constitution was not confined to a mere incorporation of the members of the club, including as it did shareholders who were not members of the club. Referring to the excerpt from the *Trebanog* judgment quoted above, McWilliam J. considered the facts of the case and in particular noted that under the articles of association of the company (which was limited by guarantee, not shares), the members of the club and of the company were identical, "and must be so". McWilliam J. stated:

> "In the present case, unlike the National Sporting Club case, the company is limited by guarantee and not by shares so that there is no question of members of the company not being members of the club . . . it is clear that the directors of the company constitute the governing body of the club and that the members of the club and of the company are identical. It does not appear to be possible to have any member of the company who is not a member of the club. Accordingly, I am of opinion that this ground of objection is not one upon which the club must be refused a renewal of its certificate of registration."[27]

13–10 A third party, whether it be an individual or a company, cannot manage or control a club in a "manner antagonistic" to the interests of the members of the club. An individual or a company can act as trustee or agent for a club once the

---

[25] [1940] 1 All E.R. 454 at 457.
[26] [1984] I.L.R.M. 246.
[27] *Ibid.* at 248.

property of the club is held for and on behalf of the members of the club. A certificate of registration can be granted to a club which is a limited company, but to support the contention that it constitutes a bona fide club, the company should be limited by guarantee and not by shares. All its shareholders must be members of the club and it must not be possible for non-members to become shareholders.

Rules of Club

A club is not eligible for the grant or renewal of a certificate of registration unless its rules comply with the Registration of Clubs Acts 1904 to 1995. The requirement that the constitution of a club must contain certain provisions is a statutory requirement and where the constitution is not in accordance with the statutory provisions, such failure may result in the refusal to grant or renew the certificate of registration. **13–11**

The provisions contained in the Registration of Clubs Acts 1904 to 1995 are imperative. However, where an application is made for the grant or renewal of a certificate of registration and the rules of the club are not in conformity with the registration of clubs code, the court is entitled to adjourn the application in order to permit the applicant to mend its hand. In *Re Rossmore Golf Club* Davitt J. stated:

> "It is true that the Act makes no provision for any adjournment of the hearing of the application save for the purpose of inquiry. I can hardly think, however, that the legislature ever intended that the hearing could not be adjourned for any other reason, such for instance as to permit or secure the attendance of an essential witness, or for the convenience of the parties or the Court. ... In my opinion, the learned Circuit Judge was quite entitled in the exercise of his discretion to adjourn the hearing of this application to enable the club to comply with the requirements of the relevant statutes. In exercising its discretion to grant any such adjournment, or allow any such amendment, it is always possible for a Court to do so upon terms, and to have due regard to the position of any objector who, but for such amendment or adjournment, would have been in a position to succeed."[28]

Section 4 of the Registration of Clubs (Ireland) Act 1904 provides that in order for any club to be eligible for registration, its constitution must contain the rules enumerated in the section. **13–12**

The rules of the club must contain the following provisions:

1. Committee

   The business and affairs of the club shall be under the management of a committee or governing body elected for not less than a year by the general body of members, and subject in whole or in a specified proportion to annual

[28] [1950] 16 Ir. Jur. Rep. 52 at 56 and 57.

re-election. The constitution of the committee should be specified in the rules. The entire of the committee, or a specified proportion thereof, should be subject to annual re-election in accordance with the rules.[29] A person can remain on the committee for more than a year if he is an officer who is not subject to annual re-election as provided for in the rules.

2. Interest in the Sale of Liquor

No member of the committee or governing body, and no manager or servant employed in the club may have any personal interest in the sale of excisable liquor therein or in the profits arising from such sale.[30]

Section 4 specifically prohibits any member of the committee and any employee of the club from having either an interest in the sale of intoxicating liquor or an interest in the profits arising from the sale. This would appear to preclude the employment of a publican, or an employee of a brewery company on condition that intoxicating liquor is to be supplied exclusively by either the publican or the brewery company to the club. In *Lynam v. O'Reilly*[31] the manager of the Phoenix Club became "practically supreme". He received the profits from membership fees, bar, billiards and card rooms in lieu of his services. O'Brien L.C.J. was satisfied that the property in the intoxicating liquor resided in the manager and that as he sold it without a licence, he rendered himself "liable to the penalties prescribed by law".[32]

13–13 3. Periodical Meetings

The committee or governing body must hold periodical meetings.[33] As a certificate of registration continues in force for one year, it is not sufficient if only one meeting a year is held. The statutory provision contemplates that the rules specify that the committee should meet at stated periods, such as monthly or quarterly.

4. Notice of Proposed Members

The names and addresses of persons proposed as ordinary members of the club must be displayed on a conspicuous place (*i.e.* the club notice board) in the club premises for at least a week before their election, and an interval of not less than two weeks is to elapse between nomination and election of ordinary members.[34] The time limits referred to in section 4 should be complied with.

---

[29] Registration of Clubs (Ireland) Act 1904, s.4.
[30] *Ibid.*
[31] Above, n.4.
[32] *Ibid.* at 56.
[33] Registration of Clubs (Ireland) Act 1904, s.4.
[34] *Ibid.*

5. Members: Election

All members should be elected by the whole body of members or by the committee or governing body, with or without specially added members.[35] This provision appears to suggest that a quorum of members is not sufficient. The rules should not contain this provision word for word with all the alternatives open but should specify whether the members are to be elected either by the whole body of members or by the committee. The customary provision is that new members will be elected by the commitee. In some cases, the committee will add a number of members to their number for this purpose.

6. Defined Subscription 13–14

There should be a defined subscription payable by members in advance.[36] In *Re Dublin Postal Services Cricket Club*[37] it was held that the annual subscription cannot be a nominal one: Judge Shannon granted the certificate of registration, subject to compliance with a condition that the annual subscription be raised to the sum of 15 shillings and that the rule in question be altered accordingly. He stated in the course of his judgment:

> "... while respectable members of the humbler classes were equally entitled to have clubs as any other class in the community ... a yearly subscription of five shillings approached too closely to being a merely nominal one ...".[38]

Not only must the subscription be more than nominal: it must be defined in the rules. The rules must specifically provide for a certain subscription or provide the means whereby the level of the annual subscription is to be set. The rule must also specify that the subscription is to be paid in advance. Thus, on an application for the grant of a certificate of registration, the secretary should be in a position to state that all persons who have become members of the club have already paid their defined subscription.[39] The amount of the subscription can, of course, be varied from time to time but it must be payable in advance, usually at the commencement of each financial year operated by the club.

7. Accounts

Correct accounts and books must be kept, showing the financial affairs and receipts and disbursements of the club.[40] Clubs usually retain an accountant to keep the club accounts.

---

[35] Registration of Clubs (Ireland) Act 1904, s.4.
[36] *Ibid.*
[37] (1936) 70 I.L.T.R. 226.
[38] *Ibid.* at 227.
[39] Registration of Clubs (Ireland) Act 1904, s.4.
[40] *Ibid.*

8. Visitors

A visitor must not be supplied with excisable liquor on the club premises unless on the invitation and in the company of a member. That member must, upon the admission of such visitor to the club premises, or immediately upon his being supplied with such liquor, enter his own name and the name and address of the visitor in a book which shall be kept for the purpose, and which shall show the date of each visit.[41] A registered club must keep a visitors' book and comply strictly with this requirement.

13–15 9. Liquor Outside Club Premises

No excisable liquors may be sold or supplied for consumption outside the premises of the club, except to members of the club between the hours of 8 a.m. and 10 p.m.[42] Thus, visitors cannot be supplied with excisable liquor outside the premises and service to members outside is confined to the above times.

10. Honorary or Temporary Members

No persons may become honorary or temporary members of the club, or be relieved of the payment of the regular entrance fee or subscription, except those possessing certain qualifications defined in the rules, and subject to the conditions and regulations prescribed therein.[43] The registration of clubs code provides for the admission of persons as honorary or temporary members: but these persons must possess special qualifications, the purpose of such provisions being to prohibit persons becoming temporary members solely for the purposes of consuming intoxicating liquor. For example, temporary members should be members of an associate club or a club which is involved in a similar activity to the applicant club. The 1904 Act envisages the service of intoxicating liquor to persons who are playing a friendly match with the applicant club. Members of another club can become temporary members for the purposes of being admitted onto the club premises and being served with intoxicating liquor. The special qualifications referred to must be defined in the rules. There will be different qualifications regarding temporary members and honorary members.

11. Liquor to Young Persons

No excisable liquors may be sold or supplied on the club premises to any person under the age of 18 years.[44]

---

[41] Registration of Clubs (Ireland) Act 1904, s.4.
[42] *Ibid.*
[43] *Ibid.*
[44] *Ibid.*, as substituted by the Intoxicating Liquor Act 1988, s.42(1).

12. Membership of Young Persons 13–16

No person under the age of 18 years shall be admitted as a member of the club unless the club is one primarily devoted to some athletic purpose.[45] The insertion of this rule could appear inappropriate in the rules of a club which is not primarily devoted to some athletic purpose. Having regard, however, to the present tendency of clubs to expand their activities, it is recommended that this paragraph be included.

13. No excisable liquor may be supplied or consumed on club premises by any person (other than a member of the club lodging in the club premises) during the prohibited hours which apply in respect of registered clubs.[46] The entire text of section 56 of the Intoxicating Liquor Act 1927, as amended by section 26 of the Intoxicating Liquor Act 1988 and section 5 of the Intoxicating Liquor Act 1995, should be inserted into the rules.

Duration of Certificate of Registration

A certificate of registration remains in force until the annual licensing District Court held next after the grant of such certificate, and shall then expire.[47] This, however, is subject to the power of a court to cancel a certificate of registration pursuant to section 9 of the Registration of Clubs (Ireland) Act 1904. A certificate of registration can continue in force and effect for up to six months after its expiry: section 3(5) of the 1904 Act provides that where an application for renewal of a certificate of registration has been applied for, the current certificate remains in force pending the final decision of the court "but not exceeding three months". The court has a discretion to extend such time to a further period not exceeding three months. An application to extend the duration of the certificate of registration for the first three month period and the second three month period should be made to the court in order to empower it to exercise its discretion, otherwise the certificate of registration will lapse. 13–17

Registrar of Clubs

The Registrar of Clubs is the District Court clerk of the court area in which the club premises are situated.[48] The District Court clerk is obliged to keep a register 13–18

---

[45] Registration of Clubs (Ireland) Act 1904, s.4.

[46] Intoxicating Liquor Act 1927, s.56, as amended by the Intoxicating Liquor Act 1988, s.26, and by the Intoxicating Liquor Act 1995, s.5.

[47] Registration of Clubs (Ireland) Act 1904, s.3(3), as amended by the Courts (No. 2) Act 1986, s.9.

[48] District Court Rules 1948, r. 109, provides: "The Registrar of Clubs for the purposes of the Registration of Clubs (Ireland) Act 1904, shall be the Clerk of the Court area in which the club premises are situate" (S.I. No. 431 of 1947).

of clubs in which he enters the name of each registered club situate within his district. The register should show the date of such certificate, whether it is granted for the first time or on renewal, the address of the premises to which the certificate applies, and the names and addresses of the officials and the committee of management or governing body of the club.[49]

The register should also contain details as to whether the club is tenant or proprietor and occupier of the premises. The register and a copy of the rules lodged with the registrar should be open to inspection by the Garda Síochána, the Revenue Commissioners and any member of the public. Notice of application for the grant or renewal of the certificate of registration is made to the District Court clerk who is obliged on receiving notice of the application "forthwith" to give notice of the application to the Superintendent of the Garda Síochána for the Garda district in which the club premises is situate. As the Circuit Court is the court of first instance in an application for the grant of an original certificate of registration, the registrar forwards the appropriate statutory documentation already lodged with him by the secretary of the club, to the appropriate county registrar.

The Registrar of Clubs is also obliged to make an entry in the register of a conviction under section 8 of the 1904 Act or of an order made pursuant to section 9 of the 1904 Act.

Application for Grant or Renewal of Certificate of Registration

13–19 The court is obliged as soon as may be to hear an application for the grant or renewal of a certificate of registration and having first heard the applicant, if there are objectors, to hear the objectors to the application. The court is entitled to "order such inquiry as it thinks fit and thereafter shall grant or refuse the application".[50] In either application, the court may order costs and expenses to be paid by the "unsuccessful party".[51]

The word "court", for the purposes of an application for the grant of an original certificate of registration of a club, means the Circuit Court.[52] Applications for the grant of an original certificate of registration are made to the registrar in accordance with the 1904 Act, but "shall be heard and determined by the Circuit Court in lieu of the court prescribed by the said Act".[53] Although an application for the renewal of a certificate of registration continues to be made to the registrar of clubs, it is determined by the annual licensing District Court which can be adjourned for a period of up to six months.

---

[49] Registration of Clubs (Ireland) Act 1904, s.1(1).
[50] *Ibid.*, s.3(3).
[51] *Ibid.*, s.3(4)
[52] Intoxicating Liquor (General) Act 1924, s.19.
[53] *Ibid.*, s.23(1).

Grant

In determining an application for the grant of a certificate of registration, a court should have regard to the general object of the Registration of Clubs Acts 1904 to 1995. In *Re Rossmore Golf Club* Judge Davitt stated: 13–20

> "What is the general object to be secured by the Clubs Act of 1904? It seems to me that it was to prevent the mischief of the existence of establishments which, though in reality mere unlicensed drinking houses, by masquerading as clubs were enabled to evade the control of the licensing laws. It was to ensure that only genuine reputable clubs should by registration acquire the right to supply liquor to their members subject to the restrictions contained in the Act; and that the police should, by means of information contained in the register and the club rules lodged with the registrar, be facilitated in their control of such establishments, the prevention, detection and punishment of abuses, and the enforcement generally of the law."[54]

The court granted an adjournment of that application to permit the applicant to amend the rules so that they would conform with the requirements of the Registration of Clubs (Ireland) Act 1904. Judge Davitt noted that rules of court dealing with applications for the grant and renewal of certificates of registration were to be made under section 23(2) of the Intoxicating Liquor Act 1924 and he pointed out that such rules of court had not been made at that time.

At the date of writing, no rules of court have been made setting forth the procedure for the making of an application for the grant of a certificate of registration. Rule 83 of the proposed District Court Rules provides for rules governing the registration of clubs and the granting of club authorisations.

Where the rules of an applicant club are not in conformity with the provisions of the Registration of Clubs Acts 1904 to 1995, the court is entitled to direct the deletion of the repugnant part of these rules.[55]

Discretion of Court

The court is obliged, once it has heard the application and objections, to grant or refuse the application.[56] Where the secretary of the club making application for the certificate of registration has satisfied the jurisdictional requirements laid down in sections 2, 3 and 4 of the 1904 Act, and where the rules are in compliance with the Act, the court must direct the issue of the certificate of registration. 13–21

Section 3(1) of the Registration of Clubs (Ireland) Act 1904, as amended by section 44 of the Intoxicating Liquor Act 1988, provides that where no objections are taken to the grant or renewal of the certificate of registration, "the

---

[54] Above, n.28, at 56.

[55] *Re The Grocers' Assistants' Association Club* (1936) 70 I.L.T.R. 234

[56] Registration of Clubs (Ireland) Act 1904, s.3(3).

Court shall, if satisfied that the application has been duly made as aforesaid and that the rules of the club are in conformity with the provisions of this Act, grant the application". So, the court has no discretion, and once the application has been made in accordance with the Registration of Clubs Acts 1904 to 1995 and where the rules are in conformity with the statute as amended, it must grant the application. Discretion only comes into play when objections to the grant or renewal have been made.

Where there are objections, however, the court is only entitled to take into account those grounds of objection provided for in section 5 of the 1904 Act as amended. Finlay P. considered the interpretation of section 5 of the 1904 Act in *Comhaltas Ceoltoirí Éireann*. He referred to section 5 and stated that:

> "This provision I am satisfied prevents the court on an application for the grant or renewal of a certificate from exercising any general discretion and confines it to considering objections coming within the enumerated categories."[57]

The grounds of objection to the grant and renewal of a certificate of registration are dealt with below in chapter 21, "Objections", at paragraphs 21–67 to 21–73. The category of objectors to the grant of a certificate of registration and its renewal differ. The grounds of objection which can be relied upon by an objector on the grant and renewal of a certificate of registration are the same.

Renewal

13–22 An application to renew a certificate of registration is made at the annual licensing sessions. Where a club neglects to make application for renewal of its certificate of registration at the annual licensing sessions in accordance with the requirements of the Registration of Clubs Acts 1904 to 1995, the court will not grant a renewal of its certificate of registration thereafter, unless it is satisfied "that such failure was due to inadvertance".[58] Thus, the applicant must prove that the failure to renew was unintentional.

Appeal

13–23 Section 11(1) of the Registration of Clubs (Ireland) Act 1904 provides that the decision of the court in dealing with an application for an original certificate or for the renewal of a certificate, or in cancelling a certificate, shall be subject to appeal.

---

[57] Unreported, High Court, Finlay P., December 14, 1977, at p. 1.
[58] Registration of Clubs (Ireland) Act 1904, s.3(6).

Cancellation

A court may cancel the certificate of registration on application by a competent objector in either of two specified circumstances, namely, where a conviction under section 8 of the 1904 Act has been obtained or where the court makes an order pursuant to the provisions of section 9(1) of the 1904 Act. 13–24

The application to cancel the certificate is made to the District Court by a competent objector as the Circuit Court has jurisdiction only to deal with the grant of an original certificate of registration.

Section 9(1) of the 1904 Act provides that on summary complaint by a competent objector to the grant or renewal of a certificate of registration, the court may make an order that on certain grounds, to be specified in the order, a registered club is being so managed or carried on as to constitute a ground of objection to its renewal.[59] Where this order is made, the court may "after such further inquiry as it may think necessary" cancel the certificate of the club for the period for which it still has to run.[60]

The court will have regard to the grounds specified in the order which must indicate that the club has been managed in such a manner as to constitute a ground of objection to the renewal of the certificate. It may cancel the certificate of registration where a conviction has taken place but it will take into account the magnitude of the offence.

Where the certificate of registration is cancelled pursuant to section 9(2) of the 1904 Act, the club can apply to be re-registered. In *Lees v. Lovie*[61] it was held that where a certificate of registration was cancelled, the club could never be registered again under the Act.

However, the equivalent English legislation did not make provision for the subsequent re-registration of the club. Section 9(2) of the 1904 Act provides, *inter alia*, "for the renewal of the certificate at the date to which it would have been competent to do so had the certificate not been cancelled".

Club Premises

Where a court has cancelled the certificate of a club pursuant to the provisions of section 9 of the 1904 Act, it is entitled to order that the premises occupied by the club shall not be used for the purposes of any club which requires registration under the Act for a specified period. This specified period can 13–25

---

[59] It should be noted that where a court makes an order pursuant to the provisions of s. 9(1) of the 1904 Act, the appropriate course is that the District Court judge issues a summons pursuant to the provisions of s. 11(3) of the 1904 Act which provides:

> "If on a summary complaint being made in respect of a club the court grants a summons, the summons shall be served on the secretary and on such other person, if any, as the court may direct."

[60] Registration of Clubs (Ireland) Act 1904, s.9(2).

[61] [1912] 2 K.B. 425 at 428.

extend to 12 months, in the case of a first order, or in the case of a second or subsequent order, up to five years. The court, however, may "for good cause shown" cancel or vary such order.[62]

Sale of Intoxicating Liquor

13–26 The registration of clubs code permits the sale of intoxicating liquor to members of the club and also to members of the public in certain defined circumstances. In order that a club may be eligible to be registered under the Registration of Clubs Acts 1904 to 1995, the rules of the club must provide for the times during which intoxicating liquor may be supplied to persons.[63] Members of the club lodging in the club premises are entitled to be served with intoxicating liquor outside permitted hours. Members of the club and their visitors can be served with intoxicating liquor during permitted hours. Persons who are not members of the club cannot be served with intoxicating liquor outside the premises of the club although members may be served outside the premises between 8 a.m. to 10 p.m. Section 27 of the Intoxicating Liquor Act 1988 amends section 7 of the Intoxcating Liquor Act 1962 by extending the drinking-up time in a club from 10 minutes to 30 minutes. The hours during which a club may sell intoxicating liquor are dealt with in chapter 22, "Trading Hours", at paragraphs 22–23 *et seq.*

Club Authorisation: Club Members

13–27 The supply of excisable liquors outside permitted hours is allowed where a "club authorisation" is granted by the District Court. However a club authorisation is confined "to members of the club", and does not permit the supply of excisable liquors to a visitor or non-member even upon the invitation or in the company of a member. Section 21 of the Intoxicating Liquor (General) Act 1924 as amended by section 8 of the Intoxicating Liquor Act 1962 provides for the grant of what is commonly referred to as a "club extension".

STATUTORY PROVISION

13–28 Section 21 of the Intoxicating Liquor (General) Act 1924, as amended by section 8 of the Intoxicating Liquor Act 1962, provides:

> "(1) A Justice of the District Court may on the application of the secretary of a registered club authorise such club, notwithstanding the provisions contained in its rules pursuant to this Part of this Act, to supply excisable liquors to

[62] Registration of Clubs (Ireland) Act 1904, s.9(3).
[63] Intoxicating Liquor Act 1927, s.56.

members of the club during any one period, specified in the authorisation and not exceeding six hours in duration, during which such supply of excisable liquor would be prohibited by the rules of the club.

(2) The supply of excisable liquors in a registered club to members of the club during any period covered by an authorisation under this section shall be lawful and shall not be deemed to be a breach of the rules of the club.

(3) Not more than fifteen authorisations shall be granted under this section to any one club in any year."

The supply of intoxicating liquor to persons other than members during the period covered by the authorisation is not expressly permitted, despite the provisions contained in the Act of 1904 providing for the supply of intoxicating liquor to a visitor in the company of a member where he has been introduced onto the premises in accordance with the club rules. It could be argued that the intention of the legislature was to allow the supply of liquor, where an authorisation is obtained after permitted hours, to members and visitors who are introduced to the premises in accordance with the Registration of Clubs Acts 1904 to 1995.

There is no statutory prohibition on the grant of a club authorisation on a Sunday, or Christmas Day, Good Friday or St Patrick's Day. The District Court has no jurisdiction to grant a club authorisation for a period exceeding six hours. **13–29**

It is unclear as to whether the "year" referred to in section 21(3) of the 1924 Act refers to a calendar or a licensing year. The Interpretation Act 1937 refers to year as "calendar year" but the likely intention of the legislature was that "year" would be construed in accordance with the duration of the certificate of registration, *i.e.* from one annual licensing session to the next annual licensing session. **13–30**

There is no requirement to notify the Garda Síochána or any other person of this application nor is provision made for objection. The discretion of the District Court in dealing with this application has never been judicially considered. However, in *The State (Hennessy) and Chariot Inns Ltd v. Commons* Finlay P. stated: **13–31**

> "A consideration of the entire code of licensing laws seems to suggest that, where they intended that there should be specific grounds upon which a District Justice should exercise his discretion to grant or refuse any form of licence, the legislature (present and past) have set out those grounds most clearly and, in most cases, have required that an order of the Court should specifically state the grounds for refusal in the event of a refusal of an application."[64]

[64] [1976] I.R. 238 at 245.

The registration of clubs code should be distinguished from the licensing code in that the grant of a certificate of registration does not constitute the grant of a licence. As can be seen from the Registration of Clubs (Ireland) Act 1904, however, the category of objectors entitled to object to the grant and to the renewal of a certificate of registration is clearly set forth, as are the grounds of objection. So, following Finlay P.'s reasoning in the *Hennessy* case the discretion of the District Court judge is confined to inquiring whether the club has satisfied the requirements stipulated in section 21 of the 1924 Act.

Club Authorisation: Members of the Public

13–32 The terms of this jurisdiction (see above, paragraph 13–27) may be constrasted with that conferred upon the court by section 14 of the Intoxicating Liquor Act 1962 which authorises the sale and supply of intoxicating liquors to members of the public, on the occasion of a special event.

STATUTORY PROVISION

13–33 Section 14 of the Intoxicating Liquor Act 1962 provides:

> "(1) A Justice of the District Court may, on the application of the secretary of a registered club (within the meaning of the Registration of Clubs Acts) the main object of which is the promotion of any outdoor pastime, sport, game or recreation among its members, authorise, notwithstanding the provisions contained in the rules of the club pursuant to those Acts, the sale or supply by or with the consent of the club to any person for consumption in the buildings or grounds of the club and the consumption in the buildings or ground of the club by any person, of excisable liquor at such times as may be specified in the authorisation on the occasion of a special event in the club and that, in the opinion of the Court, is likely to attract a considerable number of people to the club.
>
> (2) An authorisation shall not be granted under this section in respect of a club in relation to more than one event in a year and the period of the authorisation shall not exceed five consecutive days, but it shall not authorise the supply or consumption of excisable liquor on any day during that period on which the event to which it relates is not taking place.
>
> (3) The sale, supply and consumption of excisable liquors in the buildings or grounds of a club pursuant to an authorisation under this section shall be lawful and shall be deemed not to be a breach of the rules of this club."

As in the previous case there is no provision for notification of any party nor does the section provide for objection to the application. So, the court is confined to considering the objects of the club and whether the event is a special event which is likely to attract a considerable number of people to the club.

This provision can be contrasted with the ordinary club authorisation as the grant of this authorisation permits the supply of intoxicating liquor to any member of the public.

Special Event

The expression "special event" in the context of its application to an occasional licence was considered in *Rahill and Goode v. Brady* in the High Court where Butler J. stated: **13–34**

> "However, giving the words of the [section] their ordinary and natural meaning, as I must in the absence of definition, I am satisfied that an event must be special either intrinsically because of its own character or from the nature of the place where it is held. In the latter case it must be different from the ordinary use of the premises although it may be intrinsically commonplace."[65]

The Supreme Court affirmed the decision of Butler J., Ó Dálaigh C.J. stating that a special event is one which is not usual or common but which is "singular".

The expression, where it is used in the context of an application to supply intoxicating liquors to members of the public by the secretary of a registered club, is not defined by section 14 of the 1962 Act. The question arises as to whether the special event must be a special sporting event, being an event in accordance with the objects of the club, or whether it must be special in the sense of being different from the ordinary use of the club and its grounds. This has not been decided by the Superior Courts. Judge Smith, on appeal from the District Court, granted an authorisation to the secretaries of three sporting clubs, where the special event was the Athy Agricultural Show.[66]

The authorisation provides for the sale or supply of excisable liquors to all members of the public, whether in the club buildings, or in its grounds.

The sale or supply of intoxicating liquor is not confined to the club itself and the club may consent to the sale of intoxicating liquor by another person.

Only one application per year will be granted: the event can take place over a period of five consecutive days, but if the event to which the authorisation relates does not occur on one or more days during that period, the sale of intoxicating liquor during that time is not lawful.

Declaratory Procedure

An application can be made for an order declaring a proposed club premises to be fit and convenient for the purposes of an application for a certificate of registration. Sections 15 and 17 of the Intoxicating Liquor Act 1960 apply in **13–35**

[65] [1971] I.R. 69 at 73.
[66] *Ex tempore* judgment delivered in Trim Circuit Court, May 26, 1995.

respect of the acquisition, construction and alteration of proposed club premises and is dealt with in chapter 20, "Declaratory Jurisdiction", at paragraphs 20–42 *et seq.*

Club: Offences

13–36 The Registration of Clubs Acts 1904 to 1995 deal with offences and penalties applicable to a registered and an unregistered club. These offences are listed in Appendix C2 below.

Power of Search by Garda Síochána

13–37 A member of the Garda Síochána may enter onto a club premises, search the premises and take names and addresses of persons found therein, if he is of the opinion that there are reasonable grounds for supposing that the club is being managed so as to constitute a ground of objection to the renewal of the certificate of registration or that an offence is being committed.

Section 43(1) of the Intoxicating Liquor Act 1988 provides:

> "If any member of the Garda Síochána is of opinion that there are reasonable grounds for supposing that any club registered under the Registration of Clubs (Ireland) Act, 1904 is so managed or carried on as to constitute a ground of objection to the renewal of its certificate under that Act, or that an offence under that Act has been or is being committed in any such club, or that any excisable liquor is sold or supplied, or kept for sale or supply, on the premises of a club which is not registered under that Act, he may enter and search the premises of such club and take the names and addresses of any persons found therein."

This brings registered clubs into line with the provisions relating to on-licensed and off-licensed premises permitting the Garda Síochána a right of entry onto such premises for the purposes of detecting offences.

CHAPTER 14

NIGHTCLUBS

Introduction

Nightclubs are a relatively recent trend in Ireland, replacing the very popular but "dry" ballrooms of the 1950s. The licensing code does not specifically deal with this phenomenon: there is no such thing as a nightclub licence. **14–1**

Nightclubs by their nature operate from the late evening to the early hours of the following morning, attracting the majority of their customers after usual permitted licensing hours. Accordingly, an applicant night club owner must, in addition to holding an intoxicating liquor licence, apply to the court for a special exemption order excepting him from the statutory provisions prohibiting the service of intoxicating liquor after hours. A special exemption order can only be granted in respect of a premises which is a hotel or a restaurant for the purposes of the Intoxicating Liquor Act 1927.[1] Practitioners should note that the holder of a special restaurant licence is not entitled to apply for a special exemption order.[2]

In addition to this, a person who wishes to operate his premises as a nightclub is obliged to apply for a public dancing licence under the Public Dance Halls Act 1935.

It is possible for various types of establishment to operate nightclubs on their premises. The operation of a nightclub is contingent upon obtaining and renewing various different licences, certificates and special exemption orders. This chapter deals with those requirements which the proprietors of such premises must satisfy prior to the lawful operation of a nightclub thereon. **14–2**

---

[1] Intoxicating Liquor Act 1927, s.5, as amended. See below, chap. 22, "Trading Hours", for other premises which qualify.
[2] Intoxicating Liquor Act 1988, s.22.

1. Hotels

14–3 The holder of an on-licence for a premises which is a hotel for the purposes of the Intoxicating Liquor Act 1927 is entitled to apply for a special exemption order, exempting him from the statutory provisions relating to prohibited hours.[3] The criteria set out below must be satisfied before a hotelier can operate a nightclub.

(a) Licence

14–4 The hotelier must hold an on-licence. Whether the licence is an unrestricted publican's licence or the conditional licence issued pursuant to section 2(2) of the Licensing (Ireland) Act 1902, which is commonly referred to as a hotel licence, does not matter. Section 5 of the Intoxicating Liquor Act 1927 stipulates, *inter alia*, that the licence must be an on-licence for premises "which are an hotel". The expression "hotel" is defined by section 1 of the Intoxicating Liquor Act 1927 as "licensed premises structurally adapted for use and bona fide used as a hotel or a hotel and restaurant and having not less than ten apartments set apart and exclusively used for the sleeping accommodation of travellers".

Accordingly, the licensee of premises to which an ordinary publican's licence attaches and which comes within this statutory definition is entitled to apply for special exemption orders without the necessity of operating a restaurant.

(b) Special Exemption Order

14–5 The holder of an on-licence is confined to carrying on business in his premises within the hours permitted by the Intoxicating Liquor Act 1927, as amended, but he may operate outside such hours by permission of the court. He applies to the District Court for a special exemption order "exempting him on any special occasion from the provisions of this Act relating to prohibited hours in respect of the said premises".[4] A hotelier, provided that his premises is a hotel for the purposes of the Intoxicating Liquor Act 1927, is entitled to serve intoxicating liquor up until half an hour past midnight, in conjunction with a meal, in the portion of the premises usually set apart for the service of meals.[5] He must apply for a special exemption order if he wishes to serve intoxicating liquor, with a meal, beyond 12.30 a.m. The District Court in practice grants a special exemption order up to 1.30 a.m. and this has been extended to 2 a.m. in some parts of Dublin.

---

[3] See above, chap. 8, "Hotels".
[4] Intoxicating Liquor Act 1927, s.5(1), as amended by the Intoxicating Liquor Act 1943, s.6.
[5] Intoxicating Liquor Act 1927, s.13.

A special exemption order will be granted in respect of a special occasion as defined by section 5(5) of the Intoxicating Liquor Act 1927: such special occasion includes the occasion of a dance held in a "ballroom" licensed under the Public Dance Halls Act 1935. A special exemption order must be sought in respect of each and every separate special occasion to be held on the premises. If a number of different functions are being held in the premises, a special exemption order must be sought in respect of each particular function. A special exemption order will not be granted in respect of any function proposed to be held on a Sunday.[6]

(c) Public Dancing Licence

As a special exemption order is only granted for a special occasion, the applicant must prove that the occasion is "special" or he must apply for a public dancing licence.[7] **14–6**

On an application for a public dancing licence, the area or areas which will be used for public dancing must be specified on the plans produced in court.

2. Public House with Full Restaurant Certificate

The holder of a publican's licence can apply to exempt himself from prohibited hours if the premises are a restaurant for the purposes of the Intoxicating Liquor Act 1927. **14–7**

(a) Licence

The licence must be an on-licence, but there is nothing in the licensing code preventing the holder of a restricted licence, namely a six-day licence or an early closing licence, from holding a restaurant certificate or applying for special exemption orders, with the exception that the holder of a six-day licence is not entitled to serve intoxicating liquor on any Sunday.[8] **14–8**

(b) Restaurant Certificate

To be in a position to apply for special exemption orders, the publican will have to prove that the premises are a restaurant for the purposes of the Intoxicating Liquor Act 1927. The word "restaurant", as defined by section 1 of the Intoxicating Liquor Act 1927, means "licensed premises certified under this **14–9**

---

[6] Intoxicating Liquor Act 1927, s.5(3).

[7] For a definition of "special occasion", see below, chap. 23, "Exemption Orders and Occasional Licences", at paras. 23–30 to 23–32.

[8] Intoxicating Liquor Act 1927, s.13, as inserted by s.5 of the 1960 Act and amended by s.4 of the 1962 Act, s.28 of the Intoxicating Liquor Act 1988 and s.4 of the Intoxicating Liquor Act 1995.

Act to be a restaurant for the purposes of this Act". A restaurant certificate issues in respect of a premises which the court certifies has been "structurally adapted for use and bona fide and mainly used as a restaurant, refreshment house, or other place for supplying substantial meals to the public".[9]

In *Application of Patrick Walsh*[10] Gannon J. referred to special exemption orders as "a permitted departure from the statutory requirements which qualify him to have his licence and his certificate in the case of a restaurant".[11] He held that the supply of meals at private dinners, public dances or discos could not be taken into account in deciding whether a restaurant business was carried on for the purpose of section 12 of the 1927 Act.

A publican cannot therefore rely upon his nightclub trade where he seeks to satisfy the court that his premises are a restaurant for the purposes of the 1927 Act.

14–10 **Limited Restaurant Certificate** Where a premises is certified to be a restaurant for the purposes of section 13 of the Intoxicating Liquor Act 1927, the licensee is entitled to supply intoxicating liquor with meals during hours otherwise prohibited in the restaurant portion of his premises.[12] The certificate is commonly known as the limited restaurant certificate. Such a premises is not a restaurant as defined by section 1 of the Intoxicating Liquor Act 1927, and the licensee is therefore not entitled to apply for special exemption orders under section 5 of the Intoxicating Liquor Act 1927, as amended.

(c) Special Exemption Order

14–11 Armed with his on-licence, restaurant certificate and public dancing licence, the publican may apply to the court for a special exemption order which will allow him to supply intoxicating liquor to the public during otherwise prohibited hours.

(d) Public Dancing Licence

14–12 Once the premises are certified as a restaurant, it becomes necessary to apply for a public dancing licence so that the licensee can rely on the meaning of "special occasion" under section 5 of the Intoxicating Liquor Act 1927, as amended. A substantial meal must be served at the dance, the price of which must be included in the price of admission to the dance.

---

[9] Intoxicating Liquor Act 1927, s.12.
[10] Unreported, High Court, Gannon J., November 30, 1981.
[11] *Ibid.* at p. 14.
[12] See above, n.8.

3. Special Restaurant Licence

The holder of a special restaurant licence is expressly prohibited from applying for a special exemption order.[13] He must therefore confine himself to the permitted hours provided for in section 14 of the Intoxicating Liquor Act 1988. There is nothing to prevent him from applying for a public dancing licence, however, but the time during which such dancing must take place cannot be extended by order of the court pursuant to a special exemption order. **14–13**

4. Wine Retailer's On-Licence

When the restaurant certificate jurisdiction was introduced in 1927,[14] it was restricted to applicants for certificates of the court leading respectively to the grant of a new on-licence or the transfer or renewal thereof.[15] As a wine retailer's on-licence does not require the production of a certificate of the court for its grant or renewal, section 8 of the Intoxicating Liquor Act 1943 introduced an amendment to section 12 of the Intoxicating Liquor Act 1927 to provide for the grant of a restaurant certificate in respect of a premises to which a wine retailer's on-licence attached. Most nightclubs in Ireland operate with wine retailers' on-licences, restaurant certificates and public dancing licences. **14–14**

(a) Licence

The application for the wine retailer's on-licence is made to the Revenue Commissioners on proof of a minimum valuation of the premises, which depends upon the population of the place within which the premises is situate; and proof that the premises is a refreshment house.[16] **14–15**

(b) Restaurant Certificate

The holder of a wine retailer's on-licence is entitled, by virtue of section 12(1A) of the Intoxicating Liquor Act 1927, to apply at any time to the District Court for an order that his premises are a restaurant for the purposes of the Intoxicating Liquor Act. If the court certifies that the premises are within the definition of restaurant contained in the Intoxicating Liquor Act 1927, the licensee is entitled to serve intoxicating liquor with meals in that portion of the premises usually set apart for the supply of meals up until 12.30 a.m. on the morning of the following day.[17] **14–16**

---

[13] Intoxicating Liquor Act 1988, s.22.
[14] Intoxicating Liquor Act 1927.
[15] *Ibid.*, s.12.
[16] See above, chap. 4, "Licences to Sell Intoxicating Liquor by Retail", at para. 4–39.
[17] See above, n.8.

(c) Special Exemption Order

14–17 Whenever a disco takes place in a nightclub, the licensee must conform to the usual permitted hours. He will be entitled to open his premises up until 12.30 a.m. of the morning following the night on which a disco is held if he serves food and confines the celebration to that part of the premises where meals are usually served. If, however, he applies for a special exemption order, then he can keep his premises open until the time permitted by the court, provided he abides by the conditions imposed by the court, including the service of substantial meals.

(d) Public Dancing Licence

14–18 In the usual course, the applicant seeks a public dancing licence to bring himself within the provisions of section 5(5) of the Intoxicating Liquor Act 1927, and thereby qualify and be entitled to apply for special exemption orders.

Part IV

THE COURTS: LICENSING JURISDICTION

CHAPTER 15

CHANGES IN THE CHARACTER, SCOPE AND ATTRIBUTES OF A LICENCE

Introduction

The legislature has made provision for the conversion of a licence of a certain character into a licence of a different character. Two statutes make express provision for the change in character of a licence. In addition, a substantial body of case law has arisen from the numerous applications to convert the character of licences in situations which fall outside these statutory provisions. The attempts to create off-licences in place of on-licences have increased, especially since the early 1980s when supermarkets began to replace the pub/grocery as the main outlet for household shopping. **15–1**

A. Change in Character: Statutory Provision

1. Grant of Full Licence for Premises having a Restricted Licence

The grant of a full licence in substitution for a restricted licence is provided for in section 27 of the Intoxicating Liquor Act 1960. The provision is one of the exceptions to the general prohibitory terms of the Licensing (Ireland) Act 1902 (see above, chapter 6, "Public House Licence"). **15–2**

Policy

15–3 The intention of the legislature was to permit the holder of a restricted licence to convert his licence into a full licence on the extinguishment of another restricted licence or licences, or a full licence. The policy of the 1902 Act was continued in that it is only possible to apply for the grant of a full licence in place of a restricted licence where one or more other licences is/are tendered for extinguishment.

STATUTORY PROVISION

15–4 Section 27 of the Intoxicating Liquor Act 1960 provides:

"(1) In this section—

"full licence" means a publican's licence within the meaning of Part II of the Act of 1910 which is neither a six-day licence nor an early-closing licence;

"restricted licence" means—

(a) a publican's licence which is not a full licence, or
(b) a beerhouse licence within the meaning of Part II of the Act of 1910.

(2) Where a person who holds a restricted licence in respect of any premises (in this subsection and in subsection (3) of this section referred to as the relevant premises) shows to the satisfaction of the District Court on application thereto at any sitting thereof for the Court area in which the relevant premises are situate that, in relation to

(a) another restricted licence in respect of premises situate in that Court area, or
(b) each of two other restricted licences in respect of premises both of which are situate elsewhere than in that Court area, or
(c) a full licence

either—

(i) he is the holder thereof, or
(ii) he has procured the consent of the holder thereof to the extinguishing thereof if and when a full licence in respect of the relevant premises is granted pursuant to this section,

the Court shall cause a certificate to be given to that person entitling him to receive a full licence in respect of the relevant premises.

(3) Upon the grant pursuant to an application under subsection (2) of this section of the full licence in respect of the relevant premises—

(a) the restricted licence in respect of the relevant premises shall be extinguished, and
(b) the other licence or licences, as the case may be, to which the application related shall be extinguished and the other premises or each of the other premises, as the case may be, to which the application related shall, for the purposes of the Act of 1902, be deemed never to have been licensed."

JURISDICTIONAL REQUIREMENTS

1. The Applicant. The applicant must be: 15–5

   (a) The holder of a restricted licence.

   (b) (i) The holder of the licences to be tendered for extinguishment, or

   (ii) he must be in a position to prove that he has procured the consent of the holder of such licences to their extinguishment if and when the full licence is granted.

2. Restricted Licence. The existing licence must be a restricted licence. This means one of the following:

   (a) a six-day licence[1];

   (b) an early closing licence[2];

   (c) a beerhouse licence.[3]

3. Licence or Licences to be Extinguished 15–6

   (a) Where an applicant wishes to apply for a full publican's licence in place of a restricted licence, he must be in a position to tender any of the following for extinguishment:

   (i) a restricted licence which is attached to premises situated in the same District Court licensing area;

   (ii) if no restricted licence is available for extinguishment in the same District Court licensing area, he must prove that there are two restricted licences attached to premises and they are not in the same District Court licensing area. These licences, as in the case of an application under section 13 of the Intoxicating Liquor Act 1960 can attach to premises situated anywhere in the State. Unlike section 13, there is no requirement that each of the restricted licences be of the same character. It is possible, therefore, for an applicant to tender an early closing licence and a six-day licence for extinguishment in order to obtain the full licence.

   (iii) if an applicant cannot bring himself within the preceding two options, he can obtain a full seven-day publican's on-licence relating to premises situate anywhere in the State, for extinguishment.

---

1 A six-day licence is granted subject to a condition that the holder shall keep his premises closed during the whole of Sunday: Intoxicating Liquor Act 1927, s.8.

2 An early closing licence is a licence granted subject to a condition that the holder shall close his premises one hour earlier than that at which such premises would otherwise have to be closed: Intoxicating Liquor Act 1927, s.9.

3 A beerhouse licence is an on-licence taken out by a retailer of beer. It entitles the holder to sell beer, cider and perry.

(b) He must prove that the licence or licences is/are not a hotel licence granted under section 2(2) of the Licensing (Ireland) Act 1902, or a greyhound racetrack licence or a special restaurant licence.[4]

4. Venue

This application, although for an on-licence, is not made to the Circuit Court: the statute specifically provides that the District Court is the appropriate venue. The application is to "any sitting" of the District Court.[5] There is no provision in the statute for notification of notice parties such as the Garda Síochána or even the District Court clerk, nor for publication of the application. This can be contrasted with all other applications to court for certificates for on-licences. The statute does not require the applicant to give notice of his intention to apply. The intention of the legislature is that as the applicant is the holder of a restricted licence, it is unnecessary to notify the public or the usual statutory notice parties: the application is made *ex parte*.

15–7 In *Application of Thomas J. Dunne,* Walsh J. compared the provisions contained in section 27 of the Intoxicating Liquor Act 1960 with those contained in section 19 of that Act and stated: "I have no doubt that the provisions of section 27 are obligatory and that no discretion rests in the court".[6] Compliance with section 24 of the Fire Services Act 1981 as to notifying the fire officer is obligatory.

STATUTORY CONSEQUENCES

15–8 1. Existing Licence

The existing licence, *i.e.* the restricted licence attaching to the premises, will be extinguished by operation of law upon the grant of the new full licence. In *Doyle v. Hearne (No. 2)*[7] Finlay C.J. was satisfied that the grant of a new seven-day licence under section 27(5) of the 1927 Act constituted an automatic extinguishment of the old licence.

2. Other Licence or Licences

The licence or licences proved in court as being available for extinguishment will be extinguished upon the grant of the new licence.

---

[4] Intoxicating Liquor Act 1962, s.20, as amended by the Intoxicating Liquor Act 1988, s.23.
[5] But see the Intoxicating Liquor Act 1962, s.20: the reference to the Circuit Court in relation to a s.27 application is incorrect.
[6] [1968] I.R. 105 at 118.
[7] [1988] I.R. 317.

3. Old Premises 15–9

The premises to which the licence or licences attached cannot be re-licensed pursuant to section 2(1) of the 1902 Act, as amended by section 23 of the Intoxicating Liquor Act 1960, on proof that they were licensed within the appropriate period.

4. New Licence 15–10

Section 27 of the 1960 Act does not make the grant of a new licence conditional upon a transfer of any endorsements which may be recorded on the old licences. The new licence, therefore, is a clean licence and any convictions recorded on the old licence(s) are not transferred. In *Doyle v. Hearne (No. 2)*[8] Finlay C.J. accepts that the new licence granted by the Revenue Commissioners would be "a licence freed from any subsisting endorsements which had attached to the restricted licence ...".

There is no provision for objections in the statute: once the statutory proofs are complied with, the licence must issue.

2. Grant of New Off-Licences in Lieu of an On-Licence in a County Borough Area

Where the holder of an on-licence can show that the public house trade is not his main business, he can apply at the annual licensing sessions for an off-licence, *i.e.* a spirit retailer's off-licence and a beer retailer's off-licence. Schedule 1 to the Finance (1909–10) Act 1910 provides that an on-licence entitles the holder to sell intoxicating liquor for consumption on and off the premises. This application can only be made where the premises are situate in a county borough. 15–11

This application is commonly referred to as an application for the reduction of an on-licence to an off-licence. In fact, it is an application by the holder of an on-licence, at the annual licensing sessions at renewal stage for a certificate granting a new spirit retailer's off-licence or a new beer retailer's off-licence or both, in lieu of a certificate for the renewal of an on-licence. If the application is successful, the applicant is automatically entitled to a wine retailer's off-licence.

STATUTORY PROVISION

Section 62 of the Intoxicating Liquor Act 1927, as amended by section 18 of the Intoxicating Liquor Act 1943 and section 9 of the Courts (No. 2) Act 1986, provides: 15–12

---

[8] *Ibid.* at 325.

"(1) The holder of an on-licence (in this section referred to as the on-licence) in respect of premises situate in a county borough may apply at any annual licensing District Court that in lieu of the renewal of the on-licence there be granted to him in respect of the said premises a certificate for a new spirit retailer's off-licence or a certificate for a new beer retailer's off-licence or certificates for both such new licences.

(2) When an application under the foregoing sub-section is made the Justice of the District Court, if he is satisfied that the renewal of the on-licence might have been granted and that the sale of intoxicating liquor for consumption on the premises is not the principal business carried on in the premises to which the on-licence is attached, may, if he so thinks fit, grant to such applicant the certificate or certificates so applied for by him.

(3) When an application under sub-section (1) of this section is granted, a new licence or new licences shall notwithstanding anything to the contrary contained in any other Act be granted to the applicant in accordance with the certificate or certificates granted to him in pursuance of such application.

(4) When a new licence or licences is or are granted under the foregoing sub-section no new on-licence shall at any time thereafter be granted in respect of the premises to which such new licence or licences is or are attached.

(5) When an application under sub-section (1) of this section is refused, such application shall be treated as an application for the renewal of the on-licence and dealt with accordingly.

(6) In this section, the expressions "spirit retailer's off-licence" and "beer retailer's off-licence" have the same meanings as such expressions respectively have in the Finance (1909–10) Act, 1910,"

JURISDICTIONAL REQUIREMENTS

15–13 1. Applicant

An applicant must be the holder of a current, valid on-licence, due for renewal at the next annual licensing District Court which attaches to premises situate in a County Borough.

2. Renewal

The applicant must satisfy the court that the licence would have qualified for renewal in the ordinary course. This means that the premises must have been licensed in the year preceding the annual licensing District Court at which the application is made.

15–14 3. Principal Business

The applicant must prove that the sale of intoxicating liquor for consumption on the premises is not the principal business carried on in the premises to which the licence attaches. The main business at the date of the application must be sales for consumption off the premises. Where the court is not satisfied that sales constitute the principal business carried on in the premises to which the on-licence attaches and accordingly refuses the application for the off-licence, the application is treated as an application for the renewal of an on-licence. Thus, section 4(2) of the Courts (No. 2) Act 1986, comes into effect and the applicant applies to the Revenue Commissioners for the renewal of the licence.

4. Venue

The venue is the annual licensing District Court and the application can be made only at the annual licensing sessions in September, not at any sitting of the District Court.

STATUTORY CONSEQUENCES

1. New Licences 15–15

Where the application is successful, a new off-licence or licences shall be granted in accordance with the certificate(s) granted by the District Court.

2. Old Premises

Once a new off-licence has been granted in respect of the premises pursuant to section 62 of the 1927 Act, as amended, that Act forbids the grant of a new on-licence "at any time thereafter". This is quite a stringent stipulation: not only does it prevent the revival of the on-licence in respect of the premises, but an application for an on-licence pursuant to any of the other jurisdictional exceptions to the 1902 Act cannot be made in respect of that premises once section 62 of the 1927 Act has been invoked successfully.

Hotel: Public Bar

Contrary to popular belief, section 9 of the Intoxicating Liquor Act 1960 is not a licensing jurisdiction. In other words, the grant of public bar facilities, under section 19, does not convert the conditional licence known as a hotel licence which is granted under section 2(2) of the Licensing (Ireland) Act 1902 from being a hotel licence into an unrestricted publican's licence. It merely removes the prohibition contained in section 2(2) of the Licensing (Ireland) Act 1902 against having public bar facilities in a hotel. The application which the licensed hotelier makes is an application for the extinguishment of an ordinary seven-day licence. 15–16

Consequence of Section 19 Order

When a section 19 order is made, it is thereafter lawful to have a public bar for the sale of intoxicating liquor in the hotel. The order, however, does not change 15–17 the nature of the licence granted in respect of the premises: the licence continues to be a licence granted under section 2(2) of the Licensing (Ireland) Act 1902, the essential difference being that the condition against having a public bar in the hotel is now removed.

A licence granted under section 2(2) of the 1902 Act cannot be proffered for extinguishment in substitution for the grant of a licence pursuant to the jurisdictional exceptions to the general prohibitory terms of the Licensing (Ireland) Act 1902.[9] The removal of the statutory prohibition on having public bar facilities following a successful section 19 application does not alter the position.

B. Change in Character: No Statutory Provision

Introduction

15–18 Attempts have been made to invoke jurisdictional exceptions to the terms of the 1902 Act and to apply for a licence different in character to that already held by an applicant. The courts have only recently permitted this and then only in exceptional circumstances. The type of applications which have been made can be divided into three categories:

1. Conversion to Licence More Comprehensive in Character

(a) Off-licence to an On-Licence

15–19 After the coming into force of the Licensing (Ireland) Act 1902, attempts were made to invoke certain jurisdictional exceptions to the Act and seek licences "more comprehensive in character and quality" than those previously held.[10] The judiciary roundly rejected such attempts.

In *R. (Collins) v. Donegal Justices*[11] an attempt was made to obtain a publican's licence in respect of a premises to which a spirit grocer's licence attached. O'Brien L.C.J. stated:

> "… I do not think that the first sub-section of section 2 has the very general effect ascribed to it by the plaintiff's counsel. If the applicant's contention be well founded, it would be possible for the thousands of spirit groceries in the country to be converted into ordinary public houses, and thereby give an impetus to and develop the very evil the Act was intended to redress. This consideration reasonably leads to the conclusion that the word "licence" is to be read

---

[9] Intoxicating Liquor Act 1962, s.20, as amended by the Intoxicating Liquor Act 1988, s.23.
[10] *per* O'Brien L.C.J., *R. (Collins) v. Donegal Justices* (1902) 36 I.L.T.R. 229.
[11] *Ibid.*

distributively, and that the rule of construction, *reddendo singula singulis*, is to be applied — *i.e.* that on each application for a licence, regard must be had to the character of the licence already attached to the premises ... The *status quo* was to be preserved, not extended."[12]

Gibson J. was of the same view, saying:

"If the Act is to have the interpretation suggested and argued for by the applicant's counsel, it should be called the spirit grocers' relief Act."[13]

Both O'Brien L.C.J. and Gibson J. were satisfied that, from a reading of the statute, it was not the intention of the legislature to put the holders of spirit grocers' and inferior licences in the same position as publicans. O'Brien L.C.J. contrasted the public house and the spirit grocer in a much quoted sentence:

"Now, the public house was the great source of supply of drink to the public, though a spirit grocer's may be fraught with special danger to the limited class of women who are addicted to drink, and who might avail themselves to a more or less secret way of getting drink."[14]

The Supreme Court endorsed the judgment in the *Collins* case in *R. (Henderson) v. Louth Justices*, Cherry L.J. stating:

"The statute was intended to preserve existing interests, to preserve the *status quo*, and not to confer upon licensed persons rights different from those they enjoyed at the passing of the Act."[15]

(b) Off-Licence to Off-Licences

In *Re Margaret McLaughlin*[16] an application for a spirit retailer's off-licence and a beer retailer's off-licence pursuant to section 2(1) of the 1902 Act was made where only one licence existed in respect of the premises, namely a spirit retailer's off-licence. The application was refused on appeal by Judge Moonan who said:

"Accordingly it is clear that any difference whatever in the new licence is a bar to granting it."[17]

(c) Restricted Licence to Full or More Comprehensive Licence

In upholding the principle in the *Collins* case, Palles C.B., in *R. (Dorrian) v. Greer*,[18] refused to sanction the grant of a publican's six-day licence, where the 15–20

[12] *Ibid.* at 229.
[13] *Ibid.* at 230.
[14] *Ibid.* at 229.
[15] (1911) 45 I.L.T.R. 8, 73 at 74.
[16] (1939) 73 I.L.T.R. 251.
[17] *Ibid.* at 251.
[18] (1903) 3 N.I.J.R. 302.

licence which previously attached to the premises was an early closing six-day licence. The Chief Baron noted that the words in section 2(1) must be read distributively with reference to each particular class of licence. He referred to four classes of publicans' licences:

1. six-day early closing licences;
2. six-day licences;
3. seven-day licences; and
4. seven-day early closing licences.

He noted that "there was something entirely distinct in each of these classes of licence, and each of them differed in character",[19] noting also that it was apparent from the 1902 Act that the legislature "distrusted the hitherto licensing authorities, and desired to limit their powers". He concluded that the logical construction of the section was to read it distributively, both as regards "on" and "off" licences and as regards the various kinds of licences which came under the description of "on" licences.[20]

In *The State (Tuomey) v. The Circuit Court Judge of the Midland Circuit*[21] an application for a new seven-day licence in lieu of an existing six-day licence in respect of premises situate at Market Square, Abbeyleix, was granted by the Circuit Court judge. The President of the High Court was satisfied that this order was made without jurisdiction; an order of certiorari issued, and the certificate granted by the Circuit Court judge was quashed.

It is not possible to convert a licence into a licence more comprehensive in quality and character than the existing licence.

2. Conversion to Licence of Lesser Character

15–21 The courts have accepted that in certain circumstances it is possible to succeed in an application for the grant of an off-licence where the licence proffered for extinguishment is an on-licence. Prior to the decision in *Re Application of Power Supermarkets Ltd*[22] it was generally believed that it was necessary in all cases to tender for extinguishment a licence of the same character. In *Re Application of Power Supermarkets Ltd*[23] the applicant wished to secure an off-licence but was unable to obtain off-licences for extinguishment in the parish in which the premises were situate.

---

[19] *Ibid.* at 303.
[20] *Ibid.* at 303 and 304.
[21] [1932] I.R. 95.
[22] [1988] I.R. 206 (the "Killarney case").
[23] [1981] I.L.R.M. 270 (the "Carlow case").

The applicant was advised to apply for an on-licence and tender an on-licence within the same parish for extinguishment. The applicant then applied for a declaration as to the fitness and convenience of the proposed supermarket for the purposes of receiving an on-licence. In order to render the proposed premises suitable for the sale of intoxicating liquor for consumption on and off the premises, the applicant proposed to install a small bar. The application was successful before Judge Sheridan in the Circuit Court but was reversed on appeal. McWilliam J. was of the opinion that the food department of a supermarket was not fit and convenient to receive an on-licence.

In *Application of Power Supermarkets Ltd*[24] the applicant obtained a declaration as to the fitness and convenience of a supermarket in Waterford where it was proposed to have "a very small bar"; the applicant also undertook to "reduce" the publican's licence, when granted, to an off-licence under section 62 of the Intoxicating Liquor Act 1927. Ellis J. held that the court could not take into account the undertakings of the applicant. He stated:

> "It does not seem to me either proper, fit, suitable or convenient that a supermarket foodstore premises should have a publican's on-licence attached to it."[25]

Following these setbacks, John Cassidy, S.C., devised a new strategy and advised that the applicant apply for an off-licence, and offer a licence of a greater character, *i.e.* an on-licence, for extinguishment.

Walsh J., giving the judgment of the Supreme Court in *Re Application of Power Supermarkets Ltd*,[26] was satisfied in the circumstances of the case that the production of an on-licence for extinguishment was sufficient compliance with the statutory requirements governing the grant of an off-licence. In that case, the application for the off-licence was made to the District Court, pursuant to the provisions of section 4 of the Licensing (Ireland) Act 1902.[27] The licence available for extinguishment was a publican's licence. A question which the court was asked to address in the case stated to the Supreme Court was whether the licence sought must be of the same character as the licence being extinguished. Walsh J. stated:

> "No such requirement is made by the Act of 1902. There is judicial authority for holding that the section cannot be availed of to obtain an on-licence by surrendering an off-licence, see *R. (Collins) v. Donegal Justices* [1903] 2 I.R. 533. The Circuit Court judge held, and in my opinion correctly so, that the Act did permit the granting of an off-licence upon the extinguishment of an on-licence provided the other requirements of the Act of 1902 were met."[28]

---

[24] Unreported, High Court, Ellis J., June 3, 1981 (the "Waterford" case).
[25] *Ibid.* at p. 11.
[26] Above, n.22.
[27] The judgment incorrectly refers to the application as being made under s.2 of the 1902 Act.
[28] Above, n.22, at 209.

15–22 None of the jurisdictional exceptions to the prohibitory terms of the 1902 Act which are contained in that Act contain the proviso that the licence to be extinguished must be a licence of the same character as that being sought. Since this decision, in a substantial number of applications for off-licences, the licence proffered for extinguishment has been an on-licence. Because of the increase in the supermarket and off-licence business in the country, fewer off-licences are now available for extinguishment. Off-licences are a rare and precious commodity: the big supermarket chains and a number of other traders throughout the country have since obtained off-licences where an on-licence was tendered for extinguishment. Walsh J. in the *Power Supermarkets* (Killarney) case pronounced himself satisfied that the granting of off-licences, where an on-licence has been tendered for extinguishment, led to the reduction in the overall number of on-licences.

It must be borne in mind, however, where an on-licence is tendered for extinguishment, that an application for off-licences can only be made if no express statutory provision requires that the existing licence be of the same character as the off-licences which are the subject of the application.

Since the *Power Supermarkets* (Killarney) case, applications have been made for off-licences where an on-licence is offered for extinguishment, the jurisdictions invoked being sections 3 and 4 of the Licensing (Ireland) Act 1902.

The view has recently been expressed that the holder of an on-licence might invoke section 2(1) of the 1902 Act to obtain a new off-licence in substitution therefor. Blayney J. noted in *O'Rourke and Flanagan v. Grittar*[29] that an applicant for a new off-licence in place of an existing on-licence "might come within the exception to the prohibition in section 2 of the 1902 Act against the granting of new licences". He stated:

> "... since an on-licence is defined in the Intoxicating Liquor Act, 1927, as meaning 'a licence for the sale of intoxicating liquor for consumption either on or off the premises', it would appear very likely that the holder of such a licence would be able to acquire a new off-licence on the ground that his premises came within the exception in s. 2(1) of the Act of 1902, that is, that they are premises which are now licensed".[30]

If the legislature had intended such a result, there would have been no reason to enact Section 62 of the Intoxicating Liquor Act, 1927 (which provides for the grant of an off-licence where an on-licence exists). The whole nature and purpose of section 2(1) of the 1902 Act is to "revive" a pre-existing business once an applicant can prove that he comes within the appropriate statutory time period as provided for by section 23 of the Intoxicating Liquor Act 1960.

It is unlikely that section 6 of the Licensing (Ireland) Act 1902 can be invoked where an applicant seeks a new off-licence in place of an existing on-licence: the proviso requires the court to be satisfied that the grant of the

[29] [1995] I.R. 541.
[30] *Ibid.* at 567.

new licence would render the "said" licensed premises more suitable for business carried on therein.

3. Conversion to Licence of Different Character where Statutory Prohibition

As seen above, the Supreme Court in the *Power Supermarkets* (Killarney) case[31] has decided that where there is no statutory requirement that the licence sought must be of the same character as the licence being extinguished, then the production of an on-licence for extinguishment is sufficient compliance with the statutory requirements for the grant of an off-licence. Later statutory exceptions to the prohibitory terms of the 1902 Act, which provide for the grant of a new licence on the proffering for extinguishment of a licence or licences, require that the licence or licences to be extinguished be of the same character as the licence sought. This is in contrast to the provisions relating to the grant of new licences contained in the Licensing (Ireland) Act 1902. An application for a new off-licence, where an on-licence is offered for extinguishment and an application for an on-licence where off-licences are offered for extinguishment will not succeed in the following circumstances: **15–23**

1. Where the application is for a licence for more convenient premises in a rural area under section 21 of the Intoxicating Liquor Act 1943. Section 21(2)(a) provides: **15–24**

   > the licence (in this sub-section referred to as a new licence) to which the applicant is declared by the said certificate to be entitled and which is granted to him in pursuance of that certificate shall be a licence of the same character in all respects (including conditions inserted therein) as the licence (in this sub-section referred to as the old licence) attached to the existing premises".

2. In the case of an application for a new licence in respect of premises substituted for destroyed premises under section 22 of the Intoxicating Liquor Act 1943. Section 22(2)(a) provides:

   > The licence (in this sub-section referred to as the new licence) to which the applicant is declared by the said certificate to be entitled and which is granted to him in pursuance of that certificate shall be a licence of the same character in all respects (including conditions inserted therein) as the licence (in this sub-section referred to as the old licence) which was attached to the original premises when they were burnt down or otherwise destroyed or rendered uninhabitable."

3. In the case of an application for a new licence in substitution for premises demolished by a local authority under sections 6 and 7 of the Intoxicating Liquor Act 1953. Section 7(3)(a) provides:

[31] Above, n.22.

> The licence granted in pursuance of this section shall be of the same character and be subject to the same conditions as the licence attached to the former premises."

4. In the case of an application for a new licence in a rural area in substitution for two existing licences under section 13 of the Intoxicating Liquor Act 1960. Section 13(2)(a) provides:

> The licence granted in pursuance of the section shall be of the same character and subject to the same conditions as the licences attached to the existing premises."

5. In the case of an application for a new licence in substitution for a demolished premises under section 14 of the Intoxicating Liquor Act 1960. Section 14(2)(a) requires that the licence shall

> "be a licence of the same character in all respects (including conditions inserted therein) as the [old] licence".

15–25 In *O'Rourke and Flanagan v. Grittar*,[32] where the application before the District Court was for an off-licence in respect of premises in County Kildare (a rural area), the owner of a chain of supermarkets profferred two on-licences for extinguishment. The application was made pursuant to section 13 of the Intoxicating Liquor Act 1960 which requires the extinguishment of two licences of the same character. The District Court judge sought the opinion of the High Court on the correct interpretation of section 13(1)(b) and section 13(2)(a) of the Intoxicating Liquor Act 1960. Gannon J. referred to Walsh J.'s judgment in the *Power Supermarkets* (Killarney) case and stated:

> "... Walsh J. pointed out there is no express requirement in the Act of 1902 that the licence applied for under s. 2 of that Act must be of the same character as the licence for which it is substituted. Nevertheless, there is substantial judicial authority to support that argument, although the cases cited refer only to attempts to substitute a new on-licence for an off-licence."[33]

Implicit in this reference is the suggestion that this judicial authority was distinguished by Walsh J. in reaching his decision in the *Power Supermarkets* (Killarney) case.

Gannon J. referred to the expression "of the same character" used in the statutes referred to above and continued:

> "It seems to me that when the legislature has adopted in its legislation a method of expression chosen by the judiciary to interpret the legislation it would not be reasonable that the courts would construe in a different way the later legislation which makes use of the same mode of expression. . . .

---

[32] Above, n.29.
[33] *Ibid.* at 551.

> "... in considering the prescribed requirements of s. 13 of the Act of 1960, I do not think the question for consideration is whether the extinguished licences are sufficient to authorise the certificate for a different licence. It seems to me that if a licence can properly be described as "greater" or "less" or "more extensive" than another, it does not comply with the requirement of being the same. In such a case, the greater would of course "be sufficient" but that is not what the legislation requires."[34]

On appeal, the Supreme Court was somewhat more sympathetic to the applicant's submissions that the policy of section 13 of the Intoxicating Liquor Act 1960 was to "encourage the extinguishment of as many as possible of redundant publicans' licences that then existed in rural areas throughout the State". The appeal, however, was unsuccessful. In *O'Rourke and Flanagan v. Grittar* (Supreme Court) O'Flaherty J. in his dissenting judgment, stated: 15–26

> "While I am inclined to accept that it did not occur to the legislators when enacting the Act of 1960 that two on-licences could be extinguished in favour of one off-licence in a rural area — for the simple reason that such would not have made much sense in the commerce of the time — I believe that it should be regarded as implicit in the legislative intention that the greater should include the lesser. Therefore, I accept the argument advanced by Mr Landy, S.C on behalf of [Grittar], that an on-licence has twin characters — that of an on-licence and that of an off-licence and, accordingly, on the extinguishment of two on-licences it should be possible to obtain an off-licence."[35]

The Chief Justice refused the application as did Blayney J. who was satisfied that were it not for the very specific terms of the statute, the applicant's submissions, to the effect that the greater included the lesser, and that on-licences could also be considered to be off-licences, would carry great weight. However, he was satisfied that as the section expressly requires that the licence granted should be of the same character as the licence to be extinguished "and since it cannot be disputed that an on-licence and an off-licence are licences of a different character, an off-licence cannot be granted on the extinction of two on-licences".[36] He came to the conclusion that:

> "This is a somewhat unreal result and one which may not have been intended as the policy of the legislature since 1902 has been to restrict the number of licences, and in particular, the number of publicans' licences."[37]

The Chief Justice was satisfied that the provisions of section 13 were quite clear: it was a fundamental requirement of the statute that the licences to be extinguished be of the same character as the licence sought, or that the licence to be granted under section 13 should be of the same character and subject to the same conditions as the licences attached to the existing premises. He stated:

---

[34] *Ibid.* at 551 and 552.
[35] *Ibid.*, at 564.
[36] *Ibid.* at 566.
[37] *Ibid.*

> "An 'on-licence' is of completely different character to an 'off-licence'; it permits the sale of intoxicating liquors for consumption on and off the premises whereas the 'off-licence' only permits the sale of intoxicating liquors for consumption off the premises. This is a fundamental difference between the characters of both licences."[38]

Applications for licences (whether more or less comprehensive in quality than the existing licences) pursuant to the jurisdictional exceptions introduced since the Intoxicating Liquor Act 1943, cannot succeed where the legislation expressly requires that the new licence be of the same character and subject to the same conditions as the old licence.

4. Conversion of Restricted Licence to Off-Licence

15–27 The question arises whether an application for an off-licence under the 1902 Act will succeed where a restricted licence is tendered for extinguishment.

A restricted licence is either an early closing on-licence or a six day on-licence.[39] A restricted licence is not a licence of the same character, or subject to the same conditions as an off-licence. The application will not succeed where the statute expressly provides that the licence to be granted is to be of the same character and subject to the same conditions.

If an application were to be made for off-licences under, say, section 4 of the Licensing (Ireland) Act 1902, it is questionable whether the restrictive licence could be said to be greater or more extensive than the licence being sought.[40]

---

[38] *Ibid.* at 563.
[39] Intoxicating Liquor Act 1927, ss.8 and 9.
[40] See *R. (Dorrian) v. Greer*, above, n.18.

CHAPTER 16

JURISDICTION

Introduction

All licences for the sale of intoxicating liquor, whether by retail or in wholesale quantities, are granted by an officer of the Revenue Commissioners.[1] In the case of the most common types of retail licence, such as publicans' licences and off-licences, it is necessary to produce to the Revenue Commissioners a certificate granted by a court of competent jurisdiction certifying that the applicant is entitled to receive a licence. **16–1**

Various statutes use the expression "licensing authority" being the person or the body granting a new licence. The expression was considered in *Application of Oshawa Ltd* where it was noted that the functions of the licensing authority are divided between the courts and the administration. O'Flaherty J. stated:

> "The court investigates any objections, the suitability of the proposed licensee and the premises and must see that there is compliance with the law; once a certificate issues then it is for the Revenue Commissioners to grant the appropriate licence."[2]

---

[1] Collector of Customs and Excise.

[2] [1994] 2 I.R. 425 at 434.

16–2 Once the application is successful and the court makes the order entitling the applicant to receive the licence, the county registrar or District Court clerk, as the case may be, issues a certificate which is presented to the Revenue Commissioners for the purpose of obtaining the licence. The contents of this certificate will state, *inter alia*, that the applicant is entitled to a licence, the type of licence to which he is entitled, the place at which he is authorised to carry on the licensed trade and the jurisdiction relied upon by the court to authorise the issue of the certificate. Where the certificate relates to an off-licence, it will also certify the rateable valuation of the premises, and the period during which the premises have been in the exclusive occupation of the applicant.[3]

Once the certificate has been obtained, it should be presented, together with the appropriate excise duty, to the "proper officers of excise in Ireland" in order that the licence will issue.[4] Since the enactment of section 242 of the Finance Act 1992 the production of a tax clearance certificate, in addition to the certificate and the excise duty, is now a necessary precondition to the issue of a licence. This chapter discusses the functions and jurisdiction of those bodies involved in the grant, transfer and renewal of licences.

Jurisdiction of the Courts

16–3 Before the enactment of the Courts of Justice Act 1924 the justices at petty sessions and the justices at quarter sessions had jurisdiction in relation to all licensing matters. The justices at petty sessions dealt with renewal and temporary transfers of on-licences and the grant, renewal and transfer of off-licences. The justices at quarter sessions dealt with the grant and transfer of on-licences and appeals from justices at petty sessions.

The District Court and the Circuit Court are now the courts of first instance in licensing applications. The Superior Courts function as a court of appeal whether on the facts or on a point of law by way of appeal or case stated. The court of first instance may also refer a question of law by way of consultative case stated; it is preferable that evidence be heard before the question of law is raised for determination by the Superior Courts.[5] The succeeding paragraphs deal with the jurisdiction of each court in relation to various licensing applications.

[3] An off-licence usually comprises three separate and distinct licences, *i.e.* the beer retailer's off-licence, the wine retailer's off-licence and the spirit retailer's off-licence. The requirement as to rateable valuation and exclusive occupation only relates to beer retailers' off-licences.

[4] Licensing (Ireland) Act 1833, s.6.

[5] *Doyle v. Hearne (No. 1)* [1987] I.R. 601.

The District Court

General

The Courts of Justice Act 1924 conferred on the District Court the jurisdiction previously vested in the justices or a justice of the peace sitting at petty sessions. Section 77(C) of the Courts of Justice Act 1924 conferred jurisdiction upon the District Court to grant certificates in respect of off-licences. 16–4

STATUTORY PROVISION

Section 77 of the Courts of Justice Act 1924 provides: 16–5

> "77 — The District Court shall have and exercise all powers, jurisdictions, and authorities which immediately before the 6th day of December, 1922, were vested by statute or otherwise in Justices or a Justice of the Peace sitting at Petty Session and also (by way of addition and not of exception) the following jurisdictions.
>
> (C) — In granting certificates for spirit and other licences — all licensing jurisdiction heretofore exercised by Justices of the Peace at Petty Sessions or at Quarter Sessions or by Courts of Quarter Sessions or by Recorders or by Justices of the Peace out of Petty Sessions except the power of granting new licences conferred on the Circuit Court by Section 50 of this Act."

Section 33 of the Courts (Supplemental Provisions) Act 1961 extended the jurisdiction of the District Court to encompass the grant of a music and singing licence, thereby overruling Hanna J.'s judgment in *Re Bailey.*[6] In that case, it was held that section 77(C) of the 1924 Act must be given a meaning which excluded licences for which no certificate is given, such as a music and singing licence.

1. Grant

The District Court acts as the court of first instance in the following applications: 16–6

1. An application for a certificate authorising the applicant to sell beer and/or spirits to the public for consumption off the premises where sold. Section 1 of the Beer Retailers' and Spirit Grocers' Retail Licences (Ireland) Act 1900 confers upon the licensing justices a free and unqualified discretion either to refuse or grant a certificate for any new excise or other licence for the

[6] [1933] I.R. 722.

sale of beer or spirits by retail to be consumed off the premises. This Act, as applied by section 77(C) of the Courts of Justice Act 1924, and section 48 of the Courts (Supplemental Provisions) Act 1961, continued the jurisdiction enjoyed by justices of the peace at petty sessions to grant off-licences. An application for an off-licence can be made at any time during the licensing year but must be made at a sitting of the District Court for the court area within which the premises the subject of the application is situate.[7]

16–7 2. An application for a certificate for a new spirit retailer's off-licence or a certificate for a new beer retailer's off-licence or certificates for both such new licences in lieu of the renewal of an on-licence.[8] This application is made to the annual licensing District Court. Where a District Court judge is satisfied that the sale of intoxicating liquor for consumption on premises to which an on-licence attaches is not the principal business carried on in that premises, he is entitled to grant an off-licence in substitution for the existing on-licence to the applicant.

3. An application for a full publican's licence in respect of a premises to which a restricted licence is attached. A restricted licence is a six-day and/or early closing licence or a beer house on-licence.[9] This is the only occasion where the District Court may grant a certificate in respect of an on-licence.

4. An application for an order extinguishing an ordinary seven-day licence in order to permit a hotel to have a public bar for the sale of intoxicating liquor.[10] This application is brought in the District Court where the holder already has a licence in respect of a hotel which was granted under section 2(2) of the 1902 Act and where no previous order under section 19 of the Intoxicating Liquor Act 1960 has been made.

16–8 5. An application for a certificate entitling the applicant to apply for a wholesale beer dealer's licence.[11] The application for a wholesale dealer's licence in spirits and wine is made directly to the Revenue Commissioners and there is no need to produce a certificate.

6. An application for the grant of a temporary public dancing licence and an annual public dancing licence.[12] An application for a public dancing licence where no such licence exists at the time of the application may be made at any time to a judge of the District Court. An application to renew a public

---

[7] District Court Rules 1948, r. 98 (S.I. No. 431 of 1947) as substituted by District Court Rules 1955, r. 11 (S.I. No. 83 of 1955). See below, chap. 17, "Practice and Procedure".

[8] Intoxicating Liquor Act 1927, s.62, as amended by the Intoxicating Liquor Act 1943, s.18 and the Courts (No. 2) Act 1986, s.9.

[9] Intoxicating Liquor Act 1960, s.27.

[10] *Ibid.*, s.19.

[11] Courts of Justice Act 1924, s.77(C), as applied by the Courts (Supplemental Provisions) Act 1961, s.48.

[12] Public Dance Halls Act 1935, s.2.

dancing licence must be made at the annual licensing District Court and at no other time.[13]

7. An application for a music and singing licence. This application is made to the annual licensing District Court, or any adjournment thereof or at any special session convened with 14 days' previous notice.[14]

8. An application for the grant of a full restaurant certificate and a limited restaurant certificate. The application by the holder of a wine retailer's on-licence for a restaurant certificate may be made at any sitting of the District Court.[15] Where the holder of a publican's licence applies to the District Court for a restaurant certificate, such application must be made in conjunction with an application for a certificate for the transfer or renewal of an on-licence. Section 12(1) of the Intoxicating Liquor Act 1927 refers to "a certificate for the transfer . . . of an on-licence". An application for a certificate of transfer is made at the annual licensing District Court, so the application for the restaurant certificate which is brought in conjunction with this application must also be made at the annual licensing District Court. Section 48 of the Intoxicating Liquor Act 1988 added a further subsection to section 12 of the Intoxicating Liquor Act 1927 and provided for the grant of a restaurant certificate by the District Court "following application pursuant to section 4 of the Courts (No. 2) Act 1986, to an officer of the Revenue Commissioners for the renewal of an on-licence without the production of a certificate of the District Court". It is clear from this provision that the application for the restaurant certificate must be connected with the application for renewal. The application should, therefore, be made at the annual licensing District Court or at an adjourned sitting thereof.

9. An application for the grant of a certificate of registration for a club, where the application is not for the grant of an "original" certificate of registration.[16] Where, for example, there are alterations to a club house premises which are minor or are not substantial, the District Court has jurisdiction to grant a new certificate of registration in respect of the altered clubhouse premises. However, where there are substantial alterations, it is appropriate to apply for the grant of an original certificate of registration in respect of the new and different premises. This application is made to the Circuit Court. 16–9

10. An application to the Revenue Commissioners for a wine retailer's on-licence to which an objection has been lodged is heard by the District Court.[17] Where an officer of the Garda Síochána (not below the rank of

---

[13] *Ibid.*, s.2(4).

[14] Public Health Acts Amendment Act 1890, s.51(2) as applied by the Courts (Supplemental Provisions) Act 1961, s.33.

[15] Intoxicating Liquor Act 1927, s.12(1)(A) as amended by the Intoxicating Liquor Act 1943, s.8.

[16] Intoxicating Liquor (General) Act 1924, s.19.

[17] Refreshment Houses (Ireland) Act 1860, ss.13, 14.

inspector) objects to the first granting by the Revenue Commissioners of a wine retailer's on-licence under section 14 of the Refreshment Houses (Ireland) Act 1860, the District Court judge for the court area in which the premises sought to be licensed are situate, shall "proceed to consider, examine on oath into, and adjudicate upon the truth, sufficiency and validity of any such objection".

2. Renewal

16–10 1. Until the enactment of the Courts (No. 2) Act 1986, it was necessary to apply to the District Court for a certificate in order to renew a licence which required a court certificate for its grant.[18] Section 4(2) of the Courts (No. 2) Act 1986 provides that where an applicant requires to renew his licence, a court certificate is not required, save in certain cases listed in section 4(5) where the District Court continues to exercise jurisdiction to grant the appropriate certificate. The production to the Revenue Commissioners of a certificate of the court is required in the following cases:

(i) where notice of objection to the renewal of the licence has been lodged with the court within the time prescribed in rules of court;

(ii) where the licence is one which is renewable by virtue of the provisions of Section 30(1)(b) of the Intoxicating Liquor Act 1960[19];

(iii) where it is proposed to insert an early closing condition or a condition that the licence holder shall not trade on a Sunday, in the licence.[20]

Except in the cases enumerated, the District Court no longer issues the certificate which was a necessary precondition to the renewal of the licence.

2. An application for the renewal of a certificate of registration for a club is made to the annual licensing District Court.[21] A certificate of registration remains in force until the annual licensing District Court next following the grant of such certificate and shall then expire.[22]

---

[18] Spirits (Ireland) Act 1854, s.11.
[19] *i.e.* where the licence has expired and where the court transfers same to a person who does not hold the lowest estate or tenancy in the premises.
[20] Courts (No. 2) Act 1986, s.4(5).
[21] Registration of Clubs (Ireland) Act 1904, s.3, as amended by the Intoxicating Liquor Act 1988, s.44.
[22] Intoxicating Liquor (General) Act 1924, s.19.

3. Transfer

An application for an ad interim transfer is made at any sitting of the District Court for the court area within which the premises are situate, although the court may grant the application at any sitting of the District Court in any area in its district.[23] An application for a certificate of transfer (otherwise known as the confirmation of transfer) is made at the annual licensing District Court.[24] The District Court also has jurisdiction to hear an application for an ad interim transfer of a beer retailer's off-licence and a spirit retailer's off-licence.[25] The application for the certificate of transfer of an off-licence is made at the annual licensing District Court for the court area within which the premises are situate.[26] **16–11**

4. Declaratory Jurisdiction

An application for a declaratory order pursuant to the provisions of sections 15 and 16 of the Intoxicating Liquor Act 1960 is made to the District Court.[27] **16–12**

The Circuit Court

General

The licensing jurisdiction formerly vested in the justices at quarter sessions was transferred to the Circuit Court originally by virtue of section 50 of the Courts of Justice Act 1924 which was repealed by section 3, Schedule 1 to the Courts (Supplemental Provisions) Act 1961, and thereafter by section 22(3)(a) and section 24 of the Courts (Supplemental Provisions) Act 1961. **16–13**

Section 50 of the Courts of Justice Act 1924 provided:

> "The Circuit Court shall have jurisdiction in all cases of application for a new licence entitling the applicant to sell intoxicating liquor for consumption on the premises."

Section 24 of the Courts (Supplemental Provisions) Act 1961, conferred full original jurisdiction on the Circuit Court in all applications for new on-licences. In *The State (Attorney General) v. Durcan*, Davitt P. stated:

---

[23] Public House (Ireland) Act 1855, s.1 and the District Court Rules 1948, r. 97, as amended by the District Court Rules 1955, r. 12.
[24] Licensing Act (Ireland) 1874, s.12. and the District Court Rules 1948, r. 100.
[25] Intoxicating Liquor Act 1960, s.29.
[26] Licensing Act (Ireland) 1874, s.12, and the District Court Rules 1948, r. 100.
[27] Intoxicating Liquor Act 1960, ss.15, 16.

"This original jurisdiction is conferred without qualification or limitation, and it seems to me that it must necessarily include jurisdiction to determine all questions which have to be determined in deciding whether an application for a certificate leading to a new on-licence should or should not be granted."[28]

STATUTORY PROVISION

16–14 Section 24 of the Courts (Supplemental Provisions) Act 1961 provides:

> "(1) In this section "on-licence" has the same meaning as in the Licensing Acts, 1833 to 1960.
>
> (2) The Circuit Court shall have jurisdiction in all cases of applications for new on-licences.
>
> (3) The jurisdiction conferred on the Circuit Court by this section shall be exercised by the judge of the circuit in which the premises in respect of which the new on-licence is sought are situate.
>
> (4) Where the Circuit Court grants under this section a new on-licence, then, notwithstanding anything contained in any enactment, the licence shall not require to be confirmed at any subsequent sitting of the Circuit Court."

1. Grant

16–15 The Circuit Court is the court of first instance in the following applications

1. an application for a certificate leading to the grant of a publican's licence, and a hotel licence;
2. an application for an order permitting public bar facilities in respect of a hotel which was licensed by virtue of section 2(2) of the 1902 Act[29];
3. an application for a certificate leading to the grant of a special restaurant licence[30];
4. an application for a certificate leading to the grant of a licence in respect of holiday camp premises[31];
5. an application for the grant of an original certificate of registration for a club[32];

---

[28] [1964] I.R. 279.
[29] Intoxicating Liquor Act 1960, s.19(3).
[30] Intoxicating Liquor Act 1988, s.8.
[31] Tourist Traffic Act 1952, s.44(1).
[32] Intoxicating Liquor (General) Act 1924, s.19.

6. an application for a restaurant certificate in conjunction with an application for a certificate leading to the grant of a new on-licence in respect of a public house.[33]

2. Declaratory Jurisdiction

The Circuit Court has jurisdiction to determine an application for a declaration as to the fitness and convenience of a proposed licensed premises, the suitability of proposed registered club premises, and the suitability of licensed premises for a restaurant certificate or a limited restaurant certificate.[34] **16–16**

3. Appeal

The Circuit Court is the court of appeal in licensing cases where the District Court is the court of first instance.[35] **16–17**

An appeal in a criminal case under the Licensing Acts or the Registration of Clubs Acts is also made to the Circuit Court. Section 59 of the Courts of Justice Act 1936 provides, *inter alia*, that:

> "every appeal which lies to the Circuit Court from an order of the District Court in a criminal case under the Licensing (Ireland) Acts, 1833 to 1927, or under the Registration of Clubs Acts, 1904 to 1927, shall lie to the judge of the Circuit Court within whose circuit is situate the licensed premises or the club premises on or in respect of which the offence the subject of such order was committed or to which such order otherwise relates".

The right of a licensee to appeal a conviction from the District Court to the Circuit Court is contained in section 7 of the Courts (No. 2) Act 1986, which amends section 27 of the Intoxicating Liquor Act 1927 by substitution.

STATUTORY PROVISION

Section 27(1) of the Intoxicating Liquor Act 1927 as amended by section 7 of the Courts (No. 2) Act 1986 provides: **16–18**

> "Whenever the holder of any licence for the sale of intoxicating liquor is convicted by a Justice of the District Court of an offence to which this Part of this Act applies, an appeal shall lie from such conviction to the Judge of the Circuit Court within whose circuit the district or any part of the district of such Justice is situate and the decision of such Judge shall be final and not appealable."

---

[33] Intoxicating Liquor Act 1927, s.12.
[34] Intoxicating Liquor Act 1960, ss.15, 16, and the Intoxicating Liquor Act 1953, s.8.
[35] Courts of Justice Act 1924, s.87.

The Circuit Court judge on appeal has discretion, even where he affirms the conviction, to make an order declaring that a conviction relating to prohibited hours shall not be recorded on a licence.

Refusal of Application

(a) Grounds of Refusal

16–19 Where the court of first instance refuses to grant the application, the grounds of refusal must be specified.[36] Where an application for a certificate entitling an applicant to receive a new licence is refused, the court must,

> "by order in writing, to be duly entered by the Clerk of the Peace, prohibit such licence to be issued, and therein declare the reason or ground of such prohibition."[37]

Similary, where an application to renew a licence is refused, the District Court judge must,

> "in the event of thereupon refusing such application, make an order accordingly, and cause an entry thereof to be made by the clerk, together with the grounds of refusal, in like manner as the justices assembed at quarter sessions are required to do by the Licensing (Ireland) Act, 1833."[38]

Where the court omits to state in its order the grounds of refusal as required by statute, a writ of mandamus will issue directing it to re-hear and determine the application.[39]

Even if the court refuses the application upon a statutory ground and is not asked at the hearing to state the ground or grounds for refusal, a re-hearing will be ordered.[40] It follows that if the order states, as a ground of refusal, a ground which should not have been taken into account by the court, that the order is bad.[41] In *R. (Marshall) v. Tyrone Justices*,[42] it was held that the order of the Justices was bad on its face, as the reasons for their refusal did not reference the objections they had jurisdiction to entertain. It was held by the Court of Appeal that the Justices had no jurisdiction to refuse an application for a spirit grocer's licence on the ground of the unsuitability of the premises in their locality.

However, where an order does not specifically set out the grounds for

---

[36] Licensing (Ireland) Act 1833, s.4; Licensing (Ireland) Act 1855, s.1; Beerhouses (Ireland) Act 1864, s.13; and the Licensing Act 1872, s.82.

[37] Licensing (Ireland) Act 1833, s.4.

[38] Licensing (Ireland) Act 1855, s.1.

[39] *R. v. Sykes* [1875] 1 Q.B.D. 52.

[40] *Smith, ex p.* [1878] 3 Q.B.D. 374.

[41] O'Connor, *Irish Justice of the Peace* (2nd ed., 1915) Vol. II, p. 690.

[42] [1895] 2 I.R. 174.

refusing the application but merely refuses the application "on the grounds named", this has been held to satisfy the statutory requirements. In *R. (Leslie) v. Monaghan Justices*,[43] Palles C.B. held that the expression "refused on the grounds named" meant on all grounds taken together and not on each one separately. The prosecutor contended that the order was bad on its face as it did not set out the grounds upon which the application was refused. Palles C.B., however, considered that the words "refused on the grounds named" constituted the decision of the court and they must mean on all grounds mentioned in the notice of objection.

In *O'Reilly v. Judge Cassidy and others*,[44] the Circuit Court Judge's alleged failure to state the grounds on which the renewal was refused was one of the grounds relied upon in an application for an order of judical review directing the Circuit Court judge to rehear and determine an appeal against the grant by the District Court judge of a certificate of renewal. Flood J. in delivering judgment made an order striking out this ground and did not deal with the point when delivering judgment. It is unlikely that this would have succeeded as the Circuit Court judge referred to the statutory grounds of objection when refusing the renewal. **16–20**

In *Coldwell v. The Circuit Judge of the County and City of Dublin*,[45] the Circuit Court judge refused an application for the grant of a hotel licence under section 2(2) of the Licensing (Ireland) Act 1902. He failed to set forth the grounds of such refusal in the order. The High Court made absolute a conditional order of certiorari holding that the order of the Circuit Court judge was ambiguous and bad on its face because the grounds of refusal did not appear in the order as was required by section 4 of the Licensing Act 1833. Sullivan P. stated:

> "The learned Judge may have refused to entertain the application, holding that the case was not a fit one in which to grant a licence out of the Annual Licensing Sessions, or he may have heard the application on its merits and refused it, in which case the grounds of such refusal should appear on the face of the Order."[46]

The Judge continued:

> "I therefore hold that the Order is bad on its face, and as it might, if allowed to stand, prejudicially affect the prosecutrix, it must be quashed."[47]

In *The State (Quirke) v. Circuit Court Judge of County Tipperary*,[48] the High Court held that the grounds of refusal to renew the licence in the District Court **16–21**

---

[43] (1901) 35 I.L.T.R. 35.
[44] [1995] 1 I.L.R.M. 306.
[45] (1926) 60 I.L.T.R. 89.
[46] *Ibid.* at 92.
[47] *Ibid.*
[48] (1931) 65 I.L.T.R. 157.

were sufficient as they were based on the character of the applicant and the manner in which the house had been conducted during the past year. Sullivan P. stated:

> "It was argued that that order is irregular in form and invalid as it states that the certificate was refused on the ground of the character of the appellant, although the character of the appellant was not mentioned in the notice of objection served by the Guard. I think that if a person holding a hotel licence reduces the number of rooms below that required by the Act, or maintains a public bar on his premises, these are matters which touch his character as a licensed trader. It was therefore quite legitimate to base the refusal of the licence on the ground of the character of the applicant."[49]

(b) Appeal

16–22 Where an application for grant or renewal is refused, the aggrieved party may appeal. Section 87 of the Courts of Justice Act 1924 provides that in licensing cases, the applicant or a person entitled by law to object may appeal pursuant to such provisions as may be prescribed by the rules made under the Act.[50] The right of an objector to appeal was confirmed in *Re O'Brien and the Intoxicating Liquor Act, 1943*.[51]

In *O'Connor v. Fahy and The Attorney General*[52] it was held that there was a right of appeal to the High Court from the Circuit Court in all cases, save where expressly excluded. In this case, the appellant appealed to the High Court on circuit against the refusal of the Circuit Court judge to grant a six-day publican's licence. As a preliminary point, counsel for the superintendent and the Attorney General argued that there was no jurisdiction in the High Court to hear the matter since there was no right of appeal from the Circuit Court in licensing matters. Haugh J. stated that there was a right of appeal to the High Court and that a licensing case was a civil case.

Where the court of first instance refuses a certificate for the renewal or transfer of a licence, the licence remains in force and effect until the final determination of the appeal once the appellant deposits the amount of the excise duty chargeable on a renewal of the licence with the proper officer of Customs and Excise.[53]

Where an appeal against the refusal of the certificate is taken by the aggrieved party he cannot, however, rely upon the omission of the court of first instance to state the grounds of refusal in the order. Even where the order of the court of first instance is "erroneous or informal" the court of appeal must

---

[49] *Ibid.* at 159.
[50] Licensing (Ireland) Act 1860, s.1; Beerhouses (Ireland) Act 1864, s.13; and the Licensing Act 1872, s.82.
[51] [1951] Ir. Jur. Rep. 8.
[52] (1943) 77 I.L.T.R. 152.
[53] Intoxicating Liquor Act 1927, s.60.

determine the "matter" of such appeal "notwithstanding such omission, error or informality".[54]

Acting within Jurisdiction

A court in granting its order must act within the jurisdiction conferred upon it. 16–23
In *The State (Davidson) v. District Justice Farrell and Circuit Judge Conroy*,[55] Maguire C.J. cited with approval the following passage from the Simonds edition of *Halsbury's Laws of England*:

> "Want of jurisdiction may arise from the nature of the subject matter; so that the inferior tribunal had no authority to enter on the inquiry or upon some part of it. It may also arise from the absence of some essential preliminary proceeding. Thus, although the inferior tribunal may have jurisdiction over the subject matter of the inquiry, it may be a condition precedent to the exercise of its jurisdiction that the proceedings should be begun within a specified time, or that some step should have been previously taken by the person who institutes proceedings before the tribunal."[56]

In the *Davisdon* case Kingsmill Moore J. stated:

> "A magistrate or other inferior Court cannot wrongfully extend the ambit of their jurisdiction by deciding that a case falls within their jurisdiction when it does not, unless it appears that there has been given to him, or it, as part of the jurisdiction, the power to decide, authoritatively as opposed to incidentally, whether the case does or does not fall within jurisdiction. It may be that the jurisdiction of a magistrate to entertain a case depends on the existence or non-existence of a certain state of facts. Before he entertains the case, he must endeavour to ascertain whether such facts do or do not exist. If such ascertainment is merely incidental to establishing whether he had jurisdiction or not, and if he comes to a wrong determination, then the superior Court, if on extrinsic evidence it appears that such determination was wrong, either in law, or because it was without or against the weight of evidence, may grant *certiorari*. But if the jurisdiction of the magistrate, by virtue of the statute giving him jurisdiction, extends to determining *as part of his decision, and not as a mere preliminary incidental to entertaining the case* the existence or non-existence of the state of facts, then his erroneous decision cannot be challenged by *certiorari*."[57]

The jurisdiction conferred by statute must therefore be examined. In *R. (McClinchy) v. Greer*[58] the prosecutor sought to make absolute a conditional order for a writ of mandamus directed to the Collector of Inland Revenue, 16–24

---

[54] Licensing (Ireland) Act 1860, s.1.
[55] [1960] I.R. 438.
[56] (3rd ed., 1955), Vol. 11, para. 268.
[57] *The State (Davidson) v. District Justice Farrell and Circuit Judge Conroy*, above, n.55, at 453.
[58] [1904] I.R. 494.

ordering him to issue an ordinary publican's licence to the prosecutor. The respondent's contention was that the premises were not previously licensed and did not come within any of the exceptions in the Licensing (Ireland) Act 1902. Consequently, the justices had no jurisdiction to enter into consideration of the application for a certificate, as a result of which the order and certificate were wholly void. Palles C.B. agreed with this contention and held that there was no jurisdiction to consider the application and that the certificate was void. He stated:

> ". . . it is settled law that the absence of jurisdiction to make an order by an inferior Court good on its face can be shown, although it has not been quashed on *certiorari*, if such absence of jurisdiction is not founded on *bias* or interest intrinsic in the tribunal. In such a case, the order is void *ab initio*. The *certiorari* does not in such a case make that void which when made was voidable only. It does no more than remove from the records of the inferior Court that which was null and void from its inception."[59]

16–25 The question whether a court acted within or in excess of its jurisdiction in granting a licence pursuant to the provisions of section 2(1) of the Licensing (Ireland) Act 1902, was considered in *The State (Attorney General) v. Judge Durcan*.[60] Here the Circuit Court judge granted an order entitling the applicant to receive a publican's licence on the mistaken assumption that the premises had been licensed within the previous five years. Davitt P. referred to *Halsbury's Laws of England*[61]:

> "The case is more difficult where the jurisdiction of the inferior tribunal depends, not upon some preliminary proceeding, but upon the existence of some particular fact. If the fact is collateral to the actual matter which the inferior tribunal has to try, that tribunal cannot, by a wrong decision with regard to it, give itself jurisdiction which it would not otherwise possess, unless by statute the inferior tribunal is given power to determine conclusively questions relating to its own jurisdiction. The inferior tribunal must, indeed, decide as to the collateral fact, in the first instance; but the superior court may upon *certiorari* inquire into the correctness of the decision and may quash the proceedings in the lower court if such decision is erroneous. On the other hand, if the fact in question is not collateral, but a part of the very issue which the lower court has to inquire into, *certiorari* will not be granted, although the lower court may have arrived at an erroneous conclusion with regard to it".[62]

Davitt P. noted that the licensing jurisdiction of the Circuit Court was conferred without qualification or limitation and that this must necessarily

---

[59] *Ibid.* at 497.
[60] Above, n.28.
[61] Above, n.56, pp. 142-43, para. 270.
[62] Above, n.60, at 286 and 287.

include jurisdiction to determine all questions in deciding whether an application for a certificate leading to a new on-licence should or should not be granted:

> "It seems to me that the prohibition contained in s.2, para.1, of the Licensing (Ireland) Act, 1902 (as amended), cannot deprive the Circuit Court of jurisdiction conclusively to determine, subject to the right of appeal to this Court, whether the premises in question were or were not licensed within the requisite five year period. I take the view that if the learned Circuit Court Judge was wrong in considering that the premises in question had been licensed within the five year period he erred in the exercise of his jurisdiction, and that his order cannot be questioned by this Court on *certiorari*."[63]

In *The State (Attorney General) v. Judge McGivern*,[64] Ó Dálaigh J. considered the jurisdiction of a judge of the District Court in relation to the grant of a special exemption order. He stated: 16–26

> "In our opinion there is nothing in the structure of the subsection to indicate that the Oireachtas is subtracting from the substantive jurisdiction of the Justice the determination of what is a special occasion and placing it among the pre-existing absolutes to jurisdiction. . . . Matters collateral to jurisdiction are usually distinguished by their clear cut and identifiable character, arising from the terms used or from appended definitions. . . . Their very imprecision is of itself a mark that their meaning is being committed to the Justice as part of his substantive jurisdiction and that they are not being set apart as a condition precedent to jurisdiction. . . . The determination by the Justice whether an occasion is a special occasion . . . is not preliminary to, but part of his substantive jurisdiction".[65]

Thus, an error made by a judge in respect of a matter which is not preliminary to or collateral to jurisdiction is not reviewable on certiorari.

A number of cases deal with the question of whether a court of limited jurisdiction has acted in excess of jurisdiction in renewing licences and whether such orders were void. This area of law is abstruse, complex and can be contradictory. In a number of these cases the superior courts seem concerned with the drastic consequences which would ensue if it were held on the facts of each particular case that the orders of the inferior court were void. 16–27

In *The State (Reddy) v. District Justice Johnson*,[66] a certificate in the usual form entitling the applicant to the renewal of his public house licence was granted by the District Court judge on September 28, 1979. Six months after the expiry of six calendar months from the making of this order, the prosecutor applied for an order of certiorari directed to the District Court judge for the

[63] *Ibid.* at 290.
[64] Unreported, Supreme Court, July 25, 1961.
[65] *Ibid.* at pp. 7 and 8.
[66] Unreported, High Court, McWilliam J., July 31, 1980.

purposes of quashing the order. The prosecutor/objectors alleged that no licensed trade had been carried on in the premises for the past three years and that the applicant for renewal had sold the premises some considerable time before the annual licensing sittings at which the licence was renewed.

It was contended on behalf of the prosecutor that the applicant for renewal did not own any interest in or occupy the premises in respect of which the licence was granted at the time of the application for renewal. McWilliam J. refused the prosecutor's application noting that no objection to the renewal of the licence had been made at the annual licensing sittings. In particular, the Judge relied upon the judgment of Holmes J. in *R. (Murphy) v. Cork Justices* where Holmes J. said:

> "With every desire to come to a different conclusion, I can find no warrant, either in the licensing statutes or in the general law, for holding that the certificate of the Justices involves a declaration that the grantee of the licence has a possessory interest in the licensed premises; and, if this be so, it suggests the conclusion that every licence is given on the implied condition that it shall operate if and so long as the licensee is entitled to such an interest."[67]

McWilliam J. interpreted this passage to mean:

> "Although it was not the basis of the decision in the case, this very interesting passage seems to me to indicate that the certificate of the District Justice was given within his jurisdiction, but that the effect of the certificate may be open to question on either of the grounds put forward by the objector".[68]

He referred to the case of *Murphy v. Crean*[69] in which it was reaffirmed that there can be no property in a licence apart from the premises in which the business is carried on by the licensee, and the well-known principle of Palles C.B. as follows:

> "There is another elementary principle . . . viz. that a licence, being an authority to a named person to carry on trade in a specified house, cannot continue to exist if the occupation of the house ceases to be in that named person, unless some other person acquires statutable authority under a justices' order of transfer to trade under that licence."[70]

McWilliam J. was satisfied that even if the District Court judge erred in the exercise of his jurisdiction, his order could not be questioned on certiorari. Following this decision, it would appear that where a court makes an order entitling a person with no interest or estate in the premises to the renewal of the licence, such order is not void, even though the person to whom the certificate was granted could not possibly carry on business on foot of the licence as he does not possess the required estate or interest in the premises.

---

67 [1895] 2 I.R. 104 at 115.
68 *The State (Reddy) v. District Justice Johnson*, above, n.66, at p. 12.
69 [1915] 1 I.R. 111.
70 *Ibid.* at 142 and 143.

In *Application of Doreen Riordan*[71] Finlay P. held that where a District Court judge granted certificates renewing a licence from the years 1974 to 1978, despite the fact that the licence should have been forfeited in 1974, such orders were made within his jurisdiction, even though they were based on the erroneous assumption that the licence had not been forfeited. He noted that the order of forfeiture was not made by the appropriate District Court clerk and felt that as a matter of justice it would be unfair, because of the neglect of the statutory duty on the part of an officer of the State, that the Garda Síochána should now be permitted to obtain a declaration of the court as to the invalidity of the licence. **16–28**

The President, relying upon the *Durcan* case,[72] was satisfied that the mistaken assumption regarding the licence was an error which was made within jurisdiction, and was not capable, therefore, of being reviewed on certiorari.

In *Application of Declan Bannerton*,[73] the applicant contended that orders of renewal of a hotel licence granted under section 2(2) of the Licensing (Ireland) Act 1902 even though made in error, as there was no evidence of registration with Bord Fáilte, were nevertheless valid and subsisting orders and could not now be contradicted. In the High Court Barron J. held that there was a basic distinction between this case and the *Riordan*[74] case: **16–29**

> "In *Riordan's case* the orders which were made in error were made in error as to a vitiating element which arose once and for all. Once the licence was forfeit, then no further order could validly have been made in respect of that licence. However, once an order within jurisdiction was made and was not quashed on *certiorari* or reversed on appeal then the vitiating element, i.e. the forfeiture of the licence, was deemed never to have existed. The effect of the orders was to declare that the licence had never been forfeit. In the present case, the vitiating element is one which continues from year to year. The orders which were made in error and which have not been quashed on *certiorari* nor reversed on appeal are in effect declarations that the hotel was registered at the date of the making of each order in the register of hotels kept by Bord Fáilte Éireann. However, this proof is one which arises each year."[75]

Barron J. was satisfied that the complainant could assert that the licence could not be renewed in the absence of proof that the hotel was currently registered in the register of hotels kept by Bord Fáilte, although he did not express a view as to whether the previous orders renewing the licence were made within or in excess of jurisdiction.

Finlay C.J. on appeal also distinguished the facts of the *Riordan* case and was not satisfied that it would be proper or possible to exempt the applicant

---

[71] [1981] I.L.R.M. 2.
[72] Above, n.28.
[73] [1986] I.R. 758.
[74] Above, n.71.
[75] Above, n.73, at 666.

from the consequences of section 20 of the Intoxicating Liquor Act 1960 (now repealed), namely the necessity to obtain a Bord Fáilte certificate as a condition of renewal of a licence.

16–30 In *Application of Catherine Allen*,[76] Gerard Allen was the holder of a publican's licence in respect of premises which he owned. The licence was renewed by him every year until September 1980. In 1970, he had, however, assigned the premises to his mother, Catherine Allen, and no application for transfer had been made. At the annual licensing court in September 1980, Mrs Allen applied for a certificate of transfer of the publican's licence. The District Court stated a case for the opinion of High Court as follows: "Must I regard the renewal certificates and licences issued during the year 1970 as valid?" McWilliam J. answered the question in the negative.[77]

Some of the cases are difficult to reconcile. The question of whether the inferior tribunal makes an order which is based on an error of fact or makes the order within or in excess of its jurisdiction seems to differ according to the circumstances of each case.

Reviewable Order

16–31 Once a judge makes an order, he is *functus officio* in respect of that order. He cannot grant an order or licence subject to having the matter re-entered by any of the parties. In *Sheehan v. Reilly*,[78] a public dancing licence and a music and singing licence were granted subject to the condition that the solicitor for the objectors had liberty to have the matter re-entered on 48 hours' notice to the licence holder and the Garda Síochána. Barron J. held that the respondent was not entitled to grant what was in effect a reviewable licence.

Function of County Registrar

16–32 The county registrar must transmit details of orders made by the court to the District Court clerk. These include the following details[79]:

(a) name and address of the owner of the licensed premises;

(b) name and address of the licensee;

[76] Unreported, High Court, McWilliam J., 1981.
[77] The Allens had managed to obtain two other licences for the purpose of applying for a new licence. Their predicament, therefore, was not as serious as that of Mrs Riordan.
[78] [1992] 1 I.R. 368.
[79] Licensing Act (Ireland) 1874, s.15.

(c) situation and description of every licence granted in the district.[80]

He also issues the certificate entitling the applicant to receive his licence.[81]

Function of District Court Clerk

The District Court clerk is obliged to keep a register of every licence granted in his district.[82] This register must contain the particulars sent to him by the county registrar in exercise of his functions under section 15 of the Licensing Act (Ireland) 1874. The particulars of all certificates given by the District Court judge must be included in the register. These certificates include the following: 16–33

1. a certificate of renewal and transfer of an on-licence;
2. a certificate of grant, transfer and renewal of a spirit and beer retailer's off-licence;
3. a certificate of grant, transfer and renewal of a wholesale beer dealer's licence.[83]

The details contained in the register include:

(a) the address of the premises in respect of which the court certificate was granted;

(b) the name and address of the owner of the premises;

(c) the holder of such certificate.[84]

The District Court clerk must also enter the following matters on the register:

1. forfeiture of a licence;
2. exemption orders granted;
3. disqualification of premises;
4. records of convictions;
5. all other matters relating to licences (*e.g.* orders of ad interim transfer).[85]

The District Court clerk must amend the register if so directed by order of the District Court but only upon a successful application of an applicant to have

---

[80] Licensing (Ireland) Act 1833, s.10, and the Licensing Act (Ireland) 1874, s.15.
[81] *Ibid.*, s.5.
[82] Licensing Act (Ireland) 1874, s.16.
[83] *Ibid.*
[84] *Ibid.*
[85] *Ibid.*

his name entered as owner of a premises.[86] This applies, for example, where a company changes its name and the ad interim transfer application is not appropriate.

Function of Excise Authorities

16–34 Although the Excise Authorities comprise part of the licensing authority,[87] their function is limited. In *Application of Doreen Riordan*[88] Finlay P. quoted from the judgment of Holmes J. in *R. (Murphy) v. Cork Justices*[89] where he had dealt with the question of whether there had been a decision by a competent tribunal that the person to whom the licence was given was qualified to receive it. Holmes J. stated:

> "Now I think it is clear that as far as the Excise licence is concerned the issue of it decides nothing of the kind. It is merely a ministerial act which the proper officer is obliged to do upon receiving the certificate of the Justices and being tendered the amount of the duty."[90]

Finlay P. in the *Riordan* case, approved of Holmes J.'s description of the function of the excise authority in relation to the issue of the licence and stated that:

> ". . . it seems clear that they have no obligation to enquire at the time when they do issue the licence as to whether the applicant for it has survived from the time at which he was granted the certificate of renewal as from the time at which he made the application and tendered them the licence duty. If they have no obligation or right, as I see it, to make that enquiry, it would follow, it seems to me, that it could not be a consequence of a delay on the part of the Excise Authorities in the issue of the actual licence paper that if the applicant had died in the intervening period that licence would be in some way invalid or void."[91]

In that case, an application to the Collector of Customs and Excise for the issue of a licence pursuant to the certificate granted by the court appears to have been made shortly after the granting of the certificate and probably before the death of Mr Riordan. Because the Excise Authorities have no statutory obligation to inquire whether or not the applicant was alive prior to issuing the licence, the issue of the licence in the circumstances of the *Riordan* case could not be questioned.

---

86 *Ibid.*, s.16.
87 *per* O'Flaherty J. in *Application of Oshawa Ltd*, above, n.2.
88 Above, n.71.
89 Above, n.67.
90 *Application of Doreen Riordan*, above, n.71, at 10.
91 *Ibid.*

Chapter 17

PRACTICE AND PROCEDURE

Introduction

17–1 The Licensing (Ireland) Act 1833, as amended, in particular by section 9 of the Courts (No. 2) Act 1986, sets out the procedure for the grant by the court of a certificate entitling an applicant to receive an on-licence.

In *Re McLoughlin's Licensing Application*[1] Davitt P., President of the Circuit Court, stated:

> "The procedure for obtaining a new licence derives from the provisions of Sections 2, 3, 4 and 5 of the Licensing Act, 1833. These provide for the giving to the appropriate persons notice of a person's intention to apply for the licence: for the making of objections by authorised persons to the grant of the licence, grounded upon one or more of what have come to be called the three statutory grounds of objection; and for the examination into, and adjudication on, such objections for the Licensing Authority. They provide that the Licensing Authority shall, if it be satisfied of the truth and sufficiency of an objection and if it

[1] Unreported, Davitt P., Circuit Court, March 10, 1961.

> deems it improper to entrust the applicant with a licence, make an Order in writing prohibiting the issue of the licence and declaring its reasons for such prohibition. An applicant who correctly followed the procedure laid down, and succeeded in persuading the Licensing Authority to overrule any objections made, became entitled to the benefit of Section 5. That provides that, upon the application being disposed of by the Licensing Authority, the applicant was entitled to a Certificate on foot of which the licence would be granted by the Revenue authorities."

The amendments effected by the 1986 Act supersede various procedural requirements contained in Order 42 of the Circuit Court Rules 1950.[2] Statutory procedural requirements have been held to be mandatory. Failure to comply with these requirements goes to the jurisdiction of the court. In *R. (Byrne) v. Divisional Justices of Dublin (Loughrey's Case)*,[3] Andrews J. rejected submissions that the procedural provisions of the Beerhouses (Ireland) Act 1864 were merely directory and not mandatory. He stated: **17–2**

> "I entertain no doubt that the enactment in this section relating to the giving of the 21 days' notice is mandatory, and that compliance with it is a condition precedent to the exercise of the jurisdiction to grant the certificate."[4]

It is interesting to note that the chief magistrate considered adjourning the sessions to permit 21 days to elapse before the hearing of the application but then proceeded to grant the application notwithstanding short service. The Court of Appeal did not consider whether the chief magistrate had jurisdiction to do this.

Andrews J. was satisfied that the requirements as to notice laid down by the legislature could not be dispensed with:

> ". . . and it is equally clear that the reason of requiring notice to be given was to enable the person to whom it was given to make the necessary inquiries, and ascertain whether there was any objection to the application for a certificate. I do not feel at liberty to substitute a 'reasonable time' for the fixed period of 21 days; to do so, would be to alter the Act, and would produce great uncertainty in the proceedings of every licensing sessions in Ireland ... I am of opinion that s.4 of the Act of 1864 is mandatory, both as regards the giving of the notice and the time within which it is thereby required to be given, and, that the mandatory requirements of that section not having been complied with by the applicant in this case, the magistrate had no jurisdiction to grant the certificate applied for."[5]

In the same case, Gibson J. held that the notice prescribed by statute was a condition precedent to the magistrate's jurisdiction. He stated:

---

[2] S.I. No. 179 of 1950.
[3] (1904) 37 I.L.T.R. 250.
[4] *Ibid.* at 251.
[5] *Ibid.*

> "The Justices have no jurisdiction to adjudicate on the sufficiency of the notice or to relax the observance of the statutory condition."[6]

17–3 The test in construing whether a time limit contained in a statutory provision is mandatory or directory is to ascertain the intention of the legislature when the time limit was imposed.[7] The view taken by courts of first instance in licensing cases is that statutory notice periods are mandatory and failure to comply therewith goes to the jurisdiction of the court.

Where procedural requirements contained in the rules differ from statutory procedural requirements, the statutory requirements must be followed. Those procedural matters which are not, however, governed by statute but by the rules, may be abridged at the discretion of the court. Order 59, rule 6 of the Circuit Court Rules 1950 provides:

> "The Court may, upon such terms (if any) as it may think reasonable, enlarge or abridge any of the times fixed by these Rules for taking any step or doing any act in any proceeding, and may also, upon such terms as to costs or otherwise as it shall think fit, declare any step taken or act done to be sufficient, even though not taken or done within the time or in the manner prescribed by these Rules."

1. ON-LICENCE

A. Application

1. Grant

(a) General[8]

17–4 **Venue** The sittings of the Circuit Court held in the town nearest to the premises to which the application relates provided that this town is located in the county in which such premises are situate.[9]

Circuit Court judges have been disposed to permit the application to be made in another town on the circuit, provided special application is made in advance and provided all necessary statutory requirements as to notice and publication will be satisfied.

---

6 *R. (Byrne) v. Divisional Justices of Dublin (Loughrey's Case)*, above, n.3.

7 *Irish Refining plc v. Commissioner of Valuation and Judge Fawsitt and Cork County Council* [1990] 1 I.R. 568.

8 "Grant of a Full On-Licence in Substitution for Restricted Licence" is dealt with at para. 17–14 below.

9 Licensing (Ireland) Act, 1833, s.2, and Ord. 42, r. 1 of the Circuit Court Rules 1950.

Contents of Notice

1. The notice must be in writing and state the applicant's intention to apply to the court for a certificate enabling him to obtain an excise licence to sell intoxicating liquor. 17–5

2. This notice must be signed by the applicant. In *R. (Murphy) v. Donegal Justices*,[10] the original notice was signed by the applicant, but those notices which were served on the notice parties were signed by the applicant's solicitor as agent for the applicant. The application was refused. The court ordered that a writ of mandamus should issue directing the justices to rehear the application. The note of judgment taken in the case is very concise:

   > "The Court held that the case was governed by *In re Whitley* and made absolute the conditional order with costs."[11]

   However, it seems that the *Whitley*[12] case may be distinguished. In *Whitley* the court held that since there was nothing in the Companies Act 1862 to show that the legislature intended anything special as to the mode of signature of the memorandum of association, the ordinary rule that signature by an agent was sufficient, applied. Thus, there was no specific statutory requirement for personal signature. Section 2 of the Licensing (Ireland) Act 1833, however, requires that the notice shall be "signed by such person" being of course the applicant. It is therefore prudent to ensure that all notices are personally signed by the applicant.

3. Where the applicant is a corporation, the corporate seal must be affixed to the notice over the signature of the director and secretary.

4. The notice must specify the applicant's place of residence. In *R. (O'Donoghue) v. County Court Judge and Justices of Co. Cork*,[13] O'Brien L.C.J. held that the applicant was obliged to state a place of abode in the notice of application, *i.e.* a "residence" or "home" as distinguished from a business address.

5. The address of the premises must be included in the notice. If the premises is situate in a city or town, the notice should state the street, square, lane, or other description together with the number of the premises. If not, the notice should describe the premises in detail, referring to the road or highway on or adjacent to which the premises lies, specifying the townland, parish, barony, half-barony and county in which the premises are situate. The parish should be the civil parish and this information can be ascertained from the Ordnance Survey Office. 17–6

---

[10] (1896) 30 I.L.T.R. 6.
[11] *Ibid.* at 7.
[12] *Re Whitley Partners Ltd* [1886] 32 Ch.D. 337.
[13] (1911) 45 I.L.T.R. 37

In *R. (O'Donoghue) v. County Court Judge and Justices of Co. Cork,*[14] where it was held that as the licensed premises were in the country, the notice of application was bad because it omitted to state the townland and barony in which the premises were situate. In *R. (Rogers) v. Antrim Justices*[15] it was held that premises in a town are sufficiently described as being in that town, notwithstanding that the townland is not specified. Where the premises are in the country, however, the civil parish, townland and barony should be specified.[16]

6. The notice must specify the sitting of the court at which the application is to be made, noting the courthouse and the date of commencement of the sessions.

7. The statutory provisions under which the application is made must be stated. This means the particular jurisdiction which the applicant is invoking[17] and is not a reference to the general section under which the county registrar issues the certificate in the case of a successful application, (namely, section 5 of the 1833 Act). It is important before settling the notice to ascertain clearly the section or sections upon which the applicant will be relying in court to show jurisdiction.

   Where there is a failure to indicate the correct jurisdiction, a collective citation may be sufficient. In *Application of Declan Bannerton*[18] counsel for the applicant urged before the Supreme Court that the failure to refer to the correct jurisdictional section in an application for a new licence for hotel premises barred the complainant from proving that the licence was a licence granted pursuant to section 2(2) of the 1902 Act, *i.e.* a "hotel licence." The Chief Justice rejected the submission and considered that as a collective citation of the Licensing Acts was recited in the heading of the notice of application, this was sufficient to invoke a particular section of one of the Acts included in the citation. In the judgment, the Chief Justice stated:

   > "As appears from the recital of the heading of the application already contained in this judgment, section 2, paragraph 2, of the Act of 1902 was not referred to at all in the head of this notice, though the Act of 1902 would, of course, be included in the collective citation of the Licensing Acts, 1833 to 1962."[19]

   He continued:

   > "It seems to me much more correct in these proceedings now to assume that the

---

[14] *Ibid.*
[15] [1900] 2 I.R. 388.
[16] All the above requirements are contained in s.2 of the 1833 Act and are also incorporated into the Circuit Court Rules 1950, Ord. 42.
[17] *e.g.* Licensing (Ireland) Act 1902, s.4, for city premises, or Intoxicating Liquor Act, 1960, s.13, for a premises situate in a rural area.
[18] [1986] I.L.R.M. 471 (Sup. Ct.).
[19] *Ibid.* at 473 and 474.

Circuit Court in 1978 acted within its jurisdiction, even though the application may not have complied in full with the Circuit Court Rules. . .".[20]

Thus, where a section grounding jurisdiction is not specifically invoked in the title of a notice of application, this will not vitiate the notice, once the collective citation is quoted.

Notice Parties Notice must be given to the following persons or bodies: 17–7

1. Superintendent of the Garda Síochána for the area within which the applicant resides. The superintendent is a statutory notice party.[21] In *R. (O'Donoghue) v. County Court Judge and Justices of Co. Cork*,[22] it was held by the King's Bench Division that an applicant for a publican's licence was obliged to serve the notice of application on the inspector of police in the district in which the applicant resided. In giving judgment, O'Brien L.C.J. stated that compliance with section 9 of the 1854 Act was "clearly a condition precedent to the granting of the application".[23]
2. Fire authority for the functional area within which the premises are situate.[24]
3. Officer in charge of the Garda Síochána of the district in which the premises are situate.[25]
4. Judge of the District Court within whose district the premises are situate.[26]
5. County registrar for the county in which the premises are situate.[27]

Notice Period The Circuit Court Rules 1950, Order 42, rule 5, provide: 17–8

> "Save in Dublin Circuit, such notice shall be served at least 21 days before the first day of the Sitting of the Court at which the application is to be made.
>
> In the Dublin Circuit, such notice shall be served at least 21 days before the day upon which such application is intended to be made, and shall operate to set down the application for hearing upon any day after the expiration of the said time upon which the application may come on for hearing in its order in the list."

The practice in the Dublin Circuit is that the county registrar will fix one day for taking licensing applications and the Circuit Court office will, on request,

[20] *Ibid.* at 474 and 475.
[21] Spirits (Ireland) Act 1854, s.9.
[22] Above, n.13.
[23] *Ibid.* at 38.
[24] Fire Services Act 1981, s.24.
[25] Circuit Court Rules 1950, Ord. 42, r. 4(i).
[26] *Ibid.*, Ord. 42, r. 4(ii), and Licensing (Ireland) Act 1883, s.2.
[27] Circuit Court Rules, Ord. 42, r. 4(iii), and Licensing (Ireland) Act 1883, s.2.

indicate that day. The notice of application should be served on all notice parties at least 21 days before that date. This occurs approximately every four to five weeks, save during the long vacation.

In circuits other than Dublin, the 21-day period is measured by reference to the commencement date of the sessions on the circuit in which the premises is situate.

It should be noted that section 9 of the Courts (No. 2) Act 1986 deleted the requirement contained in section 2 of the Licensing (Ireland) Act 1833, to give 21 days notice to the judge of the District Court and the county registrar. The requirement to give notice still remains but an applicant is not now obliged by statute to give 21 days' notice to the District Court judge or the county registrar. The Circuit Court Rules, however, apply and the court has a discretion to abridge the time for service. The notice periods required are as follows:

17–9 1. Superintendent of the Garda Síochána where the applicant resides: 21 days at least before the date on which the application is intended to be made.[28]

2. Fire authority for the functional area within which the premises are situate: one month's notice in writing or such shorter period of notice as the fire officer may in the special circumstances of the case agree to accept.[29]

3. Officer in charge of the Garda Síochána for the district in which the premises are situate:

   (i) in the Dublin Circuit, 21 days before the date upon which such application is intended to be made;

   (ii) in the rest of the country, at least 21 days before the first day of the sitting of the court at which the application is to be made.[30]

4. Judge of the District Court within whose district the premises are situate:

   (i) in the Dublin Circuit, 21 days before the date upon which such application is intended to be made;

   (ii) in the rest of the country, at least 21 days before the first day of the sitting of the court at which the application is to be made.[31]

5. County registrar for the county within which the premises are situate:

   (i) in the Dublin Circuit, 21 days before the date upon which such application is intended to be made;

   (ii) in the rest of the country, at least 21 days before the first day of the sitting of the court at which the application is to be made.[32]

---

[28] Spirits (Ireland) Act 1854, s.9.
[29] Fire Services Act 1981, s.24
[30] Circuit Court Rules 1950, Ord. 42, r. 5.
[31] *Ibid.*
[32] *Ibid.*

In calculating the 21-day period, neither the day of the commencement of the sessions nor the day of service of the notice of application may be taken into account. In *Re O'Connor*,[33] a notice served on March 5 where the sessions commenced on March 26 was held to be late.

It is clear that the court has jurisdiction to abridge time for service of the notice on the District Court judge, the county registrar, and on the superintendent of the Garda Síochána where the premises are situate. The fire officer is statutorily entitled to accept short notice.

Publication The notice of application must be advertised in a newspaper circulating in the place in which the premises are situate at least 21 days before the application will be heard. Section 9 of the Courts (No. 2) Act 1986 amends section 10 of the Licensing Act (Ireland) 1874 by substitution and provides: 17–10

> "Every person intending to apply for a new licence or for the transfer of a licence shall, at least 21 days before the intended application is to be heard, cause to be inserted or advertised in a newspaper circulating in the place in which the premises concerned are situate, a notice duly complying with the requirements of section 2 of the Licensing (Ireland) Act, 1833".

This statutory provision overrules the requirement in Order 42, rule 6, of the Circuit Court Rules 1950 which stipulated that notice of the application be published not more than four and not less than two weeks before the first day of the commencement of the appropriate sessions or, in the Dublin Circuit, before the date upon which the application was intended to be made.

It is questionable whether the court has jurisdiction to adjourn a case which has been returned for the first day of the sessions in order to satisfy the statutory requirements as to time.

If a national daily newspaper is used, the applicant is advised to be in a position to prove that the particular edition in which the advertisement appeared was available for sale in retail newsagents in the general neighbourhood of the proposed new licensed premises. It should be noted that a copy of the entire newspaper is required. It is not sufficient simply to cut out the advertisement and affix the name and date of the newspaper. If the entire newspaper is not lodged, the county registrar may not be able to determine the edition of the newspaper in which the notice was published.

Thus, in a licensing application before a Circuit Court judge sitting in a provincial town, where it is proved that a notice has been inserted in a national newspaper, it must be shown that the edition circulated in the area in which the premises are situate.

Plans The Circuit Court Rules provide that on the hearing of an application, the applicant shall produce a map or plan of the premises.[34] In practice, this 17–11

[33] (1867) 1 I.L.T. & S.J. 178.
[34] Circuit Court Rules 1950, Ord. 42, r. 8.

plan is lodged with the county registrar at the time, or as soon as possible after, the notice of application is served on the county registrar. The plans are also served on the Garda Síochána and the fire authorities.

The plans required are as follows:

1. location plan illustrating precisely the position of the premises in relation to neighbouring premises in the general area within which the premises sought to be licensed are situate which is usually taken from the most recent Ordnance Survey of the area ;
2. site plan;
3. the layout of all floors in the premises sought to be licensed, including areas not intended to be used for business, such as residential accommodation. All the salient features of the premises should be shown, including the user or intended user of every apartment and the manner in which they are furnished, *e.g.* wall seating, moveable seating, fire exits, counters, shelving, storage, lavatories, and so on;
4. elevations from all points of the compass;
5. the area proposed to be licensed should be delineated with a red verge line;
6. all the above should, if possible, be contained on one sheet of paper. This requirement was laid down by the late Deale J., when he was President of the Circuit Court.

In 1968, he wrote to the various court registrars apprising them of his requirements:

Kilrose, Sorrento Road, Dalkey,
Co. Dublin.
17th July, 1968.

Dear Mr. O'Neill,

The maps lodged with these applications have been recently becoming less and less satisfactory, and now applicants are frequently lodging three, four and even five sheets along with architects working drawings. These numerous papers are unmanageable in Court, and in the Court files afterwards.

Henceforth what will be required is one large sheet only, showing:

(a) a small scale locataion map of the premises, outlined in red to show the limits of the proposed licence.

(b) plans of various floors, if necessary on a small scale so as to fit all in on sheet.

(c) small front elevation drawing.

(d) Colouring of various parts where needed to show old from new, or changes.

(e) Legend explaining colouring.

(f) where the licence is intended to be for buildings only - i.e. excluding yards, gardens, grounds and the like, (b) above should be surrounded with red line to correspond with (a) above.

Any maps not complying with the foregoing should be returned to the Applicant's Solicitor with a note of the foregoing requirements.

Do you think you could now conveniently circularise all Solicitors in the County telling them of these requirements?

YOURS SINCERELY,
Kenneth Deale.

Patrick J. O'Neill Esq.,
County Registrar,
Courthouse.[35]

In more recent times, however, and mainly because of the size of premises proposed to be licensed, it has become the practice to prepare a booklet of plans with all the above details included.

In *Re Brannigan*,[36] Haugh J in the High Court adjourned an appeal to permit alterations to be made to maps in relation to a part of the applicant's application. This facilitated the provision of further and substantially different plans. This would appear to be an acknowledgement by the Superior Courts that in an application for a certificate leading to the grant of a publican's on-licence, plans can be amended during the course of an application.

The requirement to deposit plans in an application for a certificate leading to the grant of an on-licence is not a statutory requirement: it is therefore not mandatory. The requirement to deposit plans with the superintendent at declaratory stage is a statutory requirement. In *Application of Terence J. Maguire*,[37] Murnaghan J. held that failure to deposit a copy of the plan with the superintendent in an application for a declaratory order under section 15 of the Intoxicating Liquor Act 1960 (which was substantially the same as that relied upon in court) was fatal to the application. **17–12**

Proofs The applicant must produce the following: **17–13**

1. plans;
2. newspaper carrying the statutory advertisement outlined in red;
3. affidavits of service of notice of application on all notice parties;

[35] Reproduced by kind permission of Mr Niall O'Neill, Solicitor, Naas.
[36] [1947] 13 Ir. Jur. Rep. 1.
[37] Unreported, High Court, Murnaghan J., April 4, 1963.

4. notice of application;
5. planning permission: proof of planning permission for the building as a licensed premises must be available at some stage before the court will sanction the issue of a certificate leading to the grant of a licence[38];
6. further proofs required by the relevant jurisdictional section.

(b) Grant of a Full On-Licence in substitution for Restricted Licence

17–14 Section 27 of the Intoxicating Liquor Act 1960 provides for the grant of a new on-licence in substitution for a restricted licence: this is the only case where the Circuit Court is not the venue for the grant of a new licence. It is important to note that the statute specifically provides that the application should be made in the District Court and to "any sitting" there. There is no provision in the statute for notification of notice parties such as the Garda Síochána or even the District Court clerk. This can be contrasted with the requirements for an application for a new licence where no restricted licence is held. The statute does not require that the applicant "duly give notice" of his intention to apply nor is publication of the application required. It is probable that as the applicant already holds a restricted licence in respect of a premises, the legislature deemed it unnecessary to require him to notify the public or the usual statutory notice parties. The application is made *ex parte* so an objection cannot arise. A literal interpretation of section 24 of the Fire Services Act 1981 would require notification of the fire officer. It is arguable whether the legislature intended this.

2. Renewal

17–15 An application for the renewal of a publican's licence is made to the Revenue Commissioners. The licence will not issue without a court certificate in certain circumstances (discussed below, in chapter 19, "Renewal", at paragraphs 19–5 to 19–7).[39]

The notice of application for renewal must be submitted to the Collector of Customs and Excise together with the following:

1. the appropriate excise duty: this is now calculated in accordance with the annual turnover of the business[40];
2. a tax clearance certificate.[41]

---

[38] *Re Kitterick* (1971) 105 I.L.T.R. 105.
[39] Courts (No. 2) Act 1986, s.4, which came into force on July 22, 1988.
[40] Finance Act 1992, s.155.
[41] Finance (1909–10) Act 1910, s.49, as amended by the Finance Act 1992, s.156.

Notice Parties Every publican is obliged to notify the fire authority one month in advance of his application to the Revenue Commissioners. The fire officer may agree a shorter period of notice: **17–16**

> "In any case where a certificate is not required for the renewal of a licence (other than an off-licence) under the *Licensing Acts, 1833* to *1986*, the applicant for such renewal shall give one month's notice in writing (or such shorter period of notice as the fire authority may in the special circumstances of the case agree to accept) of the application to the fire authority in the functional area of which the premises are situated, and if the fire authority objects to such application, such fire authority may appear, be heard and adduce evidence in respect of the application for a certificate provided for by *section 4(7)* or *4(8)* (as the case may be) of the *Courts (No. 2) Act, 1986*."[42]

The requirement to notify the fire authority of the application to renew is statutory and cannot be disregarded and this is so even where no objection by any party is lodged to the renewal.

3. Transfer

An application to transfer a publican's licence from one person to another is made to the District Court. The Public House (Ireland) Act 1855 provides for the grant of a temporary transfer of a licence to a person until the annual licensing sessions to be held next after the expiration of one calendar month.[43] A temporary transfer is commonly known as an "ad interim transfer". **17–17**

The application to confirm the temporary transfer (application for a certificate of transfer) is made at the annual licensing sessions.[44]

(a) Ad Interim Transfer

The District Court Rules 1948, as amended by the District Court Rules 1955 regulate the procedural requirements for an ad interim transfer. **17–18**

Venue An application for an ad interim transfer may be made at any sitting of the District Court for the court area within which the premises are situate.[45] The Rules also provide that where there are special circumstances, the application may be made at any sitting of the District Court in any court area in the district in which the relevant District Court judge sits.[46]

---

[42] Fire Services Act 1981, s.24(2), as inserted by the Courts (No. 2) Act 1986, s.9.
[43] Public House (Ireland) Act 1855, s.1.
[44] Licensing Act (Ireland) 1874, s.12, District Court Rules 1948, r. 100.
[45] District Court Rules 1948, r. 97(1) (S.I. No. 431 of 1947), as amended by the District Court Rules 1955, r. 12 (S.I. No. 83 of 1955).
[46] *Ibid.*, r. 97(2).

17–19 **Notice of Application** The notice of application need not be couched in any formal language but should specify:

1. the name of the applicant;
2. his address;
3. a full description of the licensed premises to which the application relates; and
4. the name of the present licensee.

Notice Parties

1. Superintendent of the Garda Síochána in charge of the district within which the premises are situate[47];
2. District Court clerk of the court area within which premises are situate.[48]

The fire officer is *not* a notice party.

17–20 **Notice Period** The notice to be given is "reasonable notice".[49] In practice, 48 hours is regarded as reasonable notice. The notice is interpreted by reference to such matters as whether the applicant is known to the local gardaí or whether time should be allowed for an inquiry as to whether he can satisfy the Public House (Ireland) Act 1855.

Publication There is no requirement to publish this application.

Proofs[50] The applicant must produce the following:

1. the notice of application;
2. affidavits of service of notice of application on all notice parties;
3. document of title upon which the applicant grounds his application or, where applicable, the original probate or grant of administration upon which the applicant relies;
4. current licence or a certified copy licence or certified copy receipt showing the payment of the current licence duty.[51]

---

[47] District Court Rules 1948, r. 98.
[48] *Ibid.*
[49] *Ibid.*
[50] As will be seen below, in chap. 18, "Transfer", at paragraph 18–17, the court must hear evidence on oath from the applicant.
[51] District Court Rules 1948, r. 97(3).

(b) Certificate of Transfer

The procedure relating to the grant of a certificate of transfer is governed by sections 2 to 6 of the Licensing (Ireland) Act 1833, as amended, and by the District Court Rules 1948. **17–21**

Venue The annual licensing District Court for the court area within which the premises are situate.[52] A District Court judge has general powers of adjournment conferred by section 27 of the Courts of Justice Act 1953. Thus, he is entitled to adjourn the annual licensing District Court once the application is before him.

Notice The contents of the notice of application must comply with the requirements of section 2 of the Licensing (Ireland) Act 1833. As in an application for a certificate leading to the grant of a new on-licence, this application must be preceded by a notice which is similar in its terms. It should: **17–22**

1. be signed by the applicant;
2. specify the name and address of the applicant;
3. give detailed particulars of the location of the premises as in an application for a new on-licence[53];
4. give the date of the annual licensing District Court;
5. if no temporary transfer was previously obtained in respect of the premises, state the name of the existing or previous licence holder.

Notice Parties

1. Officer in charge of the Garda Síochána of the district in which the applicant resides.[54] **17–23**
2. Local superintendent of the Garda Síochána[55] (generally assumed to be the superintendent of the Garda Síochána for the area within which the premises are situate).
3. Clerk of the District Court area in which the licensed premises are situate.[56]
4. It is not clear whether the fire officer for the functional area within which the premises are situate should be notified. Section 24 of the Fire Services Act 1981 provides for notification to the fire officer in the event, *inter alia*, of an application for:

   "a certificate for the grant or renewal of a licence . . .".

---

[52] Licensing Act (Ireland) 1874, s.12, and District Court Rules 1948, r. 100.
[53] Licensing (Ireland) Act 1833, s.2.
[54] Spirits (Ireland) Act 1854, s.9.
[55] District Court Rules 1948, r. 101(2).
[56] *Ibid.*, r. 101(2), as substituted by District Court Rules 1955, r.13.

Although the section does not mention "transfer", the practice is to notify the fire officer.

17–24 **Notice Period** The notice period for all notice parties (except the fire officer) is 21 days before the date of the annual licensing District Court.[57] Section 9 of the Spirits (Ireland) Act 1854 provides that the superintendent of the Garda Síochána for the area within which the applicant resides must receive 21 days' notice of the making of the application. The fire officer is given one month's notice (or such shorter period as may be agreed between the parties).

Publication The notice of application is advertised in a newspaper circulating in the area in which the premises is situate. This notice must comply with the requirements of section 2 of the Licensing (Ireland) Act 1833.[58] The statutory provision refers to an application "for a new licence, or for the transfer of a licence".[59]

Where the 21-day period has not expired, it is the practice of the annual licensing District Court to adjourn the application to permit applicants to comply with the statutory notice period.

Proofs The applicant must produce:

1. documents of title;
2. licence;
3. affidavits of service of notice of application on all notice parties;
4. newspaper carrying the statutory advertisement outlined in red;
5. notice of application.

B. Objection

1. Grant

17–25 Section 4 of the Licensing (Ireland) Act 1833, as amended by section 31 of the Intoxicating Liquor Act 1960, provides for objections to the grant of applications for new on-licences. James O'Connor, in his book *The Irish Justice of the Peace*, writes:

> "The statute contemplates either that a written objection shall be sent in beforehand, or that an objection shall be made orally at the sessions."[60]

---

[57] District Court Rules 1948, r. 101(2) as substituted by District Court Rules 1955, r. 13.
[58] Licensing Act (Ireland) 1874, s.10 as substituted by the Courts (No. 2) Act 1986, s.9.
[59] *Ibid.*
[60] (2nd. ed., 1915), Vol. II, p. 684.

Unlike the objection to the renewal of an on-licence, there is no statutory provision requiring prior notification of such objection. However, to avoid adjournment, it is advisable to give the applicant adequate notice of the grounds of objection.

Section 3 of the 1833 Act provides that the applicant's name is to be called and that demand is made "whether anyone has or knows of any objection to or why such application should not be allowed or licence granted".

The notice of objection should specify the names and addresses of the objectors, and the grounds of objection upon which they intend to rely. The statutory grounds of objection upon which objectors may rely are contained in section 4 of the 1833 Act.[61]

2. Renewal

Section 14 of the Licensing Act (Ireland) 1874, as amended by section 9 of the Courts (No. 2) Act 1986, provides: **17–26**

> "The justices shall not entertain any objection to the signing of such certificate, or receive any evidence in respect to same, unless a written notice of intention to oppose be served on the applicant, stating in general terms the grounds on which the renewal of such licence is to be opposed."

The provisions contained in section 14 which allowed the court to adjourn the application where no notice of objection was served, have been repealed by the 1986 Act. The intention of the legislature, therefore, is that the notice period of 21 days in the District Court (Renewal of Intoxicating Liquor Licences) Rules 1988[62] (which were made under the 1986 Act) is mandatory.

The procedure governing objections to the renewal of on-licences is prescribed in section 4 of the Courts (No. 2) Act 1986, and the District Court Rules made thereunder, which came into force on July 13, 1988.[63]

Contents of Notice The form of notice to be used is set out in the District Court Rules 1988, at rule 5(2). The form is signed by the objector or his solicitor. **17–27**

Notice Parties All objectors, including the fire officer, must serve the notice of objection in the form referred to above, on the holder of the licence. The District Court clerk must receive the original notice of objection, together with a statutory declaration of service.

Notice Period Section 4(5) of the Courts (No. 2) Act 1986 requires that the notice of objection is lodged with the District Court within the time prescribed in the District Court Rules 1988 just referred to. The fire officer must serve

---

[61] See below, chap. 21, "Objections".
[62] S.I. No. 145 of 1988.
[63] *Ibid.*

notice of objection on the holder of the licence at least seven days prior to the date of the annual licensing District Court. He should lodge the original notice, together with a statutory declaration of service, with the District Court clerk at least four days prior to the date of the annual licensing District Court.

All other objectors must serve the notice of objection on the holder of the licence at least 21 days prior to the date of the annual licensing District Court. The original of the notice of objection, together with the statutory declaration of service, should be lodged with the District Court clerk at least 10 days prior to the date of the annual licensing District Court.

17–28 **Objections on Grounds of Unfitness of Premises** If an objector wishes to object on the grounds of the unfitness of the licensed premises, then he must give notice in writing of his objection to the holder of the licence, not less than 12 months before the hearing of the application.[64]

Particulars of Objection It was decided by the High Court in *O'Donovan v. Kelly*[65] that an objector is bound to reply fully to particulars to his objections which are raised by the applicant for the renewal of the licence. This case concerned an objection by the Garda Síochána to the renewal of an off-licence in respect of a premises at Phibsboro. In the District Court, Judge Hogan expressed the view that:

> "bearing in mind the consequences of such an objection being upheld, and in the interests of natural justice, that it is only fair that the Respondent be entitled to know to the fullest extent what he has to defend (or it be made known to him what case he has to meet)".

Carroll J. held that Judge Hogan was correct in requiring the Garda Síochána to reply fully to the following particulars:

1. the basis on which it was maintained that the applicant was not a fit and proper person to hold the licence;
2. particulars of any allegations which the gardaí intended to make about the running of the premises, specifying the date or dates in question, the alleged actions or omissions of the applicant relied on and the nature of the evidence it was intended to adduce;
3. particulars including names and addresses of the civilian witnesses proposed to be called by the State at the hearing of the objection;
4. copies of all statements taken from the witnesses.

The practice of the District Court is to require that detailed particulars of all objections to renewal of licences be supplied by objectors before the hearing of the case.

---

[64] Intoxicating Liquor Act 1960, s.32(2).
[65] Unreported, High Court, Carroll J., November 13, 1990.

3. Transfer

(a) Ad Interim Transfer

It was accepted by Henchy J. in *The State (Doyle) v. Carr* that opposition to an ad interim transfer can "come only from the Garda Síochána".[66] 17–29

(b) Certificate of Transfer

An objection to the grant of a certificate of transfer, like an objection to the grant of an original licence, may be made orally at the annual licensing sessions, or in writing beforehand. There are no rules or statutory provisions governing the procedure for making objections. Although section 24 of the Fire Services Act 1981 does not use the expression "transfer", it is arguable that the fire officer is a competent objector. 17–30

If objection is made in writing, the name and address of the objector should be specified, as should the grounds of objection on which he proposes to rely; either the objector or his solicitor should sign the notice of objection.

2. OFF-LICENCE

A. Application

1. Grant

Although the expression "off-licence" is used in the singular in relation to the right to sell intoxicating liquor for consumption off the premises, the majority of off-licensed premises have the benefit of three distinct off-licences, namely: 17–31

1. spirit retailer's off-licence;
2. wine retailer's off-licence;
3. beer retailer's off-licence.

When an application is made to court for an off-licence, the notice generally requests off-licences for the sale of spirits and beer only, as the holder of either a spirit retailer's off-licence or a beer retailer's off-licence may apply to the Revenue Commissioners for a wine retailer's off-licence and obtain the licence without a court certificate.[67]

---

[66] [1970] I.R 87 at 92.
[67] Intoxicating Liquor Act 1962, s.28.

The procedure relating to the grant of off-licences is contained in rules 93 and 94 of the District Court Rules 1948, as amended. These rules derive from earlier statutory provisions and the wording of the District Court Rules follows the statutes closely. The Beerhouses (Ireland) Act 1864 sets forth the procedure which applies to beer retailer's off-licences. Applications for certificates leading to the grant of spirit retailers' off-licences "shall be made in the manner and subject to the like conditions as to appeals against the same and otherwise (so far as the same are applicable) as are prescribed by the Beerhouses (Ireland) Act, 1864".[68]

It is necessary, in the course of presenting an application for an off-licence, to satisfy the court that the granting of the certificate sought is not prohibited by the Licensing (Ireland) Act 1902. This can be done by showing that the application comes within one of the exceptions to the general prohibitory terms contained therein. Otherwise, the applicant must prove that he is entitled to invoke exceptions created by subsequent statutes such as the Intoxicating Liquor Act 1943 or the Intoxicating Liquor Act 1960 and that such jurisdiction applies equally to off-licences as to on-licences.

The notice of application must specify the section or sections of the statute relied upon to ground jurisdiction in the application before the court.

Although there is no rule or statutory provision requiring the filing or service of a map or plan of the premises, the general practice is to make a plan available at the hearing, to lodge it with the notice of application and serve a copy upon the local Garda superintendent.

17–32 **Venue** Rule 11 of the District Court Rules 1955 provides:

> "An application for the grant of a Certificate for a licence to sell spirits or beer in retail quantity for consumption off the premises or an application for the grant of a Certificate for a wholesale beer dealer's licence may be made at any sitting of the District Court for the Court area in which the premises for which the licence is required are situated."[69]

17–33 **Contents of Notice** The application must be preceded by a notice stating the intention of the applicant to make the application. It must be signed by the applicant or, if the applicant is a corporate body, the director and secretary and the corporate seal should be impressed on the notice, duly witnessed in accordance with law.[70] The notice should contain the following details:

1. the nature of the licence or licences for which the applicant requires a court certificate;

---

[68] Licensing Act 1872, s.82.
[69] Though note that the Beer Retailers' and Grocers' Retail Licences (Ireland) Act 1900, s.2, has not been repealed.
[70] District Court Rules 1948, r. 94.

2. the place of residence of the applicant;

3. the situation and place of the premises where the applicant intends to carry on the business, specifying the townland and county in which it is situate, and if the premises are situate in a city or town, the street, square, or other description of the house with the number of the house, if it has a number. The civil parish and barony should also be specified;

4. where the applicant has, within the two years preceding the application, held a licence as a spirit grocer or beer retailer, the notice shall give full particulars of the premises in respect of which the applicant held such a licence. In the case of a supermarket chain holding many licences, it is necessary to set out a description of all of these in a schedule to the notice of application;

5. in every case where the applicant has been at any time previously licensed for the sale of wine, spirits, beer, ale, cider or other excisable liquors to be consumed on the premises or off the premises, the notice should set forth the last place of business where such intoxicating liquor has been sold, together with the date at which such person has given up or otherwise discontinued the sale thereof[71];

6. the annual rateable valuation of the premises.[72] This is only necessary where the application is for the grant of a certificate for a beer retailer's off-licence;

7. the period during which the premises have been in the exclusive occupation of the applicant.[73]

Notice Parties

1. Clerk of the court area in which the premises for which a licence is required are situate.[74] 17–34

2. Superintendent of the Garda Síochána in the garda district in which the applicant resides.[75]

3. Local superintendent of the Garda Síochána.[76]

The fire officer is *not* a notice party.

Notice Period All notice parties must receive 21 days' notice in writing.[77]

---

[71] Beerhouses (Ireland) Act 1864, s.4.
[72] Beer Licences Regulation (Ireland) Act 1877, s.2.
[73] *Ibid.* This must be at least three months immediately preceding the date of the certificate of the court.
[74] District Court Rules 1948, r. 94(1).
[75] Beerhouses (Ireland) Act 1864, s.4, and Licensing Act 1872, s.82.
[76] District Court Rules 1948, r. 94(1).
[77] Beerhouses (Ireland) Act 1864, s.4, and the Licensing Act 1872, s.82.

17–35 **Publication** Section 10 of the Licensing Act (Ireland) 1874, as substituted by section 9 of the Courts (No. 2) Act 1986, requires an applicant for a new licence or for the transfer of a licence to advertise in a paper circulating in the place in which his premises are situate a notice conforming with the requirements of section 2 of the Licensing (Ireland) Act 1833. Section 37 of the 1874 Act defines "licence" as

> "any licence for the sale of any intoxicating liquor granted by an officer of excise in Ireland upon production . . . of a certificate of justices, under the provisions of any Act now or hereafter requiring such certificate, but shall not include an excise license as defined in section 81 of the principal Act, or a wholesale beer dealer's license, as hereinafter defined".

The "principal" Act referred to is the Licensing Act 1872. Section 81 of that Act defines "excise license" as a spirit grocer's licence. This licence was replaced by the spirit retailer's off-licence by virtue of the Finance (1909–10) Act 1910.

Accordingly, an applicant for a beer retailer's off-licence is obliged by the 1872 Act, to publish a notice of his intention to make the application .

The position with regard to an applicant for a spirit retailer's off-licence is not so clear. As section 82 of the Licensing Act 1872 requires that "all applications for certificates for spirit grocers' licences are to be made in the manner and subject to the like conditions as applications under the 1864 Act", in practice an application for both licences is advertised.

2. Renewal

17–36 Applications for the renewal of off-licences are made to the Revenue Commissioners. Where a notice of objection to the renewal of a spirit retailer's off-licence or a beer retailer's off-licence is lodged, a certificate of the court is required. The form of certificates required are referred to below, in chapter 7, "Off-Licences" at paragraph 7–5 to 7–16. Where an objection is lodged by the superintendent of the Garda Síochána to the grant by the Revenue Commissioners of a wine retailer's off-licence, then the applicant is summoned to the District Court to "show cause" against such objection.

The notice of application for the renewal of a spirit retailer's off-licence should be accompanied by:

1. the appropriate excise duty;
2. a tax clearance certificate.

The notice of application for renewal of a beer retailer's off-licence, in addition to the above matters, should be accompanied by:

1. a statutory declaration that the conditions in section 2 of the Beer Licences Regulation (Ireland) Act 1877 concerning the rateable valuation of the premises have been met;

2. a statutory declaration that the premises have been in the exclusive occupation of the licence holder for at least three months preceding the date of the application for renewal.

Unlike the renewal of an on-licence, the applicant for the renewal of an off-licence need not notify the fire officer in advance of his application.

3. Transfer

(a) Ad Interim Transfer

The provisions of section 1 of the Public House (Ireland) Act 1855 apply in relation to the grant of off-licences for which a certificate of the court must be obtained.[78] **17–37**

Venue Any sitting of the District Court for the court area in which such premises is situate.[79]

Contents of Notice The name of the applicant is specified in the notice together with his address, a full description of the premises and the identity of the licensee. **17–38**

Notice Parties

1. Superintendent of the Garda Síochána in charge of the district within which the premises are situate.[80]
2. District Court clerk of the court area in which the licensed premises are situate.[81]

The fire officer is *not* a notice party.

Notice Period The notice period as provided for in rule 98 of the Rules of the District Court 1948 is "reasonable notice". The usual notice given is 48 hours.

Publication There is no requirement to publish notice of this application.

[78] Intoxicating Liquor Act 1960, s.29.
[79] District Court Rules 1948, r. 97.
[80] *Ibid.*, r. 98.
[81] *Ibid.*

(b) Certificate of Transfer

17–39 **Venue** The annual licensing District Court for the court area in which the premises are situate.[82]

Contents of Notice The notice of application is similar to the notice required for the grant of a new off-licence, except where the application is for a transfer on the occasion of the death or removal of the previous licence holder which occurred immediately prior to the application. In this case, a certificate as to the exclusive occupation of the premises for a period of three months prior to the date of the application is not required.[83]

Notice Parties

1. Clerk of the court area in which the premises for which a licence is required are situate.[84]
2. Superintendent of the Garda Síochána in the garda district in which the applicant resides.[85]

The fire officer is *not* a notice party.

Notice Period All notice parties must receive 21 days' notice in writing.[86]

Publication The provisions relating to publication are the same as those which apply in respect of an application for the grant of a new off-licence.

B. Objection

Grant, Renewal and Transfer

17–40 The same considerations which apply to objections to the grant, renewal and transfer of an on-licence apply in respect of off-licences, although it should be noted that the fire officer is not a competent objector.[87]

---

[82] Licensing Act (Ireland) 1874, s.12, and District Court Rules 1948, r. 100.
[83] Beer Retailers' and Spirit Grocers' Retail Licences (Ireland) Act 1900, s.3.
[84] District Court Rules 1948, r. 94(1).
[85] Beerhouses (Ireland) Act 1864, s.4, and Licensing Act 1872, s. 82.
[86] Beerhouses (Ireland) Act 1864, s.4, and District Court Rules 1948, r. 94(1).
[87] Fire Services Act 1981, s.24.

3. WHOLESALE BEER DEALER'S LICENCE

A. Application

1. Grant

Venue Any sitting of the District Court for the court area in which the premises are situate.[88] **17–41**

Contents of the Notice The applicant must provide the following information:

1. his name and address;
2. the identity of the premises. This address should be specified with sufficient particularity to satisfy the District Court Rules 1948, r. 94;
3. the rateable valuation of the premises;
4. the period for which premises have been in the exclusive occupation of the applicant[89];
5. the notice of application should be signed by the applicant[90];
6. where the applicant was previously licensed for the sale of wine, spirits, beer, ale, cider or other excisable liquors to be consumed on the premises or elsewhere, the notice should set forth the last date of business where those liquors were sold, together with the date at which the applicant had given up or otherwise discontinued the sale thereof.

Notice Parties

1. District Court clerk of the court area in which the premises are situate. **17–42**
2. Superintendent of the Garda Síochána of the district within which the applicant resides.[91]
3. Local superintendent.[92]

The fire officer is *not* a notice party.

---

[88] District Court Rules 1948, r. 93, as substituted by the District Court Rules 1955, r. 11, and the Courts of Justice Act 1924, s.77(C), as applied by the Courts (Supplemental Provisions) Act 1961, s.48. Note: the Beer Retailers' and Spirit Grocers' Retail Licences (Ireland) Act 1900, s.3, does not apply.

[89] District Court Rules 1948, r. 94(4).

[90] Beerhouses (Ireland) Act 1864, s.4, as applied by the Licensing Act (Ireland) 1874, s.8.

[91] *Ibid.*

[92] District Court Rules 1948, r. 94.

Notice Period

1. The District Court clerk should receive 48 hours' notice.[93]
2. Every applicant should give "21 days' notice in writing" to the Garda Síochána.[94]

Publication There is no requirement to publish notice of this application.[95]

Proofs The applicant must produce the following:

1. notice of application;
2. affidavits of service of notice of application on all notice parties;
3. certificate of rateable valuation;
4. proof of exclusive occupation within the past three months.[96]

2. Renewal

17–43 The licence is renewed by the Revenue Commissioners. The following details must be submitted by way of statutory declaration:

1. rateable valuation of the premises;
2. confirmation that the premises were in the exclusive occupation of the applicant for three months preceding the date of the application for renewal;

The excise duty must be paid and a tax clearance certificate must be presented.

3. Transfer

17–44 An application for an ad interim transfer of a wholesale beer dealer's licence cannot be made: in all other respects the considerations relating to the grant of a certificate of transfer of a wholesale beer dealer's licence are the same as those applicable in respect of off-licences.[97]

---

[93] *Ibid.*, r. 12.
[94] Beerhouses (Ireland) Act 1864, s.4.
[95] Licensing Act (Ireland) 1874, ss.10 and 37.
[96] District Court Rules 1948, r. 94(4).
[97] Beerhouses (Ireland) Act 1864, s.4, as applied by the Licensing Act (Ireland) 1874, s.8.

B. Objection

The same considerations which apply to objections to the grant, renewal and certificate of transfer of an off-licence (see above, paragraph 17–40) apply in respect of wholesale beer dealer's licences. **17–45**

4. HOTEL LICENCE

A. Application

1. Grant

A hotel licence is a restricted publican's licence which is granted subject to conditions specified in section 2(2) of the Licensing (Ireland) Act 1902. The procedure which governs the grant, renewal and transfer of hotel licences is the same as that which applies to on-licences described at paragraphs 17–4 to 17–24 above. The statute regulating the procedure applicable to the grant, renewal and transfer of an on-licence is the Licensing (Ireland) Act 1833. **17–46**

Applicants frequently adduce evidence at the application for a grant of a hotel licence that Bord Fáilte is satisfied with the structure of the premises; a Bord Fáilte certificate is not necessary until the licence is due for renewal.

2. Renewal

A certificate of registration with Bord Fáilte must be submitted to the Revenue Commissioners where the licence is granted under section 2(2) of the 1902 Act after July 4, 1960, and where the applicant applies to renew a licence in respect of which effect was given to section 42(1) of the Tourist Traffic Act 1952.[98] **17–47**

3. Transfer

It is not necessary to submit a Bord Fáilte certificate where an applicant is applying for a certificate of transfer of either of the licences referred to at paragraph 17–47 above. **17–48**

---

98 Courts (No. 2) Act 1986, s.4(9).

B. Objection

17–49 The procedure is similar to that applying to publicans' on-licences (see paragraphs 17–25 to 17–30).

Public Bar

A. Application

Venue

17–50 1. District Court at any sitting thereof for the court area in which the hotel premises are situate.[99]

2. Circuit Court, if the application is made in conjunction with an application for a new hotel licence under section 2(2) of the 1902 Act.[100]

Notice of Application The applicant should specify:

1. his intention to apply;
2. his place of abode;
3. the situation and place of the hotel premises;
4. the sitting of the court at which the application is to be made;
5. whether the application is made pursuant to section 19(1) or (3) of the Intoxicating Liquor Act 1960.

There is no statutory requirement that the application be signed by the applicant.

17–51 **Notice Parties** There are no statutory notice parties to this application. However, the practice is to give notice to the Garda Síochána and the District Court clerk or where the application is to the Circuit Court in conjunction with an application for a "hotel licence" certificate, the county registrar.

Notice Period The practice is to give 48 hours' notice to the Garda Síochána. The District Court clerk usually receives 48 hours' notice although rule 12 of the District Court Rules 1948 does not apply as the application is made *ex parte*.[101] Where the application is made to the Circuit Court, the notice parties usually receive the same notice as on an application for the hotel or publican's licence.

---

99 Intoxicating Liquor Act 1960, s.19(1).
100 *Ibid.*, s.19(3).
101 *Application of Thomas J. Dunne* [1968] I.R. 105.

Publication There is no requirement to publish the notice of application.

Proofs The applicant must produce the following:

1. a hotel licence where appropriate. Otherwise, a certificate entitling the applicant to receive a hotel licence;
2. notice of application;
3. affidavits of service of notice of application on all notice parties;
4. plans.

B. Objection

No provision is made in the statute for objections. 17–52

5. LICENCE FOR HOLIDAY CAMP PREMISES[102]

A. Application

1. Grant

Venue Circuit Court.[103] 17–53

Contents of Notice As this is an application for an on-licence, those details required in an application for the grant of an on-licence should be set forth.[104]

Notice and Publication Section 44(1) of the Tourist Traffic Act 1952 provides that where an applicant "duly gives notice of his intention to apply for an on-licence in respect of specified premises . . . "; the requirements relating to notice and publication of an application for an on-licence apply accordingly.

Application for Order Varying the Premises to which the Licence Relates 17–54
The procedure is similar to an application for the grant of the certificate entitling the applicant to receive an on-licence in respect of the premises.

---

[102] This licence was created by Part VI of the Tourist Traffic Act 1952.
[103] Tourist Traffic Act 1952, s.44(1).
[104] See above, paras. 17–4 to 17–13.

2. Renewal

17–55 An applicant for the renewal of a holiday camp licence follows the same procedure as the applicant renewing an ordinary on-licence, although the certificate which is granted by the court where an objection is disallowed confirms as follows:

1. the good character of the licensee;
2. the peaceable and orderly manner in which the licensed premises were conducted in the year ending on the expiry of the licence;
3. the orderly manner in which the holiday camp in which the premises are situate was conducted in the year ending on the expiry of the licence.

3. Transfer

17–56 There is no statutory provision for the transfer of this licence: it is, however, an on-licence so the provisions relating to transfers which apply to the ordinary on-licence apply by implication.

B. Objection

17–57 The procedure governing objections to the grant, renewal and transfer of this licence are the same as those which apply to the on-licence.

6. RESTAURANTS

17–58 This section examines the procedure regarding the following:

(a) Full Restaurant Certificate

(b) Limited Restaurant Certificate

(c) Special Restaurant Licence

(a) Full Restaurant Certificate

A. Application

1. Grant

Venue

1. Annual licensing District Court where the applicant holds a full publican's licence, following an application to renew the publican's licence. **17–59**

STATUTORY PROVISION

Section 12(1B) of the Intoxicating Liquor Act 1927, as inserted by section 48 of the Intoxicating Liquor Act 1988, provides:

> "Where, following application pursuant to section 4 of the Courts (No. 2) Act 1986, to an officer of the Revenue Commissioners for the renewal of an on-licence without the production of a certificate of the District Court, the applicant applies to the Court to certify that the premises in respect of which the renewal of the on-licence is sought are a restaurant for the purposes of this Act, the provisions of subsection (1) of this section shall apply and have effect as if that application to the Court were an application, in accordance with that subsection, for a restaurant certificate."

The applicant must prove that he has made an application for the renewal of his on-licence.[105]

2. Annual licensing District Court where an application is made for a certificate of transfer of an on-licence.[106]
3. Any sitting of the District Court, where an applicant is the holder of a wine retailer's on-licence.[107]
4. Any sitting of the Circuit Court where the application for the restaurant certificate is made in conjunction with an application for a certificate leading to the grant of a new on-licence.

---

105 See definition of "restaurant" in s.1 of the Intoxicating Liquor Act 1927: "licensed premises certified under this Act to be a restaurant for the purpose of this Act": see also Intoxicating Liquor Act 1943.

106 District Court Rules 1948, r. 100.

107 Intoxicating Liquor Act 1927, s.12(1A).

17–60 **Contents of Notice** The applicant must provide the following information:

1. state his intention to apply;
2. his place of residence;
3. the situation and place of the premises for which the certificate is required;
4. the nature of the restaurant certificate which he seeks, *i.e.* full restaurant certificate;
5. the sitting of the court at which the application is to be made;
6. the Act and section of the Act under which the application is to be made;
7. the nature of the on-licence attaching to the premises.

Notice Parties

1. Officer in charge of the Garda Síochána for the licensing area.[108]
2. District Court clerk.[109]
3. Where the application is made to the Circuit Court, the county registrar is, as a matter of practice, notified.

The fire officer is *not* a notice party.

Notice Period

1. The Garda Síochána receive at least 10 days' notice before the date on which the application is proposed to be made. This notification is made in writing.[110]
2. The District Court clerk should receive at least 48 hours' notice in writing.

Publication There is no statutory requirement to publish the notice of application.

2. Renewal[111]

17–61 **Venue** Annual licensing District Court.[112] The procedural requirements which obtain in respect of the grant of a restaurant certificate apply to its

---

108 Intoxicating Liquor Act 1927, s.12(2).
109 District Court Rules 1948, r. 12.
110 Intoxicating Liquor Act 1927, s.12(2).
111 The application is, in fact, an application for a new restaurant certificate in respect of premises previously certified as a restaurant.
112 Section 12(3) of the 1927 Act provides: "every restaurant certificate shall unless sooner revoked under this section, remain in force until the next annual licensing district court for the licensing area".

renewal: a restaurant certificate expires at the annual licensing District Court and the applicant must apply for a fresh order of the court certifying that the premises are a restaurant for the purposes of the Intoxicating Liquor Act 1927.

3. Transfer

The court does not transfer a restaurant certificate to another person: it has already certified that the premises are a restaurant until the next annual licensing District Court for the licensing area. **17–62**

B. Objection

The only person who can object is the officer in charge of the Garda Síochána. This objection is made at the annual licensing District Court and on the occasion of an application to the Circuit Court in conjunction with an application for a new licence. The Garda Síochána are entitled to make application at any time for an order revoking the restaurant certificate.[113] There are no procedural provisions for formal notification of objection by the Garda Síochána. **17–63**

(b) Limited Restaurant Certificate

A. Application

1. Grant

Section 12A of the Intoxicating Liquor Act 1927, which was inserted by section 9 of the Intoxicating Liquor Act 1960, introduced a new form of restaurant certificate into the licensing code known as the limited restaurant certificate. **17–64**

Venue

1. The District Court, at any time, where the premises are already licensed.[114]
2. The Circuit Court, at any time, in conjunction with an application for a new licence.[115]

---

[113] Intoxicating Liquor Act 1927, s.12(4).
[114] *Ibid.*, s.12A.
[115] *Ibid.*

17–65 **Contents of Notice** The applicant must provide the following information:

1. state his intention to apply for a limited restaurant certificate;
2. the nature of the restaurant certificate required;
3. his place of residence;
4. the situation and place of premises;
5. the portion of the premises, the subject of the application;
6. the sitting of the court at which the application is to be made;
7. the Act and section of the Act under which the application is to be made;
8. the nature of the licence attaching to the premises.

Notice Parties

1. Officer in charge of the Garda Síochána for the licensing area.
2. District Court clerk.

The fire officer is *not* a notice party.

Notice Period

1. The Garda Síochána receive at least 10 days' notice of the making of the application.[116]
2. The District Court clerk receives 48 hours' notice.[117]

Publication There is no requirement to publish this application.

2. Renewal and Transfer

17–66 The provisions relating to renewal and transfer are the same as those which obtain in respect of the full restaurant certificate (see above, paragraphs 17-61 and 17–62).

B. Objection

17–67 The only persons who can object are the Garda Síochána. The provisions relating to objections are similar to those which obtain in respect of full restaurant certificates (see above, paragraph 17-63).

---

[116] Intoxicating Liquor Act 1927, s.12A(2) as inserted by the Intoxicating Liquor Act 1960, s.9.
[117] District Court Rules 1948, r. 12.

(c) Special Restaurant Licence

A. Application

1. Grant

This licence is, by virtue of the provisions of section 7(2) of the Intoxicating Liquor Act 1988, deemed "for the purposes of the Finance (1909–10) Act 1910 to be a retailer's on-licence", and the procedural provisions applicable to on-licences apply. **17–68**

Venue The Circuit Court.[118] Section 8(1) of the 1988 Act refers to the "Circuit Court" so the Circuit Court Rules 1950, Order 42 apply. This provides that the application is made "at the sittings of the Court held in the town nearest to the premises to which the application relates, and in the county in which such premises are situate".

Notice Parties, Notice Period and Publication Section 8(1) of the 1988 Act provides that an applicant must "duly" give notice of his intention to apply. As a special restaurant licence is deemed to be an on-licence for the purposes of the Finance (1909–10) Act 1910, the procedural requirements affecting notification and publication are the same as those which relate to an on-licence although the contents of the notice must include a reference that the applicant is the owner and occupier of the premises. **17–69**

Proofs The proofs are similar to an application for an on-licence although the grant of a special restaurant licence does not involve the extinguishment of another licence. The following should be noted:

1. plans: where there is a waiting area, the plans must show that it does not exceed 20 per cent of the dining area and the seating capacity of the restaurant does not exceed 250 persons[119];
2. the applicant must adduce evidence that a Bord Fáilte certificate is in force in respect of the restaurant.

---

[118] Intoxicating Liquor Act 1988, s.8(1).
[119] Special Restaurant Licence (Standards) Regulations 1988 (S.I. No. 147 of 1988).

2. Renewal

17–70 The application to the Revenue Commissioners must be accompanied by a Bord Fáilte certificate within the meaning of the Intoxicating Liquor Act 1988.[120] A tax clearance certifice and the appropriate excise duty must also be presented.

Every applicant for renewal is obliged to notify the fire officer in accordance with section 24 of the Fire Services Act 1981,[121] and the fire officer must receive one month's notice, or such shorter period as may be agreed between the parties.

3. Transfer

17–71 As this licence is deemed to be retailer's on-licence for the purposes of the Finance (1909–10) Act 1910, the rules relating to ad interim transfer and the certificate of transfer which affect on-licences apply. There is no statutory provision requiring the production of a Bord Fáilte certificate to the Revenue Commissioners when applying for a licence after the grant of a certificate of transfer.

B. Objection

1. Grant

17–72 The procedure is the same as that which applies to objections to the grant of an on-licence: see above, paragraph 17–25.

2. Renewal

17–73 The procedure is the same as for an on-licence. Section 10 of the Intoxicating Liquor Act 1988 lists the category of objectors to the renewal of the special restaurant licence. Objections should be preceded by the issue and service of the notice provided for in the District Court Rules 1988 at least 21 days prior to the date of the annual licensing sessions. The original notice of objection together with a declaration of service is lodged with the District Court clerk 10 days prior to the annual licensing District Court. The fire officer must comply with the provisions in the 1988 Rules if he wishes to object.[122]

---

[120] Courts (No. 2) Act 1986, s.4(9A), as inserted by s.18 of the Intoxicating Liquor Act 1988.

[121] See the Intoxicating Liquor Act 1988, s.20, which provides that the Fire Services Act 1981, s.24 shall apply in relation to every application for the grant or renewal of a special restaurant licence.

[122] Courts (No. 2) Act 1986, s.4(5), and the Special Restaurant Licence (Standards) Regulations 1988, above, n.119.

Objectors must give notice of objection 12 months in advance of the hearing of the application, where the objection is made under section 32(2) of the Intoxicating Liquor Act 1960 on the grounds of the unfitness of the premises.

3. Transfer

The provisions relating to the ad interim transfer and certificate of transfer are the same as those which obtain in respect of an on-licence (see above, paragraphs 17–29 to 17–30). **17–74**

Application to Revenue Commissioners

On the grant of the Circuit Court certificate entitling the applicant to the licence, the applicant must present the tax clearance certificate, the certificate of the court and the sum of £3,000 to the Revenue Commissioners before the licence will issue.

7. CLUBS

A. Application

1. Grant of Certificate of Registration

The Registration of Clubs Acts 1904 to 1995 regulate the procedure with which the secretary of a club must comply on an application for the grant or renewal of a certificate of registration. In *Re Rossmore Golf Club*,[123] Davitt J. held that the provisions of sections 2, 3 and 4 of the 1904 Act relating to the grant of a certificate of registration were imperative in the sense that they must be complied with before such certificate can issue. However, he found that these provisions are not imperative in the sense that if they are not complied with by an applicant in the first instance, the application must necessarily fail. Accordingly, the statutory provisions do not preclude the court from granting an adjournment or permitting an amendment of the application in order to enable the applicant to effect compliance with the section. The judge stated: **17–75**

> "Upon close examination of the Act as a whole I am of opinion that it was not the intention of the legislature that a genuine, reputable club which is willing

[123] [1950] 16 Ir. Jur. Rep. 52.

> and anxious to comply with all the requirements of the law should, through defects … occasioned, perhaps, by mistake, inadvertance, or even ignorance, be necessarily involved in failure with its inevitable consequences of much inconvenience and the useless expenditure of time and money."[124]

The Intoxicating Liquor (General) Act 1924 transferred the jurisdiction to grant applications for original certificates of registration from the District Court to the Circuit Court. Section 23(2) provides that the jurisdiction is to be exercised "in manner to be prescribed by rules of court, by the Circuit Judge of the circuit in which the premises of the club are situate". At the time of writing, no such rules have been made.

17–76 **Venue** The Circuit Court of the circuit in which the premises of the club are situate. The application for the grant of the original certificate of registration "shall continue" to be made to the "registrar" in accordance with the Registration of Clubs (Ireland) Act 1904, as amended.[125] Section 1 of the 1904 Act provides for the keeping of the register of clubs by the "Petty Sessions Clerk (hereinafter called 'the Registrar')". Rule 109(1) of the District Court Rules 1948, provide that the registrar of clubs, for the purposes of the Registration of Clubs (Ireland) Act 1904 "shall be the Clerk of the Court Area in which the club premises are situate". Although the application is made to the District Court clerk in his capacity of registrar of clubs, he forwards the notice of application and all accompanying documents to the county registrar. The application is then listed before the Circuit Court judge for the county within which the club premises is situate and is heard and determined by him.

17–77 **Registrar of Clubs** To comprehend fully the statutory procedural requirements contained in the Registration of Clubs (Ireland) Act 1904, as amended, the statutory obligations placed upon the registrar and the records he is bound by statute to maintain should be considered. The registrar must do the following:

1. keep a register of clubs;
2. enter the name of each club situate within his district in the register;
3. record the date of each certificate of registration;
4. record whether the certificate of registration was granted for the first time or on renewal;
5. record the address of the premises to which the certificate relates;
6. record the names and addresses of the officials of the committee of management or governing body of the club;

[124] *Re Rossmore Golf Club*, above, at 56.
[125] See the Intoxicating Liquor (General) Act 1924, s.23(1).

7. record whether the club is the tenant of the premises, or the proprietor and occupier of the premises.

The register is in statutory form and may be inspected on payment of a fee.

Contents of Notice The applicant must provide the following information:

1. state his intention to apply for a certificate of registration;
2. the application should be signed by the chairman or secretary of the club;
3. the name and objects of the club should be specified;
4. the address of the premises to be occupied by the club should be specified.

Documents to be Lodged with District Court Clerk

1. The notice of application. **17–78**
2. Two copies of the rules of the club.
3. A list containing the names and addresses of officials and the committee of management or the governing body.
4. The list containing the names of the members of the club.
5. The statutory peace commissioner's certificate (see Appendix A).

Documentation to be lodged with the County Registrar

1. Notice of application.
2. Plans.
3. Affidavits of service of notice of application on all notice parties.
4. *Daily* newspaper carrying the statutory advertisement.

Notice Parties

1. District Court clerk who notifies the superintendent of the Garda Síochána.[126] **17–79**
2. As a matter of practice, the applicant notifies the superintendent of the Garda Síochána himself.
3. County registrar.

[126] Registration of Clubs (Ireland) Act 1904, s.3, as amended by the Intoxicating Liquor Act 1988, s.44.

4. Fire authority.[127]

As a matter of practice, a copy of the plans and the rules of the club are lodged by the applicant with the superintendent of the Garda Síochána.

Notice Period

1. The fire officer is the only person entitled to a notice period regulated by statute. He is entitled to receive at least one month's notice or a shorter period if agreed between the parties.[128]
2. The District Court clerk is a statutory notice party but the statute does not require that he is notified within a particular specified time limit. However, section 3(10) of the Registration of Clubs (Ireland) Act 1904 provides that objections should be lodged with the registrar within 10 days of receipt or publication of the notice of application. It is clear therefore, that the notice of application should be served on the District Court, in excess of the 10-day period in order to permit the competent objectors to bring objections within the 10-day period.

The practice is to serve all notice parties at least 21 days prior to the date of the hearing of the application. There is no court rule providing for the service of notice in applications for an original certificate of registration.

This failure to specify a period of notice on an application for a new certificate as opposed to renewal may be a *casus omissus* in the statute.

Publication Section 2(1) of the 1904 Act stipulates that the notice of application be published once in a *daily* newspaper circulating in the locality. It is not sufficient to publish in a local weekly newspaper. Again, no statutory time period is provided. The practice is that the notice of application be published 21 days prior to the date of the intended hearing. Care should be taken to ensure that the edition of the newspaper is one that circulates in the locality in which the premises are situate.

2. Renewal of Certificate of Registration

17–80 All applications, except those for an original certificate of registration, are heard and determined by the District Court.[129]

[127] Fire Services Act 1981, s.24
[128] *Ibid.*
[129] Intoxicating Liquor (General) Act 1924, s.23(1).

Venue As a certificate of registration remains in force until the annual licensing District Court next held after the grant of such certificate,[130] the application for renewal takes place at the annual licensing District Court.

Practitioners should note that where a renewal is sought, the current certificate remains in force pending the final decision of the court or for up to three months, whichever is the longer, unless the court, in its discretion, extends such time to a further period not exceeding three months.[131]

Contents of Notice The contents of an application for renewal of a certificate of registration are similar to and must comply with the "same incidents and publication as in the case of an original application for registration".[132] 17–81

Notice Parties

1. District Court clerk.[133]
2. Superintendent of the Garda Síochána.
3. Fire officer.[134]

Notice Period The period of notice on application for the renewal of a certificate of registration is 21 days. Section 2(2) of the 1904 Act provides:

> "The secretary of any club desiring a renewal of the certificate shall, at a date not later than 21 days prior to its expiry, make application to the registrar for such renewal in the same manner and subject to the same incidents and publication as in the case of an original application for registration".

In addition, the fire officer is notified one month in advance.[135]

Publication As in the case of an application for a certificate of registration (see above, paragraph 17–79).

B. Objection

Grant and Renewal of Certificate of Registration

Objections to the grant and renewal of the certificate of registration are regulated by statute. The categories of person entitled to object to the grant or 17–82

---

[130] Registration of Clubs (Ireland) Act 1904, s.3(3), as substituted by the Courts (No. 2) Act 1986, s.9.
[131] Registration of Clubs (Ireland) Act 1904, s.3(5).
[132] *Ibid.*, s.2(2).
[133] *Ibid.*, s.3, as amended by the Intoxicating Liquor Act 1988, s.44.
[134] Fire Services Act 1981, s.24.
[135] *Ibid.*, s.24(1).

renewal of a certificate of registration are different, but competent objectors to both the grant and renewal are obliged to do the following:

1. lodge objections with the registrar of clubs within 10 days of the receipt or publication of the notice of application;
2. at the same time, send a copy of the objections to the secretary of the club.[136]

17–83 **Contents of Notice** There is no statutory provision, but practice suggests that the notice of objection should be signed by the objector or his solicitor and should specify the grounds of objection upon which the objector intends to rely.

Notice Parties

1. The secretary of the applicant club.
2. The registrar of clubs.[137]

Notice Period An objector is obliged to lodge objections with the registrar "within ten days of the receipt or publication or the notice of application". A copy of these objections should be sent to the secretary of the club "at the same time".[138]

8. DECLARATORY JURISDICTION

A. Application

1. Declaratory Order

(a) On-Licence

17–84 This procedure relates to declaratory applications in respect of on-licences, including hotel licences. The declaratory jurisdiction does not apply to special restaurant licences.[139]

17–85 **Venue** All applications are made to the Circuit Court.

---

[136] Registration of Clubs (Ireland) Act 1904, s.3(1) and (2), as substituted by the Intoxicating Liquor Act 1988, s.44.
[137] Registration of Clubs (Ireland) Act 1904, s.3(2).
[138] *Ibid.*
[139] Intoxicating Liquor Act 1988, s.19.

Contents of Notice The applicant must provide the following information:

1. state his intention to apply;
2. his place of abode;
3. he must identify the premises to be acquired, constructed or altered in as much detail as if the application were for a certificate;
4. general practice requires that the procedure stipulated in respect of an application for a certificate should also be followed and the notice of application and copies should be signed by the applicant;
5. the applicant should specify the sitting of the court at which the application is to be made;
6. the Act and section of the Act under which the application is intended to be made, together with the declaratory jurisdiction to be invoked.

Notice Parties

1. Superintendent of the Garda Síochána within whose district it is proposed to locate the premises. It is a statutory requirement that the superintendent of the Garda Síochána be served with a copy of the plans of the premises.[140]
2. There is no statutory requirement to notify the county registrar, but the practice is to notify him 21 days in advance.
3. The District Court judge may be notified but this is not a statutory requirement.
4. There is no statutory requirement to notify the fire authority at declaratory stage, but it is prudent to do so in case it may subsequently require substantial alterations.

Plans The application is accompanied by a plan of the premises.[141] In *Application of Terence J. Maguire*,[142] objection was taken that the plans upon which the applicant based his application in the High Court on appeal had not been deposited with the superintendent as was required by section 15(3)(c) of the Intoxicating Liquor Act 1960. The appeal proceeded on the basis of a set of plans which were different to those lodged with the original application in the Circuit Court, and copies of the plans were sent to the Chief State Solicitor two days before the hearing of the appeal. Murnaghan J. stated: 17–86

[140] Intoxicating Liquor Act 1960, 15(3).
[141] *Ibid.*, s.15(4).
[142] Unreported, High Court, Murnaghan J., April 4, 1963.

> "It is, I think, the common experience in licensing appeals that alterations are made in the original plans as a result of something that transpired at the hearing in the Circuit Court and that amended plans are relied upon in the High Court. The applicant's counsel sought to justify the altered plans in this case by reliance on this practice. The provisions of Section 15(3)(c) are mandatory and failure to deposit with the Superintendent a copy of the plan which is substantially the one relied upon in Court is fatal to the application. The purpose of depositing a copy of the plans with the Superintendent is to enable him to consider the proposed alterations and to assist the Court by objecting to the application in a proper case."

In this case, the judge considered whether the plans lodged with the superintendent were substantially the same as the plans before the High Court. He was satisfied that there were substantial differences. This position may, however, be contrasted with the position relating to an application for a certificate. The requirement to deposit plans in these applications is not statutory but it is required by the rules.[143]

17–87 **Notice Period** 21 days' notice in writing of intention to make the application.[144]

Publication The applicant should insert notice of intention to make the application "at least 21 days before the making of the intended application, in a newspaper circulating in the place in which it is proposed to have the premises".[145]

Proofs The applicant must produce the following:

1. notice of application;
2. affidavits of service of notice of application on all notice parties;
3. plans;
4. newspaper carrying the statutory advertisement;
5. evidence of title, where required;
6. proofs required by the statutory provision grounding jurisdiction.

(b) Off-Licences

17–88 **Venue** The application is made to the District Court in the area within which the premises are situate.

143 Circuit Court Rules 1950, Ord. 42, r. 8: "on the hearing of the application, the applicant shall produce a map or plan of the premises".
144 Intoxicating Liquor Act 1960, s.15(3)(b).
145 *Ibid.*, s.15(3)(a).

Contents of Notice As the application is for a declaration that the proposed premises are fit and convenient to be licensed, the applicant must provide the following information:

1. state his intention to apply;
2. his place of abode;
3. he must identify the premises to be acquired, constructed or altered in as much detail as if the application were for a certificate;
4. the notice of application and copies should be signed by the applicant;
5. the sitting of the court at which the application is to be made should be specified;
6. the Act and section of the Act under which the application is intended to be made, together with the declaratory jurisdiction to be invoked.

Notice Parties

1. Superintendent of the Garda Síochána within whose district the proposed premises are/will be situate.[146] The superintendent, as in the case for an on-licence, should be served with a copy of the plans. 17–89
2. There is no statutory requirement to notify the District Court clerk, but he is notified as a matter of practice.

There is *no* requirement to notify the fire officer.

Notice Period 21 days' notice in writing of intention to make the application.

Publication The application is advertised at least 21 days before the making of the intended application, in a newspaper circulating in the place in which the proposed premises are/will be situate.[147]

Proofs The applicant must produce the following:

1. notice of application;
2. affidavits of service of the notice of application on all notice parties;
3. plans of the proposed premises;
4. newspaper carrying the statutory advertisement;

[146] See above, n.140.
[147] Intoxicating Liquor Act 1960, s.15(3)(a).

5. evidence of title;
6. proofs required by the section grounding jurisdiction.

(c) Application to Extend Duration

17–90 The Intoxicating Liquor Act 1960, section 15(6), provides that a declaratory order shall remain in force "for two years from the grant of the application or for such longer period as the Court granting the application may in any particular case think proper to provide". A practice has grown up of making an application to extend the duration of the declaratory order where the premises have not been built within the time provided for by the court granting the declaratory application. Reference to a declaratory order is deemed to be a reference to "declarations which are in force".[148]

An attempt was made recently to extend the duration of a declaratory order after the expiry of the time granted by the court making the declaratory order. This application, which was made in the Circuit Court in Naas, failed before Judge Smith, who held that such an application should be made during the pendency of the declaratory order and prior to its expiry.[149]

17–91 **Venue** That court which granted the application for the declaratory order. Accordingly, if an application for a declaratory order fails before the Circuit Court but is successful on appeal to the High Court, the application for the extension of its duration will be made in the High Court.

Contents of Notice The notice should be in the form of a notice of motion grounded upon an affidavit of the applicant or his architect explaining the reasons for the failure to complete the construction or alteration within the time provided for by the court. The affidavit should refer to or exhibit the declaratory order and should deal with the proposed completion date of the building.

Notice Parties The Garda Síochána and the county registrar or District Court clerk, as appropriate.

Notice Period Four clear days between the service of the notice of motion and the day named in the notice for hearing of the motion.[150]

Publication There is no requirement to publish this application.

---

148 *Ibid.*, s.17(6).
149 *Application of Bresc Inns Ltd* Circuit Court, Judge Smith, February 25, 1995.
150 Circuit Court Rules 1950, Ord. 51, r. 2.

Proofs The applicant must produce the following:

1. notice of motion;
2. affidavits of service of notice of motion;
3. affidavit grounding application and exhibiting or referring to declaratory order.

(d) Clubs

This is an application for a declaration that proposed premises would be suitable for the grant or renewal of a certificate of registration and for a declaration that the number of registered clubs of similar character which have premises in the same district would not be such as to require the refusal of the application. 17–92

Venue

1. The Circuit Court where the application is for a declaratory order leading to the grant of an original certificate of registration. 17–93
2. The District Court where the application is for a declaratory order leading to the renewal of the certificate of registration.

Section 15(2) of the 1960 Act confers jurisdiction on the District Court to approve plans of premises proposed to be acquired, constructed or altered by an existing registered club. In practice where minor alterations are contemplated by an existing registered club in respect of its premises which are already the subject of a certificate of registration, such application is made to the District Court at renewal stage. However, where substantial alterations are contemplated or where the club proposes to acquire or construct an alternative premises, the practice is to make the application to the Circuit Court.

Contents of Notice The secretary of the club should provide the following information in the notice of application: 17–94

1. state his intention to apply;
2. state whether or not the club is an existing registered club,;
3. the place of abode of the secretary;
4. the club premises to be acquired, constructed and/or altered should be described and identified in detail;
5. the name and objects of the club should be clearly identified;
6. the notice of application should be signed by the secretary;
7. the sitting of the court at which the application is to be made must be identified;

8. the sections grounding jurisdiction under the Registration of Clubs Acts 1904 to 1995, together with the declaratory jurisdiction, should be invoked.

Notice Parties

1. The District Court clerk is notified in his capacity as registrar of clubs.
2. The county registrar is notified at least 21 clear days in advance of the making of the application. There is no statutory provision requiring such notification but he is invariably notified.
3. The superintendent of the Garda Síochána within whose district it is proposed that the premises are/will be situate.[151]

The fire officer is *not* a statutory notice party, but as a matter of practice he is notified.

17–95 **Accompanying Documentation** As the application is for an order pursuant to the provisions of section 15(2) of the 1960 Act, it is not necessary to lodge the documentation required prior to the grant of a certificate of registration. The court, however, in the case of an objection may require evidence that the club or the proposed club is a bona fide club and that it has or will have sufficient members as required by the registration of clubs code.

Notice Period 21 days' notice in writing of intention to make the application.[152]

Publication 21 days before the making of the intended application in a newspaper circulating in the place within which it is proposed to locate the premises.[153]

Proofs The applicant must produce the following:

1. notice of application;
2. affidavits of service of notice;
3. plans;
4. newspaper carrying the statutory advertisement;

The 1960 Act does not require the club or proposed club to prove an estate or interest in the proposed premises or that it has an agreement in relation to same. This can be contrasted with an application under section 15(1) of the 1960 Act. However, a court may make the declaratory order subject to the condition that at certificate stage the club would be in a position to show that it is owner or tenant of the club house or has club premises.

---

[151] Intoxicating Liquor Act 1960, s.15(3)(b).
[152] *Ibid.*
[153] *Ibid.*

(e) Restaurants

The declaratory jurisdiction does not apply to special restaurant licences.[154] However, Section 16 of the Intoxicating Liquor Act 1960 provides for the grant of a declaration as to the suitability of licensed premises for a full restaurant certificate and a limited restaurant certificate. 17–96

Full Restaurant Certificate and Limited Restaurant Certificate

Venue The court to which it is proposed to apply for a grant of the restaurant certificate or the limited restaurant certificate.

Contents of Notice The applicant should provide the following information: 17–97

1. state his intention to apply;
2. his place of abode;
3. he should identify in detail the premises to be acquired, constructed or altered;
4. he should identify the sitting of the court at which it is intended to make the application;
5. he should specify the type of restaurant certificate which he requires;
6. he should specify, where he is seeking a limited restaurant certificate, the portion of the premises to which the certificate is to apply.

Notice Parties

1. The superintendent of the Garda Síochána within whose district it is proposed to locate the premises.[155] 17–98
2. County registrar or District Court clerk, as the case may be. This is not a statutory requirement but it is the practice to do so.

There is *no* requirement to notify the fire authority.

Notice Period

1. Ten days' notice in writing of the intention to make the application should be given to the superintendent of the Garda Síochána.
2. The other notice parties should, as a matter of convenience, be given similar notice of the making of the application.

---

[154] Intoxicating Liquor Act 1988, s.19.
[155] Intoxicating Liquor Act 1960, s.16(3).

Plans The application is accompanied by a plan of the premises.[156]

Publication There is no requirement to publish this application.

Proofs The applicant must produce the following:

1. notice of application;
2. affidavits of services of notice of application on all notice parties;
3. plans.

B. Objection

17–99 Section 15 of the Intoxicating Liquor Act 1960 provides for the making of objections "in like manner" to an application for the grant of a certificate entitling the applicant to receive a licence and an application for a certificate of registration and an application for a restaurant certificate. As in the case of an application for a restaurant certificate, the only notice party in a section 16 application is the superintendent of the Garda Síochána: there is no statutory provision for objection. Section 15(5) of the Intoxicating Liquor Act 1960 provides for objections as follows:

1. any person who would be entitled to object to an application for the grant of a certificate entitling the applicant to receive a licence in respect of the premises shall be entitled to object in like manner to an application for a declaratory order;
2. any person who would be entitled to object to an application for the grant or renewal of a certificate of registration under the Registration of Clubs (Ireland) Act 1904 applicable to the premises shall be entitled to object in like manner to an application for a declaratory order;

Thus, the procedures regulating objections to the grant of an on-licence, the grant or renewal of a certificate of registration and the grant of a restaurant certificate apply in relation to objections to the grant of a declaratory order.

2. Grant of Certificates where a Declaratory Order has already been made

17–100 Where an applicant seeks a certificate leading to the grant of an on-licence, off-licence, a full restaurant certificate or a limited restaurant certificate, or a

[156] Intoxicating Liquor Act 1960, s.16(4).

certificate of registration in respect of a club premises and has already obtained a declaratory order as provided for under any of the declaratory jurisdictions above mentioned, he must, in addition to the necessary jurisdictional proofs, prove at certificate stage that the declaratory order was made and that the premises have been acquired, constructed and/or altered in substantial accordance with the terms of the declaration. He must also show that the application for the certificate has been made within the period stipulated by the court granting the declaratory order.

9. PUBLIC DANCING LICENCES

A. Application

1. Grant of Temporary Dancing Licence[157]

Venue Any sitting of the District Court for the court area in which the premises are situate.[158] **17–101**

Contents of Notice The following details should be included in the notice of application:

1. the applicant's name;
2. his place of residence;
3. the address of the premises the subject of the application;
4. the sitting of the court at which the application is to be made;
5. the period for which the licence is sought;
6. the place to which the application relates;
7. whether or not the premises are licensed for the sale of intoxicating liquor.

Notice Parties

1. Fire officer.[159] **17–102**
2. Superintendent within whose district the place to which the application relates is situate.[160]
3. District Court clerk.[161]

---

[157] *i.e.* licence not exceeding one month.
[158] District Court Rules 1948, r. 108(2).
[159] Fire Services Act 1981, s.24.
[160] Public Dance Halls Act 1935, s.3.
[161] District Court Rules 1948, r. 12.

Notice Period

1. The fire authority should receive one month's notice or such shorter period as may be agreed between the parties.
2. The superintendent of the Garda Síochána should receive 48 hours' notice.[162]
3. The District Court clerk should receive 48 hours' notice of the making of the application.[163]

Publication There is *no* requirement to publish this application.

Proofs The applicant must produce the following:

1. notice of application;
2. affidavits of service of notice of application on all notice parties;
3. certificate of public liability insurance;
4. a plan of the premises may be required to identify the area which is the subject of the application.

2. Grant of Annual Public Dancing Licence

Venue

17–103 1. Any sitting of the District Court for the court area in which the premises are situate where no such licence is already in existence.
2. At the annual licensing District Court and at no other time where an annual public dancing licence exists in relation to the premises.[164]

Contents of Notice The applicant should provide the following information:

1. his name;
2. his place of residence;
3. the address of the premises;
4. the sitting of the court at which the application is to be made;
5. the portion/portions of the premises intended for public dancing;
5. whether or not the premises are licensed for the sale of intoxicating liquor.

---

162 Public Dance Halls Act 1935, s.3.
163 District Court Rules 1948, r. 12.
164 Public Dance Halls Act 1935, s.2(4).

Notice Parties

1. Fire officer.[165] 17–104
2. Local authority for the area within which the place for which the licence sought is situate.[166]
3. Superintendent within whose district the place to which the application relates is situate.[167]
4. District Court clerk of the court area within which the premises are situate.[168]

Notice Period

1. Fire officer: one month's notice or such shorter period as may be agreed with the authority.[169]
2. Local authority: at least one month's notice in writing.[170]
3. Garda superintendent: at least one month's notice in writing.[171]
4. District Court clerk: 48 hours' notice of the making of the application.[172]

Publication The notice of application should be published in a newspaper circulating in the district in which the place to which such application relates is situate, at least one month before the hearing of the application.[173] 17–105

Proofs The applicant must produce the following:

1. notice of application;
2. affidavits of service of notice of application on all notice parties;
3. plans: the place to which the application refers should be identified with a coloured verge line;
4. newspaper carrying the statutory advertisement;
5. certificate of public liability insurance;
6. evidence of consent of fire officer to the application. This is not a statutory requirement but in practice the court insists on such evidence.

---

165 Fire Services Act 1981, s.24.
166 Public Dance Halls Act 1935, s.3(2)(b).
167 *Ibid.*
168 District Court Rules 1948, r. 12.
169 Fire Services Act 1981, s.24.
170 Public Dance Halls Act 1935, s.3(2)(b).
171 *Ibid.*
172 District Court Rules 1948, r. 12.
173 Public Dance Halls Act 1935, s.3(1).

3. Renewal[174]

17–106 **Venue** Annual licensing District Court and at no other time.[175]

4. Transfer

17–107 A public dancing licence is not transferable from the licensee to another person. An application for a public dancing licence by a new applicant, with the consent of the existing licensee, may be made at any time.[176]

Venue Any sitting of the District Court. There are no statutory requirements as to procedure: but if the application is for the grant of a licence exceeding one month, then the procedural regulations for the application for an annual public dancing licence apply.

B. Objection

Grant and Renewal

17–108 There is no statutory provision regulating the form of objections to applications for the grant of public dancing licences. In practice, any member of the Garda Síochána or any person who appears to the judge during the hearing of the application to be interested may appear and is heard in opposition.

10. MUSIC AND SINGING LICENCES

A. Application

1. Grant of Temporary Music and Singing Licence[177]

17–109 **Venue** Any sitting of the District Court for the court area within which the premises is situate.[178]

---

174 The application is in fact for a new public dancing licence.
175 Public Dance Halls Act 1935, s.2(4), and District Court Rules 1948, r. 108(1).
176 Public Dance Halls Act 1935, s.8(2).
177 Not exceeding 14 days.
178 District Court Rules 1948, r. 108(2).

Contents of Notice The applicant should provide the following information:

1. his name;
2. his place of residence;
3. the address of the premises, and the place to which the application relates;
4. the sitting of the court at which the application is to be made;
5. the period for which the licence is sought;
6. whether or not the premises are licensed for the sale of intoxicating liquor.

Notice Parties

1. Fire officer.[179] **17–110**
2. District Court clerk.[180]

There is no statutory requirement to notify the Garda Síochána, but in practice they are notified.

Notice Period

1. The fire officer receives one month's notice or such shorter period as may be agreed with him.[181]
2. The District Court clerk should receive at least 48 hours' notice.[182]

Publication There is no requirement to publish this application.

2. Grant of Annual Music and Singing Licence

Venue An application for the grant of the music and singing licence may be made at the annual licensing sessions, or any adjournment thereof or any special session convened with 14 days previous notice.[183] **17–111**

Contents of Notice The applicant should specify the following:

1. his name;
2. his place of residence;

---

[179] Fire Services Act 1981, s.24.
[180] District Court Rules 1948, rr. 12 and 108(3).
[181] Fire Services Act 1981, s.24.
[182] District Court Rules 1948, rr. 12 and 108(3).
[183] Public Health Acts Amendment Act 1890, s.51(2) and (11), and District Court Rules 1948, r. 108.

3. the address of the premises;
4. the place to which the application relates should be identified;
5. the sitting of the court at which the application is to be made;
6. whether or not the premises are licensed for the sale of intoxicating liquor.

Notice Parties

1. Fire officer.[184]
2. Superintendent of the Garda Síochána.[185]
3. District Court clerk.[186]

Notice Period

17–112 1. The fire officer: one month's notice or such shorter period as may be agreed between the parties.[187]
2. Superintendent of the Garda Síochána: 14 days.[188]
3. District Court clerk: 14 days before the date of the hearing of the application.[189]

Publication There is no requirement to publish this application.

Proofs The applicant must produce the following:

1. the notice of application;
2. affidavits of service of the notice of application on all notice parties;
3. plans of the premises specifying the place for which the licence is sought;
4. some courts require production of a certificate of public liability insurance: it is prudent for practitioners to check with the appropriate District Court clerk.

---

184 Fire Services Act 1981, s.24.
185 Public Health Acts Amendment Act 1890, s.51(4).
186 *Ibid.*
187 Fire Services Act 1981, s.24.
188 Public Health Acts Amendment Act 1890, s.51(4).
189 *Ibid.*

Renewal

The licence expires, as a matter of practice, at each annual licensing sessions although section 51 of the Public Health Acts Amendment 1890 provides that every licence shall be in force for one year or for such shorter period as the judge on the grant of the licence shall determine, unless the same shall have been previously revoked. Practitioners should note that the usual form of licence issued by the District Court clerk has, as one of the conditions, that the licence remains in force until the next annual licensing sessions. The application to renew is made at the annual licensing sessions and the procedural requirements which relate to the grant of an annual music and singing licence apply. **17–113**

Transfer

Section 51(3) of the 1890 Act empowers a District Court judge "from time to time" to "transfer any such licence to such persons as he thinks fit". **17–114**

The procedural requirements relating to the grant of a licence other than a temporary music and singing licence apply, although it is questionable as to whether the fire officer is a notice party at transfer stage.

B. Objection

As with objections to public dancing licences, there are no procedural requirements regulating objections to the grant, transfer and renewal of music and singing licences. **17–115**

11. SPECIAL EXEMPTION ORDER

Venue The District Court.[190] An application can be made to any judge of the District Court for a special exemption order. **17–116**

Notice of Application The applicant should provide the following information:

1. his name;
2. his place of residence;

[190] Intoxicating Liquor Act 1927, s.5(1).

3. identify the place to which the application relates;
4. the occasion for which the special exemption order is sought;
5. the times during which the special occasion is to take place and, in particular, the prohibited hours from which the applicant seeks the exemption.

Notice Parties

17–117 1. The officer in charge of the Garda Síochána.[191]

2. The District Court clerk.[192]

Notice Period

1. The Garda Síochána should receive notice "not less than 48 hours before the making of the application".[193]
2. The District Court clerk should receive 48 hours' notice.[194]

The fire officer is *not* a notice party.

Publication There is no requirement to publish this application.

Proofs The applicant must produce the following:

1. notice of application;
2. affidavits of service of the notice of application on all notice parties.

12. OCCASIONAL LICENCE

17–118 **Venue** The application is made to the judge of the District Court.[195]

Notice of Application The applicant should provide the following information:

1. the applicant's name;
2. his place of residence;
3. that he is the holder of an on-licence;

---

191 Intoxicating Liquor Act 1927, s.5(4).
192 District Court Rules 1948, r. 12.
193 Intoxicating Liquor Act 1927, s.5(4).
194 District Court Rules 1948, r. 12.
195 Intoxicating Liquor Act 1962, s.11(1).

4. identify the premises to which the on-licence attaches;
5. identify the unlicensed place which is the subject of the application;
6. identify the special event to which the application relates;
7. specify the times and, where relevant, the days during which the applicant requires to sell intoxicating liquor.

Notice Parties

1. The officer in charge of the Garda Síochána should receive a notice in writing of the applicant's intention to make the application, setting out the applicant's name and address, and the place, occasion and time for which the occasional licence to which the application relates is required.[196]
2. The District Court clerk.[197]

The fire officer is *not* a statutory notice party but the practice is to notify him.

Notice Period

1. Garda Síochána: not less than 48 hours before the making of the application.[198] **17–119**
2. District Court clerk: at least 48 hours' notice of the making of the application.[199]

Some District Court judges require as a matter of practice that the fire officer be notified of the making of the application. This is not a statutory requirement but it is becoming a rule of practice; practitioners should check with the appropriate District Court clerk.

Publication There is no requirement to publish this application.

Proofs The application must produce the following:

1. notice of application;
2. affidavits of service of notice of application on all notice parties;
3. evidence that the applicant is the holder of an on-licence;
4. evidence that the event is a "special event".

---

[196] Intoxicating Liquor Act 1962, s.11(7).
[197] District Court Rules 1948, r. 12.
[198] Intoxicating Liquor Act 1962, s.11(7).
[199] District Court Rules 1948, r. 12.

13. AREA EXEMPTION ORDER

17–120 **Venue** The District Court.[200]

Contents of Notice The applicant should provide the following information:

1. his name;
2. his address;
3. the address of the premises in respect of which he is the holder of a licence;
4. the special event or events the subject of the application;
5. the locality in which, or near which, the special event is to take place;
6. the time during which the order is sought;
7. the section grounding jurisdiction pursuant to which the application is being made.

Notice Parties

1. The officer in charge of the Garda Síochána for the locality to which the application relates.[201]
2. The District Court clerk.[202]

The fire officer is *not* a statutory notice party.

Notice Period

17–121 1. The Garda Síochána should receive at least seven days' notice.[203]
2. The District Court clerk should receive 48 hours' notice.[204]

Publication The notice of application should be published in a newspaper circulating in the locality, not less than seven days before the date on which the application is proposed to be made.[205]

---

[200] Intoxicating Liquor Act 1962, s.10(1).
[201] *Ibid.*, s.10(3).
[202] District Court Rules 1948, r. 12.
[203] See above, n.201.
[204] District Court Rules 1948, r. 12.
[205] Intoxicating Liquor Act 1962, s.10(3).

Proofs The applicant must produce the following:

1. notice of application;
2. affidavits of service of notice of application on all notice parties;
3. evidence of approval of a majority of the holders of licences in the locality;
4. evidence that the event is a special event;
5. newspaper carrying the statutory advertisement;
6. evidence that the applicant is the holder of a licence;
7. evidence that his premises are not situate in the County Borough of Dublin.

14. GENERAL EXEMPTION ORDER

Venue The District Court.[206] **17–122**

Contents of Notice The applicant should provide the following information:

1. his name;
2. his address;
3. identify the premises to which the applicant's on-licence attaches;
4. identify the location of the public market or fair or the place where persons follow a lawful trade or calling;
5. identify the time for which the order is sought;
6. the section grounding jurisdiction pursuant to which the application is being made.

Notice Parties

1. The officer in charge of the Garda Síochána for the licensing area.[207] **17–123**
2. The District Court clerk.[208]

The fire officer is *not* a statutory notice party.

---

[206] Intoxicating Liquor Act 1927, s.4(1).
[207] *Ibid.*, s.4(8).
[208] District Court Rules 1948, r. 12.

Notice Period

1. Garda Síochána: at least one week before the making of the application.[209]
2. District Court clerk: 48 hours before the making of the application.[210]

Publication There is no requirement to publish this application.

Proofs The applicant must produce the following:

1. notice of application;
2. affidavits of service of notice of application on all notice parties;
3. evidence that the applicant is the holder of an on-licence.

15. EXEMPTIONS for licensed business on SUNDAY AFTERNOONS and the AFTERNOONS of ST. PATRICK'S DAY

17–124 **Venue** The District Court.[211]

Contents of Notice The applicant should provide the following information:

1. his name;
2. his address;
3. the premises to which his on-licence attaches;
4. state that the premises are not situate in a county or other borough;
5. that the application has the approval of a majority of the holders of licences in respect of premises situate in the locality;
6. the applicant should identify the holders of licences situate in the locality;
7. the section grounding jurisdiction pursuant to which the application is being made;
8. the time and date to which the application relates.

---

[209] Intoxicating Liquor Act 1927, s.4(8).
[210] District Court Rules 1948, r. 12.
[211] Intoxicating Liquor Act 1962, s.16(1).

Notice Parties

1. Officer in charge of the Garda Síochána for the locality to which the application relates.[212] 17–125
2. District Court clerk.[213]

There is *no* statutory requirement to notify the fire officer.

Notice Period

1. The Garda Síochána should receive at least 10 days' notice in writing before the date on which the application is intended to be made.[214]
2. The District Court clerk receives 48 hours' notice of the making of the intended application.[215]

Publication The notice of application should be published in a newspaper circulating in the locality not less than seven days before the date on which the application is proposed to be made.[216]

Proofs The applicant must produce the following:

1. notice of application;
2. affidavits of service of notice of application on all notice parties;
3. newspaper carrying the statutory advertisement;
4. evidence that the applicant is the holder of a licence (but not a six-day licence);
5. evidence that the locality is not a county or other borough;
6. evidence of approval of a majority of licence holders in the locality.

16. EXEMPTIONS for unlicensed business on SUNDAY MORNINGS and the mornings of ST PATRICK'S DAY

Venue The District Court.[217] 17–126

---

[212] *Ibid.*, s.16(7).
[213] District Court Rules 1948, r. 12.
[214] Intoxicating Liquor Act 1962, s.16(7).
[215] District Court Rules 1948, r. 12.
[216] Intoxicating Liquor Act 1962, s.16(7).
[217] *Ibid.*, s.17(1).

Contents of Notice The applicant must provide the following information:

1. his name;
2. his address;
3. the premises to which his licence attaches;
4. state that the premises are not situate in a county or other borough;
5. state that the application has the approval of a majority of the holders of such licences in respect of premises situate in the locality;
6. identify these licences;
7. the section grounding jurisdiction pursuant to which the application is brought;
8. the time and date to which the application relates.

Notice Parties

17–127

1. Officer in charge of the Garda Síochána for the locality to which the application relates.[218]
2. District Court clerk.[219]

The fire officer is *not* a statutory notice party.

Notice Period

1. Garda Síochána: at least 10 days' notice.[220]
2. District Court clerk: 48 hours' notice.[221]

Publication The notice of application must be published in a newspaper circulating in the locality not less than seven days before the date on which it is proposed to make the application.[222]

Proofs The applicant must produce the following:

1. notice of application;
2. affidavits of service of notice of application on all the notice parties;
3. newspaper carrying the statutory advertisement;

---

218 *Ibid.*, s.17(7).
219 District Court Rules 1948, r. 12.
220 Intoxicating Liquor Act 1962, s.17(7).
221 District Court Rules 1948, r. 12.
222 Intoxicating Liquor Act 1962, s.17(7).

4. evidence that the applicant is the holder of a licence (other than a hotel licence);
5. evidence that the locality is not situate in a county or other borough;
6. evidence of approval of a majority of the holders of licences in respect of premises situate in the locality.

17. CLUB AUTHORISATION

Venue The District Court.[223] 17–128

Contents of Notice The secretary of the club should include the following details in the notice of application:

1. his name;
2. his address;
3. the name of the club and its address;
4. the period for which the order is sought;
5. the notice of application may include details of the club function to which the authorisation relates, but this is not a statutory requirement;
5. the number of authorisations already granted to the club during the year.

Notice Parties There is no statutory provision for notification of any party: however, the District Court Rules 1948 require notification of the following persons:

1. Garda superintendent in charge of the district where the club is situate.[224]
2. District Court clerk.[225]

The fire officer is *not* a statutory notice party.

Notice Period

1. Garda Síochána: at least 48 hours before the making of the application.[226]
2. District Court clerk: at least 48 hours before the making of the application.[227]

---

[223] Intoxicating Liquor (General) Act, 1924, s.21.
[224] District Court Rules 1948, r. 109(2)
[225] *Ibid.*, r. 12.
[226] *Ibid.*, r. 109(2).
[227] *Ibid.*, r. 12.

Publication There is no requirement to publish the notice of application.

Proofs The applicant must produce the following:

1. notice of application;
2. affidavits of service of notice of application on all the notice parties

18. AUTHORISATION for SPECIAL EVENT in SPORTS CLUB

17–129 **Venue** The District Court.[228]

Contents of Notice The secretary of the registered club should specify the following:

1. his name;
2. his address;
3. the objects of the club;
4. the address of the club;
5. the period to which the order is to relate;
6. the special event in the club which is likely to attract a considerable number of people.

17–130 **Notice Parties** There is no statutory provision for notification of any party: in practice the following parties are notified.

1. District Court clerk[229];
2. Garda Síochána are sometimes notified but there is no statutory obligation to do so.

The fire officer is *not* a statutory notice party.

Notice Period District Court clerk: 48 hours.[230]

Publication There is no requirement to publish this application.

---

[228] Intoxicating Liquor Act, 1962, s.14(1).
[229] District Court Rules 1948, r. 12.
[230] *Ibid.*

Proofs The applicant must produce the following:

1. notice of application;
2. affidavits of service of notice of application on all notice parties.

19. FESTIVAL CLUB

This application will either be for a special exemption order, where the premises to which the application relates is a licensed premises, or an occasional licence, where the premises to which the application relates is not a licensed premises. The procedure in respect of both types of applications is dealt with above, at paragraphs 17–116 to 17–119. **17–131**

20. THEATRES

1. Theatre with Patent

Pursuant to the provisions of the Dublin Theatres Act 1786, a theatre cannot operate without a royal patent, now given by the Department of An Taoiseach. The last patent which issued in respect of a theatre was for the Gate Theatre in the 1950s. Each patent must be renewed every 21 years. The procedure for any new theatre wishing to apply for a patent appears to be redundant as the Department of An Taoiseach is not issuing new patents for theatres. **17–132**

2. Theatre: Places of Public Entertainment

Since the early 1990s, the Revenue Commissioners have been issuing theatre licences in respect of certain unpatented premises. These premises have the benefit of a music and singing licence granted pursuant to the provisions of section 51 of the Public Health Acts Amendment Act 1890, obtained in the District Court. The decision as to whether or not a theatre licence will issue is made by the Revenue Commissioners. The procedure is for an officer of Customs and Excise to visit the premises: the Revenue Commissioners also consult with the Arts Council in deciding whether to issue the licence. **17–133**

CHAPTER 18

TRANSFER

Introduction

18–1 A licence to sell intoxicating liquor cannot simply be transferred by the holder thereof to another person: the transfer of a licence can be effected only by an order of the court. The endorsement of a licence by the named licensee, or a purported transfer of the licence by conveyance or deed, will not effect a valid transfer. The licensing code provides for the temporary transfer of a licence by endorsement thereon, by order of the court. A certificate of transfer resulting in the grant of a licence by the Revenue Commissioners to a person other than the previous holder of the licence must also be made by order of the court.

Where the licensee sells or assigns his interest in the premises to another, the purchaser or assignee must thereupon apply to the court for an order permitting him to trade. If this application is made during the currency of the licence, the District Court will grant a temporary transfer of the licence to such person by marking the statutory form of endorsement on the back of the licence. An application for a certificate of transfer is then made at the annual licensing sessions.

18–2 The proposed transferee must be in possession of the premises to which the licence attaches. In *R. (Cox) v. Recorder of Dublin*, Fitzgibbon L.J. stated:

> "I hold it an essential condition to the grant of a licence that the person to be licensed should be, *de facto* and *de jure*, upon receiving his licence, entitled to the possession of the premises, and ready to carry on the business there, then, and thenceforward."[1]

Where a licensee transfers the lowest estate in the licensed premises to another, the licence becomes inoperable until either the licence is transferred to the purchaser or assignee by order of a court of competent jurisdiction, or the licensee resumes legal possession and occupation of the licensed premises.

It has long been an established principle of the licensing code that there is no property in a licence separate from the premises to which the licence attaches.[2] A licence, therefore, cannot be transferred from one premises to another. In *Murphy v. Crean* Palles C.B. stated:

> "There is not in the whole licensing code any provision for the transfer of a licence from one house to another house."[3]

The District Court is the court of first instance in all applications for the transfer of an intoxicating liquor licence. There are two main classes of transfer: **18–3**

1. an ad interim or temporary transfer which is endorsed by a District Court judge on the back of a licence and which gives the transferee temporary authority to trade until the next annual licensing sessions;
2. a certificate of transfer whereby the District Court judge, at the annual licensing sessions, grants a certificate entitling the transferee to the grant of a licence in his own name for the full licensing year up until the following September 30. This certificate of transfer is sometimes referred to as a "confirmation" of transfer.[4]

The grant of an ad interim transfer is not a condition precedent to the grant of a certificate of transfer: the authority to trade, however, can derive only from an order of the court.

Gibson J. in *R. (Duggan) v. Fermanagh Justices* stated:

> ". . . the possession of a licence [*i.e.* grant by virtue of an ad interim transfer] . . . does not constitute any necessary part of the assignee's right to apply for a full licence at Licensing Sessions."[5]

An application for the transfer of a licence cannot succeed unless that licence is an existing licence. In *Murphy v. Crean*, Palles C.B. stated: **18–4**

[1] [1885–86] 16 L.R.I. 424 at 438. See also *Re M'Fadden* (1904) 38 I.L.T.R. 264.
[2] *Kelly v. Montague* [1892–93] 29 L.R.I. 429.
[3] [1915] I.R. 111 at 142.
[4] District Court Rules 1948, r. 100 (S.I. No. 431 of 1947).
[5] [1909] 2 I.R. 132 at 160.

"If the house in which it is desired to carry on a publican's business be not licensed in the then current year, the application must be for an original licence. . . ".[6]

A licence which has lapsed cannot be transferred; the correct application is for a new licence. In *R. (Slevin) v. Longford Justices*[7] Samuels J. held that there was no jurisdiction to grant a transfer after a licence had ceased to exist.[8] In *R. (O'Connor) v. Recorder of Dublin*, May L.C.J. stated:

"Upon these enactments it is clear that a transfer could only be made of an existing licence. The transferee being thereby enabled to carry on the business of his predecessor until the expiration of that license and no longer. The endorsement to be made by justices at petty sessions or by a divisional justice in Dublin could only be made upon a licence during the current year of its existence and not upon a licence which was expired; and, therefore, it seems manifest that the divisional justice was right in declining to make the endorsement required."[9]

18–5 Section 115 of the Finance Act 1995 provides for the continuation in force of the licence beyond its latest expiry date where a licence has been granted in respect of the previous licensing period, in circumstances where an application has been made for a tax clearance certificate, or where the application has been refused and an appeal has been lodged. The continuation in force of the licence is conditional upon the payment of the appropriate excise duty. As the licence is deemed to be in force once these conditions have been satisfied, there is no reason why the court cannot grant a transfer of such licence to another person.

A. Ad Interim Transfer

Temporary Authority to Trade

18–6 Where a person purchases or takes a lease of a licensed premises, intending to sell excisable liquor therein, he must take immediate steps to acquire statutory authority to trade. He cannot apply for a licence in his own name by means of a certificate of transfer from the existing licensee to himself until the annual licensing sessions. The legislature, therefore, provided the statutory machinery whereby the magistrates, now the judge of the District Court, could, by endorsement thereon, temporarily transfer the vendor's or former licensee's licence to the person now in possession, giving him temporary authority to trade

[6] Above, n.3, at 142.
[7] [1923] 2 I.R. 79.
[8] The judgment of the King's Bench Division was upheld by the Court of Appeal.
[9] (1879) 13 I.L.T.R. 141 at 142.

until the next licensing sessions immediately following the expiration of one month from the date of the order. This type of order is generally described as an ad interim transfer.

The Public House (Ireland) Act 1855, which is also known as the Transfer of Licences (Ireland) Act 1855, provides for the temporary transfer of a licence within the licensing year in certain circumstances.[10] The statute had applied only to on-licences but by virtue of section 29 of the Intoxicating Liquor Act 1960, the provisions of the 1855 Act now apply to off-licences for the grant of which a certificate of the court is required.[11]

STATUTORY PROVISION

Section 1 of the Public House (Ireland) Act 1855 provides: **18–7**

> "1. Upon the Death of any Person duly licensed to carry on the Business of a Licensed Victualler, and to sell Excisable Liquors by Retail, to be consumed on the Premises, in *Ireland*, or upon the Removal of any such Person from the House or Premises at which he is authorized by any such Licence to carry on such Business as aforesaid in *Ireland*, or the Sale of or Assignment of his Interest therein by Operation of Law or otherwise, it shall be lawful for the Justices of the Peace of the District within which any such licensed House or Premises shall be situated, assembled at Petty Sessions, or the Justices in any Liberty, City, Town, or Place within which any such licensed House or Premises shall be situated, assembled at Petty Sessions, at any Time when no Quarter Sessions shall be holden for any such County, Riding, Division, Liberty, City, Town, or Place, (if they shall think proper so to do, after examining upon Oath all necessary Parties) to transfer, by Endorsement thereon, any and every such Licence as aforesaid then in force, to any Person, not disqualified by Law, to whom it shall be proposed at the Time of such Application to transfer any such Licence, to use, exercise, and carry on the Business of a Licensed Victualler at the same House and on the same Premises, and there to sell such Exciseable Liquors as might theretofore have been lawfully sold and retailed therein; and thereupon it shall be lawful for such Person so to use, exercise, and carry on the said Business of such House and Premises, until the Quarter Sessions of the Peace which shall be holden of such same County, Riding, Division, Liberty, City, Town, or Place next after the Expiration of One Calendar Month from the Time of such Transfer, and no longer."

Rules 97, 98 and 99 of the District Court Rules 1948 provide for the circumstances in which an ad interim transfer can be granted and the procedure which an applicant must follow.

---

[10] See *per* Finlay C.J. in *Fitzpatrick v. McCormack* [1986] I.R. 380 at 385.

[11] Intoxicating Liquor Act 1960, s.29, provides as follows: "the provisions of section 1 (which relates to the interim transfer of licences by the court) of the Public House (Ireland) Act 1855, shall apply in relation to off-licences for the grant of which the production of a certificate of the Court is required".

Although rule 97(1), of the District Court Rules 1948 derives from section 1 of the Act of 1855, it expands on the category of contingencies in which an application for a temporary transfer may be made to include "the incapacity of any person duly licensed to sell intoxicating liquors".

An application for an ad interim transfer can only be made in the following circumstances:

(a) upon the death of a person duly licensed to sell excisable liquors by retail to be consumed on or off the premises;

(b) the incapacity of such person;

(c) the removal of such person from the house or premises;

(d) the sale of the interest of such person in the premises;

(e) the assignment of such person's interest therein, by operation of law or otherwise.

Transfer upon a Transfer

(a) Within the same year

18–8 A question which often arises is whether application can be made for several ad interim transfers within a licensing year. The interpretation of section 1 of the Public House (Ireland) Act 1855 has given rise to much confusion and an abundance of case law.

The contrasting judgments given by Palles C.B. in the cases of *Re Deighan*[12] and *R. (Oates) v. Sligo Justices*,[13] have muddied the waters. Finlay C.J. in *Fitzpatrick v. McCormack,*[14] while acknowledging Palles C.B.'s reputation in Irish jurisprudence, refused to apply the principles expressed in the *Deighan* case to the facts before him.

In the *Deighan* case (above), Palles C.B. held that the person to whom a licence had been transferred by endorsement on an ad interim basis under section 1 of the 1855 Act could not give any other person a right to a subsequent ad interim transfer, without first applying for confirmation or a certificate of transfer. In other words a person who is an ad interim transferee of a licence is not a duly licensed person within the meaning of section 1 of the 1855 Act.

In *Dumigan v. Walsh*[15] the Solicitor General conceded that because of the decision in the *Deighan* case he could not argue that a person who obtained an ad interim transfer was a licensed person. O'Brien L.C.J. stated:

---

[12] (1897) 31 I.L.T.R. 45.
[13] [1901] 2 I.R. 352.
[14] Above, n.10.
[15] [1904] 2 I.R. 298.

> "Mr Magrath, who opened the case on behalf of the appellant Dumigan, contended, citing *Deighan's case*, in the Court of Appeal, that what Doherty got from the magistrates at Petty Sessions was not a transfer of Dumigan's license, but a mere authority to carry on the business of publican. Speaking for myself alone, I must say that, having regard to the language of the 1st section of the 18 and 19 Vict., c.114, and to the form of the order of the magistrates, I entertained some doubt as to the soundness of Mr Magrath's contention; but whilst my opinion was still wavering, and before it had at all crystallized into settled conviction, the Solicitor-General very candidly admitted that Mr Magrath's proposition was established to be correct by the decision of the Court of Appeal in D*eighan's* case; that he had argued the case himself, and that it was decided on the basis that under 18 and 19 Vict., c. 114, s.1, the *ad interim* order of the magistrates is not a transfer of the licence, but a mere authority to carry on the business for a limited time."[16]

Judge Webb in *Application of Langan*,[17] held that the justices had no jurisdiction to make a transfer from an ad interim transferee who was not a person "duly licensed". In *R. (Minahane) v. Cork Justices*,[18] Madden J. stated: **18–9**

> "If, indeed, the effect of the *ad interim* transfer were to convert the transferee into the person duly licensed in respect of the premises, it might be contended that this procedure was a necessary part of affecting the transfer of the licence, and not merely a temporary protection pending a completed transfer. But such an argument was not possible since the decision of the Court of Appeal in *In re Deighan* . . . [and] *Dumigan v. Walsh*."[19]

However, the case of *R. (Oates) v. Sligo Justices*,[20] where Palles C.B. overruled his own judgment in the *Deighan*[21] case is not referred to in any of the above cases, nor was it referred to in the Supreme Court judgment in *Fitzpatrick v. McCormack*.[22]

In the *Oates* case, an application was made to discharge a conditional order for certiorari directed to the respondent justices to quash an order refusing Mrs Oates' application for a confirmation of the transfer of a publican's licence to her on the ground of excess of jurisdiction. No submissions were made on behalf of the prosecutor and counsel for the respondent indicated that the Crown "would desire that a uniform practice should be established throughout the country" citing, *inter alia*, the *Langan* case.[23] Palles C.B. contradicted his earlier decision in the *Deighan* case and held that an ad interim transferee was

---

[16] *Ibid.* at 307.
[17] (1895) 29 I.L.T.R. 100.
[18] Unreported, June 30, 1904, referred to in (1904–1905) 39 I.L.T. & S.J. p. 443.
[19] *Ibid.* at p. 444.
[20] Above, n.13.
[21] Above, n.12.
[22] Above, n.10 (although it was opened in the *Duggan* case).
[23] Above, n.17.

a person "duly licensed" within the meaning of section 1 of the 1855 Act. He stated:

> "We are all of opinion that this is a plain case, and that Clancy, at the date of the transfer by him, was a person duly licensed within section 1 of 18 and 19 Vict. c.114. If we were to hold otherwise, it would be impossible that any public house could be transferred, or sold, twice within the same twelve months."[24]

18–10 In *R. (Duggan) v. Fermanagh Justices*[25] an application by Duggan for a certificate of transfer at quarter sessions was refused where he was the second tenant to have obtained an ad interim transfer within the licensing year. O'Brien L.C.J. held that the previous tenant was not a duly licensed person and the refusal of the application was correct. Kenny J. dissented, holding that the tenant's claim need not be based upon a direct and immediate dealing with a licensed person and that Duggan was entitled to the ad interim order and the certificate of transfer. He stated:

> "There is no sale or assignment, direct and immediate from a 'licensed person' to Duggan, nor has he acquired ownership directly and immediately upon the removal of a licensed person. If it be necessary for us to construe the Act . . . of 1855 as contemplating only such a direct and immediate dealing as this, Duggan could not support his claim. In my opinion, that is not the proper interpretation to place upon [this] statute . . . I consider that by the use of the word 'upon' the event is not restricted to a link in the title immediately following on the assignment by or removal of the licensed person, but that it may extend to a more remote dealing with the premises and licence. As has been suggested at the bar, I think that the word 'upon' may be given the meaning of 'after' or 'subsequently to' or 'consequent upon' . . .".[26]

The views of Palles C.B. in *Oates* and Kenny J. in *Duggan* are eminently practical: given that Finlay C.J. distinguished *Deighan* and *Dumigan v. Walsh* in *Fitzpatrick v. McCormack*, it is possible that their views would be followed.

(b) Position of Landlord

18–11 The question which then arises is whether it is necessary for the holder of the lowest estate and interest in the premises to apply for an ad interim transfer when he does not intend to carry on business in the premises but merely wishes to let them to some other person. This can happen when the previous tenant quits the premises and the landlord goes into possession, not with the intention to trade, but to secure another tenant. It is arguable that there is no need for the landlord himself to make an application for an ad interim transfer. In *Brown v.*

---

[24] *R. (Oates) v. Sligo Justices*, above, n.13, at 354, *per* Palles C.B.
[25] Above, n.5.
[26] *Ibid.* at 145 and 146.

Watson, the widow of the licence holder closed the premises after his death and did not attempt to carry on the business; FitzGibbon L.J. stated:

> "The defendant was not bound to take out *an interim* transfer, or a temporary licence in her own name, provided she acted with reasonable diligence and in a reasonable manner in assigning the premises to some proper person, and on the completion of the assignment was ready and willing to transfer the licence."[27]

Where the landlord does not intend to trade, the licence is inoperable until the court grants an ad interim transfer to another tenant. In *R. (Murphy) v. Cork Justices*,[28] Holmes J. noted the principles laid down in *Brennan v. Dorney*[29] where it was held that no right to the benefit of a publican's licence can exist apart from the ownership and possession of the licensed premises, and that the rightful possession of the licensed premises carries with it the right of transfer or renewal, subject to the statutory requirements applicable to such cases. He stated:

> "It seems to me to follow that if the estate or interest which entitles the publican to posession were to terminate either by assignment or otherwise, during the currency of the annual licence, and if he were allowed to remain in the licensed house as permissive occupant, he would not be entitled to carry on the business. The license would still be valid and available for the protection of the assignee on his complying with the statutory conditions but would cease to have any other operation."[30]

The licence therefore remains inoperable insofar as the landlord is concerned but once authority to trade has been granted by the court, then the person to whom that order is granted is entitled to trade thereunder.

(c) Status of ad interim transferee

Although in the *Oates*[31] case, Palles C.B. in effect held that an ad interim transferee was a person "duly licensed" for the purpose of section 1 of the 1855 Act, the Supreme Court in *Fitzpatrick v. McCormack*[32] did not go as far. Here a husband and wife were joint owners of a public house to which there was attached a liquor licence which had been issued to the husband. The husband assigned his interest in the property to his wife and an application was made to the District Court for an ad interim transfer of the licence. This application was granted by the District Court judge. At the same sitting of the District Court, 18–12

[27] (1903) 37 I.L.T.R. 246 at 249 and 250.
[28] [1895] 2 I.R. 104.
[29] [1888–89] 21 L.R. Ir. 353.
[30] Above, n.28, at 113.
[31] Above, n.13.
[32] Above, n.10.

but subsequent to the grant of an ad interim transfer to the wife, the husband pleaded guilty and was convicted and fined in relation to various charges regarding the conduct of the premises.

The District Court judge directed that the convictions should not be endorsed on the licence. Thereafter, the District Court clerk wrote to the solicitor who acted for the husband and wife, requesting him to return the licence for the purposes of endorsing each conviction thereon, and stating that he proposed to inform the revenue authorities of what would have been the consequent forfeiture of the licence. The plaintiffs issued proceedings against the District Court clerk, claiming a declaration that the husband was not the holder of the licence at the time when he was convicted of the offences and a declaration that the convictions were not recordable upon the licence.

The claim was dismissed in the High Court, but on appeal to the Supreme Court it was held that once the ad interim transfer had been granted, the wife became the holder of the licence: thus, as Stella Fitzpatrick was the holder of the licence at the time her husband was convicted, such endorsements could not be recorded on the licence. Finlay C.J. stated:

> "I am satisfied that if the matter were free of authority and if as a matter of law the simple task of the Court was to define the meaning of "holder of any licence for the sale of intoxicating liquor", one would be disposed to lean heavily in favour of the obvious interpretation as being that it was the person who had the legal right to possession of the actual licence document. Furthermore, having regard to the provisions of s.1 of the Act of 1855, one would lean equally heavily in favour of interpreting the consequence of what is there described as a "transfer by endorsement" of the licence to a person, as being that that person became lawfully entitled to possession of the licence. . . . The intention would appear to be that the licence, having been handed into the possession of the person to whom the transfer is made, carries on the face of it the authority to that person to trade under it."[33]

However, he noted that in the decisions of *Re Deighan*[34] and *Dumigan v. Walsh*[35] there was no discussion about the concept or idea of a licence holder as distinct from a licensed person. He continued:

> "It seems to me that a licensed person could not be considered to be a person other than one to whom the excise, pursuant to a certificate of the Court, had issued a licence. . . . Having regard to the terms of Part III of the Act of 1927, however, if the contention made on behalf of the defendant were correct, namely, that the transferee under the order made under s.1 of the Act of 1855, namely, Stella Fitzpatrick, is not the holder of a licence, then the extraordinarily anomalous position arises that she is wholly immune from the consequences of recording and forfeiture which flow from repeated convictions."[36]

---

[33] *Fitzpatrick v. McCormack*, above, n.10, at 387 and 388.
[34] Above, n.12.
[35] Above, n.15.
[36] *Fitzpatrick v. McCormack*, above, n.10, at 391.

Thus, an ad interim transferee can be convicted of offences against the licensing code committed during the time he holds the licence by virtue of an ad interim transfer.

Entitlement

The entitlement to an ad interim transfer is prescribed in section 1 of the 1855 Act and rule 97 of the District Court Rules 1948. In order for an application for an ad interim transfer to succeed, one of the following must have occurred, namely: **18–13**

1. The death of a person duly licensed to sell excisable liquors by retail to be consumed on or off the premises.

   Where the licensee dies his heirs, administrators, executors or assigns may carry on the business until the next sitting of the District Court in the area, 14 days after the death.[37] After that time, the District Court judge may grant a temporary transfer of the licence to a person nominated by the deceased's executor or administrator or, in their absence, to a person having an interest in the licensed premises, which transfer survives until the annual licensing District Court. The court has a discretion to extend this period for up to two years.[38]

2. The incapacity of such person.

   Incapacity refers to illness or any other reason causing the licensee's inability to carry on the trade.

3. The removal of such person from the house or premises.

   In *R. (O'Brien) v. Tipperary Justices*[39] it was held that removal does not include ejectment of a tenant by a landlord. However, O'Brien J. dissented, stating:

   > "... the very frame of (the 1855 Act) shows that the word 'removal' ... should be construed as referring to something more than the case of a sale or assignment ... and as referring to every case in which the licensed party has to leave or remove ... in consequence of ... effluxion of time, eviction or surrender; otherwise it would be difficult to give any construction to the word "removal" that would account for its being used".[40]

---

[37] Intoxicating Liquor (General) Act 1924, s.7(5).
[38] Intoxicating Liquor Act 1962, s.34.
[39] [1879–80] 4 L.R. Ir. 259.
[40] *Ibid.* at 268.

Madden J. in *R. (Duggan) v. Fermanagh Justices* accepts that the giving up of possession voluntarily by the tenant is a "removal".[41] Note also *Daly v. Scanlon*[42] where a District Court judge held that where a licensee was ejected from his licensed premises for non-payment of rent and refused to transfer the licence pursuant to a lease covenant, there was no jurisdiction to grant an application for an ad interim transfer.

4. Sale of the interest of such person in the premises.
5. The assignment of such person's interest therein by operation of law or otherwise.

According to Kenny J., the sale or assignment does not have to be immediate or direct, although his was the minority view.[43]

Duration

18–14 The District Court has jurisdiction to grant an ad interim transfer until "the Quarter Sessions of the Peace which shall be holden for the same county, riding, division, liberty, city, town, or place next after the expiration of one calendar month from the time of such transfer and no longer".[44] This is usually the next annual licensing sessions after the grant of the ad interim transfer. The annual licensing sessions are usually held at the end of each September.

If an ad interim transfer is granted sometime during September, the District Court judge sitting at the annual licensing District Court may grant an adjournment to permit the ad interim transferee to give the necessary notices required for a certificate of transfer.[45] It is conceivable that the ad interim transferee can apply at the following annual licensing District Court for a certificate of transfer, as the endorsement of the District Court judge under section 1 of the Act of 1855 permits an ad interim transferee to trade until the annual licensing sessions held next after the expiration of one calendar month from the time of the ad interim transfer.

The scheme of rule 99 of the District Court Rules 1948, however, is to deal expressly with the situation where the next annual licensing court is held within a period of one month after the date of the grant of a temporary transfer. It provides that the judge sitting at the next annual licensing District Court may adjourn any application for the renewal of the licence which has been duly lodged to a specified sitting of the court upon the application for renewal being so adjourned. The person to whom the temporary transfer has been granted may make application for a certificate by way of confirmation of transfer and for

---

[41] Above, n.5, at 151.
[42] (1933) 67 I.L.T.R. 190.
[43] Above, n.5, at 145.
[44] Public House (Ireland) Act 1855, s.1.
[45] District Court Rules 1948, r. 99.

that purpose may give the notice and publish the advertisement required by rule 101 of the District Court Rules 1948. Such application may be listed for hearing at the adjourned sitting of the annual licensing District Court and the judge, upon being satisfied that the notice and advertisement are in order may, if he thinks fit, grant the application for a certificate.

Rule 104(1) of the District Court Rules 1948 provides that where a certificate of transfer is granted, any application which may have been made for renewal of the licence should not proceed and it is not necessary for the transferee to obtain a certificate of renewal of the licence in addition to the certificate of transfer.

Tax Clearance Certificate

Where a "connected party" makes an application for an ad interim transfer **18–15**
within the licensing year both the original holder of the licence and the applicant must have their tax affairs in order so that a tax clearance certificate will issue in the name of the applicant. If the transferor is connected with the applicant and the former's tax affairs are not in order, then the Revenue Commissioners will not issue a tax clearance certificate.

Application to Court: Proofs

The proofs necessary in an application for an ad interim transfer were consid- **18–16**
ered in detail by Henchy J. in *The State (Doyle) v. Carr.*[46] He held that the District Court judge must be satisfied of three things:

1. that the required notice has been given;
2. that there is some need for the transfer arising from the death or incapacity of the licensee, or his removal from the premises, or the sale or assignment of his interest in the premises; and
3. that the applicant is not disqualified by law from holding the licence.

The District Court judge has no discretion to consider any other matters:

> "It is in the context of those limited proofs that one must construe the power given to the District Justice in rule 97(1) by the words "if he shall think proper so to do after examination on oath of the necessary parties".[47]

In *The State (Hennessy) and Chariot Inns Ltd v. Commons*[48] Finlay P., whose decision was upheld by the Supreme Court, held that the discretion of the

---

[46] [1970] I.R. 87 at 90.
[47] *Ibid.* at 91.
[48] [1976] I.R. 238.

District Court judge was not absolute but was confined to determining whether the applicant had satisfied the specific proofs required by the section (section 1 of the Public House (Ireland) Act 1855) and that the character and reputation of an applicant who was not a disqualified person were not factors relevant to the determination of an application for an ad interim transfer. In the *Hennessy* case, the District Court judge had refused the application for the ad interim transfer upon the grounds that the main controlling interest in the applicant company was vested in a person having convictions under the Licensing Acts. On that basis he held that the company did not have a suitable character and should not be entitled to an ad interim transfer.

Examination on Oath

18–17 The provisions of section 1 of the Public House (Ireland) Act 1855 requiring the examination of "necessary parties" upon oath is a mandatory requirement. The District Court is not entitled to grant an ad interim transfer without complying with this statutory provision. In *The State (Doyle) v. Carr*,[49] Henchy J. noted that the applicant for the ad interim transfer was not examined in the District Court:

> "But in a case such as this, where there is no public notification of the intended application, where opposition to the application could come only from the Garda Síochána, where the entitlement of the applicant to transfer may be established by second best evidence, I consider that the scope and purpose of the statutory requirement of a *viva voce* examination on oath show that it is a peremptory rather than a directory provision and that, even if it were held to be merely directory, it could not be said that a total disregard of such a direction is tantamount to a substantial compliance with it."[50]

Failure to hear an applicant results in the making of an order without jurisdiction.

Disqualified Persons

18–18 Certain persons are disqualified by law from holding a licence.[51] The District Court judge cannot grant an ad interim transfer to a disqualified person. However, the character and reputation of an applicant for an ad interim transfer who is not a disqualified person are not factors which are relevant to the determination of the application. The District Court judge may not, in the

---

[49] Above, n.46.
[50] *Ibid.* at 92.
[51] See above, chap. 3, "The Licensee", at para. 3–19.

exercise of his discretion consider such factors, if the proofs are in order. In *The State (Hennessy) and Chariot Inns Ltd v. Commons*, Finlay P. stated:

> "I am aware that this construction leaves open the possibility that a person of known bad character could be authorised to carry on the business of a licensee from the date of his application for an ad interim transfer, until the next annual licensing sessions, and that the District Justice would have no power to prevent what might be considered the public mischief thus arising. If this does represent a *casus omissis* in the licensing code, then it is not one which I am entitled to fill on any ground of public policy. It is, of course, relevant to consider that an applicant for an ad interim transfer does not in fact become an actual licensee on the authorities; he only gets a limited and strictly temporary authority to trade and if he is a person of bad character or unsuitable to hold a licence, at the next licensing session he must face the significant danger that he will lose his licence, by failing to have the transfer confirmed, and thus would suffer what would be substantial commercial loss."[52]

Endorsement on Licence

The endorsement is placed on the back of the licence. The District Court judge has a discretion to endorse the ad interim transfer on a certified copy of the licence, or on a certified copy of the receipt from the Customs and Excise confirming the payment of the current licence duty. He may dispense with the requirement of the endorsement on the licence if he is satisfied that the licence has been wrongfully withheld from the person entitled to possession thereof.[53] **18–19**

Conditional Grant

If an applicant for an ad interim transfer at the time of making his application to the court is not in a position to produce the original document(s) of title, grant of probate or administration upon which he relies, the court may grant the application subject to the subsequent production of such document(s) of title, grant of probate or administration.[54] The District Court regularly grants such applications on an undertaking to stamp the appropriate document of title. **18–20**

---

[52] Above, n.48, at 247.
[53] District Court Rules 1948, r. 97(3).
[54] *Ibid.*, r. 97(4).

B. Certificate of Transfer

18–21 The form of the certificate of transfer is set out at page 95 of the District Court Rules 1948, as amended.[55] The operative part of the certificate itself does not use the word "transfer" but simply certifies that the person named is entitled to receive a licence in respect of the premises designated therein. The form is signed by the clerk of the District Court following a successful application to the court at the annual licensing sessions, or where appropriate, an adjournment thereof. The rules governing an application for a certificate of transfer are contained in rules 100, 101, 102, 103 and 104 of the District Court Rules 1948. These rules are titled, somewhat confusingly, "Confirmation of transfers: on-licences and off-licences" as the word confirmation implies that it is necessary to confirm an ad interim transfer. There is no question of confirming an ad interim transfer: either an ad interim transfer is either made or not made. If it is made, it stands and is effective until the next annual licensing sessions occurring one month after the making of the order, subject to section 34 of the Intoxicating Liquor Act 1962.[56] An ad interim order, or a "protection order", cannot be and is never confirmed. Adding to the confusion is the use of the word "transfer": in the body of the certificate which issues upon a successful application for a transfer, the word "transfer" is not used. The certificate does no more than certify that the successful applicant under rule 100 is entitled to the licence sought.

The order made by the court at the annual licensing sessions is to direct the issue of a certificate entitling the applicant to a new licence. In *R. (Duggan) v. Fermanagh Justices*, Gibson J. said:

> ". . . a confirmation application is one for a new licence under the Act of 1833, free from the third objection [under section 4 of that Act] in the case of a holder of goodwill . . . the function of Sessions in October , though described as confirmation, is, in substance and reality, the granting of a new licence under the Act of 1833. I therefore concur with Mr O'Connor that in Ireland there is no such thing as the judicial transfer at Quarter Sessions of a licence; what is given is a new licence."[57]

---

[55] Form 26, issued pursuant to the District Court Rules 1948, r. 104.

[56] This section provides for the temporary transfer to a person nominated by an executor or administrator and the court can grant a temporary transfer to a person nominated by the executor or administrator of any person having an interest in the premises to which the licence relates up to "the sitting of such Annual Licensing District Court in the year, or in the second year . . . after the sitting aforesaid".

[57] Above, n.5, at 161.

Status of Transferee

When the successful applicant presents the court certificate to the Collector of Customs and Excise he obtains a new licence in his own name in respect of the premises identified in the certificate. He is the new licensee. So much for the heading of and the anomaly created by rules 100 *et seq*. Ignoring therefore, the expression "confirmation of transfer" and "certificate by way of transfer", where the purchaser of a public house or any licensed premises wishes to apply to have the licence in his own name, he must apply for the certificate to the District Court at the annual licensing sessions or any adjournment thereof irrespective of whether he has already obtained an ad interim transfer. **18–22**

Deletion of Endorsements

It is of the greatest importance for practitioners to note that on making an application for a certificate of transfer, the provisions of section 30 of the Intoxicating Liquor Act 1927 should be invoked. **18–23**

STATUTORY PROVISION

Section 30(1) of the Intoxicating Liquor Act 1927, provides as follows:

> "Whenever, on an application for a certificate for the transfer of a licence for the sale of intoxicating liquor by retail, the applicant at the time of such application satisfies the Court that the transfer is desired for the purpose of giving effect to a *bona fide* sale for money or money's worth of such licence and the premises to which the same is attached, the Court shall, if it grants such certificate, direct in and by such certificate, that all (if any) offences then recorded on such licence under this Part of this Act shall at the time of such transfer cease to be so recorded, and whenever such direction is so given every such offence shall at the time of the transfer of such licence pursuant to such certificate cease to be recorded on such licence and such licence shall be so transferred freed and discharged from the records of such offences and shall thereafter have effect for all purposes as if such offences had never been recorded thereon."

Unless this application is made to the court in conjunction with the application for the certificate of transfer, the offences shall continue to be recorded on the licence. The applicant must satisfy the court that he is a bona fide purchaser and that the transaction is a bona fide commercial transaction. A bona fide sale for money or money's worth is generally understood to include the transfer by lease of the lowest estate in the property for genuine consideration. The particulars of a direction under section 30 must be entered in the register of licences.[58]

[58] Intoxicating Liquor Act 1927, s.30(4).

Where an order under section 30 is made and the original licence holder applies within five years for a certificate of transfer in respect of the same licence or another licence, the court must direct that all offences which were recorded on the original licence be recorded on the licence in respect of which the certificate of transfer is sought. An applicant for a certificate of transfer is obliged to disclose to the court at the time of his application details of any convictions which were recorded on the licence originally held by him.[59]

Application to Court

18–24 An applicant for a certificate of transfer must attend in person (unless the judge is satisfied that there is good reason for his non-attendance) at the annual licensing District Court.[60] Rule 100 of the District Court Rules 1948 provides that the application is made at the annual licensing sessions.[61] The applicant must prove title: the court may grant the application subject to the subsequent production of such title, grant of probate or administration, as the case may be. The certificate of transfer shall not, however, be given to the applicant until he produces the document in question.[62] Rule 103(c) provides that:

> ". . . It shall be lawful for the person to whom a temporary transfer has been granted under the provisions of Rule 97 hereof to trade until such document is produced; . . .".

An applicant for a certificate of transfer, where an ad interim transfer has not been obtained, is not entitled to trade until the application for the certificate is granted. The District Court judge may at any time order that the grant of the certificate of transfer be revoked where the applicant has failed to produce title or a grant of probate or administration.

Once a certificate of transfer is granted, it is not necessary to apply for a renewal of the licence.

Rule 104(1) of the District Court Rules 1948 provides:

> "If a certificate by way of transfer of a licence is granted, any application which may have been made for renewal of the licence shall not be proceeded with, and it shall not be necessary for the transferee to obtain a certificate by way of renewal of the licence in addition to a certificate by way of transfer."

Once the application is granted, the District Court clerk is obliged to give to the applicant the certificate (contained in Form 26 of the District Court Rules 1948) entitling him to receive a licence.[63]

---

[59] Intoxicating Liquor Act 1927, s.30(2) and (3).
[60] District Court Rules 1948, r. 103.
[61] Licensing Act (Ireland) 1874, s.12. Previously this application was made at any of the four sittings of the quarter sessions.
[62] District Court Rules 1948, r. 103(c).
[63] *Ibid.*, r. 104(2).

Off-Licence

Where an application is made for a certificate of transfer of an off-licence, the District Court judge must sign the appropriate certificate certifying to the good character of the applicant, the rating of the premises, and if the transfer arises otherwise than on the death or removal of the person in occupation immediately prior to the transfer, the period during which the premises were in the exclusive occupation of the applicant.[64] 18–25

Refusal

If an applicant is refused a certificate of transfer, the judge must state the grounds of refusal in the certificate of refusal, which must be signed by him.[65] Where an application for a certificate of transfer is refused and the applicant appeals against the refusal to the Circuit Court, the licence continues in full force and effect pending the outcome of the appeal, if the appellant pays the appropriate excise duty. 18–26

Section 60 of the Intoxicating Liquor Act 1927 provides for the continuance of a licence pending an appeal against refusal to grant a certificate of transfer. 18–27

STATUTORY PROVISION

Section 60 of the Intoxicating Liquor Act 1927:

> "(1) Whenever the Justice of the District Court shall refuse an application for a certificate for a transfer or a renewal of any licence for the sale of intoxicating liquor by retail and the applicant for such certificate shall lawfully appeal against such refusal to the Circuit Court and shall prosecute such appeal with due diligence, such licence shall subject to the provisions of this section, continue in full force and effect until the first opportunity on which such an appeal could be heard by the Circuit Court and, if that Court shall so direct, for such further time (if any) as shall elapse before the final determination of such appeal.
>
> (2) A licence shall not continue in force under the foregoing subsection after the expiration of the term for which the same was granted unless, on or before such expiration, the appellant deposits with the proper officer of customs and excise the amount of the excise duty chargeable on a renewal of such licence."

The question may arise, however, as to the applicant's right to trade pending the hearing of the application for the certificate of transfer. If the applicant has already obtained an ad interim transfer, then he is entitled to trade until the determination of the application. If he makes an application in the first instance

[64] *Ibid.*, r. 104(3).
[65] *Ibid.*, r. 105.

for a certificate of transfer at the annual licensing District Court, there is no authority to trade pending the hearing of the application.

Licence on Foot of Certificate of Transfer

18–28 Section 6 of the Licensing (Ireland) Act 1833 provides for the grant of a licence by the "proper Officers of Excise in Ireland" "to any person, though not licensed in the year preceding".

C. Other Forms of Transfer

18–29 Other forms of transfer (set forth below) are provided for by statute. An application for transfer in these cases may only be made in the circumstances set forth in the legislation.

1. Transfer of Licence held by Nominee of a Body Corporate

STATUTORY PROVISION

18–30 By virtue of section 28 of the Intoxicating Liquor Act 1960 a body corporate holding its licence through a nominee is entitled to apply to the District Court to substitute another nominee:

> "A licence held by a nominee of a body corporate in respect of premises in which the lowest estate or tenancy is held by the body corporate may, on application by the body corporate to the Court at any sitting thereof for the Court area within which the premises are situate, be transferred, by endorsement made by the Court on the licence or, if the licence is not available, on a copy thereof, to such other person as a body corporate may nominate."

There seems no reason why the body corporate cannot make an application under section 28 to transfer the licence to itself, and not to a nominee.

This transfer does not need to be "confirmed" at the next annual licensing District Court. The application may be made at any sitting of the District Court. A time limit during which the notice must be lodged is not specified, so the rules of the District Court apply, and the usual 48 hours notice is given to the District Court clerk, with reasonable notice to the local Garda superintendant in charge of the district in which the premises are situate.

2. Transfer of the Licence where the Holder ceases to carry on Business

Section 30(1) of the Intoxicating Liquor Act 1960 provides for a situation where the holder of the licence ceases to carry on the business, leaves the State or cannot be found. It does not apply where the holder of the license is a nominee nor does it apply where the reason for the cessation of business is death, transfer of the premises or forfeiture of the licence. When an application has been made, the District Court can either: **18–31**

1. transfer the licence to the applicant in accordance with the provisions of section 1 of the Public House (Ireland) Act 1855, if the licence has not expired;
2. if the licence has expired, the court may, if the application is made within one year after such expiry, grant the applicant the certificate or certificates[66] required to be produced before a renewal of the licence is granted in respect of the premises. Section 30(1)(b) of the statute provides that "for the purposes of the application and of the grant of the renewal of the licence by the Revenue Commissioners, the applicant shall be deemed to be the holder of the lowest estate or tenancy in the premises". This applies only where the licence has expired. Further, the licence is deemed to have been renewed immediately after it has expired.[67]

Section 30(2) provides that an application to the court shall not be granted if the holder of the licence objects, or where the court does not consider that the applicant is, in the circumstances, a suitable person.

Where either an application for a transfer or a renewal as above, is granted, and a further application to the court for a certificate leading to the renewal of the licence is necessary, the holder of the licence is deemed for the court application and the related application to the Revenue Commissioners, to be the holder of the lowest estate or tenancy of the premises.[68]

Where the holder of the lowest estate is a person other than the holder of the licence, he may apply under section 30(5) of the Intoxicating Liquor Act 1960 for any of the above orders and a certificate of transfer.[69]

It should be noted that a licence in respect of any premises which has been transferred or renewed by virtue of subsection 1 of section 30 of the Intoxicating Liquor Act 1960 and is held by a person other than the holder of the lowest estate or tenancy in the premises, shall not be capable of being extinguished under or for the purposes of section 4 of the Licensing (Ireland) Act 1902,

---

[66] *i.e.* leading to the renewal of an off-licence.
[67] Intoxicating Liquor Act 1960, s.30(3).
[68] *Ibid.*, s.30(4); see also Courts (No. 2) Act 1986, s.5(b).
[69] *Ibid.*, s.30(5).

section 11 of the Intoxicating Liquor Act 1927, section 21 or section 31 of the Intoxicating Liquor Act 1943, or section 13 or section 19 of the Intoxicating Liquor Act 1960.[70]

18–32 Ó Dálaigh C.J. in *Re Application of Gorman*[71] considered that section 30 of the Intoxicating Liquor Act 1960 was "an ill-considered mode of amendment" as it appeared to authorise the court to grant a certificate in a form which, in some cases, would not accord with the facts.

For example, where the licence has expired and the application to court is made within one year after expiry, the court is entitled to grant a certificate to be produced to the Revenue Commissioners and which certifies, *inter alia*, that in "the past year" the house has been conducted in a "peaceable and orderly manner". Ó Dálaigh C.J. pointed out that while it was clear that in certain cases there would have been some business conducted "in the past year", the section contemplates an application for a renewal in cases where no business has been carried on "in the past year". He stated:

> "it seems to me that a District Justice, having certified as to the applicant's good character, might properly recite the provision of s.30 of the Act of 1960"

and added that, as no business had been carried on "in the past year", he was unable to certify the manner in which the business had been conducted.[72] He expressed the view that section 30 of the Intoxicating Liquor Act 1960 was not a general dispensation in respect of the requirements on renewals but that its operation was confined to the very special circumstances mentioned in section 30(1) of the 1960 Act.

3. Temporary Transfer to Person nominated by an Executor or Administrator

18–33 Section 34 of the Intoxicating Liquor Act 1962 provides for a temporary transfer of a licence to a person nominated by an executor or administrator of the deceased licensee. In this case, application is made by the executor or administrator or by any person having an interest in the premises to which the licence relates, to transfer temporarily the on-licence or the off-licence to a person nominated by such executor or administrator or such other persons.

---

[70] *Ibid.*, s.30(6).
[71] [1971] I.R. 1 at 7.
[72] *Ibid.* at 7.

STATUTORY PROVISION

Section 34 of the 1962 Act provides as follows:

> "(1) The power of a Justice of the District Court under the Licensing Acts to transfer temporarily an on-licence or an off-licence upon the death of the holder of the licence shall include power to transfer the licence to any person (being a person approved of by the Court and not disqualified by law) nominated by the executor or administrator of the holder or, if there is no executor or administrator, by any person having an interest in the premises to which the licence relates, and the transfer shall operate to authorise the person to whom the transfer is transferred to carry on in the premises to which the licence relates the business authorised by the licence until the date of the sitting of the annual licensing District Court in the Court area in which the premises are situate held next after the expiration of one month from the date of the transfer, or if the Court should then, or on any subsequent application to it, think fit to so order, until the sitting of such annual licensing District Court in the year or in the second year (as the Court may think fit to order) after the sitting aforesaid.
>
> (2) Where a licence has been transferred by virtue of sub-section 1 of this section, the licence may, on application by the nominator of the transferee to the Court at any sitting thereof for the District Court District within which the premises are situate, be transferred, by endorsement made by the Court on the licence or, if the licence is not available on a copy thereof, to such other person (being a person approved of by the Court and not disqualified by law) as the nominator may nominate."

A District Court judge has jurisdiction to transfer the licence temporarily to the person nominated until the annual licensing District Court of the year in which the application was made, or indeed until the sitting of the annual licensing District Court of the following year.

Such person nominated does not have to satisfy the three requirements laid down by Henchy J. in *The State (Doyle) v. Carr*.[73] He must not however be a disqualified person. In contrast to the case of an ad interim transfer, the nominee must be a person "approved of by the court". The provision was enacted in order to give an executor or personal representative time to ensure that the affairs of a deceased and his estate are put in order. The statutory provision does not stipulate that a certificate of transfer must be obtained. Where, however, the lowest estate or interest in the licensed premises is acquired by an applicant, he will seek a certificate of transfer.

The provision allows for a number of transfers to be made within a licensing year or indeed within the two years stipulated by section 34 of the Intoxicating Liquor Act 1962.

---

[73] Above, n.46.

CHAPTER 19

RENEWAL

Introduction

19–1 Under the Finance (1909–10) Act 1910 all retailer's licences expire on September 30 each year.[1] Although Carroll J. stated in *The State (Pheasantry Ltd) v. District Justice Donnelly*:

> "There is no constitutional right to a liquor licence or a renewal thereof. There are only such rights as are given by statute subject to the limitations and conditions prescribed by statute . . ."[2]

an applicant who applies for the renewal of his licence is treated differently by statute and by the courts from the applicant who has not held a licence in the previous year. The grounds of objection to an application to renew an existing licence are not as extensive as those which apply in the case of an application for the grant of a new licence. Since the coming into force of the Courts (No. 2) Act 1986,[3] an applicant does not now have to apply to the annual licensing District Court for a certificate as to his good character and the peaceable and orderly manner in which the premises was conducted in the previous year, save in certain exceptional circumstances which are referred to in section 4(5) of that Act.

A licence, when granted, operates from the date of its grant and expires thereafter in accordance with section 49 of the Finance (1909–10) Act 1910 as

---

[1] Though see s.115 of the Finance Act 1995 which extends the duration of the licence where an application for a tax clearance certificate has been made before a certain date and has not been issued by September 30.

[2] [1982] I.L.R.M. 512 at 516.

[3] July 22, 1988, by virtue of the Courts (No. 2) Act (Commencement) Order 1988 (S.I. No. 176 of 1988).

amended; it is, when granted, a new licence, although the licence, "in general justice and substance, does continue from year to year".[4]

Application to Renew

An application to renew a retail licence is made to the Collector of Customs and Excise on behalf of the Revenue Commissioners. Until the Courts (No. 2) Act 1986, an applicant who wished to renew his retail licence was obliged to produce the appropriate excise duty and a certificate "to the good character of such a person, and to the peaceable and orderly manner in which such house had been conducted in the past year".[5] **19–2**

STATUTORY PROVISION

Section 4(2) of the Courts (No. 2) Act 1986 provides:

> "Subject to *subsection (5)* of this section, where a renewal is required of a licence for premises which have been licensed in the immediately preceding year, it shall not be necessary to produce a certificate of the District Court to an officer of the Revenue Commissioners empowered to grant a renewal of such a licence."

Thus, save in certain exceptional circumstances, it is not now necessary to apply for the above District Court certificate. This provision applies to all licences for the grant of which either a Circuit Court or District Court certificate is required.[6]

An applicant for the renewal of off-licences, certain hotel licences, an on-licence for a holiday camp and a special restaurant licence must produce various other documentation to the Revenue Commissioners.[7]

In an application for the renewal of a licence, the applicant must inform the Revenue Commissioners, if applicable:

1. that the licence was transferred or renewed under section 30 of the Intoxicating Liquor Act 1960;
2. that he is applying for a restricted licence;
3. that the licence is a holiday camp licence;
4. that the licence is a hotel licence granted under section 2(2) of the Licensing (Ireland) Act 1902 and granted after July 4, 1960.

---

[4] *R. (Murphy) v. Cork Justices* [1895] 2 I.R. 104, *per* O'Brien J. at 112.
[5] Spirits (Ireland) Act 1854, s.11.
[6] These licences are discussed above at chap. 4, "Licences to Sell Intoxicating Liquor by Retail".
[7] Courts (No. 2) Act 1986, s.4.

Court Certificate Necessary

19–3 The Courts (No. 2) Act 1986 provides for certain circumstances whereby an applicant for renewal is obliged to seek a certificate of the court. Section 4(7) of the 1986 Act provides that where a certificate is required, it must certify as to:

> "(a) the good character of the licensee,
>
> (b) the peaceable and orderly manner in which the licensed premises were conducted in the year ending on the expiry of the licence . . . ".

An applicant for renewal must present, *inter alia*, the court certificate to the Revenue Commissioners, in the circumstances enumerated in Section 4(5) of the Courts (No. 2) Act, 1986.

STATUTORY PROVISION

19–4 Section 4(5) of the Courts (No. 2) Act 1986 provides:

> "Notwithstanding *subsection (2)* of this section, a licence shall not be renewable on expiry without the production of a certificate of the District Court for the district court area within which the premises concerned are situate where—
>
> (a) a notice of objection to such renewal has been lodged with the Court within the time prescribed in rules of court, or
>
> (b) the licence is one which is renewable by virtue of the provisions of section 30(1)(b) of the Act of 1960, or
>
> (c) it is proposed to insert a condition in the licence in pursuance of section 8 or section 9 of the Act of 1927."

(a) Objection to Renewal

19–5 The District Court (Renewal of Intoxicating Liquor Licences) Rules 1988[8] contain the rules of court referred to in subsection (5)(a) of section 4 of the 1986 Act. They set forth the venue at which an objection is to be made, the form of the notice of objection, the persons upon whom and the time by which such notice must be served. The District Court clerk is then obliged to notify the Collector of Customs and Excise of the objection. If the objector is not a member of the Garda Síochána, he must also notify the superintendent of the Garda Síochána for the area.

Where the objection is allowed and there is no appeal against the order, the District Court clerk must send a certified copy of the order to the Collector of Customs and Excise. Where the objection is disallowed and no notice of appeal

[8] S.I. No. 145 of 1988.

is duly lodged, the District Court clerk forwards the certificate for the renewal of the licence to the Collector of Customs and Excise. Where there is a notice of appeal against the order of the District Court, the District Court clerk notifies the Collector of Customs and Excise.

(b) Intoxicating Liquor Act 1960, Section 30(1)(b)

Where the holder of a licence ceases to be resident in the State or cannot be found, the court is entitled, *inter alia*, pursuant to section 30 of the Intoxicating Liquor Act 1960 to grant a certificate entitling the applicant to a renewal of the licence, but only where it has expired and the application for the certificate is made to the court within one year of expiry. The Revenue Commissioners cannot renew a licence under such circumstances without the production of a court certificate or certificates. The licence may be granted to a person who is not the holder of the lowest estate or tenancy in the premises: the court must consider whether the applicant is a suitable person to receive the certificate. In this manner the legislature preserves the discretion of the court to grant or refuse a certificate leading to the renewal of a licence. **19–6**

(c) Restricted Licence

Likewise, where an applicant for renewal wishes to convert his on-licence to a restricted licence, namely an early closing licence or a six day licence, he must first obtain the certificate referred to in section 4(7) of the 1986 Act before the Revenue Commissioners may grant him the restricted licence. The legislature cannot delegate the power of inserting conditions into a previously unrestricted licence to the Revenue Commissioners. Where an on-licence has been converted into a restricted licence by order of the court, whether by way of grant, transfer or renewal, the Revenue Commissioners may thereafter issue a restricted licence and renew it on an annual basis; the holder is not required to seek a certificate of the court for the renewal of the restricted licence.[9] **19–7**

Requirement to Notify Fire Authority

Where an applicant for renewal is not obliged to obtain a certificate of the court as a precondition to securing a renewal of his licence, he is nonetheless obliged by statute to notify the fire authority of his intention to renew the licence a month before making his application. **19–8**

---

[9] Intoxicating Liquor Act 1927, ss.8, 9.

STATUTORY PROVISION

The Schedule to the Courts (No. 2) Act 1986 inserted a new subsection in section 24 of the Fire Services Act 1981, as follows:

> "(2) In any case where a certificate is not required for the renewal of a licence (other than an off-licence) under the *Licensing Acts, 1833* to *1986*, the applicant for such renewal shall give one month's notice in writing (or such shorter period of notice as the fire authority may in the special circumstances of the case agree to accept) of the application to the fire authority in the functional area of which the premises are situated, and if the fire authority object to such application, such fire authority may appear, be heard, and adduce evidence in respect of the application for a certificate provided for by *section 4(7)* or *4(8)* (as the case may be) of the *Courts (No. 2) Act 1986*."

It must be noted that this mandatory statutory requirement does not apply to an applicant who wishes to renew his off-licence. An applicant for the renewal of the special restaurant licence must duly notify the fire officer.[10] Although the requirement to notify the fire officer is mandatory, the fire officer may agree a shorter notice period.

Tax Clearance Certificate

19–9 The Revenue Commissioners may not renew a licence unless the application for renewal is accompanied by, *inter alia*, a tax clearance certificate which has been issued in accordance with section 242 of the Finance Act 1992. This provision was introduced by section 156 of the Finance Act 1992 which amended section 49 of the Finance (1909–10) Act 1910 by adding a proviso to subsection 1 thereof. It applies to licences commencing on or after October 1, 1992: the reference to section 4 of the Courts (No. 2) Act 1986 relates to an application to renew a licence.

Duration of Licence

19–10 By virtue of the Finance (1909–10) Act 1910 licences to sell intoxicating liquor by retail expire on September 30 each year. However, in the circumstances detailed below a licence may continue in force beyond that date:

(a) Where an ad interim transfer is obtained during the month of September, such transfer entitles the holder thereof to trade until the annual licensing sessions to be held "next after the expiration of one calendar month from

---

[10] Intoxicating Liquor Act 1988, s.20.

the time of such transfer and no longer".[11] It is conceivable that the annual licensing sessions may occur the following September.

(b) Where the annual licensing District Court refuses an application either for a certificate of transfer or a certificate leading to the renewal of a licence and an appeal is lodged against such refusal, the licence can continue in full force and effect until the appeal is determined by the Circuit Court.[12] The appeal must be prosecuted with "due diligence" and the licence cannot continue in force unless "on or before such expiration" the appellant deposits with the Collector of Customs and Excise the amount of excise duty which is chargeable on the renewal.[13] If the refusal is confirmed by the Circuit Court, then the appropriate proportion of excise duty is returned to the applicant: if the applicant is successful in the Circuit Court in overturning the District Court's refusal, then the excise duty is retained by the Collector of Customs and Excise. It is clear from section 60 of the 1927 Act that payment of the excise duty must take place prior to or on the date of the expiration of the licence: if this is not done, then the licence does not continue in force. It is strange that the legislature did not see fit to make a similar provision in a case where the District Court disallows an objection to the renewal of a licence and a notice of appeal against such order is lodged with the District Court clerk in accordance with the rules of court.[14] In such a case where a publican neglects to apply for his tax clearance certificate not less than four months prior to the commencement date of the licence, even if he deposits the appropriate excise duty with the Collector of Customs and Excise prior to or on the date of the expiration of his licence, his licence cannot be deemed to continue pending an appeal to the Circuit Court since the facts necessary to ensure the continuance of the licence in accordance with section 60 of the Intoxicating Liquor Act 1927 do not exist. However, where an application for a tax clearance certificate is made on or before the appropriate time, a licence can continue in force beyond its expiry date.

(c) Since the entry into force of the Finance Act 1992,[15] an applicant who intends to renew his licence is obliged to produce a tax clearance certificate in accordance with section 242 of that Act. Section 115 of the Finance Act 1995 amended section 49 of the Finance (1909–10) Act 1910 which provides for the grant of retail licences and their date of expiration. Section 49(1A) of the Finance (1909–10) Act 1910 provides for the continuation in force of a licence beyond its "latest expiry date" in circumstances where a tax clearance certificate has been applied for but has not yet issued. The **19–11**

[11] Public House (Ireland) Act 1855, s.1.
[12] Intoxicating Liquor Act 1927, s.60.
[13] *Ibid.*, s.60(2).
[14] District Court (Renewal of Intoxicating Liquor Licences) Rules 1988 (S.I. No. 145 of 1988).
[15] May 28, 1992.

application for the tax clearance certificate must be made "not less than four months prior to the commencement date of such a licence in each subsequent year".[16] As a licence expires on September 30 each year, the application for a tax clearance certificate must be made prior to June 1 and during the currency of the licence in respect of which the application for renewal is to be made. Where the tax clearance certificate has been duly applied for but it is not issued after the date of the expiry of the licence, the section provides for the continuation of the licence pending the issue or refusal of the tax clearance certificate. Where the tax clearance certificate has been refused and an appeal against such refusal has been duly made in accordance with section 242(6) of the Finance Act 1992, then the licence continues in force until the final determination of that appeal.

However, these provisions only apply where the amount of duty that would be payable on the granting of the licence is duly deposited with the Collector of Customs and Excise. Strangely enough, there is no specific requirement that the amount of duty be lodged prior to or on the date of the expiration of the licence. The licence continues in force and expires only upon the grant of the new licence, that is upon the renewal of the licence. Where an application for a tax clearance certificate is refused or on appeal the refusal is upheld, the licence expires not later than seven days after the refusal or the determination of the appeal and the proportion of the excise duty paid by the applicant is returned.

Trading without a Licence

19–12 No person is entitled to sell, expose for sale, or keep for sale, by retail, any intoxicating liquor without being duly licensed so to sell the same, or do so at any place where he is not authorised by his licence to sell the same.[17] Breach of this provision attracts a fine of £50 and in default of payment of such fine, imprisonment for a term not exceeding six months.[18] A conviction under section 7 of the Intoxicating Liquor (General) Act 1924 can also result in the forfeiture of the licence.

STATUTORY PROVISION

Section 7(3) of the Intoxicating Liquor (General) Act 1924 provides:

> "In addition to any other penalty imposed by this section, any person convicted of a second or any subsequent offence under this section . . . shall, if he be the holder of a licence of any description for the sale of intoxicating liquor by retail, forfeit such licence."

---

[16] Finance (1909–10) Act 1910, s.49(1A).
[17] Intoxicating Liquor (General) Act 1924, s.7.
[18] *Ibid.*, s.7(2).

It is unlikely that this subsection operates to invalidate a licence which is granted after a person has been convicted of a second or subsequent offence under section 7 of the 1924 Act. However, it is clear that the legislature regards the sale of intoxicating liquor without a licence as a serious offence. A difficulty arises where a tax clearance certificate has issued to an applicant for renewal prior to the date of the expiry of his licence, and a notice of objection to the renewal of his licence is lodged by an objector. If the annual licensing District Court disallows the objection and an appeal is lodged, even if he lodges the appropriate excise duty with the Collector of Customs and Excise, he would prima facie appear to be trading illegally until the determination of that appeal in his favour, and the subsequent grant of the licence.

It is clear from *D.P.P. (O'Halloran) v. Cronin*[19] that "an intoxicating liquor licence is dated the day it is issued and takes effect from that date" and that a licence when issued has no retrospective effect. In that case the licence had not been renewed due to the delay on the part of the Revenue Commissioners in issuing the tax clearance certificate. Geoghegan J. rejected the submission of the defendant that the previous licence could be deemed to continue in force until a tax clearance certificate was issued or refused: **19–13**

> ". . . it is a clear feature of the Licensing Acts that a person cannot sell intoxicating liquor without either the appropriate excise licence or an express right under statute to trade".[20]

The judgment in the *Cronin* case led to the amendment of section 49(1A) of the Finance (1909–10) Act 1910, by section 115 of the Finance Act 1995, by permitting a licence to continue in force beyond September 30 once an application for a tax clearance certificate has been made in time. Geoghegan J. pointed to the lacuna which existed prior to the amendment, namely that a licence at that time could only be deemed to continue in force where an application for a tax clearance certificate had been refused and an appeal against such refusal was lodged.

It seems unjust that Mr Cronin should be penalised for trading without a licence, where the delay in obtaining same was to some extent the fault of the Revenue Commissioners.

In *Application of Doreen Riordan*[21] the Garda Síochána objected to the granting of an ad interim transfer of a licence to the applicant on the basis that the licence had become forfeited by operation of law. The licence, which had been held by the applicant's husband should have been forfeited seven years previously because of recordable offences. The District Court clerk did not record the offences on the licence. Finlay P. referred to "an omission and a neglect of statutory duty on the part of an officer of the State" and said:

---

[19] Unreported, High Court, Geoghegan J., February 10, 1995.
[20] *Ibid.* at p. 9.
[21] [1981] I.L.R.M. 2.

> "As a matter of justice, therefore, it seems to me extremely undesirable for it now to be possible that the State through the Garda Síochána should be permitted in effect to obtain a declaration of the court retrospective by the full of seven years as to the invalidity of the licensing of these premises since 1973 when that has occurred by reason of an omission or default on the part of one of their servants."[22]

Section 115 of the Finance Act 1995 prolongs the duration of the licence once the application for the tax clearance certificate is made on or before the time therein stipulated.

Applicant

19–14 The power of the officers of Customs and Excise to renew a licence is contained in section 1 of the Licensing (Ireland) Act 1833, which provides, *inter alia*, as follows:

> ". . . it shall and may be lawful for the proper Officers of Excise in *Ireland* to grant to the same Persons and at and for the same Houses as shall have been licensed in the Year last immediately preceding, and whose Licence shall not have been withdrawn or annulled . . . ".

So, the Revenue Commissioners are empowered to issue a licence to the person who was the licensee for the preceding year: in other words, a licence can only be renewed in the name of the previous licensee.

Rule 104 of the District Court Rules 1948 dispenses with the necessity of making an application for a renewal where a certificate of transfer has been granted by the annual licensing District Court: an application for renewal does not arise where the court has transferred the licence to some other person.

The Revenue Commissioners cannot renew the licence in the name of the ad interim transferee since he is not, as is provided for in section 1 of the Licensing (Ireland) Act 1833, a person "as shall have been licensed in the year last immediately preceding". In *Fitzpatrick v. McCormack*, Finlay C.J. stated:

> "It seems to me that a licensed person could not be considered to be a person other than one to whom the excise, pursuant to a certificate of the court, had issued a licence."[23]

He must first obtain a "confirmation" of that transfer by way of a court certificate which is then presented to the Revenue Commissioners who will issue a new licence in his name.

Thus, where an applicant has obtained a certificate of transfer, he is entitled to the grant of a licence from the Revenue Commissioners once he has satisfied

---

[22] *Ibid.* at 5.
[23] [1986] I.R. 380 at 391.

the other statutory conditions for obtaining a licence. Thereafter, he is a licensed person for the purposes of applying for a renewal of his licence.

Premises

Confusion has arisen as to whether the District Court is entitled to grant a certificate leading to the renewal of a licence where the premises to which the licence attaches has been altered.[24] The suggestion is that where there is no substantial alteration, then the court has jurisdiction to issue a certificate. If this is correct, then it would be a matter of fact for each individual District Court judge to determine whether or not the alterations which have occurred to the premises are substantial: the result would be that licences could be granted by the Revenue Commissioners in respect of different and altered premises. **19–15**

The power of the District Court to exercise such a discretion is questionable since the enactment of the Courts of Justice Act 1924 which conferred new licensing jurisdiction on various courts.

Section 1 of the Licensing (Ireland) Act 1833 empowers the Customs and Excise to grant a licence to an applicant "at and for the same houses as shall have been licensed in the year last immediately preceding". The Revenue Commissioners cannot grant a licence in circumstances where the premises are not the same as those previously licensed, unless a certificate of the Circuit Court has been obtained in respect of the altered premises.

When to Apply

An application to renew a publican's licence should be made prior to the date of expiry of the existing licence. Otherwise, the applicant will run the risk, in certain circumstances, of being prosecuted for trading without a licence. **19–16**

In *Connolly v. Collector of Customs and Excise*[25] Blayney J. refused to direct the defendant to issue a licence retrospectively as the excise duty in respect of the year for which the licence was being sought had not been paid during that particular year. This was despite the fact that the applicant had obtained, on appeal to the Circuit Court, a certificate as to his good character and the peaceable and orderly conduct of the premises during that year. He had also tendered, and the Collector of Customs and Excise had accepted, the appropriate excise duty in respect of that year. Blayney J. stated:

> "In my opinion the clear intention of the section [section 1 of the Licensing (Ireland) Act 1833] is that the renewal of the licence is to be given to the person

---

[24] See also below, chap. 21, "Objections", para. 21–36.
[25] (1988–93) 4 I.T.R. 419.

who was the licensee during the previous year, that is to say during the year prior to the date of the application for renewal."[26]

Blayney J. construed the expression "licensed in the year immediately preceding" as referring to the date of the application for the renewal and not the date preceding the year in respect of which the application for the licence was being made. If the *Connolly* case (above) is correct, it can be seen that the most prudent course to adopt is to apply for the renewal of the licence during the currency of the existing licence.[27]

Failure to Renew

19–17 Where a licence expires and the applicant has not applied to renew it during the currency of the licence, the District Court may grant a certificate leading to the renewal of the licence even though such application was not made at the annual licensing District Court.

STATUTORY PROVISION

Section 12(2) of the Licensing Act (Ireland) 1874 provides, *inter alia*:

> "Where under the provisions of this Act or any Act now in force or hereafter to be passed, the production of a certificate by justices presiding at petty sessions . . . is required previous to the grant or transfer of any licence . . . such certificate shall not (save as hereinafter provided) be granted except at an annual licensing petty sessions: provided always, that in such cases as may seem fit to such Justices sitting in petty sessions . . . a certificate may, notwithstanding the preceding provisions, be granted at any time other than that fixed for annual licensing petty sessions, and in like manner as heretofore . . . ".

The question arises as to whether the Courts (No. 2) Act 1986, dispensing as it did with the requirement of producing a justice's certificate, save in certain exceptional circumstances, impliedly repealed the provisions of section 12(2) of the Licensing Act (Ireland) 1874 thereby depriving the court of the discretion to grant a certificate in such cases as it deemed appropriate. In other words, if an applicant neglects to apply for renewal during the currency of his licence, is he now prevented from applying to the District Court for a certificate pursuant to section 12(2) of the 1874 Act by reason of the fact that he is not obliged to produce a certificate of the court as a condition for the renewal of his licence?

19–18 On reading section 11 of the Spirits (Ireland) Act 1854 which introduced the requirement to produce a justice's certificate before the licence could be renewed, it seems reasonable to infer that a renewal application can be made within a year following the expiration of the preceding licence. However, an

---

[26] *Ibid.* at 423.
[27] At the time of writing, the *Connolly* case is under appeal to the Supreme Court.

applicant should be mindful of the definition of "new licence" in section 37 of the Licensing Act (Ireland) 1874, as "a licence granted in respect of premises in respect of which a similar licence has not theretofore been granted, or, if granted, has been annulled, or has not been in force during the preceding six months". So, if a period of six months has been allowed to elapse since the expiry of the licence, then the applicant is seeking, not the renewal of his licence, but what is in effect a new licence and in these circumstances, the certificate must be obtained from a judge of the Circuit Court.

In *R. (Robinson) v. Londonderry Justices*[28] Palles C.B. was satisfied that an application for the certificate leading to the renewal of a licence need not be made at the annual licensing sessions but could be made, by virtue of section 12(2) of the 1874 Act "at any time other than that fixed for annual licensing petty sessions". In that case a licence had existed in respect of the premises during the preceding six months.

Excise Duty

An applicant for renewal who pays his excise duty by cheque should ensure **19–19** that there are sufficient funds in his bank account to meet same. If the cheque is dishonoured after the issue of the licence, the licence is voided. Section 23 of the Finance Act 1936 provides that where the excise duty is paid by cheque and "if such cheque is dishonoured, such licence shall be void as from the grant thereof".

Conclusion

The licensee who wishes to renew his licence should be alert: he must ensure **19–20** that his application for a tax clearance certificate has been lodged well and truly in time; again, he must notify the fire officer in accordance with law of his intention to renew; if he has not obtained his tax clearance certificate prior to the expiry of his licence he must ensure payment of the appropriate excise duty to the Collector of Customs and Excise. If his application for a tax clearance certificate is refused, he must ensure that he brings his appeal in accordance with the procedure laid down in section 242 of the Finance Act 1992.

By dispensing with the necessity of obtaining a court certificate for the renewal of a licence, the legislature intended to remove the inconvenience whereby all publicans were required to apply to the District Court at the annual licensing sessions for a certificate leading to renewal of the licence, thereby relieving the heavy work load of the court and indeed the District Court clerk. To an extent this has been achieved, but the onus placed on the publican by the legislature is great.

---

[28] (1911) 45 I.L.T.R. 171.

CHAPTER 20

DECLARATORY JURISDICTION

Introduction

20–1 Although first introduced to the licensing code by Part VI, Chapter II of the Tourist Traffic Act 1952 and thereafter by sections 8 and 9 of the Intoxicating Liquor Act 1953, the declaratory jurisdiction did not become of general application until the enactment of the Intoxicating Liquor Act 1960.[1] This procedure allows an applicant to obtain the initial approval of the court on the basis of plans lodged with the county registrar or District Court clerk, before going to the expense of proceeding with the scheme and running the risk of failing in his application for the relevant certificate, either on the ground of failure to comply with jurisdictional requirements or because of a successful objection. The declaratory jurisdiction can be invoked by an applicant seeking an on-licence or an off-licence; it also applies in respect of a club seeking a certificate of registration and certain restaurants.

20–2 In *Re Thomas Hill, Applicant*[2] the applicant sought a certificate for a new publican's licence for the sale of intoxicating liquor by retail in premises which,

---

[1] July 4, 1960.

[2] [1945] 11 Ir. Jur. Rep. 69.

at the date of the application, consisted of a vacant site upon which the foundations for a substantial building to comprise a public house had recently been laid. The applicant had entered into an agreement for the extinguishment of a seven-day publican's on-licence should the application be granted. In refusing the application on the ground that it was premature, Judge McCarthy stated:

> "I have no doubt that the plans prepared are excellent, and that the Applicant is a fit and proper person.... In my view, an applicant, coming in as this applicant has, says, in effect, 'I will spend a certain amount, and if the Court says or does something which I may, if I choose, regard as a judicial blessing on my initial effort and encouragement to proceed, I will continue to build'. I could not give, or suggest that there should be given, a preference or possibility of preference to any person because he has decided that now is the best time, and I do not think that the Court should be asked to limit his risk, as against another person who, not applying now, might be prepared to risk building a complete structure before applying at a later date."[3]

The proposal to expand the declaratory jurisdiction and make it of general application was strongly urged by Judge Conroy in submissions which he made to the Intoxicating Liquor Commission of 1957. The Commission noted that "he said he was speaking from personal experience of the hardships which followed refusal of an application after an applicant had gone to the expense of constructing premises for use as a public house".[4]

A. General Declaratory Jurisdiction

The general declaratory jurisdiction is contained in sections 15 and 16 of the Intoxicating Liquor Act 1960. It is invoked by a person who shows that he proposes to acquire, construct or alter premises and to apply to the Circuit Court or the District Court, as may be appropriate, for the grant of a certificate entitling him to receive a licence in respect of the premises. It is accordingly not necessary for the person invoking this jurisdiction: 20–3

(a) to have title to the premises;

(b) to show that he has commenced construction of or alteration of the premises.

The jurisdiction involves two applications to the court, *i.e.* the declaratory application and once the work has been carried out in accordance with the declaratory order, an application under section 17 of the Intoxicating Liquor

[3] *Ibid.* at 71.

[4] Reports of the Commission of Inquiry into the Operation of the Laws Relating to the Sale and Supply of Intoxicating Liquor 1957, p. 16.

Act 1960 for the grant of a certificate entitling the applicant to receive a licence in respect of the premises. The application for the certificate will be granted where an applicant shows that he has substantially complied with the terms of the declaratory order, and no objection on the ground of his character is made or is successful.

Licences in respect of which Declaratory Jurisdiction does not Apply

20–4 The declaratory jurisdiction may not be invoked in respect of the following licences:

(a) Special Restaurant Licence

20–5 Section 19 of the Intoxicating Liquor Act 1988 provides:

> "Sections 15 and 17 of the Act of 1960 shall not apply in relation to any application to the Circuit Court for a certificate entitling the applicant to receive a special restaurant licence under this Act".

(b) Licences for the Sale of Intoxicating Liquor

20–6 Where the production of a certificate of the District Court or the Circuit Court is not required for the grant of a licence, for example, a wine retailers's on-licence and a wine retailer's off-licence and a theatre licence, then the declaratory jurisdiction is not appropriate.

(c) Public Dancing Licence

20–7 The declaratory jurisdiction does not apply in respect of a public dancing licence. In *Application of Chariot Inns Ltd,*[5] where section 6 of the Licensing (Ireland) Act 1902 was invoked, the court granted a declaration that the proposed premises were fit and convenient to receive a publican's licence and a restaurant certificate. In that case, the objectors indicated to the court that they had no real objection to the grant of a publican's licence in respect of the existing licensed premises and the proposed extensions, or to the grant of a restaurant certificate for the entire premises. Their concern was the inconvenience that would be caused by "late night dancers and revellers". Johnson J., however, pointed out that this was not a matter for him to decide. He stated:

> "I think their objections may very well be justified in the long term but having regard to the present situation that is not something I have to deal with."[6]

---

[5] Unreported, High Court, Johnson J., April 12, 1991.
[6] *Ibid.* at p. 3.

Thus, an applicant can be exposed to the risk of expending considerable sums of money in developing the function room and night club business as the declaratory jurisdiction is not available in such a case.

(d) Music and Singing Licence

An applicant for a music and singing licence must incur the expense of acquiring and/or constructing and/or altering his premises for the purposes of making such an application and still runs the risk of a refusal of his application if an objection succeeds. 20–8

Licences in respect of which Declaratory Jurisdiction applies

Section 15(1) of the Intoxicating Liquor Act 1960 permits the making of an application for a declaratory order where it is proposed to acquire, construct or alter premises and thereafter apply to the Circuit Court or the District Court, as may be appropriate, for a certificate entitling the applicant to a licence in respect of the premises. The section applies to the following licences: 20–9

(a) Publican's Licence

The application for the declaratory order and the certificate is made to the Circuit Court. 20–10

(b) Off-Licences

The application for the declaratory order and the certificate is made to the District Court. 20–11

(c) Hotel Licence

The application for the declaratory order and the certificate is made to the Circuit Court. 20–12

In *Application of Daniel Rice*[7] counsel for the objectors argued that the application for a declaratory order must fail, as the applicant could not satisfy the minimum rateable valuation requirement nor could he show that the premises had 10 or more rooms set aside for the sleeping accommodation of travellers. He argued that the declaratory jurisdiction was not intended to apply to a hotel premises. Haugh J. was satisfied that as section 15 of the 1960 Act clearly dealt with any unbuilt premises it applied to "and was meant to apply to intended hotels".[8]

---

[7] (1962) 96 I.L.T.R. 197.
[8] *Ibid.* at 198.

(d) Holiday Camp Premises

20–13 The statute conferring jurisdiction upon the Circuit Court to grant a certificate entitling an applicant to receive an on-licence in respect of a holiday camp[9] does not provide for a declaratory procedure. This is in marked contrast to the provisions of section 41 of the Tourist Traffic Act 1952 which introduced the declaratory procedure in respect of certain types of hotels, and section 8 of the Intoxicating Liquor Act 1953 which provides for a declaratory order in respect of a local authority site. Section 15 of the Intoxicating Liquor Act 1960 does not apply in respect of an application under section 8 of the 1953 Act; however it does not exclude an application in respect of holiday camp premises from its ambit. It refers, *inter alia*, to an application for the grant of a certificate entitling an applicant to receive a licence in respect of premises and it would seem to follow that the declaratory jurisdiction applies in respect of proposed holiday camp premises.

Duration of Declaratory Order

20–14 A declaratory order remains in force "for two years from the grant of the application or for such longer period as the Court granting the application may in any particular case think proper to provide".[10] For some time after the passing of the 1960 Act, it was thought that an application to extend the duration of a declaratory order for a period in excess of the statutory two years must be made when the declaratory order was granted.

However, in *Application of Eoghan O'Catháin*,[11] shortly before the expiration of the statutory period of two years, the High Court (which had granted a declaratory order on appeal from the Circuit Court), directed an extension for a further year. Since then, the Circuit Court and District Court have consistently entertained applications for the extension of the life of a declaratory order where the order was originally made by one or other of those courts in the first instance. An application for an extension of the period of a declaratory order may only be made to the court during the currency of the period originally granted by the court: if the declaratory order is allowed to lapse in time it cannot be revived by order of the court.

STATUTORY PROVISION

20–15 Section 15(1) of the Intoxicating Liquor Act 1960 provides:

> "Where a person proposes to acquire, construct or alter premises (not being premises in relation to which an application may be brought under section 8 of

---

[9] Tourist Traffic Act 1952, s.44.
[10] Intoxicating Liquor Act 1960, s.15(6).
[11] Unreported, High Court, Record No. 1, 1965.

the Intoxicating Liquor Act, 1953) and to apply to the Circuit Court or the District Court, as may be appropriate, for the grant of a certificate entitling him to receive a licence in respect of the premises, he may apply to that Court for a declaration that the premises would be fit and convenient to be so licensed, and, if he shows to the satisfaction of the Court—

(a) that, if the acquisition, construction or alteration, as the case may be, of the premises were then completed and the application for the grant of the certificate aforesaid were then made and no objection on the ground of the character, misconduct or unfitness of the applicant were made on the hearing of the application, it would be proper, having regard to the provisions of the Licensing Acts, 1833 to 1960, to grant the application and

(b) in any case where the applicant proposes to construct premises, that he is the holder of the lowest estate or tenancy in the site on which it is proposed to construct the premises or, if he is not such holder, that the holder thereof has agreed to convey the lowest estate or tenancy in the site to the applicant if and when a declaration under this section is made in relation to the site,

the Court, if it is so satisfied, may grant the application on such terms as the Court may think fit."

Substantive Application

The court must consider the declaratory application as though it were an application for a certificate, or, as Murnaghan J. stated in *Re Thomas Joseph Cummins*: **20–16**

> "In these circumstances I have to consider the notional position created by clause (a) of section 15(1) . . . that, if the acquisition, construction or alteration, as the case may be, of the premises were then completed and the application for the grant of the certificate aforesaid were then made and no objection on the ground of character, misconduct or unfitness of the applicant were made on the hearing of the application, it would be proper, having regard to the provisions of the Licensing Acts, 1833 to 1960, to grant the application. . .' and if I am so satisfied I may grant the application for a declaration on such terms as I may consider fit."[12]

The application for the declaratory order, therefore, becomes the substantive application and the proofs necessary to show jurisdiction to grant a certificate must be adduced at declaratory stage. For example, in an application under section 4 of the Licensing (Ireland) Act 1902, the necessary increase in population and evidence from the Ordnance Survey is proved at declaratory stage.

This can cause difficulties, particularly in an application under section 3 of the Licensing (Ireland) Act 1902. This provides for the grant of a new licence for premises in the immediate vicinity of premises to which a licence which

[12] [1964] I.R. 67 at 68 and 69.

became extinguished or surrendered by virtue of the expiration of a lease was attached.

Where he does not wish to run the risk of his application for a certificate being refused after the expiry of the lease and consequent surrender or extinguishment of the licence, the applicant may apply to the court for a declaratory order and indicate that at certificate stage, the lease will have expired and the licence will be extinguished, as required by section 3. It is questionable, however, whether this would satisfy the "notional position".

20–17 The legislature appears to have catered for this notional position where a licence is being sought in substitution for a licence which previously attached to a demolished premises. Section 14(3) of the 1960 Act provides as follows:

> "Where, before the demolition of the original premises, an application in relation to the new premises or (if the new premises have not been constructed) the proposed new premises is made to the Court under section 15 of this Act, the original premises shall be deemed, for the purposes of that section, but not otherwise, to have been demolished, but an application under section 17 of this Act in respect of the new premises shall not be granted unless the Court (being otherwise satisfied, having regard to the provisions of that section, to grant the application) is satisfied that the original premises have been demolished."

So, an applicant who invokes the jurisdictional exception contained in section 14 of the 1960 Act does not have to incur the expense of demolishing the premises until after the declaratory order has been granted: evidence of demolition in a section 14 application where a declaratory order has already been made can be adduced at certificate stage.

No such express statutory protection exists in respect of section 3 of the 1902 Act, so the question as to whether an applicant is obliged to prove that a lease has expired and a licence has become extinguished or surrendered by virtue of such expiry at the declaratory stage, arises. The court, however, has a very wide discretion under section 15 of the 1960 Act. It could be argued that when granting the declaratory application on such terms as it "may think fit", the court may impose a condition that the lease will have expired and the appropriate licence surrendered or extinguished prior to the making of the certificate application.

Application to Court

JURISDICTIONAL REQUIREMENTS

20–18 1. Premises

Acquire The applicant must prove that he intends to acquire the premises which are the subject of the application. He need not prove that he has acquired the premises, but an agreement with the present owner of the premises to acquire them once the declaratory order has been granted is sufficient proof.

Construct The statute requires proof, where the applicant proposes to construct premises, of either of the following:

(i) That the applicant is the holder of the lowest estate and tenancy in the site upon which it is proposed to construct the premises. This means that he has either purchased the freehold or has entered into a lease or tenancy of the site.

(ii) If the applicant is not the owner, he must show that he has entered into an agreement with the holder of the lowest estate or tenancy in the site that such estate or tenancy will be conveyed to the applicant upon a successful declaratory application.

Alter If an applicant proposes to alter existing licensed premises and make a declaratory application, he must prove one of the following:

(i) where he owns the premises, evidence of such ownership by way of the appropriate stamped title documentation;

(ii) where he proposes to acquire the premises and then alter them, evidence that he has entered into an agreement with the owner of the premises for the conveyance of the lowest estate or tenancy in the premises to him once the declaratory order has been made.

2. Venue **20–19**

Where the application relates to an on-licence, the venue is the Circuit Court. Where the application relates to a spirit or beer retailer's off-licence or both, the application is made to the District Court.

3. Fit and Convenient

This expression is also considered by the court in an application under section 13 of the Intoxicating Liquor Act 1960 which relates to the grant of a new licence in a rural area. In considering the question of fitness and convenience, the courts take into account both the structure itself and its location *vis-à-vis* neighbouring houses, churches and schools. Finlay J. has construed "unfitness" as dealing with the premises themselves and "inconvenience" as meaning and including the location of the premises.[13]

McWilliam J. held in *Re Application of Power Supermarkets Ltd*[14] that a supermarket premises is not "fit and convenient" to receive a publican's licence. In that case, Power Supermarkets in Carlow sought a declaration that the entire food department of part of premises known as Hanover House, Carlow, would be fit and convenient to be licensed for the sale of intoxicat-

[13] *Re Centennial Properties Ltd.*, unreported, High Court, Finlay P., December 20, 1983.
[14] [1981] I.L.R.M. 270 (the "Carlow case").

ing liquor for consumption on and off its premises, if altered and constructed in accordance with plans produced to the court. The jurisdiction invoked was section 4 of the Licensing (Ireland) Act 1902. It was accepted that the applicant could not seek the grant of a certificate for an off-licence in lieu of an on-licence, as section 62 of the Intoxicating Liquor Act 1927 did not make provision for the grant of an off-licence in substitution for an on-licence where the premises were not situate in a county borough.

In evidence, the applicant conceded that although it was seeking an ordinary publican's licence, its intention was to concentrate on the normal supermarket business of sale for consumption off the premises. It was proposed that the entire of the food department of the supermarket be licensed for the sale of intoxicating liquor for consumption on the premises but that a small area would be constructed as a bar and that the applicant would confine the consumption of intoxicating liquor on the premises to the bar.

McWilliam J. held that such an arrangement was not "fit and convenient" within the meaning of section 15(1) of the 1960 Act. He stated:

> "I am of opinion that, at the moment, most people would consider that a licence for the consumption on every part of a grocery department such as this is not fitting, proper or suitable and that many, probably a majority, would consider that any bar in a grocery department such as this is not fitting, proper or suitable either."[15]

In *Re Application of Power Supermarkets Ltd*, Ellis J. referred to McWilliam J.'s judgment stating:

> "The question of whether the licence if granted is intended only to remain attached to the premises for a temporary or a short period is not a factor to which this Court properly should have regard . . . it does not seem to me either proper, fit, suitable or convenient that a supermarket or food store premises should have a publican's on-licence attached to it...".[16]

This case was decided a number of years before the case of *Re Application of Power Supermarkets Ltd*[17] where the Supreme Court was satisfied that an application under section 4 of the 1902 Act for an off-licence could succeed where an on-licence was tendered for extinguishment.

20–20 If an applicant wishes to license a supermarket or a premises which is to be used for the sale of intoxicating liquor for consumption off the premises, he should apply for an off-licence, not an on-licence. The suitability and fitness of the premises itself concerns matters such as its physical layout, internal fixtures and fittings, fire safety features, lavatory provision, heating, lighting and ventilation.[18]

---

[15] *Ibid.* at 273.
[16] Unreported, High Court, Ellis J., June 3, 1981 (the "Waterford case").
[17] [1988] I.R. 206 (the "Killarney case").
[18] *Re Centennial Properties Ltd*, above, n.13, at p. 4.

In determining the question of "inconvenience", the court has regard to environmental matters such as whether a proposed public house might cause nuisance to residents in adjoining dwellings. In *Re Application of Thomas Flynn*, Teevan J. stated:

> "The adjoining houses are so disposed that several of them would be immediately adjacent to the applicant's premises — certainly to the car park portion — and, if constructed according to the submitted plans, the public house and car park will be wedged violently into the group of residences occupied by the neighbour/objectors. There must be in consequence a very serious impairment of their privacy and comfort in their homes."[19]

An objection based upon the fitness of the premises from the point of view of public safety was upheld by Budd J. in *Re Thomas O'Brien, Applicant.*[20]

In *Centennial*[21] Finlay J. refused the application as the proposed premises would have been situated in close proximity to a housing development containing young families and a large open space developed for school sport, recreational activities and general community activity.

4. Plans

Section 15 of the 1960 Act imposes a mandatory requirement that the superintendent of the Garda Síochána receive a copy of the plans of the premises. Section 15(3)(c) does not stipulate a time within which the plans must be deposited with the Superintendent. However, they must be deposited prior to the making of the application and that plan must be substantially the one relied upon in court. In *Application of Terence J. Maguire*,[22] objection was taken that the plans upon which the applicant based his appeal to the High Court had not been deposited with the superintendent as required by section 15(3)(c) of the 1960 Act. The appeal to the High Court was opened and proceeded on a set of plans other than those lodged with the original application. Copies of the new plans were sent to the Chief State Solicitor two days before the hearing of the appeal. Murnaghan J. considered whether the plans lodged with the superintendent were substantially the same as the plans before the High Court and was satisfied that there were essential differences stating: **20–21**

> "It is, I think, the common experience in licensing appeals that alterations are made in the original plans as a result of something that transpired at the hearing in the Circuit Court and that amended plans are relied upon in the High Court. The applicant's counsel sought to justify the altered plans in this case by reliance on this practice. The provisions of section 15(3)(c) are mandatory and failure to deposit with the Superintendent a copy of the plan which is substantially the

---

[19] [1963] I.R. 301 at 315.
[20] (1974) 108 I.L.T.R. 141.
[21] Above, n.13.
[22] Unreported, High Court, Murnaghan J., April 4, 1963.

> one relied upon in court is fatal to the application. The purpose of depositing a copy of the plan with the Superintendent is to enable him to consider the proposed alterations and to assist the court by objecting to the application in its proper case."

Procedure The procedure which an applicant for a declaratory order must follow is contained in subsections 3 and 4 of section 15 of the Intoxicating Liquor Act 1960. This procedure is dealt with in detail in chapter 17, "Practice and Procedure". It should be noted that as the procedural requirements are statutory, the court has no jurisdiction to abridge or amend same, whether they relate to publication of the notice of application or service of the notice or plans.

20–22 5. Rateable Valuation

Proof of a minimum rateable valuation is required in certain licensing applications. Where an applicant seeks a declaratory order under section 15 of the 1960 Act and the provisions of section 5 of the 1902 Act as to rateable valuation apply, he need not adduce evidence that the premises has a minimum rateable valuation. Section 31 of the Intoxicating Liquor Act 1962 provides:

> "An application under section 15 of the Act of 1960 in respect of any premises may be granted notwithstanding the fact that it is not shown to the satisfaction of the Court that the premises comply with the provisions of section 5 of the Act of 1902, but an application to which both the said section 5 and subsection 1 of section 17 of the Act of 1960 refer in respect of any premises shall not be granted unless it is shown to the satisfaction of the Court that the premises comply with the provisions of the said section 5."

Therefore, if an application is made for a declaratory order in respect of proposed premises where the jurisdictional section requires proof of a certain rateable valuation under section 5 of the 1902 Act, no evidence of rateable valuation need be adduced. Proof of valuation in accordance with section 5 must be adduced at certificate stage.

A provisional certificate of rateable valuation is sufficient for the purposes of the application for the certificate.

In construing section 5 of the 1902 Act, section 21 of the Intoxicating Liquor Act 1943 and section 13 of the 1960 Act, the term "rateable valuation" is deemed to include a provisional valuation issued by the Commissioner of Valuation.[23] In *Application of Thomas Kiernan*,[24] the applicant could not prove that the premises were valued or even provisionally valued at declaratory stage. He could not rely on the exemption in section 31 of the 1962 Act as section 5 of the 1902 Act did not apply.

---

[23] Intoxicating Liquor Act 1960, s.33(2).

[24] [1965] 31 Ir. Jur. Rep. 4.

The premises in question were not completed and the Commissioner refused to issue a certificate of provisional valuation in respect of intended buildings not then existing. Ó Dálaigh C.J. stated:

> "Indeed, in ordinary circumstances a Court asked for a Declaration under Section 15, where the new licence is to be sought under Section 13, will have no difficulty in satisfying itself that the rateable valuation of the premises to be erected will not be less than £10. The plans of the proposed premises required to be lodged with the application would show at a glance whether or not the rateable valuation provision was satisfied and, in any event, if the matter be in doubt, the Court is expressly empowered to make its Declaration upon such terms as it thinks fit, and one of these terms could be that the rateable valuation would be not less than £10."[25]

Ó Dálaigh C.J. was satisfied that if proof of valuation as required by section 13 of the 1960 Act were insisted on at declaratory stage, this would defeat the plain object of the Act and treat the words of section 15, dealing with the proposal to construct a premises, as if they were not part of the section.

Rateable Valuation: Beer Retailer's Off-licence Where an application is made for a declaratory order in respect of premises for which it is proposed to apply for a beer retailer's off-licence, the *Kiernan* decision (see above) applies. Proof of valuation at declaratory stage is not essential and the court may make the grant of the declaratory order conditional upon obtaining a certificate of rateable valuation at certificate stage. Proof of valuation at certificate stage is, however, essential unless the applicant can rely on section 33(2) of the Intoxicating Liquor Act 1960 where he invokes a jurisdictional exception referred to in that section.[26]

6. Planning Permission

The court is entitled to grant a declaratory order where full planning permission has not been obtained in respect of the proposed premises. It is prudent, however, to obtain full planning permission in respect of a proposed premises prior to seeking a declaration of fitness and convenience. If planning permission has not been secured prior to the grant of the declaratory order, then the possibility of the planning application being refused and the declaratory order becoming redundant arises. The plans submitted to the planning authority and upon which planning permission is granted should be the same as the plans accompanying the declaratory application. 20–23

The court is not obliged to require proof of compliance with planning requirements before it grants the declaratory order. Walsh J. in *Application of Thomas Kitterick*[27] was satisfied that the critical time in so far as the actual

---

[25] *Ibid.* at 10.
[26] Beer Licences (Ireland) Act 1877, s.2.
[27] (1970) 105 I.L.T.R. 105.

premises are concerned, is the point at which the licence is applied for under section 17 and that if premises were erected in violation of planning requirements: "it appears to me to be quite contrary to the policy of the court that a licence should be granted notwithstanding the illegality". In considering a case stated from the High Court as to whether the court required proof of compliance with planning requirements at declaratory stage, Walsh J. responded in the negative, noting that there were two courses open to a court at declaratory stage:

> "It may require to be satisfied that the plans as submitted to it have already received the approval of all the necessary authorities so that if a building were erected in accordance with those plans it would not infringe any statutory provision. In such a case the Court might grant the Declaration sought but nonetheless still have the power under section 17 to refuse to grant the licence if the premises were in the meanwhile substantially altered from the plans originally approved by the Court even though such alterations were carried out as the result of the further requirements of the planning or other authorities. The other course open to the Court is to grant the application upon the terms that the plans as approved by the Court must be submitted for and obtain the approval of the planning and other relevant authorities in the form in which the Court has approved them or in substantial accordance therewith."[28]

The court, then, has a discretion as to whether or not it requires to be satisfied that full planning permission be obtained in respect of the proposed premises at declaratory stage.

OBJECTIONS

20–24 Any person who may object to an application for the grant of a certificate entitling the applicant to a licence in respect of the premises is entitled to object in like manner to an application for a declaratory order.[29]

The objectors are entitled to rely upon those grounds of objection which are available in an application for a certificate leading to the grant of a licence. An objector in an application for a certificate is not obliged formally to notify the applicant of his objection in advance. This applies also in a declaratory application. An objection to the character, misconduct or unfitness of the applicant is not available to an objector if the application for the certificate is made under section 21 of the Intoxicating Liquor Act 1943, *i.e.* for the grant of a new licence in respect of more convenient premises in a rural area. Thus, it follows that the question of character is not a matter which should be considered by the court in a declaratory application where section 21 of the 1943 Act is invoked.

The court may take both existing licensed premises and premises or proposed premises which have the benefit of a declaratory order which is still in

---

[28] *Ibid.* at 109.
[29] Intoxicating Liquor Act 1960, s.15(5).

force into account for the purposes of an objection to a declaratory order or a certificate.[30] So, if a person objects on the ground that there are sufficient licensed premises existing in the neighbourhood, he may refer to a site or sites which are the subject of a declaratory order, and the court must take these into account.

Application for Certificate where Declaratory Order Granted

Where a declaratory order has been obtained and the premises are constructed in accordance with its terms within the time stipulated, an applicant may apply to court for a certificate entitling him to receive a licence in respect of the premises. The applicant for the certificate need not be the same person as the applicant who obtained the declaratory order. The only objection which can be made at certificate stage is to the character, misconduct or unfitness of the applicant. 20–25

STATUTORY PROVISION

Section 17(1) of the Intoxicating Liquor Act 1960, as amended by section 32 of the Intoxicating Liquor Act 1962 provides: 20–26

> "If, on the hearing of an application for the grant of a certificate entitling the applicant to receive a licence in respect of any premises, it is shown to the satisfaction of the Court—
>
> (a) that a declaration has been made by the Court under subsection (1) of section 15 of this Act,
> (b) that the premises have been acquired, constructed or altered in substantial accordance with the terms of the declaration, and
> (c) where the application is made pursuant to any provision of the Licensing Acts that provides for the extinguishing of one or more existing licences on the grant of the licence—
>   (i) that the licence or each of the licences in respect of which it was shown to the satisfaction of the Court on the application for the declaration that the applicant was the holder thereof or had secured the consent of the holder to the extinguishing thereof is in force, or
>   (ii) if such licence or licences or any of them is or are not in force, that the licence or licences not in force has not or have not been forfeited or extinguished and the premises to which it or they related have not been deemed, by virtue of any provision of the Licensing Acts, never to have been licensed,
>
> it shall not be open to the Court to refuse the application—
>
> I. in a case where it is made pursuant to section 21 of the Act of 1943, on any ground, and

---

[30] *Ibid.*, s.15(7).

II. in any other case, on any ground other than the character, misconduct or unfitness of the applicant,

and where, as respects a licence or licences and the premises to which it or they related, it is shown to the satisfaction of the Court that it or they comply with the provisions of sub-paragraph (ii) of paragraph (c) of this subsection, the licence or licences shall be deemed, for the purposes of the provisions of the Licensing Acts relating to the granting of licences, but not otherwise, to be in force and to relate to the premises to which it or they related and, on the grant of the new licence, shall accordingly be extinguished and the premises to which it or they related shall be deemed never to have been licensed."

JURISDICTIONAL REQUIREMENTS

20–27 1. Who May Apply

An objector may object on the grounds of the character, misconduct or unfitness of the applicant at declaratory stage: the retention of this ground of objection at certificate stage is an indication that it is open to a different person to bring the certificate application. For example, a person who has obtained a declaratory order may wish to sell the site with the benefit of the declaratory order and the purchaser is entitled to make the certificate application, once he can prove substantial compliance with the terms of the declaration, subject to any objections at certificate stage.

2. Declaratory Order

The applicant proves that a declaratory order has been made. As the duration of the declaratory order is specified in the court order, the application for the certificate must be brought within the period of time so specified. Section 17(6) of the Intoxicating Liquor Act 1960 provides that "references to declarations are references to declarations that are in force".

3. Substantial Accordance

The premises must be completed in "substantial accordance with the terms of the declaration".[31] At declaratory stage, the court has a discretion to impose terms with which the applicant must comply prior to the application for the certificate. These conditions relate to matters such as rateable valuation, planning permission, etc. The premises, as built, must be substantially the same as those outlined on the plans at declaratory stage. If there are essential differences, the court cannot grant the certificate application, where the applicant seeks to rely upon the declaratory order.

---

[31] *Ibid.*, at 17(4).

4. Existing Licence 20–28

Before the coming into force of section 17(1)(c)(ii) of the Intoxicating Liquor Act 1960 (as inserted by section 32 of the Intoxicating Liquor Act 1962) difficulties arose where objections to certificates under section 17 were taken on the ground that the licence to be proferred for extinguishment was not in force at the time of the making of the section 17 application, even though it had been at the declaratory stage. In *Re Downey, Applicant*,[32] the Garda Síochána objected to a section 17 application on the grounds that the licence for which the certificate was sought, would not be in substitution for an existing licence as required by section 4 of the Licensing (Ireland) Act 1902. They contended that as the licence had been handed in at declaratory stage and had not since been renewed, the requirements of the statute could not be satisfied. Davitt P. stated:

> "I do not think that there is really any conflict between the provisions of section 15 and section 17, taken together, of the 1960 Act, and section 4 of the 1902 Act. The two applications can properly be regarded as in reality two stages of the same application — an application for a certificate leading to a licence. I do not think anyone could really be in any doubt that when the matter is looked at in this way the new licence has been granted in substitution for an existing licence in accordance with the provisions of section 4 of the Act of 1902. If section 15 and section 17 of the 1960 Act are in conflict with section 4 of the 1902 Act, then there is an implied amendment to section 4 to the extent of the inconsistency."

Section 17(1)(c) of the 1960 Act, which was substituted by section 32 of the Intoxicating Liquor Act 1962, put the matter beyond doubt.

Thus, where an applicant is invoking a jurisdictional exception to the terms of the 1902 Act which provides that he must arrange for the extinguishment of a licence or licences, he must prove: 20–29

(a) That such licence or licences is or are in force at the time of the making of the application for the certificate under section 17 of the 1960 Act.

(b) If the licence or licences are not in force, that evidence was adduced at declaratory stage that the applicant was the holder of or had secured the consent of the holder of the licence or licences to its or their extinguishment on the granting of the declaratory order. Thus, once the declaratory order is granted, the licence holder is not obliged to continue trading, and the licence remains on the court file.

(c) If the licence/licences is/are in force at the section 17 stage, that it/they has/have not been forfeited: a licence may become forfeit if a number of recordable convictions are endorsed thereon or where the holder of the licence commits an offence which leads automatically to forfeiture.

---

[32] Unreported, High Court, Davitt P., July 25, 1962.

Where a licence becomes forfeit by virtue of convictions sustained pursuant to the provisions of Part III of the Intoxicating Liquor Act 1927, no new licence can at any time thereafter be granted in respect of the premises to which such licence attached, or any part thereof.[33]

(d) That the licence or licences has/have not been extinguished: the reference to extinguishment is a reference to the extinguishment of a licence upon the grant of another licence. The intention is that the licence which was proffered in evidence at declaratory stage, could not, after the making of the declaratory order, be used for the purposes of another application and thereafter extinguished. In other words, the same licence cannot be used for more than one application unless the first application is unsuccessful and the licence is still in force.

If, at the time of making application for the certificate, the licence or licences referred to at the declaratory stage is or are not in force, the court is entitled to deem such licence or licences to be in force for the purposes of the section 17 application. However, on the grant of the new licence, pursuant to a successful certificate application, the licence or licences referred to shall be extinguished.

PROCEDURE

20–30 Section 18 of the Intoxicating Liquor Act 1960 provides that premises must be described by reference to a map in an application for a declaratory order or a certificate. The procedure to be followed by the applicant in the certificate application is similar to the application for a certificate leading to the grant of a new on-licence or off-licence.

Discretion of Court

20–31 Once the jurisdictional requirements are satisfied, the court is obliged to grant the certificate unless it is prevented from so doing by reason of the character, misconduct or unfitness of the applicant. Davitt P. in the *Downey*[34] case described the court's discretion:

> "If he were to refuse the application he could refuse it only on the ground of the applicant's character, etc. He had no jurisdiction to refuse it on any other ground, once he was satisfied that the premises had been completed in substantial accordance with his previous declaration."

STATUTORY CONSEQUENCES

20–32 The premises to which the licence or licences which are to become extinguished on the grant of the new licence are deemed never to have been licensed. This

---

[33] Intoxicating Liquor Act 1927, s.28.
[34] Above, n.32.

means that an application to revive the licence which previously attached to the premises, on the ground that the premises were licensed within the previous five years, cannot succeed.

B. Tourist Traffic Act 1952, Chapter II

Sections 41 and 42 of the Tourist Traffic Act 1952 provided for the grant of a declaratory order and a certificate in respect of certain proposed hotel premises. The renewal of the licence subsequently granted was conditional on: 20–33

1. proof that the premises are registered in the register of hotels kept by Bord Fáilte; and
2. proof, *inter alia*, that the receipts from the sale of intoxicating liquor in the preceding year were less than one third of the total receipts in that year from all the business carried on by the licence holder in the premises.

This section was rarely, if ever, invoked. The provisions were repealed by section 3 of the Intoxicating Liquor Act 1960.

C. Site Acquired by Local Authority

Introduction

The main provisions concerning the grant of a licence in substitution for a licence which is attached to premises demolished or about to be demolished by a local authority are dealt with above, in chapter 6, "Public House Licence" at paragraph 6–122 *et seq*. Sections 8 and 9 of the Intoxicating Liquor Act 1953 provide for the granting of a declaration as to the fitness and convenience of such proposed premises and the consequent granting of the certificate. 20–34

STATUTORY PROVISION

Section 8(1) of the Intoxicating Liquor Act 1953 provides: 20–35

> "Where the holder of a certificate under section 6 proposes to construct premises upon the approved site and to apply to have the premises licensed for the sale of intoxicating liquor, he may apply to the Court for a declaration that the proposed premises would be fit and convenient to be so licensed, and that either—
>
> (a) the premises when constructed will be premises to which subsection (2) of section 7 applies, or

(b) the existence of a licence for the premises would not be unreasonably detrimental to the business being carried on at the date of the application under this section in any licensed premises in the neighbourhood,

and the Court, if it is so satisfied, may grant the application on such terms as the Court may think fit.

(2) Where the local authority propose to construct premises upon a site approved by them as a site for licensed premises in substitution for licensed premises which, after the passing of this Act, have been or are to be demolished by them or by their direction in exercise of any of their functions and to lease the premises for use as a licensed premises, the local authority may apply to the Court for a declaration under subsection (1)."

Application to Court

JURISDICTIONAL REQUIREMENTS

20–36 1. Who May Apply

(a) The holder of a certificate under section 6 of the 1953 Act.

(b) The local authority. The local authority may make an application where the original premises have been or are about to be demolished and where they wish to lease the premises for use as a licensed premises.

2. New Premises

(a) The new premises must be erected on the site of the previously licensed premises.

(b) Where the local authority has issued a certificate that this site is not available as a site for licensed premises, the new premises may be located in an area within the bailiwick of the local authority, once the court is satisfied that the relocation is unlikely of itself to have a materially adverse effect on the business carried on in the neighbouring premises.

If the court is of the view that the new location is likely to have a materially adverse effect on business carried on in the neighbouring premises, it is obliged to assess whether the grant of a licence for the new premises would be unreasonably detrimental to such businesses.

PROCEDURE

20–37 The procedure is similar to an application for a declaratory order under section 15 of the Intoxicating Liquor Act 1960.The application must be accompanied by a plan of the premises and the Garda superintendent in charge of the area must receive a copy of the plan.

OBJECTIONS

As in an application for a declaratory order for an on-licence, any person who would be entitled to object to an application for a certificate entitling the applicant to a licence under section 7 of the 1953 Act, shall be entitled to object "in like manner" to the application under section 8.[35] **20–38**

Duration of Declaratory Order

The declaratory order remains in force for three years from the date of grant of the application. **20–39**

Application for Certificate where Declaratory Order granted

Section 9 of the Intoxicating Liquor Act 1953 provides for the licensing of premises built in accordance with plans approved by the court. The applicant must prove that the premises have been constructed in substantial accordance with the terms of the declaratory order. **20–40**

OBJECTIONS

Once the applicant can prove that the premises are constructed in accordance with the terms of the declaratory order, the court is not entitled to consider objections grounded upon: **20–41**

1. the unfitness or inconvenience of the premises; or
2. the detriment to any business then being carried on in the neighbourhood.

D. Certificate of Registration

The declaratory jurisdiction contained in section 15(2) of the Intoxicating Liquor Act 1960 applies both to an unregistered club which wishes to seek a declaration of suitability in respect of its premises or to a registered club seeking a declaration of suitability in respect of other or altered premises. **20–42**

---

[35] Intoxicating Liquor Act 1953, s.8(5).

STATUTORY PROVISION

20–43 Section 15(2) of the Intoxicating Liquor Act 1960 provides:

"Where a club proposes to acquire, construct or alter premises for its occupation and to apply to the Circuit Court or District Court, as may be appropriate, for the grant or renewal of a certificate of registration under the Act of 1904 applicable to those premises, it may apply to that Court for a declaration—

(a) that the premises would be suitable for the grant or renewal, as the case may be, of the certificate of registration, under the Act of 1904 applicable thereto and
(b) if the application is for the grant of such certificate, that the number of clubs registered under the Act of 1904 which are of the character of the club so applying and have premises in the district in which the premises the subject matter of the application are situate would not be such as to require the refusal of the application,

and the Court, if it is so satisfied, may grant the application on such terms as it may think fit."

Application to Court

JURISDICTIONAL REQUIREMENTS

20–44 1. Applicant

The applicant is generally the secretary or chairman of the club.

2. Venue

The subsection refers to an application to the Circuit Court or the District Court, as may be appropriate. Regard must be had to the provisions of the Registration of Clubs (Ireland) Act 1904 and the Intoxicating Liquor (General) Act 1924 in interpreting section 15(2) of the 1960 Act with regard to the appropriate venue for the making of the various declaratory applications.

An examination of the 1904 Act and the 1924 Act is essential. Section 23(1) of the 1924 Act provides that an application for the grant of an original certificate of registration should be heard and determined by the Circuit Court. Thus, an unregistered club must apply to the Circuit Court for a certificate of registration. However, a certificate of registration "is applicable" to club premises,[36] so if the location of the club premises to which the certificate is applicable changes, or if the identity of such club premises is substantially altered, then it may be necessary to apply to the Circuit Court for the certificate of registration in respect of the new or altered premises.

[36] Registration of Clubs (Ireland) Act 1904, s.1.

An application to the District Court for a declaratory order in advance of an application for the renewal of a certificate of registration may be made where the alteration envisaged is not so substantial as to require the grant of a new certificate of registration.

It is the writer's view, therefore, that the applications as listed hereunder be determined by the following courts:

- District Court: application by registered club for declaration approving alterations to premises of existing registered club.
- Circuit Court: application by club previously unregistered for declaration in respect of premises which it proposes to acquire, construct or alter.
- Circuit Court: application for declaration where registered club proposes to leave the premises presently occupied by it and to remove to different premises.
- Circuit Court: (a) application for declaration that a premises adjoining the premises presently occupied by the club are suitable for the grant of a certificate; or (b) application by a registered club that certain alterations of a substantial nature which change the character of the premises presently occupied by it render the premises more suitable for the grant of a certificate of registration.

3. Suitability **20–45**

The applicant must prove that the premises would be suitable for the grant or renewal of the certificate of registration. The expression "suitable" was considered by McWilliam J. in *Re Application of Power Supermarkets Ltd,*[37] when he compared it to the expression used in section 15(1) of the 1960 Act, namely "fit and convenient". McWilliam J. noted the meaning given by the *Concise Oxford Dictionary* (1951) and *Chambers Twentieth Century Dictionary* (1972) to both expressions and stated: "I conclude that there is not any difference between the two expressions". In this regard, the court, in considering whether a proposed club premises is suitable to receive a certificate of registration, must have regard not only to the premises itself but also to its location from the point of view of neighbouring residents and other facilities.

4. Other Registered Clubs in the District **20–46**

An applicant must also prove that the number of registered clubs of similar character which have premises in the same district are not such as to require the refusal of the application. The court does not take licensed premises or unregistered clubs into account in assessing this. It considers only clubs in

[37] [1981] I.L.R.M. 270 at 273 (the "Carlow case")

the district whose main objects correspond with those of the applicant club, and proposed club premises which have the benefit of a declaratory order. For example, it is clear that a G.A.A. club is not of the same character as a rugby club. If there is or are a number of clubs in the district which are of the same character, this does not mean that the application will be automatically refused as the court has an absolute discretion as to whether the amount of such clubs in the area are such as to require the refusal of the application.

5. District

The term "district" is not defined but as the registrar of clubs is the District Court clerk, the term "district" is the District Court licensing area within which the proposed club premises are situate.

PROCEDURE

20–47 The procedure is set forth at section 15(3) of the 1960 Act and dealt with above, chapter 17, "Practice and Procedure", at paragraphs 17–92 *et seq.* The procedure is mandatory and the plans must be deposited with the Garda superintendent. Section 18 of the Intoxicating Liquor Act 1960 provides that premises are to be described in a declaratory or certificate application by reference to a map.

OBJECTIONS

20–48 Section 15(5) of the Intoxicating Liquor Act 1960 provides that any person who would be entitled to object to an application for the grant or renewal of a certificate of registration under the 1904 Act in relation to the premises should be entitled to object "in like manner" to an application under section 15(2).

So, the objectors must lodge a notice of objection within 10 days of the publication of the newspaper with the District Court clerk and the secretary of the club. As the court in a declaratory application makes in effect two declarations it is arguable that it must confine itself to those two matters and not the other grounds of objection provided for in the Registration of Clubs Acts 1904 to 1995.

Category of Objectors

20–49 1. Where a club applies for a declaratory order in respect of the grant of a certificate of registration, the following persons may object:

(a) superintendent of the Garda Síochána for the Garda district in which the proposed club premises is situate;

(b) any person resident in the parish in which the proposed club premises is situate.

2. Where the club proposes to apply for the renewal of a certificate of registration any person may lodge an objection.

Procedure for Objections

Where an objector wishes to object to a declaratory order in respect of the grant or renewal of the certificate of registration, he must comply with the requirements of section 3 of the Registration of Clubs (Ireland) Act 1904 and lodge the objections within the time specified therein. Section 3, as amended by section 44 of the Intoxicating Liquor Act 1988, provides that the objections are to be lodged with the registrar of clubs within ten days of the receipt of publication of the notice of application and at the same time, a copy of the objections should be sent to the secretary of the club. The registrar of clubs should also be notified. Where a court is considering the number of registered clubs of the same character as the applicant club and which have premises in the same district, it takes into account declaratory orders which have been granted under section 15(2) of the 1960 Act, in respect of premises which have not yet received a certificate of registration.[38] **20–50**

Application for Certificate where Declaratory Order granted

Introduction

Where a declaratory order has been granted pursuant to section 15(2) of the Intoxicating Liquor Act 1960, the court is not entitled to consider objections grounded upon the unsuitability of the premises or upon the number of registered clubs of the same character as the applicant's club and which have premises situate in the same district. **20–51**

STATUTORY PROVISION

Section 17(2) of the Intoxicating Liquor Act 1960 provides: **20–52**

> "If, on the hearing of an application for a grant or renewal of a certificate of registration under the Act of 1904 applicable to any premises, it is shown to the satisfaction of the Court hearing the application that a declaration has been made by the Court under subsection (2) of section 15 of this Act and that the premises have been acquired, constructed or altered in substantial accordance with the terms of the declaration, the Court shall not receive any objection to the application grounded upon the unsuitability of the premises or upon the number of clubs registered under the Act of 1904 which are of the character of the club making the application and have premises situate in the district in which the premises the subject of the application are situate."

[38] Intoxicating Liquor Act 1960, s.15(7).

Discretion of Court

20–53 The court is precluded from considering the suitability of the premises, once it is satisfied that the premises have been acquired, constructed or altered in substantial accordance with the terms of the declaratory order. Further, the court is not entitled to consider other clubs of the same character which are situated in the district, even if such clubs have become established since the granting of the declaratory order.

OBJECTIONS

20–54 Objections to an application under section 17 of the 1960 Act, whether they are for the grant or renewal of a certificate of registration, can be made on the other grounds specified in section 5 of the 1904 Act. A situation can arise that a club goes to the expense of acquiring and constructing a club premises, having obtained a declaratory order but can still be refused a certificate of registration in respect of the premises. The application can be refused, for example, on the ground that the supply of excisable liquor would not be under the control of the members of the committee. It is open to the court to adjourn the application to permit the club to amend its rules in order to bring them into conformity with the code.[39] However, a club, having obtained a declaratory order, is not in as secure a position in relation to objections as an applicant for an on-licence.

PROCEDURE

20–55 The procedure to be followed is similar to an application for the grant or renewal of a certificate of registration.[40]

E. Restaurant Certificate

Introduction

20–56 Section 16 of the Intoxicating Liquor Act 1960 provides for the grant of a declaration as to suitability of licensed premises to receive what is known as a full restaurant certificate or a limited restaurant certificate. The application is for an order declaring that the premises or portion of the premises is structurally adapted for use as a restaurant. Proof of actual user of the premises or portion thereof must be established for the court to grant the certificate application.[41]

---

[39] *Re Rossmore Golf Club* [1950] 16 Ir. Jur. Rep. 52.
[40] See above, chap. 17, "Practice and Procedure", at paras. 17–75 *et seq.*

The main proof required at declaratory stage is as to the suitability of the structure.

1. Full Restaurant Certificate

STATUTORY PROVISION

Section 16(1) of the Intoxicating Liquor Act 1960 provides: 20–57

> "Where a person proposes to acquire, construct or alter premises and to apply for the grant of a restaurant certificate, within the meaning of section 12 of the Act of 1927, in relation to the premises, he may apply to the Court to which it is proposed to apply for the grant of the restaurant certificate for a declaration that the premises would be structurally adapted for use as a restaurant, refreshment house or other place for supplying substantial meals to the public, and the Court, if it is so satisfied, may grant the application on such terms as it may think fit."

Application to Court

JURISDICTIONAL REQUIREMENTS

1. Premises 20–58

   The premises as referred to in section 16 means "licensed premises".[42] A restaurant certificate attaches to a premises to which an "on-licence" attaches.[43]

2. Venue

   The application for the declaratory order is made to the court "to which it is proposed to apply for the grant of the restaurant certificate".

   (i) *Publican's Licence* Where the applicant proposes to acquire the premises and to ultimately apply for a certificate of transfer of the premises, there is nothing to prevent a section 16 declaratory application in the District Court prior to their acquisition: the application for the restaurant certificate is made in conjunction with the application for the transfer at the annual licensing District Court or an adjourned sitting thereof. If he wishes to alter the interior of his premises and apply for a restaurant

---

[41] *Whelan v. Tobin* [1976–77] I.L.R.M. 199.

[42] Intoxicating Liquor Act 1927, s.1.

[43] The expression "on-licence" means a licence for the sale of intoxicating liquor for consumption either on or off the premises or a wine retailer's on-licence within the meaning of the Finance (1909–10) Act 1910 (s.12(1A) of the Intoxicating Liquor Act 1927, as inserted by s.8 of the Intoxicating Liquor Act 1943).

certificate, he can apply to the District Court for a declaratory order in advance of an application for a restaurant certificate at the annual licensing sessions, following an application to renew the licence. Where a person proposes to construct or alter premises, he applies to the Circuit Court for a declaration as to the fitness and convenience of the proposed construction or alterations. He brings his section 16 application contemporaneously.

(ii) *Wine Retailer's On-Licence* An applicant can apply to the District Court at any time for a declaration that the premises to which the wine on-licence attaches would be structurally adapted for use as a restaurant.

20–59 3. Premises structurally adapted for use as a restaurant

(i) The court takes into account matters such as kitchen facilities, storage facilities, size and location of restaurant itself and the proximity to its kitchen, and in a public house those other areas of public resort which are used for the service of food, such as the lounge and/or bar.

(ii) The word "premises" referred to in section 16(1) of the 1960 Act relates to the entire of the area the subject matter of the declaratory order, which will include all the area which is to be licensed.

4. Discretion of the Court

The court can grant the order on such terms as it thinks fit.

PROCEDURE

The procedure, which is regulated by statute, is dealt with in chapter 17, "Practice and Procedure", at paragraph 17–96 *et seq*. It is mandatory and the court cannot intervene. Furthermore, the applicant is obliged to deposit a copy of the plans of the premises with the superintendent of the Garda Síochána within whose district it is proposed to have the premises. The application to the court should be accompanied by such plan of the premises.

Duration of Declaratory Order

20–60 As in previous cases, the duration of the declaratory order is two years from the date of the grant of the application or for such longer period as the court granting the application may in any particular case think proper to provide.[44]

[44] Intoxicating Liquor Act 1960, s.16(5).

Certification of Restaurant Premises where Declaratory Order granted

An application for a restaurant certificate, where the applicant has already obtained a declaratory order under section 16(1), can be refused on the grounds that the premises are not bona fide and mainly used as a restaurant. This creates something of an anomaly where the application under section 17 relates to the grant of a licence and a restaurant certificate. The applicant will wish to proceed with the application for the licence in order that he can open his premises and start trading. If his premises is not open and trading at the time of the making of the application for the restaurant certificate, where a declaratory order has been obtained, he will not be in a position to prove that the premises are bona fide and mainly used as a restaurant. **20–61**

Quite often, therefore, the applicant is obliged to move his application for the grant of the licence under section 17(1) of the Intoxicating Liquor Act 1960, to adduce evidence in relation to the restaurant business, to concede that such evidence is not sufficient for the purposes of a restaurant certificate application and to apply to adjourn the restaurant certificate application until he is in a position to prove that the premises are "bona fide and mainly used as a restaurant".

STATUTORY PROVISION

Section 17(4) of the Intoxicating Liquor Act 1960 provides: **20–62**

> "If on the hearing of an application for the grant of a restaurant certificate, within the meaning of section 12 of the Act of 1927, in relation to any premises it is shown to the satisfaction of the Court that a declaration has been made under subsection (1) of section 16 of this Act and that the premises have been acquired, constructed or altered in substantial accordance with the terms of the declaration, it shall not be open to the Court to refuse the application on any ground other than that the premises are not *bona fide* and mainly used as a restaurant, refreshment house, or other place for supplying substantial meals to the public."

JURISDICTIONAL REQUIREMENTS

1. Substantial Compliance **20–63**

The applicant must prove that the premises have been acquired or constructed or altered in "substantial" accordance with the terms of the declaration. As in other declaratory applications the terms will be those which the court has seen fit to insert in the order itself, and the order will have reference to the plans which were before the court at declaratory stage. If there is any substantial deviation from either, then the applicant cannot bring himself within section 17(4) of the Intoxicating Liquor Act 1960. Once the applicant can prove such substantial compliance, the court must grant the application unless it is satisfied that the premises are not bona fide and mainly used as a restaurant. The court will, in accordance with section 12 of the 1927 Act, hear the superintendent of the Garda Síochána on this point.

2. Declaratory Order

The applicant must prove at the time of the making of the application under section 17(4), that the declaratory order is still in force.

3. User as a Restaurant

Evidence that the premises are mainly used as a restaurant is required.

OBJECTIONS

20–64 No provision is made for objectors with the exception of the local superintendent of the Garda Síochána who is a notice party. This reflects section 12 of the Intoxicating Liquor Act 1927.

2. Limited Restaurant Certificate

Introduction

20–65 A limited restaurant certificate certifies that a portion of the premises as specified in plans before the court is a restaurant for the purposes of section 13 of the Intoxicating Liquor Act 1927. This means that where a defined restaurant in a premises to which an on-licence attaches is serving food, intoxicating liquor can be served after hours.[45] Certification of an area under section 12A of the 1927 Act does not permit the holder of the licence to apply for special exemption orders.

STATUTORY PROVISION

20–66 Section 16(2) of the Intoxicating Liquor Act 1960 provides:

> "Where a person proposes to acquire, construct or alter premises and to apply for the grant of a limited restaurant certificate, within the meaning of section 12A of the Act of 1927 in relation to any portion of the premises, he may apply to the Court to which it is proposed to apply for the grant of the limited restaurant certificate for a declaration that—
>
> (a) that portion of the premises will be structurally adapted for use as a restaurant, refreshment house or other place for supplying substantial meals to the public,

[45] Intoxicating Liqour Act 1927, s.13, as amended by the Intoxicating Liquor Act 1988, s.28.

(b) that portion of the premises would not include a public bar, or part of a room in another part of which there would be a public bar, and
(c) there would be public access to that portion of the premises otherwise than through a public bar,

and the Court, if it is so satisfied, may grant the application on such terms as it may think fit."

Application to Court

JURISDICTIONAL REQUIREMENTS

1. Structurally Adopted For Use

The applicant must prove structural suitability only in relation to that portion of the premises which it is proposed to use as a restaurant. This of course includes the ancillary kitchen and storage facilities. **20–67**

2. Public Bar

The applicant must also prove that the portion of the premises to which the application relates does not contain a public bar or part of a room in another part of which there is a public bar, so the apartment must be self-contained and independent from the lounge and bar contained in the premises.

The plans must show that the public can enter into that portion of the premises through an entrance that does not involve walking through a public bar. The applicant does not have to prove that access from a public bar to that portion is impossible: however, he must prove that the public has another means of access than through the public bar.

A "public bar" is defined in section 16(6) of the Intoxicating Liquor Act 1960 as "any place exclusively or mainly used for the sale and consumption of intoxicating liquor". The legislature was trying to prevent a situation whereby persons who were consuming intoxicating liquor without being served or supplied with a meal, would benefit from the provisions as to extended hours enjoyed by customers in the restaurant.

Duration

The declaratory order expires after two years, unless the court granting the application makes it for a longer period.[46] **20–68**

[46] Intoxicating Liquor Act 1960, s.16(5).

Certificate Application where Declaratory Order granted

20–69 The anomaly referred to in the introduction arises where an applicant cannot bring an application pursuant to the provisions of section 17(5) unless he can establish an existing user.

STATUTORY PROVISION

Section 17(5) of the Intoxicating Liquor Act 1960 provides:

> "If, on the hearing of an application for the grant of a limited restaurant certificate, within the meaning of section 12A of the Act of 1927, in relation to any portion of a premises it is shown to the satisfaction of the court that a declaration has been made under subsection (2) of section 16 of this Act and that the premises have been acquired, constructed or altered in substantial accordance with the terms of the declaration, it shall not be open to the Court to refuse the application on any ground other than that that portion of the premises is not *bona fide* and mainly used as a restaurant, refreshment house or other place for supplying substantial meals to the public."

JURISDICTIONAL REQUIREMENTS

20–70 1. Substantial Compliance

Where the applicant can prove substantial compliance as required by the subsection, the court may only refuse the application where it is not satisfied that the premises are bona fide and mainly used as a restaurant. It may then refuse a section 17 application or, it is submitted, adjourn it until the applicant can adduce sufficient evidence to satisfy the court that the portion of the premises to which the application relates is:

(a) already used as a restaurant; and

(b) mainly used as a restaurant.

2. Declaratory Order

The applicant may only make his application pursuant to section 17(5) of the 1960 Act where he can show that a declaratory order was granted by the court and is still in force.[47]

---

[47] Intoxicating Liquor Act 1960, s.17(6).

CHAPTER 21

OBJECTIONS

Discretion of the Court

An applicant for a certificate entitling him to receive a licence assumes the onus of establishing that the court has jurisdiction to grant his application. If he succeeds in establishing jurisdiction and there is no objection to his application by any person or body competent to object, the certificate sought will be granted. The court is not entitled to refuse the application of its own motion once the jurisdictional requirements are satisfied, in the absence of sustainanble objections. In *R. (Perry) v. Tyrone Justices* Gibson J. described the function of the court: **21–1**

"In Ireland an applicant . . . on complying with the statutory conditions, must get his licence as a matter of right; and in the absence of a prescribed objection he is, by statutory presumption, deemed to be unobjectionable. The Court has no discretion; its duty is throughout strictly judicial; and there is nothing to show that the essence of justice can be violated by allowing the characters of objector, witness and judge to be combined and confounded in the same person or persons."[1]

The *Perry* case must be read with reference to the appropriate legislative provisions which apply to different licences. For example, in determining an application for the grant of a certificate for a new beer retailer's or spirit retailer's licence, a court has a "free and unqualified discretion . . . on any grounds appearing to them sufficient" to refuse or grant the application.[2] This discretion must be exercised in accordance with the objectives of the licensing code. In *Re Application of Power Supermarkets Ltd*, Walsh J stated:

"The discretion given to the learned Circuit Court judge by section 1 of the Act of 1900 does not give him an absolute or an unqualified or an arbitrary power to grant or refuse a licence. The discretion must be exercised in accordance with the objectives of the licensing code save where some provisions of the code, such as section 13(1)(ii) of the Intoxicating Liquor Act, 1960, . . . expressly permits the taking into account of the detrimental effect of a new licence on competitors in the neighbourhood. The discretion must be exercised in the spirit of the statute, otherwise the decision would not fall within the limits and the objects intended by the legislature. . . . The discretion to be exercised pursuant to section 1 of the Act of 1900, although an unqualified one, must still be exercised judicially within the spirit of the Licensing Acts and have regard to the objectives of the statutes and the evils which the licensing code was intended to combat. In addition, the Acts were intended to ensure the proper management by suitable persons of premises suitable to be licensed. To decide that a licence ought not be granted because the competition it would offer to existing licences would be economically disadvantageous to the holders of those licences is not a ground which is contemplated by the code and therefore is not one which can be said to be an exercise of judicial discretion. . . . The Circuit judge is not entitled to take into account matters extraneous to the statutes."[3]

21–2 Where an objection has not been made by a person entitled by statute to object, but facts are revealed which would have justified a police objection, it is open to the court to adjourn the application and direct the District Court clerk to bring the circumstances to the attention of the police.[4]

In an application for the transfer of an on-licence the court is not entitled of its own motion to refuse the application if there is no objection. Kenny J. stated in the *Perry* case:

---

[1] (1904) 38 I.L.T.R. 26 at 31.
[2] Beer Retailers' and Spirit Grocers' Retail Licences (Ireland) Act 1900, s.1.
[3] [1988] I.R. 206 at 210–211 (the "Killarney case").
[4] *R. (Morgan) v. Tyrone Justices* [1896] 2 I.R. 318.

> "It is not into the sufficiency and validity of the *application* the Justices are to inquire, but of the *objection*, and it is for that purpose they are to examine the applicant. So careful was the legislature in dealing with the application, that the section contemplates a probable adjournment after the objection is made and recorded, presumably with the object of enabling the applicant to consider, and, if he can, meet it."[5]

The courts have displayed a tendency to interpret the court's discretion restrictively. In *The State (Hennessy) and Chariot Inns Ltd v. Commons*[6] Finlay P. considered the extent and nature of the discretion conferred by the statutory provisions and the District Court Rules relating to the grant of an ad interim transfer on a District Court judge:

> "A consideration of the entire code of licensing laws seems to suggest that, where they intended that there should be specific grounds upon which a District Justice should exercise his discretion to grant or refuse any form of licence, the legislatures (present and past) have set out those grounds most clearly and, in most cases, have required that the order of the court should specifically state the grounds for refusal in the event of a refusal of an application."[7]

Section 1 of the Public House (Ireland) Act 1855 provides that upon the death or removal of any person duly licensed to sell excisable liquors by retail for consumption on the licensed premises, or on the sale or assignment of his interest, it shall be lawful for a District Court judge, if he "shall think proper so to do", to transfer by endorsement the licence to any person who is not disqualified, after examining all necessary parties on oath. Finlay P. stated: **21–3**

> "The phrase contained in that section [1 of the 1855 Act] 'if they shall think proper so to do' must, in my view, be construed as conferring originally upon the . . . District Justice a discretion only based on the question as to whether the applicant has satisfied all three of what Mr. Justice Henchy in *The State (Doyle) v. Carr* [1970] I.R. 87 has described as the three necessary proofs."[8]

In the Supreme Court Kenny J. stated:

> "In this case the District Justice was not entitled to make any inquiry into the character of the applicant."[9]

Where no objection is taken to the grant or renewal of a certificate of registration in respect of a club, the court, once it is satisfied that the application complies with the statutory requirements as to notice and publication, etc., and that the rules of the club are in conformity with the provisions of the Registration of Clubs Acts 1904 to 1995, "shall grant the application".

---

5 Above, n.1, at 32.
6 [1976] I.R. 238.
7 *Ibid.* at 245.
8 *Ibid.* at 247.
9 *Ibid.* at 253.

21–4 The existence of judicial discretion in certain circumstances is evident in some of the statutory exceptions to the general prohibitory terms of the Licensing (Ireland) Act 1902. Section 4 of the 1902 Act provides for the grant of a licence where the jurisdictional requirements have been satisfied "and the licensing authority (the court) are satisfied that the restrictions in this Act on the granting of licences may be relaxed". Section 6 of the 1902 Act confers jurisdiction to grant a new licence for extended premises "where the licensing authority thinks fit".

A consideration of certain jurisdictional provisions shows an intention, in particular cases, to allow the court discretion, irrespective of whether objection has been formally made by a competent objector. Some of these provisions refer to the court's "absolute discretion" although the ambit of such discretion is limited by reference to the grounds of objection specified in the particular statutes.

The discretion of a court in relation to the grant of a music and singing licence and a public dancing licence is untrammelled. A District Court judge in considering either application is entitled to take into account any matter which may appear to him to be relevant, in addition to the particular grounds set forth in section 2(2) of the Public Dance Halls Act 1935.

In *Application of Michael Quinn*,[10] Henchy J. described the discretion given to the District Court judge in an application for a public dancing licence as "wide and imprecise" to be contrasted with "the narrow and clearly expressed discretion given by other statutes for the purpose of deciding whether certain kinds of licences should issue or not".[11] He refers to section 11(1) of the Betting Act 1931, which provides that "a certificate of suitability of premises may be refused on any one or more of the following grounds and on no other ground whatsoever", and he notes that unless one of those grounds specified in section 11(1) existed, "the issuing authority has no discretion to refuse to grant a certificate". Each statutory provision, therefore, should be reviewed in order to ascertain the ambit of the discretion, if any, which the court is entitled to exercise.

Onus on Objectors

21–5 The applicant must satisfy the jurisdictional requirements before the court can proceed to adjudicate on objections raised by the objectors.

Save in certain specific statutory provisions, such as section 13 of the Intoxicating Liquor Act 1960, the onus then rests upon an objector to put forward his objections.[12]

---

[10] [1974] I.R. 19.

[11] *Ibid.* at 24.

[12] *Application of Catherine Bonner* (1947) 81 I.L.T.R. 143 and *Re Katherine Hodgins* (1948) 82 I.L.T.R. 19.

Where No Statutory Right to Object

The general rule is that where a statute does not make provision for the service of the notice of application or for its publication, the court must, subject to the fulfilment by the applicant of the conditions contained in the appropriate statutory provision, make the order sought. In *Application of Thomas J. Dunne*[13] Walsh J. noted that section 19 of the Intoxicating Liquor Act 1960 made no provision whatever for the giving of notice or for the hearing of objections. He stated: 21–6

> "This, in my view, is a very strong indication that the extinguishment of a licence in applications under section 19 of the Act of 1960 was not intended to be a matter of discretion. This was also emphasised by the fact that such an application could be made at any sitting of the District Court."[14]

He also referred to section 27 of the 1960 Act which enables the owner of a six-day licence to convert it into a seven-day licence and which does not require the giving of notice to any party, or publication of the notice of application. He continued:

> "I have no doubt that the provisions of section 27 are obligatory and that no discretion rests in the court."[15]

Similarly, there is no requirement to publish an application for a restaurant certificate although the Garda Síochána must receive 10 days' notice of the making of the application. An applicant for a special exemption order is not required to notify any person other than the officer in charge of the Garda Síochána and the statute does not provide for the making of objection by any other party. In contrast, in an application for an occasional licence any person whom the District Court judge considers to have a bona fide interest is entitled to appear and give evidence.

In *Jaggers Restaurant Ltd. v. Ahearne*,[16] Finlay C.J. introduced the concept of "fair procedure" where a statute does not make provision for the making of an objection by the owners of licensed premises in the neighbourhood. In that case an application for a declaratory order was made, the jurisdictional provision invoked being section 14 of the Intoxicating Liquor Act 1960. This required the applicant to prove, *inter alia*, that if the substituted premises were located in the immediate vicinity of the demolished site, the location of the new premises on the "new" site, rather than on the site of the original premises, "is unlikely of itself to have a materially adverse effect on the business carried on in any licensed premises in the neighbourhood". He stated: 21–7

---

[13] [1968] I.R. 105.
[14] *Ibid.* at 117.
[15] *Ibid.* at 118.
[16] [1988] I.R. 308.

> "with regard to the balance of the matters which fall for determination by the Court under section 14 of the Act of 1960 that the ordinary rules consonant with natural justice of the right of persons affected by the decision to be heard apply. Since in the instant case one of the matters which the applicant must prove is that the location of the premises in Fleet Street rather than on the site of the original premises in Sean McDermott Street is unlikely to have a materially adverse effect on the business carried on in any licensed premises in the neighbourhood, it must inevitably follow that the owner of any licensed premises carrying on business in the neighbourhood must have an immediate and obvious interest and right to oppose the licence in order to assert what by the sub-section is clearly intended to be a protection of his business interests."[17]

This does not mean that any person who would be affected by the decision of the court to grant the order sought has *locus standi* to object. Where the statute confers jurisdiction upon a court to consider matters extraneous to or different from those grounds of objection enumerated in the Licensing (Ireland) Act 1833, the court can consider objections by persons who would be "affected by the decision" but such persons have a right to object and be heard as objectors only in the context of such additional or extraneous matters to be considered by the court.

Finlay C.J. in *Jaggers v. Ahearne* held that if the objection was founded upon the statutory grounds contained in section 4 of the 1833 Act, it was only then that the question of the objector being an inhabitant of the civil parish within which the premises were situate arose.

So, where an objector can advance the argument that the existence of a licence in respect of the new premises would be unreasonably detrimental to his business, or that the shift in location of the other premises is likely to have a materially adverse effect on his business carried on in his premises, then he does not have to prove that he is an inhabitant of the parish in order to establish his *locus standi*. This applies in the following cases:

21–8
1. an application for a licence for a more convenient premises in a rural area under section 21 of the Intoxicating Liquor Act 1943;
2. an application under section 7 of the Intoxicating Liquor Act 1953 which provides for the grant of a new licence in respect of premises substituted for premises demolished by a local authority;
3. an application for the grant of a new licence in substitution for two existing licences in a rural area under section 13 of the Intoxicating Liquor Act 1960; and
4. an application under section 14 of the Intoxicating Liquor Act 1960 as in the *Jaggers*[18] case.

---

[17] *Ibid.* at 315.
[18] *Ibid.*

In *Cashman v. Clifford*,[19] the applicant sought leave to apply for an order of judical review in respect of a ruling of the District Court judge refusing him liberty to appear and adduce evidence in opposition to the application. The matter came before the District Court by way of an appeal from the grant of a certificate of personal fitness under the Betting Act 1931. Section 13(5)(a) of the Betting Act 1931 provides that the superintendent of the Garda Síochána and the Revenue Commissioners "and no other person" shall be entitled to be heard and adduce evidence in opposition to the appeal. Barron J. acceded to the applicant's application that the words "and no other person" be severed from the section. The severing of such words from the section, however, did not give the applicant the right to be heard or the right to adduce evidence in opposition to the appeal. Such a right is given only by statute and "the applicant does not seek to be given a similar statutory right. Nor could the Court give him one". Although Barron J. noted that the Oireachtas did not give a person other than the superintendent and the Revenue Commissioners the right to be heard, he stated: 21–9

> "It is now a matter for the District Court within the exercise of its jurisdiction to determine what rights, if any, it will accord to the applicant on the hearing of the notice party's appeal before it."[20]

So, the court cannot confer a right to object upon a person who has no statutory right to do so. The court in exercising its discretion in accordance with law, and with reference to the law relating to the grant of the particular licence concerned, may determine the rights, if any, held by a person who is not a statutory objector to be heard in connection therewith. For a discussion as to the notice (if any) which an objector is required to give to an applicant, see above, chapter 17, "Practice and Procedure".

A. On-Licence

1. Grant

(a) Objectors

1. Church Warden.[21] 21–10
2. Justice of the Peace.
3. Inhabitant of the parish within which the premises in question is situate. To

---

[19] [1989] I.R. 121.
[20] *Ibid.* at 125.
[21] A church warden is an elected lay official, usually one of two, of a parish. This provision had more relevance in 1833.

inhabit means "to dwell in".[22] An inhabitant of a parish is a person who resides within the parish and does not include a person who carries on business therein.

In *R. (Gallagher) v Tyrone Justices*,[23] the court interpreted residence to include place of business. There, the notice of application was served upon a justice in a place where he daily transacted his business, rather than at the place where he "ate and slept". It was held that the notice was properly served, the place of business being a residence within the meaning of the section. Although this case was opened before the Supreme Court in the *Jaggers* case,[24] Finlay C.J., in his judgment, did not specifically interpret the expression "inhabitant of said parish". The *Jaggers* judgment recognises a distinction between an inhabitant of the civil parish and a person who carries on the licensed business in any licensed premises "in the neighbourhood of the new premises". In this case it was held that where a person seeks to object to the grant of a licence on the statutory grounds contained in section 4 of the 1833 Act, he must be an inhabitant of the civil parish within which the premises are situate. Thus, a person carrying on business in the parish is not entitled to object on the grounds set forth in section 4, unless he is also an inhabitant of the parish.

The question arises as to whether a company, whose registered offices are situate in the parish within which the premises are situate, can object. Section 2 of the 1833 Act requires that an applicant, in giving notice of his intention to make an application for a certificate leading to the grant of a new licence, sets forth his "place of abode". As a company is entitled to hold a licence[25] it would seem to be inconsistent if it was prevented from exercising the right of objection accorded to an individual. This aspect has not been considered by the Superior Courts.

21–11 4. A person who carries on licensed business in any licensed premises in the neighbourhood of the premises the subject-matter of the application. The most frequent category of objectors are the licensees of premises located in the neighbourhood of the premises sought to be licensed. These persons have *locus standi* if they can bring themselves within the concept of "fair procedure" as enunciated by Finlay C.J. in the *Jaggers* case.[26] In this case, the applicant applied to the Circuit Court for the grant of a certificate leading to a new licence, invoking section 14 of the 1960 Act. He was opposed by a number of local publicans who appealed the grant by the Circuit Court judge to the High Court. The applicant company challenged the *locus standi* of the objectors. Section 14 of the 1960 Act provides, *inter alia*, that the

---

[22] *The Oxford English Dictionary* (2nd ed., 1989).
[23] [1901] 2 I.R. 497.
[24] Above, n.16.
[25] *The State (Hennessy) and Chariot Inns Ltd v. Commons*, above, n.6.
[26] Above, n.16, at 315.

court may prohibit the issuing of a licence on the grounds of the unfitness of either the applicant or the premises, where objection is made in that regard pursuant to section 4 of the Licensing (Ireland) Act 1833. The questions raised in the case stated by the High Court included:

(i) in order lawfully to object and to lawfully maintain the appeal in the case was it necessary that any objector appellant be an inhabitant of a particular civil parish?

(ii) in order lawfully to object and lawfully to maintain the appeal in the case, was it sufficient that an objector appellant be merely a person who carries on the licensed business in any licensed premises in the neighbourhood of the new premises?

These questions were answered by the Supreme Court as follows:

(i) No.

(ii) Yes.

In the course of his judgment, the Chief Justice, with whom the other four members of the Court agreed, stated:

> "In order lawfully to oppose this application and to maintain an appeal against the granting of it by the Circuit Court, it is not necessary that a person so opposing or appealing should be an inhabitant of the civil parish of St Andrew provided that he is a person who carries on the licensed business in any licensed premises in the neighbourhood of the new premises. If, on the other hand, a person were seeking to object to the granting of a licence under section 14, not on the failure of the applicant to establish any of the proofs necessary for him to prove, but rather on the statutory grounds contained in section 4 of the Act of 1833 as to the character, misconduct or unfitness of the applicant or as to the unfitness of the new premises, such person would have to be an inhabitant of the civil parish of St Andrew."[27]

So, if an objector relies upon the grounds contained in section 4 of the 1833 Act and no other provisions, then he must be an inhabitant of the parish in which the premises in question are situate. If, however, he is objecting on another ground, such as that the grant of a licence for a new premises will materially affect his trade, then it is sufficient for him to show that he carries on business in a premises situate in the neighbourhood. 21–12

In the *Jaggers* case, Finlay C.J. accepted that the publicans in the neighbourhood had a right, conferred on them by section 14 of the 1960 Act , to object, but that this right was restricted to the protection of the business interest recognised by section 14.

The licensing code provides for the protection of the business interests of publicans in the neighbourhood in several cases. For example, some provi-

[27] *Jaggers v. Ahearne*, above, n.16, at 315 and 316.

sions in the code require the courts to consider whether the grant of a new licence would be "unreasonably detrimental" to business carried on in licensed premises in the neighbourhood.[28]

21–13 *Parish/Neighbourhood* A parish is usually regarded for the purposes of the licensing code as the "civil parish" which was originally an ecclesiastical division of land for the administration of the Anglican church under the Manors, etc. (Ireland) Act 1825.[29] These parish boundaries appeared on Ordnance Survey maps and became areas for civil and administrative purposes.[30] On the other hand, the expression "neighbourhood", which is also used in the licensing code, is a more nebulous concept. The definition of neighbourhood as contained in the *Concise Oxford Dictionary* (8th ed.) is "a district, especially one forming a community within a town or city". This expression appears to encompass a smaller area than a civil parish. In considering an objection to an application for a publican's licence on the ground that the number of previously licensed premises in the "neighbourhood" was sufficient, Lynch J., in *Re Tivoli Cinema Ltd,*[31] considered all licensed premises within a radius of 250 yards. He noted that there were 14 public houses within 250 yards of the Tivoli theatre and six within 250 yards of the premises whose licence was extinguished and which was situated 510 yards by road from the theatre "as well as a scatter of other licensed premises in the general area".[32] He was satisfied that both premises were within the immediate vicinity of one another: in considering the objection as to the number of previously licensed premises in the neighbourhood, he took into account not only the area within a radius of 250 yards of the premises, the subject-matter of the application, but also the area within a 250 yards radius of the premises whose licence was to be extinguished.

21–14 5. Officer in charge of the Garda Síochána for the Garda district within which the applicant resides.[33]

6. Superintendent of the Garda Síochána in the district in which the premises are situate. Order 42, rule 4 of the Circuit Court Rules 1950 provides that the officer in charge of the Garda Síochána of the district in which the premises are situate should receive notice.[34]

---

[28] Intoxicating Liquor Act 1943, s.21; Intoxicating Liquor Act 1953, ss.6–9; Intoxicating Liquor Act 1960, s.13.

[29] 6 Geo. 4, c .99: "Tables of Manors, Parishes, And Townlands in Ireland, and to make provision for ascertaining the boundaries of the same".

[30] These original maps are stored in the ordnance survey archives and are commonly referred to as the "bound volumes". The names of the parishes are contained in *The Index to the Townlands and Towns, Parishes and Baronies of Ireland 1851* (Genealogical Publishing Company or Census of Ireland, 1871).

[31] [1992] 1 I.R. 412.

[32] *Ibid.* at 422.

[33] Spirits (Ireland) Act 1854, s.10.

[34] S.I. No. 179 of 1950.

7. The health authority, within the meaning of the Health Acts 1947 to 1958, in the functional area in which the premises are situate is also a competent objector.[35]

8. The fire authority for the functional area within which the premises are situate is a competent objector.[36] The Fire Services Act 1981 was enacted after the Stardust disaster in 1981. The practice of the courts is to require fire safety certification or evidence from the fire officer that he is not objecting to the application.

(b) Grounds of Objection

The grounds of objection to the grant of an on-licence fall under three principal headings as follows: 21–15

(a) objections under section 4 of the Licensing (Ireland) Act 1833;

(b) other statutory objections;

(c) objections based on jurisdiction.

(i) The Licensing (Ireland) Act 1833, section 4 The grounds of objection contained in section 4 of the 1833 Act are common to practically all applications for on-licences.

STATUTORY PROVISION

Section 4 of the Licensing (Ireland) Act 1833 as amended by section 31 of the Intoxicating Liquor Act 1960 provides as follows: 21–16

> "It shall and may be lawful for any Justice of the Peace of said city, town or county, Churchwarden or other inhabitant of said parish, or the health authority within the meaning of the Health Acts 1947 to 1958, in whose functional area the house is situate, previously to transmit or then and there to deliver in writing to said Clerk of the Peace, or orally to state to said Justices in Sessions assembled, any matter or objection to such application, whether grounded upon the character, misconduct, or unfitness of the Applicant, unfitness or inconvenience of the house or place, or number of previously licensed houses in the neighbourhood".

(a) Character, Misconduct or Unfitness of Applicant 21–17

When considering the character of the applicant, the court is entitled to hear evidence of previous convictions for breaches of the licensing code.[37] In

[35] Licensing (Ireland) Act 1833, s.4 as amended by the Intoxicating Liquor Act 1960, s.31.
[36] Fire Services Act 1981, s.24.
[37] *R. v. Birmingham Justices* (1876) 40 J.P. 132.

Application of Neighbourhood Public House Ltd[38] Costello J. considered that an offer by an applicant to pay a substantial sum of money to the chairman of an objecting residents' association and subsequently to members of the residents' association themselves in exchange for the withdrawing of their objections, constituted misconduct within the meaning of section 4 of the 1833 Act.

In *Re Centennial Properties Ltd*[39] Finlay P. rejected a contention made by the objectors that difficulty or delay in obtaining costs awarded to them in relation to a previous application for a licence by a company, of which one of the directors of the applicant company was also a director, constituted unfitness.

Palles C.B. in *R. (Leslie) v. Monaghan Justices*, considered the question of "unfitness" of the applicant:

> "That does not mean moral unfitness, nor does it involve any imputation on his character. It certainly involves the fitness of the applicant to carry on the trade of a licensed publican. There is no trade that requires in the interest of the public more constant and strict supervision than the trade of a publican, and one of the objects of the statute is to ensure the applicant's constant supervision."[40]

Here Palles C.B. was satisfied that the applicant was unfit to hold a licence as he knew nothing about the trade and did not intend to supervise the business. Proof of an intention to delegate the management of a public house does not of itself constitute unfitness. In *Re Thomas O'Brien, Applicant*[41] the objector contended that the applicant did not intend to run the premises himself but through a manager. Budd J. rejected this objection, stating:

> ". . . it is quite a usual method of running a public house to appoint a competent manager. Moreover a check is kept upon the proper running of such establishments because objection can be made to the renewal of a licence at the time for renewal."[42]

Palles C.B. noted that non-residence of an applicant in the premises in question, "does not necessarily mean unfitness, but it may be an element of unfitness . . .".[43]

A substantial percentage of publicans do not now reside in their public houses, although for security purposes a manager or other member of the staff may reside therein. The test is whether or not the premises are adequately supervised by the applicant. Gibson J. in the *Perry*[44] case

---

[38] Unreported, High Court, Costello J., May 11, 1978.
[39] Unreported, High Court, Finlay P., December 20, 1983.
[40] (1901) 35 I.L.T.R. 35 at 37.
[41] (1974) 108 I.L.T.R. 141.
[42] *Ibid.* at 143.
[43] *R. (Leslie) v. Monaghan Justices*, above, n.40, at 37.
[44] *R. (Perry) v. Tyrone Justices*, above, n.1.

doubted whether the refusal of the applicant to give an undertaking to reside upon the premises during the week "would by itself constitute unfitness" although Kenny J. noted that a commercial traveller who would not undertake to reside on the premises might not be able to supervise the business sufficiently.

(b) Character, Misconduct or Unfitness of Company

A court is entitled to consider an objection to the character, misconduct or unfitness of an applicant which is a corporate entity. In *R. (Cottingham) v. Cork Justices*, Palles C.B. said:

> "I cannot see why a public company cannot have a character . . . 'Character' means 'reputation'. Reputation is acquired by conduct. The conduct of the authorised agents of a company is *its* conduct.[45]

The applicant company should prove that its directors or any of them or an experienced manager maintains constant supervision of the premises. A nominee, who is quite often a director of the company, is sometimes appointed by the company. Occasionally, the Gardaí require that a nominee be appointed in order that he, as an identifiable person, is charged with the conduct and supervision of the public house.

(c) Unfitness or Inconvenience of the House or Place[46] 21–18

An objection can be made by the Health Authority on the ground that the premises do not meet the standards required in the Health Acts. Similarly, the fire authority may object on the grounds that the premises are unsuitable within the meaning of the Fire Services Act 1981. Finlay P. in the *Centennial*[47] case regarded unfitness and inconvenience disjunctively. He construed "unfitness" as "dealing with the premises themselves". Inconvenience was interpreted as meaning and including the location of the premises. Fitness of premises involves a suitable physical layout with adequate internal fittings and fixtures and lavatory facilities. In the *Centennial* case, the applicant succeeded in rebutting every ground of objection raised but failed to obtain a declaratory order on the basis of the inconvenience of the premises. It was established in evidence that the premises would be located close to a housing estate containing young married people starting families and a high proportion of teenagers and children. Furthermore, it was situated close to a large open space devoted to leisure and sport and to a community school. Finlay P. stated:

> "Having regard to all these features, I have come to the conclusion that it has been established to my satisfaction as a matter of probability that the location

[45] [1906] 2 I.R. 415 at 422 and 423.
[46] See also above, chap. 20, "Declaratory Jurisdiction".
[47] Above, n.39.

of a licensed premises at this particular site, having regard to the features I have mentioned, is not a convenient site . . . ".[48]

In *Application of Nutgrove Inns Ltd* Barron J. refused the application on the grounds of the inconvenience of the premises stating:

"There is the closeness of the park and the playing fields, the homes for senior citizens and, most importantly, the teenage drinking problem which already exists and which could only get worse with all its attendant evils, some of which are already apparent."[49]

In the *Leslie* case, Palles C.B. in construing section 4 of the 1833 Act stated:

"the reasonable possibility of exercising police control over a public-house is a matter which may be taken into consideration".[50]

21–19 However, in *R. (Marshall) v. Tyrone Justices*[51] Palles C.B. in an application for a spirit grocer's licence stated that "the character . . . of suitability is not 'the neighbourhood' but the premises". This judgment was given prior to the enactment of the Beer Retailers' and Spirit Grocers' Retail Licences (Ireland) Act 1900 which confers on the court a "free and unqualified discretion".

Teevan J. in *Re Application of Thomas Flynn*,[52] noted that the "subject" might be wider for public house licences than for off-licences. He stated:

"I think it proper that a Court, invested with some, if restricted, discretion in the matter of certifying premises suitable for licensing, should take into consideration whether the operation of the licence is likely to be seriously detrimental to the quiet enjoyment of adjoining property."[53]

Here he was satisfied that the proposed public house and projected trade would be a considerable nuisance to the adjoining residents: he also expressed the view that a court was entitled, in determining the question of the unfitness or inconvenience of the new premises, to have regard to environmental concerns.

A court can also take into account whether or not car parking facilities are provided for the patrons. In the *Flynn* case, Teevan J. stated:

"I have already found that from every point of view the car park is an essential appurtenance to the public house."[54]

He continued:

"In modern conditions and in the case of new premises, it is a factor which may,

---

48 *Ibid.* at p. 5.
49 Unreported, High Court, Barron J., July 19, 1984, at p. 6.
50 Above, n.40, at 36.
51 (1894) 28 I.L.T.R. 133.
52 [1963] I.R. 301.
53 *Ibid.* at 315.
54 *Ibid.* at 316.

and in some cases should, be taken into consideration in assessing fitness and convenience of premises."[55]

This statement, however, must be considered in conjunction with the requirements of the planning authorities regarding the provision of car parking facilities. In the centre of Dublin city, the planning authority do not require publicans to provide car parking facilities for their patrons. In *Re Thomas O'Brien, applicant*,[56] the court upheld an objection based on the unfitness or inconvenience of premises on the grounds that the proposed site would endanger public safety. The question of whether an applicant has obtained planning permission for all the various proposed uses in respect of the premises is a matter which will be considered by the court in determining "fitness". In *Re Fox Court Developments Ltd*,[57] Keane J. was satisfied that both the existing and contemplated user of the premises were valid in planning terms.

(d) Number of Previously Licensed Houses in the Neighbourhood **21–20**

This is a question of fact and the court must consider the concept of "neighbourhood". The expression "neighbourhood" is not defined in the licensing code although in assessing whether or not the number of previously licensed premises in the neighbourhood was sufficient, Lynch J. in the *Tivoli*[58] case considered, *inter alia*, the existing licensed premises within a radius of 250 yards of both premises and was satisfied that the number of licensed premises in the area was sufficient for the ordinary licensed trade in such area.

Finlay P., in *Centennial*, was satisfied that this particular ground of objection "has to be a negative indication"; in other words that the number of licensed premises would not contra-indicate the issuing of a licence. So, it is not necessary to prove an actual overcrowding in existing licensed premises. He stated:

> "I myself in my experience pay a limited regard only to the sort of evidence that asserts that on particular days at particular times the witness found it hard to get a drink in some premises. That is always going to happen. It does not prove anything in particular."[59]

Demand In the *Centennial* case, Finlay P. held that having regard to the existence of seven hundred odd houses in the nearby housing estate: **21–21**

> "I am satisfied that the number of licensed premises . . . would not contra-indicate the issuing of a licence."[60]

---

[55] *Ibid.* at 317.
[56] Above, at n.41.
[57] [1989] I.L.R.M. 806.
[58] Above, n.31.
[59] *Re Centennial Properties Ltd*, above, n.39, at p. 6.
[60] *Ibid.*

The demand which must be proved by the applicant is "existing demand". The fact that there may be a demand in the future from a proposed shopping centre or housing estate is not a matter with which the court concerns itself.

In *Re Thomas J. Cummins*[61] Murnaghan J. accepted that there would be more and more development in and about Rochestown Avenue as time went on "but I am for the moment concerned with the position which now exists". He continued:

> "While it has been suggested in the course of the evidence that the area is one which is in the process of development, a view that I would be prepared to accept, yet for the purpose of considering the present objection I must only have regard to the situation in the neighbourhood of Granitefield as I find it at the moment."[62]

In the *Nutgrove Inns* case Barron J. upheld an objection based on the sufficiency of licensed premises. He stated:

> "The reality of this aspect of the case is that although there has been a large increase in the population over the years the new and existing licensed premises have opened and expanded to meet the constant increase in demand."[63]

Matters taken into account by Teevan J. in *Re Slattery*[64] when he refused the application on the grounds that the existing facilities were sufficient "at least for the present" were as follows:

(i) that there was a sufficient increase in population;

(ii) that there was an increase in the number of licensed houses and an enlargement of old licensed houses;

(iii) that certain of the objectors' public houses contained unused licensed space;

(iv) that people tended to leave their drinking to the last half hour or so;

(v) that customers preferred to compress their drinking into Friday and Saturday nights and Sunday opening hours.

21–22 **(ii) Other Statutory Objections** Various statutes provide for grounds of objection in addition to or which replace those contained in section 4 of the Licensing (Ireland) Act 1833. For example, section 13 of the Intoxicating Liquor Act 1960 provides for an objection to an application in a rural area based on the ground that the existence of a licence for the new premises would be unreasonably detrimental to the business then being carried on in premises in

---

61 [1964] I.R. 67.
62 *Ibid.* at 71.
63 Above, n.49, at pp. 5 and 6.
64 Unreported, High Court, Teevan J., July 24, 1959.

the neighbourhood licensed for the sale by retail of intoxicating liquor. This objection can be made by a person who can show that the interest which the legislature specifically intended to protect is under attack.

It should be noted that certain jurisdictions do not make provision for one or other of the grounds of objection as set forth in the 1833 Act. Section 7 of the Intoxicating Liquor Act 1953 which provides for the grant of a licence in substitution for premises demolished by a local authority does not list as a ground of objection, the number of previously licensed premises in the neighbourhood. An objector to an application under section 21 of the 1943 Act (which provides for the grant of a new licence for more convenient premises in a rural area) is not entitled to raise the character, misconduct or unfitness of the applicant as a ground of objection. Further, section 17 of the Intoxicating Liquor Act 1960, as inserted by section 32 of the Intoxicating Liquor Act 1962, provides that in a certificate application where section 21 of the 1943 Act is invoked and where a declaratory order has already been made, the court is not entitled to refuse the certificate application on any ground. This is in contrast to section 17(1)(c)(ii)(II) of the 1960 Act which provides that in all other applications for certificates where declaratory orders have been granted, an objection can be raised at certificate stage regarding the character, misconduct or unfitness of the applicant. In the *Jaggers*[65] case, Finlay J. noted that the grounds of objection provided for in section 14 of the Intoxicating Liquor Act 1960 were not "co-extensive" with those contained in section 4 of the 1833 Act.[66]

(iii) Objections Based on Jurisdiction An objection can be raised as to jurisdiction, *i.e.* that the premises sought to be licensed are rated at an annual valuation below the statutory minimum. Another such objection is that the applicant's premises are within a mile of another licensed premises to which an on-licence first granted on or before July 4, 1960, attaches, and which is of the same character as the licence sought.[67] 21–23

2. Renewal

(a) Objectors

(i) Any person The Spirits (Ireland) Act 1854 does not prescribe the category of persons entitled to object to the renewal of a publican's licence. This is in marked contrast to the provisions contained in the Licensing (Ireland) Act 1833 providing for the grant of a certificate entitling the applicant to receive a 21–24

[65] Above, n.16.
[66] See above, chap. 6, "Public House Licences", for a detailed treatment of specific statutory objections.
[67] Intoxicating Liquor Act 1962, s.20(2).

new publican's licence. There is no direct authority on the subject. The Minister for Justice, in introducing the amendment to section 3 of the Registration of Clubs (Ireland) Act 1904, contained in section 44 of the Intoxicating Liquor Act 1988, providing for objections to the renewal of club certificates by "any person", explained that this provision was intended to "bring clubs into line with licensed premises generally so far as objection to certificates is concerned".[68]

Mr. James O'Connor in his book on *The Licensing Laws of Ireland*[69] refers to the case of *Boulter v. Kent Justices*[70] as authority for the proposition that an objection to the renewal of an on-licence can be made by any member of the community. Further the legislature has recognised the right of "any person" to object at renewal stage by providing for an objection to renewal of a licence on the ground of the unfitness of the premises to which it relates.[71] The application for renewal of the publican's licence is now made directly to the Revenue Commissioners and a certificate of the court is necessary only in certain circumstances, enumerated in the Courts (No. 2) Act 1986 and dealt with in chapter 19, "Renewal". A certificate of the court is required where a notice of objection to the renewal of the licence is lodged within the time prescribed by the rules of court. In practice, objectors to the renewal of a licence comprise members of the community and local Garda Síochána.

21–25 **(ii) Fire Authority** There is one specific statutory notice party at renewal stage, *i.e.* the fire officer who must be notified one month in advance of the making of the application (or such shorter period as may be agreed between the parties).[72]

(b) Grounds of Objection

21–26 Section 11 of the Spirits (Ireland) Act 1854, which provided for the renewal of licences upon the production to the Collector of Customs and Excise of a certificate of the court as to the good character of the applicant and the peaceable and orderly manner in which the premises were conducted in the past year, was repealed by section 9 of the Courts (No. 2) Act 1986. The certificate referred to in section 11 is, however, required to be produced to an officer of the Revenue Commissioners where a notice of objection to such renewal has been lodged with the court within the time prescribed by the rules of court. The certificate which must be presented to the Revenue Commissioners where notice of objection has been served and where an applicant is seeking the renewal of his licence is in the following form:

---

[68] See *Dáil Debates*, second stage, p. 2014, vol. 379(b).
[69] (Dublin, 1904).
[70] [1897] A.C. 556.
[71] Intoxicating Liquor Act 1960, s.32.
[72] Fire Services Act 1981, s.24(2), as inserted by the Courts (No. 2) Act 1986, s.9.

"(a) the good character of the licensee,

(b) the peaceable and orderly manner in which the licensed premises were conducted in the year ending on the expiry of the licence. . . .".[73]

The District Court clerk is obliged, pursuant to the District Court (Renewal of Intoxicating Liquor Licences) Rules 1988,[74] to send notification of the lodgment of the notice of objection to the Collector of Customs and Excise for the district in which the premises are situate. Where the objector is not a member of the Garda Síochána, the clerk is also obliged to notify the superintendent for the area. The Collector of Customs and Excise must be notified of the order made by the court in respect of the objection. The grounds of objection to renewal are listed below.

(i) Unfitness of Premises to be Licensed This ground of objection is also open to objectors at renewal stage. An objection cannot be entertained by the court unless the objector has given "notice in writing of the intention to make the objection together with particulars in writing of the unfitness alleged" not less than 12 months before the hearing of the application to the licence holder.[75] This statutory time limit must be complied with. The intention of the legislature in imposing such time limit was to give a licence holder sufficient time to bring his premises up to the standard fit for licensing. **21–27**

(ii) Good Character of Licensee

Character In *Leader v. Yell*[76] William J. held that character meant "general reputation in the estimation of his neighbours" and though a man was living in a state of concubinage, where there was no evidence of "open and notorious profligacy", a man may still be of good character where he is generally regarded as such. **21–28**

Refusal to Serve A refusal to serve or to supply customers with intoxicating liquor may in certain circumstances constitute a ground of objection to the renewal of his licence. In *R. (Delaney) v. Queens County Justices*,[77] a publican refused to supply intoxicating liquor to certain persons who were boycotted and he demanded excessive charges from others. These facts were held to constitute evidence to support the judge's refusal of a renewal certificate. **21–29**

However, James O'Connor in *The Irish Justice of the Peace*,[78] expressed the view that if a refusal to serve arises from a fear on the part of the publican that his serving unpopular persons with liquor might injure his business, then such

[73] Courts (No. 2) Act, 1986, s.4(7).
[74] S.I. No. 145 of 1988.
[75] Intoxicating Liquor Act 1960, s.32, as amended by the Courts (No. 2) Act, 1986, s.9.
[76] 16 C.B. (NS) 584.
[77] [1887] 20 L.R. Ir. 167.
[78] Vol. II (2nd ed., 1915).

refusal affords "no ground whatever" for witholding the renewal as "a man may be of good character without being heroic enough to face public odium".[79] A "capricious refusal" to serve customers might be made a cause of objection to the renewal of his licence at the annual licensing sessions: the refusal, for example, of some publicans to serve females in parts of their licensed premises may constitute a ground of objection to the renewal of the licence.

If the equal status legislation which is being mooted at the date of writing comes into force, a publican's right to refuse may be severely curtailed.

21–30 *Breach of Undertaking* A licence cannot be granted subject to an undertaking[80]: in other words, the court is not entitled to grant a licence which is conditional upon compliance with a condition or conditions. Giving an undertaking in court has no legal validity.

However, the breach of an undertaking which is given by an applicant to the court can support a decision that the applicant is not of "good character" for the purposes of the licensing code. In *R. (Bourke) v. Dublin Justices*,[81] various undertakings were given by Mr. Bourke to the court. One such undertaking was to remove a public bar which he had opened and to conduct his premises as a hotel. He failed to remove the bar or conduct the premises as so undertaken. As the undertaking had been given by him in exchange for the withdrawal of objections to his application, Palles C.B. was of the view that there was evidence of a valid contract between Mr Bourke and the objectors. He stated:

> "I have arrived at the conclusion that I cannot say that such conduct is not capable of affecting and derogating from the good reputation as a licensed publican which, on the evidence and admissions, I must hold that Mr Bourke would otherwise have had."[82]

FitzGibbon L.J. was satisfied that everyone who knew of the breach of the undertaking by Mr Bourke "had his estimate of Bourke's character unfavourably affected".[83]

(iii) Peaceable and Orderly Conduct of Premises in Past Year

21–31 *Breaches of Law* Evidence of breaches of the licensing code by previous tenants of the premises can be adduced where it is established that "the house, apart from the person, may be of a disorderly character".[84] Permitting drunkenness or violent conduct on licensed premises and supplying intoxicating liquor to disorderly persons and permitting licensed premises to be used for

---

79 *Ibid.* at p. 709.
80 *R. v. Beesly* [1912] 3 K.B. 583.
81 [1903] 2 I.R. 429.
82 *Ibid.* at 438.
83 *Ibid.* at 442.
84 *R. v. Miskin Higher Justices* [1893] 1 Q.B.D. 275 at 278.

certain disorderly purposes which are specified in section 14 of the Licensing Act 1872 are recordable offences. Evidence of these convictions and evidence of convictions under sections 13 and 14 of the Licensing Act 1872, are admissible and will be taken into account by a Court in determining whether or not the premises have been run in a peaceable and orderly manner.

No Trading carried on in the Past Year The jurisdiction of the court to grant the renewal of a licence where no trade, or merely token trading has been carried on in the previous licensing year, has been addressed in a large number of cases. An oft quoted statement of Holmes J. in *R. (Lambe) v. Armagh Justices* indicates the attitude of the courts to the granting of certificates where trading has not been carried on in the previous year: **21–32**

> "What are the Justices to certify? Is it not to the peaceable and orderly manner in which a licensed house has been conducted in the past year? Can these words apply to a house shut up and empty, or to a house only occupied as a private residence, or to a house used exclusively for carrying on a wholly different trade? To ask these questions is to answer them. In all business there may be cessations and interruptions, rebuilding or repairing the premises, death, illness, want of means, many other causes may keep up the shutters and close the door for a time; but the trade is not abandoned. Christian L.J. once remarked, that a barrister may be said to be practising the law, or pursuing his profession, as well when travelling in Switzerland during his vacation, as when attending the Four Courts in Term time. But, what, if he were to sell his law books and establish himself as a hotel keeper in Zermatt? He no longer pursues his profession, although he is still a titular barrister."[85]

Here, the applicant had given an undertaking to the justices that he would not use the licensed premises as an ordinary public house. The premises were in fact used for storage and bottling in connection with the applicant's main offices in another street where the business of wholesale wine and spirit merchants was carried on. Holmes J. was of opinion that the certificates were given "without jurisdiction, and that the licences issued in pursuance of them were absolutely void".[86] He noted that in five successive years the applicant had obtained a certificate from the Justices that the licensed premises were conducted in a peaceable and orderly manner, "when, in point of fact, they were not conducted at all".[87]

Where an applicant did not trade in a premises until September 22 (three days prior to the hearing before the magistrates) and then applied for the renewal of her licence, it was held that in the absence of any circumstances, such as those enumerated in the judgment of Holmes J. in the *Lambe*[88] case, to explain why the premises had not been opened, the renewal certificate should have been

[85] [1897] 2 I.R. 57 at 68.
[86] *Ibid.* at 69.
[87] *Ibid.*
[88] *Ibid.*

refused.[89] The reason given in *R. (Carberry) v. Louth Justices*[90] as to why the premises had not been opened during the year was that the landlord had been unable to procure a tenant for the premises. The court quashed the order of the justices granting the renewal certificate on the grounds that same was made without and in excess of jurisdiction. In *R. (Roe) v. Roscommon Justices*, Holmes J. stated:

> "I cannot profitably add anything on this branch of the licensing law to what I said in [*Lambe's* case]; but to prevent misapprehension I should like to repeat the observations I then made as to temporary interruptions of business. Such an interruption may last the greater part or even the whole of the year; and yet it may be shown that it was a necessary incident in a continuing trade. But in the present case neither at Petty Sessions nor at Quarter Sessions nor even in this Court has there been any explanation of the premises not having been used as a public house."[91]

21–33 The test, therefore, is that where there is a temporary interruption or abandonment of trade, even if same lasts "the greater part or even the whole of the year", once the applicant can show that such interruption was a necessary incident in a continuing trade, the court may grant the certificate. In *Application of Gorman,*[92] where no trade has been carried on in the year and neither the corporation nor its nominee had any intention of using the licence or engaging in the licensed business, evidence of peaceable and orderly trading could not be established. Ó Dálaigh J. stated:

> "One can sympathise with the desire of the Corporation to be in a position to recoup the sum paid by them in respect of the licence by keeping the licence alive in order to dispose of it for value. Their problem is one which, if it is to be solved, must be solved by the Oireachtas."[93]

He referred to *Roche v. Quinn*[94] where the High Court held that the closing of a licensed premises from September 9, 1927, to September 14, 1928, except during the hours from 11 a.m. to 3.30 p.m. on September 11, 1928, "was not an interruption in trading which was a necessary incident in a continuing trade".

There was no trading and no intention to trade in the *Gorman* case: but it is conceivable that a situation could arise where, despite the fact that there had been no trading within the past year, the court could renew the licence on the basis that such cessation or interruption in trading constituted merely an interruption in a continuing trade.

---

[89] *R. (Roe) v. Roscommon Justices* [1905] 2 I.R. 101
[90] (1916) 50 I.L.T.R. 84.
[91] Above, n.89, at 118.
[92] [1971] I.R. 1.
[93] *Ibid.* at 9.
[94] [1929] I.R. 553.

Evidence of Different Trade In *R. (Morell) v. Antrim Justices*,[95] evidence was adduced that there was a large trade in sending out and delivering spirits for consumption off the premises from time to time: the only evidence of the public house trade was that some six half-glasses of whiskey had been sold and consumed on the premises during the preceding year. The court rejected the argument that as the licence entitled the holder to sell intoxicating liquor for consumption on or off the premises and there was "slight" evidence of sale for consumption on the premises, the applicant was entitled to the certificate. Palles C.B. stated: 21–34

> "It has also been decided that the character of the conduct of the licensed house is not part of what are sometimes called the *merits* of the application, but is a matter preliminary to the jurisdiction of the Justices."[96]

He was satisfied that "in substance and reality" the applicant had not carried on the trade as a licensed house. He referred to the judgment of Fitzgibbon L.J. in *R. (Cox) v. Recorder of Dublin* where he stated:

> "The public must be thought of as well as the publican, and unless they have been accommodated during the year, the certificate that the house has been 'conducted' as the statute contemplated, namely, as a house used for the sale of spirits, etc., to be consumed on the premises, cannot properly be given."[97]

So, although a publican's licence permits the sale and supply of liquor both on and off the premises, if the off-licence business is carried on to the exclusion of the on-licence business, the jurisdiction of the court to grant the certificate of renewal is questionable.

Where Premises are Destroyed Where the premises to which the licence attached have been burned down or destroyed, the question arises as to whether the court is entitled to issue a certificate. In *R. (Dudgeon) v. Antrim Justices*,[98] the King's Bench overturned the order of the County Court judge and refused to issue the certificates where the premises had been destroyed by fire. This case concerned a large number of licensed premises in the town of Lisburn which were destroyed by fire in August 1920, and where the renewal of all licences were obtained in September/October 1920. The applications for renewal for the following year, however, were refused: "the Court is satisfied that in every instance the houses had ceased to exist and there was no trading in the year".[99] 21–35

Judge Sheridan in *Breen v. Keane*[100] expressed himself dissatisfied with the decision in the *Dudgeon* case. He was satisfied that the case law, with the

---

[95] [1900] 2 I.R. 492.
[96] *Ibid.* at 499.
[97] [1885–86] 16 L.R. Ir. 424 at 438.
[98] (1922) 56 I.L.T.R. 134.
[99] *Ibid.* at 135.
[100] [1981] I.L.R.M. 279.

exception of *Dudgeon*, permitted the issue of the certificates even where the licence had ceased trading for over a year "once the court is satisfied that he has intentions to rebuild and no intention to abandon the licence".[101]

21–36 *Alteration of Premises* Where the structure of a premises has been altered and the applicant seeks a certificate for the renewal of the licence, the court cannot grant the certificate. In *Macklin v. Greacen* Griffin J. noted:

> "... as the premises to which the original licence attached had been extensively altered by the bomb attack in 1974, it is likely that the renewals of the licence thereafter were invalid on that ground ...".[102]

Where an applicant extends his premises by adding various apartments, extra lavatories or by extending his bar area, he is obliged to apply for a new licence to incorporate such extension or alterations. Prior to the enactment of the Courts of Justice Act 1924, the justices had jurisdiction both to grant and renew publicans' licences and they did renew licences for altered premises, the test then being whether the premises were "substantially the same" as the premises previously licensed. However, Section 50 of the Courts of Justice Act 1924[103] and section 24 of the Courts (Supplemental Provisions) Act 1961 conferred upon the Circuit Court judge the power to grant new on-licences. A District Court judge can issue a certificate of renewal in respect of the premises which was licensed in the immediately preceding year only and is not entitled to grant a new licence in respect of altered premises. The Circuit Court makes this order, directing the grant of a new licence, the jurisdiction invoked being section 6 of the Licensing (Ireland) Act 1902.[104]

21–37 **(iv) Jurisdiction** It is also possible to object to the renewal of a licence on the grounds that the court has no jurisdiction to make the order sought. The following grounds of objection can be advanced.

(a) *That the premises are not licensed* An application cannot be made to renew a licence where the licence has lapsed and an application to renew same has not been made within six months of the expiry of the licence.[105] Nor can a licence be renewed where it has been forfeited. Where a licence becomes forfeit by virtue of convictions sustained under Part III of the Intoxicating Liquor Act 1927, no new licence can be granted in respect of the premises or any part thereof.[106]

---

101 *Ibid.* at 285.
102 [1982] ILRM 182 at 183.
103 Repealed by s.3 of the Courts (Supplemental Provisions) Act 1961.
104 See also chap. 2, "Characteristics of a Licence" and chap. 6, "Jurisdiction".
105 Licensing Act (Ireland) 1874, s.12(2) and s.37.
106 Intoxicating Liquor Act 1927, s.28.

(b) *Where the applicant is not in possession of the premises* No right to the benefit of a publican's licence can exist separate from the ownership and possession of the licensed premises, and the rightful possession of the licensed premises carries with it the right to the transfer or renewal of the licence attaching thereto.[107] Although Holmes J. in *R. (Murphy) v. Cork Justices* stated: 21–38

> "I can find no warrant, either in the licensing statutes or in the general law, for holding that the certificate of the Justices involves a declaration that the grantee of the licence has a possessory interest in the licensed premises . . . ".[108]

He noted that the licence is granted on the implied condition that it shall operate if and so long as the licensee has a possessory interest.

In *Murphy v. Crean*[109] Palles C.B. held that as a licence is an authority to a named person to carry on trade in a specified house, it cannot continue to exist if the occupation of that house ceases to be in that named person, unless some other person obtains a transfer of the licence. In *State (Reddy) v. District Justice Johnson*,[110] McWilliam J. held that the District Court judge was acting within jurisdiction when he granted a certificate of renewal where the applicant did not have possession of the premises. He stated:

> "even if he erred in the exercise of his jurisdiction, his order cannot be questioned by this Court on *certiorari*."[111]

It is questionable however, whether the Revenue Commissioners can renew a licence in such circumstances where no certificate of the court is requied.

3. Transfer

(a) Ad Interim Transfer

(i) Objectors An applicant for an ad interim transfer is obliged to give reasonable notice to the superintendent of the Garda Síochána[112] who is a competent objector to such application. There is, however, no requirement to notify any further party other than the District Court clerk. Nor is an applicant obliged to advertise the application and the statute makes no references to objectors. In *The State (Doyle) v. Carr*,[113] Henchy J. in the course of his judgment noted that "opposition to the application could come only from the Garda Síochána". 21–39

---

[107] *Brennan v. Dorney* [1888–89] 21 L.R. Ir. 353.
[108] [1895] 2 I.R. 104 at 115.
[109] [1915] 1 I.R. 111 at 142.
[110] Unreported, High Court, McWilliam J., July 31, 1980.
[111] *Ibid.* at p. 13.
[112] District Court Rules 1948, r. 96.
[113] [1970] I.R. 87.

21–40 **(ii) Grounds of Objection** The court can only consider three matters in an application for an ad interim transfer. Henchy J. listed these in *The State (Doyle) v. Carr*:

1. that the required notification has been given;
2. that there is some need for the transfer arising from the death or incapacity of the licensee, or from his removal from the premises, or arising from the sale or assignment of his interest in the premises;
3. that the applicant is not disqualified by law from holding the licence.[114]

The court is not entitled to inquire into or consider the character or suitability of the applicant[115]; it must confine itself to considering the three matters set forth above and it cannot have regard to the suitability of the premises, the number of existing licensed premises in the area, or the public demand for a licensed premises in the area. An objection on the ground of failure to comply with the requirements of the rules can be disposed of where the court so sees fit.[116]

(b) Certificate of Transfer

21–41 **(i) Objectors** An application for a certificate of transfer is an application for the grant of a licence to a person "who shall not have been duly licensed in the preceding year".[117] Those persons, therefore, who are entitled to object to the grant of a new licence can object to an application for a certificate of transfer. There is however one potential exception to this: section 24 of the Fire Services Act 1981 confers an entitlement to object upon the fire officer only in the case of an application for "a certificate for the grant or renewal of a licence . . . under the Licensing Acts". It is not clear whether this applies to an application to transfer a licence.

21–42 **(ii) Grounds of Objection** The grounds of objection to an application for a certificate of transfer are contained in section 4 of the Licensing (Ireland) Act 1833. Those grounds of objection are as follows:

(a) the character, misconduct or unfitness of the applicant,

(b) unfitness or inconvenience of the house or place,

(c) the number of previously licensed houses in the neighbourhood.

Where, however, an application for a certificate of transfer is preceded by an ad interim transfer the third ground of objection does not lie.

---

[114] *Ibid.* at 90–91. See also above, chap. 3, "The Licensee".
[115] *The State (Hennessy) and Chariot Inns Ltd v. Commons*, above, n.6.
[116] District Court Rules 1948, r. 13.
[117] Licensing (Ireland) Act 1833, s.2.

This is the effect of *R. (Clitheroe) v. Recorder of Dublin.*[118] Here, the Recorder of Dublin refused a certificate of transfer on the ground of the number of previously licensed houses in the neighbourhood. The Queen's Bench Division overturned his decision, holding that although sections 2 to 5 of the 1833 Act applied to applications for certificates of transfer, in construing these sections regard must be had to the nature of the application. As an application for a transfer was an application in respect of a house that was "previously licensed", in consequence, an objection on the basis of the number of previously licensed houses could not have been intended to apply to such an application. O'Brien J. stated:

> "It would, in my opinion, be consistent with the provisions of [section 4 of the 1833 Act] to hold that the excessive number of previously licensed houses in the neighbourhood would be a valid ground for refusing an application in respect of a house not previously licensed, (the granting of which would increase the number, already too great), but that such an objection should not prevail where the application was made in respect of a house already licensed."[119]

May C.J. stated:

> ". . . existing vested interests should not be extinguished, even with a legitimate object, without compensation."[120]

An applicant for a certificate of transfer can only rely on the *Clitheroe* case where he can show that he has already obtained an ad interim transfer in respect of the premises. In *R. (Cox) v. Recorder of Dublin*, Morris C.J. summed up the position of the applicant in the *Clitheroe* case:

> "[He] had obtained a legal assignment of the premises; he was in possession of them; he had got an assignment of the licence — an actual working licence; he had obtained a temporary transfer of the licence, and the application to the Recorder was for the confirmation of that transfer."[121]

So, where an applicant for a certificate of transfer has already obtained an ad interim transfer, an objector cannot rely on the last ground of objection mentioned in section 4 of the Licensing (Ireland) Act 1833, *i.e.* the number of previously licensed houses in the neighbourhood. **21–43**

118 (1877) 11 I.L.T.R. 85
119 *Ibid.* at 88.
120 *Ibid.* at 87.
121 Above, n.97, at 436.

4. Declaratory Order

(a) Objectors

21–44 Any person who would be entitled to object to an application for the grant of a certificate entitling the applicant to receive a licence in respect of the premises may object to the declaratory application.[122]

(b) Grounds of Objection

21–45 A competent objector is entitled to object "in like manner" as in an application for a certificate leading to the grant of a licence. The grounds of objection which are open to an applicant in an application for a certificate apply in a declaratory application. A further ground of objection open to an objector is that the applicant has not complied with the mandatory procedural requirements of section 15 of the Intoxicating Liquor Act 1960.

B. Off-Licence

1. Grant

21–46 The off-licence generally consists of three licences; a wine retailer's off-licence, a spirit retailer's off-licence, and a beer retailer's off-licence. A certificate of the court is not necessary for the grant or renewal of a wine retailer's off-licence: the holder of a beer retailer's off-licence and a spirit retailer's off-licence is automatically entitled to apply for a wine retailer's off-licence.[123] The only statutory objector to the grant of a wine retailer's off-licence is the superintendent of the Garda Síochána for the district within which the premises are situated. The grounds of objection are specified in section 13 of the Refreshment Houses (Ireland) Act 1860.

This part of the chapter discusses objections in respect of those licences for which a court certificate is required, namely, the spirit retailer's off-licence and beer retailer's off-licence. Objections to these licences will be dealt with under the single heading of off-licence, as the category of objectors to and the grounds of objections which relate to the grant and renewal of both licences are similar, save in one respect referred to below, at paragraph 21–53.

[122] Intoxicating Liquor Act 1960, s.15(5).
[123] Intoxicating Liquor Act 1927, s.61, and Intoxicating Liquor Act 1962, s.28.

(a) Objectors

1. Section 1 of the Beer Retailers' and Spirit Grocers' Retail Licences (Ireland) Act 1900 provides for objection to the grant of a new licence for the sale of beer or spirits off the premises "by any resident or owner of property in the parish wherein are situate the house and premises in respect of which such certificate is applied for". "Owner of property" can include licensed publicans or the holders of off-licences and other retail units in the parish. This provision is much broader than that contained in section 4 of the Licensing (Ireland) Act 1833 governing objections to the grant of a new on-licence, which confines the making of objections to inhabitants of the parish. **21–47**
2. The Garda superintendent for the District in which the applicant resides.[124]
3. The fire officer is not a notice party and so is not a competent objector.

(b) Grounds of Objection

(i) Spirit Retailer's Off-Licence The certificate sought in an application for a spirit retailers's off-licence relates to the good character of the applicant and the suitability of the premises.[125] **21–48**

(ii) Beer Retailer's Off-Licence An applicant for the grant of a beer retailer's off-licence must produce a certificate of the court as to his good character and the suitability of the premises, that they are rated, if in a city or town with a population exceeding 10,000 at £15 or upwards; if elsewhere, at £8 or upwards and that they have been in the exclusive occupation of the applicant for a period of at least three months prior to the certificate.[126]

Discretion of Court In granting an off-licence the District Court judge has a "free and unqualified discretion"[127] to refuse or grant a certificate, on any grounds "appearing [to them] sufficient". The court's discretion must, however, be exercised in accordance with the policy of the licensing code, and not to safeguard the interests of existing licence holders. In *Re Application of Power Supermarkets Ltd,*[128] Walsh J. noted that the Circuit Court judge had found as a fact that since the applicant commenced business, some of the objectors had **21–49**

---

[124] Beerhouses (Ireland) Act 1864, s.5.
[125] Licensing Act (Ireland) 1874, s.9.
[126] Beerhouses (Ireland) Act 1864, s.3; Licensing Act (Ireland) 1874, s.8; Beer Licences Regulation Ireland Act 1877, s.2; Beer Retailers' and Spirit Grocers' Licences (Ireland) Act 1900, s.3.
[127] Beer Retailers' and Spirit Grocers' Retail Licences (Ireland) Act, 1900.
[128] Above, n.3.

lost business; that the turnover of at least six of the objectors had fallen by an average of one third and that this fall was directly attributable to the new competition created by the applicant. It was found that the objectors turnover would decline "even to the point of some of them being forced out of business".[129] The applicant contended that the benefit and convenience of the public was the paramount consideration in the exercise of the judge's discretion and that it transcended any question of detriment to the existing off-licence traders. Walsh J. stated:

> "The discretion given to the learned Circuit Court judge by section 1 of the Act of 1900 . . . must be exercised in accordance with the objectives of the licensing code. . . . The Act of 1902 which applies to both on-licences and off-licences was introduced for the purpose of preventing the granting of further licences save within the grounds permitted by that Act. The object of the Act was to safeguard the public interest by preventing a proliferation of licensed premises. The object of the Act of 1902 was not to shelter existing publicans from competition."[130]

In specifying the matters which a judge must take into account in deciding whether or not to grant a licence, Walsh J. indicated that the court should consider:

> ". . . the wants of the neighbourhood with reference both to its population, means of inspection by the proper authorities, and the suitability of the applicant and other considerations which relate to the objectives of the licensing code".[131]

21–50 1. Character of Applicant

This ground of objection is dealt with at paragraph 21–17.

2. Suitability

In *R. (Marshall) v. Tyrone Justices*[132] the court held that in determining whether or not a premises were suitable, all considerations of the neighbourhood which do not affect the premises themselves were to be excluded. Fitzgibbon L.J. dissented, stating: "locality cannot be separated from the premises". It is conceivable that the court would come to a different conclusion in the present day, given that this case was decided prior to the coming into force of the Beer Retailers' and Spirit Grocers' Retail Licences (Ireland) Act 1900 which gives the judges a free and unqualified discretion subject to the limitations imposed by the *Power Supermarkets Ltd* case.[133]

---

[129] *Ibid.* at 210.
[130] *Ibid.*
[131] *Ibid.* at 211.
[132] Above, n.51.
[133] Above, n.3. Note that the *Marshall* case was distinguished in *Re Application of Thomas Flynn*, above, n.52, by Teevan J. where the application was for an on-licence.

3. Jurisdiction 21–51

Objections to jurisdiction can be made where an applicant for a beer retailer's off-licence cannot prove the appropriate rateable valuation or that he has been in exclusive occupation of the premises for at least three months prior to the granting of the certificate. Failure to comply with the procedural requirements contained in section 4 of the Beerhouses (Ireland) Act 1864 can be used as a ground of objection. The court may adjourn an application, where although no objection has been made, it feels that the attention of the police should be drawn to a particular matter relating thereto.[134]

2. Renewal

(a) Objectors

The only statutory objector is the superintendent of the Garda Síochána of the district within which the applicant resides.[135] Note that "any person" may object to an application for the renewal of a licence under section 32 of the Intoxicating Liquor Act 1960 on the grounds of the unfitness of the premises by notifying the applicant 12 months in advance of the hearing. The fire officer is not a statutory notice party. 21–52

(b) Grounds of Objection

(i) Spirit Retailer's Off-Licence At renewal stage, where objection is made, a certificate of the court is required as to the good character of the applicant and the peaceable and orderly conduct of the house during the past year.[136] The suitability of the premises is not a matter to which the court can have regard at renewal stage, unless an objection is made in accordance with section 32 of the Intoxicating Liquor Act 1960. 21–53

(ii) Beer Retailer's Off-Licence In the case of a beer retailer's off-licence, objection can be taken to the good character of the applicant and/or the peaceable and orderly conduct of the house during the past year and jurisdictional matters such as the rating and exclusive occupation of the premises by the applicant.

---

[134] *R. (Morgan) v. Tyrone Justices*, above, n.4.
[135] Beerhouses (Ireland) Act, 1864, s.5, and the Licensing Act, 1872, s.82
[136] Licensing Act 1872. s.82

3. Transfer

(a) Ad Interim Transfer

21–54 As section 1 of the Public House (Ireland) Act 1855 now applies to off-licences,[137] an application can be made to the District Court for the ad interim transfer of an off-licence.

(i) Objectors As in the case of an on-licence, the superintendent is the only competent objector.

(ii) Grounds of Objection The superintendent's objections are limited to the grounds set forth in section 1 of the Public House (Ireland) Act 1855 which are dealt with, above, at paragraph 21–40.

(b) Certificate of Transfer

21–55 **(i) Objectors** Those persons competent to object to the grant of an off-licence can object to its transfer.

(c) Grounds of Objection

21–56 **(i) Spirit Retailer's Off-Licence** The certificate sought by an applicant is as to his good character and the suitability of the premises.[138]

(ii) Beer Retailer's Off-Licence The certificate is as to the good character of the applicant, the rating of the premises and if the transfer arises other than upon the death and removal of the person in occupation immediately prior to the transfer as to exclusive occupation of the premises.

Where an applicant for a certificate of transfer has within the preceding two years had a licence as a spirit grocer or beer retailer, the certificate must also be as to the peaceable and orderly manner in which he carried on business during the previous year.

4. Declaratory Order

21–57 An objection to an application for a declaratory order can be made by any person who would be entitled to object to the application for the grant of the certificate and such a person objects "in like manner" as he would if the application were for a certificate.[139]

---

137 Intoxicating Liquor Act 1960, s.29.
138 Licensing Act 1872, s.82 and the Licensing Act (Ireland) 1874, s.9.
139 Intoxicating Liquor Act 1960, s.15.

C. Hotel Licence

1. Grant

(a) Objectors

A hotel licence is an on-licence and the category of competent objectors is the same. In *Application of George Doyle*,[140] Judge McCarthy rejected the contention of counsel for the applicant that objections to hotel licences under section 4 of the 1833 Act should be limited to hotel proprietors. 21–58

(b) Grounds of Objection

Similarly, the statutory grounds of objection contained in section 4 of the 1833 Act are available to persons who are objecting to the grant of a hotel licence. These grounds are as to the character, misconduct or unfitness of the applicant, the unfitness or inconvenience of the premises and the sufficiency of licensed premises in the neighbourhood. In *Application of George Doyle*, Maguire P. held that the granting of the licence would not unduly increase the facilities in the neighbourhood stating: 21–59

> "In my opinion, furthermore, a hotel caters for a somewhat different type of customer from those catered for by the ordinary existing licensed premises."[141]

Haugh J. in *Application of Tormey*,[142] was satisfied that a trial judge must admit evidence concerning all the licensed premises in the area, "whether they are licensed hotels, public houses or off-licences, and he must consider such evidence". However, the weight which the court should accord to such evidence differs according to the circumstances of the case. The Judge continued:

> "If he thought that the aim of the applicant was to cater merely for the hotel's own clientele, he should not attach much weight to the existence of public houses in the area. If he thought, however, that the aim of the applicant was to get a hotel licence for what might be called "publican purposes", so as to make his hotel half a hotel and half a public house, he should attach great weight to the existence of previously licensed public houses in the area. This is the commonsense approach to the problem and I think, the correct one."[143]

In that case, Haugh J. accepted the applicant's evidence that the licence was sought not for the passer-by trade but as an additional amenity for the guests in the applicant's hotel and he affirmed the order of the Circuit Court judge granting the application.

---

[140] [1946] I.R. 125.
[141] *Ibid.* at 129.
[142] Unreported, High Court, Haugh J., January 15, 1954.
[143] *Ibid.*

Given the introduction of the jurisdiction permitting the hotelier to have a public bar on his premises, the distinction between hotel and public house premises may not be as pronounced in present times.

21–60 Where plans do not indicate the actual use contemplated by the applicant, this does not necessarily require the refusal of the application. In *Re Fox Court Developments Ltd*[144] the plans did not indicate the contemplated use of the ground floor and basement. Keane J. stated:

> "It is clear that the only purpose of the lodging of plans is to enable the Court to ascertain whether the premises will be fit and convenient to be licensed and to identify the precise area which is to be licensed. The fact that certain users are indicated on those plans does not mean that the applicant is forever thereafter inhibited from putting them to a different use."[145]

The court in assessing an objection as to the unfitness or inconvenience of the premises, must however still be satisfied that the premises as set forth on the plans before the court are suitable to be licensed. In the *Fox Court* case, the court was satisfied that the premises as outlined on the plans were fit and convenient to be licensed as a hotel.

The size of a public bar in a public house can be taken into account by a court when assessing an objection as to the unfitness or inconvenience of the premises.[146] The existence of a public bar where there is no section 19 order, or where there is an insufficient number of bedrooms both go to the jurisdiction of the court, as the "hotel" cannot be said to answer the statutory description.

Section 19 Order: Public Bar

21–61 As can be seen above, in chapter 8, "Hotel", at paragraph 8–26 *et seq.*, an application to the District Court for public bar facilities is made *ex parte* and no person can object, on any ground.

2. Renewal

21–62 As in the case of the renewal of a publican's on-licence, the category of objectors and grounds of objections are the same. An objection to the renewal of a hotel licence can be based on the ground that the court has no jurisdiction to issue a certificate as the hotel has ceased to come within the statutory definition in section 2(2) of the Licensing (Ireland) Act 1902.

---

[144] Above, n.57.
[145] *Ibid.* at 809.
[146] *Doyle v. Foley*, unreported, Supreme Court, June 3, 1965.

3. Transfer

The provisions relating to transfer are the same as those pertaining to a publican's licence. 21–63

4. Declaratory Order

In *Application of Daniel Rice*[147] an objection to the use of the declaratory jurisdiction by a hotelier was rejected: the court held that the declaratory jurisdiction was appropriate where the applicant sought a hotel licence pursuant to section 2 (2) of the 1902 Act. 21–64

D. Clubs

1. Grant of Certificate of Registration

(a) Objectors

Section 3 of the Registration of Clubs (Ireland) Act 1904, as amended by section 44 of the Intoxicating Liquor Act 1988, sets forth the category of objectors to the grant or renewal of a certificate of registration, the procedure which must be complied with by a prospective objector and the time limit during which he must make his objection. The competent objectors are listed below: 21–65

1. The superintendent of the Garda Síochána for the Garda district in which the club is situate. Section 3 requires the registrar of clubs (the District Court clerk) to notify the superintendent when he receives notice of the application for the grant of the certificate of registration.
2. Any person resident in the parish in which the club premises are situated.

For grounds of objection, see below, paragraph 21–67.

2. Renewal of Certificate of Registration

(a) Objectors

Section 44 of the Intoxicating Liquor Act 1988 amended the provisions of section 3 of the 1904 Act to permit objection to be made to the renewal of a certificate of registration by "any person". The Minister for Justice, Mr Collins 21–66

[147] (1962) 96 I.L.T.R. 197.

in his address to the Dáil prior to the entry into force of the 1988 Act stated that he wished to bring the provisions relating to the renewal of certificates of registration in line with provisions relating to the renewal of publicans' licences.

(b) Grounds of Objection to Grant and Renewal of Certificate of Registration

21–67 The court is not entitled to exercise a general discretion in an application for the grant or renewal of a certificate of registration. It must confine itself to considering objections coming within the enumerated categories set forth at section 5 of the Registration of Clubs (Ireland) Act 1904 as amended.

Davitt J. in *Re Rossmore Golf Club*[148] was satisfied that the purpose of the provisions on objections was to ensure that the objectives of the 1904 Act should not be defeated and not to make it difficult, troublesome or expensive for a reputable club to obtain a certificate of registration, when it was willing and anxious to comply with all necessary legal requirements. He noted that the object of the Act of 1904 was to ensure that only genuine, reputable clubs should by registration acquire the right to supply liquor to their members stating:

> "It seems to me quite clear from the Act, and particularly from section 5, that the purpose of the provisions in relation to objections was, not to enable parishioners or police to make it difficult, troublesome or expensive for a genuine, reputable club to obtain a certificate of registration, when it was willing and anxious to comply with all necessary legal requirements . . .".[149]

21–68 Section 5 of the Registration of Clubs (Ireland) Act 1904 provides that: "the Court shall not consider any objection to the grant or renewal of a certificate of registration unless it is taken upon one or more of the following grounds": In *Comhaltas Ceoltóirí Éireann*[150] Finlay P. stated:

> "This provision I am satisfied prevents the Court on an application for the grant or renewal of a certificate from exercising any general discretion and confines it to considering objections within the enumerated categories."[151]

21–69 The grounds of objection are set forth in section 5 of the Registration of Clubs (Ireland) Act 1904 as amended by section 46 of the Intoxicating Liquor Act 1988; other grounds of objection are contained in section 24 of the Intoxicating Liquor (General) Act 1924, and section 59 of the Intoxicating Liquor Act 1927. Objections can be taken on the following grounds:

1. The character of the chairman or secretary or of any official or member of the committee of management or governing body.

---

[148] [1950] 16 Ir. Jur. Rep. 52.
[149] *Ibid.* at 56.
[150] Unreported, High Court, Finlay P., December 14, 1977.
[151] *Ibid.* at p. 1.

2. The suitability of the premises. A club premises is unsuitable if it is not exclusively in the possession and occupation of the club, and where persons who are not members have the right to use and occupy side by side with the club members, the buildings which the club as licensee might also use and occupy. In *Re Butlins Mosney Holiday Camp* Judge Fawsitt stated:

> "The club's possession — if such it be — of these buildings is such that in law it could not maintain trespass. The occupancy of the said three buildings by the club is not protected by any legislation known to the Court. In the light of these facts and circumstances, [I cannot] properly find that the said 'club buildings' are suitable premises for a club seeking registration under the Registration of Clubs (Ireland) Act 1904, and amending Acts."[152]

Judge Fawsitt noted that the 1904 Act did not expressly lay down that a club should have a premises. He continued:

> ". . . common sense, however, teaches that every club must have a headquarters at which members will assemble from time to time to manage the affairs of the club."[153]

He pointed to section 2(1) of the 1904 Act which requires the secretary to lodge an application with the registrar stating, *inter alia*, the address of the premises occupied by the club.

> "In my opinion every club, an applicant for registration under the Act of 1904, must have not only a postal address but must be in occupation of premises, that is to say of a house or building, or of part of a house or building, and the description of the situation or location of such premises must appear in the register of clubs, together with the name of the club."[154]

He was not satisfied that the buildings were suitable in circumstances where the club was neither the owner nor tenant of any premises, but only had a licence to use and occupy three separate buildings.

Where numerous persons who are not members of the club are entitled to and do resort to club premises, it is open to a court to refuse to grant a certificate of registration or a renewal thereof on the ground that the premises are unsuitable. In *Re Grocers' Assistants' Association Club*,[155] many social events were conducted and attended by non-members of the applicant club in the club premises. Judge Shannon refused the application on the grounds that the premises were not suitable because of the dances held there at which non-members were present. In *Re Butler Street Recreation Club* an application for a certificate of registration was refused on the grounds that there was an "entire lack of business acumen and an entire lack of organisation and management so essential for a registered club".[156]

---

[152] (1948) 82 I.L.T.R. 93 at 97.
[153] *Ibid.* at 96.
[154] *Ibid.*
[155] (1936) 70 I.L.T.R. 234.
[156] (1940) 74 I.L.T.R. 195 at 197.

21–70 3. That the application by the club, or its rules, or any of them, are in any respect not in conformity with the provisions of the Act. Proof of this by an objector does not prevent the court from adjourning the application for the certificate of its renewal for the purposes of permitting an amendment. Judge Davitt stated in the *Rossmore Golf Club* case:

> ". . . I can find nothing in the Act to show that the legislature intended to prohibit any such adjournment or amendment. The Act provides no comprehensive code of procedure for the hearing by the Court of such applications, nor does it provide for the making of any rules of procedure. As we have seen, such latter mentioned provision was made by the Act of 1924 but was never implemented."[157]

He continued:

> "In exercising its discretion to grant any such adjournment or allow any such amendment, it is always possible for a Court to do so upon terms and to have due regard to the position of any objector who, but for such amendment or adjournment, would have been in a position to succeed."[158]

4. That the club has ceased to exist, or that its members number less than 150.

21–71 5. That it is not conducted in good faith as a club or that it is kept or habitually used for any unlawful purpose, or mainly for the supply of excisable liquor. Where a club premises is habitually used in plain contravention of the provisions of the Planning Acts, this can constitute habitual use for an unlawful purpose. Finlay P., in *Comhaltas Ceoltóirí Éireann*.[159] decided that a District Court judge can consider objections that a club is habitually used in contravention of a condition attached to the planning permission. He stated:

> "As I have already indicated I take the view that this is unlawful user of the premises and must come within the ambit of section 5(e)."

The President, however, did indicate that the District Judge has an "entire discretion" as to the validity and strength of such objection where proceedings have been instituted by the Planning Authority or where a conviction has been obtained and alternatively where there have been no such proceedings or convictions.[160]

6. That there is frequent drunkenness on the club premises, or that intoxicated persons are frequently seen to leave the club premises, or that the club is conducted in a disorderly manner.

[157] Above, n.148, at 56.
[158] *Ibid.* at 57.
[159] Above, n.150.
[160] *Ibid.* at p. 3.

7. That illegal sales of excisable liquor have taken place on the club premises. Evidence of sale of intoxicating liquor to persons other than members or persons who are not brought onto the club premises in accordance with the club rules or evidence of the sale during hours which are not permitted by the Registration of Clubs Acts 1904 to 1995 can be adduced in support of this objection. 21–72

8. That persons who are not members are habitually admitted to the club merely for the purpose of obtaining excisable liquor.

9. That the club occupies premises in respect of which, within 12 months of the formation of the club, a licence for the sale of excisable liquor has been forfeited, or a certificate under the Licensing (Ireland) Acts 1833 to 1995, in respect of the renewal of any such licences has been refused or in respect of which an order has been made that they shall not be used for the purposes of a club.

10. That the supply of excisable liquor to the club is not under the control of the members or the committee appointed by the members. Proof that the club permits a person who is not employed by the club to supply excisable liquor and to obtain a profit from such sale would be sufficient evidence to support this ground of objection. 21–73

11. That the rules of the club are habitually broken.

12. That the rules have been changed so as no longer to conform with the Registration of Clubs Acts 1904 to 1995.

13. That the number of registered clubs of the same character as the applicant club having premises in the district in which such club proposes to have its premises, is sufficient to meet the requirements of that district.

14. That the club and the premises thereof are likely to be used mainly for the purpose of supplying intoxicating liquor to the members thereof and their visitors.

15. That the rules of the club for the admission of honorary or temporary members are, in the opinion of the court, unsatisfactory or unsuitable. The registration of clubs code provides for the inclusion of members of the club as temporary members. However, the court must be satisfied that the code is not being abused by the admission of members of the general public for a limited period (such as a day) for the purpose of consuming intoxicating liquor under the guise that they are temporary members.

3. Declaratory Order

Any person who would be entitled to object to an application for the grant or renewal of a certificate of registration under the 1904 Act applicable to the 21–74 premises is entitled to object in like manner to an application for a declaratory order.[161] However, where a club applies for a certificate of registration having first obtained a declaratory order, an objector cannot object to this application on the grounds of the unsuitability of the premises, or the existence of several registered clubs of the same character as the club making the application and which have premises in the district in which the applicant club has premises. The other grounds of objection which are available to an objector to an application for the grant of a certificate of registration, may be relied upon where the application is for a certificate of registration, a declaratory order having been granted. It is unlikely that the grounds of objection enumerated at paragraphs 21–67 to 21–71 other than 2 and 13 listed are available at declaratory stage.

E. Restaurant Certificate

21–75 A restaurant certificate remains in force until the next annual licensing sessions following its grant. On its expiry, an application for a new restaurant certificate must be made.

1. Grant of Full Restaurant Certificate

(a) Objectors

21–76 The only statutory objector to the grant of a restaurant certificate, whether it be a full restaurant certificate or a limited restaurant certificate, is the officer in charge of the Garda Síochána for the licensing area in which the premises are situate. Section 12(2) of the Intoxicating Liquor Act 1927 provides:

> "The Court shall not entertain an application for a restaurant certificate unless and until satisfied that not less than ten days before the date on which the application is proposed to be made notice in writing of the intention to make the application was given to the officer in charge of the Garda Síochána for the licensing area."

There is no requirement to notify any other party and there is no statutory provision for the making of objections. Further, there is no requirement to publish the notice of application. It seems clear that the only competent objector is the superintendent of the Garda Síochána, and the court is not entitled to consider objections from any other person in relation to the application.

---

[161] Intoxicating Liquor Act 1960, s.15(5).

(b) Grounds of Objection

In *Application of Patrick Walsh*,[162] the Garda superintendent did not formally object to the application but had stated in evidence before the District Court: "I am not formally objecting. I am leaving it to the Court." It was held that in the absence of such objection, it 21–77

> "is not obligatory on the court to grant the application with no more than the absence of objection by the officer in charge".

So, the mere fact that the superintendent does not object does not preclude the court from inquiring into whether the applicant satisfies the requirements of section 12 or section 12A of the 1927 Act.

The grounds of objection are as follows:

1. That the premises are not structurally adapted for use as a restaurant.
2. That the premises are not bona fide and mainly used as a restaurant. Proof of an intention in the future to use the premises as a restaurant is not sufficient. There must be an established user.[163] Section 12 of the 1927 Act uses the word "mainly": proof that the restaurant business is merely a subsidiary part of the entire of the business carried on in the premises is not sufficient compliance with section 12 of the 1927 Act.
3. Non-compliance with statutory requirements as to notification to the Garda Síochána.

2. Grant of Limited Restaurant Certificate

(a) Objectors

The only statutory objector is the superintendent of the Garda Síochána as in the case of a full restaurant certificate. 21–78

(b) Grounds of Objection

1. That the portion of the premises, the subject of the application, is not structurally adapted for use as a restaurant. 21–79
2. That the portion of the premises, the subject of the application, is not bona fide and mainly used as a restaurant.

[162] Unreported, High Court, Gannon J. November 30, 1981.
[163] *Whelan v. Tobin* [1976–77] I.L.R.M. 199.

3. That the portion of the premises for which the restaurant certificate is being sought includes a public bar, or part of a room in another part of which there is a public bar.
4. That there is public access to that portion of the premises for which the restaurant certificate is being sought through a public bar.
5. That there has been a failure to comply with the statutory requirements as to notification.

3. Renewal and Transfer of Restaurant Certificate

21–80 There is no provision in the licensing code for the renewal or transfer of a restaurant certificate. The correct application is for a new restaurant certificate.

4. Declaratory Order

(a) Objectors

21–81 As in the certificate application, the only statutory notice party is the Superintendent of the Garda Síochána for the licensing area in which the premises are situate.[164]

(b) Grounds of Objection

21–82 The grounds of objection to an application for a declaration as to the suitability of premises for a full or limited restaurant certificate are the same as those which arise in an application for the certificate, save that an objector cannot object on the ground that the premises or portion thereof are not mainly used as a restaurant: existing user does not have to be proved. However, where the applicant, having received a declaratory order, proceeds to seek the restaurant certificate, the objector is confined to objecting on the grounds that the premises is not bona fide and mainly used as a restaurant.

[164] Intoxicating Liquor Act 1960, s.16(3).

F. Special Restaurant Licence

1. Grant

(a) Objectors

The category of objectors to the grant of a special restaurant licence is the same as for the grant of an on-licence.[165] **21–83**

(b) Grounds of Objection

1. The character, misconduct or unfitness of the applicant. **21–84**
2. The unfitness or inconvenience of the premises.
3. That there has been a failure to comply with the requirements as to due notice and publication as required by the Intoxicating Liquor Act 1988.
4. That the applicant is not the owner and occupier of the restaurant.
5. That the applicant has not shown that a Bord Fáilte certificate is in force in respect of the restaurant.

2. Renewal

(a) Objectors

1. The superintendent of the Garda Síochána for the Garda district in which the restaurant is situate. **21–85**
2. Any inhabitant of the parish in which the premises are situate.
3. The health authority within the meaning of the Health Acts in whose functional area the restaurant is situate.
4. The fire authority in whose functional area the restaurant is situate.

(b) Grounds of Objection

The grounds of objection at renewal stage are similar to those which relate to the on-licence. In addition, a competent objector may object on the ground that the premises concerned have not been bona fide and solely used as a restaurant within the meaning of the Intoxicating Liquor Act 1988 since the grant of the **21–86**

[165] See above, paras. 21–10 to 21–14, and see the Intoxicating Liquor Act 1988, s.8.

licence or the latest renewal thereof. This ground of objection can be contrasted with the ground of objection available in an application for a restaurant certificate. The premises to which a special restaurant licence attaches must be "solely" as opposed to "mainly" used as a restaurant.

3. Transfer

21–87 The provisions relating to objections to the transfer of a special restaurant licence are the same as those pertaining to the transfer of the on-licence.

4. Declaratory Order

21–88 The declaratory jurisdiction does not apply to a special restaurant licence.

G. Music and Singing Licence

21–89 The District Court has a discretion to impose whatever conditions and restrictions it sees fit, although a licence cannot be granted subject to the condition that objectors are at liberty to have the matter re-entered on notice to the licence holder. In *Sheehan v. Reilly*,[166] it was held that once the licence was granted by the respondent District Court judge, he was *functus officio*, and was not entitled to grant a reviewable licence. A music and singing licence can be transferred "from time to time" by the District Court judge "as he thinks fit".[167] It is not renewed, rather, a new licence is granted on its expiry.

1. Temporary Music and Singing Licence

(a) Objectors

21–90 1. The only statutory objector to the grant of a temporary music and singing licence is the fire officer. The court is entitled to grant a temporary music and singing licence for a period not exceeding fourteen days "notwithstanding that no notices shall have been given under this section".[168]

2. Any person who appears to the court to be interested in the application.[169]

---

[166] [1992] 1 I.R. 368.
[167] Public Health Acts Amendment Act 1890, s.51(3).
[168] *Ibid.*, s.51(11).
[169] Courts (Supplemental Provisions) Act 1961, s.33.

(b) Grounds of Objection

1. Unsuitability of the premises *vis-à-vis* fire safety. **21–91**
2. Any ground of objection which may appear to the court to be relevant and in particular those matters set forth at section 2 of the Public Dance Halls Act 1935, which are dealt with as grounds of objection to the grant of an annual music and singing licence.

2. Annual Music and Singing Licence

(a) Objectors

1. The superintendent of the Garda Síochána within whose district the place to which the application relates is situate.[170] **21–92**
2. Any person who appears to the court hearing the application to be interested therein.[171]
3. The fire officer.

(b) Grounds of Objection

1. The character and financial and other circumstances of the applicant. **21–93**
2. The suitability of the place to which the application relates.
3. The facilities for music and singing existing in the neighbourhood at the time of such application.
4. The parking facilities in the neighbourhood of such place.
5. The probable age of the persons who would be likely to make use of the place for music and singing.
6. Whether the situation of the premises is likely to make supervision by the Garda Síochána of the management of and proceedings in such place difficult.
7. The hours during which the applicant proposes that music and singing should be permitted.
8. Failure to comply with the statutory requirements as to notification.
9. As the District Court judge is entitled to take into account "any other matters which may appear to him to be relevant", an objector may advance other

---

[170] Public Health Acts Amendment Act 1890, s.51(4).
[171] Courts (Supplemental Provisions) Act 1961, s.33.

grounds of objection and it is then a matter for the court to decide whether or not such other ground or grounds is or are relevant. The District Court has extremely wide discretion in an application for a public dancing licence and a music and singing licence. In *Application of Michael Quinn* Griffin J. stated:

> "In my opinion, the general words "in addition to any other matter which may appear to him to be relevant" are not in any way limited by the words which subsequently appear in the sub-section and the District Justice is, by the subsection, given a wide discretion as to the matters which he may take into account as being relevant."[172]

H. Public Dancing Licence

21–94 Unlike the application for the music and singing licence, an applicant for a public dancing licence must advertise his application at least one month prior to the hearing of the application. However, in both these applications, the court is entitled to hear evidence in opposition to the application by "any person who appears to the Justice hearing such application to be interested".

1. Temporary Public Dancing Licence

(a) Objectors

21–95 1. The fire officer.

2. Any member of the Garda Síochána.

3. Any person who appears in court to be interested in the application.

(b) Grounds of Objection

21–96 1. Unsuitability of premises *vis-à-vis* fire safety.

2. Any ground of objection which may appear to be relevant.

[172] Above, n.10, at 31.

2. Annual Public Dancing Licence

(a) Objectors

1. Any person who appears to the court to be interested in the application. **21–97**
2. Any member of the Garda Síochána.
3. The fire officer.

(b) Grounds of Objection

The grounds of objection to the grant of a public dancing licence are set forth in section 2(2) of the Public Dance Halls Act 1904 and they are identical to the grounds which a court is entitled to consider in an application for a music and singing licence. The District Court judge again has a very wide discretion and can take into account "any matter which may appear to him to be relevant". **21–98**

Further grounds of objection open to an objector are as follows:

1. that there has been a failure to comply with the statutory requirements as to publication and notice to be given to statutory notice parties;
2. that there has been a failure by the applicant to secure appropriate public liability cover in respect of the premises. As all public dancing licence applications are now granted on condition that sufficient public liability insurance has been obtained, it has become the practice of the court to insist on the production of an appropriate certificate of public liability insurance before the application will be granted.

Objector's Right of Appeal

An objector's right to appeal to the High Court was confirmed by Gavan Duffy P. in *Re O'Brien and the Intoxicating Liquor Act, 1942* where he held, *inter alia*: **21–99**

> "When the Circuit Court grants a certificate for a new licence under section 21 of the Intoxicating Liquor Act 1943, notwithstanding objection made, the objector may appeal to the High Court under section 38 of the Courts of Justice Act, 1936."[173]

A question arises as to the *locus standi* of objectors who do not appear and object in the court of first instance and who attempt to object at appeal stage.

In the *Centennial*[174] case, the *locus standi* of certain objectors was chal-

[173] [1951] 17 Ir. Jur. Rep. 8 at 8.
[174] *Re Centennial Properties Ltd*, above, n.39.

lenged on the grounds that they had not appeared in the lower court, although it was acknowledged that other objectors were properly heard before the appellate court. Finlay P. stated:

> "Before the case was entered upon, a preliminary issue arose as to the *locus standi* and right to be heard of certain objectors who were inhabitants of the parish in which the proposed premises would be located and who had not appeared at the Circuit Court hearing from which this is an Appeal. It was submitted on behalf of the Applicants that I should deny to these persons any right of audience because only persons who had been objectors and in that sense parties to the original Application before the Circuit Court could be heard on the Appeal. I have already ruled in this case, having heard submissions on behalf of the Applicant that:
>
> 1. having regard to the fact that there is an Appeal properly before me and brought by an objector who did appear in the Circuit Court namely Joseph Kilbride & Son Ltd;
> 2. having regard to the fact that under section 13 of the Act of 1960, I am obliged to exercise discretion as to whether even when the statutory proofs have been complied with I should grant or refuse an application on the grounds set out in section 13(1) and (2); and
> 3. being satisfied that those objectors had failed to appear in the Circuit Court due to a *bona fide* mistake, that I had jurisdiction to hear them on the hearing of this appeal and it was in the interests of justice I should do so."[175]

Finlay J.'s decision might have been different had no objector appeared in the Circuit Court and if such objections at appellate stage constituted an attempt to have a full rehearing of a case which had not been opposed in the court of first instance.

General

21–100 This chapter has dealt with the various objections which may be taken by competent objectors to the grant, renewal and transfer of various licences. A study of the statutory provisions relating to the grant, for example, of occasional licences or special exemption orders which are dealt with at chapter 23, will reveal whether an objector has *locus standi* to object to a particular application and the grounds of objection open to a competent objector. By way of example, the only statutory notice party in an application for a special exemption order is the officer in charge of the Garda Síochána for the licensing area within which the premises are situated. No other person is given a statutory right to object and it is therefore questionable whether the District Court is entitled to permit

---

[175] *Ibid.* at pp. 1 and 2.

evidence to be heard from any other person. By contrast, any person appearing to the District Court judge to have a bona fide interest in an application for an occasional licence is entitled to appear and give evidence on the hearing of this application.

A court's discretion, therefore, must be exercised having reference to the matters specifically set forth in the statute and is confined thereto. It follows also that a court is not entitled to confer a right upon persons who have been given no statutory right to do so.

Part V

RIGHTS AND OBLIGATIONS: ENFORCEMENT

Chapter 22

TRADING HOURS

Introduction

The hours during which licensed premises are permitted to trade are restricted by the licensing code and, in particular, by the Intoxicating Liquor Act 1927 as amended. The times during which intoxicating liquor can be supplied in a premises to which a special restaurant licence attaches is regulated by the Intoxicating Liquor Act 1988. The registration of clubs code similarly restricts the hours during which intoxicating liquor may be supplied in a registered club. Some premises, such as hotels and restaurants, are entitled to serve intoxicating liquor beyond ordinary permitted hours, in conjunction with the service of meals. Some licensed premises may open for business other than the sale of intoxicating liquor outside normal permitted licensing hours. Further, the holder of a licence for a restaurant and a hotel and various other premises may **22–1** apply to the court for an order permitting him to keep his premises open for the sale of intoxicating liquor after ordinary permitted hours: this order is known as a special exemption order.

A licensee may supply intoxicating liquor at any time to his private friends in any part of the licensed premises other than the part in which the sale of intoxicating liquor generally takes place.[1] He is also entitled to sell intoxicating liquor at any hour on his licensed premises to a person lodging therein save in certain circumstances.[2]

An essential condition to the grant of a licence is that upon receiving his licence, the holder should be ready to carry on the business "there, then, and thenceforward".[3] In *R. (Cox) v. The Recorder of Dublin*, FitzGibbon L.J. noted that the public must be thought of as well as the publican,

> "and unless they have been accommodated during the year, the certificate that the house has been "conducted" as the statute contemplated, namely, as a house used for the sale of spirits, etc., to be consumed on the premises, cannot properly be given".[4]

A licence permits the sale of intoxicating liquor to the public within the hours permitted by the licensing code. Failure to accommodate the public by not conducting licensed business on the premises during those permitted hours may result in the refusal to grant a certificate as to the peaceable and orderly manner in which the house has been conducted in the past year where an objection has been lodged.

Permitted Persons

22–2 It is not an offence for certain persons to be on a licensed premises during prohibited hours. The following persons are lawfully entitled to be upon a licensed premises during prohibited hours:

1. the holder of the licence or the owner of the premises;
2. a person who is resident permanently or temporarily on the premises;
3. a person to whom intoxicating liquor may lawfully be sold or supplied on the premises at that time;
4. a person carrying out repairs to the premises.
5. an employee of the holder of the licence or of the owner of the premises who is on the premises in the ordinary course of his employment;
6. an officer of Customs and Excise in the course of his duty.[5]

---

[1] Intoxicating Liquor Act 1927, s.14(b).
[2] *Ibid.*, s.14(e).
[3] *R. (Cox) v. The Recorder of Dublin* [1885–86] 16 L.R. Ir. 424.
[4] *Ibid.* at 438.
[5] Intoxicating Liquor Act 1927, s.17, as amended by the Intoxicating Liquor Act 1988, s.51.

Prohibited Hours

STATUTORY PROVISION

Section 2 of the Intoxicating Liquor Act 1927, as amended by section 25 of the Intoxicating Liquor Act 1988 and section 2 of the Intoxicating Liquor Act 1995, provides: 22–3

"(1) Save as is otherwise provided by this Act, it shall not be lawful for any person to sell or expose for sale any intoxicating liquor, or to open or keep open any premises for the sale of intoxicating liquor, or to permit any intoxicating liquor to be consumed on licensed premises —

(a) on any weekday, before the hour of half-past ten o'clock in the morning, or
  (i) during a period of summer time, after the hour of half-past eleven o'clock in the evening, or
  (ii) during a period which is not a period of summer time, after the hour of eleven o'clock in the evening, or
(b) on any Sunday, before the hour of half-past twelve o'clock in the afternoon, or between the hours of two o'clock and four o'clock in the afternoon or after the hour of eleven o'clock in the evening, or
(c) on St. Patrick's Day, where that day falls on a weekday, before the hour of half-past twelve o'clock in the afternoon or after the hour of eleven o'clock in the evening, or
(d) at any time on Christmas Day or Good Friday,

Provided that where, in any year the 23rd or 24th day of December falls on a Sunday, then the provisions of this subsection which relate to a weekday during a period which is not a period of summertime shall apply for such a Sunday as if it were a weekday."

These general hours during which trading is permitted apply in respect of public houses, off-licensed premises and hotels. The provisions do not apply to a premises to which a special restaurant licence or a theatre licence attaches nor do they apply to a registered club, which is governed by the Registration of Clubs Acts 1904 to 1995. The general hours during which trading is permitted are detailed below. 22–4

1. Weekdays in summer time[6]:

   10.30 a.m. to 11.30 p.m.

[6] The expression "period of summer time" is defined in s.1(1) of the 1927 Act as meaning "a period appointed by or under the Summer Time Act 1925, to be a period of summer time". This definition is adopted in s.56(3) of the 1927 Act, introduced by s.26 of the Intoxicating Liquor Act 1988. However, the Summer Time Act 1925 was repealed by the Standard Time Act 1968 which provides that for the purposes of the Licensing Acts, summer time commences at 3 a.m. on the Sunday following the third Saturday in April or, if that day is Easter Sunday, at 3 a.m. on the Sunday following the second Saturday in April and in either case ending at 3 a.m. on the Sunday following the first Saturday in October.

2. Weekdays for the rest of the year:

   10.30 a.m. to 11.00 p.m.

3. Sunday:

   12.30 p.m. to 2.00 p.m.

   4.00 p.m. to 11.00 p.m.

4. St Patrick's Day (if it falls on a weekday, otherwise Sunday hours apply)

   12.30 p.m. to 11.00 p.m.

5. Christmas Day:

   Trading prohibited all day.

6. Good Friday:

   Trading prohibited all day.

7. Sundays which fall on December 23 or 24 in any year:

   10.30 a.m. to 11 p.m.

Holy Hour

22–5 Until the enactment of the Intoxicating Liquor Act 1988 all licensed premises in Dublin and Cork were obliged to close between 2.30 p.m. and 3.30 p.m. on weekdays. This was known as the "Holy Hour". The Holy Hour was abolished by the omission of a reference to it in section 25 of the Intoxicating Liquor Act 1988 which amended section 2 of the Intoxicating Liquor Act 1927.

Drinking-Up Time

22–6 The Licensing Acts provide for the consumption of intoxicating liquor on licensed premises after permitted hours, but only for a period of up to 30 minutes after normal closing hours.[7] The then Minister for Justice, when introducing the Intoxicating Liquor Bill 1988, at its second stage,[8] stated that the extension in the drinking up time from 10 minutes to 30 minutes would result in people being "able to drink in a more relaxed manner at closing times".[9]

---

[7] Intoxicating Liquor Act 1962, s.7, as amended by the Intoxicating Liquor Act 1988, s.27.
[8] Mr Gerry Collins, *Dáil Éireann Official Report*, Vol. 379(b), April 26, 1988, p. 1992.
[9] *Ibid.* at p. 2003.

STATUTORY PROVISION

Section 7 of the Intoxicating Liquor Act 1962, as amended by section 27 of the Intoxicating Liquor Act 1988, provides:

"(1)(a) Nothing in the Licensing Acts shall operate to prohibit a person from being on, or consuming, or permitting the consumption of, intoxicating liquor on, premises in respect of which an on-licence within the meaning of the Act of 1927 is in force during the period of thirty minutes commencing at the beginning of a period during which the sale of intoxicating liquor on licensed premises is prohibited.

(b) For the purposes of paragraph (a) of this subsection a period during which the sale of intoxicating liquor in licensed premises is permitted by or under any provision of the Licensing Acts (other than section 2 of the Act of 1927) shall be deemed to be a period during which such sale is prohibited on such premises".

Drinking up time only relates to premises to which an on-licence is attached: it applies therefore to all on-licences including a wine retailers' on-licence and restricted licences, but it does not apply to off-licences.[10]

However, the sale (as opposed to the consumption) of intoxicating liquor during this period is not permitted.

Offences

It is an offence to: 22–7

1. sell intoxicating liquor;
2. expose for sale any intoxicating liquor;
3. open a premises for the sale of intoxicating liquor;
4. keep open any premises for the sale of intoxicating liquor;
5. permit any intoxicating liquor to be consumed on licensed premises;
6. permit a person to be on licensed premises;

on any day, either before or after permitted hours specified above.[11]

---

[10] But see below, chap. 22, "Trading Hours", at paras. 22–40.

[11] Intoxicating Liquor Act 1988, s.25, which substituted a new section 2 in the Intoxicating Liquor Act 1927 which in turn was amended by the Intoxicating Liquor Act 1995, s.2; Intoxicating Liquor Act 1962, s.29, as amended by the Intoxicating Liquor Act 1988, s.51.

Ancillary Business

(a) Ancillary non-licensed business which may be carried on during specified hours

22–8 A licensed premises may, however, open its doors before permitted hours but only to carry on non-licensed business, and then only during the following times:

Weekdays: On-Licence 7.30 a.m. to 10.30 a.m.

Weekdays: Off-Licence 9 a.m. to 10.30 a.m.

Sundays which fall on December 23 or 24 in any year: On-Licence 7.30 a.m. to 10.30 a.m.

Sundays which fall on December 23 or 24 in any year: Off-Licence 9 a.m. to 10.30 a.m.[12]

(b) Ancillary non-licensed business which may be carried on at any time

22–9 Some licensed premises may carry on non-licensed business during hours prohibited under the licensing code. These are hotels, restaurants (including premises with special restaurant licences), airports, holiday camps, Áras Mhic Dhiarmuida Bus Station and premises which are structurally adapted for holding dramatic performances, concerts, lectures, dances, cinematographic exhibitions or other public entertainments and are bona fide used only for the purpose of holding all or any such entertainments or as a restaurant.[13]

A. Public House Licence

22–10 The general hours of trading listed above, at paragraph 22–4, apply to a public house. A public house may not open for non-licensed business during hours prohibited under the licensing code, subject to what is stated above at paragraph 22–8, unless the portion of the premises in which the non-licensed business is carried on is structurally separate from the remainder of the premises. Thus, the holder of an on-licence whose premises do not comply with this requirement

[12] Intoxicating Liquor Act 1927, s.3(1), as amended by the Intoxicating Liquor Act 1960, s.8, the Intoxicating Liquor Act 1962, s.3, and the Intoxicating Liquor Act 1995, s.3.

[13] Intoxicating Liquor Act 1927, s.3; Intoxicating Liquor Act 1943, s.28; Tourist Traffic Act 1952, s.53; Intoxicating Liquor Act 1953, s.5; Intoxicating Liquor Act 1988, s.14.

is entitled to open the premises between 7.30 a.m. and 10.30 a.m. on weekdays and on Sundays which fall on either December 23 or 24 to facilitate the conduct of his non-licensed business. However, he cannot open the premises on a (normal) Sunday before the hours permitted under the licensing code. The holder of a publican's licence may carry on a non-licensed business at any time in his licensed premises if the portion of the premises in which the non-licensed business is carried on is structurally separate from the portion where the licensed business is carried on.[14]

In *R. (Richardson) v. Sweeney*,[15] the High Court held that a door did not constitute structural separation for the purposes of the licensing code. In rejecting the argument that a door constituted a sufficient structural separation of licensed premises from unlicensed premises, Kenny J. was satisfied that the requirement that the separation must be of a "structural" character meant that the object of the statute[16] was to: 22–11

> "... as far as possible deprive a publican who was trying to evade the Licensing Acts of facilities for supplying liquor at prohibited hours in that part of the licensed premises where he was carrying on, say, a drapery or grocery trade".[17]

He continued:

> "If this door was not locked, or if it was ajar, I presume the justices would not have come to this conclusion. If so, then structural separation depends on the volition and pleasure of the publican, and exists or does not exist as he pleases. ... In my opinion structural separation must be such as not to admit of a possible communication between the two businesses, and a locked door, the key of which is in the publican's pocket, does not fulfil that condition."[18]

A removable wire net-work frame, firmly secured by bolts, separating licensed premises from a room in which billiards were played and tobacco was sold, is not a sufficient structural separation. In *Toppin v. Coleman*[19] O'Brien L.C.J. noted that the structure which took about 15 minutes to put up and the same number of minutes to take down was not a structural separation. He further pointed out that where its removal at any given time depended upon the volition of the owner of the public house or of his servants and having regard to its "moveability from time to time", that this afforded a means of defeating the intention of the legislation.

---

[14] Intoxicating Liquor Act 1927, s.3(1)(b).
[15] (1908) 42 I.L.T.R. 174.
[16] Intoxicating Liquors Act 1906, now repealed.
[17] *R. (Richardson) v. Sweeney*, above, n.15, at 176.
[18] *Ibid.* at 176.
[19] [1910] 2 I.R. 200.

Exemptions

22–12 The exemptions from prohibited hours which are available to a publican are detailed below.

(a) Exemptions for Sunday Afternoons

22–13 The District Court may grant an exemption order to the holders of licences situate in an area other than a County or other Borough if it is satisfied that owing to circumstances in the locality, it is desirable to do so for a Sunday afternoon.[20] An application may also be made to authorise an exemption from prohibited hours between the hours of 12 p.m. and 12.30 p.m. on St Patrick's Day.

(b) Exemptions for Unlicensed Business on Sunday Mornings

22–14 Similarly, a District Court judge is entitled to make an order permitting the carrying on of non-licensed business during any one period specified in the order, not exceeding 45 minutes in duration, on Sunday mornings and the morning of St Patrick's Day.[21]

(c) General Exemption Orders

22–15 The holder of a publican's licence, except in the County Borough of Dublin, can apply for a general exemption order. The general exemption order for the accommodation of persons following a lawful trade or calling entitles the holder of the licence to serve intoxicating liquor after the hour of 7 a.m., but only up to normal permitted closing hours. A general exemption order cannot be granted on a Sunday, Christmas Day or Good Friday.[22] Section 15 of the Intoxicating Liquor Act 1962 prevents the grant of a new general exemption order for a premises in the County Borough of Dublin. A number of public houses in Dublin hold general exemption orders which were granted prior to April 19, 1962. This entitles them to apply for the renewal of such order at every annual licensing sessions.

(d) Special Exemption Orders

22–16 A publican may apply for a special exemption order if his premises have been certified by the District Court as a restaurant or if they are a hotel for the purposes of the Intoxicating Liquor Act 1927.[23]

---

[20] Intoxicating Liquor Act 1962, s.16.
[21] *Ibid.*, s.17.
[22] Intoxicating Liquor Act 1927, s.4(7).
[23] See below, para. 22–35.

(e) Private Friends of Licensee

A publican may supply intoxicating liquor to his friends at his own expense in that portion of his premises which is not generally used for the sale of intoxicating liquor. 22–17

STATUTORY PROVISION

Section 14(b) of the Intoxicating Liquor Act 1927, provides:

> "Nothing in this Act shall be deemed to prohibit or restrict—
>
> the supplying at any time of intoxicating liquor on licensed premises to any private friends of the holder of the licence *bona fide* entertained by him at his own expense in any part of such licensed premises other than the part in which the sale of intoxicating liquor generally takes place."

Such friends must be entertained at the expense of the licensee. Where it was found that the son of a licence holder who acted as manager of his father's business, bona fide entertained his friends after closing hours, it was held that no offence had been committed.[24]

(f) Lodgers

The holder of an on-licence is entitled to sell intoxicating liquor on any part of his licensed premises at any hour to any persons lodging on his premises. 22–18

STATUTORY PROVISION

Section 14(e) of the Intoxicating Liquor Act 1927, as amended by section 10 of the Intoxicating Liquor Act 1943, provides as follows:

> "Nothing in this Act shall be deemed to prohibit or restrict—
>
> the sale of intoxicating liquor by the holder of an on-licence at any hour on licensed premises to a person then lodging in such premises, save that on Good Friday no intoxicating liquor may be so sold to any such person except at and for consumption with a meal consumed by such person in such premises."

In *Attorney General v. Egan*[25] it was held that a licensee is not entitled to supply intoxicating liquor to a lodger and permit it to be consumed by such lodger and his guests during prohibited hours.

Persons who are resident permanently or temporarily on a licensed premises do not commit an offence if they are found on the licensed premises.[26] However,

---

[24] *Armstrong v. Donovan* (1902) 3 N.I.J.R. 15.
[25] [1943] I.R. 357.
[26] Intoxicating Liquor Act 1927, s.17, as amended by the Intoxicating Liquor Act 1960, s.12.

a person falsely representing himself to be a lodger in order to obtain intoxicating liquor during prohibited hours is liable to a fine not exceeding £5.[27]

B. Restricted Licences

22–19 Restricted licences, namely six-day licences and early closing licences, are issued pursuant to sections 8 and 9 respectively of the Intoxicating Liquor Act 1927, and their very description indicates that limits are imposed upon them as regards days and times for trading. The condition inserted in the six-day licence is that the premises in respect of which the licence is granted must be kept closed during the whole of every Sunday. An early closing licence contains an early closing condition stipulating that the licensee shall close his premises one hour earlier at night than that at which he would otherwise be obliged to close the premises. Subject to the conditions contained in the court certificate and the licence itself, the same trading hours apply to the holders of these licences as apply to ordinary publicans.

However, if the holder of an early closing licence has a restaurant certificate, he is entitled to avail of the extended hours provided for by section 13 of the Intoxicating Liquor Act 1927 as amended by section 28 of the Intoxicating Liquor Act 1988 and section 4 of the Intoxicating Liquor Act 1995. The exemptions introduced by the 1995 Act, which provide that a Sunday which falls on either December 23 or 24 of any year, do not apply to six-day licences. The provisions relating to the full publican's licence in respect of exemptions for friends and lodgers, however, apply to restricted licences.

C. Off-Licence

22–20 The hours during which the holder of an off-licence may sell, expose for sale and open his licensed premises for the sale of intoxicating liquor are the same as those prescribed for premises to which an on-licence attaches and are referred to above, at paragraph 22–4. On weekdays the premises may open to sell intoxicating liquor from 10.30 a.m. to 11.30 p.m. in summer time and 11 p.m. in winter time. On a Sunday, the premises may open at 12.30 p.m. and must close at 2 p.m. The premises may then re-open at 4 p.m. and close at 11 p.m. On St Patrick's Day, where that day falls on a weekday, the premises may open at 12.30 p.m. and close at 11 p.m. The premises must be closed all day on Christmas Day and on Good Friday. Where December 23 or 24 falls on a Sunday, permitted opening hours are from 10.30 a.m. to 11 p.m.

---

[27] Intoxicating Liquor Act 1927, s.18.

Where the holder of an off-licence wishes to open his premises for non-licensed business, *i.e.* where the premises is a supermarket and he wishes to sell groceries and products other than intoxicating liquor, he is entitled to carry on such non-licensed business between 9 a.m. and 10.30 a.m. but he can only do this on weekdays and not on a Sunday, unless that Sunday falls on either December 23 or 24 of any year.[28] He may not sell any intoxicating liquor between 9 a.m. and 10.30 a.m. on weekdays. The provision in section 3(1)(b)(ii) of the Intoxicating Liquor Act 1927 which permits an off-licence business to carry on non-licensed business between 2.30 p.m. and 3.30 p.m. on weekdays were replaced by section 3 of the Intoxicating Liquor Act 1995 which deleted a reference to the Holy Hour and the holder of an off-licence may trade during this time by virtue of section 2(3) of the 1927 Act as amended.

Structural Separation

Where the holder of an off-licence structurally separates the area in which he sells intoxicating liquor from the area where he sells his other supermarket products, he may keep those premises which are structurally separate from the licensed area open at times normally prohibited by the licensing code.[29] The courts are satisfied with the practice which has grown up in recent times to separate areas in which intoxicating liquor is sold from areas in which non-licensed business is carried on by way of a steel roller shutter. The above provisions only apply in respect of premises to which a beer retailer's off-licence or spirit retailer's off-licence is attached. 22–21

Where any business other than the sale of intoxicating liquor is carried on in a premises to which a wine retailer's off-licence only is attached, the premises may open at times other than permitted hours, but only for the carrying on of such non-licensed business. This applies to chemists and druggists and not in respect of premises to which a spirit retailer's off-licence and a beer retailer's off-licence also attach.[30] 22–22

D. Permitted Hours in a Registered Club

The hours during which intoxicating liquor may be supplied and consumed on club premises are set forth in section 56 of the Intoxicating Liquor Act 1927, as amended by section 26 of the Intoxicating Liquor Act 1988 and section 5 of the Intoxicating Liquor Act 1995. The Registration of Clubs (Ireland) Act 1904 22–23

[28] Intoxicating Liquor Act 1927, s.3, as amended by the Intoxicating Liquor Act 1960, s.8, the Intoxicating Liquor Act 1962, s.3, and the Intoxicating Liquor Act 1995, s.3.
[29] Intoxicating Liquor Act 1927, s.3(1).
[30] *Ibid.*, s.3, as amended by the Intoxicating Liquor Act 1960, s.8.

requires that the rules of the club must state the times during which intoxicating liquor can lawfully be supplied. A club may supply intoxicating liquor to members of the club, outside the premises of the club, between the hours of 8 a.m. and 10 p.m.[31] Where a substantial meal is being served, intoxicating liquor can be supplied in conjunction with such meal during certain extended hours so specified.

STATUTORY PROVISION

22–24 Section 56(1) and (1A) of the Intoxicating Liquor Act 1927, as amended by section 26 of the Intoxicating Liquor Act 1988 and section 5 of the Intoxicating Liquor Act 1995, provides:

> "(1) In order that a club may be eligible to be registered under the Registration of Clubs Acts, 1904 to 1988, the rules of the club shall (in addition to the matters mentioned in section 4 of the Registration of Clubs (Ireland) Act, 1904) provide that, subject to the exceptions specified in subsections (1A), (2) and (3) of this section, no excisable liquor shall be supplied for consumption on the club premises to any person (other than a member of the club lodging on the club premises) or be consumed on the club premises by any person (other than a member of the club lodging in the club premises) —
>
> (a) on any weekday, before the hour of half-past ten o'clock in the morning, or
>   (i) during a period of summer time, after the hour of half-past eleven o'clock in the evening, or
>   (ii) during a period which is not a period of summer time, after the hour of eleven o'clock in the evening, or
>
> (b) on any Sunday, before the hour of half-past twelve o'clock in the afternoon or between the hours of two o'clock and four o'clock in the afternoon or after the hour of eleven o'clock in the evening, or
>
> (c) on St. Patrick's Day, where that day falls on a weekday, before the hour of half past twelve o'clock in the afternoon or after the hour of eleven o'clock in the evening, or
>
> (d) at any time on Christmas Day or Good Friday.
>
> (1A) Where in any year the 23rd or 24th day of December falls on a Sunday, then the provisions of subsection (1) of this section which relate to a weekday during a period which is not a period of summer time shall apply to such a Sunday as if it were such a weekday."

22–25 A member of the club who is lodging in the club premises is entitled to be supplied with intoxicating liquor and may consume same, on the club premises, at any time. All other persons, including members of the club, who are not lodging therein can only be supplied with intoxicating liquor on the club premises during the following times:

---

[31] Registration of Clubs (Ireland) Act 1904, s.4.

1. Weekdays in summer time:

   10.30 a.m. to 11.30 p.m.

2. Weekdays for the rest of the year:

   10.30 a.m. to 11 p.m.

3. Sunday:

   12.30 p.m. to 2 p.m.

   4 p.m. to 11 p.m.

4. St Patrick's Day (provided that day falls on a weekday, otherwise Sunday hours apply):

   12.30 p.m. to 11 p.m.

5. Christmas Day and Good Friday: no intoxicating liquor can be served

6. Sundays which fall on December 23 or 24 in any year:

   10.30 a.m. to 11 p.m.

No intoxicating liquor can be served during the above prohibited hours to any person other than a member of the club lodging in the club premises.

Permitted Hours Where a Meal is Being Served

Intoxicating liquor may be consumed other than during normal permitted hours but only in conjunction with the service of a substantial meal. **22–26**

STATUTORY PROVISION

Section 56(2) of the Intoxicating Liquor Act 1927, as amended by section 26 of the Intoxicating Liquor Act 1988 and section 5 of the Intoxicating Liquor Act 1995, provides:

> "Nothing contained in the Registration of Clubs Acts, 1904 to 1986, or contained by virtue only of the operation of subsection (1) of this section, in the rules of a club registered under those Acts shall operate to prohibit the supplying for consumption on the club premises of excisable liquor to any person or the consumption of excisable liquor on the club premises by any person —
>
> (a) during a period of summer time, between the hours of half-past eleven o'clock in the evening on any weekday and half-past twelve o'clock in the morning on the following day, or
> (b) during a period which is not a period of summer time, between the hours of eleven o'clock in the evening on any weekday and half-past twelve o'clock in the morning on the following day, or
> (c) on any Sunday, between the hours of two o'clock and three o'clock in the afternoon, or

(d) on Christmas Day, between the hours of one o'clock and three o'clock in the afternoon or the hours of seven o'clock and ten o'clock in the evening,

if, in each case, the excisable liquor is —

(i) ordered by that person at the same time as a substantial meal is ordered by him,
(ii) consumed at the same time as and with the meal,
(iii)supplied and consumed in the portion of the club premises usually set apart for the supply of meals, and
(iv)paid for at the same time as the meal is paid for,

Provided that where in any year the 23rd or 24th day of December falls on a Sunday, then the provisions of this sub-section which relate to a weekday during a period which is not a period of summer time shall apply to such a Sunday as if it were a weekday."

22–27 Intoxicating liquor may be served in conjunction with a meal during the following periods:

1. Weekdays in summer time:

   11.30 p.m. to 12.30 a.m. on the morning of the following day.

2. Weekdays for the rest of the year:

   11.00 p.m. to 12.30 a.m. on the morning of the following day.

3. Sundays:

   2 p.m. to 3 p.m.

4. Christmas Day

   1 p.m. to 3 p.m.

   7 p.m. to 10 p.m.

5. Sundays which fall on December 23 or 24 in any year

   11 p.m. to 12.30 a.m. on the morning of the following day.

   Thus, intoxicating liquor may be served on Christmas Day to a person other than a member lodging on the premises, but only in conjunction with the service of a meal.

The expressions "period of summer time", "ordinary weekday" and "Sunday" are defined in section 1 of the Intoxicating Liquor Act 1927.[32]

[32] "Summer time": see above, n.6. Intoxicating Liquor Act 1927, s.1, defines "Weekday" and "Sunday". "Weekday": any day which is not a Sunday, is not Good Friday, Christmas Day or St Patrick's Day; "Sunday": does not include a Sunday which is Christmas Day.

Extension of Permitted Hours

22–28 As in the case of a licensed premises, a registered club may apply to the District Court for an order extending the hours during which it is entitled to supply and serve intoxicating liquor. Unlike the special exemption order, however, there is a limit to the number of such extensions. The statute does not prohibit the grant of a club authorisation in respect of Sunday or a Christmas Day, St Patrick's Day or a Good Friday.

STATUTORY PROVISION

Section 21 of the Intoxicating Liquor (General) Act 1924, as amended by section 8 of the Intoxicating Liquor Act 1962, provides:

> "(1) A Justice of the District Court may on the application of the secretary of a registered club authorise such club, notwithstanding the provisions contained in its rules pursuant to this Part of this Act, to supply excisable liquors to members of the club during any one period, specified in the authorisation and not exceeding six hours in duration, during which such supply of excisable liquors would be prohibited by the rules of the club.
>
> (2) The supply of excisable liquors in a registered club to members of the club during any period covered by an authorisation under this section shall be lawful and shall not be deemed to be a breach of the rules of the club.
>
> (3) Not more than fifteen authorisations shall be granted under this section to any one club in any year."

A club authorisation permits the supply of excisable liquor to members of the club outside permitted hours.

A sports club may apply for an authorisation for a special event in the club.[33] Only one authorisation a year is permitted although it makes it lawful to supply intoxicating liquors to members of the public on the club premises or in its grounds.

Drinking-Up Time

22–29 The drinking-up time permitted in a registered club, as in a licensed premises, has been extended from 10 minutes to 30 minutes.

STATUTORY PROVISION

Section 7(2)(a) of the Intoxicating Liquor Act 1962, as amended by section 27 of the Intoxicating Liquor Act 1988, provides:

---

[33] Intoxicating Liquor Act 1962, s.14.

"Nothing in the Registration of Clubs Acts, or contained, by virtue only of subsection (1) of section 56 of the Act of 1927, in the rules of a club registered under those Acts shall operate to prohibit the consumption of excisable liquor on the club premises by any person during the period of thirty minutes commencing at the beginning of a period during which the supplying of excisable liquor on such premises is prohibited."

E. Hotels and Restaurants

22–30 Hotels and restaurants are permitted additional trading hours to supply intoxicating liquor with meals to their customers, subject to certain statutory conditions. The holder of a licence for a premises which is a hotel or restaurant within the meaning of the Intoxicating Liquor Act 1927 is entitled to serve intoxicating liquor with food during the hours specified in section 13 of the Intoxicating Liquor Act 1927 as amended. These additional hours do not apply in relation to a premises to which a special restaurant licence attaches. The holder of a limited restaurant certificate may serve food and intoxicating liquor during these additional hours, but only on that portion of the premises to which the certificate relates.[34]

The holder of a licence for a restaurant premises (other than one to which a limited restaurant certificate attaches) and a hotel premises may also apply for a special exemption order.

Additional Permitted Hours with Meals

STATUTORY PROVISION

22–31 Section 13 of the Intoxicating Liquor Act 1927, as amended by section 28 of the Intoxicating Liquor Act 1988 and section 4 of the Intoxicating Liquor Act 1995, provides:

"Nothing in this Act shall operate to prohibit the holder of an on-licence in respect of premises which are for the time being a hotel or restaurant from supplying intoxicating liquor to any person on the premises or from permitting intoxicating liquor to be consumed on the premises —

(a) during a period of summer time, between the hours of half-past eleven o'clock in the evening on any weekday and half-past twelve o'clock in the morning on the following day, or
(b) during a period which is not a period of summer time, between the hours of eleven o'clock in the evening on any weekday and half-past twelve o'clock in the morning on the following day, or

---

[34] Intoxicating Liquor Act 1927, s.12A(6).

(c) unless his licence is a six-day licence, on any Sunday between the hours of two o'clock and three o'clock in the afternoon, or
(d) on Christmas Day, between the hours of one o'clock and three o'clock in the afternoon or the hours of seven o'clock and ten o'clock in the evening,

if, in each case, the intoxicating liquor is —

(i) ordered by that person at the same time as a substantial meal is ordered by him,
(ii) consumed at the same time as and with the meal,
(iii) supplied and consumed in that portion of the premises usually set apart for the supply of meals, and
(iv) paid for at the same time as the meal is paid for,

Provided that where in any year the 23rd or 24th day of December falls on a Sunday, then, except in the case of a six-day licence, the provisions of this section which relates to a weekday during a period which is not a period of summer time shall apply to such a Sunday as if it were a weekday."

The additional hours during which the hotelier or restaurateur may supply or permit intoxicating liquor to be consumed on the premises with a meal may be summarised as follows: 22–32

1. Weekdays in summer time:

   11.30 p.m. to 12.30 a.m. on the morning of the following day.

2. Weekdays for the rest of the year:

   11 p.m. to 12.30 a.m. on the morning of the following day.

3. Sunday (unless his licence is a six-day licence):

   2 p.m. to 3 p.m.

4. Christmas Day:

   1.00 p.m. to 3.00 p.m.

   7.00 p.m. to 10.00 p.m.

5. Sundays which fall on December 23 or 24 in any year:

   11 p.m. to 12.30 a.m. on the morning of the following day.

There are no extended hours for the service of intoxicating liquor with meals on St Patrick's Day or on a Good Friday.

Once a hotel is a licensed premises "structurally adapted for use and bona fide used as a hotel or a hotel and restaurant and having not less than ten apartments set apart and exclusively used for the sleeping accommodation of travellers",[35] 22–33

[35] Intoxicating Liquor Act 1927, s.1.

then it is entitled to avail of the extra permitted hours. It is not necessary for the premises to have a hotel licence under section 2(2) of the Licensing (Ireland) Act 1902 or the Tourist Traffic Act 1952. So, a premises to which a publican's licence attaches and which comes within the definition of hotel as set forth in section 1 of the Intoxicating Liquor Act 1927 is entitled to avail of this exemption from permitted hours.

A premises to which a special restaurant licence attaches, however, is not entitled to avail of the above exemption as it is not a restaurant within the meaning of section 1 of the 1927 Act, which provides that "the word 'restaurant' means licensed premises certified under this Act to be a restaurant for the purposes of this Act". A premises to which a limited restaurant certificate attaches may avail of the extra permitted hours but only on that portion of the premises which has been certified to be a restaurant. The holder of a wine retailer's on-licence for premises which are a restaurant may serve wine with food during the extra permitted hours.

Non-licensed Business

22–34 Non-licensed business may be carried on at any time in premises which are a hotel or restaurant for the purposes of the Intoxicating Liquor Act 1927.[36] Therefore, a hotel or restaurant may be open at all times for business such as the serving of meals, but may serve intoxicating liquor only during permitted hours.

Special Exemption Order

22–35 The holder of an on-licence for premises which are a hotel or a restaurant for the purposes of the Intoxicating Liquor Act 1927 may apply for a special exemption order. This order will exempt him on any special occasion from the provisions of the Intoxicating Liquor Act 1927 relating to prohibited hours in respect of the said premises. There is no limit (unlike club authorisations) to the number of special exemption orders which may be granted during the year. However, a special exemption order may not be granted for any time on a Sunday, or for any time between 1 a.m. and 10 a.m. on Monday morning. A special exemption order may be sought between 12.01 a.m. and 1 a.m. on a Monday morning.[37] A restaurateur or a hotelier cannot serve intoxicating liquor, with food, after 11 p.m. on any Sunday, except where December 23 or 24 falls on a Sunday in any year.

[36] Intoxicating Liquor Act 1927, s.3(3).
[37] *Ibid.*, s.5(3), as amended by Intoxicating Liquor Act 1988, s.29.

The extent of the time period is a matter for the discretion of the District Court and the usual practice is to grant a special exemption order up until 1.30 a.m. or sometimes 2 a.m. on a weekday.

It should be noted that a provision in a public dancing licence permitting public dancing to extend beyond a time authorised in a special exemption order does not in law permit persons to be upon licensed premises at hours not expressly permitted by a special exemption order.

Lodgers and Private Friends

A hotelier and restaurateur may entertain private friends at his own expense in the part of the licensed premises other than the part in which the sale of intoxicating liquor generally takes place. A hotelier is entitled to sell intoxicating liquor at any hour on his licensed premises to a person lodging in such premises. The same provisions apply to restaurateurs. **22–36**

Drinking-Up Time

Section 7(1)(b) of the Intoxicating Liquor Act 1962 provides that the "drinking up time" provisions of the licensing code do not apply during the additional permitted hours provisions described in this chapter or where a special exemption order has been granted. **22–37**

F. Special Restaurant Licence

The special restaurant licence was created by the Intoxicating Liquor Act 1988. Section 14 of that Act sets out special trading hours in respect of premises to which a special restaurant licence attaches. **22–38**

STATUTORY PROVISION

Section 14 of the Intoxicating Liquor Act 1988, as amended by section 6 of the Intoxicating Liquor Act 1995, provides:

> "(1) It shall not be lawful for any person, in any premises to which a special restaurant licence applies, to —
>
> (a) sell or expose for sale, or
> (b) open or keep open the premises for the sale of, or
> (c) permit the consumption on the premises of,
> any intoxicating liquor —
> (i) on any weekday, or on a Sunday which falls on the 23rd or 24th day of

December in any year, between the hours of half-past twelve o'clock in the morning and half-past twelve o'clock in the afternoon, or

(ii) on any Sunday, other than a Sunday to which paragraph (i) of this subsection relates, between the hours of half-past twelve o'clock in the morning and half-past twelve o'clock in the afternoon, or between the hours of three o'clock and six o'clock in the afternoon, or between the hours of eleven o'clock in the evening and half-past twelve o'clock in the afternoon of the next following day, or

(iii) on Christmas Day, between the hours of half-past twelve o'clock in the morning and one o'clock in the afternoon or between the hours of three o'clock in the afternoon and seven o'clock in the evening or between the hours of ten o'clock in the evening and half-past twelve o'clock in the afternoon of the next following day, or

(iv) at any time on Good Friday or between the hours of twelve o'clock midnight and half-past twelve o'clock in the morning of the next following Saturday".

Permitted Hours

22–39 1. Weekdays (throughout the year):

12.30 p.m. to 12.30 a.m. on the morning of the following day.

2. Sunday:

12.30 a.m. to 3 p.m.

6 p.m. to 11 p.m.

3. Christmas Day:

1 p.m. to 3 p.m.

3 p.m. to 7 p.m.

7 p.m. to 10 p.m.

4. Good Friday:

Must be closed all day up to 12.30 a.m. on Easter Saturday

5. Sundays which fall on December 23 or 24 in any year:

12.30 p.m. to 12.30 a.m. on the morning of the following day.

There is no prohibition against opening on St Patrick's Day.

Drinking-Up Time

It is unlikely that the holder of a special restaurant licence is entitled to avail of section 7 of the Intoxicating Liquor Act 1962, as amended by section 27 of the Intoxicating Liquor Act 1988, and allow 30 minutes drinking-up time after the normal permitted hours as the licence does not come within the definition of "on-licence" contained in section 1 of the Intoxicating Liquor Act 1927. However, the argument could be advanced that as a special restaurant licence is deemed to be a retailer's on-licence for the purpose of the Finance (1909–10) Act 1910, although its does not authorise off-sales, then the provisions of section 7 apply. **22–40**

Non-Licensed Business

The holder of a special restaurant licence may open his premises at any time for the service of food but intoxicating liquor may only be served during permitted hours.[38] **22–41**

Extended Hours

Although a special restaurant licence is deemed for the purposes of the Finance (1909–10) Act 1910 to be a retailer's on-licence,[39] the holder is not entitled to apply for a special exemption order under section 5 of the Intoxicating Liquor Act 1927. **22–42**

Lodgers and Private Friends

It is questionable whether a special restaurant licence is an on-licence for the purposes of the Intoxicating Liquor Act 1927 or whether the holder of a special restaurant licence is entitled to sell intoxicating liquor at any hour on licensed premises to a person lodging in his premises so as to come within the exemption as to lodgers in section 14(e) of the Intoxicating Liquor Act 1927. If so, the supply of intoxicating liquor must take place in conjunction with the consumption of a meal.[40] Although a special restaurant licence is an on-licence, it only authorises the sale of intoxicating liquor in conjunction with the consumption of a meal. It is, however, a licensed premises and private friends can be supplied with intoxicating liquor in accordance with section 14(b) of the Intoxicating Liqour Act 1927. **22–43**

---

[38] Intoxicating Liquor Act 1988, s.14(2).
[39] *Ibid.*, s.7(2).
[40] Intoxicating Liquor Act 1988, s.7(1), and the Intoxicating Liquor Act 1927, s.14, as amended by the Intoxicating Liquor Act 1943, s.10.

G. Theatre Licence

22–44 The provisions of the Intoxicating Liquor Act 1927 relating to prohibited hours do not apply to a theatre. Section 21(2) provides that the expression "permitted time" means a period beginning "half an hour before the commencement of a performance in the theatre in respect of which the expression is used and ending half an hour after the termination of such performance".

Thus, intoxicating liquor may be sold during any hour of the day or night but the sale may not commence more than 30 minutes before the commencement of the show, and it may not extend later than 30 minutes after its conclusion.

STATUTORY PROVISION

Section 21(3) of the Intoxicating Liquor Act 1927 provides:

> "It shall not be lawful to sell or expose for sale by retail any intoxicating liquor in any theatre—
>
> (a) at any time other than during a permitted time, or
> (b) to any person other than persons who either —
> (i) are then employed in the theatre, or
> (ii) have engaged or paid for seats in the theatre for the performance taking or which took place during the permitted time or either of the permitted times then current, or
> (c) in any part of the theatre which is then accessible to persons other than those persons to whom intoxicating liquor may then be sold in such theatre."

So, intoxicating liquor can be sold from 30 minutes before the commencement of a show, throughout the show, and up to 30 minutes after the conclusion of the show.

Non-licensed Business

22–45 Non-licensed business may be carried on at any time in a premises to which a theatre licence is attached but the sale of intoxicating liquor is confined to the permitted times.[41]

[41] Intoxicating Liquor Act 1927, s.3(3).

Extended Hours

The holder of a theatre licence does not come within the provisions of section 5 of the Intoxicating Liquor Act 1927 and is therefore not entitled to apply for extended hours during which intoxicating liquor can be served. 22–46

Lodgers and Private friends

Section 14(b) of the Intoxicating Liquor Act 1927 provides for the supply of intoxicating liquor at the licence holder's expense to friends and this applies to a theatre which is a "licensed" premises. However, section 14(e), as amended by section 10 of the Intoxicating Liquor Act 1943 does not apply to a theatre as it is not an "on-licence" for the purposes of the Intoxicating Liquor Act 1927 so the sale of intoxicating liquor to a lodger is not premitted. 22–47

H. Wine Retailer's On-Licence

In *Lohan v. Fusco*[42] the Supreme Court held that non-certificated licences were to be treated in the same way as certificated licences, for the purposes of prohibited hours. In other words, the provisions relating to prohibited hours contained in the licensing code also apply to the licences issued by the Collector Customs and Excise without a court certificate, such as a wine retailer's on-licence. 22–48

I. Aerodromes

Section 27 of the Intoxicating Liquor Act 1943 distinguishes between travellers and intending travellers and members of the public for the purposes of trading hours. 22–49

The ordinary permitted hours apply in respect of an aerodrome premises for the supply of intoxicating liquor to members of the public. The licensee may also apply for special exemption orders.[43] In addition, section 26 of the Intoxicating Liquor Act 1943 permits the sale of intoxicating liquor in licensed aerodrome premises "at any time" to be consumed in the said premises by persons who have travelled by air or who intend to travel by air from an aerodrome.

---

[42] [1967] I.R. 11.
[43] Intoxicating Liquor Act 1943, s.28(2).

J. Passenger Aircraft

22–50 Intoxicating liquor may be sold to and consumed by passengers in an aircraft while such aircraft is in flight.

K. Áras Mhic Dhiarmada Bus Station

22–51 The on-licence granted to this premises permits the sale and consumption of intoxicating liquor during the same trading hours applicable to an ordinary on-licence.[44] The licensee may apply for special exemption orders and intoxicating liquor may be supplied with a meal beyond normal closing hours.[45] However, mixed trading cannot be carried on.[46]

L. Greyhound Race Tracks

22–52 Licences granted in respect of greyhound race tracks[47] authorise the sale and consumption of intoxicating liquor at the track, the keeping open of premises at the track for such sale, the permitting of such consumption on the occasion of a greyhound race meeting, sale or trials at such track during the period:

1. beginning 30 minutes before the commencement of the race meeting, sale or trials as the case may be; and
2. ending in the case of a race meeting, 30 minutes after the time at which the last race of the meeting starts and in the case of a sale or trials at the conclusion of the sale or trials as the case may be.

M. Military Canteens

22–53 Section 23(b) of the Intoxicating Liquor Act 1927 provides that licences for the sale and consumption of intoxicating liquor in military canteens (under the authority of the Minister for Defence) are not subject to the provisions relating to prohibited hours contained in Part II of the Intoxicating Liquor Act 1927. Accordingly, intoxicating liquor may be sold at any time on those premises.

---

44 Intoxicating Liquor Act 1953, s.2.
45 *Ibid.*, s.5.
46 *Ibid.*
47 Intoxicating Liquor Act 1962, s.18(2), as amended by the Intoxicating Liquor Act 1988, s.49.

N. Railway Restaurant Cars

Section 14(d) of the Intoxicating Liquor Act 1927 provides that licences authorising the sale and consumption of intoxicating liquor on a railway restaurant car are not subject to the provisions relating to prohibited hours contained in Part II of the Intoxicating Liquor Act 1927. Accordingly, intoxicating liquor may be sold at any time. **22–54**

O. Passenger Vessels

Licences authorising the sale and consumption of intoxicating liquor in passenger vessels are not subject to the provisions relating to prohibited hours contained in Part II of the Intoxicating Liquor Act 1927.[48] Accordingly, intoxicating liquor may be sold at any time. **22–55**

P. National Concert Hall

The licence granted under section 2 of the Intoxicating Liquor (National Concert Hall) Act 1983 authorises the sale of intoxicating liquor to persons attending or taking part in a function at the National Concert Hall and persons employed at the National Concert Hall during the period beginning 30 minutes before the commencement of a function and ending one hour after its conclusion.[49] **22–56**

The licence is granted to the National Concert Hall Company for such time as the National Concert Hall is operated by it.

Q. Licensed Racecourse

A licence granted for the sale of intoxicating liquor at a racecourse for consumption at the racecourse to persons attending the race-fixture is operative during the period beginning from the time the racegoing public are permitted admission (but not before 10.30 a.m.) and ending one hour after the conclusion of the last race of the race-fixture.[50] A racecourse licence is not subject to the **22–57**

---

[48] Intoxicating Liquor Act 1927, s.14(c).
[49] Intoxicating Liquor (National Concert Hall) Act 1983, s.2(2).
[50] Irish Horseracing Industry Act 1994, s.65.

prohibited hours provisions contained in Part II of the Intoxicating Liquor Act 1927.[51]

R. Holiday Camp Premises

22–58 The normal permitted hours provisions apply, although intoxicating liquor may also be served on the following occasions to persons bona fide lodging in the holiday camp:

1. Christmas Day: between 7.30 p.m. and 10 p.m.
2. Good Friday: between 6 p.m. and 9 p.m. once it is ordered and consumed with a meal and supplied and consumed in the portion of the premises usually set aside for the supply of meals.[52]

Lodgers can be supplied with intoxicating liquor at any time, although section 7(2) of the Intoxicating Liquor Act 1960 restricts the time during which a lodger may consume intoxicating liquor on St Patrick's Day or Sundays (other than a Sunday which is Christmas Day). Section 14 of the Intoxicating Liquor Act 1927 does not apply to holiday camp premises, so it is questionable whether the supplying of intoxicating liquor to private friends is authorised. The premises is treated in the same way as a restaurant or a hotel. Intoxicating liquor may be served to non-residents during the hours specified in section 13 of the Intoxicating Liquor Act 1927 but only where it is ordered and consumed at the same time as and with a meal and is supplied and consumed in the portion of the premises usually set aside for the supply of meals.[53] Non-licensed business may be carried on at any time.[54] The licensee may apply for special exemption orders.[55]

S. Wholesale Dealer's Licence

22–59 Wholesale dealing is not affected by the provisions relating to prohibited hours contained in Part II of the Intoxicating Liquor Act 1927 in any premises which are not licensed premises.[56]

---

[51] *Ibid.*, s.66.
[52] Intoxicating Liquor Act 1960, s.7.
[53] *Ibid.*
[54] Tourist Traffic Act 1952, s.53.
[55] *Ibid.*, s.52.
[56] Intoxicating Liquor Act 1927, s.23(c).

CHAPTER 23

EXEMPTION ORDERS AND OCCASIONAL LICENCES

Introduction

Breach of the statutory provisions relating to prohibited hours and selling intoxicating liquor without a licence can result in the ultimate forfeiture of a licence. The legislature has, however, made provision for extending the hours during which intoxicating liquor may be served in a licensed premises in certain circumstances. Provision has also been made to permit the sale of intoxicating liquor in premises which are not licensed for the sale of intoxicating liquor. The courts have tended to interpret the circumstances during which a person is entitled to avail of any of these exemptions in a restrictive manner. **23–1**

This area of law reflects our national characteristics and customs. The provisions for general exemption orders reflect the fact that historically Ireland was an agriculture-based society where many of these activities were conducted outside normal trading hours. The ethos "can't work with a drought" is prevalent in the extended opening hours provided for in respect of these different activities. In 1962, legislation recognised that the original aims of the licensing code were not intended to benefit city dwellers and accordingly it was provided that new general exemption orders could not be granted in the Dublin area.[1] The provisions of the licensing code which prohibit the sale of intoxicating liquor on Christmas Day, St Patrick's Day or Good Friday reflect our religious outlook, as does the prohibition against the granting of exemption orders on

[1] Intoxicating Liquor Act 1962, s.15.

Sundays. Many of the exemption orders are designed to cater for "special events" or "special occasions" which are part and parcel of Irish life.

However, the present statutory scheme is open to the criticism that it does not cater for the way in which our society has developed since the mid 1960s. The special exemption order has now come to form the cornerstone of the nightclub and entertainment business. In order to operate the late opening and drinking hours upon which these businesses thrive, the licensed premises must be either a hotel or a restaurant for the purposes of the Intoxicating Liquor Act 1927, and a special exemption order must have been obtained in respect of the event. The only statutory notice party for an application for a special exemption order is the superintendent of the Garda Síochána and the supervision of this area is a matter for him. In contrast, the category of persons who may appear and object to an application for an occasional licence is extremely wide; any person with a bona fide interest in the application may appear and give evidence.[2]

This chapter deals with exemptions which apply in respect of licensed premises and the statutory provisions which permit the sale of intoxicating liquor on unlicensed premises.

A. Licensed Premises

1. Area Exemption Order

23–2 This is an exemption order for special events: it exempts the holder of a licence, in certain instances, from complying with the requirements relating to prohibited hours in respect of his licensed premises. The order is granted by a District Court judge. An application for an area exemption order cannot be made by the holder of a licence whose premises are situate in the County Borough of Dublin. The purpose of the order is to provide for special events such as local festivals in a locality.

A "special event" has "the meaning of something of a peculiar or restricted kind which is not generally prevalent".[3] Thus, a special event must be something which is unusual and takes place infrequently.

STATUTORY PROVISION

23–3 Section 10 of the Intoxicating Liquor Act 1962 provides:

> "(1) Subject to the provisions of this section, where, on application to a Justice of the District Court by the holder of a licence in respect of premises situate in

[2] *Ibid.*, s.11(6).
[3] *Rahill and Goode v. Brady* [1971] I.R. 69 at 88, *per* Budd J.

any locality not in the county borough of Dublin, it is shown to the satisfaction of the Court that the application has the approval of a majority of the holders of licences in respect of premises so situate and is in respect of a period during which a special event or special events will take place in or near that locality of such kind that, in the opinion of the Court, the period will be one during which a considerable number of persons will be likely to be attracted to that locality, the Court, if it is satisfied that it is desirable to do so for the accommodation of those persons, may, after hearing the officer in charge of the Garda Síochána for that locality, make an order, subject to such conditions as it thinks proper, exempting the holders of licences in respect of premises so situate from the provisions of the Licensing Acts relating to prohibited hours in respect of those premises at such times, and on such days during the period as it thinks fit: provided that, where the period aforesaid exceeds nine days, the exemption shall be limited to such times and days as it thinks fit during a period or periods (not exceeding three) comprising in all not more than nine days."

JURISDICTIONAL REQUIREMENTS

1. Venue 23–4

   The District Court.

2. Applicant

   (a) The application must be made by the holder of a licence.[4] The statute does not restrict the application to the holder of an on-licence and the holder of a greyhound racetrack licence is entitled to apply,[5] as is the holder of a spirit or beer retailer's off-licence.

   (b) The applicant must show that his application has the approval of the majority of the holders of licences in respect of premises situate in the locality.

3. The Event

   (a) The applicant must show that the event or events are special and that they will take place in or near the locality.

   (b) The court must be satisfied that the event will attract a "considerable number of persons". A weekly incursion of people, equal in number to about one quarter of the resident population of an important tourist centre, does not constitute a special occasion. In *Application of Daniel C. McSweeney* Judge O'Briain refused the application for an area exemption order stating:

---

[4] See *Fitzpatrick v. McCormack* [1986] I.R. 380 for a definition of "holder".

[5] Intoxicating Liquor Act 1962, ss.1, 10.

"What might be 'a large number of persons' in a small village would hardly be so in a fair sized town. The population of Killarney I am told is 6,000 persons and the average incursion of 1,500 people on a Sunday, into this famous resort – many of them non-drinkers – could hardly be said to create a large crowd or special occasion."[6]

(c) The court must be satisfied that the area exemption order is necessary for the accommodation of those extra persons who would be likely to be attracted to the special event.

COURT ORDER

23–5 1. Where the period of the area exemption order exceeds nine days, the Court must limit the order during a period or periods (up to three) comprising in all not more than nine days.

2. The court cannot grant more than three area exemption orders in any particular year in respect of any particular locality.[7]

3. The court may revoke an area exemption order where it is shown that the application to revoke the order is approved by the majority of holders of on-licences in the locality in respect of which the area exemption order was made. However, the order to revoke must be made prior to the commencement of the area exemption order.[8]

STATUTORY CONSEQUENCES

An area exemption order operates to exempt a person in respect of whom the order has been granted from penalties relating to prohibited hours only, but not other penalties under the Licensing Acts.[9]

General

23–6 Any person is entitled to appear and give evidence in respect of the application.[10] Unlike the general exemption order, the applicant for an area exemption order must advertise his intention to apply seven days in advance of the proposed hearing date.[11] The holder of a six-day licence cannot obtain a general exemption order exempting him from prohibited hours on a Sunday.[12] Whereas

---

[6] [1953–54] 19–20 Ir. Jur. Rep. 32 at 35.
[7] Intoxicating Liquor Act 1962, s.10(4).
[8] *Ibid.*, s.10(7).
[9] *Ibid.*, s.10(5).
[10] *Ibid.*, s.10(2).
[11] *Ibid.*, s.10(3).
[12] *Ibid.*, s.10(6).

a general exemption order is intended to facilitate certain categories of traders and agrarian markets or fairs, an area exemption order is intended to facilitate the holding of festivities in a locality which is not situate in the County Borough of Dublin. The number of licence holders which constitutes a majority in an area has never been considered; this depends upon the definition of the area in the application. An applicant for a general exemption order must hold an on-licence whereas in the case of an area exemption order, the application may be made by the holder of an off-licence.

No provision is made in the licensing code for drinking-up time where an area exemption order has been granted.

2. General Exemption Order

A general exemption order is granted by a District Court judge to the holder of a licence whose premises is situate in the vicinity of a market or fair, where the court is satisfied that it is necessary to accommodate a "considerable" number of persons attending such market or fair. The same considerations apply where the licensed premises is situate in the vicinity of a place, such as a fishing harbour or a daily fruit, fish or vegetable market, such as the Corporation Market in Chancery Place or the Smithfield market in Dublin. 23–7

Section 4 of the Intoxicating Liquor Act 1927 conferred jurisdiction on the District Court to grant general exemption orders: section 15(3) of the Intoxicating Liquor Act 1962 restricted the grant of a general exemption order to premises not situate in the County Borough of Dublin, unless a general exemption order was in force in respect of the premises on April 19, 1962, or at any time during the two years immediately preceding that date.

STATUTORY PROVISION

Section 4 of the Intoxicating Liquor Act 1927, as amended by section 10 of the Intoxicating Liquor Act 1960, provides: 23–8

> "(1) The Justice of the District Court upon its being proved to his satisfaction that it is necessary or desirable so to do for the accommodation of any considerable number of persons attending any public market or fair or following any lawful trade or calling, may after hearing the officer in charge of the Garda Síochána for the licensing area grant (if he so thinks fit) to any holder of an on-licence in respect of premises situate in the vicinity of such market or fair, or of the place where such persons follow such lawful trade or calling, an order (in this Act referred to as a general exemption order) exempting such holder from the provisions of this Act relating to prohibited hours in respect of the said premises on such days and during such times (except between the hours of one and two o'clock in the morning) and upon such terms as may be specified in such order."

JURISDICTIONAL REQUIREMENTS

23–9 1. Venue

The application is made to a District Court judge.

2. Applicant

The applicant must be the holder of an on-licence. On the authority of *Fitzpatrick v. McCormack*[13] a licensee and an interim transferee may apply for a general exemption order.

3. Vicinity

"Vicinity" in the context of a rural area will be construed less restrictively than where the application relates to an urban area. In *R. (Yeates) v. Donegal Justices*,[14] the justices granted general exemption orders to 11 publicans in a village near where a fish curing and packing industry was carried on. None of the public houses were nearer than half a mile from the fish curing and packing station. The court (which comprised Palles C.B., Kenny and Wright JJ.) held that the premises were in the vicinity of the fish curing and packing operation, as there were no nearer houses in which the staff in that plant could obtain refreshment.

4. Garda Síochána

The court must hear the officer in charge of the Garda Síochána for the licensing area. It is a matter for the court, notwithstanding any evidence given by the Garda Síochána, to decide whether or not to grant the application.

COURT ORDER

23–10 1. The order must contain a condition that the holder supplies food and non-alcoholic refreshment to any person who requires same.

2. The District Court judge is entitled to withdraw a general exemption order at any time. Generally the applicant will be permitted to make representations as to why this should not be done, although the statute makes no provision for this. The District Court judge has a discretion to alter the general exemption order either by extending or restricting the hours.

---

[13] Above, n.4.
[14] (1911) 45 I.L.T.R. 158.

STATUTORY CONSEQUENCES

1. Where a general exemption order is granted, the holder is exempt during the hours specified in the order from the statutory provisions relating to prohibited hours during such period. However, he is not exempt from other offences which can be committed pursuant to the Licensing Acts, such as supplying underage persons with drink. **23–11**
2. A general exemption order (if not withdrawn earlier) expires at the next annual licensing sessions. If the applicant wishes to apply for a further general exemption order, he must do so at the annual licensing District Court.

Obligations of Licence Holder

A notice must be displayed outside the premises "in a conspicuous place" and it must specify the periods of exemption specified in the order of the District Court.[15] A notice falsely representing that the licence holder is the holder of a general exemption order or which falsely states the periods of exemption attracts a penalty not exceeding £10. **23–12**

Prohibited Times

The District Court judge may use his discretion as to the hours during which a general exemption order relates, but he must have regard to those hours which are expressly prohibited by statute. A general exemption order cannot be granted during the following hours: **23–13**

1. 1 a.m. and 2 a.m.[16];
2. where a general exemption order is granted for the accommodation of persons attending a public market or fair, or persons lawfully fishing in tidal waters, it cannot be granted before 5 a.m. or after 11.30 p.m. in summertime or after 11 p.m. in wintertime[17];
3. a general exemption order for the accommodation of persons following any lawful trade or calling (other than fishing in tidal waters) will not be granted before 7 a.m. or after 11.30 p.m. in summertime or 11 p.m. in wintertime[18];
4. a general exemption order will not be granted for any time on a Sunday, St Patrick's Day, Christmas Day or Good Friday.[19]

[15] The penalty for breach of this provision is a fine not exceeding £5; Intoxicating Liquor Act 1927, s.4(4).
[16] *Ibid.*, s.4(1).
[17] Intoxicating Liquor Act 1962, s.15.
[18] *Ibid.*
[19] Intoxicating Liquor Act 1927, s.4(7).

General

23–14 The court is conferred with a wide discretion: it can limit the sale of intoxicating liquor to those persons for whose benefit the general exemption order was granted. However, unless this is made a condition of the general exemption order, the licence holder may rely on the order to sell to any member of the public. In *Gamble v. Greene*, Andrews J. stated:

> ". . . here the licensed premises are open, and they are allowed to be open for the refreshment of anybody who comes in, if the true interpretation is that the reason they are allowed to be open is that it is for the accommodation of persons attending the fair. We think it is quite open to interpret this particular exemption order as that the words "for the accommodation of persons attending the fair" are given as the reason why the opening is allowed, and not that these words are used to exclude all other persons."[20]

It is open to the District Court to exclude certain sections of the public from being served.[21] Although the court has a discretion as to whether or not to grant the general exemption order, and as to the terms pursuant to which the general exemption order is granted, there is no provision in the statute requiring the applicant to notify any person other than the Garda Síochána, nor is there a requirement to publish the application. There is no provision for objection by the public to the application. Like the area exemption order drinking up time after the time specified in a general exemption order is not permitted.

3. Exemption for Licensed Business on the Afternoons of Sunday and St Patrick's Day

23–15 An exemption under section 16 of the Intoxicating Liquor Act 1962 permits licence holders in a rural area to open their premises at 12 noon on Sundays and on St Patrick's Day for licensed business. The exception is limited in that it only applies between the hours of 12 p.m. and 12.30 p.m. This provision is designed to accommodate rural life where large numbers of people in the vicinity of the church habitually congregate after religious worship.

The District Court judge may not make an order in respect of a period during which or part of which a considerable number of people in the locality to which the exemption would relate would be likely to be at church.[22]

---

[20] (1910) 44 I.L.T.R. 14 at 16.
[21] *Ibid.*
[22] Intoxicating Liquor Act 1962, s.16(2).

STATUTORY PROVISION

Section 16 of the Intoxicating Liquor Act 1962 provides: **23–16**

> "(1) Subject to the provisions of this section, where, on application to a Justice of the District Court by the holder of a licence (not being a six-day licence) in respect of premises situate in any locality not in a county or other borough, it is shown to the satisfaction of the Court that the application has the approval of a majority of the holders of such licences in respect of premises so situate, the Court may, if it is satisfied that, owing to circumstances in the locality, it is desirable to do so, make an order exempting the holders of all such licences in respect of premises so situate from the provisions of the Licensing Acts relating to prohibited hours in respect of those premises for the period between the hours of twelve o'clock and half past twelve o'clock in the afternoon of Sundays and St Patrick's Day."

JURISDICTIONAL REQUIREMENTS

1. Venue **23–17**

   The District Court.

2. Applicant

   The applicant can be the holder of an on-licence or an off-licence but the holder of a six-day licence cannot apply.

3. Premises

   The premises must not be situate in a county or other borough.

4. Approval

   The application must have the approval of the majority of the holders of "such licences" in respect of premises situate in the locality of the applicant premises.

COURT ORDER

1. The court may grant the order where it is satisfied that, owing to circumstances in the locality it is desirable to do so. This discretion must be exercised taking into account the prohibition against making an order where a considerable number of people in the locality will be attending Mass during the half hour in respect of which the order is sought. **23–18**

2. The District Court judge may revoke the order on the application of any person appearing to have a bona fide interest in the matter, but he must hear the applicant before this is done.[23] In contrast to the area exemption order and the general exemption order, any person is entitled to apply to revoke

[23] Intoxicating Liquor Act 1962, s.16(5).

the Sunday afternoon and St Patrick's Day exemption order. A person who is applying to revoke the order must advertise his intention so to do.[24]

STATUTORY CONSEQUENCES

23–19 1. The premises may be opened for licensed business between 12 p.m. and 12.30 p.m. on a Sunday and St Patrick's Day, *i.e.* half an hour earlier than normal.

2. The order remains in force until the date specified in the order or the date of the annual licensing District Court, whichever is the earlier.[25]

3. The order exempts the holder of the licence from any penalty for contravention of provisions relating to prohibited hours only, but not from any other penalty.[26]

4. Where the application is successful, the exemption benefits the holders of all "such licences" in the locality.

General

23–20 Any person who appears to the court to have a bona fide interest in the matter is entitled to appear and give evidence.[27]

As in the case of an area exemption order, this application must be advertised. The advertisement must be made at least 10 days before the date on which it is proposed to make the application.[28]

4. Exemption for Unlicensed Business on the Mornings of Sunday and St Patrick's Day

23–21 Section 17 of the Intoxicating Liquor Act 1962 provides for an exemption for unlicensed business on the mornings of Sunday and St Patrick's Day. The provision does not apply to premises which are situate in a county or other borough. The aim is to cater for situations where people dwelling in a rural area who attend church can obtain groceries and other provisions which may only be available in the locality in a licensed premises, after church. The District Court cannot make the order in respect of a period during which a considerable number of persons in the locality are likely to be at church.[29]

---

[24] Intoxicating Liquor Act 1962, s.16(7).
[25] *Ibid.*, s.16(4).
[26] *Ibid.*, s.16(6).
[27] *Ibid.*, s.16(3).
[28] *Ibid.*, s.16(7). Note: in the case of an area exemption order, the application must be advertised seven days in advance of the hearing date.
[29] *Ibid.*, s.17(2).

STATUTORY PROVISION

Section 17 of the Intoxicating Liquor Act 1962 provides: **23–22**

> "(1) Subject to the provisions of this section, where, on application to a Justice of the District Court by the holder of a licence (not being a licence granted by virtue of paragraph (2) of section 2 of the Act of 1902) in respect of premises situate in any locality not in a county or other borough, it is shown to the satisfaction of the Court that the application has the approval of a majority of the holders of such licences in respect of premises so situate, the Court may, if it is satisfied that, owing to circumstances in the locality it is desirable to do so, make an order permitting the holders of all such licences in respect of premises so situate to open or keep open the premises for the purpose of carrying on any business other than the sale or supply of intoxicating liquor during any one period specified in the order and not exceeding forty-five minutes in duration on the mornings of Sundays and St Patrick's Day."

JURISDICTIONAL REQUIREMENTS

1. Venue **23–23**

   The District Court.

2. Applicant

   The applicant can be the holder of an on-licence or an off-licence, but the holder of a licence which was granted pursuant to the provisions of section 2(2) of the Licensing (Ireland) Act 1902, commonly called a hotel licence, is not entitled to apply. An application by the holder of a six-day licence is not expressly prohibited.

3. The premises must not be situate in a county or other borough.

4. The applicant must show that his application has the approval of the majority of the holders of "such" licences attached to premises situate in the locality. So, an application by the holder of off-licences must obtain the approval of the holders of other off-licences and the holder of an on-licence must obtain the approval of other publicans.

COURT ORDER

1. The order of the court remains in force until the next annual licensing District Court or such date as specified in the order unless revoked earlier.[30] **23–24**

2. The order may be revoked by the District Court judge on the application of any person who appears to the court to have a bona fide interest in the matter.

[30] Intoxicating Liquor Act 1962, s.17(4).

3. The court may also amend the order.[31] A person who wishes to apply to revoke or amend the order must notify the Garda Síochána and advertise his intention to make the application.[32]

STATUTORY CONSEQUENCES

23–25 1. The grant of this application permits the opening of all licensed premises in the locality for unlicensed business during the period specified in the order.

2. The opening or keeping open of the premises pursuant to the order is not deemed to be an opening or keeping open of the premises for the sale of intoxicating liquor.[33]

3. The unlicensed business cannot be conducted for a period exceeding 45 minutes on the morning of Sundays and St Patrick's Day.

General

23–26 An objection may be made by any person who appears to the court to have a bona fide interest in the matter.[34]

The applicant must notify the Garda Síochána and advertise his intention to make the application 10 days before the proposed hearing date.[35]

5. Special Exemption Order

23–27 A special exemption order is granted by a District Court judge to the holder of an on-licence for premises which are a hotel or restaurant: it entitles the applicant to an exemption on a special occasion from those provisions of the Licensing Acts which relate to prohibited hours. The District Court judge is entitled to impose such conditions as he thinks proper and fit when granting the order. Premises which operate as nightclubs regularly apply for special exemption orders.

STATUTORY PROVISION

23–28 Section 5 of the Intoxicating Liquor Act 1927, as amended by section 10 of the Intoxicating Liquor Act 1960, section 12 of the Intoxicating Liquor Act 1962 and section 29 of the Intoxicating Liquor Act 1988, provides:

---

[31] Intoxicating Liquor Act 1962, s.17(5).
[32] *Ibid.*, s.17(7).
[33] *Ibid.*, s.17(6).
[34] *Ibid.*, s.17(5).
[35] *Ibid.*, s.17(7).

"(1) If the holder of an on-licence for premises which are an hotel or a restaurant and are situate in a county borough applies to the Justice of the District Court for an order (in this Act referred to as an special exemption order) exempting him on any special occasion from the provisions of this Act relating to prohibited hours in respect of the said premises, such Justice may, if he thinks fit so to do after hearing the officer in charge of the Garda Síochána for the licensing area, grant to the applicant upon such conditions as he thinks proper an order so exempting him during the hours and on the special occasion to be specified in such order.

(2) Any person to whom a special exemption order has been granted shall, if and so long as he complies with the conditions upon which the same has been granted, be exempt during the time to which such order applies from any penalty for contravention of the provisions of this Act relating to prohibited hours in respect of the premises to which the order relates but not from any other penalty under this or any other Act.

(3) No special exemption order shall be granted for any time on a Sunday or for any time between one o'clock and half-past ten o'clock in the morning on a Monday.

(4) A special exemption order shall not be granted unless the applicant therefor has, not less than forty-eight hours before making the application, served upon the officer in charge of the Garda Síochána for the licensing area a notice of his intention to apply for the order, setting out his name and address and the place, occasion, and time for which the order is sought.

(5) In this section "special occasion" means —

(a) (i) the occasion of a special event that is organised for the entertainment of the members of a particular association, organisation, or other like group, or

(ii) the occasion of a private function

in the premises in relation to which the special exemption order is sought and at which a substantial meal (the price (if any) of which is included in the price (if any) of admission to the event) is served to the persons attending the event,

(b) the occasion of a dance that is held in a ballroom licensed under the Public Dance Halls Act, 1935, and forming part of the premises in relation to which the special exemption order is sought being a dance at which a substantial meal (the price (if any) of which is included in the price (if any) of admission to the dance) is served to the persons attending the dance, or

(c) the occasion of a dance that is held in such a ballroom on a day that, in the opinion of the Court, is a day of special festivity generally or in the locality in which the premises are situate.

(6) Special exemption orders shall not be granted pursuant to paragraph (c) of subsection (5) of this section for any premises in respect of more than six different days in the year.

(7) Special exemption orders shall contain as one of the terms thereof a condition that intoxicating liquor shall not be sold at the event to which the order relates during the hours specified in the Order to persons other than

those attending the event and that members of the public, other than persons attending the event, shall not be admitted to the part of the premises in which intoxicating liquor is being supplied or consumed pursuant to the order.

(8) Notwithstanding the provisions of subsection (3) of this section, a special exemption order may be granted for a Sunday that is New Year's Day, New Year's Eve or St. Patrick's Day.

(9) It shall be a condition of a special exemption order that the special event, private function or dance in relation to which it is granted be held in compliance with the relevant provisions of subsection (5) of this section."

JURISDICTIONAL REQUIREMENTS

23–29 1. Venue

The application is made to a District Court judge.

2. Applicant

The applicant must hold an on-licence in respect of premises which are a hotel or restaurant for the purposes of the Intoxicating Liquor Act 1927. The word "hotel" for the purposes of the Intoxicating Liquor Act 1927 means:

> "licensed premises structurally adapted for use and bona fide used as a hotel or a hotel and restaurant and having not less than ten apartments set apart and exclusively used for the sleeping accommodation of travellers".[36]

A restaurant is a licensed premises certified under the Intoxicating Liquor Act 1927 to be a restaurant for the purposes of the Intoxicating Liquor Act 1927, namely, premises which:

> "are structurally adapted for use and bona fide and mainly used as a restaurant, refreshment house, or other place for supplying substantial meals to the public".[37]

The holder of a licence for a premises which has the benefit of a limited restaurant certificate cannot apply for a special exemption order as the premises does not satisfy the definition of restaurant for the purposes of the Intoxicating Liquor Act 1927.

The holder of a licence for a licensed aerodrome or a licensed omnibus station or a licensed holiday camp may apply for a special exemption order.[38] A special exemption order may not be granted to the holder of a special restaurant licence in respect of the premises to which such licence relates.[39]

---

[36] Intoxicating Liquor Act 1927, s.1.
[37] *Ibid.*, s.12.
[38] Intoxicating Liquor Act 1943, s.28; Intoxicating Liquor Act 1953, s.5; Tourist Traffic Act 1952, s.52.
[39] Intoxicating Liquor Act 1988, s.22.

3. Garda Síochána **23–30**

The District Court judge must hear the officer in charge of the Garda Síochána for the licensing area.

4. Special Occasion

The applicant must prove that the event for which he seeks the special exemption order is a special occasion within the meaning of section 5(5) of the 1927 Act. A "special occasion" is defined by section 5 of the Intoxicating Liquor Act 1927, as amended by section 11 of the Intoxicating Liquor Act 1960 and section 12 of the Intoxicating Liquor Act 1962. The applicant must prove to the court that the occasion for which he seeks the special exemption order is one of the following:

(i) A special event which is organised for the entertainment of members of a particular group to whom a substantial meal is served. The interpretation of the expression "special event" in the context of the grant of a special exemption order differs from the interpretation given to the expression in the context of an occasional licence. As the licensee is obliged to confine the sale of intoxicating liquor at the special event during the hours specified in the order to those persons attending the event, then the event need only be special insofar as the particular association or organisation is concerned.

(ii) A private function at which a substantial meal is served.

(iii) A dance which is held in a "ballroom" which has been licensed under the Public Dance Halls Act 1935. The ballroom must form part of the premises in relation to which the special exemption order is sought. A substantial meal must be served to the persons attending the dance. Prior to the amendment to section 5 of the Intoxicating Liquor Act 1927 effected by section 12 of the Intoxicating Liquor Act 1962 it was unclear whether a dance could, as a matter of law, constitute a special occasion.

In *The State (Attorney General) v. Judge McGivern*,[40] the Supreme Court rejected the argument that a dance could be a special occasion only if the dance was of a special type such as a dance at an "old boys" school union. The Supreme Court held that a dance could, as a matter of law, constitute a special occasion. It was then a matter for the District Court judge to decide in his discretion whether any particular dance constituted a special occasion: he was not entitled to hold that a dance simpliciter could never constitute a special occasion. Section 12 of the Intoxicating Liquor Act 1962 defines the position with more certainty. The amendment introduced by section 12 makes all dances held in a **23–31**

[40] Unreported, Supreme Court, July 25, 1961.

place or premises licensed under the Public Dance Halls Act 1935, where such place or premises form part of the premises in relation to which the special exemption order is sought, special occasions. Accordingly, the discretion left to the District Court judge as noted by Walsh J. in *Murray v. O'Colmain*, is "simply to decide whether or not the meal in question amounts to a substantial meal".[41]

23–32 It has been decided that "disco dancing" where there is no band or orchestra, is a dance within the meaning of the section. In *Flannery v. Colleran*, O'Higgins J. stated:

> "A dance within this Section is simply the occasion on which dancing takes place. Dancing itself is to move with measured steps, especially to music. It does not seem to me to matter from what source the music comes or indeed whether in fact any music is provided. In this case, I have no doubt that the provision of music by tapes or gramaphone records on an occasion when people dance constitutes a dance within the meaning of the appropriate statutory provisions."[42]

(iv) A dance held in a ballroom licensed under the Public Dance Halls Act 1935 at which a substantial meal is not being served can be a special occasion where, in the opinion of the court, it is held on a day of special festivity. This can be a day of national festivity or a day of local festivity. Only six special exemption orders can be granted in respect of this special occasion, each to be granted on different days in the year.

23–33 5. Substantial Meal

On special occasions where a substantial meal must be served, it is not necessary to charge for the meal. However, if a charge is made it must be included in the admission price. As Walsh J. stated in *Murray v. O'Colmain*:

> "In other words it is open to the owner of the ballroom in question who is holding the dance to advertise the fact that he is providing the meal free and open to him in fact to provide it free of charge".[43]

Further, the District Court judge is not entitled to consider whether or not the meal is good value or not: his function is to determine whether or not the meal is a substantial meal. A substantial meal does not require waiter or waitress service.[44] The expression "substantial meal" is defined in section 9 of the Intoxicating Liquor Act 1962 as follows:

[41] [1981] I.L.R.M. 137.
[42] Unreported, Supreme Court, March 21, 1980.
[43] Above, n.41, at 139.
[44] *Ibid.*

"For the purposes of the Licensing Acts and the Registration of Clubs Acts a meal served in any premises after the commencement of this Act shall not be deemed to be a substantial meal unless —

(a) the meal is such as might be expected to be served as a main midday or main evening meal or as a main course at either such meal, and
(b) the meal is of a kind for which —
 (i) having regard to the prices charged for meals in the premises at times other than prohibited hours, or
 (ii) if meals are not normally served in the premises having regard to all the circumstances,
 it would be reasonable to charge a sum that is not less than —
 I. the sum (if any) that for the time being stands fixed under subsection (2) of this section. . . ."

Subsection (2) provides that the Minister for Justice may from time to time by order fix such a sum. This sum was fixed by virtue of S.I. No. 211 of 1979 at not less than £2.[45]

In *Attorney General (Friel) v. McDaid*,[46] the defendant was prosecuted for certain breaches of the licensing code. On one occasion, the Gardaí found 15 men standing in the hallway drinking from glasses, some of which contained beer and stout, at 12.15 a.m. on a Sunday morning. A number of men with glasses in their hands went out to the yard and later returned to the kitchen where they were seen with chicken legs in their hands. There was no evidence of cooking in the kitchen, but one or two attendants were serving sandwiches. In the restaurant, 15 men were sitting at the tables drinking beer and stout and there were no meals on any of the tables; on one table some seven or eight soiled plates were piled with remains of sandwiches and chicken bones. The defendant said in evidence before the District Court judge that the persons in the restaurant had finished their meals, that everyone who was served with intoxicating liquor after 11.30 p.m. was supplied with a meal, consisting either of sandwiches or a more substantial meal. The District Court judge considered that sandwiches and chicken served with intoxicating liquor constituted a substantial meal. Davitt P. was satisfied that there was a gross breach of the licensing laws on each occasion. He stated: 23–34

"I do not consider that a bottle of stout in one hand and a sandwich or leg of chicken in the other constitutes a substantial meal."

[45] Intoxicating Liquor Act 1962 (Section 9) Order 1979.
[46] Unreported, High Court, May 17, 1966.

STATUTORY CONSEQUENCES

23–35 1. Where a special exemption order has been granted, the holder of the licence does not commit an offence against the prohibited hours provisions during the times referred to in the order; but he is not exempt in respect of offences against any other provisions of the Licensing Acts.

2. Intoxicating liquor may not be sold at the event to which the special exemption order relates to persons other than those attending the event. Members of the public may not be admitted to that part of the premises in which intoxicating liquor is being consumed pursuant to the order.

Prohibited Times

23–36 A special exemption order cannot be granted during the following times:

1. any time on a Sunday,[47]
2. any time between 1 a.m. and 10.30 a.m. in the morning of a Monday.[48]

There is nothing to prevent the grant of a special exemption order from 12.01 a.m. to 12.59 a.m. on a Monday morning. In *Murray v. O'Colmain*, Walsh J. stated:

> "With regard to the informal submissions made by the Superintendent before the Circuit Judge that the Oireachtas never contemplated special exemption orders being made in respect of a period beginning immediately after the expiration of Sunday, one can say without much fear of contradiction that if the Oireachtas had any such reservation in mind that it would have said so. Having gone to the trouble of expressly excluding the granting of these special exemption orders in respect of any part of Sunday, one would expect that if it was intended to carry it over until somewhere after the commencement of Monday the legislation would have said so."[49]

In *Murray v. O'Colmain*, the special occasion in question was a dance which was to be held from 10 p.m. on a Sunday to 2 a.m. on a Monday. Walsh J. noted that the District Court judge was prevented from granting special exemption orders in respect of any part of the Sunday. Accordingly, the only special exemption order he could grant was a special exemption order from 12.01 a.m. on the Monday to 2 a.m. on the Monday. He stated:

> "There is no obligation on a District Justice to grant a special exemption order in respect of the whole of a special occasion even when he is not inhibited by

---

[47] Intoxicating Liquor Act 1927, s.5(3), as amended by the Intoxicating Liquor Act 1988, s.29.
[48] *Ibid.*
[49] Above, n.41, at 140.

the provisions relating to Sunday. Therefore it cannot be assumed that the special exemption order can be granted only in respect of the whole of and not of part of the special occasion".[50]

The subsequent enactment of section 29 of the Intoxicating Liquor Act 1988 prohibits the grant of special exemption orders from 1 a.m. onwards on a Monday morning.

There are three exceptions to the general prohibition against having special exemption orders on a Sunday, *i.e.* where New Year's Day, New Year's Eve or St Patrick's Day fall on a Sunday.[51]

General

No provision is made in the licensing code for drinking up time where a special exemption order has been granted. **23–37**

B. Unlicensed Premises

Occasional Licence

Section 11 of the Intoxicating Liquor Act 1962, confers jurisdiction on the District Court to grant a licence in respect of an unlicensed premises for a particular event, where that event is a "special event". Section 11 replaces earlier statutory provisions relating to occasional licences and subsection (11) repeals those provisions.[52] An occasional licence operates to exempt the person to whom it is granted from the provisions of the Licensing Acts relating to the sale and supply of intoxicating liquor at the place and during the time for which the licence is granted. This is conditional upon the licensee complying with the conditions subject to which the licence is granted and provided that special event for which the licence is granted is held in compliance with section 11(2) and (10) of the Intoxicating Liquor Act 1962. **23–38**

The provisions of the Licensing Acts 1833 to 1995 relating to endorsement and forfeiture do not apply where the offence is committed on the premises for which the occasional licence was obtained.[53] Unless an occasional licence is granted in respect of a day of special festivity, there is no limit to the number of occasional licences which can be granted; the limitation is merely that the number of days for which an occasional licence is granted shall not exceed six.[54]

---

[50] *Ibid.*

[51] Intoxicating Liquor Act 1927, s.5(8).

[52] Revenue Act 1862, s.13; Revenue Act 1863, s.20; Revenue (No. 1) Act 1864, s.5; Intoxicating Liquor Act 1927, s.6.

[53] Intoxicating Liquor Act 1962, s.11(9).

[54] *Ibid.*, s.11(1), as amended by the Intoxicating Liquor Act 1977, s.1.

The grant of an occasional licence does not prevent the holder of the on-licence from carrying on his licensed business in the premises to which the on-licence attaches.

STATUTORY PROVISION

23–39 Section 11 of the Intoxicating Liquor Act 1962, as amended by section 1 of the Intoxicating Liquor Act 1977, provides:

> (1) Subject to the provisions of this section, on application to a Justice of the District Court by the holder of an on-licence, the Court may, if it so thinks fit, and is satisfied that a special event is being held at any place to which no licence for the sale of intoxicating liquor is attached grant to the applicant a licence (in this section referred to as an occasional licence) authorising him to sell at that place during such times and on such days (not exceeding six) as may be specified in the licence such intoxicating liquor as he is authorised to sell by the on-licence aforesaid.
>
> (2) (a) An occasional licence shall not be granted for dinner unless it is organised as a special function for the entertainment of the members of a particular association, organisation or other like group.
>
> (b) An occasional licence shall not be granted for a dance unless —
>
> (i) it is held elsewhere than in the open air or in a tent, marquee or other such structure, and
>
> (ii) either—
>
> I. it is organised as a special function for the entertainment of the members of a particular association, organisation or other like group and a substantial meal (the price (if any) of which is included in the price of admission (if any) to the dance) is served to the persons attending the dance, or
>
> II. it is held wholly or partly on a day that, in the opinion of the Court, is a day of special festivity generally or in the locality in which the place to which the licence relates is situate."

JURISDICTIONAL REQUIREMENTS

23–40 1. Venue

The District Court.

2. Applicant

The application can be made by the holder of a publican's licence, hotel licence, a six day licence, or an early closing licence. It cannot be made by the holder of an off-licence or off-licences, and section 21 of the Intoxicating Liquor Act 1988 provides that the holder of a special restaurant licence cannot apply for an occasional licence.

3. Special Event

The applicant must prove that the event is a "special event". The expression "special event" is not defined in the Intoxicating Liquor Act 1962. It has been interpreted restrictively by the Superior Courts. In *Rahill and Goode v. Brady*, Butler J. in the High Court, stated:

> "However, giving the words of section 11 of the Act of 1962 their ordinary and natural meaning, as I must in the absence of definition, I am satisfied that an event must be special either intrinsically because of its own character or from the nature of the place where it is held. In the latter case it must be different from the ordinary use of the premises although it may be intrinsically commonplace."[55]

He held that bi-weekly sales of cattle and pigs in a county town at a place normally used for that place only were not special events within the meaning of the section.

In the Supreme Court, Ó Dálaigh C.J. stated: 23–41

> "A special event then is one which is not usual or common, but which is singular. In determining whether an event is special or not is it therefore necessary to inquire: – 'Is it usual or common, or is it singular?' This inquiry brings into view as one element the frequency of the event. Events that are usual or common are not special events; while a singular event is a special event. It should be repeated: the frequency of the event becomes a factor when we are considering whether the event is a 'special event', but not by reason of the designation 'occasional licence' to which I attach no particular importance."[56]

So, a special event is not only a particular or identifiable event; it must also have a distinguishing quality or feature. Budd J. was satisfied that the legislature intended to restrict the occasions on which such licences could be granted and that ordinary every-day user of the premises sought to be licensed was not to be regarded as a special event. He stated:

> "Having regard, therefore, to what I believe is the ordinary meaning of the word 'special', to what is to be gleaned from the Act as a whole as to the meaning of the term 'special event', to what is to be deduced from the nature and user of this mart premises and what the term would seem to mean from the viewpoint of the owners and those attending the premises, it would seem to me that the combined force of all these considerations leads to the view that the term 'special event' has the meaning of something of a peculiar or restricted kind which is not generally prevalent. It follows, accordingly, that the sales of pigs and cattle occurring weekly throughout the year in a place designed and used exclusively for that purpose cannot be a 'special event."[57]

---

[55] Above, n.3, at 73.
[56] *Ibid.* at 83.
[57] *Ibid.* at 88.

23–42 A wedding is not a special event for the purposes of the licensing code. Gannon J. held in *Re William Barrett*, that the interpretation of whether an event is special or not:

> "must be considered in relation to the persons for whose benefit the Licensee will carry on his trade as well as in relation to the place at which that trade may be conducted . . . [for] the event to be special in the sense of 'being something unusual or out of the ordinary or distinct from something generally prevalent or common' must be considered as it might effect not merely the intended guests of the wedding nor even the people of the locality".[58]

As the effect of the grant of an occasional licence is to authorise the holder of an on-licence to sell such intoxicating liquor as he is authorised to sell by the on-licence at an otherwise unlicensed place, the public at large must benefit from the conduct of the trade.

23–43 If the event is a dinner, the applicant must prove that it is organised as a special function for the entertainment of members of a particular association, organisation or other like group.

If the event is a dance, he must prove that the dance is not held in the open air or in a tent or marquee or other such structure and either:

(a) that it is organised as a special function for the entertainment of the members of a particular association, organisation or other like group, and a substantial meal (the price (if any) of which is included in the price of admission (if any) to the dance) is served to the persons attending the dance, or

(b) it is held wholly or partly on a day that, in the opinion of the court, is a day of special festivity generally or in the locality in which the place to which the licence relates is situate.[59]

An occasional licence will be granted for a temporary structure or a marquee if the special event is a dinner, but not if it is a dance.

STATUTORY CONSEQUENCES

23–44 1. The holder of an on-licence may sell such intoxicating liquor as he is authorised to sell by the on-licence during such times and on such days (not exceeding six) as may be specified in the occasional licence.

2. Where the special event is held wholly or partly on a day of special festivity referred to above, the holder cannot obtain an occasional licence in respect of any premises for more than six different days in a year.[60]

---

[58] Unreported, High Court, Gannon J., May 8, 1984.
[59] Intoxicating Liquor Act 1962, s.11(2).
[60] *Ibid.*, s.11(3).

3. Where the occasional licence is granted in respect of a dinner or a dance which constitutes a "special event" for the purposes of section 11, the sale of intoxicating liquor is confined to persons attending the dinner or dance in question.[61] Where the special event is not a dinner or a dance, intoxicating liquor may be served to the general public but not before 8 a.m. or after 10 p.m.
4. The licence operates to exempt the person to whom it is granted from the provisions of the Licensing Acts relating to the sale and supply of intoxicating liquor at the place and during the time for which the licence is granted, but only if and so long as he complies with the conditions subject to which it was granted. Further, the special event must fall within the provisions of section 11(2) of the Intoxicating Liquor Act 1962.[62]

Prohibited Times

1. An occasional licence may not be granted in respect of any Sunday, Christmas Day or Good Friday.[63] 23–45
2. Where the special event is not a dinner or a dance, an occasional licence may not be granted before 8 a.m. in the morning or after 10 p.m. in the evening.[64]

General

Any person who appears to the court to have a bona fide interest is entitled to appear and give evidence at the hearing of the application for the occasional licence.[65] 23–46

No provision is made in the licensing code for drinking up time where an occasional licence has been granted.

Section 11(3) of the 1962 Act limits the number of occasional licences which can be granted for a day of special festivity. Section 11(1) stipulates a maximum number of days in respect of which the order may operate. It should be noted that under the Interpretation Act 1937, "year" must be taken as meaning a calendar year. Accordingly, the provisions relating to occasional licences, although they may be thought to refer to the licensing year, do not in fact do so. The holder of an occasional licence is not subject to criminal sanction under the licensing code. This facilitates the obtaining of an occasional licence where licence holders in the area might initially be reluctant to seek one. The effective

---

[61] *Ibid.*, s.11(4).
[62] *Ibid.*, s.11(8).
[63] *Ibid.*, s.11(5).
[64] *Ibid.*, s.11(10).
[65] *Ibid.*, s.11(6).

sanction, however, is the refusal of a subsequent occassional licence where a previous breach is proved. A surprising omission is the absence of a requirement to advertise the application notwithstanding that any person who appears to have a bona fide interest may give evidence. Although there are no provisions in the Fire Services Act 1981 for giving the fire officer notice of the application, the practice in the District Court is to require that the fire officer be notified of the application.

C. Licensed and Unlicensed Premises

Festival Club

23–47 Section 13 of the Intoxicating Liquor Act 1962 provides for the grant of an occasional licence or a special exemption order in respect of social functions held for members of a club which are organised in connection with a festival which consists in the presentation of performances of music, dancing, plays, concerts or the showing of films. A special exemption order will be granted in respect of a licensed premises; an occasional licence will be granted in respect of an unlicensed premises. The applicant does not have to prove that a substantial meal is to be served to persons attending the function.[66] However, the sale of intoxicating liquor must be confined to members of the club which is arranging the function and to persons holding an invitation to the function issued in accordance with section 13(2) of the Intoxicating Liquor Act 1962.

STATUTORY PROVISION

23–48 Section 13 of the Intoxicating Liquor Act 1962 provides:

"(1) Where on application to it under section 11 of this Act or section 5 of the Act of 1927 the District Court is satisfied that —

(a) a festival consisting wholly or mainly of the presentation of performances of music, dancing or plays or showing of films or of any combination of such performances or showings is being held, and
(b) a *bona fide* club has been formed by the organisers of the festival the members of which are either persons performing at the festival or persons paying a single subscription the payment of which entitles them to attend each event of the festival or each event of a particular class, being a class constituting a significant part of the festival, or one event, at least, on each of the five or more consecutive days, and
(c) a social function is being held at a place that is either a place to which no licence for the sale of intoxicating liquor is attached or is a hotel or restaurant

[66] *Ibid.*, s.13(1).

by the members of the club, being a function that takes place during the period of the festival or a function that begins on the last day of the festival and ends on that day or on the day following that day,

the Court may, notwithstanding anything contained in section 11 of this Act, or section 5 of the Act of 1927, and irrespective of whether or not a substantial meal is to be served to persons attending the function, grant, upon such conditions as it thinks proper, either an occasional licence or a special exemption order, as may be appropriate, authorising the person making the application (being, in the case of an application for an occasional licence, the holder of an on-licence and, in the case of an application for a special exemption order, the holder of an on-licence for the premises to which the application relates) to sell at the place at which the function is being held, during such times and (subject to subsection (5) of section 11 of this Act or subsection (3) of section 5 of the Act of 1927) on such day or days as may be specified in the licence or order, as the case may be, such intoxicating liquor as he is authorised to sell by the on-licence aforesaid.

(2) It shall be a condition of an occasional licence or special exemption order granted in relation to a social function by virtue of this section that the sale of intoxicating liquor pursuant to the licence or order be confined to members of the club by whom the function is being held and to persons holding an invitation to the function (being a written invitation stating the name of the person invited issued not later than twenty-four hours before the commencement of the function) from the organisers of the festival during which the function is being held, that a list of the names of the members of the club and the persons invited to the function be kept by the organisers of the festival, that the list be open to inspection by the Garda Síochána and that the function be held in compliance with the relevant provisions of section 11 of this Act and section 5 of the Act of 1927 and of this section."

JURISDICTIONAL REQUIREMENTS

1. Venue **23–49**

   The District Court.

2. Applicant

   The applicant must be the holder of an on-licence.

3. The Event

   (a) The applicant must show that a "festival" as defined in section 13(1)(a) is being held;

   (b) the court must be satisfied that a bona fide club has been formed by the organisers of the festival and that the members of the club are either persons performing at the festival or persons who have paid a single subscription which entitles them to attend each event of the festival or each event of a particular class;

(c) the applicant must show that a social function is being held at the place (whether it is licensed or unlicensed) and that it takes place in accordance with section 13(1)(c) of the Intoxicating Liquor Act 1962;

(d) the applicant must show that the organisers of the festival during which the function is being held support the application;

(e) any invitation issued to persons who attend the function for which the order or licence is obtained must have been received at least 24 hours before the commencement of the function.

STATUTORY CONSEQUENCES

23–50 1. An occasional licence may not be granted in respect of any Sunday, Christmas Day, or Good Friday.[67]

2. A special exemption order will not be granted for a licensed premises for any time on a Sunday or for any time between 1 a.m. and 10.30 a.m. on a Monday.[68]

3. The occasional licence or special exemption order operates to permit the sale of intoxicating liquor to members of the club which has arranged the function and persons holding an invitation to the function in accordance with section 13(2) of the Intoxicating Liquor Act 1962.

4. Not more than one special exemption order or occasional licence can be granted on any day in relation to any festival.[69]

---

[67] Intoxicating Liquor Act 1962, s.13(1).
[68] *Ibid.*
[69] *Ibid.*, s.13(4).

CHAPTER 24

OFFENCES

Introduction

Throughout the entire history of the licensing code, the legislature has sought to regulate the licensed trade by the imposition of penalties on the holder of a licence for the commission of offences. Offences which the legislature regards as serious can result in the endorsement and indeed forfeiture of a licence. Many offences have been created by the licensing statutes during the last two centuries and it is beyond the scope of this work to consider each single offence. For ease of reference Appendix C1, below, lists offences under the Licensing Acts which are categorised as follows: **24–1**

(a) the offence;

(b) the statute pursuant to which it was created;

(c) the fine or penalty imposed;

(d) whether the offence is recordable;

(e) whether a conviction or convictions results in a forfeiture of the licence.

Appendix C2 lists offences under the Registration of Clubs Acts 1904 to 1905 and Appendix C3 sets forth offences in places of public entertainment.

A. Licensed Premises

24–2 Offences under the Licensing Acts can be grouped under seven broad headings as set out in Appendix C1.

1. Unlicensed Activities

The offences listed under this category may attract substantial monetary penalties and imprisonment. The offence of occupying an unlicensed drinking premises is an endorsable offence which can ultimately result in the forfeiture of a licence where the occupier is the holder of a licence to sell intoxicating liquor by retail.[1] The sale or exposing for sale of intoxicating liquor without a licence by the holder of a retail licence results in the forfeiture of a licence on a second or subsequent offence.[2]

The sale of intoxicating liquor without the required licence is regarded with the utmost seriousness by the legislature. Note, however that a prosecution for unlicensed sales will not succeed where a licence holder has applied at the appropriate time for a tax clearance certificate pursuant to the provisions of section 242 of the Finance Act 1992 at or before the time specified as his current licence continues in force for a certain period. Once an application for a tax clearance certificate has been duly made, the licence to which it relates continues in force after September 30 (the date of the expiry of the licence) until the grant or refusal of the tax clearance certificate or, where an appeal has been duly lodged, a specified period after the determination of such appeal.

2. Prohibited Hours

24–3 If a licence holder permits a person who is not an exempted person to be on his premises during prohibited hours, or sells intoxicating liquor on his premises during prohibited hours, he commits an offence which can be recorded on his licence at the discretion of the court.[3] The fines are substantial.

Six-Point Summons

24–4 A prosecution for breach of the licensing laws relating to prohibited hours takes the form of what is generally known as the six-point summons. If, at a time

---

1 Intoxicating Liquor Act 1962, s.26.
2 Intoxicating Liquor (General) Act 1924, s.7.
3 Intoxicating Liquor Act 1927, s.25, as amended by the Courts (No. 2) Act 1986.

when the sale of intoxicating liquor on the licensed premises is prohibited by law and when the premises are required to be closed, the licence holder:

1. sells intoxicating liquor;
2. exposes intoxicating liquor for sale;
3. opens the premises for the sale of intoxicating liquor;
4. keeps the premises open for the sale of intoxicating liquor;
5. permits intoxicating liquor to be consumed on the premises;
6. permits persons to be on the premises,

he commits an offence and is liable to prosecution.

The first five offences are created by section 2 of the Intoxicating Liquor Act 1927, as amended by section 25 of the Intoxicating Liquor Act 1988. The sixth offence was created by section 29 of the Intoxicating Liquor Act 1962, as amended by section 51 of the Intoxicating Liquor Act 1988. Although all these offences can arise out of the same transaction, the defendant may be convicted of more than one.

In *McCarthy v. Murphy*[4] Keane J. noted that the offences created by section 2 of the 1927 Act (counts 1 to 5), and the offence created by section 29 of the 1962 Act (count 6) were separate and distinct offences and that a licensee who was found guilty of an offence under section 2 of the 1927 Act was not necessarily guilty of an offence under section 29 of the 1962 Act. He stated: 24–5

> "The two offences being separate and distinct there seems no reason in principle why, where evidence is adduced which would support a conviction in respect of both offences, the defendant should not be convicted of both."[5]

In *The State (Armstrong) v. Donnelly*,[6] it was held that the offences contained in counts 5 and 6 are not of necessity offences which must always arise together: they are not a duplication and therefore a separate conviction for each is not precluded.

Permitting Consumption of Intoxicating Liquor on a Licensed Premises

Count 5, which is the offence of permitting the unlawful consumption of intoxicating liquor on a licensed premises does not impose absolute liability on the holder of a licence. In *Attorney General v. Carroll*, Hanna J. stated: 24–6

> "Now, under these circumstances did the publican in law 'permit' the consumption of the stout by the guests of the lodger? I think he did 'permit' it within the

[4] [1981] I.L.R.M. 213.
[5] *Ibid.* at 215.
[6] [1985] I.R. 636.

meaning of the Act. My reasons are as follows: From the publican's point of view, short of sharing in the stout himself, I do not see how he could have done anything more in fact to permit, suffer or allow the act. He was aware of all the circumstances in connection with the consumption of the drink, and suffered these persons to carry on their drinking in his presence – himself being one of the party – without protest or prevention or making any reasonable effort to carry out his duty under the Act."[7]

He expresses the test as follows:

"I am satisfied that the publican 'permits' in law the consumption of intoxicating liquor on his premises, if he does not take reasonable steps to prevent it. Here there was neither protest nor any attempt at prevention, but acquiescence and full knowledge."[8]

Permitting Persons to be on Licensed Premises

24–7 Count 6 on the six-point summons is an offence which was created by section 29 of the Intoxicating Liquor Act 1962. In *Duncan v. Gleeson*, Pringle J. stated:

"In my opinion, the onus remains on the prosecution to prove that the defendant permitted drink to be consumed, or persons to be on the premises after the permitted hours and the ten minutes allowed by section 7 of the Act of 1962; and that if the court is satisfied that the defendant took all reasonable steps to clear the premises on the expiry of the permitted hours and during the ten minute extension, the charges should be dismissed."[9]

24–8 Accordingly, whether the offence of "permitting" has been committed depends on the efforts made by the publican to clear the premises. In *McHale v. Cole*,[10] Judge McGivern referred to the words of section 29 of the 1962 Act and said:

"I must be satisfied that the licensee permitted the people to be on his premises. They must be there with his permission. The section contemplates the publican permitting people to be on his premises during the closing hours or failing to take the proper steps to clear the premises at closing time."[11]

In that case he was satisfied that every conceivable effort was made to clear the house and accordingly he dismissed the summonses and reversed the conviction.

In *Attorney General. v. Greeny*,[12] it was held that the District Court judge could not reasonably hold that the respondent publican could not clear the

[7] [1932] I.R. 1.
[8] *Ibid.* at 10.
[9] [1969] I.R. 116 at 120.
[10] (1966) 100 I.L.T.R. 83.
[11] *Ibid.* at 84.
[12] (1971) 105 I.L.T.R. 7.

premises by 11 p.m. or that he was unable to prevent or control the consumption of intoxicating liquor.

Open for Sale

Count 3 on the six-point summons was created by section 2 of the Intoxicating Liquor Act 1927. In *Davis v. Lennon*[13] Judge Davitt held that having persons within the premises does not *per se* render the defendant liable to conviction for having the premises open for sale, unless there was some means of access for customers to the interior of the premises from the outside. **24–9**

Lodgers

An offence is not committed if the sale of intoxicating liquor occurs during prohibited hours to persons who are resident permanently or temporarily on the premises.[14] This does not extend to the guest of such persons. In *Attorney General v. Egan* Maguire J. stated: **24–10**

> "I take the view that it would be inconsistent with the spirit of the [1927] Act that an exception which favours the lodger should be extended to the friends of the lodger."[15]

3. Underage Persons

Part IV of the Intoxicating Liquor Act 1988 introduced provisions relating to persons under the age of 18 years and repealed earlier provisions which created offences concerning young persons.[16] The expression "knowingly" which was contained in those sections is not used in Part IV of the Intoxicating Liquor Act 1988. Accordingly, Part IV imposes a higher duty of care on the licence holder and his servants or agents to ensure that an offence relating to underage drinking is not committed, than was the case under prior statutes. A number of offences under Part IV are endorsable. Where an offence is committed by a servant or agent of the holder of the licence without his knowledge and contrary to his express orders and directions, the licence holder cannot be convicted.[17] **24–11**

The sale and provision of intoxicating liquor to persons under the age of 18 years is prohibited under sections 31 and 32 of the Intoxicating Liquor Act 1988

---

13 [1939] 5 Ir. Jur. Rep. 44.
14 Intoxicating Liquor Act 1927, s.17, as substituted by the Intoxicating Liquor Act 1960, s.12.
15 [1943] I.R. 357 at 364.
16 Intoxicating Liquor Act 1988, s.4, repealed the Children Act 1908, s.120, and the Intoxicating Liquor (General) Act 1924, ss.10, 11, 12 and 25.
17 *Emary v. Nolloth* [1903] 2 K.B. 264.

respectively. An offence under section 31 of the 1988 is endorsable for the purposes of Part III of the Intoxicating Liquor Act 1927.[18] It is a defence in a prosecution under section 31 to prove that an age card was produced or that the accused had reasonable grounds for believing that the young person was over 18 years. The District Court and the Circuit Court on appeal have no discretion in relation to the endorsement of a licence for an offence under section 31. A licence holder may not permit a person under the age of 15 years to be in the bar of the premises without a parent or guardian.[19] Permitting a person under the age of 18 years to be on that part of a licensed premises which is used in consequence of a special exemption order is an endorsable offence.[20] It is a defence to such a charge under section 35(7) for the licensee to prove that he used all due diligence to prevent the underage person from being admitted to the premises or that such person produced an age card or that the licensee, his servants or agents, had reasonable grounds for believing that such person was over the age of 18 years.[21] Section 36 of the Intoxicating Liquor Act 1988 imposes a restriction on persons under the age of 18 years being on premises used for the sale of intoxicating liquor for consumption off the premises. Again, the offence is endorsable and the defence to the charge is similar to that available in respect of an offence under section 35 of the 1988 Act.[22]

The employment of a person under the age of 18 years (or 16 years in certain cases) is prohibited by section 38 of the 1988 Act, and the offence is endorsable for the purposes of Part III of the Intoxicating Liquor Act 1927.

4. Manufacture, Storage, Possession, Processing and Offering for Sale of Intoxicating Liquor

24–12 The sale of adulterated or illegally distilled liquor or liquor in incorrect measures constitutes an offence: some of these offences are endorsable and others can result in the forfeiture of a licence.

5. Other Substantive Offences: By Licensed Persons

24–13 Breach of the terms of a licence, the supply of intoxicating liquor on credit, permitting drunken or disorderly conduct on a premises, or using premises for a purpose other than as a licensed premises, may constitute an offence resulting in some instances in the forfeiture of a licence.

---

[18] Intoxicating Liquor Act 1988, ss.31(3).
[19] *Ibid.*, s.34. Note, however, that a conviction under this section does not give rise to an endorsement.
[20] *Ibid.*, s.35.
[21] *Ibid.*, s.35(7).
[22] *Ibid.*, s.36(7).

6. Other Substantive Offences: General

The only offence in this category which can result in the forfeiture of a licence is the making of an internal communication between a licensed premises and an area which is used for public entertainment or resort, or as a refreshment house. A conviction on this charge leads to automatic forfeiture of the licence. A "licensed premises" for this purpose is a premises to which a licence granted on foot of a court certificate attaches. **24–14**

7. Procedural, Enforcement and Miscellaneous Offences

These are listed below in Appendix C. **24–15**

General Defences

Certain defences may be available in addition to those already mentioned. For example, the defendant can apply to dismiss the summons on the grounds of delay where an application for the issue of the summons is not made within six months of the date of the alleged offence. **24–16**

A possible defence open to an employer is to show that he should not be held vicariously liable for offences committed by his servants or agents. Where the manager of a licensed premises contravenes the provisions relating to prohibited hours and acts outside the scope of his employment, the licence holder will not be convicted of the offence of permitting intoxicating liquor to be consumed on licensed premises during prohibited hours.[23]

In *Devlin v. Nugent*,[24] liquor was supplied by the hall porter employed in a licensed premises during prohibited hours. It was held that he was acting without authority and outside the scope of his employment. In *Herlihy v. McFeely*,[25] it was held that a licensee is not relieved of liability in an offence under section 29 of the Intoxicating Liquor Act 1962 where he delegates control to a resident manageress, who permits persons to be upon the premises during prohibited hours. Judge McWilliam referred to the case of *Emary v. Nolloth* and noted Lord Alverstone's statement:

> "If the offence is prohibited in itself, knowledge on the part of the licensee is immaterial. . . . Then comes the class of case in which the licensee is charged with knowingly allowing, permitting or suffering an offence to be committed:

[23] *O'Halloran v. Taylor* (1926) 60 I.L.T.R. 6 and *Finnerty v. Carroll* [1941] 7 Ir. Jur. Rep. 58.
[24] (1942) 76 I.L.T.R. 117.
[25] (1976) 110 I.L.T.R. 6.

> in those cases knowledge is essential; but . . . if the licensee delegated his authority to someone else..and the person left in charge commits the offence, the licensee is responsible for permitting it . . . ".[26]

Following the decision in *Emary v. Nolloth*, McWilliam J. held that as the defendant delegated the authority for the entire management of the premises to the manageress, he was not entitled to have the charge dismissed.

24–17 A nominee who participates in the running of the licensed premises can be prosecuted as principal offender.[27] Where, however, the nominee has "no hand, act or part" in the running of the premises, and did not aid or abet the commission of the offences as charged, he has a defence. In *D.P.P. v. Roberts* Finlay C.J. stated:

> "At common law, a person is not criminally responsible for the unauthorised act of its servants or agents. Even when a statutory provision can be so construed the offence of 'permitting' by its very definition postulates something in the nature of guilty knowledge."[28]

However, Finlay C.J. in that case queried Barrington J.'s statement in *McMahon v. Murtagh Properties Ltd*[29] that a nominee participating in the running of the business of a licensed premises could be prosecuted for aiding and abetting the commission of an offence, insofar as that would be interpreted as indicating that such a person could not be prosecuted as a principal offender. He stated:

> "*Prima facie* it would appear that section 2 of the Act of 1927 provides for the commission of an offence by any person involved in licensed trading after hours, irrespective of whether he is the holder of a licence or not."[30]

In the *Roberts* case, the defendant who held the licence as nominee took no part in the business. The Supreme Court held that while the concept of a nominee holding a licence on behalf of a body corporate would ordinarily give the impression that the nominee warranted to control the servants, agents or officers of the company so as to ensure compliance with the law, this was not sufficient to render a person guilty of a criminal offence which the statute did not make one of strict liability. Griffin and Hederman JJ. dissented, Griffin J. noting that there was an exception to the rule that an accused person could not be convicted of a criminal offence unless he had a guilty mind. The exception was that in respect of offences under the licensing law:

---

[26] Above, n.17, at 269.
[27] *D.P.P. v. Roberts* [1987] I.R. 268.
[28] *Ibid.* at 274.
[29] [1982] I.L.R.M. 342.
[30] *D.P.P. v. Roberts*, above, n.27, at 275.

> "a principle has been established that a licensee cannot avoid criminal liability for breaches of the licensing laws by those to whom he has in reality delegated his powers, duties and obligations under the Acts – duties and responsibilities which, by accepting the licence, he incurred and were imposed on him under the Acts".[31]

B. Clubs

Cancellation of Certificate of Registration

Unlike the provisions which relate to a licensed premises, there is nothing in the registration of clubs code which provides for the endorsement or forfeiture of a certificate of registration. However, a District Court judge is entitled to cancel a certificate of registration, on application by a "competent objector", where the club is being managed as to constitute a ground of objection to the renewal of its certificate. **24–18**

Section 9(1) of the Registration of Clubs (Ireland) Act 1904 provides that a competent objector may make a summary complaint and the court can convict or make an order that the club is being managed so as to constitute a ground of objection to renewal. The court may then, "having regard to the magnitude of the offence or to the grounds specified as aforesaid", cancel the certificate for the outstanding period.[32]

The court may also direct that the club premises may not be used for the purposes of any club which requires registration "for up to 12 months for a first order, and up to five years for a second or subsequent order".[33]

STATUTORY PROVISION

Section 9(1) of the Registration of Clubs (Ireland) Act 1904 provides: **24–19**

> "On summary complaint by or at the instance of any person competent to lodge objections to the grant or renewal of a certificate of registration it shall be lawful for the court to make an order that, on grounds to be specified therein, a registered club is being so managed or carried on as to constitute a ground of objection to the renewal of its certificate as hereinbefore provided."

These grounds are as follows:

1. that it is not conducted in good faith as a club, or that it is kept or habitually used for any unlawful purpose, or mainly for the supply of excisable liquor;

---

[31] *Ibid.* at 279.
[32] Registration of Clubs (Ireland) Act 1904, s.9(2).
[33] *Ibid.*, s.9(3).

2. the character of the chairman, secretary or member of the committee;
3. the suitability of the premises;
4. that the club has ceased to exist or that the number of members is less than 150;
5. that illegal sales of excisable liquor have taken place on the club premises;
6. that there is frequent drunkenness on the club premises, or that persons in a state of intoxication are frequently seen to leave the club premises, or that the club is conducted in a disorderly manner;
7. that persons who are not members are habitually admitted to the club merely for the purpose of obtaining excisable liquor;
8. that the supply of excisable liquor is not under the control of members or the committee appointed by its members;
9. that any of the rules of the club are habitually broken;
10. that the rules have been changed so as not to be in conformity with the provisions of the 1904 Act as amended;

An offence can be committed by an unregistered club and by a registered club. Some of these offences are dealt with below: for a more comprehensive list see Appendix C2, below

1. Registered Club

Advertising a Function

24–20 It is an offence to publish an advertisement relating to any function to be held on the premises of a registered club, save in accordance with section 45(2) of the Intoxicating Liquor Act 1988. The offence may be committed by the registered club and by every person entered in the register of clubs as an official or member of the committee of management or governing body of the club at the time the advertisement is published, or by any person who published or caused the advertisement to be published.[34] An official or member of the committee may defend a prosecution by proof that the advertisement was issued without his consent or connivance or that he exercised all due diligence to prevent its publication. A person who published the advertisement or who caused it to be published may defend the prosecution where he can prove:

> "that he is a person whose business it is to publish or arrange for the publication of advertisements and that he received the advertisement in question for publication in the ordinary course of business and did not know and had no

[34] Intoxicating Liquor Act 1988, s.45.

reason to suspect that its publication would constitute an offence under the said subsection (1)".[35]

No offence is committed where the advertisement is published inside the premises of the registered club in which the function is to be held nor if the advertisement relates to a function involving any sport, game or physical recreation which does not take place outside the hours during which excisable liquor may be supplied and consumed on the club premises in accordance with the club rules. It seems clear that a club cannot externally advertise a function which does not involve a sport, game or physical recreation. The expression "function" is not defined but it usually involves dancing and music.

Any function which takes place outside normal permitted hours is expressly prohibited. A club is not entitled to advertise occasions for which it has obtained club authorisations.

"Advertisement" includes all forms of advertising, *i.e.* in a newspaper or periodical, by the display of notices, by means of circulars or other documents, or by exhibition of photographs, or by cinematograph film, or by way of sound broadcasting or television, or by inclusion in a cable programme service.[36]

Prohibited Hours

It is an offence to supply intoxicating liquor for consumption on club premises outside permitted hours. **24–21**

STATUTORY PROVISION

Section 58 of the Intoxicating Liquor Act 1927, as amended by section 51 of the Intoxicating Liquor Act 1988, provides:

(1) If any excisable liquor is supplied for consumption on the premises of a club registered under the Registration of Clubs (Ireland) Act, 1904, or is consumed on the premises of any such club by any person in contravention of the rules of such club relating to the supplying and consumption of excisable liquor on the premises of such club, such club shall be guilty of an offence under this section and shall be liable on summary conviction thereof, in the case of a first offence, to a fine not exceeding £300 or, in the case of a second or any subsequent offence, to a fine not exceeding £500.

(2) Proceedings under this section may be brought against a club in the name under which it is registered under the Registration of Clubs (Ireland) Act, 1904, and any summons or other document required to be served on a club for the purpose or in the course of such proceedings may be served on the secretary of the club and any warrant for the recovery of the amount of a fine imposed on the club under this section may be executed against the goods and chattels of the club."

---

[35] *Ibid.*, s.45(4).
[36] *Ibid.*, s.45(6).

24–22 In *Newman v. Jones*,[37] the club steward was instructed by the members of the committee to serve intoxicating liquor only to members and affiliated members of the club but he disobeyed this instruction. Despite the fact that the money taken by the steward went into the coffers of the club, the court held that no offence had been committed by the club; the trustees were not responsible for the acts of the steward since he acted contrary to their orders and without their knowledge or consent.

Unlike the provisions which relate to a licensed premises, there is no provision for endorsement or forfeiture of the club certificate where an offence under section 58 has been committed. However, a District Court judge may cancel the certificate of registration on application by a competent objector and may make an order finding that illegal sales of excisable liquor have taken place on the club premises.

Service of Summons

24–23 If an offence has been committed by a club, the summons may be served on the club by leaving it with an employee of the club at the club's principal office, or by sending the summons by registered letter to the principal office.[38]

2. Unregistered Club

24–24 The sale, supply or purchase of liquor on the premises of an unregistered club is an offence. The offender, whether he sells or supplies the liquor or authorises its sale or supply or whether he pays for it can be fined and imprisoned.[39] The keeping of liquor for supply or sale on the premises of an unregistered club is an offence exposing every officer and member of the club to liability.[40] If a certificate of registration lapses, is cancelled or is not renewed, the club can be prosecuted pursuant to section 9 of the Registration of Clubs (Ireland) Act 1904.

C. Places of Public Entertainment

24–25 An offence can be committed in respect of a premises which is licensed under the Public Health Act Amendment Act 1890 or the Public Dance Halls Act 1935. It is an offence to use an unlicensed place for public dancing, music or singing where a licence is required. Offences under the provisions are listed below, in Appendix C3.

---

[37] [1886] 17 Q.B.D. 132.
[38] District Court Rules 1948, r. 48(2).
[39] Registration of Clubs (Ireland) Act 1904, s.7(1).
[40] *Ibid.*, s.7(2).

Chapter 25

ENDORSEMENT

Introduction

Convictions on liquor licences are recorded by the District Court, and on appeal by the Circuit Court.[1] Part III of the Intoxicating Liquor Act 1927 provided for the endorsement of a licence in respect of certain offences. These offences are listed in the First Schedule to that Act. Further endorsable offences were introduced by subsequent legislation.[2] Section 35 of the Intoxicating Liquor Act 1927 precludes the application of the Probation of Offenders Act 1907 to endorsable offences. This can have grave consequences for the holder of a licence, as a licence with three current endorsements is forfeit, with the result that no new licence can at any time thereafter be granted in respect of that premises or any part thereof.[3] Because of the serious implications for the publican, the legislature has given the court a discretion, where a number of offences are committed on the same day, to order that some, but not all, be recorded.[4] **25–1**

Further, in 1986 the legislature restored the discretion of the District Court and, on appeal, the Circuit Court to decide *not* to endorse a licence in respect of offences relating to prohibited hours.[5] Part III of the 1927 Act applies to all licences for the sale of intoxicating liquor by retail even where the grant of such licence does not depend upon obtaining a certificate of the court. In *Lohan v.*

[1] Intoxicating Liquor Act 1927, s.27.
[2] *e.g.* the offence of permitting persons to be on licensed premises during prohibited hours was introduced by s.29 of the Intoxicating Liquor Act 1962.
[3] Intoxicating Liquor Act 1927, s.28.
[4] *Ibid.*, s.29.
[5] *Ibid.*, s.25, as amended by the Courts (No. 2) Act 1986, s.6; and Intoxicating Liquor Act 1927, s.27, as amended by the Courts (No. 2) Act 1986, s.7.

Fusco the Supreme Court held that the provisions of section 25(1) of the 1927 Act applied to a wine retailer's on-licence, FitzGerald J. stating:

> "In ordinary language the respondents are holders of "licences" which entitle them to sell intoxicating liquor. The definition of licence in the Act of 1874 restricted the meaning of the word "licence" in the Licensing (Ireland) Act, 1833 to 1924, to such as were "certificated" but that restriction has been removed by the Act of 1927 as amended by the Act of 1943."[6]

The summons charging the holder of a licence with an endorsable offence must state that "such holder will be required to produce such licence to the Court at such trial".[7] At the trial the court "shall require such holder to produce such licence and deliver the same to the registrar, clerk, or other principal officer of the Court".[8]

Two or More Offences on the Same Day

(a) Discretion to Record

25–2 Section 29 of the Intoxicating Liquor Act 1927 gives the court a discretion, when entering a number of convictions in respect of offences committed on the same day to order that some, but not all, of them be recorded. This discretion is generally exercised by the District Court on a six-point summons. The usual order is to convict in respect of one count on the summons and if the judge exercises his discretion under section 29 of the 1927 Act only that one conviction is recorded. The power to record "one or more . . . but not all" convictions arises in respect of all endorsable offences to which Part III of the 1927 Act applies, but only if committed on the same day.

25–3 In *The State (Armstrong) v. Donnelly*[9] the Supreme Court was satisfied from "a careful reading of that section" that a person convicted of more than one offence arising on the same day, who has not any previous convictions entered against him can, in the discretion of the court, be left free of any recorded convictions". To ensure this result, the court must exercise its discretion by directing that any other conviction entered in respect of the same date be not recorded. Finlay J. stated:

> "The section is not to be construed as imposing an obligation on the court in the exercise of its discretion to record one conviction in every case, but merely provides that the exemption from recording cannot be applied by the court to all the convictions entered. Read, therefore, in my view, with section 25(4) [the

---

[6] [1967] I.R. 11 at 27.
[7] Intoxicating Liquor Act 1927, s.32(1).
[8] *Ibid.*
[9] [1985] I.R. 636.

> "First Bite" provision[10]], the court may, if it decides to exercise its discretion, in the case of a person without any previous conviction, leave the legal effect of its decision that the first conviction, by virtue of section 25(4) is not recorded in any event and that the court in exercise of its discretion under section 29 countermands the recording of any other conviction entered in respect of the same date."[11]

In *Attorney General (O'Muireadhaigh) v. Boles*[12] it was held that section 29 does not apply in respect of two or more convictions imposed by the court on the same day in respect of offences committed on different days.

(b) Separate and Distinct Offences

In *McCarthy v. Murphy*,[13] Keane J. held that the charge of permitting persons to be on the licensed premises during prohibited hours and the charge of permitting consumption of intoxicating liquor on the licensed premises on the same occasion are separate and distinct offences. He stated: 25–4

> "A licensee who permits a workman carrying out repairs to the premises . . . to be on the premises during the prohibited hours commits no offence. If, however, he permits that person to consume intoxicating liquor on the premises during the prohibited hours, he commits an offence. A licensee who is found guilty of one of the two offences under consideration is not necessarily guilty of the other offence. The two offences being separate and distinct there seems no reason in principle why, where evidence is adduced which would support a conviction in respect of both offences, the defendant should not be convicted of both."[14]

In the *Armstrong*[15] case, Finlay C.J. approved of Keane J.'s conclusions and in respect of the offences in the case before him he pronounced himself satisfied that those were not of necessity offences "which must always arise together and are not in any sense a duplication of offences".

It should be noted that the offence of permitting consumption of intoxicating liquor during prohibited hours was created by section 2 of the 1927 Act, and the offence of permitting persons to be on the premises during prohibited hours was created by section 29 of the Intoxicating Liquor Act 1962.

(c) "First Bite"

Where a licence holder is convicted for the first time of an endorsable offence in relation to a particular premises, he is entitled to avail of the "first bite" 25–5

[10] See below, para. 25–5 for an explanation of the "first bite" principle which applied in this case.
[11] *State (Armstrong) v. Donnelly*, above, n.9, at 641.
[12] [1963] I.R. 420.
[13] [1981] I.L.R.M. 213.
[14] *Ibid.* at 215.
[15] Above, n.9.

principle, *i.e.* that the conviction is not recorded on the licence. This applies to all endorsable offences, including those which attract a mandatory endorsement.

STATUTORY PROVISION

Section 25(4) of the Intoxicating Liquor Act 1927, as inserted by section 37(1) of the Intoxicating Liquor Act 1960, provides as follows:

> "Notwithstanding anything contained in sub-section (1) of this section, where a person is convicted in relation to any premises in respect of which he holds a licence for the sale of intoxicating liquor by retail of an offence to which this Part of this Act applies and the conviction is the first conviction of that person in relation to those premises of an offence to which this Part of this Act applies, the conviction shall not be recorded on the licence."

25–6 Where, however, a licensee is convicted of two offences which relate to one transaction or incident but the court does not exercise its discretion under section 29 of the Intoxicating Liquor Act 1927, the first bite provision cannot be availed of to preclude the recording of both convictions. In *The State (Armstrong) v. Donnelly*,[16] the prosecutor applied to the respondent District Court judge for a certificate of no objection to the transfer to the prosecutor of a wine retailer's on-licence held by a company. Prior to this application, the company had been convicted of two offences relating to incidents which occurred on November 23 to 24, 1982, and two further offences relating to incidents which occurred on November 26 to 27, 1982, all of which were recordable offences.

The District Court judge refused to exercise his discretion[17] to order that one of each of the two convictions imposed for offences committed on the same day should not be recorded on the licence. Three of the convictions were endorsed on the licence as the Prosecutor was entitled to avail of the first bite principle. Mr Armstrong then applied to the court for a certificate of no objection to the transfer to him of the wine retailer's on-licence held by the company. The District Court judge refused the application on the ground that as a result of the endorsements, the licence had been forfeited pursuant to section 28 of the 1927 Act and therefore could not be transferred. The issue to be determined by the Supreme Court was whether the first bite principle should be construed to exclude first time convictions of any person in respect of a single date from compulsory recording, or whether it should be construed as excluding only the first conviction imposed on any person from mandatory recording. The latter interpretation would require any second or subsequent conviction imposed in respect of an offence on the same date as the first offence to be

---

[16] *Ibid.*
[17] Conferred by the Intoxicating Liquor Act 1927, s.29.

mandatorily recorded, subject to the discretion vested in the District Court by section 29 of the 1927 Act.

Finlay C.J. held:

> "In my view it is impossible to construe "conviction" throughout that sub-section [Section 25(4)] in the plural without doing violence to the meaning of the words contained in it. Whilst . . . it may be possible to speak of "first convictions", it is not, in my view, possible to construe "second" and "third" and "every subsequent" "convictions" without altering and doing violence to the meaning of the sub-section. There arises, therefore, a relatively strong presumption to be implied from the section to which sub-section (4) was added that the plural meaning of the word 'conviction' is not to be implied".[18]

Accordingly, where two convictions are sustained in respect of a single date, the holder of the licence may use the "first bite" principle in respect of the first conviction only.

Where a previous endorsement has been recorded but has expired, a licence holder cannot avail of the "first bite" provision.[19]

Conviction: Where Court has Discretion not to Endorse

Section 6 of the Courts (No. 2) Act 1986 restored the discretion of the District Court *not* to record convictions by amending section 25 of the 1927 Act relating to offences concerning prohibited hours. 25–7

STATUTORY PROVISION

Section 25(1) of the Intoxicating Liquor Act 1927, as amended by section 6 of the Courts (No. 2) Act 1986, provides:

> "Subject to the provisions of sub-section 1(A) of this section, whenever the holder of any licence for the sale of intoxicating liquor by retail is convicted of an offence to which this Part of this Act applies, the conviction subject to subsection (4) of this section shall, if the person so convicted is the holder of one such licence only, be recorded on such licence or, if such person is the holder of two or more such licences in respect of the same premises, be recorded on all such licences or, if such person is the holder of two or more such licences which do not all relate to the same premises, be recorded on such one or more of those licences as relate to the premises in respect of which the offence was committed.
>
> 1(A) In the case of a conviction for any offence relating to prohibited hours, the provisions of subsection (1) of this section shall apply only if the Court in its discretion so thinks proper."

[18] *The State (Armstrong) v. Donnelly*, above, n.9, at 641.
[19] *D.P.P. v. Farrell* (1980) 114 I.L.T.R.106.

STATUTORY PROVISION

25–8 Section 27 of the Intoxicating Liquor Act 1927, as amended by section 7 of the Courts (No. 2) Act 1986, confers discretion upon the Circuit Court on appeal.

> "(1) Whenever the holder of any licence for the sale of intoxicating liquor is convicted by a Justice of the District Court of an offence to which this part of this Act applies, an appeal shall lie from such conviction to the Judge of the Circuit Court within whose circuit the District or any part of the District of such Justice is situate, and the decision of such Judge shall be final and not appealable.
>
> (2) On the hearing of an appeal under subsection (1) of this section from a conviction for an offence relating to prohibited hours, the Judge of the Circuit Court may, although affirming the conviction, make, if in his discretion he so thinks proper, an order declaring that such conviction shall not be recorded on such licence and, whenever such an order is so made, such conviction shall not be so recorded and shall for all purposes be deemed never to have been so recorded and, accordingly, any forfeiture occasioned by the recording of such conviction shall be deemed to be cancelled."

Accordingly, a District Court judge and on appeal a Circuit Court judge, has a discretionary power not to record a conviction which relates to prohibited hours.

The licence which is endorsed is the licence which attaches to the premises in respect of which the offence was committed. If more than one licence is attached to such premises, all licences are endorsed.[20]

Conviction: Where Court must Endorse

25–9 Part III of the Intoxicating Liquor Act 1927 requires the District Court and on appeal, the Circuit Court, to record convictions on licences in respect of "offences to which this Part of this Act applies". As explained, a court may only exercise a discretion not to endorse in two circumstances, namely, where the offence relates to prohibited hours or where two or more endorsable offences were committed on the same day. In all other cases, the court must record particulars of the conviction on the licence unless the "first bite" provision applies. The latter offences include the following:

1. any offence against any of the enactments mentioned in the First Schedule to the Intoxicating Liquor Act 1927. These offences include the following:
   (a) permitting drunkenness or violent conduct on licensed premises and supplying intoxicating liquor to disorderly persons;

---

[20] *i.e.* if the licences are off-licences.

(b) permitting licensed premises to be used for certain disorderly purposes;

(c) harbouring and bribing, etc., of the police by licensed persons;

(d) permitting gaming on licensed premises;

(e) obstructing entry of the police to a licensed premises;

(f) prohibition on sale of intoxicating liquor by credit[21];

2. offences against any enactments for the time being in force relating to the adulteration of intoxicating liquor;
3. the sale of intoxicating liquor by retail without being duly licensed or at a place where a person is not authorised by his licence to sell intoxicating liquor[22];
4. offences relating to persons under 18 on licensed premises[23];
5. offences relating to special restaurant licences[24];
6. offences under the Betting Acts.

Duration of Endorsement

Where a conviction is recorded, the first conviction remains so recorded for a period of two years from the date of conviction, the second for a four-year period and the third and subsequent convictions for six years. **25–10**

STATUTORY PROVISION

Section 25(2) and (3) of the Intoxicating Liquor Act 1927[25] provides:

> "(2) Whenever a conviction of the holder of a licence is under this section recorded on such licence such conviction shall, in the case of the first conviction so recorded on such licence after the passing of this Act, continue so recorded for the period of two years from the date of the conviction and, in the case of the second conviction so recorded on such licence after the passing of this Act, continue so recorded for the period of four years from the date of the conviction and, in the case of the third conviction and of every subsequent conviction so recorded on such licence after the passing of this Act, continue so recorded for the period of six years from the date of the conviction.

[21] Payment by a credit card is not a sale on credit. See *Re Charge Card Services Ltd* [1988] 3 W.L.R. 764 (C.A.).
[22] Intoxicating Liquor (General) Act 1924, s.7.
[23] Intoxicating Liquor Act 1988, Part IV.
[24] *Ibid.*, Part II.
[25] Intoxicating Liquor Act 1927, s.25(2) was amended by the Intoxicating Liquor Act 1960, s.37(1)(b), and the Courts (No. 2) Act 1986, s.6.

(3) Every conviction recorded on a licence under this section shall, at the expiration of the period during which under the foregoing sub-section the same is to continue recorded, cease for all purposes to be so recorded."

Where the period of an endorsement is spent, despite the wording of section 25(3), the consequences for a subsequent endorsement cannot be considered without regard to the previous conviction recorded on the licence. Accordingly, if a two year endorsement is spent, a subsequent endorsement remains recorded for four years and even where such subsequent endorsement has ceased to be recorded, an endorsement which is later in time again must remain recorded on the licence for six years. In *D.P.P. v. Farrell* Judge Sheridan stated:

"A clear distinction emerges from the various sections of the code between a conviction on the one hand and the recording of a conviction on the other. In my view, notwithstanding section 25(3) of the 1927 Act, the conviction remains even when the endorsement ceases for all purposes to be recorded. It was open to the Legislature to provide that the person shall be deemed never to have been convicted which phrase occurs twice in the very next sub-sections namely, section 37(2)(a) and (2)(b) of the 1960 Act... In my view, it would be straining the sub-section far too far to admit such construction . . .".[26]

Omission to Record Conviction on Licence

25–11 The District Court clerk is obliged by virtue of section 32(2) of the Intoxicating Liquor Act 1927, to endorse the date and other particulars of a conviction on a licence. If a conviction occasions the forfeiture of a licence, the licence should be retained by the District Court clerk who must also send a notice of such forfeiture to the Revenue Commissioners. The District Court clerk must enter details of convictions in the register of licences.

In *The State (Armstrong) v. Donnelly*, Finlay C.J. considered the obligation of the District Court Clerk under the section:

". . . I have no doubt that there is a clear and direct mandatory obligation on the District Court, through the agency of the clerk to that court, to comply with the statutory provisions and to endorse on each licence, on the occasion of each conviction, a conviction which by law falls to be endorsed thereon."[27]

STATUTORY PROVISION

25–12 Section 31 of the Intoxicating Liquor Act 1927 provides that an omission to record a conviction does not affect the validity of the conviction or forfeiture:

"An omission to record on a licence a conviction which is by this Act required

---

[26] Above, n.19, at 108.
[27] Above, n.9, at 642.

> to be recorded thereon shall not prejudice or affect the validity or effect of such conviction or (unless such omission is made by order of a Court under this Act) relieve the convicted person from any consequence which would ensue from such conviction if it had been so recorded."

In the *Armstrong* case, Finlay C.J. was informed that as a matter of practice the recording of convictions on a licence in the Metropolitan District Court was neither expressly ordered in the order of conviction nor was it carried out by the clerk of the Court. He stated:

> "I am satisfied that if this practice in the Metropolitan District Court still continues, it is a matter of urgent necessity that it should be altered and the statute complied with".[28]

In *Application of Doreen Riordan*,[29] Finlay P. held that section 31 of the 1927 Act does not invalidate an order of a court of record, even where the order was based on an error within rather than in excess of that court's jurisdiction. In that case, a licence had become forfeited by operation of law, but nonetheless it was renewed annually over the following five years. Finlay P. stated: 25–13

> "The question which I must ask myself however, is as to whether this section could be construed so as to make a total variation in what I understand to be the continuing force and effect of an apparently valid order of a Court of Record or could be said to be a qualification or exception to the general principles with regard to orders made by inferior courts within their jurisdiction even when they are based on an error within that jurisdiction. I am satisfied that so to construe it would be quite unwarranted by the terms of the section itself and would be inconsistent with what I would deem to be an obligation strictly to construe a section which appears to be stringent against the individual. For these reasons I am satisfied that the more fundamental and general principle of the validity of the orders made must survive . . .".[30]

That decision was made at a time when an applicant was obliged to apply to the annual licensing District Court for a certificate as to the peaceable and orderly manner in which his premises had been conducted in the immediately preceding year and as to his good character, which he would present to the Revenue Commissioners for the issue of the licence. Since the coming into force and effect of the Courts (No. 2) Act 1986 however, the application for a certificate is unnecessary (save in the case of an objection to the renewal of a licence and the circumstances enumerated in section 4 thereof) so the licence is renewed without a court certificate. Accordingly, it is likely that the renewal of a licence by the Revenue Commissioners, which had become forfeit by operation of law will be declared to be invalid.

---

[28] *Ibid.*
[29] [1981] I.L.R.M. 2.
[30] *Ibid.* at 9.

Holder of Licence Liable to Conviction

25–14 The appropriate person to be charged and convicted of an offence under Part III of the Intoxicating Liquor Act 1927 is the holder of the licence. In *Fitzpatrick v. McCormack*,[31] it was held by the Supreme Court that an ad interim transferee was the holder of the licence for the purposes of Part III of the Intoxicating Liquor Act 1927. The Court was satisfied that the intention of the Public House (Ireland) Act 1855 was that the licence should indicate the authority of the transferee to trade under it on its face. Finlay C.J. stated:

> "Having regard to the terms of Part III of the Act of 1927, however, if the contention made on behalf of the defendant were correct, namely, that the transferee under the order made under section 1 of the Act of 1855, namely, Stella Fitzpatrick, is not the holder of a licence, then the extraordinarily anomalous position arises that she is wholly immune from the consequences of recording and forfeiture which flow from repeated convictions."[32]

Once the ad interim transfer has been granted, the ad interim transferee is subject to the penalties and restrictions created by Part III of the 1927 Act and is liable for convictions sustained from the time he becomes the ad interim transferee.

Transfer of Licensed Premises:

(a) Bona Fide Sale

25–15 Where an applicant seeks a certificate or confirmation of a transfer and proves to the court that the transaction is a bona fide transaction, then he can make a contemporaneous application under section 30 of the Intoxicating Liquor Act 1927 requesting the court to direct that any endorsements on the licence be deleted.

STATUTORY PROVISION

Section 30(1) of the Intoxicating Liquor Act 1927 provides:

> "Whenever, on an application for a certificate for the transfer of a licence for the sale of intoxicating liquor by retail, the applicant at the time of such application satisfies the Court that the transfer is desired for the purpose of giving effect to a *bona fide* sale for money or money's worth of such licence and the premises to which the same is attached, the Court shall, if it grants such certificate, direct in and by such certificate that all (if any) offences then recorded on such licence under this Part of this Act shall at the time of such

[31] [1986] I.R. 380.
[32] *Ibid*. at 391.

> transfer cease to be so recorded, and whenever such direction is so given every such offence shall at the time of the transfer of such licence pursuant to such certificate cease to be recorded on such licence and such licence shall be so transferred freed and discharged from the records of such offences and shall thereafter have effect for all purposes as if such offences had never been recorded thereon."

So, where the court makes a section 30 order, the new licence has all the advantages of a clean licence, including the first bite provisions of the licensing code. The court must be satisfied that the transfer is a bona fide transfer and not a device to evade the provisions of the 1927 Act.

(b) Original Transfer

Where an applicant for a certificate of transfer disposed of premises to a person who made a successful section 30 application, and his present application is made within five years of the original section 30 application, any offences recorded on the original licence will be recorded on the licence of the applicant for transfer, the duration of the endorsements to take effect from the date of the grant of the present certificate of transfer.[33] **25–16**

This section only applies where the holder of the licence makes a bona fide transfer of his licence to a third party and later applies for a new licence in his own name.

In *Application of Hesketh Investments Ltd*,[34] Barrington J. held that section 30(2) of the Intoxicating Liquor Act 1927 did not apply where a company was applying for a certificate of transfer and evidence was adduced that a conviction had been recorded against two directors of the company in respect of another licensed premises of which those two directors were joint licensees. He stated:

> "In the present case a newly incorporated company has acquired a licence from a *bona fide* vendor against whom there is, so far as I am aware, no recorded conviction. Yet it is suggested that there should be recorded on the licence of the company, not the recorded convictions of the transferors of the publican's business, but the recorded convictions of private individuals who are now shareholders and directors of the company. But it appears to me that this suggestion also misses the fact that the parties involved are different legal entities . . . the learned President has accepted that the present transaction is a *bona fide* sale and the issue is whether, in the light of this finding, he is *obliged* to record on the licence of the applicant company a conviction recorded against the persons who are now directors of the company when they were acting in a different capacity as owners and managers of a different business. In my view, he is not so obliged."[35]

---

[33] Intoxicating Liquor Act 1927, s.30(2).
[34] [1984] I.L.R.M. 134.
[35] *Ibid*. at 137 and 138.

Grant of New Licence

25–17 Certain sections of the licensing code preserve endorsements which attach to a licence once it is extinguished on the grant of a new licence. In *D.P.P. v. Farrell*[36] Judge Sheridan noted that the grant of the new licence, in certain cases, was conditional upon the carrying forward of endorsements recorded on the old or extinguished licence. The legislature has made statutory provision for the preservation of endorsements. A new licence granted under certain sections must contain endorsements which were recorded on the old licence. In some instances, convictions recorded on the old licence at the time of the grant of the new licence are deemed to be recorded on the new licence and to have been so recorded on the date on which the convictions were recorded on the old licence.

So, by operation of law, the endorsements on the old licence are carried forward. A conviction will only be carried forward if it was sustained at a time when the applicant for the new licence was the holder of the old licence. Licences granted pursuant to the exceptions contained in the Licensing (Ireland) Act 1902 are not caught by this condition: subsequent statutes, however, made the grant of a new licence conditional upon the preservation of endorsements on the prior licence. These are as follows:

25–18

1. Section 21 of the Intoxicating Liquor Act 1943 provides that a conviction recorded on the extinguished licence shall be carried forward but only if it became recorded on the old licence at a time when the applicant was the holder thereof.[37] This section permits the grant of a new licence for more convenient premises in a rural area.
2. Section 22 of the Intoxicating Liquor Act 1943 provides that a conviction recorded on the extinguished licence is carried forward but only where that conviction became recorded at a time when the applicant was the holder of the licence.[38] This section permits the grant of the new licence for a premises which is substituted for destroyed premises.
3. Sections 6 to 9 of the Intoxicating Liquor Act 1953 provides that any convictions recorded on a former licence are deemed to be recorded on the new licence.[39] These provisions deal with the grant of a new licence for premises in substitution for premises demolished by the Local Authority. The conviction will only be carried forward if it was sustained on the old licence during a time when the applicant was the licensee.
4. Section 13 of the Intoxicating Liquor Act 1960 provides that a conviction will only be carried forward if it became recorded on either of the old

---

[36] Above, n.19.
[37] Intoxicating Liquor Act 1943, s.21, and the Intoxicating Liquor Act 1960, s.26.
[38] Intoxicating Liquor Act 1943, s.22, and the Intoxicating Liquor Act 1960, s.26.
[39] Intoxicating Liquor Act 1953, s.7(3)(d).

licences when the applicant for the new licence was the holder of the licences at the time the convictions were recorded. If more than two convictions are recorded on the old licences, it is provided that only the latest two convictions shall be deemed to be recorded on the new licence.[40] This section permits the grant of a new licence in a rural area in substitution for two existing licences.

5. Section 14 of the Intoxicating Liquor Act 1960 provides that the grant of a new licence is conditional upon the recording of any conviction or convictions on the old licence but only if such conviction or convictions were recorded at a time when the applicant was the holder of the old licence. If the conviction is carried forward onto the new licence, it is deemed to have been recorded on the date when it became recorded on the old licence.[41] The section provides for the grant of a new licence in lieu of demolished premises.

Where the statute, however, does not make a specific provision for the carrying forward of an endorsement which was recorded on the previous licence, the new licence is granted free from endorsement. In *D.P.P. v. Farrell* (above) Judge Sheridan considered the carrying forward of endorsements upon the grant of a new licence. Noting that the legislature provided in certain instances for the imposition of endorsements on new licences he stated: **25–19**

> "It therefore cannot be said that the Legislature, in any way, were not conscious of the need, in certain instances, to impose the restrictions of endorsements in varying degrees on new licences."[42]

He referred in particular to section 6 of the Licensing (Ireland) Act 1902 and stated:

> "There is nothing in section 6 to circumscribe in any way the issue of the new licence or to make it conditional upon a transfer of existing endorsements or conditions".[43]

Finlay C.J. in *Doyle v. Hearne (No. 2)*[44] approved this *dictum*.

[40] Intoxicating Liquor Act 1960, s.13(2)(d).
[41] *Ibid.*, s.14.
[42] Above, n.19, at 109.
[43] *Ibid.*
[44] [1988] I.R. 317 at 325.

CHAPTER 26

FORFEITURE

Introduction

26–1 The licensing code provides for the forfeiture of a licence to sell intoxicating liquor by retail where the holder of the licence commits an offence or series of offences within a defined time scale. Convictions in respect of offences to which Part III of the Intoxicating Liquor Act 1927 apply result in the forfeiture of a licence where there are three convictions currently recorded on the licence. Where a licence is thus forfeited, no new licence can at any time thereafter be granted in respect of that premises.[1]

Temporary Licence

26–2 Where the District Court makes an order of forfeiture it may grant a temporary licence where an appeal against such conviction is duly made.

STATUTORY PROVISION

Section 53 of the Licensing Act 1872 provides, *inter alia*:

> "... Where a licence is forfeited on or in pursuance of a conviction for an offence, and an appeal is duly made against such conviction, the court by whom the conviction was made may by order, grant a temporary licence to be in force during the pendency of the appeal upon such conditions as they think just".

[1] Intoxicating Liquor Act 1927, s.28(2).

Appeal

Section 59 of the Courts of Justice Act 1936 provides that every appeal which lies to the Circuit Court from an order of the District Court in a criminal case under the Licensing Acts shall lie to the judge of the circuit within whose circuit the licensed premises in respect of which the offence was committed is situate or to which such order otherwise relates. **26–3**

The county registrar must notify the District Court clerk of details of the order of the Circuit Court. In his turn, the District Court clerk must enter such details in the District Court licensing register and if the order occasions a forfeiture of the licence he must send notice of such order to the proper officer of the Revenue Commissioners.[2]

A. Offences: General

Offences which lead to the forfeiture of a licence are listed below in Appendix C. This chapter reviews the principal offences leading to forfeiture and considers whether an order of forfeiture precludes the relicensing of the premises. **26–4**

1. Endorsable Offences

Offences to which Part III of the Intoxicating Liquor Act 1927 applies are recordable, *i.e.* where the holder of a licence is convicted of an offence under Part III, the conviction will be endorsed on his licence. The court must direct the endorsement of the licence unless the offence relates to prohibited hours, in which case it has a discretion or the conviction is a first conviction.[3] The endorsement is recorded on the licence attaching to the premises in respect of which the offence has been committed.[4] **26–5**

Endorsable offences to which Part III of the 1927 Act applies include offences relating to prohibited hours and offences relating to adulteration of intoxicating liquor. The Schedule to the Act of 1927 lists several offences and further endorsable offences were introduced by subsequent legislation. The main endorsable offences are listed in Appendix C, below.

Forfeiture

Where the holder of a licence with two current convictions is convicted of a recordable offence to which Part III of the Intoxicating Liquor Act 1927 relates **26–6**

---

[2] *Ibid.*, s.32(3).
[3] *Ibid.*, s.25, and see above, chap. 25.
[4] *Ibid.*

and which is ordered to be endorsed on the licence, it becomes forfeited. The forfeiture of a licence in respect of endorsable offences has the serious consequence that the premises to which the licence attached can never thereafter be licensed.

STATUTORY PROVISION

26–7 Section 28 of the Intoxicating Liquor Act 1927 provides:

> "(1) Whenever the holder of a licence for the sale of intoxicating liquor by retail is convicted of an offence to which this Part of this Act relates and such conviction is by virtue of this Part of this Act recorded on such licence, and at the time of such recording two convictions (subsequent in date to the passing of this Act) are by virtue of this Part of this Act recorded on such licence, such licence shall thereupon be forfeited.
>
> (2) Where a licence is forfeited under this section no new licence shall at any time thereafter be granted in respect of the premises or any part of the premises to which such licence was attached."

This extremely stringent provision against relicensing of a premises, or indeed any part thereof, where the licence has been forfeited, underlines the legislature's determination to prevent breaches of the licensing code.

Appeal to Circuit Court

26–8 Where a licence holder is convicted of an endorsable offence in the District Court, an appeal lies from such conviction to the Circuit Court.[5] A Circuit Court judge is empowered to affirm a conviction in respect of prohibited hours but has a discretion to order that the endorsement be deleted from the licence.[6] If the Circuit Court judge exercises this discretion in favour of the licensee, any forfeiture occasioned by the recording of such conviction is deemed to be cancelled.[7]

2. Sale of Intoxicating Liquor without Licence

26–9 The sale by retail of intoxicating liquor by an unlicensed person and the sale by retail of intoxicating liquor at a place which is not licensed are offences under the licensing code and any licence-holder who is convicted of a second or subsequent such offence forfeits his licence. This offence is not an offence to which Part III of the Intoxicating Liquor Act applies; accordingly, there is nothing to preclude the premises from being re-licensed.

---

[5] *Ibid.*, s.27(1), as amended by the Courts (No. 2) Act 1986, s.7.
[6] *Ibid.*, s.27(2), as amended by the Courts (No. 2) Act 1986, s.7.
[7] *Ibid.*

STATUTORY PROVISION

Section 7 of the Intoxicating Liquor (General) Act 1924 provides:

> "(1) From and after the passing of this Act no person shall sell, expose for sale, or keep for sale, by retail, any intoxicating liquor without being duly licensed so to sell the same, or at any place where he is not authorised by his licence to sell the same.
>
> (2) Every person who shall sell, expose for sale, or keep for sale, by retail any intoxicating liquor without being duly licensed so to sell such intoxicating liquor, and every person who shall sell, expose for sale, or keep for sale by retail any intoxicating liquor at any place where he is not authorised by his licence so to sell the same, shall be guilty of an offence under this section and shall be liable on summary conviction thereof to a penalty not exceeding fifty pounds, or in default of payment of such penalty to imprisonment for a term not exceeding six months.
>
> (3) In addition to any other penalty imposed by this section, any person convicted of a second or any subsequent offence under this section or having been convicted before the passing of this Act of an offence under section 3 of the Spirits (Ireland) Act, 1854, or section 3 of the Licensing Act, 1872, is convicted of an offence under this section shall, if he be the holder of a licence of any description for the sale of intoxicating liquor by retail, forfeit such a licence."

The licence to be forfeited need not attach to the premises in respect of which the offence was committed. This contrasts with section 25 of the Intoxicating Liquor Act 1927 which relates to endorsable offences, where the licences to be endorsed and/or forfeited must relate to the premises where the offence took place. Section 7(3) operates a forfeiture only where a conviction for a second or subsequent offence has been obtained at the time that the defendant is the holder of a licence. In other words, if the defendant is unlicensed at the time of his conviction, such conviction will not operate to forfeit a licence subsequently obtained.

3. Offences Relating to Prohibited Products

Various offences were created by the Illicit Distillation (Ireland) Act 1831 which deal with the concealing, possession, or sale of illicitly-distilled spirits. The penalties are severe and in the case of a licence-holder, a conviction results in the forfeiture of his licence. Section 27(3) of the Intoxicating Liquor (General) Act 1924 provides that the holder thereof "shall forever be disqualified from holding a licence for the sale of intoxicating liquor by retail". Section 27(5) of the 1924 Act appears to give the court discretion to impose a sentence of imprisonment for a term not exceeding six months in the case of a first offence or, in the case of a subsequent offence, a term not exceeding 12 months in lieu of a fine or forfeiture of the licence. 26–10

4. Conduct of Premises

(a) Thieves

26–11 Where a licensed person harbours thieves on his premises, the court has a discretion to order the forfeiture of the licence on a first offence. On a conviction for a second offence, the licence must be forfeited and the licensed person is disqualified from holding such licence for two years.[8]

(b) Brothel

26–12 A conviction for permitting a licensed premises to be used as a brothel results in the forfeiture of the licence and the licence holder is disqualified from ever holding any licence for the sale of intoxicating liquors.[9]

(c) Internal Communication

26–13 Section 9 of the Licensing Act 1872 provides that every person who makes or uses or allows to be made or used, any internal communication between any licensed premises and any unlicensed premises which are used for public entertainment or resort, or as a refreshment house, shall be liable to a penalty. If he is the holder of a licence, that licence shall be forfeited. In *Commissioners of Customs and Excise v. Griffith*,[10] the view taken by the majority of the court was that section 9 did not apply to internal communications existing at the time of the grant of the licence, so that an order granting a certificate entitling an applicant to receive a licence in respect of a premises which has an existing internal communication with a shopping centre cannot form the basis of a criminal prosecution. Scrutton L.J. stated:

> "The words "make or allow to be made" clearly refer to a communication made since the date of the licence, and in my view the words "use or allow to be used" refer to communications so made."[11]

A similar offence is created by section 85 of the Licensing Act 1872 in respect of a spirit grocer.

There is no statutory prohibition against re-licensing the premises.

---

8 Prevention of Crimes Act 1871, s.10.

9 Licensing Act 1872, s.15.

10 [1924] 1 K.B. 735, *per* Scrutton L.J. at 747 and Sargeant L.J. at 749.

11 *Ibid.* at 747.

5. Procedural Offences

Where the Revenue Commissioners grant the renewal of a licence on foot of false and misleading information provided by the applicant, the applicant is guilty of an offence. On conviction, the District Court has a discretion to order forfeiture of the licence.[12] 26–14

There is no express prohibition against a future application to re-licence the premises.

B. Offences: Specified Premises

1. Theatre

Section 21 of the Intoxicating Liquor Act 1927 makes provision for the forfeiture of a theatre licence in certain circumstances. 26–15

STATUTORY PROVISION

Section 21(4) provides:

> "Every person who sells or exposes for sale by retail any intoxicating liquor in a theatre in contravention of this section shall be guilty of an offence under this section and shall be liable on summary conviction thereof to a fine not exceeding fifty pounds or, in the case of a second or subsequent offence, at the discretion of the Court, to imprisonment for any term not exceeding six months and also in the case of such second or subsequent offence, in the discretion of the Court to forfeiture of the theatre licence."

If the holder of a theatre licence sells or exposes for sale by retail any intoxicating liquor at a time other than during a permitted time or to persons other than those expressly provided for in section 21(3)(b) of the 1927 Act, or in any part of the theatre which is accessible to persons other than those to whom intoxicating liquor may then be sold, an offence is committed and subsection (4) of section 21 applies. The court may order the forfeiture of the licence on a second or subsequent offence.

Forfeiture

There is nothing in the statute to limit the exercise of the court's discretion to forfeit the licence after a second or subsequent offence. If the court directs the forfeiture of the licence there is no statutory provision prohibiting the re-licensing of the premises. 26–16

[12] Courts (No. 2) Act 1986, s.4(3) and (4).

2. Off-Licence

26–17 In addition to the general statutory provisions relating to forfeiture, the legislature has made provision for the forfeiture of an off-licence in the following circumstances:

1. Section 2 of the Spirits (Ireland) Act 1845 creates an offence of selling spirits to be consumed on the premises, when the licence which attaches to the premises is an off-licence. That Act refers to the spirit grocer's licence which is now the spirit retailer's off-licence. The court has no discretion in relation to the forfeiture, which occurs on conviction for a first offence. In addition, if the licence holder opposes, obstructs or delays the entrance of a policeman onto a premises, his licence becomes forfeited. There is no statutory prohibition on the re-licensing of a premises where forfeiture occurs.
2. Section 13 of the Intoxicating Liquor (General) Act 1924 creates an offence where intoxicating liquor sold by the holder of a off-licence is consumed with "his privity or consent" on "any highway, lane or byeway adjoining or near such premises". The offence relates to the holder of a licence "of any description authorising the sale of intoxicating liquor by retail for consumption off the premises". This section does not apply to on-licences, and section 13 can be contrasted with the succeeding sections which refer to licences "of any description for the sale of intoxicating liquor by retail (whether for consumption on or off the premises)".[13] The licence becomes forfeit in the case of a subsequent offence.[14] The 1924 Act does not prohibit the re-licensing of premises where the licence becomes forfeited under this section.

3. Wine Retailer's On-Licence

26–18 Where the holder of a wine retailer's on-licence stores spirits on his premises, or sells or retails spirits, his licence "shall become null and void".[15] Where a licensed wine retailer adulterates or sells adulterated wine, or permits drunkenness or disorderly conduct on his premises, the court may adjudge that such person should be disqualified from selling wine for any term not exceeding five years.[16]

[13] Intoxicating Liquor (General) Act 1924, s.15.
[14] *Ibid.*, s.13(1).
[15] Refreshment Houses (Ireland) Act 1860, s.27.
[16] *Ibid.*, s.31.

PART VI

PRACTICAL ISSUES

CHAPTER 27

PLANNING PERMISSION

Introduction

Planning permission has assumed a particular significance in the licensing code since *Application of Thomas Kitterick.*[1] Although the planning code and the licensing code may appear to overlap in certain respects, "the planning code and the licensing code are separate and distinct codes of law".[2] The planning code authorises development, including change of user in premises. The licensing code deals with the grant and renewal of licences for the supply of alcohol in premises. The nuisances which may result as a consequence of the grant of a licence are subjected to the control of the annual licensing sessions. This chapter is intended to alert the practitioner to the principal planning issues which may arise in a licensing context. **27–1**

Breach of Planning Permission **27–2**

In *Application of Thomas Kitterick* the Supreme Court held that it was contrary to the policy of the courts to grant a licence where there was a breach of or non-compliance with the planning code. In *Re Tivoli Cinema Ltd*[3] Lynch J. held that the planning code and the licensing code were separate and distinct codes. In the *Tivoli* case the applicant applied for a certificate entitling it to receive a full seven day publican's on-licence in respect of the Tivoli theatre in Francis

[1] (1971) 105 I.L.T.R. 105
[2] *Re Tivoli Cinema Ltd* [1992] 1 I.R. 412, *per* Lynch J. at 419.
[3] *Ibid.*

Street, Dublin. One of the objections raised to the application was that as planning permission for use of the premises as a licensed premises had been granted in respect of an extremely small portion of the premises, namely, the bar, that a certificate entitling the applicant to receive a licence in respect of the entire theatre premises could not be granted. The judge took the view that this ground of objection could not succeed as he had to assume for the purposes of the application that the applicant would not contravene the planning code, and that if there was a contravention of the planning code, this was a matter for the planning authorities.

Lynch J. went on to say:

> "However, use of any part of the premises other than the bar for supplying and/or consuming intoxicating liquor would involve an unauthorised use of such other part of the premises which could be restrained under the planning code and might then be used as a ground of objection to renewal of the licence if such wrongful use were to be allowed by the applicant."[4]

He distinguished the *Kitterick*[5] case and held that in the case before him there was no evidence of a breach of planning permission. He noted, however, that acts amounting to unauthorised use of the premises or breaches of planning permission could constitute "a ground of objection to renewal" of the publican's licence. Presumably such ground of objection could come under the heading of the character of the applicant and the objectors would contend that the failure of the applicant to uphold the law was a matter which went to his character.

27–3 Since the *Kitterick* case it has been recognised that planning permission is relevant both at declaratory stage (where an applicant seeks a declaration under sections 15 or 16 of the Intoxicating Liquor Act 1960 that the court approves the grant of the licence or certificate in principle) and where the applicant seeks a certificate leading to the grant of a licence or certificate under section 17 of the 1960 Act. In a declaratory application Walsh J. considered that:

> "the primary function of the court is to be satisfied that the premises as delineated on the plans submitted and deposited in accordance with the provisions of section 15 [of the Intoxicating Liquor Act 1960], should, if erected, be physically fit and convenient to be licensed. Insofar as a court must envisage the premises as already having been completed, it must do it on the assumption that the premises are erected in accordance with law".[6]

The judge took the view that the court has a discretion as to whether or not to insist on compliance with planning permission at declaratory stage.

---

4 *Ibid.* at 419.
5 Above, n.1.
6 *Ibid.* at 108.

Application for Declaratory Order

There are two possible results at declaratory stage. First, the court may require that the plans submitted have already received the approval of all the necessary authorities so that if a building were erected in accordance with those plans it would not infringe any statutory provision. 27–4

The second possibility is that the court will grant the application prior to the grant of planning permission but subject to a condition that the terms of the planning permission to be granted will be complied with. Accordingly, if the premises are subsequently erected in violation of planning permission, although they comply with plans approved by the court at declaratory stage, the court will hold that the premises have not been constructed in substantial accordance with the terms of the original declaration. The rationale for this is that the original declaration must be construed as being subject to a condition that the premises will be erected in accordance with law.[7] If subsequent to the grant of the declaration, the premises are erected in contravention of law the court will hold that they were not constructed in compliance with the original declaration.

Walsh J. stated in *Application of Thomas Kitterick*:

> "If at that stage the premises have been erected even in strict accordance with the plans submitted to the Court originally but have been erected in violation of other statutory provisions or whose then conditions do not comply with the requirements of other statutory provisions, it appears to me to be quite contrary to the policy of the Courts that a licence should be granted notwithstanding the illegalities. When a case comes back to Court for the grant of the licence under section 17 [of the Intoxicating Liquor Act, 1960], it is the function of the Court to be satisfied that the terms of the declaration under section 15 have been complied with and to consider, if the question is raised, within that context, the legality of the construction or alteration, as the case may be. That also provides objectors with the opportunity for a judicial consideration of their views on the alteration, if any, or such other matters as may properly arise at that stage."[8]

Consequently, the apparently limited discretion granted to the court under section 17 of the 1960 Act to decide whether the premises have been erected in substantial accordance with the declaration made under section 15 must be read in the light of the wider role that Walsh J. envisaged the court should play in this matter.

Application for Certificate

Where a declaratory order has been granted and has been substantially complied with and an application is subsequently made for the grant of a certificate 27–5

[7] *Application of Thomas Kitterick*, above, n.1.
[8] *Ibid.* at 109.

entitling the applicant to a new licence or certificate pursuant to section 17 of the Intoxicating Liquor Act 1960, the court looks only at the character of the applicant and his fitness to hold the licence.

In considering the application for the grant of a certificate under section 17, the courts will countenance some deviation from the original plans presented at declaratory stage provided that the building is still constructed in substantial accordance with the terms of the declaration. Walsh J. himself envisaged that there would be "substantial accordance" if the modifications did not amount to a substantial alteration within the meaning of section 17.[9]

Use of Licensed Premises

27–6 A licensed premises can be put to various uses, only some of which have been specifically defined in either the planning code or the licensing code. The change of user of a premises to one requiring an applicant to hold a liquor licence requires planning permission, either because it does not constitute "exempted development" within the meaning of the planning code, or because of an intensification of user.

(a) Nightclub

27–7 A nightclub is not defined in either the planning code or the licensing code. This type of premises became increasingly common in the late 1960s and 1970s: it caters for persons who wish to avail of "after hours" drinking and music, singing and dancing of the discotheque variety.

Where a use is not specified in Part IV of the 1994 Planning Regulations[10] it is regarded as a separate use for which planning permission is required. As "nightclub" is not defined in the planning code, nor is it within the categories of exempted development set forth in the 1994 Planning Regulations, it is reasonable to conclude that it is to be regarded as a separate user for which planning permission will be required. Where, however, a publican converts a portion of his premises to a function room/nightclub, he might be able to argue that use of the premises to include a function room/nightclub is within the "use" for which planning permission has already been given in respect of the premises. When a change of use incorporates a use ancillary to the main user of the business, then planning permission may not be required.[11] However, this will depend on the facts of each particular case. For example, if a publican wished to convert a small family-run public house into a substantial function room/nightclub, it is likely that the planning authority would impose more stringent requirements in relation to sound level control, the number of

---

[9] *Ibid.*

[10] Local Government (Planning and Development) Regulations 1994 (S.I. No. 86 of 1994).

[11] *Robinson v. Chariot Inns Ltd* [1986] I.L.R.M. 621.

patrons attending and kitchen and lavatory facilities. The test is that the user of the function room/nightclub business must be said to be ancillary to the public house trade.

In *Robinson v. Chariot Inns Ltd* Lardner J. stated: **27–8**

> "I am satisfied . . . from my own knowledge of modern licensed premises that facilities in licensed premises have changed over the years from the old days when all that was provided was a drink, often in premises containing rudimentary seating and primitive facilities. Public houses now usually have comfortable seating and offer many and extensive facilities for their patrons, including meals and amusement facilities as well as modern toilet facilities."[12]

The judge was satisfied that the activities carried on in the respondent's premises in Ranelagh, Dublin such as cabaret, dancing or the provision of snooker tables were all ancillary to the main use as a premises licensed for the sale of intoxicating liquor.

> "It seems to me that in 1985, the provision of ancillary facilities, such as snooker tables in part of the licensed premises, as in the present case, does not necessarily change the nature of their use and is within the 'user' for which planning permission exists."[13]

This case must be read in conjunction with *Carrick Hall Holdings Ltd v. Dublin Corporation.*[14] If intensification of use amounts to a material change of use, planning permission for change of use of a premises is necessary. In that case, McWilliam J. held that intensification of use could amount to a material change of use and that an increase in vehicular traffic is relevant when deciding if there had been a material change of use.

Where a licensee introduces late night dancing onto his premises, the business will be operating outside normal permitted hours and this arguably constitutes an intensification of use.

In an application to the planning authorities for planning permission in respect of a premises which is to include a function room/nightclub, the following details should be made clear: **27–9**

1. the particular portion of the premises to be used for public dancing;
2. the size of the dance floor should be specified.

The plans presented to the planning authorities should be the same as those before the licensing court.

---

[12] *Ibid.* at 623.
[13] *Ibid.*
[14] [1983] I.L.R.M. 268.

(b) Restaurant

27–10 The use by a publican of his premises as a restaurant does not constitute exempted development. Such use may, however, be "ancillary". Accordingly, care should be taken by a purchaser who purchases licensed premises with the intention of using them as a restaurant.[15]

The increase in size or volume of the business of a restaurant can constitute an intensification of use so as to require planning for the purposes of the Planning Acts. By analogy with the *Carrick Hall* decision, where there is an increase in the scale of the restaurant operation so that the whole character of the business being carried on in the premises changes, planning permission should be sought. Where an applicant seeks a full restaurant certificate, he asks the court to certify that the premises are structurally adapted for use as a restaurant and mainly used for the supply of substantial meals to the public. It follows that the use is not ancillary to the use as a licensed premises and that planning permission must be sought.

A publican who applies for a limited restaurant certificate is in a different position: he can advance the argument that as the limited restaurant certificate only attaches to a defined portion of his premises, the public house business is the main business.

(c) Hotel

27–11 Planning permission must be sought where a premises is to be used as a hotel. Where a hotelier who holds a hotel licence granted pursuant to the provisions of section 2(2) of the Licensing (Ireland) Act 1902 (permitting the hotel to operate a hatch bar) applies for an order under section 19 of the Intoxicating Liquor Act 1960 permitting him to have public bar facilities on his premises, he must apply for planning permission where the grant of the public bar facilities changes the whole character of his business.

In *Carrick Hall Holdings Ltd v. Dublin Corporation*[16] the evidence was that once public bar facilities were obtained, the plaintiff constructed or altered the ground floor of the premises to incorporate a lounge bar and a sign proclaiming "Lounge Bar" in large letters was erected. Subsequently, there was a large increase in the licensed trade and an increase in the number of vehicles coming and going and parked on Orwell Road, Rathgar, Dublin. McWilliam J. held that intensification of use could be a material change of use and that an increase in vehicular traffic is relevant when deciding if there had been a material change of use. He was satisfied that:

---

[15] Under art. 11(3) of the 1994 Planning Regulations, the provisions within a state-controlled building of a shop or restaurant for visiting members of the public constitues exempted development for the purpose of the Planning Acts. Applying the maxim of construction *expressio unius est exclusio alterius*, other restaurants are not exempted developments insofar as the Planning Acts are concerned.

[16] Above, n.14.

"the change from a hotel licence without a public bar to an ordinary seven day licence with a public bar has changed the whole character of the business carried on in the premises and directly and for the first time caused the increase in traffic, parking, noise and other unsatisfactory changes in amenities for the local residents which I have already mentioned."[17]

(d) Full Seven-Day Publican's On-Licence

Use of a premises as a public house requires planning permission. An application for planning permission may be required where a restricted licence is converted into a full seven-day publican's on-licence. This would occur only when the character of the business previously carried on changes materially and an intensification of user occurs, or where the original planning permission stipulated a Sunday closing condition. **27–12**

(e) Theatre Licence

Under the provisions of Class II of Part IV of Schedule 1 to the 1994 Planning Regulations a change in use from a cinema, concert hall or bingo hall or skating rink or gymnasium to a theatre constitutes exempted development within the meaning of the planning code. **27–13**

(f) Music and Singing Licence

An applicant for a music and singing licence must apply for planning permission if the music and singing changes the character of the business. If the music and singing is an ancillary part of the main business of the premises, the *Robinson v. Chariot Inns Ltd*[18] principle will apply. The court tends to regard such use in the light of the modern day usage of licensed premises and will take into account that public houses now offer varied and extensive facilities for their patrons, including meals and amusement facilities. If the change of use dramatically alters the character of the business carried on, then planning permission should be sought. **27–14**

(g) Registered Club

The Registration of Clubs (Ireland) Acts 1904 to 1995 provide for the registration of private members' clubs. "Social club" was an exempted use in the 1977 Planning Regulations.[19] It is not an exempted use in the 1994 Planning Regulations. Although the registration of a club does not make it a licensed premises, it does authorise the supply of excisable liquor to members and their visitors. **27–15**

---

[17] *Ibid.* at 271.
[18] Above, n.11.
[19] Local Government (Planning and Development) Regulations 1977 (S.I. No. 65 of 1977).

As it is not an exempted develoment, planning permission is required. Section 5(e) of the 1904 Act states that one of the enumerated valid grounds of objection is that the club is kept or habitually used for any unlawful purpose or mainly for the supply of excisable liquor. In *Comhaltas Ceoltóirí Éireann*[20] Finlay P. held that this provision conferred on the court an express statutory power to refuse the grant or renewal of a certificate where such grant or renewal would facilitate an illegality. He held that if club premises were habitually used in plain contravention of the provisions of the Planning Acts, it would be used for an unlawful purpose:

> "The court is thus conferred with an express statutory power to refuse the grant or renewal of a certificate where such grant or renewal could facilitate illegality and it is unnecessary for the court to fall back upon any more general or implied power deriving from public policy. If a club premises were habitually used in plain contravention of the provisions of the Planning Acts, it would in my view be habitually used for an unlawful purpose. . . . To the general question, therefore, raised in the case before me as to whether the learned District Justice can hear and consider objections to the renewal of the certificate based on an allegation of habitual user in contravention of the Planning Acts, the answer must be 'yes'."[21]

In that case, the District Court judge was being asked to inquire into the validity of a planning permission where the alleged invalidity was a legal formality leading up to the grant of the permission, and the permission appeared clearly to be valid on its face. In the circumstances, Finlay P. held that this was an inquiry that the District Court judge was not entitled to make pursuant to the provisions of the Registration of Clubs (Ireland) Act 1904. However, as to the question whether the District Court judge could consider and hear allegations that the club was habitually used in contravention of conditions attached to the planning permission by way of objection, Finlay P. stated:

> "The user or construction of premises in breach of a condition attached to a permission granted under the Planning Acts, is of course, an offence punishable under those Acts. As I have already indicated, I take the view that this is unlawful user of the premises and must come within the ambit of section 5(e)".[22]

In conclusion, he stated that it would be open to a District Court judge to have regard in a case both to a conviction obtained in proceedings instituted by a planning authority and to the absence of any such proceeding or conviction. The court took the view that as the body charged with the enforcement of planning permission and related conditions also imposed those conditions it might be expected that this body would be the most vigilant in relation to any breach.

---

[20] Unreported, High Court, Finlay P., December 14, 1977.
[21] *Ibid.* at p. 1.
[22] *Ibid.* at pp. 2 and 3.

(h) Supermarket Premises

Where an applicant is constructing a supermarket premises for the purpose of selling intoxicating liquor for consumption off the premises, his application to the planning authority should make it clear that the premises are to be a licensed premises. **27–16**

Under article 8 of the 1994 Planning Regulations a "shop" is defined to include the retail sale of goods to the public, though it expressly excludes use as a hotel, restaurant or public house. It is arguable that where the alcohol is being sold in the normal course of retail sale by a shop, that such sale constitutes the retail sale of goods within the meaning of the definition and that planning permission for change of use from an unlicensed shop to a shop which retails intoxicating liquor is not required.

Conclusion

As a general principle when an applicant is considering the establishment or construction of a licensed premises with any of the above uses, or conversion or expansion of an existing licensed premises to include other such functions, it is advisable that the proposed use or uses be made clear to the planning authorities to enable them to make an appropriate planning decision in respect of the premises. **27–17**

CHAPTER 28

TAX CLEARANCE CERTIFICATE

Introduction

28–1 Since the coming into effect of the Finance Act 1992, the holders of various types of licences to sell intoxicating liquor, by retail and otherwise, are obliged to produce tax clearance certificates to an officer of Customs and Excise before the appropriate licence can issue.[1] The licences in question are specified in section 49 of the Finance (1909–10) Act 1910 as amended by section 156 of the Finance Act 1892 and section 79 of the Finance Act 1993.

STATUTORY PROVISION

28–2 Section 49(1) of the Finance (1909–10) Act 1910 provides:

> "The licences specified in the First Schedule to this Act shall be in such form as the Commissioners direct, and any such licence may be granted on payment of the appropriate duty by any officer of Customs and Excise authorised to grant the licence by the Commissioners, provided that, notwithstanding anything to the contrary in any other enactment, in particular, section 5 of the Licensing (Ireland) Act, 1833, section 7 of the Excise Act, 1835, the Licensing (Ireland) Act, 1902, sections 13 and 14 of the Intoxicating Liquor Act, 1960, section 4 of the Courts (No. 2) Act, 1986 and section 9 of the Intoxicating Liquor Act, 1988, any licence commencing on or after the 1st day of October, 1992, which is a spirit retailer's on-licence, a spirit retailer's off-licence or a wine retailer's on-licence as is specified in the First Schedule to this Act shall not be granted by the Commissioners unless a tax clearance certificate in relation to that licence

[1] The Act came into force on May 28, 1992.

> has been issued in accordance with *section 242* of the *Finance Act, 1992*, provided also that, notwithstanding anything to the contrary in any other enactment, any licence commencing on or after the 1st day of July, 1994, which is a wholesale dealer's licence for spirits, beer, wine or sweets, as is specified in the First Schedule to this Act shall not be granted by the Revenue Commissioners unless a tax clearance certificate in relation to that licence has been issued in accordance with section 242 (as amended by the *Finance Act 1993*) of the Finance Act, 1992."[2]

If an applicant for the grant or renewal of any of the licences specified above cannot produce a tax clearance certificate, then his licence will not be granted or renewed by the Collector of Customs and Excise. These provisions are mandatory. As a consequence of this requirement a substantial number of licences have lapsed, because of the inability of licensees to obtain a tax clearance certificate.

This legislative provision has been more effective than any other provision in the licensing code in reducing the number of licences. It has enormous financial consequences for every publican, spirit grocer and wholesale dealer in the country. There has as yet been no constitutional challenge to the validity of the Finance Act 1992. It is doubtful that a challenge on the basis that the provision infringes the licensee's right to earn a livelihood by requiring him to have his tax affairs in order before his licence will issue, would succeed. The right to earn a livelihood is not absolute.[3]

In *The State (Pheasantry Ltd) v. Donnelly*, Carroll J. stated:

> "There is no constitutional right to a liquor licence or a renewal thereof. There are only such rights as are given by statute subject to limitations and conditions prescribed by statute."[4]

Although section 49 of the Finance (1909–10) Act 1910 does not specifically use the expression "grant or renewal", it is clear that the provisos apply in respect of any licences listed below commencing after the particular date mentioned therein, irrespective of whether it is the initial grant or a renewal.

---

[2] Finance (1909–10) Act 1910, s.49, as amended by the Finance Act 1992, s.156, and the Finance Act 1993, s.79.

[3] See *Attorney General v. Paperlink Ltd* [1984] I.L.R.M. 373 at 384 where Costello J. stated: "It seems to to be inaccurate and potentially confusing to state without qualification that each citizen has the constitutional right to carry on the occupation in which he is actually earning his living . . . the freedom to exercise this constitutional right is not an absolute one and it may be subject to legitimate legal constraints." As to whether the right to earn a livelihood is a property or a personal right, see Costello J. in *Cafolla v. O'Malley* [1985] I.R. 486.

[4] [1982] I.L.R.M. 512 at 516.

Licences which Require Production of Tax Clearance Certificate

(a) Licences: Retail

28–3 1. Spirit retailer's on-licence, which includes the following:

(a) full seven-day publican's on-licence;

(b) six day publican's on-licence;

(c) early closing licence;

(d) hotel licence;

(e) special restaurant licence;

(f) licence in respect of a theatre;

(g) licence in respect of the whole or any part of any aerodrome premises;

(h) licence in respect of the whole or any particular part of any bog premises;

(i) licence in respect of any holiday camp premises or a part or parts thereof;

(j) licence in respect of any part of the bus station in Áras Mhic Dhiarmada at Store Street in Dublin;

(k) licence in respect of a greyhound race track;

(l) licence in respect of an authorised racecourse;

(m) wine retailer's on-licence;

(n) railway refreshment room licence.

2. Spirit retailer's off-licence.

(b) Licences: Wholesale Dealer

This category includes the following:

1. wholesale spirit dealer's licence;
2. wholesale beer dealer's licence;
3. wholesale wine dealer's licence;
4. wholesale sweets dealer's licence.

Expiry of Licence

28–4 Wholesale dealers' licences expire on June 30 of each year. Licences to sell intoxicating liquor by retail and manufacturers' licences expire on September 30 of each year.

The position brought about under the Finance Act 1992 did not make provision for the continuation in force of a licence after the expiry date where a tax clearance certificate had not issued prior to or on the date of the expiry, except where a tax clearance certificate had been refused and an appeal against such refusal had been made.

Accordingly, if a tax clearance certificate had not issued prior to the expiry of the licence, there was no statutory provision permitting the applicant to continue trading pending its issue, save where a determination had been made in respect of the application, or same had been refused and an appeal had been lodged against such refusal. Geoghegan J. in *D.P.P. (O'Halloran) v. Cronin* noted:

> "I would doubt that if its attention had been drawn, the Oireachtas would ever have intended the lacuna to arise which has been identified in this case. If I am right about that, then it is to be hoped that amending legislation, if necessary, with retrospective effect, will be introduced."[5]

Legislation was introduced by the Finance Act 1995 in the form of an amendment to section 49(1A) of the Finance (1909–10) Act 1910 to deal with this lacuna. In the *Cronin* case (above) the holder of a wine retailer's on-licence was prosecuted in respect of four separate offences under section 7 of the Intoxicating Liquor (General) Act 1924 which contains a general prohibition against the sale of intoxicating liquors without a licence. The defendant was prosecuted between the date of the expiry of his licence on September 30, 1992, and the issue of a new licence on January 13, 1993, following the issue of a tax clearance certificate. On a case stated Geoghegan J. answered questions put by the President of the District Court, Judge Smithwick, as follows: **28–5**

1. a licence cannot be considered as retrospectively authorising the sale of wine from the beginning of a licensing year; and
2. the previous licence is not deemed to continue in force until a tax clearance certificate is either issued or refused.

The amendment introduced by section 115 of the Finance Act 1995 to section 156 of the 1992 Act provides for the continuation in force of a licence beyond its ordinary expiry date, and the grant of a temporary licence in specified circumstances, provided that the appropriate excise duty is paid to the Collector of Customs and Excise.

---

[5] Unreported, High Court, Geoghegan J., February 10, 1995.

STATUTORY PROVISION

28–6 The Finance (1909–10) Act 1910, section 49(1A) provides:

"(a)Where in the case of a licence to which the proviso to subsection (1) of this section relates—

(i) an application in accordance with section 242 of the Finance Act, 1992, for a tax clearance certificate has been made —

(I) not less than two months prior to the commencement date of such a licence, where such a commencement date is in the year ending on the 31st day of December, 1995, or

(II) not less than four months prior to the commencement date of such a licence in each subsequent year,

and a tax clearance certificate has not yet been issued or refused, or

(ii) a tax clearance certificate has been refused and an appeal against such refusal has been made and accepted in accordance with subsection (6) of the said section 242,

and in either case, the licence could, but for the provisions relating to a tax clearance certificate have been issued, then—

(A) in a case where a licence has been granted in respect of the previous licensing period, such licence may continue in force beyond its latest expiry date pending—

(I) the issue or refusal of a tax clearance certificate, or

(II) in the case of an appeal, the final determination of that appeal, and

(B) in a case where a licence has not been granted in respect of the previous licensing period, a licence may be issued temporarily and remain in force pending —

(I) the issue or refusal of a tax clearance certificate, or

(II) in the case of an appeal, the final determination of that appeal:

Provided that the amount of the duty that would be payable on the granting of the licence is duly deposited with the proper officer of Customs and Excise.

(b) every licence issued temporarily or continued in force in accordance with paragraph (a) of this subsection shall, while it remains in force, be deemed to be a licence within the meaning of this section, and

(c) Where —

(i) a determination is made to issue a tax clearance certificate, in respect of an application referred to in subparagraph (i) of paragraph (a), or

(ii) the final determination of an appeal referred to in subparagraph (ii) of paragraph (a) is to the effect that the application for a tax clearance certificate in relation to a licence is an acceptable application,

and where the tax clearance certificate has been issued, the licence continued in force or issued temporarily under this subsection shall expire upon the grant of a licence under this section and the duty deposited shall be set against the appropriate duty payable on the grant of the licence.

(d) Where —

(i) a determination is made to refuse a tax clearance certificate, in respect of an application referred to in subparagraph (i) of paragraph (a), or

(ii) the final determination of an appeal under subparagraph (ii) of paragraph (a) is to the effect that the refusal of an application for a tax clearance certificate in relation to a licence is a valid refusal,

the licence continued in force or issued temporarily under the subsection shall expire not later than seven days after such refusal or after the determination of such appeal, and the amount of any duty deposited in excess of the proportion of that duty attributable to the period when the licence was temporarily in force shall be repaid."[6]

Application

An application for a tax clearance certificate is made to the Collector General in a form prescribed by the Revenue Commissioners: the applicant must specify the commencement date of the licence to which the application relates and where the licence is for a period of less than one year, the licensing period. A licence will continue in force after its expiry date where an application "in accordance with Section 242 of the Finance Act 1992" has been made (*i.e.* for a tax clearance certificate) "not less than four months prior to the commencement date of the licence in the succeeding year".[7] 28–7

Thus, a licensee will not be liable to prosecution under section 7 of the Intoxicating Liquor (General) Act 1924 for trading without a licence after the normal expiry date of the licence (whether this is on June 30 or September 30) provided he has made application for the tax clearance certificate four months in advance of the commencement date of the new licence. It is prudent practice for a licensee to apply for his tax clearance certificate, if he holds a retailer's licence, during the month of May of the current licensing year and where he is a wholesale dealer during the month of February of the licensing year.

Refusal

Where a tax clearance certificate has been refused and an appeal against this refusal has been made and accepted in accordance with section 242 of the Finance Act, the licence continues in force beyond its latest expiry date. Where the applicant does not appeal against the refusal or an appeal is unsuccessful, the licence continues in force for a period of seven days after such refusal or after the determination of such appeal and then expires. There is no reason why an application for an ad interim transfer in respect of the licence during this time cannot be granted as the licence is deemed to be a current, valid and subsisting licence until the seven-day period has expired: once the transfer is 28–8

---

6 Section 49(1A) was inserted by the Finance Act 1992, s.156, and amended by the Intoxicating Liquor Act 1995, s.115.

7 Finance (1909–10) Act 1910, s.49(1A).

granted in respect of a licence "then in force" it authorises the sale of intoxicating liquor until the next annual licensing District Court.[8]

Grant of Temporary Licence

28–9 The Revenue Commissioners may issue a new licence which remains in force pending the issue or refusal of a tax clearance certificate, or where an appeal has been lodged in accordance with section 242 of the Finance Act 1992, the final determination of that appeal. The temporary licence remains in force until either of the following:

1. where a tax clearance certificate issues, the temporary licence expires upon the date of the grant of the new licence,
2. where a tax clearance certificate is refused or the appeal against a refusal is unsuccessful, the temporary licence continues in force for a period of seven days after the date of such refusal or determination.

In the same way, an ad interim transfer can be granted prior to the expiration of seven days after the date of such refusal or determination.

Practitioners should note that it is vitally important to advise licensees to apply for their tax clearance certificates in sufficient time to ensure that they can continue trading after the normal date of expiry. It is also essential to ensure that where an application for a tax clearance certificate has been refused, the licensee is advised to consider lodging an appeal against such refusal promptly and in accordance with section 242 of the Finance Act 1992.

Appeal

28–10 Where an application for a tax clearance certificate is refused, the applicant may appeal the refusal. He must appeal, by notice in writing, within 30 days of the refusal. The notice of appeal is valid only if it specifies the following matters:

1. the matter or matters with which the person is aggrieved, and
2. the grounds, in detail, of the appellant's appeal in relation to each matter. Where any amount under the Finance Acts which is due to be paid and is not in dispute, this must be duly paid to the Collector of Customs and Excise.

If the appeal has not been made and accepted in accordance with section 242(6) of the Finance Act 1992, the licensee cannot avail of the protection afforded by section 49(1A) of the Finance (1909–10) Act 1910. In other words,

[8] Public House (Ireland) Act 1855, s.1.

his licence shall not be deemed to continue in force after the expiry date, which is September 30 in the case of a retail licence, and June 30 for a wholesale dealer's licence.

Applicant

The beneficial holder of the licence makes the application for the tax clearance certificate. The expression "beneficial holder of a licence" was initially defined by section 242 of the Finance Act 1992 as meaning the person named on the licence or, where that person was a nominee, the person on whose behalf the nominee held the licence. This definition, however, is superseded by the broader definition contained in section 140 of the Finance Act 1993, which amends Section 242 of the Finance Act 1992. The beneficial holder of the licence is defined as being "the person who conducts the activities under the licence". The licence permits, the licensee, his nominee or employee only to sell intoxicating liquor. It is possible that the legislature intended to target persons operating under a franchise agreement in a licensed premises. **28–11**

A tax clearance certificate will issue to persons who have complied with all the obligations imposed on them by the Tax Acts, the Capital Gains Tax Acts and the Value Added Tax Act 1972 as amended and extended, in relation to the payment of taxes, interest and penalties and the delivery of returns.[9]

A tax clearance certificate issues to the following persons:

1. an individual, where he and any partnership of which he is or was a partner in respect of the period of his partnership has complied with the above obligations;
2. a partnership, where each partner has complied with his tax obligations;
3. a company, where each person who is the beneficial owner thereof, or where a person is able, directly or indirectly, to control more than 50 per cent of the ordinary share capital of the company has or have complied with its/their tax obligations.[10]

Circumstances where Tax Clearance Certificate is required

A tax clearance certificate must be obtained in respect of the following applications: **28–12**

1. grant of a new licence;

[9] Finance Act 1992, s.242.
[10] *Ibid.*

2. renewal of a licence;
3. transfer of a licence where a certificate of transfer has been obtained.[11]

Where the applicant for transfer is a "connected person" within the meaning of section 16(3) of the Finance Act 1968, not only must he produce a tax clearance certificate, but the person who held the licence within that licensing year must also produce a tax clearance certificate. However, this only applies in respect of the following persons:

1. where the transferor is a company connected with the transferee within the meaning of section 16(3) of the Finance (Miscellaneous Provisions) Act 1968 and even where the transferor company has been wound up or dissolved without being wound up;
2. where the transferor is the company and the transferee is a partnership in which a partner is or was able, or where more than one partner is a shareholder, those partners together are or were able, directly or indirectly, either on his or their own, or with a connected person or connected persons within the meaning of section 16(3) of the 1968 Act, control more than 50 per cent of the ordinary shared capital of the company; or
3. the transferor is a partnership and the transferee is a company with similar provisions applying in relation to controlling more than 50 per cent of the ordinary share capital of the company.

Connected Person

28–13 The question whether a person is connected with another is determined by the reference to section 16(3) of the Finance (Miscellaneous Provisions) Act 1968.

STATUTORY PROVISION

Section 16(3) sets out what constitutes a connected person as follows:

> "(a) Any question whether a person is connected with another shall for the purpose of this Part be determined in accordance with the following paragraphs of this sub-section, any provision that one person is connected with another being taken as including provision that the other person is connected with the first mentioned person.
> (b) A person is connected with an individual if that person is the individual's husband or wife, or is a relative, or the husband or wife of a relative, of the individual or of the individual's husband or wife.
> (c) A person in his capacity as trustee of a settlement, is connected with any

[11] This is also known as a confirmation of a transfer.

individual who in relation to the settlement is a settlor, and with any person who is connected with such an individual.

(d) A person is connected with any person with whom he is in partnership, and with the husband or wife or a relative of any individual with whom he is in partnership,

(e) A company is connected with another company—

(i) if the same person has control of both, or a person has control of one and persons connected with him, or he and persons connected with him have control of the other; or

(ii) if a group of two or more persons has control of each company, and the groups either consist of the same persons or could be regarded as consisting of the same persons by treating (in one or more cases) a member of either group as replaced by a person with whom he is connected.

(f) A company is connected with another person, if that person has control of it or if that person and persons connected with him together have control of it.

(g) Any two or more persons acting together to secure or exercise control of a company shall be treated in relation to that company as connected with one another and with any person acting on the directions of any of them to secure or exercise control of the company."

"Relative" means brother, sister, ancestor or lineal descendant.

So, where the parties are connected, a tax clearance certificate shall not issue unless the transferor has complied with his obligations under the Tax Acts, the Capital Gains Acts and the Value Add Tax Act 1972 as amended and extended.

Section 242(3) of the Finance Act 1992 does not cover transactions between private individuals even though they are or may be connected.

Restrictive Impact

The Finance Act 1992 is one of the most powerful weapons available to the Revenue Commissioners to coerce recalcitrant publicans into regularising their fiscal affairs and settling tax arrears. It is estimated that approximately one in five publicans is in negotiation with the office of the Collector General in a bid to sort out his tax affairs and to obtain a tax clearance certificate. A substantial number of licences throughout the country have lapsed and it is envisaged that this level will, to some extent, continue. 28–14

It is ironic that in 1992, some 90 years after the enactment of the Licensing (Ireland) Act 1902, a much more effective method of securing the reduction of the number of licences (the aim of the 1902 legislation) has resulted from a measure designed to ensure tax compliance.

CHAPTER 29

DUTIES OF A SOLICITOR

Introduction

29–1 A solicitor purchasing a licensed premises on behalf of a client should, as a first step, ascertain the nature of the licence attaching to the premises. The consequence of failing to identify the type of licence and advise the client accordingly may result in an action for professional negligence.

The Law Society's Requisitions on Title, prepared under the guidance of Maeve Hayes, Solicitor, and John Cassidy, S.C., deal with a variety of matters including the type of licence attaching to the premises, whether such licence is current and valid and whether the vendor has carried out alterations to the licensed premises without obtaining a certificate from the court leading to the grant of a new licence in respect of the altered premises.

In addition to insisting on full and comprehensive replies to requisitions raised, the solicitor should inspect the District Court licensing register relating to the premises in order to confirm the nature of the licence, whether it is an ordinary seven-day publican's licence, a restricted licence, a hotel licence issued under section 2(2) of the Licensing (Ireland) Act 1902, or a special restaurant licence. The licence document which issues in respect of an ordinary publican's licence and a hotel licence are the same, as both licences are publican's licences: the licence granted under section 2(2) of the Licensing (Ireland) Act 1902 is a publican's licence but its validity is conditional upon continued compliance with the definition of hotel in section 2(2) as amended. The following words appear at the foot of the licence document issued in respect of public houses and hotels:

> "This form of licence is used for houses and certain hotels licensed under Section 2(2) of the Licensing (Ireland) Act, 1902. A hotel licence is subject to certain restrictions which do not apply to a public house."

A publican's licence which is granted to a hotel licensed under section 2(2) of the 1902 Act is granted in respect of premises which comply with the statutory requirements as to the number of bedrooms but do not contain a bar. Failure to comply with the conditions governing the hotel licence at renewal stage results in the licence ceasing "to be a protection to the holder".[1]

Further, a client should be advised that a hotel licence, unlike the unrestricted publican's licence cannot be extinguished for valuable consideration to facilitate the grant of a new licence. It must also be remembered that obtaining an order permitting public bar facilities in a hotel does not convert a hotel into a public house.[2]

Duty of Care

A solicitor owes concurrent duties under contract and tort in advising a client on licensing matters. A general duty of care arises in tort from the professional relationship between the solicitor and the client. The extent of this duty may differ from the contractual duty owed to the client. **29–2**

In *Finlay v. Murtagh*[3] Henchy J. held that a client was entitled to sue his solicitor in tort where the client suffered loss as a result of the solicitor's failure to exercise due professional care and skill, notwithstanding that the client could sue also in contract. Where the solicitor's fault arises not from the breach of the general duty of care arising from the solicitor/client relationship but from a breach of a particular and special term of the contract, the cause of action lies in contract. Henchy J. stated:

> "The modern law of tort shows that the existence of a contractual relationship which impliedly deals with a particular act or omission is not, in itself, sufficient to rule out an action in tort in respect of that act or omission."[4]

The standard expected of a solicitor is to exercise the knowledge and skill conforming to the recognised contemporary standards of his profession and if he is a specialist, such further skill and knowledge as he holds himself out to possess. In *Daniels v. Heskin* Kingsmill Moore J. stated: **29–3**

> "A doctor owes certain well recognised duties to his patient. He must possess such knowledge and skill as conforms to the recognised contemporary standards of his profession and, if he is a specialist, such further and particularised skill and knowledge as he holds himself out to possess."[5]

The general duty owed by a solicitor to his client requires the degree of care to be expected in the circumstances from a reasonably careful and skilful

---

1 *Quinn v. Bourke* [1906] 2 I.R. 94 at 102, *per* Madden J.
2 Intoxicating Liquor Act 1960. s.19.
3 [1979] I.R. 249.
4 *Ibid.* at 257 and 258.
5 [1954] I.R. 73 at 86.

solicitor. However, if there is a common practice having "inherent defects",[6] which ought to be obvious to any solicitor giving the matter due consideration, the fact that it has been widely and generally adopted over a period of time does not constitute a defence.

In *Roche v. Peilow*, Henchy J. in considering the duty of care imposed and the standard expected from a reasonably careful member of the profession, stated:

> "a person cannot be said to be acting reasonably if he automatically and mindlessly follows the practice of others when by taking thought he would have realised that the practice in question was fraught with peril for his client and was readily avoidable or remediable".[7]

Henchy J. continued:

> "The professional man is, of course, not be judged with the benefit of hindsight but if it can be said that if at the time, on giving the matter due consideration he would have realised that the impugned practice was in the circumstances incompatible with his client's interests, and if an alternative and safe course of conduct was reasonably open to him, he will be held to have been negligent".[8]

District Court Licensing Register

29–4 Where premises are clearly represented as a hotel but are not registered with Bord Fáilte, this can amount to an actionable misdescription.[9] Where an issue arises as to either the validity of the licence or the nature of the licence attaching to the premises, the District Court licensing register should be inspected by the solicitor for the purchaser. So held Finlay P. in *Taylor v. Ryan*.[10] Here, the client expressed his concern to the solicitor as to the nature of the licence attaching to the premises "in a persistent fashion". Finlay P. stated:

> "I am driven to the conclusion however that the existence of a valid licence attached to these premises was a fundamental part of the reason why the plaintiff was purchasing them and since the plaintiff himself put the defendant on notice in a persistent fashion of a doubt existing concerning the validity of the licence that it was not a sufficient precaution for this defendant to take to rely on his knowledge of the factual situation or on the knowledge of the plaintiff of the trading, custom and habits of the premises."[11]

---

[6] *O'Donovan v. Cork County Council* [1967] I.R. 173 at 193, *per* Walsh J.
[7] [1986] I.L.R.M. 189 at 197.
[8] *Ibid.*
[9] *Pierse v. Allen*, unreported, High Court, Murphy J., June 9, 1993; *Professional Negligence Law Reports* (1993), p. 486.
[10] Unreported, High Court, Finlay P., March 10, 1983; *Professional Negligence Law Reports*, p. 47.
[11] *Ibid.* at 52.

Finlay P. further noted that "a simple direct enquiry to the District Court Office" would have revealed that the licence was recorded at all material times as being a hotel licence. He was satisfied that in the peculiar circumstances of the case and because of the persistent expressions of concern by the client, an inspection of the District Court licensing register was required to meet the reasonable standard of professional care necessary.

Murphy J. has expressed the view that a solicitor acting on behalf of a purchaser of licensed premises is not required to inspect the register of licences "unless there are some circumstances giving rise to suspicion".[12] The licence issued in respect of a hotel premises and public house is identical but the nature of the publican's licence differs substantially from that of a hotel licence. A solicitor, who is deemed to be "familiar" with the Licensing Acts "and the different type of premises in respect of which such licences could be granted",[13] is advised to inspect the District Court licensing register prior to the purchase. Obtaining a photostat copy of the front of a licence is not sufficient to satisfy the standard of reasonable care expected by a solicitor acting for the prospective purchaser.[14]

In *Application of Declan Bannerton*,[15] Finlay C.J. noted that any "reasonable" investigation of the title to the premises would have revealed their licensing history and stated:

> "It seems to me, therefore, that the applicant had good reason, on proper advice, to at least suspect that it would probably be necessary, if the true facts became known to the licensing sessions, for him to register this hotel, pursuant to the provisions for registering hotels with Bord Fáilte, if he wished to continue renewing the licence."[16]

Requisitions on Title

It is essential that full replies are sought to the Law Society's Requisitions on Title. These requisitions on title are comprehensive and full replies should reveal the nature of the licence and guarantee its currency and validity. The need for comprehensive and detailed replies cannot be overemphasised. **29–5**

The negligence actions in *Kelly v. Crowley*[17] and *Taylor v. Ryan*,[18] arose from insufficiently detailed particulars being furnished to the requisitions on title and failure by the solicitors for the purchaser to obtain better particulars.

---

[12] *Kelly v. Crowley* [1985] I.R. 212 at 228.
[13] *Ibid.* at 228, *per* Murphy J.
[14] *Taylor v. Ryan*, above, n.10.
[15] [1986] I.R. 758.
[16] *Ibid.* at 767.
[17] Above, n.12.
[18] Above, n.10.

A solicitor should also, when investigating the title to the premises, ensure that covenants restricting the user of the premises do not apply, in particular covenants restricting its use as a licensed premises. In certain circumstances, it may be necessary to look behind the initial title to the premises.[19]

29–6 A solicitor should ascertain the nature of the interest held by the vendor publican in the premises. In *Kehoe v. Louth & Son*,[20] the plaintiffs were made aware that the property comprising the licensed premises was held at a yearly tenancy; they were advised by their solicitor that the tenancy was "as good as freehold" as they would have the right to acquire the freehold . It was found as a fact that this statement was not accurate. As the yearly rent was not less than the rateable valuation it would be necessary to have the premises revalued by the Valuation Commissioners in order to acquire the fee simple interest. This was not done. Although no finding of negligence was made in this case a solicitor for the purchaser should be quite clear as to the interest being acquired in the premises and the action, if any, required to acquire the full fee simple interest on purchase.

Publican's Licence

29–7 When purchasing a licensed premises, the solicitor for the purchaser should inspect the District Court licensing register to ascertain the nature of the licence. If the licence is a publican's licence, he should then investigate the register to ascertain whether any recordable convictions exist in respect of the premises. If endorsements exist he should satisfy himself that they are not current or, if current, that the number thereof would not result in forfeiture of the licence.

Hotel

29–8 Where a solicitor is purchasing a hotel premises, he should ascertain whether the premises are registered with Bord Fáilte. If the premises were licensed after July 4, 1960, registration with Bord Fáilte is an essential precondition to the renewal of the licence.

In *Application of Declan Bannerton*[21] the fact that a hotel licence had originally been granted in respect of hotel premises prior to July 4, 1960 (when the requirement of registration with Bord Fáilte was introduced)[22] did not relieve the holder of the licence from registering the premises with Bord Fáilte.

[19] See *McMullen v. Farrell* [1993] 1 I.R. 123.
[20] [1992] I.L.R.M. 282.
[21] Above, n.15.
[22] Intoxicating Liquor Act 1960, s.20.

Here, the hotel licence had lapsed and the applicant was obliged to apply for a new hotel licence after the coming into force of section 20 of the Intoxicating Liquor Act 1960. Once the premises received a new licence under section 2(2) of the Licensing (Ireland) Act 1902, section 20 of the Intoxicating Liquor Act 1960 applied.

When purchasing a hotel premises on behalf of a client, a solicitor should also ascertain that the premises come within the statutory definition contained in section 2(2) of the 1902 Act. Section 2(2) of the 1902 Act introduced the concept of the hotel into the licensing code. It provides for the grant of a publican's licence to a premises answering the description of hotel as contained therein subject to conditions, *i.e.* that the premises contain a certain number of bedrooms for the customers (the number depends on the location of the premises) and do not contain a public bar. When purchasing a hotel for a client, the solicitor should ensure that the number of bedrooms required are actually set apart and used for the sleeping accommodation of the public. User of some of the bedrooms by the staff or owners of the hotel is not sufficient: the bedrooms must be set aside for the accommodation of the public. Where a bar exists on the premises, a solicitor must ascertain that an order permitting public bar facilities on the premises has been obtained under the provisions of section 19 of the Intoxicating Liquor Act 1960, from either the District Court, or the Circuit Court in conjunction with an application for a new hotel licence. The existence of a bar on a hotel premises where no section 19 order has been obtained disentitles the holder thereof to the protection of the hotel licence and the validity of that licence is at best questionable. **29–9**

In *Kelly v. Crowley*,[23] the replies to requisitions raised by the purchaser's solicitor as to the type of licence attaching to the property, were insufficient. The reply from the vendor's solicitor referred the purchaser's solicitor to the attached licence but did not deal with the nature of the licence or the privileges attaching thereto. The purchaser's solicitor did not inspect the register of licences. The particular circumstances of the case were further complicated by the fact that the purchaser's solicitor had been instructed only two days before the auction of the premises. This, it was held, did not afford him a defence. He should have inquired from the vendor's solicitor before the auction, or from the auctioneer, as to whether the licence was a hotel licence or an unrestricted publican's licence. The plaintiffs took possession of the premises and operated them as a public house but when they sought to renew the licence at the annual licensing District Court it transpired that the licence was a hotel licence within the meaning of section 2(2) of the 1902 Act. Renewal of the licence was refused on the ground, *inter alia*, that the premises were not operated as a hotel within the meaning of the licensing laws. Murphy J. held for the plaintiff and stated: **29–10**

[23] Above, n.12.

> "In this case, I feel that I must proceed on the basis that the defendant, as a person professing to act in an important transaction on behalf of his client, involving a licence issued under the Licensing Acts, was familiar with those Acts and the different types of premises in respect of which such licences could be granted. That being so, it seems to me to follow in the absence of any evidence of some proper established professional practice to the contrary, that the defendant/solicitor should have inquired from the vendor's solicitor prior to the auction, or indeed enquired from the auctioneer at the auction itself, as to whether the licence referred to in the brochure advertising the premises was a licence granted in respect of an hotel premises or some other type of premises."[24]

Murphy J. noted that if this inquiry had been made by the vendor's solicitor of the auctioneer this "might well have been an adequate discharge of his duty to the plaintiffs". However, in the light of Finlay P.'s judgment in *Taylor v. Ryan*[25] where he refers to circumstances giving rise to suspicion as to the nature of the licence, if the purchaser's solicitor has any doubts whatever as to whether the premises are a hotel or a public house, he should inspect the District Court licensing register.

Special Restaurant Licence

29–11 Where a solicitor is purchasing a restaurant for a client, he should ascertain whether the premises has the benefit of a current restaurant licence or whether they are merely certified as being a restaurant for the purposes of the Intoxicating Liquor Act 1927. The premises will not be certified as a restaurant for such purposes unless a publican's licence or a wine retailer's on-licence attaches thereto. If the premises have the benefit of a special restaurant licence, it is important to ensure that they are also currently registered with Bord Fáilte within the meaning of section 8(2) of the Intoxicating Liquor Act 1988. The purchaser should require sight of the Bord Fáilte certificate.

Planning Permission

29–12 The Law Society's Requisitions on Title deal with queries which should be raised by a purchaser's solicitor regarding planning permission. The vendor's solicitor should take care to ensure that no misdescription or misrepresentation is made.

Similarly, the purchaser's solicitor should ensure that all replies are fully particularised. He must be satisfied that full planning permission has been obtained in respect of the entire premises, in particular where the premises have been expanded or a user has been changed. Where a licensed premises has been

---

[24] *Ibid.* at 228.
[25] Above, n.10.

extended or even reduced in area, the purchaser's solicitor should insist that a new licence is or has been issued in respect of such altered area. If this is not done the purchaser will be required to apply for a new licence in respect of the altered area.[26]

Where a hotel has recently obtained a public bar, the purchaser's solicitor should inquire as to whether such intensification of user was approved by the planning authority. 29–13

In *Carrick Hall Holdings Ltd v. Dublin Corporation*[27] it was held that a change of use of a hotel premises from a hotel without a public bar to a hotel with a public bar necessitates an application to the planning authorities.

In *Hanafin v. Gaynor*,[28] it was held that no liability attached to a solicitor who accepted an answer regarding planning permission in the requisitions on title which subsequently turned out to be false, in circumstances where he was not put on notice of any matter to arouse suspicion.

A solicitor who is purchasing a premises on behalf of a client should also request fire safety certification in respect of the premises, where relevant. Where works have been carried out on the premises which require fire safety certification, such fire safety certificate should be made available. Prior to the Planning Regulations 1992, it was necessary to ensure compliance with the relevant building regulations in force in relation to the property.[29] It may still be necessary to see whether or not those building regulations have been complied with. 29–14

Lease

A solicitor who acts on behalf of a client who wishes to lease his licensed premises to a tenant should advise his client to insist upon the production of a current tax clearance certificate before entering into the lease agreement. The tenancy agreement should contain a term that the tenant will apply for a tax clearance certificate at least four months in advance of the expiry of the licence. 29–15

The lessor should ascertain whether the proposed tenant has obtained a tax clearance certificate for the current licensing year. It would be unwise for a landlord to enter into a tenancy agreement unless the tenant is in a position to show that his tax affairs are in order: failure to produce the current tax clearance certificate may result in the refusal by the Revenue Commissioners to renew

---

26 *Re Denis Guiney, Applicant* (1941) 75 I.L.T.R. 110 where Davitt P. states "a licence attaches to a structure and not to a site".

27 [1983] I.L.R.M. 268.

28 Unreported, High Court, Egan J., May 29, 1990.

29 Local Government (Planning and Development) Regulations 1992 and Local Government (Planning and Development) (No. 2) Regulations 1992 (S.I. Nos. 209 and 222 of 1992).

the licence in the tenant's name thereby necessitating an application by the landlord to the Circuit Court to revive the licence.

So, a condition in the tenancy agreement should require the tenant to apply for a tax clearance certificate during the month of May, in the case of a retail licence, and during the month of February, in the case of a wholesale dealer's licence. In order to protect the licence, the lessee should require that the tax clearance certificate be produced to him at least one month prior to the date of the expiry of the licence. The lease should contain a clause that if a new tax clearance certificate is refused on first application or on appeal such refusal will operate to determine the tenant's interest in the premises. Only in this way will the landlord be able to ensure a transfer of the licence from the tenant: the application for the transfer must take place within seven days of the refusal, as the licence expires on the seventh day after the refusal of the certificate.

Mortgage

29–16 In *I.C.C. Bank plc v. Verling*[30] the mortgagor granted a lease to a third party without the consent of the mortgagee, as was required in the mortgage deed. Lynch J. granted a mandatory interlocutory injunction compelling the defendants to deliver up vacant possession of the licensed premises forthwith. Without giving a final decision on the issue, the judge was satisfied that the plaintiff had made out a strong prima facie case and the balance of convenience lay with granting the injunction sought.

Checklist

29–17 Where a solicitor is purchasing a licensed premises for and on behalf of a client, the matters detailed below should be considered:

1. Check the District Court licensing register to ascertain the nature of the licence attaching to the premises.
2. Check the District Court licensing register to see whether or not there are any current endorsements on the licence.
3. Check the District Court licensing register to ensure that the licence has been renewed annually.
4. Insist on detailed replies to the Law Society's Requisitions on Title. If anything arises from these requisitions which requires further investigation

[30] [1995] 1 I.L.R.M. 123.

or if the solicitor is not satisfied that the answers given to the replies are complete and accurate, further investigation should be carried out.

5. Check whether the premises have been altered and, if so, whether full planning permission has been obtained in respect of the premises.
6. Check whether there has been an intensification or change of user in the premises and if so, whether any planning permission required has been obtained.
7. Check whether a new licence has been issued in respect of altered premises.
8. Where alterations have been carried out which require fire safety certification, and/or compliance with applicable building regulations, check that such fire safety certification or building bye-law approval has been obtained.

Where a solicitor acts on behalf of a landlord, he should ensure that the tenant is in possession of or can obtain a valid tax clearance certificate and he should insert the provisions recommended above, at paragraph 29–15, in the tenancy agreement.

Where a solicitor acts on behalf of a purchaser, the solicitor should make an application pursuant to section 30 of the Intoxicating Liquor Act 1927, to delete any convictions then recorded on the licence.

APPENDICES

Appendix A

PRECEDENTS

On-Licence

1. Application for NEW PUBLICAN'S LICENCE
2. Application for a DECLARATION as to Fitness and Convenience to Receive PUBLICAN'S LICENCE
3. Notice of OBJECTION to RENEWAL of Publican's Licence

Off-Licence

1. Application for NEW OFF-LICENCE (Spirit and Beer Retailer)
2. Application for DECLARATION as to Fitness and Convenience to Receive a Retailer's Off-Licence
3. Notice of OBJECTION to RENEWAL of Spirit and Beer Retailer's Off-Licence

Licence for Hotel Premises

1. Application for a NEW Licence for HOTEL Premises
2. Application for an Order making it lawful to have a PUBLIC BAR in a HOTEL
3. Notice of OBJECTION to RENEWAL of Intoxicating Liquor Licence for Hotel

Restaurants

1. Application for SPECIAL RESTAURANT LICENCE
2. Notice of OBJECTION to RENEWAL of Special Restaurant Licence
3. Application for "FULL" RESTAURANT CERTIFICATE
4. Application for DECLARATION as to the Suitability of Licensed Premises for a "FULL" RESTAURANT CERTIFICATE
5. Application for a LIMITED RESTAURANT CERTIFICATE
6. Application for DECLARATION as to Suitability of Licensed Premises for LIMITED RESTAURANT CERTIFICATE

Registered Club

1. A. Notification (to Registrar of Clubs) for Grant of ORIGINAL CERTIFICATE of REGISTRATION for a CLUB
   B. Application to the Court for the Grant of ORIGINAL CERTIFICATE of REGISTRATION for a CLUB
2. Application for DECLARATION approving ALTERATIONS to PREMISES of EXISTING REGISTERED CLUB
3. Application for DECLARATION that certain premises which a Club proposes to ACQUIRE, CONSTRUCT OR ALTER are suitable for GRANT of a CERTIFICATE OF REGISTRATION:
   A. Unregistered Club
   B. Registered Club — NEW premises
   C. Registered Club — SUBSTANTIALLY ALTER EXISTING PREMISES or ACQUIRE premises ADJOINING existing premises
4. Application for RENEWAL of CERTIFICATE OF REGISTRATION
5. CERTIFICATE to Accompany Application by a CLUB for GRANT of Certificate of Registration or the RENEWAL of Certificate of Registration
6. Application for a CLUB AUTHORISATION
7. Application for SPECIAL EVENT in Sports Club

Transfer

1. Application for AD INTERIM TRANSFER of ON-LICENCE
2. Application for CERTIFICATE OF TRANSFER of ON-LICENCE
3. Application for AD INTERIM TRANSFER of OFF-LICENCE
4. Application for CERTIFICATE OF TRANSFER of OFF-LICENCE
5. ENDORSEMENT of TEMPORARY TRANSFER by a District Court judge

Applications for Exemptions from Prohibited Hours

1. Application for SPECIAL EXEMPTION ORDER
2. Application for GENERAL EXEMPTION ORDER
3. Application for EXEMPTION for SPECIAL EVENT(S)
4. Application for EXEMPTION for licensed business on SUNDAY AFTERNOONS and the AFTERNOON of ST PATRICK'S DAY
5. Application for OCCASIONAL LICENCE
6. Application for OCCASIONAL LICENCE where a FESTIVAL CLUB has been formed
7. Application for SPECIAL EXEMPTION ORDER where a FESTIVAL CLUB has been formed
8. Application for EXEMPTION for Unlicensed Business conducted on SUNDAY MORNINGS and the MORNING OF ST PATRICK'S DAY in licensed premises situate in any locality not in a county or other borough

Licences for Place of Public Entertainment

1. Application for ANNUAL PUBLIC DANCING LICENCE
2. Application for TEMPORARY PUBLIC DANCING LICENCE
3. Application for ANNUAL MUSIC AND SINGING LICENCE
4. Application for TEMPORARY MUSIC AND SINGING LICENCE
5. Notice of Surrender of PUBLIC DANCING LICENCE
6. Application for PUBLIC DANCING LICENCE with Consent of Licensee under Existing Licence

Other Precedents

1. REQUISITIONS ON TITLE relating to Licensed Premises
2. AGREEMENT for the Extinguishment of an ON-LICENCE
3. Sample Clauses for insertion in MORTGAGE DEED
4. Suggested RULES/CONSTITUTION for REGISTERED CLUB

ON-LICENCE

1. Application for New Publican's Licence

THE CIRCUIT COURT

________________ **CIRCUIT** **COUNTY OF** ________________

IN THE MATTER OF:
THE LICENSING ACTS 1833 TO 1995

AND IN THE MATTER OF:
THE COURTS (SUPPLEMENTAL PROVISIONS) ACT 1961

AND IN THE MATTER OF:
[SECTION, SUBSECTION, ETC., OF STATUTE CREATING JURISDICTION TO APPLY FOR A CERTIFICATE ENTITLING APPLICANT TO RECEIVE A LICENCE]

AND IN THE MATTER OF:
AN APPLICATION OF __________

Applicant ________________

TAKE NOTICE that .... whose place of abode is at .... in the County of ...., intends to apply to this Honourable Court sitting at .... in the County of .... at the sittings thereof commencing on the .... day of ...., 19......., at 10.30 o'clock in the forenoon or so soon thereafter as this application may be taken in its order in the Court list for a Certificate entitling and enabling the Applicant to receive a full Seven-Day Publican's Licence to sell intoxicating liquor by retail for consumption on premises known as .... and situate at .... [*description of premises to comply with Order 42, rule 2 of Circuit Court Rules*] in the County of ...., which said premises are more particularly described upon drawings accompanying this application.

Signed: ______________________
Applicant

____
Solicitors for the Applicant Dated this ..... day of ...., 19...

To: The County Registrar [*for the county in which the premises is situate*]

And: The District Court Clerk [*for the District Court licensing area within which the premises is situate*]

And: The Superintendent of the Garda Síochána [*for the Garda District within which the applicant resides*]

And: The Superintendent of the Garda Síochána [*for the Garda District within which the premises is situate*][1]

And: The Fire Authority [*for the functional area within which the premises is situate*]

[1] Where a body corporate is applying, notice should be given to the superintendent of the Garda Síochána for the Garda district in which the company has its registered office.

2. Application for a Declaration as to Fitness and Convenience to Receive a Publican's Licence

THE CIRCUIT COURT

________________ **CIRCUIT** **COUNTY OF** ________________

IN THE MATTER OF:
THE LICENSING ACTS 1833 TO 1995

IN THE MATTER OF:
THE INTOXICATING LIQUOR ACT 1960, SECTION 15

AND IN THE MATTER OF:
THE COURTS (SUPPLEMENTAL PROVISIONS) ACT 1961

AND IN THE MATTER OF:
[SECTION, SUBSECTION, ETC., OF STATUTE CREATING JURISDICTION TO APPLY FOR A CERTIFICATE ENTITLING APPLICANT TO RECEIVE A LICENCE]

AND IN THE MATTER OF:
AN APPLICATION OF __________

Applicant ________________

TAKE NOTICE that .... whose place of abode is at .... in the County of ...., intends to apply to this Honourable Court sitting at .... in the County of .... at the sittings thereof commencing on the .... day of ...., 19......., at 10.30 o'clock in the forenoon or so soon thereafter as this application may be taken in its order in the Court list for a Declaration that certain premises which the Applicant proposes to acquire and/or construct and/or alter (as the case may be), and known as .... and situate at [*description of premises to comply with Order 42 of the Circuit Court Rules*] in the Civil Parish of .... in the County of ...., will be fit and convenient to be licensed as a Public House when acquired and/or constructed and/or altered in accordance with the plans accompanying this application.

Signed: ______________________
Applicant

____
Solicitors for the Applicant Dated this ..... day of ...., 19...

To: The County Registrar [*for the county in which the premises is situate*]

And: The District Court Clerk [*for the District Court licensing area within which the premises is situate*]

And: The Superintendent of the Garda Síochána [*for the Garda District within which the premises is situate*]

And: The Superintendent of the Garda Síochána [*for the Garda District within which the applicant resides*][2]

And: The Fire Authority [*for the functional area within which the premises is situate*][3]

AND TO WHOM IT MAY CONCERN

[2] Where a body corporate is applying, notice should be given to the superintendent of the Garda Síochána for the Garda district in which the company has its registered office.

[3] Notification to the fire authority is not a statutory requirement, however it is advisable to notify the fire authority at declaratory stage.

3. Notice of Objection to Renewal of Publican's Licence

THE DISTRICT COURT

DISTRICT COURT AREA OF ______ **DISTRICT NO. ______**

COURTS (NO. 2) ACT 1986, SECTION 4

Objector ________________

TAKE NOTICE that the above named Objector of ...., will object at the sitting of the District Court............at .... on the ....day of ...., 19............, at .... a.m /p.m. to the renewal of ....licence attached to the premises situate at .... in the Court area and District aforesaid on the following grounds:

Signed: ________________________
Objector/Solicitor for Objector Dated this ..... day of ...., 19...

To: ________________________
Licensee

____
Address

And: District Court Clerk [*for the District Court licensing area with which the premises are situate*]

OFF-LICENCE

1. Application for New Off-Licence

THE DISTRICT COURT

DISTRICT COURT AREA OF _______ **DISTRICT OF _______**

IN THE MATTER OF:
THE LICENSING ACTS 1833 TO 1995

AND IN THE MATTER OF:
THE BEERHOUSES (IRELAND) ACT 1864, SECTION 3

AND IN THE MATTER OF:
THE LICENSING ACT (IRELAND) 1872, SECTION 82

AND IN THE MATTER OF:
THE LICENSING ACT (IRELAND) 1874, SECTIONS 9, 10 AND 37

AND IN THE MATTER OF:
THE BEER LICENCES REGULATION (IRELAND) ACT 1877, SECTION 2

AND IN THE MATTER OF:
THE BEER RETAILERS' AND SPIRIT GROCERS' RETAIL LICENCES (IRELAND) ACT 1900, SECTIONS 1, 2

AND IN THE MATTER OF:
THE COURTS OF JUSTICE ACT 1924, SECTION 77(C), AS APPLIED BY THE COURTS (SUPPLEMENTAL PROVISIONS) ACT 1961, SECTION 48

AND IN THE MATTER OF:
RULES 93, 94, DISTRICT COURT RULES 1948, AS AMENDED

AND IN THE MATTER OF:
[SECTION, SUBSECTION, ETC., OF STATUTE CREATING JURISDICTION TO APPLY FOR CERTIFICATE ENTITLING APPLICANT TO RECEIVE SPIRIT AND BEER RETAILER'S OFF-LICENCE]

AND IN THE MATTER OF:
AN APPLICATION OF _________

Applicant __________________

TAKE NOTICE that .... whose place of abode is at .... in the County of ...., intends to apply to the Court sitting at .... in the County of ...., in the Court area and District aforesaid, on the .... day of ...., 19......., at .... a.m./p.m. or so soon thereafter as this application may be taken in its order in the Court list for Certificates entitling and enabling the Applicant to obtain Excise Licences to sell:

(a) spirits; and

(b) beer

for consumption off the premises owned and occupied by the Applicant and situate at .... in the County of ......, which said premises are more particularly described on the Map and/or plans of the premises accompanying this Application

AND FURTHER TAKE NOTICE that the Rateable Valuation of the premises for which the Licences are required is £........

AND FURTHER TAKE NOTICE that the premises have been in exclusive occupation of the Applicant since the .... day of ...., 19.....

AND FURTHER TAKE NOTICE that within the preceding two years, the Applicant has held a Licence as a Spirit Grocer or Beer Retailer at the house and premises situate at ....

Signed: ________________________
Applicant

____
Solicitors for the Applicant Dated this ..... day of ...., 19...

To: The District Court Clerk [*for the District Court licensing area within which the premises is situate*]

And: The Superintendent of the Garda Síochána [*for the Garda District within which the premises is situate*]

And: The Superintendent of the Garda Síochána [*for the Garda District within which the applicant resides*]

2. Application for Declaration as to Fitness and Convenience to Receive a Retailer's Off-Licence

THE DISTRICT COURT

DISTRICT COURT AREA OF _______ **DISTRICT OF _______**

IN THE MATTER OF:

THE LICENSING ACTS 1833 TO 1995

AND IN THE MATTER OF:

THE BEERHOUSES (IRELAND) ACT 1864, SECTION 3

AND IN THE MATTER OF:

THE LICENSING ACT 1872, SECTION 82

AND IN THE MATTER OF:

THE LICENSING ACT (IRELAND) 1874, SECTIONS 9, 10, 37

AND IN THE MATTER OF:

THE BEER LICENCES REGULATION (IRELAND) ACT 1877, SECTION 2

AND IN THE MATTER OF:

THE BEER RETAILERS' AND SPIRIT GROCERS' RETAIL LICENCES (IRELAND) ACT 1900, SECTIONS 1, 2

AND IN THE MATTER OF:

THE COURTS OF JUSTICE ACT 1924, SECTION 77(C), AS APPLIED BY THE COURTS (SUPPLEMENTAL PROVISIONS) ACT 1961, SECTION 48

AND IN THE MATTER OF:

THE INTOXICATING LIQUOR ACT 1960, SECTION 15

AND IN THE MATTER OF:

RULES 93, 94, DISTRICT COURT RULES 1948, AS AMENDED

AND IN THE MATTER OF:

[SECTION, SUBSECTION, ETC., OF STATUTE CREATING JURISDICTION TO APPLY FOR CERTIFICATE ENTITLING APPLICANT TO RECEIVE SPIRIT AND BEER RETAILER'S OFF-LICENCE]

AND IN THE MATTER OF:

AN APPLICATION OF _________

Applicant __________________

TAKE NOTICE that .... whose place of abode is at .... in the County of ...., intends to apply to the Court sitting at .... in the County of ...., in the Court area and District aforesaid, on the .... day of ...., 19......., at 10.30 o'clock in the forenoon or so soon thereafter as this application may be taken in its order in the Court list for a Declaration that certain premises known as .... and situate at .... in the Court Area and District aforesaid which the Applicant proposes to acquire and/or construct and/or alter (as the case may be), would be fit and convenient to be licensed for the purposes of the sale by retail of spirits and/or beer for consumption off the premises when acquired and/or constructed and/or altered in accordance with plans accompanying this application.

Signed: __________________________

Applicant

____

Solicitors for the Applicant Dated this ..... day of ...., 19...

To: The District Court Clerk [*for the District Court licensing area within which the premises is situate*]

And: The Superintendent of the Garda Síochána [*for the Garda District within which the premises is situate*]

And: The Superintendent of the Garda Síochána [*for the Garda District within which the applicant resides*]

3. Notice of Objection to Renewal of Spirit and Beer Retailer's Off-Licence

THE DISTRICT COURT

DISTRICT COURT AREA OF _______ **DISTRICT NO. _______**

COURTS (NO. 2) ACT 1986, SECTION 4

Objector __________________

TAKE NOTICE that the above named Objector of ...., will object at the sitting of the District Court...........at .... on the ....day of ...., 19..........., at .... a.m /p.m. to the renewal of the spirt and beer retailers' off-licences attached to the premises situate at .... in the Court area and District aforesaid on the following grounds:

Signed: ____________________________
Objector/Solicitor for Objector Dated this ..... day of ...., 19...

To: __________________________
Licensee

____
Address

And: District Court Clerk [*for the District Court licensing area with which the premises are situate*]

LICENCE FOR HOTEL PREMISES

1. Application for a New Licence for Hotel Premises

THE CIRCUIT COURT

__________ **CIRCUIT** **COUNTY OF** __________

IN THE MATTER OF:

THE LICENSING ACTS 1833 TO 1995

AND IN THE MATTER OF:

THE LICENSING (IRELAND) ACT 1902, SECTION 2, PARAGRAPH 2 AS AMENDED BY THE INTOXICATING LIQUOR ACT 1960, SECTION 21

AND IN THE MATTER OF:

THE COURTS (SUPPLEMENTAL PROVISIONS) ACT 1961

AND IN THE MATTER OF:

AN APPLICATION OF __________

Applicant __________

TAKE NOTICE that .... whose place of abode is at .... in the County of ...., intends to apply to this Honourable Court sitting at .... in the County of .... at the sittings thereof commencing on the .... day of ...., 19......., at 10.30 o'clock in the forenoon or so soon thereafter as this application may be taken in its order in the Court list for a Certificate entitling and enabling the Applicant to receive a Licence for the sale of intoxicating liquor for consumption upon the premises known as .... and situate at .... [*description of premises to comply with Order 42, rule 2 of the Circuit Court Rules*] in the County of ...., which said premises are more particularly described upon drawings accompanying this application.

Signed: ____________________

Applicant

____

Solicitors for the Applicant

Dated this ..... day of ...., 19...

To: The County Registrar [*for the county in which the premises is situate*]

And: The District Court Clerk [*for the District Court licensing area within which the premises is situate*]

And: The Superintendent of the Garda Síochána [*for the Garda District within which the premises is situate*]

And: The Superintendent of the Garda Síochána [*for the Garda District within which the applicant resides*]

And: The Fire Authority [*for the functional area within which the premises is situate*]

2. Application for an Order making it lawful to have a Public Bar in a Hotel licensed under section 2, paragraph 2, of the Licensing (Ireland) Act 1902

THE DISTRICT COURT

DISTRICT COURT AREA OF _______ **DISTRICT NO. ______**

IN THE MATTER OF:
THE LICENSING ACTS, 1833 TO 1995

AND IN THE MATTER OF:
THE INTOXICATING LIQUOR ACT 1960, SECTION 19

AND IN THE MATTER OF:
AN APPLICATION OF __________

Applicant ________________

TAKE NOTICE that .... whose place of abode is at .... in the County of ...., intends to apply to the Court sitting at .... in the County of ...., in the Court area and District aforesaid on the .... day of ...., 19......., at 10.30 o'clock in the forenoon or so soon thereafter as this application may be taken in its order in the Court list for an Order pursuant to Section 19 of the Intoxicating Liquor Act, 1960, in respect of premises known as .... and situate at .... in the County of ...., in the Court Area and District aforesaid to which said premises is attached a Licence in respect of a Hotel granted under Section 2, paragraph 2 of the Licensing (Ireland) Act, 1902, and which said premises are more particularly described upon drawings accompanying this application.

AND TAKE NOTICE that the Licence to be submitted for extinguishment by Order of the Court under subsection (1) of Section 19 of the above mentioned Act of 1960 is an Ordinary Seven Day Publican's Licence presently attached to a Public House situate at .... in the County of ....

Signed: ________________________
Applicant

____
Solicitors for the Applicant Dated this ..... day of ...., 19...

To: The District Court Clerk [*for the District Court licensing area within which the premises is situate*]

And: The Superintendent of the Garda Síochána [*for the Garda District within which the premises is situate*][4]

[4] The Garda Síochána are put on notice merely as a matter of courtesy.

3. Notice of Objection to Renewal of Intoxicating Liquor Licence for Hotel

THE DISTRICT COURT

DISTRICT COURT AREA OF _______ **DISTRICT NO. _______**

COURTS (NO. 2) ACT 1986, SECTION 4

Objector ____________________

TAKE NOTICE that the above named Objector of ...., will object at the sitting of the District Court...........at .... on the .... day of ...., 19 ...., at .... a.m /p.m. to the renewal of the .... licence attached to the premises situate at .... in the Court area and District aforesaid on the following grounds:

Signed: __________________________
Objector/Solicitor for Objector Dated this ..... day of ...., 19...

To: __________________________
Licensee

____
Address

And: The District Court Clerk [*for the District Court licensing area with which the premises are situate*]

RESTAURANTS

1. Application for Special Restaurant Licence

THE CIRCUIT COURT

______________ **CIRCUIT** **COUNTY OF** ______________

IN THE MATTER OF:

THE LICENSING ACTS 1833 TO 1994

AND IN THE MATTER OF:

THE INTOXICATING LIQUOR ACT 1988, SECTION 8

AND IN THE MATTER OF:

AN APPLICATION OF ________

Applicant ______________

WHEREAS the Applicant is the owner and occupier of a Restaurant situate at .... and known as .... [*description of premises to comply with Order 42, rule 2 of Circuit Court Rules*] in the County of ....

TAKE NOTICE that the Applicant whose place of abode is at .... will apply to this Honourable Court sitting at .... in the County of .... at the sittings thereof commencing on the .... day of ...., 19......., at 10.30 o'clock in the forenoon or so soon thereafter as this application may be taken in its order in the Court list for a Certificate entitling him to receive on payment to the Revenue Commissioners of the fee specified in the said Act of 1988 a Special Restaurant Licence in respect of the Restaurant

AND TAKE NOTICE that on the hearing of the said application the Applicant will rely upon proof that there is then in force a Bord Fáilte Certificate in respect of the Restaurant.

Signed: ______________________

Applicant

____

Solicitors for the Applicant Dated this ..... day of ...., 19...

To: The County Registrar [*for the county in which the premises is situate*]

And: The District Court Clerk [*for the District Court licensing area within which the premises is situate*]

And: The Superintendent of the Garda Síochána [*for the Garda District within which the premises is situate*]

And: The Superintendent of the Garda Síochána [*for the Garda District within which the applicant resides*]

And: The Fire Authority (*for the functional area within which the premises is situate*)

2. Notice of Objection to Renewal of Special Restaurant Licence

THE DISTRICT COURT

DISTRICT COURT AREA OF ______ **DISTRICT NO. ______**

COURTS (NO. 2) ACT 1986, SECTION 4

Objector ________________

TAKE NOTICE that the above named Objector of ...., will object at the sitting of the District Court............at .... on the ....day of ...., 19............, at .... a.m /p.m. to the renewal of the special restaurant licence attached to the premises situate at .... in the Court area and District aforesaid on the following grounds:

Signed: ________________________
Objector/Solicitor for Objector Dated this ..... day of ...., 19...

To: ______________________
Licensee

____
Address

And: The District Court Clerk [*for the District Court licensing area within which the premises are situate*]

3. Application for "Full" Restaurant Certificate

THE DISTRICT COURT (or as the case may be)[5]

DISTRICT COURT AREA OF _______ **DISTRICT NO. _______**

IN THE MATTER OF:
THE LICENSING ACTS 1833 TO 1995

AND IN THE MATTER OF:
THE INTOXICATING LIQUOR ACT 1927, SECTION 12

AND IN THE MATTER OF:
AN APPLICATION OF _________

Applicant __________________

TAKE NOTICE that .... whose place of abode is at .... in the County of ...., intends to apply to the Court sitting at .... in the County of .... on the .... day of ...., 19......., at 10.30 o'clock in the forenoon or so soon thereafter as this application may be taken in its order in the Court list for an Order certifying pursuant to Section 12 of the Intoxicating Liquor Act, 1927, that premises known as .... and situate at .... in the County of ...., in the Court Area and District aforesaid, are a restaurant for the purposes of the above mentioned Act of 1927, which said premises are more particularly described upon drawings accompanying this application.

Signed: ______________________
Applicant

____
Solicitors for the Applicant Dated this ..... day of ...., 19...

To: The District Court Clerk [*for the District Court licensing area within which the premises is situate*]

And: The Superintendent of the Garda Síochána [*for the Garda District within which the premises is situate*]

[5] This application is brought before the Circuit Court on the occasion of "any application for a Certificate for a new On-Licence": see the Intoxicating Liquor Act 1927, s.12.

4. Application for Declaration as to the Suitability of Licensed Premises for a "Full" Restaurant Certificate

THE DISTRICT COURT[6]

DISTRICT COURT AREA OF _______ **DISTRICT NO. _______**

IN THE MATTER OF:

THE LICENSING ACTS 1833 TO 1995

AND IN THE MATTER OF:

THE INTOXICATING LIQUOR ACT 1927, SECTION 12

AND IN THE MATTER OF:

THE INTOXICATING LIQUOR ACT 1960, SECTION 16(1)

AND IN THE MATTER OF:

AN APPLICATION OF __________

Applicant ________________

WHEREAS ...., the above named Applicant, whose place of abode is at .... in the County of ...., proposes to acquire and/or construct and/or alter (as the case may be), licensed premises situate at [*give detailed description of premises*] in the Court Area and District aforesaid, and known as .... in accordance with plans accompanying this application and to apply to this Court for the grant of a Restaurant Certificate within the meaning of Section 12 of the Act of 1927 in relation to the premises.

TAKE NOTICE THAT the Applicant will apply to the Court sitting at .... in the County of .... on the .... day of ...., 19....., at 10.30 o'clock in the forenoon for a Declaration that the said premises would be structurally adapted for use as a restaurant, refreshment house or other place for supplying substantial meals to the public if and when the said premises are constructed/altered in accordance with the said plans.

---

[6] This application is made to the Circuit Court in conjunction with a declaratory application regarding an on-licence.

Signed: ________________________

Applicant

____

Solicitors for the Applicant Dated this ..... day of ...., 19...

To: The District Court Clerk [*for the District Court licensing area within which the premises is situate*]

And: The Superintendent of the Garda Síochána [*for the Garda District within which the premises is situate*]

5. Application for a Limited Restaurant Certificate

or

Application for a Certificate that a designated portion of a licensed premises is a Restaurant for the purposes of section 13 of the Intoxicating Liquor Act 1927

THE DISTRICT COURT[7]

DISTRICT COURT AREA OF _______ **DISTRICT NO. _______**

IN THE MATTER OF:
THE LICENSING ACTS 1833 TO 1995

AND IN THE MATTER OF:
THE INTOXICATING LIQUOR ACT 1927, SECTION 12A

AND IN THE MATTER OF:
AN APPLICATION OF _________

Applicant __________________

TAKE NOTICE that .... whose place of abode is at .... in the County of ...., intends to apply to the Court sitting at .... in the County of .... on the .... day of ...., 19......., at 10.30 o'clock in the forenoon or so soon thereafter as this application may be taken in its order in the Court list for an Order in relation to portion of the Applicant's licensed premises situate at .... in the Court Area and District aforesaid, known as ...., designated "restaurant" on the plans accompanying this application certifying that the said portion of his premises is a restaurant for the purposes of Section 13 of the above mentioned Act of 1927 as substituted and amended.

---

[7] This application is to the Circuit Court where the applicant seeks a certificate for a new on-licence.

Signed: ______________________
Applicant

____
Solicitors for the Applicant   Dated this ..... day of ...., 19...

To: The District Court Clerk [*for the District Court licensing area within which the premises is situate*]

And: The Superintendent of the Garda Síochána [*for the Garda District within which the premises is situate*]

6. Application for Declaration as to the Suitability of Licensed Premises for a "Limited" Restaurant Certificate

THE DISTRICT COURT[8]

DISTRICT COURT AREA OF ______ **DISTRICT NO. ______**

IN THE MATTER OF:

THE LICENSING ACTS 1833 TO 1995

AND IN THE MATTER OF:

THE INTOXICATING LIQUOR ACT 1927, SECTION 12A

AND IN THE MATTER OF:

THE INTOXICATING LIQUOR ACT 1960, SECTION 16(1)

AND IN THE MATTER OF:

AN APPLICATION OF ________

Applicant ________________

WHEREAS ...., the above named Applicant, ... whose place of abode is at .... in the County of ...., proposes to acquire and/or construct and/or alter (as the case may be) licensed premises situate at [*give detailed description of premises*] and known as .... in the Court Area and District aforesaid in accordance with plans accompanying this application and to apply to this Court for the grant of a limited Restaurant Certificate within the meaning of Section 12A of the Act of 1927 in relation to portion of the said premises designated "restaurant" on the said plans

TAKE NOTICE THAT the Applicant will apply to the Court sitting at .... in the County of .... at the sittings thereof commencing on the .... day of ...., 19......., at 10.30 o'clock in the forenoon or so soon thereafter as this application may be taken in its order in the Court list for a Declaration that the said portion of the Applicant's premises would be structurally adapted for use as a restaurant, refreshment house or other place for supplying substantial meals to the

[8] This application is brought before the Circuit Court on the occasion of an application pursuant to the Intoxicating Liquor Act 1960, s.15.

Signed: ______________________
Applicant

____
Solicitors for the Applicant   Dated this ..... day of ...., 19...

To: The District Court Clerk [*for the District Court licensing area within which the premises is situate*]

And: The Superintendent of the Garda Síochána [for the Garda District within which the premises is situate]

REGISTERED CLUB

1.A Notification (to Registrar of Clubs) for Grant of Original Certificate of Registration for a Club

IN THE MATTER OF:

THE REGISTRATION OF CLUBS ACTS 1904 to 1995

AND IN THE MATTER OF:

THE REGISTRATION OF CLUBS (IRELAND) ACT 1904, SECTIONS 2, 3

AND IN THE MATTER OF:

THE INTOXICATING LIQUOR (GENERAL) ACT 1924, SECTION 23

AND IN THE MATTER OF:

AN APPLICATION FOR THE GRANT OF AN ORIGINAL CERTIFICATE OF REGISTRATION

AND IN THE MATTER OF:

AN APPLICATION OF _________ CLUB SECRETARY

TAKE NOTICE that I, ..., of ...., Secretary of the above mentioned Club which occupies premises situate at ...., hereby apply for a Certificate of Registration pursuant to the Statutes mentioned in the title hereof.

This application is accompanied by:
(a) Two copies of the Rules of the Club;
(b) List containing the names and addresses of the Committee of Management of the Club;
(c) The names of all the members of the Club;
(d) A Certificate in the form as set out in the First Schedule to the above mentioned Act of 1904 [*see Registered Club Form 5, page 748*] duly signed as in the said Statute provided;
(e) £.......... stamps.

The objects of the Club are .... [*set forth objects as contained in the Club Constitution*].

Signed: ____________________

Secretary

____

Solicitors

Dated this ..... day of ...., 19 ...

To: The District Court Clerk (as Registrar of Clubs) [*for the District Court licensing area within which the Club premises is situate*][9]

[9] This notice is to be lodged with the registrar of clubs as above.

1.B Application to the Court for the Grant of Original Certificate of Registration for a Club

THE CIRCUIT COURT

________________ **CIRCUIT** **COUNTY OF** ________________

IN THE MATTER OF:
THE REGISTRATION OF CLUBS ACTS 1904 TO 1995

AND IN THE MATTER OF:
THE REGISTRATION OF CLUBS (IRELAND) ACT 1904, SECTIONS 2, 3

AND IN THE MATTER OF:
THE INTOXICATING LIQUOR (GENERAL) ACT 1924, SECTION 23

AND IN THE MATTER OF:
THE COURTS (SUPPLEMENTAL PROVISIONS) ACT 1961

AND IN THE MATTER OF:
AN APPLICATION OF _________ CLUB SECRETARY

TAKE NOTICE that an application in the following form has been made to the Registrar of Clubs:—

TAKE NOTICE that I, ..., of ...., Secretary of the above mentioned Club which occupies premises situate at ...., hereby apply for a Certificate of Registration pursuant to the Statutes mentioned in the title hereof.

This application is accompanied by:

(a) Two copies of the Rules of the Club;
(b) List containing the names and addresses of the Committee of Management of the Club;
(c) The names of all the members of the Club;
(d) A Certificate in the form as set out in the First Schedule to the above mentioned Act of 1904 [*see Registered Club Form 5, page 748*] duly signed as in the said Statute provided.
(e) £.......... stamps.

The objects of the Club are .... [*set forth objects as contained in the Club Constitution*].

Signed: ______________________
Secretary of .... Club

AND TAKE NOTICE that the said application shall be heard and determined by this Honourable Court sitting at .... in the County of .... on the .... day of ...., 19..........., at 10.30 o'clock in the forenoon or so soon thereafter as this application may be taken in its order in the Court list.

Signed: ______________________

Secretary of .... Club

To: The County Registrar [*for the county within which the premises is situate*]

And: The Superintendent of the Garda Síochána [*for the Garda District within which the premises is situate*]

And: The Fire Authority [*for the functional area within which the premises is situate*]

2. Application for Declaration approving Alterations to Premises of Existing Registered Club

THE DISTRICT COURT

DISTRICT COURT AREA OF _______ **DISTRICT NO.** _______

IN THE MATTER OF:
THE REGISTRATION OF CLUBS ACTS 1904 TO 1995

AND IN THE MATTER OF:
THE INTOXICATING LIQUOR ACT 1960, SECTION 15(2)

AND IN THE MATTER OF:
AN APPLICATION OF _________ CLUB SECRETARY

WHEREAS the above named Club is registered pursuant to the Statutes named in the title hereof and occupies premises at .... in the County of ....

AND WHEREAS the Club proposes to alter its said premises in accordance with plans accompanying this application

TAKE NOTICE that I, ..., of ...., Secretary of the above mentioned Club intend to apply to the Court sitting at .... in the County of .... in the Court Area and District aforesaid at 10.30 o'clock in the forenoon or so soon thereafter as this application may be taken in its order in the Court list for a Declaration that the premises would be suitable for the renewal of the Certificate of Registration if altered in accordance with the said plans.

Signed: ________________________
Secretary of the .... Club

____
Solicitors for the .... Club Dated this ..... day of ...., 19 ...

To: The District Court Clerk (as Registrar of Clubs) [*for the District Court licensing area within which the premises is situate*]

And: The Superintendent of the Garda Síochána [*for the Garda District within which the premises is situate*]

And: The Fire Authority [*for the functional area within which premises is situate*][10]

---

[10] Notification of the fire authority is not a statutory requirement; it is advisable, however, to notify the fire authority at the declaratory stage.

3. Application for Declaration that certain premises which a Club proposes to Acquire, Construct or Alter are suitable for Grant of a Certificate of Registration

A. Application by Unregistered Club for Declaration

THE CIRCUIT COURT

_______________ **CIRCUIT** **COUNTY OF** _______________

IN THE MATTER OF:
THE REGISTRATION OF CLUBS ACTS 1904 TO 1995

AND IN THE MATTER OF:
THE INTOXICATING LIQUOR ACT 1960, SECTION 15(2)

AND IN THE MATTER OF:
AN APPLICATION OF _________ CLUB SECRETARY

WHEREAS the above named Club is an unregistered Club and proposes to acquire/construct or alter premises to be occupied by the Club situate at .... in accordance with plans accompanying this application

AND WHEREAS the Club proposes to apply to the Court in due course for the grant of a Certificate of Registration under the Statutes named in the title hereof

TAKE NOTICE that I, ..., of ...., Secretary of the said Club intend to apply to this Honourable Court sitting at .... in the County of .... at the sessions thereof commencing on the .... day of ..., 19..... at 10.30 o'clock in the forenoon or upon such date or at such time as the Court may direct for:—

1. A Declaration that the premises would be suitable for the grant of a Certificate of Registration under the Act of 1904 applicable thereto if constructed and/or acquired and/or altered in accordance with the said plans.
2. A Declaration that the number of Clubs registered under the Act of 1904 which are of the character of the Applicant Club and have premises in the District in which the premises, the subject matter of the application, are situate, is not such as to require the refusal of this application.

Signed: ________________________
Secretary of the .... Club

____
Solicitors for the .... Club   Dated this ..... day of ...., 19 ...

To: The County Registrar [*for the county within which the premises is situate*]

And: The District Court Clerk (as Registrar of Clubs) [*for the District Court licensing area within which the premises is situate*]

And: The Superintendent of the Garda Síochána [*for the Garda District within which the premises is situate*]

And: The Fire Authority [*for the functional area within which premises is situate*][11]

[11] Notification of the fire authority is not a statutory requirement; it is advisable, however, to notify the fire authority at the declaratory stage.

3.B Registered Club — New Premises

THE CIRCUIT COURT

________________ CIRCUIT COUNTY OF ________________

IN THE MATTER OF:
THE REGISTRATION OF CLUBS ACTS 1904 TO 1995

AND IN THE MATTER OF:
THE INTOXICATING LIQUOR ACT 1960, SECTION 15(2)

AND IN THE MATTER OF:
AN APPLICATION OF _________ CLUB SECRETARY

WHEREAS the above mentioned Club is registered pursuant to the Statutes named in the title hereof

AND WHEREAS the premises to which the Certificate is applicable within the meaning of subsection (1) of section 1 of the Act of 1904, being the premises presently occupied by the Club is situate at .... and known as ....

AND WHEREAS the Club proposes to acquire, construct and/or alter alternative premises in accordance with plans accompanying this application being premises to which the said Certificate is not applicable and which are situate at .... and to apply to the Court for the grant of a Certificate of Registration under the Act of 1904 applicable to the alternative premises

TAKE NOTICE that I, ..., of ...., Secretary of ...., the said Club, intend to apply to this Honourable Court sitting at .... in the County of .... at the sessions thereof commencing on the .... day of ..., 19..... at 10.30 o'clock in the forenoon or so soon thereafter as this application may be taken in its order in the Court list for:—

1. A Declaration that the alternative premises would be suitable for the grant of a Certificate of Registration under the Act of 1904 applicable thereto if constructed and/or altered in accordance with the said plans.

2. A Declaration that the number of Clubs registered under the Act of 1904 which are of the character of the Applicant Club and have premises in the District in which the premises, the subject matter of the application, are situate is not such as to require the refusal of this application.

Signed: ________________________
Secretary of the .... Club

____
Solicitors for the .... Club Dated this ..... day of ...., 19 ...

To: The County Registrar [*for the county within which the premises is situate*]

And: District Court Clerk, as Registrar of Clubs [*for the district Court Licensing area within which the premises is situate*]

And: The Superintendent of the Garda Síochána [*for the Garda District within which the premises is situate*]

And: The Fire Authority [*for the functional area within which premises is situate*][12]

[12] Notification of the fire authority is not a statutory requirement; it is advisable, however, to notify the fire authority at the declaratory stage.

3.C Registered Club – Substantially Alter Existing Premises or Acquire Premises adjoining Existing Premises

THE CIRCUIT COURT

________________ CIRCUIT COUNTY OF ________________

IN THE MATTER OF:
THE REGISTRATION OF CLUBS ACTS 1904 TO 1995

AND IN THE MATTER OF:
THE INTOXICATING LIQUOR ACT 1960, SECTION 15(2)

AND IN THE MATTER OF:
AN APPLICATION OF _________ CLUB SECRETARY

Take notice that:—

WHEREAS the above mentioned Club is registered pursuant to the Statutes named in the title hereof

AND WHEREAS the premises to which the Certificate is applicable within the meaning of subsection (1) of section 1 of the Act of 1904, being the premises presently occupied by the Club is situate at .... and known as ....

AND WHEREAS the Club proposes to acquire other premises adjoining the Club premises situate at .... or to extend, enlarge and to alter substantially the said premises (as the case may be) in accordance with plans accompanying this application and to apply to the Court for the grant of a Certificate applicable to the premises as so enlarged, extended and altered

TAKE NOTICE that I, ..., of ...., Secretary of ...., the said Club, intend to apply to this Honourable Court sitting at .... in the County of .... at the sessions thereof commencing on the .... day of ..., 19..... at 10.30 o'clock in the forenoon or so soon thereafter as this application may be taken in its order in the Court list for:—

1. A Declaration that the premises, the subject matter of the application, would be suitable for the grant of a Certificate of Registration under the Act of 1904 applicable thereto if extended, enlarged and substantially altered in accordance with the said plans.

2. A Declaration that the number of Clubs registered under the Act of 1904 which are of the character of the Applicant Club and have premises in the District in which the premises, the subject matter of the application, are situate is not such as to require the refusal of this application.

Signed: ______________________

Secretary of the .... Club

____

Solicitors for the .... Club Dated this ..... day of ...., 19 ...

To: The County Registrar [*for the county within which the premises is situate*]

And: District Court Clerk, as Registrar of Clubs [*for the District Court licensing area within which the premises is situate*]

And: The Superintendent of the Garda Síochána [*for the Garda District within which the premises is situate*]

And: The Fire Authority [*for the functional area within which premises is situate*][13]

[13] Notification of the fire authority is not a statutory requirement; it is advisable, however, to notify the fire authority at the declaratory stage.

4. Application for Renewal of Certificate of Registration

THE DISTRICT COURT

DISTRICT COURT AREA OF _______ **DISTRICT NO. _______**

IN THE MATTER OF:
THE REGISTRATION OF CLUBS ACTS 1904 TO 1995

AND IN THE MATTER OF:
THE REGISTRATION OF CLUBS (IRELAND) ACT 1904, SECTION 2(2)

AND IN THE MATTER OF:
AN APPLICATION OF _________ CLUB SECRETARY

TAKE NOTICE that I, ..., whose place of abode is at ...., Secretary of .... Club which occupies premises situate at ...., in the Court Area and District aforesaid intend to apply to the Court sitting at .... in the County of .... in the Court Area and District aforesaid at 10.30 o'clock in the forenoon or so soon thereafter as this application may be taken in its order in the Court list for the renewal of the Certificate of Registration of the above mentioned Club.

This application is accompanied by:—
(a) Two copies of the Rules of the Club;
(b) A list containing the names and addresses of the Committee of Management of the Club;
(c) The names of all the members of the Club;
(d) A Certificate in the form as set out in the First Schedule to the above mentioned Act of 1904 [*see page 666*] duly signed as in the said Statute provided.
(e) £.......... stamps.

The objects of the Club are .... (set forth objects as contained in the Club Constitution).

Signed: ______________________
Secretary of the .... Club

____
Solicitors for the .... Club

Dated this ..... day of ...., 19 ...

To: The District Court Clerk (as Registrar of Clubs) [*for the District Court licensing area within which the Club premises is situate*]

And: The Superintendent of the Garda Síochána [*for the Garda District within which the premises is situate*]

And: The Fire Authority [*for the functional Area within which premises is situate*]

5. Certificate to Accompany the Application by a Club for Grant of a Certificate of Registration or the Renewal of a Certificate of Registration

We, Peace Commissioners, for the County (or County Borough) of .... and ...., owner of premises occupied by (or to be occupied) by the Club hereinafter mentioned, hereby certify that to the best of our knowledge and belief, the .... Club, designated in the accompanying application is to be (or, in the case of an application by an existing Club, has been and is to be) conducted as a bona fide Club and not mainly for the supply of excisable liquor.

Dated this ..... day of ...., 19 ...

[*Signature and Address of each person certifying to be inserted*]

6. Application for a Club Authorisation

THE DISTRICT COURT

DISTRICT COURT AREA OF ______ **DISTRICT NO. ______**

IN THE MATTER OF:
THE REGISTRATION OF CLUBS ACTS 1904 TO 1995

AND IN THE MATTER OF:
THE INTOXICATING LIQUOR (GENERAL) ACT 1924, SECTION 21, AS AMENDED BY THE INTOXICATING LIQUOR ACT 1962, SECTION 8

AND IN THE MATTER OF:
AN APPLICATION OF ________ CLUB SECRETARY

TAKE NOTICE that I, ..., of ...., Secretary of .... Club which Club is a duly registered Club under the above mentioned Acts, intends to apply to the Court sitting at .... in the County of .... in the Court Area and District aforesaid at 10.30 o'clock in the forenoon or so soon thereafter as this application may be taken in its order in the Court list for an Order authorising the above Club notwithstanding the provisions contained in the Club rules pursuant to the Registration of Clubs Acts to supply excisable liquors to members of the Club during the following period:—

.... [*not exceeding six hours*], being a period during which such supply of excisable liquors would be prohibited by the Rules of the aforesaid Club.

Not more than .... authorisations have been granted to the Club during the year.

Signed: ______________________
Secretary of the .... Club

____
Solicitors for the .... Club

Dated this ..... day of ...., 19 ...

To: The District Court Clerk (as Registrar of Clubs) [*for the District Court licensing area within which the Club premises is situate*]

And: Superintendent of the Garda Síochána [*for the Garda District within which the premises is situate*]

7. Application for Special Event in Sports Club

THE DISTRICT COURT

DISTRICT COURT AREA OF ______ **DISTRICT NO. ______**

IN THE MATTER OF:
THE REGISTRATION OF CLUBS ACTS 1904 to 1995

AND IN THE MATTER OF:
THE INTOXICATING LIQUOR ACT 1962, SECTION 14

AND IN THE MATTER OF:
AN APPLICATION OF ________ CLUB SECRETARY

TAKE NOTICE that I, ... of ...., Secretary of ....Club, which Club is a duly registered Club under the above-mentioned Acts intend to apply to the Court sitting at.......... in the County of .... in the Court Area and District aforesaid at 10.30 o'clock in the forenoon or as soon therafter as this application may be taken in its order in the Court list for an Order authorising the sale or supply by or with the consent of the aforementioned Club to any person for consumption in the buildings or grounds of the Club which are situate at........... by .... of excisable liquor during the following times:

.... Days [*not exceeding five consecutive days*] .... Hours

on the occasion of the following Special Event [*specify*] which is likely to attract a considerable number of people to the Club.

AND TAKE NOTICE that the objects of the aforementioned Club are .... [*must be promotion of outdoor pastime as provided for by section 14 of the Intoxicating Liquor Act 1962*].

Signed: ________________________
Secretary of the .... Club

____
Solicitors for the .... Club Dated this ..... day of ...., 19 ...

To: The District Court Clerk (as Registrar of Clubs) [*for the District Court licensing area within which the Club premises is situate*]

TRANSFER

1. Application for Ad Interim Transfer of On-Licence

THE DISTRICT COURT

DISTRICT COURT AREA OF ______ **DISTRICT NO. ______**

IN THE MATTER OF:
THE LICENSING ACTS 1833 TO 1995

AND IN THE MATTER OF:
THE PUBLIC HOUSE (IRELAND) ACT 1855, SECTION 1

AND IN THE MATTER OF:
RULE 97 OF THE DISTRICT COURT RULES 1948 (AS AMENDED)

AND IN THE MATTER OF:
AN APPLICATION OF ________

Applicant ________________

TAKE NOTICE that .... whose place of abode is at .... in the County of ...., intends to apply to the Court sitting at .... on the .... day of ...., 19......., at 10.30 o'clock in the forenoon or so soon thereafter as this application may be taken in its order in the Court list for an Order pursuant to the Statute and Rule mentioned above temporarily transferring to the Applicant the Publican's On-Licence (Ordinary) attached to the premises situate at .... in the Court Area and District aforesaid now in the name of .... by endorsement on the Licence.

Signed: ______________________
Applicant

____
Solicitors for the Applicant Dated this ..... day of ...., 19 ...

To: The District Court Clerk [*for the District Court licensing area within which the premises is situate*]

And: The Superintendent of the Garda Síochána [*for the Garda District within which the premises is situate*]

2. Application for Certificate of Transfer of On-Licence (Confirmation of Transfer)

THE DISTRICT COURT

DISTRICT COURT AREA OF ______ **DISTRICT NO. ______**

IN THE MATTER OF:
THE LICENSING ACTS, 1833 TO 1995

AND IN THE MATTER OF:
THE LICENSING ACT (IRELAND) 1874, SECTION 10, AS AMENDED BY SUBSTITUTION IN THE FIRST SCHEDULE TO THE COURTS (NO. 2) ACT 1986

AND IN THE MATTER OF:
THE LICENSING (IRELAND) ACT 1833, SECTION 6

AND IN THE MATTER OF:
AN APPLICATION OF ________

Applicant ________________

TAKE NOTICE that .... whose place of abode is at .... in the County of ...., will apply to the Annual Licensing District Court at .... on the .... day of ...., 19...., at 10.30 o'clock in the forenoon or so soon thereafter as this application may be taken in its order in the Court list for a Certificate by way of transfer entitling the Applicant to receive a Seven Day Publican's On-Licence in respect of premises known as .... and situate at .... in the Court Area and District aforesaid, such Certificate being the Certificate referred to at subsection (2) of rule 94 of the District Court Rules as amended.

Signed: ______________________
Applicant

____
Solicitors for the Applicant Dated this ..... day of ...., 19 ...

To: The District Court Clerk [*for the District Court licensing area within which the premises is situate*]

And: The Superintendent of the Garda Síochána [*for the Garda District within which the premises is situate*]

And: The Superintendent of the Garda Síochána [*for the Garda District within which applicant resides*]

And: The Fire Authority [*for the functional area within which premises is situate*][14]

[14] It is not clear whether the fire officer is a notice party to this application.

3. Application for Ad Interim Transfer of Off-Licence

THE DISTRICT COURT

DISTRICT COURT AREA OF ______ **DISTRICT NO. ______**

IN THE MATTER OF:
THE LICENSING ACTS 1833 TO 1995

AND IN THE MATTER OF:
THE PUBLIC HOUSE (IRELAND) ACT 1855, SECTION 1

AND IN THE MATTER OF:
THE INTOXICATING LIQUOR ACT 1960, SECTION 29

AND IN THE MATTER OF:
RULE 97 OF THE DISTRICT COURT RULES 1948 (AS AMENDED)

AND IN THE MATTER OF:
AN APPLICATION OF _________

Applicant _________________

TAKE NOTICE that .... whose place of abode is at .... in the County of ...., intends to apply to the Court sitting at .... on the .... day of ...., 19......., at 10.30 o'clock in the forenoon or so soon thereafter as this application may be taken in its order in the Court list for an Order pursuant to the Statute and Rule mentioned above temporarily transferring to the Applicant the Licences for the sale of spirits and beer by retail for consumption off the premises in respect of premises known as and situate at .... in the Court Area and District aforesaid now in the name of .... by endorsement on the Licence.

Signed: ______________________
Applicant

____
Solicitors for the Applicant Dated this ..... day of ...., 19 ...

To: The District Court Clerk [*for the District Court licensing area within which the premises is situate*]

And: The Superintendent of the Garda Síochána [*for the Garda District within which the premises is situate*]

4. Application for Certificate of Transfer of Off-Licence (Confirmation of Transfer)

THE DISTRICT COURT

DISTRICT COURT AREA OF ______ **DISTRICT NO. ______**

IN THE MATTER OF:

THE LICENSING ACTS, 1833 TO 1995

AND IN THE MATTER OF:

THE LICENSING ACT (IRELAND) 1874, SECTION 10, AS AMENDED BY SUBSTITUTION IN THE FIRST SCHEDULE TO THE COURTS (NO. 2) ACT 1986

AND IN THE MATTER OF:

THE LICENSING (IRELAND) ACT 1833, SECTION 6

AND IN THE MATTER OF:

RULES 100 TO 105 INCLUSIVE OF THE DISTRICT COURT RULES 1948 AS AMENDED AND SUBSTITUTED

AND IN THE MATTER OF:

AN APPLICATION OF ________

Applicant ________________

TAKE NOTICE that .... whose place of abode is at .... in the County of ...., will apply to the Annual Licensing District Court at .... on the .... day of ...., 19......., at 10.30 o'clock in the forenoon or so soon thereafter as this application may be taken in its order in the Court list for a Certificate by way of transfer entitling the Applicant to receive Licences for the sale of spirits and beer by retail for consumption off the premises in respect of premises known as .... and situate at .... in the County of .... in the Court Area and District aforesaid, such Certificate being the Certificate referred to at subsection (2) of Rule 104 of Rules of District Court as amended.

AND TAKE NOTICE that the Applicant has within the preceding two years held Licences as a Spirit Grocer and/or Beer Retailer in respect of the following premises [*here list premises where applicable*].

AND FURTHER TAKE NOTICE that the rateable valuation of the premises sought to be licensed is £........

AND FURTHER TAKE NOTICE that the said premises have been in the exclusive occupation of the Applicant since the ...... day of ...., 19......

Signed: ______________________
Applicant

____
Solicitors for the Applicant Dated this ..... day of ...., 19 ...

To: The District Court Clerk [*for the District Court licensing area within which the premises is situate*]

And: The Superintendent of the Garda Síochána [*for the Garda District within which the premises is situate*]

And: The Superintendent of the Garda Síochána [*for the Garda District within which applicant resides*].

5. Endorsement of Temporary Transfer by a District Court Judge

THE DISTRICT COURT

DISTRICT COURT AREA OF _______ **DISTRICT NO. _______**

I, ..., the undersigned, District Court Judge assigned to .... District, having first examined on Oath all necessary persons do hereby transfer this Licence to [*A.B.*] until the sitting of the Annual Licensing District Court to be held next .... after the expiration of one calendar month from the date hereof.

Signed: __________________________
Judge of the District Court Dated this ..... day of ...., 19 ...

APPLICATIONS FOR EXEMPTIONS FROM PROHIBITED HOURS

1. Application for Special Exemption Order

THE DISTRICT COURT

DISTRICT COURT AREA OF ______ **DISTRICT NO.** ______

IN THE MATTER OF:

THE LICENSING ACTS 1833 TO 1995

AND IN THE MATTER OF:

THE INTOXICATING LIQUOR ACT 1927, SECTION 5, AS AMENDED BY THE INTOXICATING LIQUOR ACT 1943, SECTION 6, AND BY THE INTOXICATING LIQUOR ACT 1962, SECTION 12

AND IN THE MATTER OF:

AN APPLICATION OF ________

Applicant __________

TAKE NOTICE that .... whose place of abode is at .... in the County of ...., intends to apply to the Court sitting at .... in the County of .... on the .... day of ...., 19......., at 10.30 o'clock in the forenoon or so soon thereafter as this application may be taken in its order in the Court list for a Special Exemption Order in respect of a special occasion being the occasion of [*here specify the occasion which must come within one or other of the definitions listed at subsection (5) of the Act 1927, paragraphs (a), (b) or (c), inserted by section 12 of the Act 1962*] exempting the Applicant from the provisions of the Licensing Acts 1833 to 1995, relating to prohibited hours between the hours of .... on the .... day of ...., 19......., and .... on the .... day of ...., 19......, in respect of premises known as .... and situate at .... in the Court Area and District aforesaid to which said premises is attached a Full Publican's Seven Day On-Licence and which said premises are a Restaurant or Hotel [*delete as appropriate*] for the purposes of the Intoxicating Liquor Act 1927, as amended.

Signed: ______________________
Applicant

____
Solicitors for the Applicant Dated the ..... day of ...., 19 ...

To: The District Court Clerk [*for the District Court licensing area within which the premises is situate*]

And: The Superintendent of the Garda Síochána [*for the Garda District within which the premises is situate*]

2. Application for General Exemption Order

THE DISTRICT COURT

DISTRICT COURT AREA OF ______ **DISTRICT NO. ______**

IN THE MATTER OF:
THE LICENSING ACTS 1833 TO 1995

AND IN THE MATTER OF:
THE INTOXICATING LIQUOR ACT 1927, SECTION 4, AS AMENDED BY THE INTOXICATING LIQUOR ACT 1962, SECTION 10

AND IN THE MATTER OF:
AN APPLICATION OF ________

Applicant__________

TAKE NOTICE that .... whose place of abode is at .... in the County of ...., the holder of a Publican's Licence (Ordinary) in respect of premises situate at ...., in the County of ......, in the Court Area and District aforesaid, being premises situate in the vicinity of ...., *a Public Market or Fair or a place where a considerable number of persons follow a lawful trade or calling [delete as appropriate)* intends to apply to the Court sitting at .... in the County of .... on the .... day of ...., 19......, at 10.30 o'clock in the forenoon or so soon thereafter as this application may be taken in its order in the Court list for a General Exemption Order exempting him from the provisions of the Intoxicating Liquor Act, 1927, as amended relating to prohibited hours in respect of the said premises on such days and during such hours as are specified in the Schedule hereto and subject to Statute and to such terms as will be specified by the Court.

SCHEDULE

Days	**Hours**

Signed: ______________________
Applicant

____
Solicitors for the Applicant Dated the ..... day of ...., 19 ...

To: The District Court Clerk [*for the District Court licensing area within which the premises is situate*]

And: The Superintendent of the Garda Síochána [*for the Garda District within which the premises is situate*]

3. Application for Exemption for Special Event(s) (Area Exemption Order)

THE DISTRICT COURT

DISTRICT COURT AREA OF _______ **DISTRICT NO. _______**

IN THE MATTER OF:

THE LICENSING ACTS 1833 TO 1995

AND IN THE MATTER OF:

THE INTOXICATING LIQUOR ACT 1962, SECTION 10

AND IN THE MATTER OF:

AN APPLICATION OF __________

Applicant___________

WHEREAS the above named Applicant is the holder of a Publican's Licence (Ordinary) in respect of premises situate at .... and known as .... [*here give full description of premises*] in the County of ....

AND WHEREAS the said premises are situate in the locality of [*here mention Town of* ....], within the meaning of the word "locality" as defined in section 10(8) of the above mentioned Act of 1962

AND WHEREAS the application has the approval of a majority of the holders of Licences in respect of premises situate within the said locality as so defined

AND WHEREAS a special event within the meaning of section 10 of the said Act of 1962 will take place in (or near) the said locality on the .... day of ...., 19......., or between the ...... day of ....., 19......... (as the case may be), and in consequence thereof a considerable number of people will be attracted to the said locality

TAKE NOTICE that I, ... the undersigned, intend to apply to the Court sitting at .... in the County of .... on the .... day of ...., 19......., at 10.30 o'clock in the forenoon or so soon thereafter as this application may be taken in its order in the Court list for an Order subject to such conditions as the Court thinks proper exempting the holders of Licences in respect of premises situate in the said locality from the provisions of the Licensing Acts, 1833 to 1995, relating to prohibited hours in respect of those premises at such times and on such days during the period of the said event as are set out in the Schedule hereto or as the Court may think fit.

SCHEDULE

Days	**Hours**

Signed: __________________________
Applicant

____
Solicitors for the Applicant Dated the ..... day of ...., 19 ...

To: The District Court Clerk [*for the District Court licensing area within which the premises is situate*]

And: The Superintendent of the Garda Síochána [*for the Garda District within which the premises is situate*]

4. Application for Exemption for Licensed Business on Sunday afternoon and on the Afternoon of St Patrick's Day by the holder of Seven Day Publican's Licences in respect of premises situate in any locality not being in a County or County Borough

THE DISTRICT COURT

DISTRICT COURT AREA OF _______ **DISTRICT NO. _______**

IN THE MATTER OF:

THE LICENSING ACTS 1833 TO 1995

AND IN THE MATTER OF:

THE INTOXICATING LIQUOR ACT 1962, SECTION 16

AND IN THE MATTER OF:

AN APPLICATION OF _________

Applicant___________

TAKE NOTICE that .... being a holder of a Licence (not being a Six Day Licence) in respect of premises situate at ...., a locality which is not a County or other Borough, intends, with the approval of a majority of holders of Full Seven Day On-Licences in respect of premises situate in the said locality to apply to the Court, having regard to the circumstances in the locality, for an Order exempting the holders of all such Licences in respect of premises so situate, from the provisions of the Licensing Acts, 1833 to 1995, relating to prohibited hours in respect of those premises for the period between the hours of 12.00 o'clock noon and 12.30 o'clock in the afternoon on Sundays and St Patrick's Day.

Signed: _________________________

Applicant

____

Solicitors for the Applicant Dated the ..... day of ...., 19 ...

To: The District Court Clerk [*for the District Court licensing area within which the premises is situate*]

And: The Superintendent of the Garda Síochána [*for the Garda District within which the premises is situate*]

5. Application for Occasional Licence

THE DISTRICT COURT

DISTRICT COURT AREA OF ______ **DISTRICT NO. ______**

IN THE MATTER OF:

THE LICENSING ACTS 1833 TO 1995

AND IN THE MATTER OF:

THE INTOXICATING LIQUOR ACT 1962, SECTION 11, AS AMENDED BY THE INTOXICATING LIQUOR ACT 1977, SECTION 1

AND IN THE MATTER OF:

AN APPLICATION OF ________

Applicant ________

TAKE NOTICE that .... whose place of abode is at .... in the County of ...., being the holder of a Publican's Licence (Ordinary) in respect of premises situate at .... in the County of .... in the Court Area and District aforesaid intends to apply to the Court sitting at .... in the County of .... on the .... day of ...., 19......., at 10.30 o'clock in the forenoon or so soon thereafter as this application may be taken in its order in the Court list for an Occasional Licence authorising the Applicant to sell intoxicating liquor at .... in the Court Area and District aforesaid being a place to which no licence for the sale of intoxicating liquor is attached during the times and on the days set out in the Schedule hereto on the occasion of ....

SCHEDULE

Days **Hours**

CONDITIONS [*in addition to statutory conditions*]

Signed: ________________________

Applicant

____

Solicitors for the Applicant Dated the ..... day of ...., 19 ...

To: The District Court Clerk [*for the District Court licensing area in which the unlicensed premises is situate*]

And: The Superintendent of the Garda Síochána [*for the Garda District in which the unlicensed premises is situate*][15]

[15] The President of the District Court has issued a practice direction requiring notification of the fire officer in an application for an occasional licence, despite the absence of a statutory requirement to do so.

6. Application for Occasional Licence where a Festival Club has been formed

THE DISTRICT COURT

DISTRICT COURT AREA OF ______ **DISTRICT NO. ______**

IN THE MATTER OF:

THE LICENSING ACTS 1833 TO 1995

AND IN THE MATTER OF:

THE INTOXICATING LIQUOR ACT 1962, SECTION 13

AND IN THE MATTER OF:

AN APPLICATION TO THE COURT PURSUANT TO THE INTOXICATING LIQUOR ACT 1962, SECTION 11

AND IN THE MATTER OF:

AN APPLICATION OF ________

Applicant __________

TAKE NOTICE that .... whose place of abode is at .... in the County of ...., the holder of Seven Day Publican's On-Licence in respect of premises situate at .... in the County of .... in the Court Area and District aforesaid intends to apply to the Court at .... in the County of .... on the .... day of ...., 19......., at 10.30 o'clock in the forenoon or so soon thereafter as this application may be taken in its order in the Court list for an Occasional Licence authorising the Applicant to sell intoxicating liquor at .... in the Court Area and District aforesaid being a place to which no Licence for the sale of intoxicating liquor is attached on the days and during the hours set out in the Schedule hereto on the occasion of the holding of a Social Function organised or supported by the Committee and organisers of the .... Festival Club.

AND FURTHER TAKE NOTICE that all the requirements of section 13 of the Intoxicating Liquor Act, 1962, have been complied with.

SCHEDULE

Days **Hours**

CONDITIONS [*in addition to statutory conditions*]

Signed: __________________________

Applicant

____

Solicitors for the Applicant Dated the ..... day of ...., 19 ...

To: The District Court Clerk [*for the District Court licensing area with which unlicensed premises is situate*]

And: The Superintendent of the Garda Síochána [*for the Garda District in which unlicensed premises is situate*]

7. Application for Special Exemption Order where a Festival Club has been formed

THE DISTRICT COURT

DISTRICT COURT AREA OF _______ **DISTRICT NO. _______**

IN THE MATTER OF:
THE LICENSING ACTS 1833 TO 1995

AND IN THE MATTER OF:
THE INTOXICATING LIQUOR ACT 1962, SECTION 13

AND IN THE MATTER OF:
AN APPLICATION TO THE COURT UNDER THE INTOXICATING LIQUOR ACT 1927, SECTION 5

AND IN THE MATTER OF:
AN APPLICATION OF __________

Applicant___________

TAKE NOTICE that .... whose place of abode is at .... in the County of ...., the holder of a Seven Day Publican's On-Licence in respect of premises situate at .... in the County of ..... in the Court Area and District aforesaid intends to apply to the Court at .... on the .... day of ...., 19....., at 10.30 o'clock in the forenoon or so soon thereafter as this application may be taken in its order in the Court list for a Special Exemption Order authorising the Applicant to sell intoxicating liquor at .... in the Court Area and District aforesaid being a licensed *Hotel* or *Restaurant* [*delete as appropriate*] on the days and during the hours set out in the Schedule hereto on the occasion of the holding of a Social Function organised or supported by the committee and organisers of the .... Festival Club

AND FURTHER TAKE NOTICE that all the requirements of section 13 of the Intoxicating Liquor Act, 1962, have been complied with.

SCHEDULE

Days	**Hours**

CONDITIONS [*in addition to statutory conditions*]

Signed: ______________________
Applicant

____
Solicitors for the Applicant Dated the ..... day of ...., 19 ...

To: The District Court Clerk [*for the District Court licensing area in which licensed premises is situate*]

And: The Superintendent of the Garda Síochána [*for the Garda District in which licensed premises is situate*]

8. Application for Exemption for Unlicensed Business conducted on Sunday mornings and the morning of St Patrick's Day on Licensed Premises situate in any locality not being in a County or other Borough

THE DISTRICT COURT

DISTRICT COURT AREA OF ______ **DISTRICT NO. ______**

IN THE MATTER OF:
THE LICENSING ACTS 1833 TO 1995

AND IN THE MATTER OF:
THE INTOXICATING LIQUOR ACT 1962, SECTION 17

AND IN THE MATTER OF:
AN APPLICATION OF ________

Applicant __________

TAKE NOTICE that .... whose place of abode is at .... in the County of ...., the holder of a .... Licence (not being a Licence granted by virtue of paragraph (2) of section 2 of the Act of 1902), in respect of premises situate at ...., within the Court Area and District aforesaid, intends to apply to the Court sitting at .... on the .... day of ...., 19......., at 10.30 o'clock in the forenoon or so soon thereafter as this application may be taken in its order in the Court list for an Order permitting the Applicant and the holders of such Licences in respect of premises situate in the locality of the Applicant's premises to wit:—

to open or keep open such premises for the purpose of carrying on any business other than the sale or supply of intoxicating liquor within the following period:—

[*Hours*]

Signed: ________________________
Applicant

____
Solicitors for the Applicant Dated the ..... day of ...., 19 ...

To: The District Court Clerk [*for the District Court licensing area in which the licensed premises is situate*]

And: The Superintendent of the Garda Síochána [*for the Garda District in which the licensed premises is situate*]

LICENCES FOR PLACE OF PUBLIC ENTERTAINMENT

1. Application for Annual Public Dancing Licence

THE DISTRICT COURT

DISTRICT COURT AREA OF ______ **DISTRICT NO. ______**

IN THE MATTER OF:
THE PUBLIC DANCE HALLS ACT 1935, SECTIONS 2, 3

IN THE MATTER OF:
THE COURTS (SUPPLEMENTAL PROVISIONS) ACT 1961

IN THE MATTER OF:
THE DISTRICT COURT RULES 1948, RULE 12

AND IN THE MATTER OF:
AN APPLICATION OF ________

Applicant__________

TAKE NOTICE that .... whose place of abode is at .... in the County of ...., will apply to the Court sitting at .... in the County of the .... day of ...., 19......., at 10.30 o'clock in the forenoon or so soon thereafter as this application may be taken in its order in the Court list for a Licence to use a particular place for public dancing, *viz.* [*here describe the premises fully and refer to Map*]

The said premises is/is not [*delete as appropriate*] licensed for the sale of intoxicating liquor and is situate in the Court Area and District aforesaid.

Signed: ________________________
Applicant

____
Solicitors for the Applicant Dated this ..... day of ...., 19 ...

To: The District Court Clerk [*for the District Court licensing area in which the premises is situate*]

And: The Superintendent of the Garda Síochána [*for the Garda District in which the premises is situate*]

And: The Fire Authority [*for the functional area within which premises is situate*]

And: The Local Authority [*for the place within which the premises is situate*]

2. Application for Temporary Public Dancing Licence or for Public Dancing Licence for a Defined Period not exceeding One Month

THE DISTRICT COURT

DISTRICT COURT AREA OF ______ **DISTRICT NO. ______**

IN THE MATTER OF:
THE PUBLIC DANCE HALLS ACT 1935, SECTIONS 3, 6

IN THE MATTER OF:
THE COURTS (SUPPLEMENTAL PROVISIONS) ACT 1961

IN THE MATTER OF:
THE DISTRICT COURT RULES 1948, RULES 12 AND 108

AND IN THE MATTER OF:
AN APPLICATION OF ________

Applicant __________

TAKE NOTICE that .... whose place of abode is at .... in the County of ...., will apply to the Court sitting at .... in the County of .... on the .... day of ...., 19......., at 10.30 o'clock in the forenoon or so soon thereafter as this application may be taken in its order in the Court list for a Licence to use a particular place namely [*here describe premises fully*] which is/is not [*delete as appropriate*] licensed for the sale of intoxicating liquor which said premises is situate in the Court Area and District aforesaid, for Public Dancing for a defined period as follows:—

From the .... day of ......, 19......., to the .... day of ...., 19......, inclusive between the hours of .... and .... (which said period does not exceed one month).

Signed: ______________________
Applicant

____
Solicitors for the Applicant

Dated this ..... day of ...., 19 ...

To: The District Court Clerk [*for the District Court licensing area in which the premises is situate*]

And: The Superintendent of the Garda Síochána [*for the Garda District in which the premises is situate*]

And: The Fire Authority [*for the functional area within which premises is situate*]

3. Application for Annual Music and Singing Licence

THE DISTRICT COURT

DISTRICT COURT AREA OF ______ **DISTRICT NO.** ______

IN THE MATTER OF:
THE PUBLIC HEALTH ACTS AMENDMENT ACT 1890, SECTION 51

IN THE MATTER OF:
THE COURTS (SUPPLEMENTAL PROVISIONS) ACT 1961

AND IN THE MATTER OF:
AN APPLICATION OF ________

Applicant __________

TAKE NOTICE that .... whose place of abode is at .... in the County of ...., will apply to the Court sitting at .... in the County of .... on the .... day of ...., 19......., at 10.30 o'clock in the forenoon or so soon thereafter as this application may be taken in its order in the Court list for a Licence to keep and use the premises known as .... [*here describe premises fully*] and situate at .... in the County of .... in the Court Area and District aforesaid, for Public Singing, Music or other public entertainment of like kind.

Signed: ______________________
Applicant

____
Solicitors for the Applicant Dated this ..... day of ...., 19 ...

To: The District Court Clerk [*for the District Court licensing area in which the premises is situate*]

And: The Superintendent of the Garda Síochána [*for the Garda District in which the premises is situate*]

And: The Fire Authority [*for the functional area within which premises is situate*]

4. Application for Temporary Music and Singing Licence or for a Music and Singing Licence for a period not exceeding 14 days

THE DISTRICT COURT

DISTRICT COURT AREA OF _______ **DISTRICT NO.** _______

IN THE MATTER OF:
THE PUBLIC HEALTH ACTS AMENDMENT ACT 1890, SECTION 51(11)

AND IN THE MATTER OF:
THE COURTS (SUPPLEMENTAL PROVISIONS) ACT 1961

AND IN THE MATTER OF:
RULES OF THE DISTRICT COURT 1948, RULE 12

AND IN THE MATTER OF:
AN APPLICATION OF __________

Applicant __________

TAKE NOTICE that .... whose place of abode is at .... in the County of ...., will apply to the Court sitting at .... in the County of .... on the .... day of ...., 19......., at 10.30 o'clock in the forenoon or so soon thereafter as this application may be taken in its order in the Court list for a Licence to keep or use the premises known as .... [*here describe premises fully*] and situate at .... in the County of ...., in the Court Area and District aforesaid for Public Singing, Music or other Public Entertainment of like kind for the following period:

From the .... day of ...., 19......, to the .... day of ...., 19........, inclusive between the hours of .... and .... (which said period does not exceed 14 days).

Signed: ________________________
Applicant

____
Solicitors for the Applicant Dated this ..... day of ...., 19 ...

To: The District Court Clerk [*for the District Court licensing area in which the premises is situate*]

And: The Superintendent of the Garda Síochána [*for the Garda District in which the premises is situate*][16]

And: The Fire Authority [*for the functional area within which premises is situate*]

[16] Notice to the Garda Síochána is not required by statute: Public Health Acts Amendment Act 1890, s. 51(11). It is merely a matter of courtesy.

5. Notice of Surrender of Public Dancing Licence

THE DISTRICT COURT

DISTRICT COURT AREA OF _______ **DISTRICT NO. _______**

IN THE MATTER OF:
THE PUBLIC DANCE HALLS ACT 1935, SECTION 7

AND IN THE MATTER OF:
AN APPLICATION OF __________

Applicant___________

TAKE NOTICE that .... whose place of abode is at .... in the County of .... being licensed to use premises known as [*specify*] and situate at .... for public dancing until [*specify expiry date*] hereby surrenders the within licence [*enclose licence*].

Signed: __________________________
Licensee

____
Solicitors for the Licensee Dated this ..... day of ...., 19 ...

To: District Court Clerk [*for the District Court licensing area in which the premises is situate*]

6. Application for Public Dancing Licence with Consent of Licensee under Existing Licence

THE DISTRICT COURT

DISTRICT COURT AREA OF ______ **DISTRICT NO.** ______

IN THE MATTER OF:
THE PUBLIC DANCE HALLS ACT 1935, SECTION 8

AND IN THE MATTER OF:
AN APPLICATION OF ________

Applicant __________

TAKE NOTICE that......... whose place of abode is at .... in the County of .... will apply to the Court sitting at .... in the County of .... on the ....day of.........., 19....., at 10.30 o'clock in the forenoon or so soon therafter as this Application may be taken in its order in the Court list for a licence to use a particular place for public dancing [*describe premises in full*].

AND TAKE NOTICE that the existing Licensee whose place of abode is at .... hereby consents to this application.

Signed: ____________________
Applicant

____
Solicitors for the Applicant Dated this ..... day of ...., 19 ...

To: The District Court Clerk [*for the District Court licensing area in which the premises is situate*]

And: The Superintendent of the Garda Síochána [*for the Garda District in which the premises is situate*][17]

And: The Fire Authority [*for the functional area within which premises is situate*]

---

[17] Notice to the Garda Síochána is not required by statute: Public Health Acts Amendment Act 1890, s. 51(11). It is merely a matter of courtesy.

OTHER PRECEDENTS

1. Requisitions on Title relating to Licensed Premises

REQUISITIONS ON TITLE[18]	REPLIES
29. FIRE SERVICE ACT 1981	
1. Have any notices been served on the Vendor under the Fire Services Act 1981?	
2. Are there any proceedings pending under the Fire Services Act 1981?	
3. Has the property ever been inspected by the Fire Authority for the functional area within which the property is situate? If so what were its requirements?	
. . .	
40. LICENSING	
1. a. Is there a current licence attached to the property?	
b. If so, please state fully and concisely the character of the licence and furnish a complete copy thereof (front and back).	
2. Is the licence a Publican's Licence (Ordinary) entitling the holder thereof to sell intoxicating liquor whether for consumption on or off the property during the ordinary hours of opening permitted by law?	
3. Specify the Statute and Section(s) pursuant to which the licence was granted.	
4. a. On what date was the licence first granted.	

[18] From the 1996 edition of *Law Society's Objections and Requisitions* reproduced with the kind permission of Ms Maeve Hayes, Conveyancing Committee, Law Society of Ireland.

REQUISITIONS ON TITLE	REPLIES
b. If this information cannot be ascertained state whether the licence was first granted prior to or subsequent to 31st July 1902.	
5. Does the licence carry the benefit of any special or general exemptions.	
6. a. Are there any conditions, restrictions or qualifications attaching to the licence.	
b. If so specify same in detail.	
7. Is the property regularly open for the conduct of the Publican's business.	
8. Furnish now plan of the property showing the exact extent of the property covered by the licence.	
9. Are there any statutory provisions relating to the structural lay-out or user of the property non-compliance with which might affect the validity of the licence or the right to renew.	
10. a. Has the property ever been altered or enlarged since the date upon which the same was first licensed.	
b. If so was an application made to the Court and an Order granted under Section 6 of the Licensing (Ireland) Act 1902 as amended by Section 24 of the Intoxicating Liquor Act 1960.	
c. If the answer to b. above is in the affirmative furnish any Order now.	
11. a. Did the applicant who was first granted the licence give any undertakings to the Court in relation to the conduct of the Licensed Premises or otherwise.	

REQUISITIONS ON TITLE	REPLIES
b. If so give details.	
12. a. Did any subsequent licensee for the time being give any undertakings to the Court or to any objectors upon any grant or renewal thereof.	
b. If so, give details.	
13. Is there any mortgage of any nature, charge, burden or equity affecting the property which would give any person other than the licensee either a legal or equitable interest in the licence?	
14. Furnish details of all convictions against the licensee for the time being since 4 July 1960 or since the date upon which the licence was first granted whichever date is the later.	
15. If it is contended that one or more of the convictions were not recordable on the licence pursuant to the provisions of Part III of the Intoxicating Liquor Act 1927 state the reason(s).	
16. Are there any convictions recorded on the licence at present?	
17. Are there any convictions recordable on the licence at this date.	
18. a. If the property was sold to a bona fide purchaser for money or monies worth at any time since 4 July 1960 or since the date upon which the licence was first granted whichever date is the later, were Orders made under Section 30 of the Intoxicating Liquor Act 1927 directing that any offences recorded at the time of such transfer should cease to be recorded.	

REQUISITIONS ON TITLE	REPLIES
b. If so give details in particular of the date or dates of such Orders.	
19. Are there any Summonses pending against the Vendor for an alleged breach or breaches of the licensing laws.	
20. Has the Vendor or his servants or agents committed any breach of the licensing laws in respect of which a Summons might issue against the Vendor.	
21. Confirm that all the proper parties have been served for renewal of the licence if applicable.	
22. Confirm that:	
a. The current licence will be endorsed by the Vendor and handed over to the Purchaser on closing.	
b. The Vendor will take all steps necessary including attendance at Court if required to facilitate the transfer of the licence to the Purchaser.	
23. a. Was compliance with any requirements of the Fire Authority outstanding at the last annual licensing sessions or has notice of any requirements been issued since that date.	
b. If so furnish Certificate from the Fire Authority confirming compliance therewith.	
24. a. Has the Vendor served one calendar month's notice on the Fire Authority of his intention to apply for the renewal of a Licence at the next Annual Licensing Sessions.	

REQUISITIONS ON TITLE	REPLIES
b. If so furnish copy and any reply received to such notice.	
41. RESTAURANT/HOTEL	
1. a. Has the property an "Hotel Licence" attached thereto which licence issued pursuant to Section 2(2) of the Licensing (Ireland) Act 1902.	
b. If so, confirm that there is no public bar on the property.	
c. If there is furnish copy of an order pursuant to Section 19 of the Intoxicating Liquor Act 1960 so authorising.	
2. On what date was the property first certified by the Court as being suitable to receive an hotel licence.	
3. State the number of apartments currently set apart and used exclusively as sleeping accommodation for travellers.	
4. If the property was certified as an hotel either under the provisions of Section 42(1) of the Tourist Traffic Act 1952 or section 20 of the Intoxicating Liquor Act 1960 furnish now the current Certificate of Registration from Bord Failte.	
5. Has Bord Failte served any notice of additional requirements which much be complied with before the next annual licensing sessions.	
6. a. Has any grant been paid to the licensee or any other person in respect of the property by Bord Failte.	
b. If so furnish details.	
9. a. Has the property been certified as	

REQUISITIONS ON TITLE	REPLIES

being suitable to receive a full or limited Restaurant Certificate pursuant to the Intoxicating Liquor Act 1927.

b. If so furnish now a copy of current certificate and confirm that the original will be furnished on closing.

42. SPECIAL RESTAURANT LICENCE

1. a. Is the Licence a Special Restaurant licence issued pursuant to Sections 8 and 9 of the Intoxicating Liquor Act 1988.

b. If so furnish now a complete copy of the current licence.

c. Confirm that the original current licence will be endorsed by the Vendor and handed over to the Purchaser on completion.

2. On what date was the licence first granted.

3. Furnish now a complete copy of the plans lodged in Court upon the grant of the Court Certificate authorising the issue of the licence.

4. a. Have any alterations been made to the property from the position as shown in the said plans which might affect the validity of the licence or might adversely affect the renewal thereof.

b. If so give full particulars now.

5. a. Has the property been extended or enlarged from the position as shown in the said Plans.

REQUISITIONS ON TITLE	REPLIES
b. If so give full particulars now.	
6. Has any application been made and an Order granted by the Court consequent upon any such extension or enlargement.	
7. Confirm that the Vendor holds a current Bord Failte Certificate within the meaning of Section 8(2) of the Intoxicating Liqour Act 1988 in respect of the property and the Vendors Restaurant business carried on therein.	
8. a. Furnish now a complete copy of such Bord Failte Certificate	
b. Confirm that the original current Bord Failte Certificate will be endorsed by the Vendor and handed over to the Purchaser on completion.	
9. a. Have any alterations been made to the property since the latest inspection thereof by or on behalf of Bord Failte in connection with the Bord Failte Certificate which might cause the Bord Failte Certificate to be cancelled or might adversely affect the renewal thereof.	
b. If so give full particulars.	
10. a. Has Bord Failte any requirements in respect of the property which are still outstanding.	
b. If so furnish details now.	
11. a. Confirm that the Vendor has not received and is not aware of any notice or intention on the part of Bord Failte to issue a notice threatening cancellation of the Bord Failte Certificate.	

REQUISITIONS ON TITLE	REPLIES
b. If such notice has been received furnish now a complete copy thereof.	
12. a. Has the Vendor given any undertaking (formally or otherwise) to the Local Health Authority Bord Failte the Fire Authority the Gardai the Courts or any other party for the purpose of obtaining the grant or renewal of the licence or any registration certification withdrawal of objection or otherwise in connection with same.	
b. If so give now full particulars and confirm that such undertaking has been fully complied with.	
13. Confirm that all proper notices have been served for the renewal of the licence if applicable.	
14. Confirm that an application has been made for the renewal of the Bord Failte Certificate if applicable.	
43. DANCING MUSIC AND SINGING	
1. a. Is there a Public Dancing Licence attached to the property.	
b. If so furnish now copy thereof and confirm that same will be handed over on closing.	
2. a. Is there a Music and Singing Licence attached to the property.	
b. If so furnish now copy thereof and confirm that same will be handed over on closing endorsed by the Vendor.	
3. In respect of the licences referred to at 1 and 2:	

REQUISITIONS ON TITLE	REPLIES
a. Did the applicant who was first granted the licence give any undertakings to the Court in relation to the conduct of the property or otherwise.	
b. If so furnish now details thereof.	
c. Did the licensee for the time being give any undertaking to the Court or to any objectors upon any grant or renewal thereof?	
d. If so furnish now details thereof.	

2. Suggested Agreement for the Extinguishment of On-Licence

AN AGREEMENT made the ...... day of ......, 1990, and made BETWEEN A.B. Publican of .... in the County of .... (hereinafter called "the Licensee") of the one part and C.D............ of .... in the County of .... (hereinafter called "the Intending Applicant") of the other part

WHEREAS the Intending Applicant intends to apply to the Circuit Court sitting at .... in the County of .... pursuant to the provisions of Section 4 of the Licensing (Ireland) Act 1902 [*or as the case may be*] for the grant of a Publican's Licence (Ordinary) in respect of premises situate at .... in the County of ....

AND WHEREAS the Statute provides, inter alia, that any new Licence shall be granted in substitution for an existing Licence held in respect of premises situate within a City or Town

AND WHEREAS for the consideration hereinafter appearing the Licensee has agreed with the Intending Applicant to surrender to the Court for extinguishment the aforementioned existing Publican's Licence so as to enable the Intending Applicant in the course of his application for a new Licence to comply with the requirements of the said Statute

NOW THIS AGREEMENT WITNESSETH that in consideration of the payment by the Intending Applicant to the Licensee of the sum of £....... in the manner hereinafter appearing, the Licensee agrees to produce, hand over and surrender his said existing Publican's Licence for extinguishment as hereinbefore provided

And the Licensee further agrees and covenants with the Intending Applicant as follows:—

1. That his said Licence is a valid, current and subsisting Licence, free from any endorsement under Part III of the Intoxicating Liquor Act 1927, as amended.
2. That the said Licence was not issued pursuant to the provisions of paragraph 2 of Section 2 of the Licensing (Ireland) Act 1902, that is to say, it is not what is known as a "Hotel Licence".
3. That the said Licence is not a special Restaurant Licence, issued pursuant to the provisions of section 8 of the Intoxicating Liquor Act 1988.
4. That the said Licence has never been forfeited.
5. That the said licence is not a greyhound racetrack licence, issued pursuant to the provisions of section 18 of the Intoxicating Liquor Act 1962.

6. That the trade of publican is and will continue to be carried on in the premises to which the Licence is attached and that the Licensee will take such steps as may be necessary to keep such Licence valid and subsisting and that same will not be allowed lapse pending its surrender to the Court in the course of the Intending Applicant's application.
7. That the Licensee will comply with the Licensing Acts, 1833 to 1995, and will do no act and will neglect no statutory obligation which will occasion the endorsement or forfeiture of the said Licence.
8. That there are no conditions or restrictions attaching to the said Licence and that same is and will continue to be an existing Licence within the meaning of Section 4 of the said Act of 1902, pending the Intending Applicant's application to the Court and any appeal therefrom.
9. That the Licensee will produce the said Licence when called upon and will attend Court on the making of the said application and give such evidence as may be necessary to lead to the grant of the Intending Applicant's application for a new Licence in substitution for the Licensee's Licence.

And the Intending Applicant agrees and covenants with the Licensee:—

1. That he will pursue his said intended application with all due diligence and take all steps that may be necessary to ensure that same is brought to a successful conclusion at the earliest date.
2. That he will pay the said consideration to the Licensee in manner following:—
   (a) as to £......... part thereof upon the signing of this agreement;
   (b) as to £........ balance thereof upon the successful conclusion of the Intending Applicant's application for a new Licence.

IN WITNESS whereof the parties have hereunto signed their names and affixed their seals the day and year first herein WRITTEN.

SIGNED, etc.

3. Sample Clauses for Insertion in Mortgage Deed[19]

A. The Mortgagor will apply or will cause application to be made at all proper times to the relevant authorities for the time being and will use his best endeavours to obtain a renewal of the Seven-Day Publican's On-Licence ("the Publican's Licence"), the Public Music and Singing Licence ("Music Licence") and the Public Dancing Licence ("Dancing Licence") during the term of the Mortgage and will pay all fees and excise duties payable thereon.

B. The Mortgagor shall comply with and observe the provisions of the Tourist Traffic Acts 1939 to 1987, the Licensing Acts 1833 to 1995, the Fire Services Act 1981 (all as amended from time to time) and in particular and without prejudice to the generality of the foregoing shall, or shall cause his servants or agents:

(i) annually or at such intervals as may be prescribed, to renew the registration of the premises with Bord Failte or any other regulatory body prescribed by statute and to comply promptly with all requirements of Bord Fáilte or such other regulatory body;

(ii) annually to give all prescribed notice and take all prescribed steps for the purposes of renewing the Publican's Licence;

(iii) to apply for and, where appropriate, renew all other licences necessary in connection with the trade carried on in the premises;

(iv) to produce to the Mortgagee for inspection, on being requested to do so, the Publican's Licence and any other licences attached to the premises or relating to the trade carried on in the premises;

(v) not to do anything whereby or by means whereof the Publican's Licence or any other Licence attached to the premises or relating to the trade carried on in the premises may be forfeited, lapse or be extinguished or become void or voidable or whereby any privileges attaching thereto may be lost or jeopardised;

(vi) to fulfil any undertaking given to any Court or any third party on the grant of the Publican's Licence;

(vii) not to give any undertaking other than such undertaking as may have to be given in the ordinary course of business to any Court or to any third party in relation to the Publican's Licence without the prior consent of the Landlord, which prior consent shall not be unreasonably withheld;

(viii) to give immediate notice to the Mortgagee of any Summons issued against the Mortgagor in respect of any alleged offence charged against the

---

[19] The kind assistance of Ms Maeve Hayes, Solicitor, Mason Hayes & Curran in the preparation of this Appendix is gratefully acknowledged.

Mortgagor in respect of the trade carried on in the premises and of any notice received by the Mortgagor of any intention to oppose the renewal of the Publican's Licence;

(ix) not to transfer, assign, surrender or otherwise dispose of any Licence and/or Certificates attaching to the premises from time to time nor take any steps to remove to any other property without the consent in writing of the Mortgagee.

MORTGAGEE'S ATTORNEY

C. Without prejudice to the obligations of the Mortgagor under the covenants hereinbefore contained the Mortgagor hereby irrevocably appoints the Mortgagor and any receiver appointed severally as his/its attorney or as attorneys of the Mortgagor to apply for and obtain the renewal of any Licence and/or Certificates attaching to the premises from time to time which are necessary for keeping the premises open for use in accordance with the permitted user herein.

ALTERNATE CLAUSE

To apply or cause application to be made to the Revenue Commissioners or appropriate authority for the time being for the issue of the Certificate of Tax Clearance entitling the Mortgagor to apply for the grant or renewal of the relevant Intoxicating Liquor Licence for use in keeping open the premises during the term of the Mortgage for the sale and consumption therein of beer, wine, spirits and excisable liquors by retail and to produce proof to the Mortgagee that such application has been made on or before the 1st of September in each calendar year, and further to produce a copy of this Certificate of Tax Clearance to the Mortgagee on or before the 31st of September of each calendar year or as soon thereafter as may be permitted by the Mortgagee, but in any event not later than 31st of October of each calendar year.

ALTERNATIVE CLAUSES

The Borrower hereby undertakes with the Mortgagee to:

(a) Carry on the business of licensed premises at the secured property to best advantage in a proper and businesslike manner and in conformity with Statutes, Regulations and Bye-Laws applicable thereto and not to permit to be done any act or thing whereby the Liquor Licence or the renewal thereof may be endangered;

(b) Insure and keep insured the Liquor Licence against loss and non-renewal in a sum of £.................. with an insurance company and on terms previously approved of by the Mortgagee and note the interest of the Mortgagee upon all policies of insurance and produce to or deposit with all policies of such insurance and the receipts of all premiums and payments, if necessary, for effecting and keeping up such policies;

(c) Procure that all monies now or hereafter payable under any policy of insurance in respect of the loss non-renewal or forfeiture of the Liquor Licence whether effected or maintained in pursuance of such clause (b) above otherwise are paid to the Mortgagee or if the same are paid to the Borrower all such moneys on trust for the Mortgagee to be applied in or towards the payment of the secured liabilities;

(d) Keep in full force and effect and so often as is necessary promptly renew the Liquor Licence and apply for and obtain any extension to or replacement of the Liquor Licence necessary or desirable in connection with the enlargement or reconstruction of the secured premises;

(e) Immediately on the execution of the Mortgage to produce to the Mortgagee the original Intoxicating Liquor Licence, the Mortgagee to retain as part of its security hereby constituted a certified copy of the Licence and forthwith on each renewal of the Liquor Licence, to produce to the Mortgagee the said original Intoxicating Liquor Licence and permit the Mortgagee to retain as part of its security a certified copy of the renewed Licence;

(f) The Mortgagor hereby irrevocably appoints the Mortgagee and any Receiver appointed severally his Attorney in his name and as his act and on his behalf to make application, execute any document and do any other act which may be necessary or desirable for the purposes of obtaining or effecting any renewal or transfer of an Intoxicating Liquor Licence.

4. Suggested Constitution for Club

NAME AND OBJECTS OF CLUB

1. The Club shall be known as ....
2. The Club Premises ("the Club House") shall be situated at ....
3. The object for which the club is established is to play and foster the game of .... [*e.g.* golf].

MEMBERSHIP

4. The Club shall consist of such number of ordinary members as the Committee shall from time to time think fit, not being less than 150 in number. In addition, but subject to these Rules, honorary members and temporary members may be admitted to Membership at the discretion of the Committee provided that the only persons who may be admitted to honorary membership shall be either persons who have or had distinguished amateur or professional [e.g. golfing] careers or rendered exceptional services to the administration of the game of [golf] or are persons who hold golfing handicaps.
5. Admission to ordinary membership shall be by ballot in accordance with Rule 6.
6. At the meeting at which the election of a candidate for ordinary membership is considered, every member of the Committee shall be entitled to vote in person for or against each candidate for admission at such election. The election shall be decided by simple majority. The decision of the Committee as to whether any candidate has been duly elected or not shall be final. Immediately upon the election of a member notice thereof shall be placed in a conspicuous place in the Club House and the elected member shall be entitled to be furnished with a copy of these Rules by which he shall in any case be bound. The membership of an elected member shall not be deemed to commence until the candidate discharges the annual membership subscription payable in respect of the calendar year in which he is elected.

SUBSCRIPTION

7. The annual membership subscription payable for the whole or any part of a year shall be payable in advance. The Committee shall be entitled to review the amounts of the annual subscriptions at any time.

8. All annual subscriptions, other than the first subscription of a new member, shall be payable on the 1st day of April in each year.

9. From and after the 1st day of April in each year a member shall not be qualified to act as a member of the Committee nor to avail himself or herself of any of the privileges of membership of the Club until his or her subscription for the current year has been paid.

HONORARY AND TEMPORARY MEMBERSHIP

10. The Secretary shall have power in the name of the Committee to declare as temporary members of Club the members of any sporting organisation or association using the Club House on any day or days for the duration of the event and for the evening on which it concludes subject to receipt in advance of a written list of the names of such members so certified in writing by the organiser of the sporting event in which they are participating.

11. (a) Honorary and Temporary members shall be entitled for the duration of their honorary or temporary membership to all the benefits and privileges of membership save that they shall not be qualified to be officers of the Club or members of the Committee or to attend or vote at general meetings of the Club and shall not be liable for an annual subscription.

(b) The Secretary shall maintain the following separate registers of members;

(i) Ordinary Members;
(ii) Honorary Members;
(iii) Temporary Members;

and said registers of members shall be kept at the Club House and available for inspection by members, members of the Garda Síochána and any other person or body entitled by law to inspect same.

COMMITTEE OF MANAGEMENT

12. The business and affairs of the Club shall be under the management of a Committee consisting of six ordinary members duly elected to be members of the Committee. No member of the Committee and no manager or servant employed in the Club shall have any personal interest in the sale of excisable liquor in the Club House or in the profits arising from such sale.

13. All nominations for the Committee must be furnished to the Secretary at least 21 days before the date of the meeting. A list of the candidates for election to the Committee shall be posted in or adjacent to the Club House 14 days before the date of the annual general meeting.

14. The Committee shall have power to appoint an ordinary member to fill any casual vacancy among the members of the Committee.

15. The Committee shall hold quarterly meetings for the purpose of transacting the business of the Club. Three members of the Committee shall be a quorum.

16. The Annual General Meeting of the Club shall be held in the month of June or as soon thereafter as may be convenient.

17. At all meetings of the Committee in the event of difference of opinion the question shall be decided by a single majority. In the event of an equality of votes the Chairman shall have a second or casting vote.

18. Full minutes shall be made in proper books of all resolutions and proceedings of the Committee and every minute signed by the Chairman of the Committee shall be sufficient evidence of the facts therein stated.

19. The Committee shall have power to make such regulations consistent with these general rules as it shall from time to time think necessary for the well being of the Club, and such regulations shall be binding on the members. Furthermore, the Committee may employ such staff and enter into such contracts as it deems necessary for the proper management of the Club House and the general conduct of the business of the Club therein.

ACCOUNTS

20. Correct accounts and books shall be kept showing the financial affairs, receipts and disbursements of the Club; and the Committee shall procure that the accuracy thereof shall be ascertained and verified at the end of each financial year by audit conducted by the Auditors for the time being of the Club.

SALE OF EXCISABLE LIQUOR

21. No excisable liquor shall be supplied for consumption in the Club House to any person:

(a) on any weekday before 10.30 a.m.; or

(i) during the period of summertime after 11.30 p.m.; or
(ii) during the period which is not a period of summertime after 11 p.m.; or

(b) on any Sunday before 12.30 p.m. or between 2 p.m. and 4 p.m. or after 11 p.m.; or

(c) on St Patrick's Day when that day falls on a weekday before 12.30 p.m. and after 11 p.m.; or
(d) on any time on Christmas Day or Good Friday;

(e) where in any year December 23 or 24 falls on a Sunday before 10.30 a.m.; or
   (i) during a period of summertime after the hours of 11.30 p.m.; or
   (ii) during a period which is not a period of summertime after the hour of 11 p.m.;

provided always that nothing herein shall operate to prohibit the Club supplying for consumption in the Club House of excisable liquor by any person:

(a) during a period of summertime between 11.30 p.m. on any weekday and 12.30 a.m. on the following day; or

(b) during any period which is not a period of summertime between 11 p.m. on any weekday and 12.30 a.m. on the following day; or

(c) on any Sunday between 2 p.m. and 3 p.m.; or

(d) on Christmas Day between 1 p.m. and 3 p.m. or 7 p.m. and 10 p.m.;

(e) where in any year December 23 or 24 falls on a Sunday then the provisions of the Registration of Clubs Code which relate to a weekday during a period of summertime shall apply to such a Sunday as if it were a weekday, if, in each case, the excisable liquor is ordered and consumed with the meal, supplied and consumed in the portion of the club premises usually set apart for the supply of meals and paid for at the same time as the meal is paid for.

22. (a) No excisable liquor shall be sold or supplied to any person under the age of 18 years and no person under the age of 18 years shall be admitted as a member of the club unless the club is primarily devoted to an athletic purpose.

(b) No excisable liquor shall be sold or supplied for consumption outside the premises of the Club, except to members of the Club between 8 a.m. and 10 p.m.

23. A visitor shall not be supplied with excisable liquor in the Club House unless on the invitation and in the company of a member , and the member shall, with the admission of such visitor to the Club House or immediately upon the visitor being supplied with such liquor, enter the members name and the name and address of the visitor in a book which shall be kept for that purpose and which shall show the date of each such visit.

24. Any provisions which are contained in this constitution which are not in conformity with any statutory provision contained in the Registration of Clubs Acts 1904 to 1995 shall be deemed to be null and void. No rule of the Club with the exception of the rules relating to the supply of intoxicating liquor on the club premises shall be altered, rescinded or added to without the consent of at least two thirds of the members present and entitled to vote at any general

meeting of the Club. All rules contained in the Club constitution which relate to the supply of intoxicating liquor on the club premises may be altered by the Committee so as to conform with the Registration of Clubs Acts 1904 to 1995 (as may be amended from time to time).

Appendix B

STATUTES

1. Licensing (Ireland) Act 1833
2. Public House (Ireland) Act 1855
3. Public Health Acts Amendment Act 1890
4. Licensing (Ireland) Act 1902
5. Registration of Clubs (Ireland) Act 1904
6. Intoxicating Liquor (General) Act 1924
7. Intoxicating Liquor Act 1927
8. Public Dance Halls Act 1935
9. Intoxicating Liquor Act 1943
10. Intoxicating Liquor Act 1953
11. Intoxicating Liquor Act 1960
12. Intoxicating Liquor Act 1962
13. Courts (No. 2) Act 1986
14. Intoxicating Liquor Act 1988
15. Intoxicating Liquor Act 1995

LICENSING (IRELAND) ACT 1833[1]

3 & 4 Will. 4, c. 68

AN ACT TO AMEND THE LAWS RELATING TO THE SALE OF WINE, SPIRITS, BEER, AND CIDER BY RETAIL IN IRELAND

I. It shall and may be lawful for the proper Officers of Excise in Ireland to grant to the same Persons and at and for the same Houses as shall have been licensed in the Year last immediately preceding, and whose Licence shall not have been withdrawn or annulled **[Deletion: by the Intoxicating Liquor Act 1943, s.32]** a Licence or Licences for the Sale of Beer, Cider, and Spirits, under the Provisions of the said recited Act, to sell in Ireland by Retail, in any House specified in such Licence, Beer, Cider, and Spirits respectively to be consumed in such House, without requiring the Production of any Certificate or other Authority from any Justice or Justices of the Peace, Magistrate, or other Person or Persons whatever, on the Persons respectively applying for such Licences complying with the Conditions of this Act; any thing in any Act or Acts heretofore made or in force at the Time of the Passing of this Act to the contrary in anywise notwithstanding.

II. Every Person in Ireland who shall not have been duly licensed in the preceding Year to sell Beer, Cider, or Spirits, to be consumed in the House where sold, and who shall intend to apply for an Excise Licence, under the Provisions of this Act and of the said recited Act, for the Sale of Beer, Cider or Spirits by Retail, to be consumed as aforesaid, shall, **[Deletion: by the Courts Act (No. 2) 1986, ss.9, 10(5), Sched. 1]** give or cause to be given to each of the Two next resident (c) Magistrates (d), and **[Deletion: by the Statute Law Revision Act 1891, s.1, Sched.]** to the Clerk of the Peace for the County or County of a City or County of a Town in which such House shall be situate, severally and respectively, a Notice in Writing (e), signed by such Person (f), stating the Intention of such Person to make such Application, and setting forth the Situation and Place of such House (g). as well in respect to the Road or Highway on or adjacent to which it lies, or otherwise, in a true and particular Manner, specifying the Town, Townland, Parish, Barony, Half Barony (h), and if in a City or Town the Street, Square, Lane, or other Description of Place, together with the Number of such House if such House shall have been numbered, and also the Place of Abode of such Person, **[Deletion: by the Statute Law Revision Act 1891, s. 1, Sched.]** and every such Clerk of the Peace shall file and keep such Notice given to him, and shall **[Deletion: by the Courts (No. 2) Act 1986, ss.9, 10(5), Sched. 1]** make out a List of the Names of

[1] Sometimes cited as Public Houses (Ireland) Act 1833.

all such Applicants, with their Place of Abode, and the Situation and Description, as contained in such Notice, of the House for which such Person shall desire to be licensed, **[Deletion: by the Statute Law Revision Act 1891, s.1, Sched.]** and transmit a Copy of such List to every Magistrate resident within such City or Town, and to the Clerk of every Petty Sessions within such County.

III. And be it further enacted, That upon a certain Day and Hour during such ensuing Quarter Sessions, to be fixed by Rule of said Court, the Names of all such Applicants, together with their Places of Abode, shall be severally called aloud, in alphabetical Order, in open Court, by the Officer of said Court, and Proclamation made of each such Application, and Demand made whether any one has or knows of any Objection to or why such Application should not be allowed or Licence granted.

IV. And be it further enacted, That it shall and may be lawful for any Justice of the Peace of said City, Town or County, Churchwarden or other Inhabitant of said Parish **or the health authority within the meaning of the Health Acts 1947 to 1958 in whose functional area the house is situate**[2] previously to transmit or then and there to deliver in writing to said Clerk of the Peace, or orally to state to said Justices in Sessions assembled, any Matter or Objection to such Application, whether grounded upon the Character, Misconduct or Unfitness of the Applicant, Unfitness or Inconvenience of the House or Place, or Number of previously licensed Houses in the Neighbourhood; and that if any such Objection shall be so transmitted or made, an Entry thereof shall then be recorded by the Clerk of the Peace; and the Justices in such Sessions assembled shall then, or at some other convenient Time to be appointed, proceed to consider, examine into, and adjudicate upon the Truth, Sufficiency, and Validity of such Objection, and for that Purpose to examine on Oath such Applicant or other Person as they may deem fit; and if such Justices shall be thereupon satisfied of the Truth and Sufficiency of such Objection, and shall deem it improper to intrust such Applicant with a Licence for such House, they shall, by Order in Writing to be duly entered by the Clerk of the Peace, prohibit such Licence to be issued and therein declare the Reason or Ground of such Prohibition.

V. And be it further enacted, That upon each Application being disposed of by the Justices attending at such Sessions it shall be lawful for the Clerk of the Peace or his Deputy, and he is hereby required to give or cause to be given to the Person entitled thereto a Certificate in the Form following:—

> I, A.B., Clerk of the Peace of do certify, that C.D. is (or C.D. and E.F. are) duly entitled to receive a Licence for the sale of Beer, Cider, or Spirits (as the case may be) by Retail at in the Parish of (or if extra-parochial, in the Townland of), in this County (County of a Town or City, as the case may be).
>
> Dated this Day of
>
> "A.B. Clerk of the Peace for ."

---

[2] Amended by the Intoxicating Liquor Act 1960, s. 31.

and every such Clerk of the Peace shall for the issuing of such Certificate be entitled to demand and receive the Sum of Two Shillings and Sixpence, and no more, as a Fee, before he shall sign or deliver such Certificate.

VI. And be it further enacted, That it shall and may be lawful for the proper Officers of Excise in Ireland, within their respective Districts, to grant, under the Provisions of the said recited Act, a Licence or Licences for the Sale of Beer, Cider, and Spirits, to sell in Ireland by Retail, in any House specified in such Licence, Beer, Cider and Spirits respectively, to be consumed in such House or elsewhere, to any Person, though not licensed the Year preceding, whom the Justices of the Peace for the City, Town, County, or District within which such House is situate, in Quarter Sessions assembled as herein-before provided, shall not deem it improper to intrust with such Licence, and to whom they shall not, by order there made, prohibit such Licence to be issued, upon the Person applying for such Licence producing such Certificate as aforesaid to such Officer of Excise, and complying with the other Conditions of this Act, **[Deletion: by the Statute Law Revision Act 1891, s.1, Sched.]** such Person first paying for such Licence or Licences the duties of excise for and in respect of such Licence or Licences, according to the Rate and in the Manner prescribed by the said recited Act, or any other Act or Acts then in force with respect to such Licences.

[s.VII deleted by the Sale of Spirits (Ireland) Act 1855, s.4]

VIII. And be it further enacted, That if any Person licensed to sell Beer, Cider, or Spirits by Retail shall, during the Continuance of such Licence or Licences, be convicted of any Misdemeanour, or of any Offence of a higher Nature, or shall be duly convicted of any Three several Offences under the Provisions of this Act or any of them, which Three Offences shall have been committed within the Space of Two Months, then and in every such Case it shall and may be lawful for the Justices of the Peace within whose Jurisdiction such Person shall be licensed to sell Spirits or Beer, assembled at any Quarter Sessions or Adjournment thereof, if they shall so think fit, by Order in open Court made upon due Notice, to annul the Licence held by such Person; and if any such Person whose Licence or Licences shall be so annulled, and on whom a Notice shall have been served of the same being annulled, signed by the said Magistrates or any Two of them, shall sell by Retail any Spirits or Beer, every such Person shall be subject to the same Penalties as Persons selling Beer, Cider, or Spirits without having obtained a Licence for that Purpose are by Law liable.

IX. And be it further enacted, That every Person licensed under this Act to sell Beer, Cider, and Spirits by Retail shall, so long as he shall continue so licensed, be entitled to take out a Licence to sell Foreign Wine by Retail in the same House or Premises in which he shall be licensed to sell Beer, Cider, and Spirits. **[Deletion: by the Statute Law Revision Act 1891, s.1, Sched.]**

X. And be it further enacted, That every Person who shall obtain a Licence to sell Spirits, Beer, or Cider by Retail, to be consumed in the House where sold, shall, within Six Days next and after he shall have so obtained such Licence, deliver or cause to be delivered to the Clerk of the Peace for the County, City or Town within which the House specified in such Licence shall be situate, a Note in Writing, under the Hand of such Person, or under the Hand of some person by him authorised in that behalf, in which shall be specified, set forth and inserted the Christian and Surname and Place of Abode of such Person, and a description of the Place where such House and Premises in which Spirits, Beer, or Cider are licensed to be sold by such Person, and the Place where such House and Premises shall be situate **[Deletion: by the Statute Law Revision Act 1891, s.1, Sched.]**; and such licensed Person shall pay or cause to be paid to such Clerk of the Peace the Sum of Two Shillings and Sixpence; and if any Person who shall have obtained such Licence as aforesaid shall not, within the Time and in the Manner herein-before directed, deliver or cause to be delivered such Note in Writing as aforesaid, every such Person shall forfeit and lose the Sum of Ten Pounds.

XI. And be it further enacted, That a List or Register of every Licence so to be granted for selling by Retail any Beer, Cider, or Perry, or Spirits, to be drank or consumed on the Premises, specifying the Name and Place of Abode of every Person licensed **[Deletion: by the Statute law Revision Act, 1891, s.1, Sched.]** and the Description and Situation of the House or Place mentioned in such licence shall be kept at the Office of the Clerk of the Peace for the County, County of a City, or County of a Town, as the Case may be; which List or Register shall at all reasonable Times be produced to and shall be open to the Inspection and Perusal of every Magistrate within whose Jurisdiction the House or Place specified in each Licence respectively shall be situate; and any Copy of or Extract from any such List or Register, which shall or may be at any Time required by any such Magistrate as aforesaid, shall be given to him by such Clerk of the Peace.

[s.XII deleted by the Finance Act 1939, s.21, Sched. 6]

XIII. And be it further enacted, That no Distiller, **[Deletion: by the Revenue (No. 2) Act 1864, s.9]** Rectifier or Compounder of Spirits, Bailiff, Gaoler, Turnkey, Constable, Sheriff, Sub-Sheriff, Sheriff's Officer, Peace Officer, or Keeper of any Turnpike Gate, nor any Person not being a Householder, shall be capable of receiving or holding a Licence to sell Beer, Cider, or Spirits by Retail, to be drank or consumed on the Premises.

XIV. And be it further enacted, That no Person selling or licensed to sell Beer or Cider, Spirits or Wine, by Retail, to be drank or consumed on the Premises, shall have or keep his House or other Place of sale open for the sale of Spirits, Wine or Beer, or shall sell or Retail Spirits, Wine, or Beer, nor shall suffer any Spirits, Wine or Beer to be drank or consumed in or at such House or other Place, at any Time between the Hours of Eleven of the Clock in the Night and Seven of the Clock in the Morning, nor at any Time before Two of the Clock in the Afternoon on any Sunday, Good Friday, Christmas Day, or any Day appointed for a Public Fast or Thanksgiving; and if any such Person shall keep his House or other Place of Sale open for selling or shall sell Spirits, Wine or Beer at any Time between the Hour of Eleven of the Clock at Night and the Hour of Seven of the Clock in the Morning, or at any Time before Two of the Clock in the Afternoon on any Sunday, Good Friday, Christmas Day, or any Day appointed for a Public Fast or Thanksgiving, such Person shall forfeit the Sum of Two Pounds for any such Offence; and every separate Sale shall be deemed a separate Offence, and all Sales on any one Day shall be deemed and considered and may be prosecuted as separate Offences: Provided always, that nothing herein contained shall extend to prohibit the Sale of Spirits, Wine, or Beer to a Traveller.

XV. And be it further enacted, That it shall and may be lawful for any Justice of the Peace, or for any Chief Constable, or for any Churchwarden or Overseer herein-after mentioned, or for any Constable authorized for the Purpose by any such Justice, within the Limits of his Jurisdiction, to enter into any House or Place kept by any Person selling or having a Licence to sell Spirits, Wine, or Beer by Retail, at any Time between the Hours of Eleven of the Clock on Saturday night and Two of the Clock in the Afternoon of Sunday, or between the Hours of Eleven of the Clock on any other Night and Seven of the Clock in the Morning, and to remove from and put out of such House or Place any Person who shall be so found within such prohibited Hours in such House or Place (not being a Lodger or Inmate of such House or Place), and who shall appear to be or to have recently been drinking, tippling or gaming therein; and if any such Person shall not, when thereto required by such Justice of the Peace, Chief or other Constable, Churchwarden, or Overseer as aforesaid, remove from and quit such House, or shall forcibly resist such Justice, Constable, Churchwarden, or Overseer, it shall and may be lawful for any Constable, Churchwarden or Overseer to apprehend and take into Custody any such Person so offending, and to carry and convey, or cause to be carried or conveyed, every and any such Person so apprehended before any Justice of the Peace within whose Jurisdiction such House or Place shall be situate, to be dealt with according to Law; and every such Person who shall so neglect or refuse to remove from or quit such House, or shall so forcibly resist such Justice, Constable, Churchwarden, or Overseer, being duly convicted of such Offence, shall thereupon for every such Offence forfeit any Sum not exceeding Twenty Shillings nor less than Five Shillings; and if any Offender so convicted shall not forthwith pay the Sum so forfeited, such Offender shall be committed to the House of Correction for any time not exceeding One Week.

XVI. And be it enacted, That if any Offender convicted in manner aforesaid shall be a Soldier on Full Pay, and attached to any Regiment in His Majesty's Service stationed or being within the Jurisdiction of such Justice, a Communication of such Conviction shall be forthwith made by such Justice to the Commanding Officer of such Regiment, and the Offender so convicted shall be detained until delivered over to the Commanding Officer, or his Order, to be amenable to Military Discipline.

XVII. And to be further enacted, That if any Person selling or licensed to sell Spirits, Wine, or Beer by Retail, or any Person aiding or assisting such Retailer, shall prevent or endeavour to prevent, by Threats or Violence or otherwise, any such Justice, or Chief or other Constable, Churchwarden, or Overseer, in that Behalf authorized under this Act, from entering any House or Place, or for searching for any such Person or Persons as aforesaid, or shall assault or otherwise resist any such Justice, or Chief or other Constable, Churchwarden, or Overseer as aforesaid, every such Person so offending shall forfeit and lose a Sum not exceeding the Sum of Ten Pounds.

XVIII. And be it further enacted, That if any Person selling or licensed to sell Spirits, Wine, or Beer shall for the Space of Ten Minutes after Demand made of Entrance delay or neglect to admit any Justice, or Chief or other Constable, Churchwarden, or Overseer as aforesaid into any House or Place of such Person, for the Purpose of making such Search as aforesaid, such Person so offending shall forfeit and lose a Sum not exceeding the Sum of Two Pounds.

XIX. And be it further enacted, That every Person selling or licensed to sell Spirits, Wine, or Beer by Retail, in whose House or Place any Person shall be found to be or to have been recently drinking, tippling, or gaming at any Hour or Time at which the Sale of Spirits or Beer is prohibited by this Act, shall upon Conviction thereof forfeit and pay the Sum of Two Pounds.

XX. And be it further enacted, That it shall be lawful for the Parishioners of the several Parishes in Ireland at Vestry assembled, once in every Year, or oftener if necessary, to appoint such Number of Persons, not exceeding Five, as to them shall seem meet, to be Overseers of Persons and Houses in which Spirits or Beer shall be sold by Retail within every such Parish respectively; and every Overseer so appointed shall have as full and ample Power and Authority for carrying the Provisions of this Act into execution within such Parish as any Constable or other Peace Officer hath or may have by virtue of this Act; and every such Overseer shall for the purposes of this Act be and be deemed and taken to be a Constable or Peace Officer.

XXI. And be it further enacted, That it shall be lawful for any One Justice acting for any County, City or Place where any Riot or Tumult shall happen, or for any Two or more Justices where any Riot or Tumult shall be apprehended and expected to take Place, to order or direct that every Person selling Spirits or Beer by Retail, and keeping any House or Place for that Purpose, situate within their respective Jurisdictions, and in or near the Place where such Riot or Tumult shall happen or be expected to take place, shall close his House or Place at any time and for such Length of Time as such Justice or Justices shall order or direct; and every Person to whom such Order shall be given, and who shall keep open such House or other Place in violation of such Order shall forfeit and lose the Sum of Two Pounds.

[ss.XXII to XXXVIII deleted by the Statute Law Revision Act 1891, s.1, Sched.]

XXXIX. And be it further enacted, That one Moiety of every Fine, Penalty and Forfeiture by this Act imposed, and not expressly directed to be otherwise applied, shall, after deducting all further necessary Charges of Levy not herein-before provided for, be paid to the Use of His Majesty, His Heirs and Successors and the other Moiety to him who shall inform, discover, or sue for the same or to the Poor of the Parish in which such Offence shall have been committed, at the Discretion of the Justices who shall award the same.

XL. Provided always, and be it further enacted, That every Provision, Clause, Matter, and Thing contained in any Statute heretofore passed repugnant to the Provisions of this Act or any of them, or for or in lieu of which Provision is hereby made (if any such there be), be and the same are hereby repealed.

PUBLIC HOUSE (IRELAND) ACT 1855[1]

18 & 19 Vict. c. 114

AN ACT FOR THE TRANSFER OF LICENCES OF PUBLIC HOUSES IN IRELAND

I. Upon the death of any person duly licensed to carry on the business of a licensed victualler, and to sell excisable liquors by retail, to be consumed on the premises, in Ireland, or upon the removal of any such person from the house or premises at which he is authorised by any such licence to carry on such business as aforesaid in Ireland, or the sale of or assignment of his interest therein by operation of law or otherwise, it shall be lawful for the justices of the peace of the district within which any such licensed house or premises shall be situated, assembled at petty sessions, or the justices in any liberty, city, town, or place within which any such licensed house or premises shall be situated, assembled at petty sessions, at any time when no quarter sessions shall be holden for any such county, riding, division, liberty, city, town, or place, (if they shall think proper so to do, after examining upon oath all necessary parties) to transfer, by endorsement thereon, any and every such licence as aforesaid then in force to any person, not disqualified by law, to whom it shall be proposed at the time of such application to transfer any such licence, to use, exercise, and carry on the business of a licensed victualler at the same house and on the same premises, and there to sell such exciseable liquors as might theretofore have been lawfully sold and retailed therein; and thereupon it shall be lawful for such person so to use, exercise, and carry on the said business at such house and premises, until the quarter sessions of the peace which shall be holden for the same county, riding, division, liberty, city, town, or place next after the expiration of one calendar month from the time of such transfer, and no longer.

II. Provided always, that nothing herein contained shall be construed to empower any justices at petty sessions to make any such transfer as aforesaid within any of the divisions assigned or to be assigned to any of the police courts already established or to be established within the district of Dublin Metropolis, but that any such application as is herein-before authorised to be made at petty sessions shall, when the licensed house and premises shall be situated within any of the said divisions of the police district of Dublin Metropolis, be made to one of the police magistrates sitting at any of the said courts, and such magistrate shall, in his discretion, make any such transfer as aforesaid, in the manner and for the time herein-before mentioned:

[1] Sometimes cited as Transfer of Licences (Ireland) Act 1855.

Provided also that any person who shall be authorized under the provisions of this Act to continue to carry on the business of a licensed victualler shall, after the obtaining such authority, and so long as the same shall continue in force, be subject to all the powers, regulations, proceedings, penalties, and provisions declared by or contained in any Act or Acts in force touching the regulation, government, or control of licensed keepers of inns, alehouses, and victualling houses, in like manner as if the same had been repeated and re-enacted in this Act; and that all penalties and forfeitures imposed by any such Act or Acts shall be applied as directed by the same respectively.

PUBLIC HEALTH ACTS AMENDMENT ACT 1890
(*Excerpts*)

53 & 54 Vict. c. 59

An Act to amend the Public Health Acts.

PART I

GENERAL

2.—(1) This Act shall be construed as one with the Public Health Acts.

(2) Part One of this Act shall extend to England and Wales and Ireland, exclusive of the administrative county of London. Parts Two, Three, Four and Five, shall extend to any district in which they are respectively adopted under the provisions of this Act.

(3) This Act may be cited as the Public Health Acts Amendment Act, 1890, and this Act and the Public Health Acts may be cited together as the Public Health Acts.

3.—The followings provisions shall have effect with regard to the adoption of the parts of this Act, which are adoptive, by local authorities:—

(1) An urban authority may adopt all or any of such parts.

(2) A rural authority may adopt Part Three so far as it is declared by this Act to be applicable to such authority, without prejudice to the provisions of this Act relating to the investing of rural authorities with urban powers.

(3) The adoption shall be by a resolution passed at a meeting of the local authority; and one calendar month at least before such meeting special notice of the meeting and of the intention to propose such resolution shall be given to every member of the authority, and the notice shall be deemed to have been duly given to a member of it, if it is either—

(a) Given in the mode in which notices to attend meetings of the authority are usually given; or

(b) Where there is no such mode, then signed by the clerk of the authority, and delivered to the member or left at his usual or last known place of abode in England, or forwarded by post in a prepaid letter, addressed to the member at his usual or last known place of abode in England.

(4) Such resolution shall be published by advertisement in some one or more

newspapers circulating within the district of the authority and by causing notice thereof to be affixed to the principal doors of every church and chapel in the place to which notices are usually fixed, and otherwise in such manner as the authority think sufficient for giving notice thereof to all persons interested, and shall come into operation at such time not less than one month after the first publication of the advertisement of the resolution as the authority may by the resolution fix, and upon its coming into operation such parts of the Act as are adopted shall extend to that district.

(5) A copy of the resolution shall be sent—

(a) Where any part of the Act is adopted, to the Local Government Board;

(b) Where Part Two is adopted, to the Board of Trade;

(c) Where Part Four is adopted, to a Secretary of State.

(6) A copy of the advertisement shall be conclusive evidence of the resolution having been passed, unless the contrary be shown; and no objection to the effect of the resolution, on the ground that notice of the intention to propose the same was not duly given, or on the ground that the resolution was not sufficiently published, shall be made after three months from the date of the first publication of the advertisement.

. . .

PART IV

Music and Dancing

51.—For the regulation of places ordinarily used for public dancing or music, or other public entertainment of the like kind, the following provisions shall have effect (namely):—

(1) After the expiration of six months from the adoption of this part of this Act, a house, room, garden, or other place, whether licensed or not for the sale of wine, spirits, beer, or other fermented or distilled liquors, shall not be kept or used for public dancing, singing, music or other public entertainment of the like kind without a licence for the purpose or purposes for which the same respectively is to be used first obtained from the licensing justices of the licensing district in which the house, room, garden, or place is situate, and for the registration thereof a fee of five shillings shall be paid by the person applying therefor.

(2) Such justices may, under the hands of a majority of them assembled at their general annual licensing meeting or at any adjournment thereof or at any special session convened with fourteen days previous notice, grant licences to such persons as they think fit to keep or use houses, rooms, gardens, or places for all or any of the purposes aforesaid upon such terms and conditions, and subject to such restrictions as they by the respective licences determine, and every licence shall be in force for one year or for such shorter period as the justices on the grant of the licence shall determine, unless the same shall have been previously revoked as herein-after provided.

(3) Such justices may from time to time at any such special session aforesaid transfer any such licence to such person as they think fit.

(4) Each person shall in each case give fourteen days notice to the clerk of the licensing justices and to the chief officer of police of the police district in which the house, room, garden, or place is situated, of his intention to apply for any such licence or for the transfer of any such licence.

(5) Any house, room, garden, or place kept or used for any of the purposes aforesaid without such licence first obtained shall be deemed a disorderly house, and the person occupying or rated as occupier of the same shall be liable to a penalty not exceeding five pounds for every day on which the same is kept or used for any of the purposes last aforesaid.

(6) There shall be affixed and kept up in some conspicuous place on the door or entrance of every house, room, garden, or place so kept or used and so licensed as aforesaid, an inscription in large capital letters in the words following:

> "Licensed in pursuance of Act of Parliament for . . ."
>
> with the addition of words showing the purpose or purposes for which the same is licensed.

(7) Any house, room, garden or place so kept or used, although so licensed as aforesaid, shall not be opened for any of the said purposes except on the days and between the hours stated in the licence.

(8) The affixing and keeping up of such inscription as aforesaid, and the observance of the days and hours of opening and closing, shall be inserted in and made a condition of every such licence.

(9) In case of any breach or disregard of any of the terms or conditions upon or subject to which the licence was granted, the holder thereof shall be liable to a penalty not exceeding twenty pounds, and to a daily penalty not exceeding five pounds, and such licence shall be liable to be revoked by the order of a court of summary jurisdiction.

(10) No notice need be given under subsection four of this section when the application is for a renewal of any existing licence held by the applicant for the same premises.

(11) The justices in any petty sessions may, if and as they think fit, grant to any person applying for the same a licence to keep or use any house, room, garden, or place for any purpose within the meaning of this section for any period not exceeding fourteen days which they shall specify in such licence, notwithstanding that no notices shall have been given under subsection four of this section.

(12) This section shall not apply within twenty miles of the cities of London or Westminster.

(13) In this section the expressions "licensing justice", "licensing district", and "clerk of the licensing justices" have respectively the same meanings as in the Licensing Acts, 1872–1874; the expression "police district" means any area for which a separate police force is maintained; and the expression "chief officer of police" means the chief constable, head constable, or other officer, by whatever name called, having the chief command of such separate police force.

LICENSING (IRELAND) ACT 1902

2 Edw. 7, c.18

AN ACT TO AMEND THE LAW RELATING TO ISSUE OF LICENCES FOR THE SALE OF INTOXICATING LIQUORS IN IRELAND.

BE IT ENACTED BY THE KING'S MOST EXCELLENT MAJESTY, BY AND WITH THE ADVICE AND CONSENT OF THE LORDS SPIRITUAL AND TEMPORAL, AND COMMONS, IN THIS PRESENT PARLIAMENT ASSEMBLED, AND BY THE AUTHORITY OF THE SAME, AS FOLLOWS:

1.—This Act shall extend to Ireland only, and may be cited as the Licensing (Ireland) Act, 1902.

2.—From and after the passing of this Act, no licence shall be granted for the sale of intoxicating liquors, whether for consumption on or off the premises, except:—

(1) For premises (not being premises which were licensed by virtue of paragraph (2) of this section) which were licensed at any time during the period of five years immediately before the day on which notice of an application for the grant of a certificate entitling the holder to receive a licence in respect of the premises is given, pursuant to rules of court, to the appropriate County Registrar or to the appropriate District Court Clerk, as the case may be; or[1]

(2) For an hotel, which expression shall refer to a house containing **at least ten, or, if situate in a county borough (which expression shall be deemed, for the purposes of this section, to include the Dublin Metropolitan District) twenty apartments**[2] set apart and used exclusively for the sleeping accommodation of travellers, and having no public bar for the sale of intoxicating liquors; or

(3) For a railway refreshment room.

3.—Where, by reason of the expiration of a lease, a licence for the sale of intoxicating liquors for consumption on **or off**[3] the premises comprised in the lease is extinguished or surrendered, the licensing authority may, notwithstanding anything in this Act, grant a licence for suitable premises in the immediate vicinity of the premises to which the licence so extinguished or surrendered was attached.

---

1 Substituted by the Intoxicating Liquor Act 1960, s.23.
2 Substituted by the Intoxicating Liquor Act 1960, s.21.
3 Inserted by the Intoxicating Liquor Act 1943, s.23.

4.—Where, owing to increase in population, there is a growth or extension of any city or town, and the licensing authority are satisfied that the restrictions in this Act on the granting of licences may be relaxed, they may grant a licence to any applicant notwithstanding that the same would be otherwise forbidden by this Act; provided that such licence shall be granted only for premises situate in the parish in which such increase in population has taken place, and in substitution for an existing licence or licences held in respect of premises situate within the city or town, as the case may be, comprising the whole or any part of the parish **or for premises situate in a parish in which the increase aforesaid has not taken place if the premises are situate in the city or town and either—**

(a) the city or town is within the parish and there is an increase in population in the area comprising the city or town, or

(b) a part only of the city or town is within the parish and there is an increase in population in the area comprising such part,

and the licence is in substitution for an existing licence or licences held in respect of premises situate in the city or town aforesaid and in the parish aforesaid.[4]

5.—In the case of applications under section two, sub-section two, and sections three and four **the rateable valuation, as defined in the Interpretation Act, 1937, of the premises shall be**[5] not less than:—

Thirty pounds in the Dublin Metropolitan Police District and the city of Belfast;

Twenty pounds in the cities of Cork, Limerick, Waterford, and Londonderry;

Fifteen pounds in the city of Kilkenny and the town of Galway;

Twelve pounds in any other town of over ten thousand inhabitants at the census ascertained next preceding the application; and

Ten pounds in all other places.

6.—Nothing in this Act shall operate to prevent the granting of new licences, where the licensing authority thinks fit, to premises attached to or adjoining premises licensed for the sale of intoxicating liquors **at any time during the period of five years immediately before the day on which notice of an application for the grant of a certificate entitling the holder thereof to receive any such new licence is given, pursuant to rules of court, to the appropriate County Registrar or to the appropriate District Court Clerk, as the case may be**[6] provided always that such new licence as last herein-before mentioned shall only be granted in order to render the said licensed premises more suitable for the business carried on therein.

---

[4] Inserted by the Intoxicating Liquor Act 1962, s.19.
[5] Substituted by the Intoxicating Liquor Act 1960, s.33(1)(a).
[6] Substituted by the Intoxicating Liquor Act 1960, s.24.

7.—Nothing in this Act shall be taken to affect the law as to the transfer or assignment of licences from one person to another or as to the renewal of licences.

8.—In this Act:

the expression "increase in population" shall be taken to mean an increase of not less than twenty-five per cent. of the population according to the last census;

the expression "licence" means any licence for the sale of intoxicating liquor granted by an officer of excise, other than a wholesale beer dealer's licence or a licence required for a military or constabulary canteen or a licence which can be granted without the production of a certificate of a recorder or justice; and

other expressions shall have respectively the same meaning as in the Licensing (Ireland) Acts, 1833 to 1900, and for this purpose this Act shall be construed with the said Acts.

9.—This Act shall continue in force until the thirty-first day of December one thousand nine hundred and seven, and no longer unless Parliament shall otherwise determine.

REGISTRATION OF CLUBS (IRELAND) ACT 1904

4 Edw., 7 c.9

AN ACT TO PROVIDE FOR THE REGISTRATION OF CLUBS IN IRELAND, AND FOR OTHER PURPOSES CONNECTED THEREWITH

BE IT ENACTED BY THE KING'S MOST EXCELLENT MAJESTY, BY AND WITH THE ADVICE AND CONSENT OF THE LORDS SPIRITUAL AND TEMPORAL, AND COMMONS, IN THIS PRESENT PARLIAMENT ASSEMBLED, AND BY THE AUTHORITY OF THE SAME, AS FOLLOWS:—

1.—(1) From and after the commencement of this Act a register shall be kept by every petty sessions clerk (hereinafter called "the registrar"), in which he shall enter the name of each club situate within his district to which a certificate of registration is granted under the provisions of this Act, which register shall be in a form prescribed by the Lord Lieutenant, and shall show the date of such certificate, whether such certificate is granted for the first time or on renewal, the address of the premises to which the certificate is applicable, and the names and addresses of the officials and the committee of management or governing body of the club, and whether the club is tenant or the proprietor and occupier of the said premises. The register and copy of the rules lodged with the registrar shall at all reasonable hours be open to inspection without fee, in the Dublin Metropolitan Police District by a superintendent of the Dublin Metropolitan Police or any constable authorised by him in writing, and elsewhere in Ireland by a District Inspector of the Royal Irish Constabulary or any constable so authorised by him, or in any place by any officer of the Inland Revenue and in any place by any person on payment of a fee of one shilling.

(2) The registration of a club under this Act shall not constitute the club licensed premises or authorise any sale of exciseable liquors therein which would otherwise be illegal.

2.—(1) The secretary of any club desiring a certificate of registration shall lodge with the registrar for the petty sessions district in which the club is situate an application signed by the chairman or secretary of the club, stating the name and object of the club and the address of the premises occupied by the club, and shall publish the notice of such application once in a daily newspaper circulating in the locality. Such application shall be accompanied by two copies of the rules of the club, by a list containing the names and addresses of the officials and committee of management or governing body and the names of the members and by a certificate in or as nearly as may be in the form set out in the First Schedule annexed hereto, which certificate shall be signed where the premises are situate within the county borough of Dublin by two justices of the peace for the said county borough, and where the premises are situate in any part of the Dublin Metropolitan Police District which is not comprised in the county borough of Dublin by two justices of the peace for the county of Dublin, and where the premises are situate elsewhere in Ireland by two justices of the peace sitting in petty sessions for the district within which such premises are situate, and shall also, where such premises are not owned by the club, be signed by the owner of such premises, or, where the owner is under any legal disability, by his legal representative.

(2) The secretary of any club desiring a renewal of the certificate shall, at a date not later than twenty-one days prior to its expiry, make application to the registrar for such renewal in the same manner and subject to the same incidents and publication as in the case of an original application for registration.

[s.2(3) deleted by the Intoxicating Liquor (General) Act 1924, s.31, Sched. 2]

3.—(1) The registrar shall forthwith give notice of such application to the superintendent of the Garda Síochána for the Garda district in which the club, the subject of the application, is situated and, if no objections are taken as hereinafter provided, the court shall, if satisfied that the application has been duly made as aforesaid and that the rules of the club are in conformity with the provisions of this Act, grant the application.

(2) It shall be competent for such superintendent of the Garda Síochána, on receiving such notice, and for any person resident in the parish in which the club premises are situated, to lodge objections to the grant of the certificate on any of the grounds of objection specified in this Act and it shall be competent for any person to lodge objections to the renewal of the certificate on any such grounds. Such objections shall be lodged by the objectors with the registrar within ten days of the receipt or publication of the notice of application, and at the same time a copy of the objections shall be sent by them to the secretary of the club applying for the grant or renewal of a certificate.[1]

(3) The court shall, as soon as may be, hear parties upon the application and objections, and may order such inquiry as it thinks fit, and thereafter shall grant or refuse the application. Upon the grant of any such application the court shall cause the entries required by this Act to be made in the register, and thereupon the registrar shall issue to the applicant, in or as nearly as may be in the form set out in the Second Schedule annexed hereto, a certificate of registration. **Such certificate so issued shall, subject to the provisions of this Act, remain in force until the annual licensing district court (within the meaning of the Intoxicating Liquor Act, 1927) held next after the grant of such certificate, and shall then expire.**[2]

(4) The court shall have power to order costs and expenses to be paid by the unsuccessful party, where objection has been taken to the granting or renewal of a certificate, in like manner as in any case of summary jurisdiction where an order is made for payment of money not being in the nature of a penalty for an offence.

[1] Substituted by the Intoxicating Liquor Act 1988, s.44.
[2] Substituted by the Courts (No. 2) Act 1986, ss.9, 10(5), Sched. 1.

(5) Notwithstanding the provisions of this Act as to the duration of a certificate, where a renewal has been applied for, the current certificate shall remain in force pending the final decision of the court, but not exceeding three months, unless the court shall in its discretion extend such time to a further period not exceeding three months.

(6) A club failing to make application for renewal of a certificate, by the date at or previous to which such application must in terms of this Act be made, shall not be granted such renewal unless the court is satisfied that such failure was due to inadvertence.

[s.3(7) repealed by the Statute Law Revision Act 1927, Sched.]

4.—In order that any club may be eligible to be registered, the rules of the club shall provide:—

(a) That the business and affairs of the club shall be under the management of a committee or governing body elected for not less than a year by the general body of members and subject in whole or in a specified proportion to annual re-election, and that no member of the committee or governing body, and no manager or servant employed in the club, shall have any personal interest in the sale of exciseable liquors therein, or in the profits arising from such sale.

(b) That the committee or governing body shall hold periodical meetings.

(c) That the names and addresses of persons proposed as ordinary members of the club shall be displayed on a conspicuous place in the club premises for at least a week before their election, and that an interval of not less than two weeks shall elapse between nomination and election of ordinary members.

(d) That all members shall be elected by the whole body of members or by the committee or governing body, with or without specially added members.

(e) That there shall be a defined subscription payable by members in advance.

(f) That correct accounts and books shall be kept showing the financial affairs and receipts and disbursements of the club.

(g) That a visitor shall not be supplied with exciseable liquor in the club premises unless on the invitation and in the company of a member, and that the member shall, upon the admission of such visitor to the club premises, or immediately upon his being supplied with liquor, enter his own name and the name and address of the visitor in a book which shall be kept for the purpose and which shall show the date of each visit.

(h) That no exciseable liquors shall be sold or supplied for consumption outside the premises of the club, except to members of the club, between the hours of eight o'clock in the morning and ten o'clock at night.

(i) That no persons shall be allowed to become honorary or temporary members of the club or be relieved of the payment of the regular entrance fee or subscription, except those possessing certain qualifications defined in the rules, and subject to conditions and regulations prescribed therein.

(j) **That no excisable liquors shall be sold or supplied in the club premises to any person under the age of eighteen years.**

(k) **That no person under the age of eighteen shall be admitted as a member of the club unless the club is one primarily devoted to some athletic purpose.**[3]

[proviso to s.4 deleted by the Intoxicating Liquor (General) Act 1924, s.31, Sched. 2]

5.—The court shall not consider any objection to the grant or renewal of a certificate unless it is taken upon one or more of the following grounds:—

(a) The character of the chairman or secretary or of any official or member of the committee of management or governing body; or

(b) The suitability of the premises; or

(c) That the application made by the club, or its rules, or any of them, are in any respect specified in such objection not in conformity with the provisions of this Act; or

(d) That the club has ceased to exist, or that the number of members is less than **one hundred and fifty,**[4] or

(e) That it is not conducted in good faith as a club, or that it is kept or habitually used for any unlawful purpose, or mainly for the supply of exciseable liquor; or

(f) That there is frequent drunkenness on the club premises, or that persons in a state of intoxication are frequently seen to leave the club premises, or that the club is conducted in a disorderly manner; or

(g) That illegal sales of exciseable liquor have taken place on the club premises; or

(h) That persons who are not members are habitually admitted to the club merely for the purpose of obtaining exciseable liquor, or

(i) That the club occupies premises in respect of which, within twelve months next preceding the formation of the club, a licence for the sale of exciseable liquors has been forfeited, or a certificate under the Licensing (Ireland) Acts, 1833 to 1900, in respect of the renewal of any such licence has been refused, or in respect of which an order has been made that they shall not be used for the purposes of a club; or

(j) That the supply of exciseable liquor to the club is not under the control of the members or the committee appointed by the members; or

---

[3] Substituted by the Intoxicating Liquor Act 1988, s.42.
[4] Amended by the Intoxicating Liquor Act 1988, s.46.

(k) That any of the rules of the club are habitually broken; or

(l) That the rules have been so changed as not to be in conformity with the provisions of the immediately preceding section of this Act.

[s.6 deleted by the Intoxicating Liquor (General) Act 1924, s.31, Sched. 2]

7.—(1) If any exciseable liquor is sold or supplied to any member or other person on the premises of an unregistered club, every person supplying or selling such liquor, every person who shall pay for such liquor and every person authorising the supply or sale of such liquor shall be liable, on summary conviction, to imprisonment with or without hard labour for a term not exceeding one month, or to a fine not exceeding fifty pounds, or to both.

(2) If any exciseable liquor is kept for supply or sale on the premises of an unregistered club, the same, and the vessels containing the same, may be seized by the police under a warrant from a justice of the peace or divisional justice of the Dublin Metropolitan Police District, granted after examination on oath of a credible witness to the fact that such liquor is so kept, and every officer and member of the club shall be liable, on summary conviction, to a fine not exceeding for a first offence seven pounds, for a second offence fifteen pounds and for a third or subsequent offence thirty pounds, unless he proves to the satisfaction of the court that such liquor was so kept without his knowledge or against his consent, and on such conviction such liquor and the vessels containing the same shall be forfeited and sold, and the proceeds thereof applied in like manner as a penal sum under the Fines Act (Ireland), 1851.

8.—If any exciseable liquor is sold or supplied in a registered club for consumption outside the premises of the club, except as provided in section 4, paragraph (h), every person supplying or selling such liquor, every person who shall pay for such liquor and every person authorising the sale or supply of such liquor shall be liable severally, on summary conviction, to a fine not exceeding for a first offence **£100 and for a second or a subsequent offence £150,**[5] unless he proves to the satisfaction of the court that such liquor was so sold or supplied without his knowledge or against his consent, and, where it is proved that such liquor has been received, delivered or distributed within the premises of the club and taken outside the premises, it shall, failing proof to the contrary, be deemed to have been so taken for consumption outside the premises.

9.—(1) On summary complaint by or at the instance of any person competent to lodge objections to the grant or renewal of a certificate of registration it shall be lawful for the court to make an order that, on grounds to be specified therein, a registered club is being so managed or carried on as to constitute a ground of objection to the renewal of its certificate as hereinbefore provided.

(2) Where such order has been made or where a conviction has taken place, under the provisions of the immediately preceding section, the registrar shall forthwith make an entry of the order of conviction in the register of clubs and lay the same

---

[5] Amended by the Intoxicating Liquor Act 1988, s.51, Sched.

before the court, and it shall be lawful for the court, if it thinks fit and after such further inquiry as it may think necessary, having regard to the magnitude of the offence or to the grounds specified as aforesaid, to cancel the certificate of the club for the period for which it may still have to run, provided always that it shall be competent for such club to apply for the renewal of the certificate at the date at which it would have been competent to do so had the certificate not been cancelled.

(3) Where the court has refused an application by any club for the renewal of a certificate, or has cancelled the certificate of a club in manner provided as aforesaid, it may, if it think fit, further pronounce an order that the premises occupied by such club shall not be used for the purposes of any club which requires registration under this Act for a specified period, which may extend to twelve months in case of a first order, or in case of a second or subsequent order to five years; Provided that any such order may, for good cause shown, be subsequently cancelled or varied by the court.

10.—Where an order has been made that a registered club is being so managed or carried on as to constitute a ground of objection to the renewal of its certificate, then, if the following grounds, or any of them, are specified in such order, videlicet:—

(1) That it is not conducted in good faith as a club, or that it is kept or habitually used for any unlawful purpose, or mainly for the supply of exciseable liquor; or

(2) That there is frequent drunkenness on the club premises, or that persons in a state of intoxication are frequently seen to leave the club premises, or that the club is conducted in a disorderly manner; or

(3) That persons who are not members are habitually admitted to the club merely for the purpose of obtaining exciseable liquor;

every person entered in the register of clubs as an official or a member of the committee of management or governing body of the club shall, unless he satisfies the court that the club was so managed or carried on without his knowledge or against his consent, be liable, on summary conviction, to a penalty not exceeding for a first offence **£300 and for a second or a subsequent offence, whether in connection with the same or another club, £500.**[6]

11.—(1) The decision of the Court in dealing with an application for an original certificate or for the renewal of a certificate or in cancelling a certificate, shall be subject to appeal in manner provided by the Summary Jurisdiction Acts, as if it was an order subject to appeal under those Acts.

(2) A justice shall not adjudicate on the hearing of any application or complaint affecting a club of which he is a member.

(3) If on a summary complaint being made in respect of a club the court grants a summons, the summons shall be served on the secretary and on such other person, if any, as the court may direct.

---

[6] Amended by the Intoxicating Liquor Act 1988, s.51, Sched.

(4) The certificate under section 2 of this Act shall not be signed by a divisional justice of the Dublin Metropolitan Police District, and any justice having signed any such certificate shall not adjudicate on the hearing of an application under section 3 of this Act.

12.—If the secretary of any club or any other person knowingly lodges with the registrar an application for registration which is false in any material particular, he shall be liable, on summary conviction, to imprisonment, with or without hard labour, for a term not exceeding three months, or to a fine not exceeding **£100,**[7] or to both.

13.—For the purposes of this Act, unless the context otherwise requires, the following expressions shall have the meanings hereinafter assigned to them, namely—

"Certificate" shall mean a certificate of registration;

"Registered club" shall mean a club holding a certificate of registration in force at the time;

"Secretary" shall include any officer of a club or other person performing the duties of a secretary;

"Court" shall mean court of summary jurisdiction, but in any part of Ireland other than the Dublin Metropolitan Police District the court shall, for the purposes of this Act, be constituted of two or more justices of the peace sitting in petty sessions for the district in which the premises are situate;

"Clerk of petty sessions" shall include in the case of the Dublin Metropolitan Police District the principal clerk at each police court.

14.—This Act shall apply to Ireland only and may be cited as the Registration of Clubs (Ireland) Act, 1904. **[Deletion: by Sched. to Statute Law Revision Act 1927].**

---

[7] Amended by the Intoxicating Liquor Act 1988, s.51, Sched.

INTOXICATING LIQUOR (GENERAL) ACT 1924

No. 62 of 1924

AN ACT TO AMEND THE LAW RELATING TO THE SALE OF INTOXICATING LIQUOR AND THE LAW RELATING TO THE MANUFACTURE AND SALE OF SPIRITS, AND IN CONNECTION THEREWITH TO AMEND THE ILLICIT DISTILLATION (IRELAND) ACT 1831, AND THE REGISTRATION OF CLUBS (IRELAND) ACT 1904, AND FOR OTHER PURPOSES RELATING TO THE MATTERS AFORESAID

BE IT ENACTED BY THE OIREACHTAS OF SAORSTÁT ÉIREANN AS FOLLOWS:

PART I

Prohibited Hours

[ss.1–6 repealed by the Intoxicating Liquor Act 1927 s.63, Sched. 2]

PART II

Licensing

7.—(1) From and after the passing of this Act no person shall sell, expose for sale, or keep for sale, by retail, any intoxicating liquor without being duly licensed so to sell the same, or at any place where he is not authorised by his licence to sell the same.

(2) Every person who shall sell, expose for sale, or keep for sale, by retail any intoxicating liquor without being duly licensed so to sell such intoxicating liquor, and every person who shall sell, expose for sale, or keep for sale, by retail any intoxicating liquor at any place where he is not authorised by his licence so to sell the same, shall be guilty of an offence under this section and shall be liable on summary conviction thereof to a penalty not exceeding fifty pounds, or in default of payment of such penalty to imprisonment for a term not exceeding six months.

(3) In addition to any other penalty imposed by this section, any person convicted of a second or any subsequent offence under this section or having been convicted before the passing of this Act of an offence under section 3 of the Spirits (Ireland) Act, 1854, or section 3 of the Licensing Act, 1872, is convicted of an offence under this section shall, if he be the holder of a licence of any description for the sale of intoxicating liquor by retail, forfeit such licence.

(4) In the case of a conviction for any offence under this section, the court may, if it thinks expedient so to do, declare all intoxicating liquor found in the possession of the person so convicted, and the vessels containing such liquor to be forfeited.

(5) No penalty shall be incurred under this section by the heirs, executors, administrators, or assigns of any licensed person who dies before the expiration of his licence, or by the trustee of any licensed person who is adjudged a bankrupt or whose affairs are liquidated by arrangement before the expiration of his licence, in respect of the sale or exposure for sale or keeping for sale of any intoxicating liquor, provided such sale or exposure for sale or keeping for sale be made on the premises specified in such licence, and takes place prior to the sitting of the Justice of the District Court in the court area in which such premises are situate next after the expiration of fourteen days from the death of the said person or the appointment of a trustee in the case of his bankruptcy or the liquidation of his affairs by arrangement, as the case may be.

8.—(1) It shall not be lawful for any licence holder to supply any intoxicating liquor for consumption on his premises or for any person to consume any intoxicating liquor on the premises in which it is purchased unless either—

(a) the intoxicating liquor is paid for in ready money before or at the time at which it is supplied, or

(b) the intoxicating liquor is ordered and consumed at the same time as a meal is ordered and consumed, and is paid for at the same time as such meal is paid for.

(2) Every licence holder who shall supply, and every person who shall consume, any intoxicating liquor in contravention of this section shall be guilty of an offence under this section and shall be liable on summary conviction thereof in the case of a first offence to a penalty not exceeding five pounds, and in the case of any subsequent offence to a penalty not exceeding ten pounds. **[Deletion: by the Intoxicating Liquor Act 1927, s.63, Sched. 2]**

9.—(1) The Minister for Justice may by order prescribe the sizes of the bottles in which any specified intoxicating liquor may be sold, and where any such order is in force it shall not be lawful to sell or supply the intoxicating liquor specified in the order in bottles of any size other than one of the sizes prescribed by the order.

(2) Every person who shall sell or supply any intoxicating liquor in contravention of this section shall be guilty of an offence under this section and shall be liable on summary conviction thereof in the case of a first offence to a penalty not exceeding five pounds, and in the case of any subsequent offence to a penalty not exceeding ten pounds.

[ss.10–12 repealed by the Intoxicating Liquor Act 1988, s.4]

13.—(1) If any purchaser of any intoxicating liquor from the holder of a licence to which this section applies drinks such liquor on the premises where the same was sold to him or on any highway, lane or byeway adjoining or near such premises, such licence holder shall, if it shall appear that such drinking was with his privity or consent, be guilty of an offence under this section, and upon summary conviction thereof shall be liable, in the case of a first offence, to a penalty not exceeding one hundred pounds, and in the case of any subsequent offence shall forfeit his licence.

(2) If any person in the employment of the holder of a licence to which this section applies permits or consents or is privy to any intoxicating liquor purchased from such licence holder being drunk on the premises where the same was sold or on any highway, lane or byeway adjoining or near such premises, such person shall be guilty of an offence under this section, and on summary conviction thereof shall be liable to a penalty not exceeding fifty pounds, or in default of payment of such penalty to imprisonment for a term not exceeding three months.

(3) Every person who drinks any intoxicating liquor purchased from the holder of a licence to which this section applies on the premises where the same was sold, or on any highway, lane or byeway adjoining or near such premises, shall be guilty of an offence under this section, and shall be liable on summary conviction thereof to a penalty not exceeding twenty pounds, or in default of payment of such penalty to imprisonment for a term not exceeding one month.

(4) If the holder of a licence to which this section applies himself takes or carries, or employs, or suffers any other person to take or carry any intoxicating liquor out of or from the premises of such licence holder for the purpose of being sold on his account or for his benefit or profit, and of being drunk or consumed in any other house, or in any tent, shed, or other building of any kind whatsoever belonging to such licence holder, or hired, used, or occupied by him or on or in any place, whether enclosed or not, and whether or not a public thoroughfare, such intoxicating liquor shall be deemed to have been drunk by the purchaser thereof on the premises of such licence holder with his privity and consent, and such licence holder shall be punishable under this section accordingly.

In any proceeding brought under or in reliance on this subsection, it shall not be necessary to prove that the premises or place or places to which such liquor is taken to be drunk belonged to, or were hired, used, or occupied by the licence holder, if proof be given to the satisfaction of the court hearing the case that such liquor was taken to be consumed thereon or therein with intent to evade the conditions of the licence.

(5) In this section the expression "premises where the same was sold" shall include any premises adjoining or near the premises where the liquor was actually sold and belonging to the same licence holder or under his control or used by his permission.

(6) This section applies to licences of any description authorising the sale of intoxicating liquor by retail for consumption off the premises.

14.—(1) Notwithstanding anything to the contrary contained in the Expiring Laws Act, 1924, the Licensing (Ireland) Act, 1902, as amended by this section shall continue in force until the Oireachtas otherwise determines.

(2) In the construction of the Licensing (Ireland) Act, 1902, the expression "increase of population" shall, from and after the passing of this Act be taken to mean an increase of the population according to the last census of not less than twenty-five per cent. over the population according to the census taken in the year 1901.

(3) In this Act and every other Act of the Oireachtas, whether passed before or after this Act, the expression "The Licensing (Ireland) Acts 1833 to 1905" shall include the Licensing (Ireland) Act, 1902.

15.—(1) This section applies to every licence of any description for the sale of intoxicating liquor by retail (whether for consumption on or off the premises) on premises—

(a) which are situate outside the City of Dublin, and

(b) which were destroyed or damaged during the period beginning on the 1st day of April, 1922, and ending on the 12th day of May, 1923, and

(c) the destruction or damage of which occurred during the course of and as an incident in the conflict between the armed forces of the Provisional Government of Ireland or of the Government of Saorstát Éireann and persons offering armed resistance to those forces, and

(d) in which the business of selling intoxicating liquor has been suspended on account of such destruction or damage.

(2) Every licence to which this section applies shall (for the purposes of renewal and of any certificates required for renewal but for no other purpose) be deemed to continue in force up to the time of the completion of the rebuilding or restoration of the licensed premises, and to be vested in the person legally entitled to the possession of such premises.

(3) Until the completion of the rebuilding or restoration of the licensed premises, it shall be competent for the person in whom a licence to which this section applies is vested to apply for any justice's certificate required for renewal, and for the court to consider such application, although the same may not be made to the annual licensing district court.

(4) Until the completion of the rebuilding or restoration of the licensed premises, any certificate as to the conduct of the business required for the purpose of renewal of a licence to which this section applies shall be a certificate in respect of the conduct of the business during the period between the date of the last renewal prior to the destruction or damage of the licensed premises and the date of such destruction or damage.

[ss.16–18 repealed by the Intoxicating Liquor Act 1927, s.63, Sched. 2]

PART III

CLUBS

19.—(1) In this Part of this Act the word "court" has the same meaning as it has in the Registration of Clubs (Ireland) Act, 1904, save that the word "court" shall, for the purposes of applications for the grant of an original certificate of registration of a club under the Registration of Clubs (Ireland) Act, 1904, as amended by this Act, mean the Circuit Court.

(2) All other words used in this Part of this Act which are also used in the Registration of Clubs (Ireland) Act, 1904, have the same meanings in this Part of this Act as they respectively have in that Act.

[s.20 repealed by the Intoxicating Liquor Act 1927, s.63, Sched. 2]

21.—(1) A Justice of the District Court may on the application of the secretary of a registered club authorise such club, notwithstanding the provisions contained in its rules pursuant to this Part of this Act, to supply excisable liquors to members of the club during any one period, specified in the authorisation and not exceeding six hours in duration, during which such supply of excisable liquors would be prohibited by the rules of the club.

(2) The supply of excisable liquors in a registered club to members of the club during any period covered by an authorization under this section shall be lawful and shall not be deemed to be a breach of the rules of the club.

(3) Not more than fifteen[1] authorizations shall be granted under this section to any one club in any year.

[s.22 repealed by the Finance Act 1939, s.21, Sched. 6]

23.—(1) All applications for the grant of an original certificate of registration under the Registration of Clubs (Ireland) Act, 1904, shall continue to be made to the registrar in accordance with that Act as amended by this Act, but shall be heard and determined by the Circuit Court in lieu of the court prescribed by the said Act.

(2) The jurisdiction conferred on the Circuit Court by this section shall be exercised, in manner to be prescribed by rules of court, by the Circuit Judge of the Circuit in which the premises of the club are situate.

24.—The objections to the grant of a certificate which may be considered by the court under section 5 of the Registration of Clubs (Ireland) Act, 1904, shall include objections taken on either or both of the following grounds, that is to say:—

(a) that the number of registered clubs of the character of the club applying for the certificate and having premises in the district in which such club proposes to have its premises, is sufficient to meet the requirements of that district;

(b) that the club and the premises thereof are likely to be used mainly for the purpose of supplying intoxicating liquor to the members thereof and their visitors.

(2) The objections to the grant or renewal of a certificate which may be considered by the court under section 5 of the Registration of Clubs (Ireland) Act, 1904, shall include an objection on the ground that some excise duty payable in respect of the club is unpaid.

[s. 25 repealed by the Intoxicating Liquor Act 1988, s.4]

---

[1] Amended by the Intoxicating Liquor Act 1962, s.8.

PART IV

ILLICIT DISTILLATION

26.—(1) Any person who sells, purchases, or has in his possession in any area or place to which this section for the time being applies, or who brings into any such area or place, or sells to any person in such area or place, any quantity of any material to which this section for the time being applies in relation to that area or place without having a permit issued under this section so to do, shall be guilty of an offence under this section, and on summary conviction thereof shall be liable in the case of a first offence to a penalty not exceeding fifty pounds, and in the case of any subsequent offence to a penalty not exceeding one hundred pounds.

(2) Where any person having a permit issued to him under this section, sells, purchases, or has in his possession in, or brings into, or sells to a person in the area or place to which the permit relates a greater quantity of the materials specified in the permit than is thereby permitted, such person shall for the purpose of this section be deemed to have sold, purchased, had in his possession in, or brought into, such area or place without a permit the excess of such materials above the quantity permitted by the permit.

(3) On any conviction under this section the court may, if it thinks expedient so to do declare all the materials in respect of which the offence was committed and the cases and vessels containing such material to be forfeited.

(4) The Minister for Justice may issue permits to persons to sell, purchase, or have possession of any specified quantity of any material to which this section for the time being applies in any specified area or place to which this section for the time being applies or to bring any specified quantity of any such material into any such specified area or place.

(5) The Minister for Justice may make regulations prescribing the terms and conditions on which permits will be issued by him under this section and may in such regulations provide for such permits being issued through members of the Garda Síochána or (with the consent of the Minister for Finance) through officers of excise, and may also, subject to the approval of the Minister for Finance, prescribe the fees (not exceeding five shillings on each permit) to be charged by him for such permits.

(6) This section shall apply to such areas and places as the Minister for Justice shall from time to time by order appoint and shall apply to such materials capable of being used as ingredients of illicitly distilled spirits as the Minister shall, in relation to any particular area or place by order from time to time appoint.

(7) Not less than one week before making an order applying this section to any area or place or to any material in relation to any area or place, the Minister for Justice shall publish notice of his intention to make the order at least twice in each of two newspapers circulating in such area or place.

27.—(1) Section 18 of the Illicit Distillation (Ireland) Act, 1831, from the words "and if any officer of excise having entered" to the end of the section, is hereby repealed, and in lieu thereof it is hereby enacted that no action shall lie against any officer of excise or any member of the Garda Síochána for or in respect of any act, matter, or thing done by him while making any such search as is mentioned in the said section 18, if such act, matter, or thing would have been lawful if done under the authority of a search warrant granted under section 17 of the said Act.

(2) In the construction and application of section 19 of the Illicit Distillation (Ireland) Act, 1831 the expression "room or place" as used in that section shall include and be deemed always to have included any building whatsoever, and any yard, garden, field, bog or other piece of ground, and any cave or other underground place, whether natural or artificial, and any boat, vessel, or other structure on, in, or under water.

(3) Where the holder of a licence for the sale of intoxicating liquor by retail is convicted of an offence against section 22, section 23, or section 24 (which impose penalties for concealing, having possession of, or selling illicitly distilled spirits) of the Illicit Distillation (Ireland) Act, 1831, such licence shall be forfeited, and the holder thereof shall for ever be disqualified for holding a licence for the sale of intoxicating liquor by retail.

(4) Every person convicted of an offence against section 30 (which imposes a penalty of ten pounds on persons giving notice to smugglers of the approach of excise officers) of the Illicit Distillation (Ireland) Act, 1831, shall be liable to a penalty of fifty pounds in lieu of the penalty mentioned in the said section, but such penalty of fifty pounds shall be capable of being mitigated under section 39 of the said Act.

(5) Any person convicted of an offence against the Illicit Distillation (Ireland) Act, 1831, may, in lieu of any penalty imposed by that Act or by this section, be sentenced to imprisonment with hard labour for a term not exceeding, in the case of a first offence, six months, or in the case of any subsequent offence, twelve months.

PART V

MISCELLANEOUS AND GENERAL

28.—(1) The sale of methylated spirits between the hours of nine o'clock in the evening of Saturday and nine o'clock on the following Monday morning is hereby prohibited.

(2) The sale of methylated spirits by retail to any person—

(a) whose name and address are not either previously known to the seller or vouched for by some person previously known to him, or

(b) who does not state the purpose for which he requires such spirits,

is hereby prohibited.

(3) Every retailer of methylated spirits shall at the time of the sale by him of any quantity of such spirits by retail, record in a book to be kept by him for that purpose—

(a) the name and address of the purchaser;

(b) the purposes for which the purchaser stated he required the spirits;

(c) the quantity of spirits so sold;

(d) the date of the sale.

(4) Any excise officer or police constable may at any time inspect and take extracts from the book kept by a retailer of methylated spirits pursuant to the foregoing subsection, and may for that purpose enter the premises of any such retailer.

(5) Every person who shall sell any methylated spirits—

(a) at any time during which the sale thereof is prohibited by this section, or

(b) to any person to whom the sale of methylated spirits is prohibited by this section, or

(c) without recording in such book as aforesaid the particulars prescribed by this section,

and every person who shall obstruct any officer of excise or any police constable in the exercise of his rights of inspection and taking extracts under this section shall be guilty of an offence under this section and shall be liable on summary conviction to a fine of not less than ten pounds nor more than one hundred pounds.

(6) Any sale of methylated spirits on the premises of a retailer of methylated spirits shall for the purposes of this section be deemed to have been made by such retailer.

(7) In this section the expression "police constable" includes any member of the Dublin Metropolitan Police and any member of the Garda Síochána.

29.—Every person who drinks any methylated spirits shall be guilty of an offence under this section and shall be liable on summary conviction thereof to imprisonment for any term not exceeding six months.

30.—All and every fine or other money penalty imposed by any of the Licensing (Ireland) Acts, 1833 to 1905, or the Illicit Distillation (Ireland) Act, 1831, the Spirits (Ireland) Act, 1854, the Spirits (Ireland) Act, 1855, or the Spirits (Ireland) Act, 1857, or authorised by any of those Acts to be imposed, shall, on and after the passing of this Act, be and the same are hereby increased to double the amounts respectively mentioned in those Acts.

31.—The enactments mentioned in the Second Schedule to this Act are hereby repealed to the extent specified in the third column of that Schedule.

32.—(1) This Act may be cited as the Intoxicating Liquor (General) Act, 1924.

(2) Parts I, II and V of this Act shall be construed as one with the Licensing (Ireland) Acts, 1833 to 1905, and may be cited with those Acts as the Licensing (Ireland) Acts, 1833 to 1924.

(3) Part III of this Act shall be construed as one with the Registration of Clubs (Ireland) Act, 1904, and may be cited with that Act as the Registration of Clubs Acts, 1904 and 1924.

[Sched. 1 repealed by the Intoxicating Liquor Act 1927, s.63, Sched. 2]

SECOND SCHEDULE

Enactments Repealed

Session and Chapter	Short Title	Extension of Repeal
7 Will. IV. & 1 Vic. cap. 25.	Dublin Police Act, 1842.	Section 6.
17 & 18 Vic. cap. 89.	Spirits (Ireland) Act, 1854.	Section 3.
35 & 36 Vic. cap. 94.	Licensing Act, 1872.	Sections 3, 5, 6, 7, 83 and 84.
37 & 38 Vic. cap. 69.	Licensing Act (Ireland), 1874.	Sections 21 and 22.
53 & 54 Vic. cap. 42.	Revenue Act, 1889.	Sections 26.
1 Edw. VII. cap. 27.	Intoxicating Liquors (Sale to Children) Act, 1901.	The whole Act.
4 Edw. VII. cap. 9.	Registration of Clubs (Ireland) Act, 1904.	Subsection (3) of section 2; proviso to section 4; and section 6.
5 Edw. VII. cap. 3.	Licensing (Ireland) Act, 1905.	The whole Act.
6 Edw. VII. cap. 39.	The Intoxicating Liquor (Ireland) Act, 1906.	Section 2 from the beginning of the section to the word "building."
No. 28 of 1924.	The Intoxicating Liquor Act, 1924.	The whole Act.

INTOXICATING LIQUOR ACT 1927

No. 15 of 1927

AN ACT TO AMEND AND IN PART CONSOLIDATE THE LAW RELATING TO THE SALE OF INTOXICATING LIQUOR, TO ENABLE THE NUMBER OF LICENCES FOR THE SALE OF INTOXICATING LIQUOR TO BE REDUCED BY THE ABOLITION FROM TIME TO TIME OF CERTAIN SUCH LICENCES, AND TO AMEND THE LAW RELATING TO THE REGISTRATION OF CLUBS

BE IT ENACTED BY THE OIREACHTAS OF SAORSTÁT ÉIREANN AS FOLLOWS:—

PART 1

PRELIMINARY

1.—(1) In this Act (except in Part V thereof) — the expression "weekday" means any day which is not a Sunday and is not Good Friday, Christmas Day, or St Patrick's Day;

the expression "ordinary weekday" means any weekday which is not a Saturday;

the word "Saturday" does not include a Saturday which is Christmas Day or St Patrick's Day;

the expression "St Patrick's Day" does not include a St Patrick's Day that falls on a Sunday;

the word "Sunday" does not include a Sunday which is Christmas Day;

the expression "period of summer time" means a period appointed by or under the Summer Time Act, 1925 (No. 8 of 1925) to be a period of summer time;

the word "town" means and includes any town having Commissioners under the Towns Improvement (Ireland) Act, 1854;

the word "hotel" means licensed premises structurally adapted for use and bona fide used as a hotel or a hotel and restaurant and having not less than ten apartments set apart and exclusively used for the sleeping accommodation of travellers;

the word "restaurant" means licensed premises certified under this Act to be a restaurant for the purposes of this Act;

the word "theatre" means a theatre or place of public entertainment licensed for the sale of intoxicating liquor under section 7 of the Excise Act, 1835;

the expression "theatre licence" means a licence for the sale of intoxicating liquor granted under section 7 of the Excise Act, 1835, in respect of a theatre;

the expression "licensing area" means a district court area prescribed by law for the purposes of the transaction of licensing business, and when used in relation to licensed premises means the District Court area as so prescribed in which the licensed premises are situate;

the expression "Justice of the District Court" when used in relation to licensed premises means the Justice of the District Court for the time being exercising jurisdiction in the licensing area in which the licensed premises are situate;

the expression "annual licensing district court" means the sitting of the District Court held pursuant to rules of court in a licensing area for the hearing of applications for certificates for renewals of licences for the sale of intoxicating liquor;

the expression "licensed premises" means (except in Part IV of this Act) premises in respect of which a licence **whether granted on production or without production of a certificate of the Circuit Court or the District Court**[1] for the sale by retail of intoxicating liquor has been granted and is in force;

the expression "on-licence" means a licence **whether granted on production or without production of a certificate of the Circuit Court or the District Court**[2] for the sale of intoxicating liquor for consumption either on or off the premises;

the expression "off-licence" means a licence **whether granted on production or without production of a certificate of the Circuit Court or the District Court**[3] for the sale of intoxicating liquor for consumption off the premises; and

the expression "the Minister" means the Minister for Justice.

(2) For the purposes of the application of this Act (except Part V thereof) to the Dublin Metropolitan area, that area shall be deemed to be a county borough, and accordingly the provisions of this Act in relation to county boroughs shall apply to the whole of the Dublin Metropolitan area, and the provisions of this Act in relation to urban county districts shall not apply to any part of the said area.

PART II

Prohibited Hours

2.—(1) Save as is otherwise provided by this Act, it shall not be lawful for any person to sell or expose for sale any intoxicating liquor, or to open or keep open any premises for the sale of intoxicating liquor, or to permit any intoxicating liquor to be consumed on licensed premises—

(a) on any weekday, before the hour of half-past ten o'clock in the morning, or

---

[1] Amended by the Intoxicating Liquor Act 1943, s.3.
[2] Amended by the Intoxicating Liquor Act 1943, s.3.
[3] Amended by the Intoxicating Liquor Act 1943, s.3.

(i) **during a period of summer time, after the hour of half-past eleven o'clock in the evening, or**

(ii) **during a period which is not a period of summer time, after the hour of eleven o'clock in the evening, or**

(b) **on any Sunday, before the hour of half-past twelve o'clock in the afternoon, or between the hours of two o'clock and four o'clock in the afternoon or after the hour of eleven o'clock in the evening, or**

(c) **on St Patrick's Day, where that day falls on a weekday, before the hour of half-past twelve o'clock in the afternoon or after the hour of eleven o'clock in the evening, or**

(d) **at any time on Christmas Day or Good Friday.**

Provided that where in any year the 23rd or 24th day of December falls on a Sunday, then the provisions of this subsection which relate to a weekday during a period which is not a period of summer time shall apply to such a Sunday as if it were a weekday.[4]

(2) Every person who shall sell or expose for sale any intoxicating liquor or open or keep open any premises for the sale of intoxicating liquor or permit any intoxicating liquor to be consumed on licensed premises in contravention of this section shall be guilty of an offence under this section and shall be liable on summary conviction thereof, in the case of a first offence, to a fine not exceeding £400, or, in the case of a second or any subsequent offence, to a fine not exceeding £800.

(3) Every reference in this Act to the provisions of this Act relating to prohibited hours shall be construed and have effect as a reference to the provisions of this section, and all references in this Act to prohibited hours or to times or hours in which the sale of intoxicating liquor is prohibited by this Act shall be construed as references to the hours during which the sale of intoxicating liquor is prohibited by this section.[5]

3.—(1) Where—

(a) **any business other than the sale of intoxicating liquor (in this section referred to as non-licensed business) is carried on in any premises to which an on-licence or an off-licence is attached (other than premises to which a wine retailer's off-licence within the meaning of the Finance (1909-10) Act, 1910, and no other off-licence is attached), and**

(b) **the portion of the premises in which the non-licensed business is carried on is not structurally separated from the remainder of the premises,**

the opening or keeping open of the premises for the purpose of carrying on the non-licensed business shall for the purposes of this Act be deemed to be an

---

4 Inserted by the Intoxicating Liquor Act 1995, s.2.
5 Inserted by the Intoxicating Liquor Act 1988, s.25.

opening or keeping open of the premises for the sale of intoxicating liquor save and except—

(i) in the case of premises to which an on-licence is attached, between the hours of half-past seven o'clock and half-past ten o'clock in the morning on weekdays, and on a Sunday that falls on the 23rd or 24th day of December in any year, and

(ii) in the case of premises to which an off-licence is attached, between the hours of nine o'clock and half-past ten o'clock in the morning on weekdays and on a Sunday that falls on the 23rd or 24th day of December in any year.[6]

[s.3(2) deleted by the Intoxicating Liquor Act 1960, s.8]

(3) This section shall not apply to any hotel, restaurant, theatre, or railway refreshment room or to any premises which are structurally adapted for holding dramatic performances, concerts, lectures, dances, cinematograph exhibitions, or other public entertainments and are bona fide used for the purpose of holding all or any such entertainments and for no other purpose except a restaurant.

4.—(1) The Justice of the District Court upon its being proved to his satisfaction that it is necessary or desirable so to do for the accommodation of any considerable number of persons attending any public market or fair or following any lawful trade or calling, may after hearing the officer in charge of the Garda Síochána for the licensing area grant (if he so thinks fit) to any holder of an on-licence in respect of premises situate in the vicinity of such market or fair, or of the place where such persons follow such lawful trade or calling, an order (in this Act referred to as a general exemption order) exempting such holder from the provisions of this Act relating to prohibited hours in respect of the said premises on such days and during such times (except between the hours of one and two o'clock in the morning) and upon such terms as may be specified in such order.

(2) Every general exemption order shall contain as one of the terms thereof a condition that the holder thereof shall during every period of exemption supply on the premises to which the order relates food and non-alcoholic drink at reasonable prices to any person demanding the same.

(3) The holder of a general exemption order shall, if and so long as he complies with the terms of such order, be exempt during every period of exemption from any penalty for contravention in respect of the premises to which the order relates of the provisions of this Act relating to prohibited hours but not from any other penalty under this or any other Act.

(4) The holder of a general exemption order shall, during every period of exemption keep affixed in a conspicuous place on the outside of the premises to which such order relates a notice, in such form as shall be approved by the Justice of the District Court, stating the several periods of exemption specified in such

---

[6] Section 3(1)(ii), as amended by the Intoxicating Liquor Act 1960, s.8, and by the Intoxicating Liquor Act 1962, s.3, and substituted by the Intoxicating Liquor Act 1995, s.3.

order, and every holder of a general exemption order who fails to comply with the provisions of this subsection shall be guilty of an offence under this subsection and shall be liable on summary conviction thereof to a penalty not exceeding five pounds.

(5) Every person who affixes or keeps affixed to his premises any notice falsely representing that he is the holder of a general exemption order or falsely stating the periods of exemption under a general exemption order of which he is the holder shall be guilty of an offence under this subsection and shall be liable on summary conviction thereof to a penalty not exceeding ten pounds.

(6) The Justice of the District Court may at any time (if it seems fit to him) withdraw any general exemption order or alter the same by way of extension or otherwise as he shall deem necessary or expedient, but not so as to render any person liable to any penalty for anything done under such order before the holder thereof was informed of such withdrawal or alteration.

(7) No general exemption order shall be granted for any time on any Sunday or St Patrick's Day, Christmas Day or Good Friday.

(8) A general exemption order shall not be granted unless the applicant therefor has, not less than one week before making the application, served upon the officer in charge of the Garda Síochána for the licensing area a notice of his intention to apply for the order setting out his name and address and the place, occasion and time for which the order is sought.

(9) In this section the word "holder" when used in relation to a general exemption order means the person to whom such order was granted under this section, and the expression "period of exemption" means a time during which the holder of a general exemption order is thereby exempted from the provisions of this Act relating to prohibited hours.

(10) A general exemption order in respect of premises shall, unless withdrawn under subsection (6) of this section or expressed to expire sooner, remain in force until the annual licensing district court for the licensing area in which the premises are situate next following the granting of the order is held and shall then expire.[7]

5.—(1) If the holder of an on-licence for premises which are an hotel or a restaurant **[Deletion: by the Intoxicating Liquor Act 1943 s.6]** applies to the Justice of the District Court for an order (in this Act referred to as a special exemption order) exempting him on any special occasion from the provisions of this Act relating to prohibited hours in respect of the said premises, such Justice may, if he thinks fit so to do after hearing the officer in charge of the Garda Síochána for the licensing area, grant to the applicant upon such conditions as he thinks proper an order so exempting him during the hours and on the special occasion to be specified in such order.

(2) Any person to whom a special exemption order has been granted shall, if and so long as he complies with the conditions upon which the same has been granted,

[7] Inserted by the Intoxicating Liquor Act 1960, s.10.

be exempt during the time to which such order applies from any penalty for contravention of the provisions of this Act relating to prohibited hours in respect of the premises to which the order relates but not from any other penalty under this or any other Act.

(3) No special exemption order shall be granted for any time on a Sunday or for any time between one o'clock and half-past ten o'clock in the morning on a Monday.[8]

(4) A special exemption order shall not be granted unless the applicant therefor has, not less than forty-eight hours before making the application, served upon the officer in charge of the Garda Síochána for the licensing area a notice of his intention to apply for the order, setting out his name and address and the place, occasion, and time for which the order is sought.

(5) In this section 'special occasion' means—

(a) (i) the occasion of a special event that is organised for the entertainment of the members of a particular association, organisation, or other like group, or

(ii) the occasion of a private function.

In the premises in relation to which the special exemption order is sought and at which a substantial meal (the price (if any) of which is included in the price (if any) of admission to the event) is served to the persons attending the event,

(b) the occasion of a dance that is held in a ballroom licensed under the Public Dance Halls Act, 1935, and forming part of the premises in relation to which the special exemption order is sought being a dance at which a substantial meal (the price (if any) of which is included in the price (if any) of admission to the dance) is served to the persons attending the dance, or

(c) the occasion of a dance that is held in such a ballroom on a day that, in the opinion of the Court, is a day of special festivity generally or in the locality in which the premises are situate.

(6) Special exemption orders shall not be granted pursuant to paragraph (c) of subsection (5) of this section for any premises in respect of more than six different days in a year.

(7) A special exemption order shall contain as one of the terms thereof a condition that intoxicating liquor shall not be sold at the event to which the order relates during the hours specified in the order to persons other than those attending the event and that members of the public, other than persons attending the event, shall not be admitted to the part of the premises in which intoxicating liquor is being supplied or consumed pursuant to the order.

(8) Notwithstanding the provisions of subsection (3) of this section, a special exemption order may be granted for a Sunday that is New Year's Day, New Year's Eve or St Patrick's Day.

---

[8] Substituted by the Intoxicating Liquor Act 1988, s.29.

(9) It shall be a condition of a special exemption order that the special event, private function or dance in relation to which it is granted be held in compliance with the relevant provisions of subsection (5) of this section.[9]

6.[10]—(1) In this section the expression "occasional licence" means an occasional licence granted under section 13 of the Revenue Act, 1862 and the several enactments amending that enactment, and the expression "licensing area" means the licensing area in which the place for which the occasional licence is desired is situate.

(2) The consent required by the said enactments for the granting of an occasional licence shall not be necessary but in lieu thereof no occasional licence shall be granted without the previous consent of the Justice of the District Court and such consent shall only be given by such Justice in open court and after hearing the officer in charge of the Garda Síochána for the licensing area.

(3) The consent of the Justice of the District Court mentioned in the foregoing subsection shall not be given unless the applicant therefor has, not less than forty-eight hours before making the application, served upon the officer in charge of the Garda Síochána for the licensing area a notice in writing of his intention to apply for such consent, setting out his name and address, and the place, occasion, and time for which the occasional licence the subject of such consent is desired.

(4) An occasional licence shall operate to exempt the person to whom the licence is granted (if and so long as he complies with the conditions on which the same is granted) from the provisions of this Act relating to prohibited hours at the place and during the time for which the licence is granted.

(5) The provisions of this or any other Act requiring an offence to be endorsed on a licence shall not apply to an offence committed in respect of an occasional licence.

7.—(1) Section 64 of the Licensing Act, 1872 (which relates to the production of licences and penalties for non-production) shall apply to all general exemption orders, special exemption orders and occasional licences.

(2) Section 33 of the Licensing Act (Ireland) 1874 (which relates to the production of licences and to penalties for non-production) shall apply to all general exemption orders, special exemption orders and occasional licences.

8.—(1) In this Act, the expression "Sunday-closing condition" means such condition as is mentioned in subsection (2) of this section and the expression "six-day licence" means an on-licence containing a Sunday-closing condition whether such licence was granted before or after the passing of this Act and whether such condition was inserted in such licence under this Act or under an enactment repealed by this Act.

(2) Where on the occasion of an application for a certificate for a new on-licence

---

[9] Amended by the Intoxicating Liquor Act 1962, s.12.

[10] Section 6 of the Intoxicating Liquor Act 1927 repealed insofar as it relates to licences authorising the sale of intoxicating liquor by s.11(11) of the Intoxicating Liquor Act 1962.

or a certificate for a transfer or renewal of an on-licence, the applicant, at the time of his application, applies to the Court to insert in his certificate a condition that he shall keep the premises in respect of which such licence is or is to be granted closed during the whole of Sunday, the Court shall cause the said condition to be inserted in such certificate and whenever such condition is so inserted in such certificate such condition shall also be inserted in the licence granted, transferred, or renewed in pursuance of such certificate.

(3) There shall be inserted in every certificate for the transfer or renewal of a six-day licence and in every licence granted in pursuance of such certificate **and in every such six day licence renewed thereafter**[11] the like Sunday-closing condition as is contained in the licence so transferred or renewed.

(4) The holder of a six-day licence shall keep the premises to which such licence relates closed during the whole of Sunday, and if such premises are situate in a county borough, the provisions of this Act relating to prohibited hours shall, in so far as such provisions relate to Sundays apply to such premises as if the same were not situate in a county borough.

(5) The notice which a licensed person is required by section 11 of the Licensing Act, 1872, to keep painted or affixed on his premises shall, in the case of a six-day licence, contain such words as the Court may order for giving notice to the public that a six-day licence has been granted in respect of the premises.

9.—(1) In this Act the expression "early closing condition" means such condition as is mentioned in subsection (2) of this section and the expression "early closing licence" means an on-licence containing an early closing condition, whether such licence was granted before or after the passing of this Act and whether such condition was inserted in such licence under this Act or under an enactment repealed by this Act.

(2) Where, on the occasion of any application for a certificate for a new on-licence, or a certificate for the transfer or renewal of an on-licence, the applicant applies to the Court to insert in his certificate a condition that he shall close the premises in respect of which such licence is or is to be granted one hour earlier at night than that at which such premises would otherwise have to be closed, the Court shall cause the said condition to be inserted in such certificate, and, whenever such condition is so inserted in such certificate, such condition shall also be inserted in the licence granted, transferred, or renewed in pursuance of such certificate.

(3) There shall be inserted in every certificate for the transfer or renewal of an early closing licence and in every licence granted in pursuance of such certificate **and in every such early closing licence renewed thereafter**[12] the like early closing condition as is contained in the licence so transferred or renewed.

(4) The holder of an early-closing licence shall close the premises to which such licence relates one hour earlier in the evening than the ordinary hour at which such premises would be closed under the provisions of this Act relating to prohibited

[11] Inserted by the Courts (No. 2) Act 1986, ss.9, 10(5), Sched. 1.

[12] Inserted by the Courts (No. 2) Act 1986, ss.9, 10(5), Sched. 1.

hours and the said provisions shall apply to such premises as if the several latest hours after which the sale or exposing for sale of intoxicating liquor is thereby prohibited were respectively one hour earlier than the hour stated in such provisions.

(5) The notice which a licensed person is required by section 11 of the Licensing Act, 1872, to keep painted or affixed on his premises shall, in the case of an early-closing licence, contain such words as the Court may order for giving notice to the public that an early-closing licence has been granted in respect of the premises.

10.—A person who takes out a licence containing a condition rendering such licence a six-day licence or a condition rendering such licence an early closing licence shall be entitled to a remission of one seventh of the duty which would otherwise be payable by him for a similar licence not containing such condition, and a person who takes out a licence containing conditions rendering such licence a six-day licence and also an early closing licence shall be entitled to a remission of two-sevenths of the duty which would otherwise be payable by him for a similar licence not containing such conditions.

[s.11 repealed by the Intoxicating Liquor Act 1960, s.3, Sched.]

12.—(1) Where on the occasion of any application for a certificate for a new on-licence or a certificate for the transfer or renewal of an on-licence, the applicant requests the Court to certify that the premises in respect of which the certificate is sought are a restaurant for the purposes of this Act, the Court, if satisfied after hearing the officer in charge of the Garda Síochána for the licensing area that such premises are structurally adapted for use and bona fide and mainly used as a restaurant, refreshment house or other place for supplying substantial meals to the public, shall grant to such applicant a certificate (in this section referred to as a restaurant certificate) certifying that such premises are a restaurant for the purposes of this Act.

(1A) A person who is the holder of a wine retailer's on-licence within the meaning of the Finance (1909–1910) Act, 1910, may, at any sitting of the justice of the District Court, apply to the Court to certify that the premises to which such licence is attached are a restaurant for the purposes of this Act and the Court, if satisfied after hearing the officer in charge of the Garda Síochána for the licensing area that such premises are structurally adapted for use and *bona fide* and mainly used as a restaurant, refreshment house or other place for supplying substantial meals to the public, shall grant to such person a certificate (in this section also referred to as a restaurant certificate) certifying that such premises are a restaurant for the purposes of this Act.[13]

(1B) Where, following application pursuant to section 4 of the Courts (No. 2) Act, 1986, to an officer of the Revenue Commissioners for the renewal of an on-licence without the production of a certificate of the District Court, the applicant applies to the Court to certify that the premises in respect of which

[13] Amended by the Intoxicating Liquor Act 1943, s.8.

the renewal of the on-licence is sought are a restaurant for the purposes of this Act, the provisions of subsection (1) of this section shall apply and have effect as if that application to the Court were an application, in accordance with that subsection, for a restaurant certificate.[14]

(2) The Court shall not entertain an application for a restaurant certificate unless and until satisfied that not less than ten days before the date on which the application is proposed to be made notice in writing of the intention to make the application was given to the officer in charge of the Garda Síochána for the licensing area.

(3) Every restaurant certificate shall unless sooner revoked under this section remain in force until the next annual licensing district court for the licensing area.

(4) A Justice of the District Court may, on the application of the officer in charge of the Garda Síochána for the licensing area, at any time revoke a restaurant certificate if he is satisfied, after hearing such officer and the holder of such certificate, that the premises to which such certificate relates have ceased to be structurally adapted for the use or to be *bona fide* or mainly used as a restaurant, refreshment house or other place for the supplying of substantial meals to the public.

(5) Every holder of a restaurant certificate shall cause such certificate to be displayed prominently in the premises to which such certificate relates.

12A.—(1) Where on application to a Justice of the District Court in relation to premises to which an on-licence is attached or on the occasion of an application for a new on-licence, the applicant requests the Court to certify that any portion of the premises to which the application relates is a restaurant for the purposes of section 13 of this Act, the Court, if satisfied, in relation to that portion of the premises, after hearing the officer in charge of the Garda Síochána for the licensing area that—

(a) it is structurally adapted for use and *bona fide* and mainly used as a restaurant, refreshment house or other place for supplying substantial meals to the public,

(b) it does not include a public bar or part of a room in another part of which there is a public bar, and

(c) there is public access to it otherwise than through a public bar,

shall grant to the applicant a certificate (in this section referred to as a limited restaurant certificate) certifying that that portion of the premises is a restaurant for the purposes of section 13 of this Act.

(2) The Court shall not entertain an application for a limited restaurant certificate unless and until satisfied that not less than ten days before the date on which the application is proposed to be made notice in writing of the intention to make the application was given to the officer in charge of the Garda Síochána for the licensing area.

(3) Every limited restaurant certificate shall unless sooner revoked under this section remain in force until the next annual licensing district court for the licensing area.

---

[14] Inserted by the Intoxicating Liquor Act 1988, s.48.

(4) A Justice of the District Court may, on the application of the officer in charge of the Garda Síochána for the licensing area, at any time revoke a limited restaurant certificate if he is satisfied, after hearing the officer and the holder of the certificate, that the portion of the premises to which the certificate relates has ceased to be structurally adapted for use or to be *bona fide* or mainly used as a restaurant, refreshment house or other place for the supplying of substantial meals to the public or that it includes a public bar or part of a room in another part of which there is a public bar or that there is no public access to it otherwise than through a public bar.

(5) Every holder of a limited restaurant certificate shall cause the certificate to be displayed prominently in the portion of the premises to which the certificate relates.

(6) Where, in relation to any portion of a licensed premises, a limited restaurant certificate is in force–

- **(a) the portion of the premises to which the certificate relates shall be deemed, for the purposes of section 13 of this Act, but not otherwise, to be premises which are for the time being a restaurant, and**
- **(b) subsection (1) of section 17 of this Act shall be construed and have effect in relation to a person who is found on those premises at a time specified in the said section 13 at which the consumption of intoxicating liquor is permitted with a meal as if references therein (other than the reference in paragraph (b)) to a licensed premises were references to a public bar in licensed premises.**

(7) In this section 'public bar' includes any place exclusively or mainly used for the sale and consumption of intoxicating liquor.[15]

13.—Nothing in this Act shall operate to prohibit the holder of an on-licence in respect of premises which are for the time being a hotel or restaurant from supplying intoxicating liquor to any person on the premises or from permitting intoxicating liquor to be consumed on the premises—

- **(a) during a period of summer time, between the hours of half-past eleven o'clock in the evening on any weekday and half- past twelve o'clock in the morning on the following day, or**
- **(b) during a period which is not a period of summer time, between the hours of eleven o'clock in the evening on any weekday and half-past twelve o'clock in the morning on the following day, or**
- **(c) unless his licence is a six-day licence, on any Sunday, between the hours of two o'clock and three o'clock in the afternoon, or**
- **(d) on Christmas Day, between the hours of one o'clock and three o'clock in the afternoon or the hours of seven o'clock and ten o'clock in the evening,**

---

[15] Inserted by the Intoxicating Liquor Act 1960, s.9.

if, in each case, the intoxicating liquor is—

(i) ordered by that person at the same time as a substantial meal is ordered by him,

(ii) consumed at the same time as and with the meal,

(iii) supplied and consumed in the portion of the premises usually set apart for the supply of meals, and

(iv) paid for at the same time as the meal is paid for.[16]

Provided that where in any year the 23rd or 24th day of December falls on a Sunday, then, except in the case of six-day licence, the provisions of this section which relate to weekday during a period which is not a period of summer time shall apply to such a Sunday as if it were such a weekday.[17]

14.—Nothing in this Act shall be deemed to prohibit or restrict—

(a) the sale at any time at a railway station of intoxicating liquor on arrival or departure of trains to passengers who have travelled or hold tickets entitling them to travel on those trains for a distance of not less than ten miles to or from such railway station, or

(aa) the sale at any time at a railway station (being a station to which persons who have recently travelled or are about to travel by ship resort for refreshment) of intoxicating liquor to passengers who have recently travelled or hold tickets entitling them, and are about, to travel by ship for a distance of not less than fifty miles, or[18]

(b) the supplying at any time of intoxicating liquor on licensed premises to any private friends of the holder of the licence *bona fide* entertained by him at his own expense in any part of such licensed premises other than the part in which the sale of intoxicating liquor generally takes place, or

(c) the sale of intoxicating liquor in passenger vessels in pursuance of the Acts in that behalf, or

(d) the sale of intoxicating liquor for consumption on a railway restaurant car in pursuance of the Acts in that behalf, or

(e) the sale of intoxicating liquor by the holder of an on-licence at any hour on licensed premises to a person then lodging in such premises, save that on Good Friday **[Deletion: by the Intoxicating Liquor Act 1943, s.10]** no intoxicating liquor may be so sold to any such person except at and for consumption with a meal consumed by such person in such premises.

[ss.15, 16 repealed by the Intoxicating Liquor Act 1960, s.3, Sched.]

17.—(1) Subject to subsections (2) and (4) of this section, a person who is

---

[16] Amended by the Intoxicating Liquor Act 1995, s.4.
[17] Inserted by the Intoxicating Liquor Act 1962, s.4.
[18] Inserted by the Intoxicating Liquor Act 1962, s.5.

found on any licensed premises during any time in which the sale of intoxicating liquor on such premises is prohibited by this Act shall, unless he is either—

(a) the holder of the licence or the owner of the premises, or

(b) resident permanently or temporarily on the premises, or

(c) a person to whom intoxicating liquor may lawfully be sold or supplied on the premises at that time, or

(d) carrying out construction, decorative, repair, replacement or maintenance work in relation to the premises or any of the fittings or equipment thereon,

(e) in the employment of the holder of the licence or of the owner of the premises and is on the premises in the ordinary course of such employment, or

(f) an officer of customs and excise in the course of his duty as an officer,

be guilty of an offence under this subsection and shall be liable on summary conviction thereof to a fine of not less than £25[19] **and not more than £50.**[20]

(2) Where any business other than the sale of intoxicating liquor (in this subsection referred to as non-licensed business) is carried on in any licensed premises and the portion of the premises in which the non-licensed business is carried on is not structurally separated from the remainder of the premises, subsection (1) of this section shall not apply in relation to the premises during any time in which the premises are lawfully open for the carrying on of the non-licensed business.

(3) Subject to subsection (4) of this section, a person who consumes intoxicating liquor on any licensed premises during any time in which the sale of intoxicating liquor on such premises is prohibited by this Act shall, unless he is a person as respects whom the relevant requirements of this Act for the lawful sale or supply of intoxicating liquor on those premises at that time are satisfied, be guilty of an offence under this subsection and shall be liable on summary conviction to a fine of not less than £25[21] **and not more than £50.**[22]

(4) A person shall not be convicted of an offence under both subsection (1) and subsection (3) of this section in respect of the same occasion.[23]

18.—Every person who by falsely representing himself to be lodging in any licensed premises buys or obtains or who attempts by such false representation to buy or obtain on such licensed premises any intoxicating liquor during a period in which the sale of intoxicating liquor on such premises is prohibited by this Act shall be guilty of an offence under this section and shall be liable on summary conviction thereof to a fine not exceeding five pounds.

---

[19] Substituted by the Intoxicating Liquor Act 1988, s.51, Sched.
[20] Substituted by the Intoxicating Liquor Act 1988, s.51, Sched.
[21] Amended by the Intoxicating Liquor Act 1988, s.51, Sched.
[22] Amended by the Intoxicating Liquor Act 1988, s.51, Sched.
[23] Substituted by the Intoxicating Liquor Act 1960, s.12.

19.—(1) Whenever the Justice of the District Court is satisfied on the written application of a Superintendent or Inspector of the Garda Síochána that in the interest of public peace and order it is expedient that the sale of intoxicating liquor should immediately cease in any town or village in the licensing area, such Justice may order the immediate closing for the remainder of that day, or for such shorter period as he may deem adequate, of all premises licensed for the sale of intoxicating liquor in such town or village.

(2) Whenever an order is made under this section, every holder of a licence in the town or village to which such order relates shall, upon the same being communicated verbally to him by a member of the Garda Síochána, immediately close his licensed premises and keep the same closed during the time mentioned in such order, and any person who fails or refuses to comply with the terms of any such order shall be guilty of an offence under this section and shall be liable on summary conviction thereof to a fine not exceeding ten pounds.

(3) Whenever an order is made under this section and any holder of a licence fails or refuses to comply with such order, any member of the Garda Síochána may use such force as may be necessary for ensuring compliance with such order.

20.—(1) No person shall be admitted to any theatre after the hour of half-past nine in the evening unless either—

(a) he has previously engaged or paid for a seat in that theatre for the performance or entertainment then in progress or about to commence, or

(b) he is employed in that theatre or has business with a person so employed.

(2) If any person is admitted to any theatre in contravention of this section, the holder of the theatre licence in respect of that theatre shall be guilty of an offence under this section and shall be liable on summary conviction thereof to a fine not exceeding five pounds.

21.—(1) The provisions of this Act in relation to prohibited hours shall not apply to a theatre.

(2) In this section the expression "permitted time" means a period beginning half an hour before the commencement of a performance in the theatre in respect of which the expression is used and ending half an hour after the termination of such performance.

(3) It shall not be lawful to sell or expose for sale by retail any intoxicating liquor in any theatre—

(a) at any time other than during a permitted time, or

(b) to any persons other than persons who either—

(i) are then employed in the theatre, or

(ii) have engaged or paid for seats in the theatre for the performance taking or which took place during the permitted time or either of the permitted times then current, or

(c) in any part of the theatre which is then accessible to persons other than those persons to whom intoxicating liquor may then be sold in such theatre.

(4) Every person who sells or exposes for sale by retail any intoxicating liquor in a theatre in contravention of this section shall be guilty of an offence under this section and shall be liable on summary conviction thereof to a fine not exceeding fifty pounds or, in the case of a second or subsequent offence, at the discretion of the Court to imprisonment for any term not exceeding six months and also in the case of such second or subsequent offence, in the discretion of the Court to forfeiture of the theatre licence.

22.—(1) Any member of the Garda Síochána may demand of any person found on any licensed premises during the time in which the sale of intoxicating liquor on such premises is prohibited by this Act the name and address of such person and, if he has ground to suppose that a name or address given by such person in response to such demand is false or misleading, may demand of such person corroborative evidence of such name or address, and if any such person fails or refuses to give on such demand his name and address or either of them or such corroborative evidence or gives a name or an address or corroborative evidence which is false or misleading such person shall be guilty of an offence under this section and shall be liable on summary conviction thereof to a fine not exceeding **£50.**[24]

(2) Any member of the Garda Síochána may arrest without warrant any person who, on his name and address or such corroborative evidence as aforesaid being lawfully demanded of him under this section, fails or refuses to give such name and address or either of them or such evidence.

(3) In the Licensing Act, 1872, and in the Licensing Act (Ireland), 1874, the word "constable" shall include any member of the Garda Síochána and the said Acts shall be construed and have effect accordingly.

(4) In section 23 of the Licensing Act (Ireland), 1874, the expression "provisions of the principal Act or this Act" shall include the provisions of this present Act, and the said section shall be construed and have effect accordingly.

23.—This Part of this Act shall not apply to—

(a) any club for the time being registered under the Registration of Clubs (Ireland) Act, 1904, or

(b) any canteen held under the authority of the Minister for Defence, or

(c) the sale of intoxicating liquor by wholesale in any premises which are not licensed premises, or

(d) the sale of medicated or methylated spirits made up in medicine and sold by registered medical practitioners or chemists and druggists, pharmaceutical chemists or registered druggists.

---

[24] Substituted by the Intoxicating Liquor Act 1988, s.51, Sched.

PART III

ENDORSEMENT OF LICENCES

24.—In this Part of this Act the expression "offences to which this Part of this Act applies" means and includes any offence against any of the enactments mentioned in the First Schedule to this Act or any enactment for the time being in force relating to the adulteration of **intoxicating liquor**[25] or any offence under the provisions of this Act relating to prohibited hours.

25.—(1) Subject to the provisions of subsection (1A) of this section[26] whenever the holder of any licence for the sale of intoxicating liquor by retail is convicted of an offence to which this Part of this Act applies the conviction **subject to subsection (4) of this section**[27] shall, if the person so convicted is the holder of one such licence only, be recorded on such licence or, if such person is the holder of two or more such licences in respect of the same premises, be recorded on all such licences, or, if such person is the holder of two or more such licences which do not all relate to the same premises, be recorded on such one or more of those licences as relate to the premises in respect of which the offence was committed.

(1A) In the case of a conviction for any offence relating to prohibited hours, the provisions of subsection (1) of this section shall apply only if the Court in its discretion so thinks proper.[28]

(2) Whenever a conviction of the holder of a licence is under this section recorded on such licence such conviction shall, in the case of the first conviction so recorded on such licence after the passing of this Act, continue so recorded for the period of **two years**[29] from the date of the conviction and, in the case of the second conviction so recorded on such licence after the passing of this Act, continue so recorded for the period of **four years**[30] from the date of the conviction and, in the case of the third conviction and of every subsequent conviction so recorded on such licence after the passing of this Act, continue so recorded for the period of **six years**[31] from the date of the conviction.

(3) Every conviction recorded on a licence under this section shall, at the expiration of the period during which under the foregoing subsection the same is to continue recorded, cease for all purposes to be so recorded.

(4) Notwithstanding anything contained in subsection (1) of this section, where a person is convicted in relation to any premises in respect of which he holds a licence for the sale of intoxicating liquor by retail of an offence to which this Part of this Act applies and the conviction is the first conviction of that

---

[25] Substituted by the Intoxicating Liquor Act 1943, s.13.
[26] Inserted by the Courts (No. 2) Act 1986, s.6.
[27] Substituted by the Intoxicating Liquor Act 1960, s.37.
[28] Inserted by the Courts (No. 2) Act 1986, s.6.
[29] Substituted by the Intoxicating Liquor Act 1960, s.37.
[30] Substituted by the Intoxicating Liquor Act 1960, s.37.
[31] Substituted by the Intoxicating Liquor Act 1960, s.37.

person in relation to those premises of an offence to which this Part of this Act applies, the conviction shall not be recorded on the licence.[32]

26.—(1) Whenever the holder of a licence for the sale of intoxicating liquor is convicted by a Justice of the District Court of an offence to which this Part of this Act applies such Justice may, if satisfied that by reason of the trivial nature of the offence such conviction ought not to be recorded on such licence, make an order stating the circumstances which reduce the offence to one of a trivial nature and declaring that such conviction shall not be recorded, and whenever such order is so made such conviction shall not be so recorded.

(2) Whenever an order is made by a Justice of the District Court under the foregoing subsection on a prosecution at the instance of a member of the Garda Siochana, an appeal shall lie at the instance of such prosecutor to the Judge of the Circuit Court within whose circuit the district or part of the district of such Justice is situate against such order, but not against the conviction in respect of which such order was made, and if such appeal is dismissed such Judge may order the costs of the appeal to be paid by such prosecutor.[33]

27.—(1) Whenever the holder of any licence for the sale of intoxicating liquor is convicted by a Justice of the District Court of an offence to which this Part of this Act applies, an appeal shall lie from such conviction to the Judge of the Circuit Court within whose circuit the District or any part of the District of such Justice is situate, and the decision of such Judge shall be final and not appealable.

(2) On the hearing of an appeal under subsection (1) of this section from a conviction for an offence relating to prohibited hours, the Judge of the Circuit Court may, although affirming the conviction, make, if in his discretion he so thinks proper, an order declaring that such conviction shall not be recorded on such licence and, whenever such an order is so made, such conviction shall not be so recorded and shall for all purposes be deemed never to have been so recorded and, accordingly, any forfeiture occasioned by the recording of such conviction shall be deemed to be cancelled.[34]

28.—(1) Whenever the holder of a licence for the sale of intoxicating liquor by retail is convicted of an offence to which this Part of this Act relates and such conviction is by virtue of this Part of this Act recorded on such licence, and at the time of such recording two convictions (subsequent in date to the passing of this Act) are by virtue of this Part of this Act recorded on such licence, such licence shall thereupon be forfeited.

(2) Where a licence is forfeited under this section no new licence shall at any time thereafter be granted in respect of the premises or any part of the premises to which such licence was attached.

---

[32] Inserted by the Intoxicating Liquor Act 1960, s.37.

[33] See s.15 of the Intoxicating Liquor Act 1943 which provides "no order shall be made after the passing of this Act under section 26 of the Act of 1927".

[34] Substituted by the Courts (No. 2) Act 1986, s.7.

29.—Whenever the holder of a licence for the sale of intoxicating liquor by retail is convicted of two or more offences to which this Part of this Act applies and such offences were committed on the same day, the Court by which such holder is so convicted or the Court by which such conviction is affirmed on appeal (as the case may be) may if it so thinks fit order that such one or more as such Court shall think fit but not all of such convictions shall not be recorded on such licence, and whenever such order is made the conviction or convictions in respect of which the order is made shall not be recorded on such licence notwithstanding the provisions of this Act, and, in the case of an order made on appeal, shall for all purposes be deemed never to have been so recorded.

30.—(1) Whenever, on an application for a certificate for the transfer of a licence for the sale of intoxicating liquor by retail, the applicant at the time of such application satisfies the Court that the transfer is desired for the purpose of giving effect to a *bona fide* sale for money or money's worth of such licence and the premises to which the same is attached, the Court shall, if it grants such certificate, direct in and by such certificate that all (if any) offences then recorded on such licence under this Part of this Act shall at the time of such transfer cease to be so recorded, and whenever such direction is so given every such offence shall at the time of the transfer of such licence pursuant to such certificate cease to be recorded on such licence and such licence shall be so transferred freed and discharged from the records of such offences and shall thereafter have effect for all purposes as if such offences had never been recorded thereon.

(2) Whenever a licence (hereinafter called the first licence) is transferred, freed and discharged under the foregoing subsection from the record of an offence and the person who was the holder of such licence immediately before such transfer (hereinafter called the first transfer) applies (whether in the same or another licensing area) within five years after such transfer for a certificate for the transfer (hereinafter called the second transfer) to him of the same or another licence (hereinafter called the second licence) the court if it grants such certificate shall in and by such certificate direct that all offences which immediately before the first transfer were recorded under this Part of this Act on the first licence shall on the second transfer be recorded on the second licence, and whenever such direction is so given every such offence shall on the second transfer be recorded on the second licence, and such record shall from and after the second transfer have effect as if the same had been made on the second licence at the time when it was made on the first licence save that for the purpose of calculating the duration under this Act of such record the period between the first transfer and the second transfer shall be omitted.

(3) It shall be the duty of every person who applies for a certificate for a transfer to which the foregoing subsection would apply to disclose to the Court at the time of application the facts by reason of which that subsection so applies, and every such person who fails or neglects to make such disclosure shall be guilty of an offence under this section and shall be liable on summary conviction thereof to a fine not exceeding fifty pounds, and also, if such person is at the date of such conviction the holder of the licence the subject of such certificate, every offence which would under the foregoing subsection have been recorded on such licence if such disclosure had been duly made shall be deemed to have been duly so recorded in accordance with that subsection.

(4) Every entry in a register of licences of a certificate for a transfer in and by which a direction is given under this section shall include the particulars of such direction.

31.—An omission to record on a licence a conviction which is by this Act required to be recorded thereon shall not prejudice or affect the validity or effect of such conviction or (unless such omission is made by order of a Court under this Act) relieve the convicted person from any consequence which would ensue from such conviction if it had been so recorded.

32.—(1) Whenever the holder of a licence for the sale of intoxicating liquor by retail is charged with an offence to which this Part of this Act applies the summons or other document bringing such holder before a Court for trial on such charge shall state that such holder will be required to produce such licence to the Court at such trial, and at such trial the Court shall require such holder to produce such licence and deliver the same to the registrar, clerk, or other principal officer of the Court.

(2) Whenever the holder of any such licence as aforesaid is convicted by or before any Court of an offence to which this Part of this Act applies the following provisions shall have effect that is to say:—

(a) the registrar, clerk, or other principal officer of the Court shall forthwith endorse on such licence the date and such other particulars as the circumstances may require of such conviction;

(b) if such principal officer is not the district court clerk by whom is kept the register of licences in which such licence is registered, such principal officer shall send to such district court clerk notice of such conviction together with all material particulars;

(c) if such conviction occasions the forfeiture of such licence, such principal officer shall retain such licence and, if he is not the district court clerk aforesaid, shall send such licence to such district court clerk;

(d) the said district court clerk shall enter in the register of licences in which such licence is registered the date and such other particulars as the circumstances may require of such conviction;

(e) if such conviction occasions the forfeiture of such licence, the said district court clerk shall send to the proper officer of the Revenue Commissioners notice of such forfeiture.

(3) Whenever an order is made by the Circuit Court on an appeal from a conviction of an offence to which this Part of this Act applies, the county registrar shall forthwith transmit to the district court clerk by whom is kept the register of licences in which such licence is registered notice of such order together with the material particulars thereof and upon receipt of such notice such district court clerk shall enter in such register such particulars of such order as circumstances require and, whenever such order occasions or affects in any way a forfeiture of such licence, shall send notice of such order to the proper officer of the Revenue Commissioners.

33.—(1) Every register of licences shall be received in any Court as evidence of all matters entered therein in pursuance of this Act and in particular of all convictions, recordings of convictions, and forfeitures of licences so entered therein.

(2) Every endorsement upon a licence of a matter required by this Act to be so endorsed shall, if such endorsement purports to be made and signed by the officer required by this Act to make the same, be evidence of the matters stated in such endorsement without proof of the signature or authority of such officer.

(3) Every copy of an entry made in a register of licences in pursuance of this Act shall, if such copy purports to be signed and certified to be a true copy by the district court clerk by whom such register is kept, be received in any Court (without proof of the signature or authority of the person by whom the same is signed and certified) as a true copy of such entry and as evidence of any matter of which such entry would be evidence.

34.—If any person defaces or obliterates or attempts to deface or obliterate any record of a conviction on his licence he shall be guilty of an offence under this section and shall be liable on summary conviction thereof to a penalty not exceeding ten pounds.

35.—The provisions of subsection (1) of section 1 of the Probation of Offenders Act, 1907, shall not apply where any person is charged before a Justice of the District Court with an offence to which this Part of this Act applies and the Court thinks that the charge is proven.

[Part IV (ss.36–54) repealed by the Intoxicating Liquor Act 1960, s.3, Sched.]

PART V

CLUBS

55.—(1) All words used in this Part of this Act which are also used in the Registration of Clubs (Ireland) Act, 1904, have the same meaning in this Part of this Act as they respectively have in that Act.

[s.55(2) repealed by the Intoxicating Liquor Act 1960, s.3, Sched.]

56.—(1) In order that a club may be eligible to be registered under the Registration of Clubs Acts, 1904 to 1986, the rules of the club shall (in addition to the matters mentioned in section 4 of the Registration of Clubs (Ireland) Act, 1904) provide that, subject to the exceptions specified in subsections (1A),[35] (2) and (3) of this section, no excisable liquor shall be supplied for consumption on the club premises to any person (other than a member of the

[35] Inserted by the Intoxicating Liquor Act 1995, s.5(1)(a).

club lodging in the club premises) or be consumed on the club premises by any person (other than a member of the club lodging in the club premises)—

(a) on any weekday, before the hour of half-past ten o'clock in the morning, or

(i) during a period of summer time, after the hour of half-past eleven o'clock in the evening, or

(ii) during a period which is not a period of summer time, after the hour of eleven o'clock in the evening, or

(b) on any Sunday, before the hour of half-past twelve o'clock in the afternoon or between the hours of two o'clock and four o'clock in the afternoon or after the hour of eleven o'clock in the evening, or

(c) on St. Patrick's Day, where that day falls on a weekday, before the hour of half-past twelve o'clock in the afternoon or after the hour of eleven o'clock in the evening, or

(d) at any time on Christmas Day or Good Friday.

(1A) Where in any year the 23rd or 24th day of December falls on a Sunday, then the provisions of subsection (1) of this section which relate to a weekday during a period which is not a period of summer time shall apply to such a Sunday as if it were such a weekday.[36]

(2) Nothing contained in the Registration of Clubs Acts, 1904 to 1986, or contained by virtue only of the operation of subsection (1) of this section, in the rules of a club registered under those Acts shall operate to prohibit the supplying for consumption on the club premises of excisable liquor to any person or the consumption of excisable liquor on the club premises by any person—

(a) during a period of summer time, between the hours of half-past eleven o'clock in the evening on any weekday and half-past twelve o'clock in the morning on the following day, or

(b) during a period which is not a period of summer time, between the hours of eleven o'clock in the evening on any weekday and half-past twelve o'clock in the morning on the following day, or

(c) on any Sunday, between the hours of two o'clock and three o'clock in the afternoon, or

(d) on Christmas Day, between the hours of one o'clock and three o'clock in the afternoon or the hours of seven o'clock and ten o'clock in the evening,

if, in each case, the excisable liquor is—

(i) ordered by that person at the same time as a substantial meal is ordered by him,

---

[36] Inserted by the Intoxicating Liquor Act 1995, s.5(1)(b).

(ii) consumed at the same time as and with the meal,

(iii) supplied and consumed in the portion of the club premises usually set apart for the supply of meals, and

(iv) paid for at the same time as the meal is paid for.

Provided that where in any year the 23rd or 24th day of December falls on a Sunday, then the provisions of this subsection which relate to a weekday during a period which is not a period of summer time shall apply to such a Sunday as if it were such a weekday.[37]

(3) In this section—

"period of summer time", "weekday" and "Sunday" have the meanings assigned to them by section 1 of this Act.[38]

[s.57 repealed by the Intoxicating Liquor Act 1960, s.3, Sched.]

58.—(1) If any excisable liquor is supplied for consumption on the premises of a club registered under the Registration of Clubs (Ireland) Act, 1904, or is consumed on the premises of any such club by any person in contravention of the rules of such club relating to the supplying and consumption of excisable liquor on the premises of such club, such club shall be guilty of an offence under this section and shall be liable on summary conviction thereof, in the case of a first offence, to a fine not exceeding **£300**[39] or, in the case of a second or any subsequent offence, to a fine not exceeding **£500.**[40]

(2) Proceedings under this section may be brought against a club in the name under which it is registered under the Registration of Clubs (Ireland) Act, 1904, and any summons or other document required to be served on a club for the purpose or in the course of such proceedings may be served on the secretary of the club and any warrant for the recovery of the amount of a fine imposed on a club under this section may be executed against the goods and chattels of the club.

59.—The objections to the grant of a certificate which may be considered by the court under section 5 of the Registration of Clubs (Ireland) Act, 1904 shall include an objection taken on the ground that the rules of the club for the admission of honorary or temporary members are in the opinion of the court unsatisfactory or unsuitable.

PART VI

MISCELLANEOUS AND GENERAL

60.—(1) Whenever the Justice of the District Court shall refuse an application for a certificate for a transfer or a renewal of any licence for the sale of intoxicating liquor by retail and the applicant for such certificate shall lawfully appeal against

---

[37] Inserted by the Intoxicating Liquor Act 1995, s.5(1)(c).
[38] Substituted by the Intoxicating Liquor Act 1988, s.26.
[39] Substituted by the Intoxicating Liquor Act 1988, s.51, Sched.
[40] Substituted by the Intoxicating Liquor Act 1988, s.51, Sched.

such refusal to the Circuit Court and shall prosecute such appeal with due diligence, such licence shall subject to the provisions of this section continue in full force and effect until the first opportunity on which such an appeal could be heard by the Circuit Court and, if that Court shall so direct, for such further time (if any) as shall elapse before the final determination of such appeal.

(2) A licence shall not continue in force under the foregoing subsection after the expiration of the term for which the same was granted unless, on or before such expiration, the appellant deposits with the proper officer of customs and excise the amount of the excise duty chargeable on a renewal of such licence.

(3) Moneys deposited with an officer of customs and excise under the foregoing subsection shall, if the refusal which is the subject of the appeal is confirmed by the Circuit Court, be repaid on such confirmation to the appellant by whom the same were deposited less such part thereof as bears to the whole of the moneys so deposited the same proportion as the time during which such licence has been continued in force by virtue of subsection (1) of this section bears to one year, and, if such refusal is reversed by the Circuit Court, shall be applied in or towards the discharge of the excise duties payable in respect of the said licence.

61.—(1) Notwithstanding anything to the contrary contained in any other Act, the Revenue Commissioners shall not grant, whether by way of new licence or of transfer or renewal of an existing licence, a wine retailer's off-licence to any person other than a person who is carrying on the business of chemist and druggist, pharmaceutical chemist, or registered druggist, or a person who is for the time being the holder of a spirit retailer's off-licence or a beer retailer's off-licence then in force.

(2) In this section the expressions "wine retailer's off-licence", "spirit retailer's off-licence" and "beer retailer's off-licence" have the same meanings as such expressions respectively have in the Finance (1909-10) Act, 1910.

62.—(1) The holder of an on-licence (in this section referred to as the on-licence) in respect of premises situate in a county borough may apply at **any annual licensing District Court**[41] that in lieu of the renewal of the on-licence there be granted to him in respect of the said premises **[Deletion: by the Courts (No. 2) Act 1986, ss.9, 10(5), Sched. 1]** a certificate for a new spirit retailer's off-licence or a certificate for a new beer retailer's off-licence or certificates for both such new licences.

(2) When an application under the foregoing subsection is made the Justice of the District Court, if he is satisfied that **[Deletion: by the Courts (No. 2) Act 1986, ss.9, 10(5), Sched. 1]** the renewal of the on-licence might have been granted and that the sale of intoxicating liquor for consumption on the premises is not the principal business carried on in the premises to which the on-licence is attached, may, if he so thinks fit, grant to such applicant the certificate or certificates so applied for by him.

(3) When an application under subsection (1) of this section is granted, a new

---

[41] Substituted by the Intoxicating Liquor Act 1943, s.18.

licence or new licences shall notwithstanding anything to the contrary contained in any other Act be granted to the applicant in accordance with the certificate or certificates granted to him in pursuance of such application.

(4) When a new licence or licences is or are granted under the foregoing subsection no new on-licence shall at any time thereafter be granted in respect of the premises to which such new licence or licences is or are attached.

(5) When an application under subsection (1) of this section is refused such application shall be treated as an application for **[Deletion: by the Courts (No. 2) Act 1986, ss.9, 10(5), Sched.1]** the renewal of the on-licence and dealt with accordingly.

(6) In this section the expressions "spirit retailer's off-licence" and "beer retailer's off-licence" have the same meanings as such expressions respectively have in the Finance (1909-10) Act, 1910.

63.—The enactments mentioned in the Second Schedule to this Act are hereby repealed to the extent specified in the third column of that Schedule.

64.—(1) This Act may be cited as the Intoxicating Liquor Act, 1927.

(2) Parts I, II, III, IV, and VI, of this Act shall be construed as one with the Licensing (Ireland) Acts, 1833 to 1924 and may be cited with those Acts as the Licensing (Ireland) Acts, 1833 to 1927.

(3) Part V of this Act shall be construed as one with the Registration of Clubs Acts, 1904 and 1924 and may be cited with those Acts as the Registration of Clubs Acts, 1904 to 1927.

FIRST SCHEDULE

ENACTMENTS, CONVICTIONS UNDER WHICH ARE TO BE RECORDED

Reference to the Enactment	Subject matter of the Enactment
The Licensing Act, 1872, section 13	Permitting drunkenness or violent conduct on licensed premises and supplying intoxicating liquor to disorderly persons.
The Licensing Act, 1872, section 14	Permitting licensed premises to be used for certain disorderly purposes.
The Licensing Act, 1872, section 16	Harbouring, bribing, and certain other acts by licensed persons in relation to constables.
The Licensing Act, 1872, section 17	Permitting gaming on licensed premises.
The Licensing Act (Ireland) 1874, section 23	Powers of constables to enter licensed premises and the penalty for obstructing such entry.
The Intoxicating Liquor (General) Act, 1924, section 8	Prohibiting the sale of intoxicating liquor on credit.
The Intoxicating Liquor (General) Act, 1924, section 10[42]	Sales of intoxicating liquor to young persons for consumption on the premises.
The Intoxicating Liquor (General) Act, 1924, section 11[43]	Sales of intoxicating liquor to young persons for consumption off the premises.
The Intoxicating Liquor (General) Act, 1924, section 12[44]	Employment of young persons to sell intoxicating liquor.

[42] Repealed by the Intoxicating Liquor Act 1988, s.4.
[43] *Ibid.*
[44] *Ibid.*

SECOND SCHEDULE

ENACTMENTS REPEALED

Session and Chapter	Short Title	Extent of Repeal
23 and 24 Vic. c. 107	The Refreshment Houses (Ireland) Act, 1860	Sections 29 and 43.
27 and 28 Vic. c. 35	The Beer Houses (Ireland) Act, 1864	Section 6 so far as it relates to the hours during which houses may not be kept open for the sale by retail of beer not to be consumed on the premises.
35 and 36 Vic. c. 94	The Licensing Act, 1872	Sections 30, 31, 33, 34, 49, 55, 56, 57, 78, 86 and 88, and section 90 so far as it relates to disqualified premises.
37 and 38 Vic. c. 69	The Licensing Act (Ireland), 1874	Sections 2, 7, 11, 27, 28 and 29.
41 and 42 Vic. c. 72	The Sale of Liquors on Sunday (Ireland) Act, 1878	The whole Act.
43 and 44 Vic. c. 20	The Inland Revenue Act, 1880	Section 44.
63 and 64 Vic. c. cclxiv	The Dublin Corporation Act, 1900	Section 61 the words "or alter the provisions of any Act now in force with respect to the sale of intoxicating liquors on Sunday, or the keeping open of any premises for that purpose".
6 Edw. VII. c. 39	The Intoxicating Liquors (Ireland) Act, 1906	The whole Act.
10 Edw. VII. and 1 Geo. V. c. 33	The Hotels and Restaurants (Dublin) Act, 1910	The whole Act.
No. 62 of 1924	The Intoxicating Liquor (General) Act, 1924	Sections 1, 2, 3, 4, 5 and 6; section 8 sub-section (2) from the words "and in any case" to the end of the sub-section; section 10 from the words "and in any case" to the end of the section; section 11 sub-section (3) from the words "and in any case" to the end of the sub-section; section 12 from the words "and in any case" to the end of the section; sections 16, 17, 18 and 20; and First Schedule.

PUBLIC DANCE HALLS ACT 1935

No. 2 of 1935

AN ACT TO MAKE PROVISION FOR THE LICENSING, CONTROL, AND SUPERVISION OF PLACES USED FOR PUBLIC DANCING, AND TO MAKE PROVISION FOR OTHER MATTERS CONNECTED WITH THE MATTERS AFORESAID

BE IT ENACTED BY THE OIREACHTAS OF SAORSTÁT ÉIREANN AS FOLLOWS:—

1.—In this Act—

the word "place" means a building (including part of a building), yard, garden, or other enclosed place, whether roofed or not roofed and whether the enclosure and the roofing (if any) are permanent or temporary;

the expression "public dancing" means dancing which is open to the public and in which persons present are entitled to participate actively;

the expression "licensing area" means a district court area prescribed by law for the purposes of the transaction of licensing business;

the expression "annual licensing district court" means the sitting of the District Court held pursuant to rules of court in a licensing area for the hearing of applications for certificates for renewals of licences for the sale of intoxicating liquor.

2.—(1) Subject to the provisions of this Act, any person may apply to the justice of the District Court exercising jurisdiction in any licensing area for a licence (in this Act referred to as a public dancing licence) to use a particular place, whether licensed or not licensed for the sale of intoxicating liquor, situate in such licensing area for public dancing, and such Justice may, if he so thinks proper, grant such license to such person.

(2) In considering an application under this section for a public dancing licence, a Justice of the District Court shall, in addition to any other matter which may appear to him to be relevant, have regard to the following matters, that is to say—

(a) the character and the financial and other circumstances of the applicant for such licence;

(b) the suitability of the place to which such application relates;

(c) the facilities for public dancing existing in the neighbourhood of such place at the time of such application;

(d) the accommodation for the parking of vehicles in the neighbourhood of such place;

(e) the probable age of the persons who would be likely to make use of such place for public dancing;

(f) whether the situation of such place is or is not such as to render difficult the supervision by the Garda Síochána of the management of and proceedings in such place;

(g) the hours during which the applicant proposes that public dancing should be permitted in such place.

(3) On the hearing of an application under this section for a public dancing licence, any member of the Garda Síochána and any person who appears to the Justice hearing such application to be interested therein may appear and be heard in opposition to such application and may adduce evidence in support of such opposition.

(4) Every application under this Act for a public dancing licence (except an application for a public dancing licence in respect of a place for which no such licence is in existence at the time of such application and an application for a public dancing licence for a defined period not exceeding one month and an application which is authorised by this Act to be made at any time) shall be made at an annual licensing district court and at no other time.

3.—(1) No application to the District Court for the grant of a public dancing licence (other than a public dancing licence for a defined period not exceeding one month) shall be made or entertained unless the person making such application has, at least one month before the hearing of such application, published a notice of his intention to make such application in a newspaper circulating in the district in which is situate the place to which such application relates.

(2) Every person applying to the District Court for the grant of a public dancing licence shall—

(a) in the case of an application for a public dancing licence for a defined period not exceeding one month, give to the Superintendent of the Garda Síochána within whose district is situate the place to which such application relates at least forty-eight hours' notice in writing of such application, and

(b) in every other case, give at least one month's notice in writing of such application to the Superintendent of the Garda Síochána within whose district, and to the local authority within whose functional area, is situate the place to which such application relates.

4.—A Justice of the District Court granting a public dancing licence may insert therein such conditions and restrictions as he shall think proper, and in particular (without prejudice to the generality of the foregoing power) may insert in such licence conditions limiting the days on which and the hours during which the place to which the licence relates may be used for public dancing.

5.—(1) Every public dancing licence shall operate to authorise the licensee thereunder and (save as is otherwise provided by this section) no other person to use the place specified in such licence, so long as such licence continues in force, for public dancing subject to the provisions of this Act and to the conditions and restrictions contained in such licence.

(2) Where the licensee under a public dancing licence dies while such licence is in force, the personal representative of such deceased licensee shall, until the happening of whichever of the following events first happens, that is to say, the expiration, revocation or surrender of such licence or the expiration of three months from the death of such deceased person, be deemed for all purposes to be the licensee under such licence and shall accordingly have all the rights, powers, and duties of such licensee under or in respect of such licence.

6.—(1) A public dancing licence may be granted for a defined period specified therein not exceeding one month and when so granted shall, unless revoked, or surrendered under this Act, be in force for the said defined period and no longer.

(2) Save as is otherwise provided by the foregoing sub-section of this section, every public dancing licence granted under this Act shall come into force immediately upon the grant thereof and, unless sooner revoked or surrendered under this Act, shall continue in force until the conclusion of the annual licensing district court held in the same licensing area next after the annual licensing district court or other sitting at which such licence was granted.

7.—The licensee under a public dancing licence may at any time surrender such licence by notice in writing sent or delivered, together with such licence, to the district court clerk for the licensing area in which the place to which such licence relates is situate.

8.—(1) A public dancing licence shall not be transferable from the licensee thereunder to another person.

(2) Where a public dancing licence (in this section referred to as the existing licence) is in force in respect of any place, an application may, with the consent of the licensee under the existing licence, be made under this Act at any time for a public dancing licence in respect of the said place to another person, and if such licence is granted the grant thereof shall operate as a revocation of the existing licence.

9.—(1) In addition and without prejudice to any right of appeal for the time being existing under any other Act, an appeal shall lie to the Circuit Court—

(a) by the applicant for a public dancing licence from an order of the District Court refusing to grant such application, and

(b) by the applicant for a public dancing licence from so much of an order of the District Court granting such licence as requires an insertion in such licence of particular conditions or restrictions, and

(c) by any person who appeared at and was heard in opposition to an application for a public dancing licence, from an order or any particular part of an order of the District Court granting such licence.

(2) The jurisdiction of the Circuit Court to hear an appeal under this section shall be exercised by the Judge of that Court having jurisdiction in the circuit in which was situate the courthouse in which the order appealed from was made.

10.—(1) No place, whether licensed or not licensed for the sale of intoxicating liquor, shall be used for public dancing unless a public dancing licence granted under this Act is in force in respect of such place.

(2) If any place is used for public dancing in contravention of this section, the occupier of such place shall be guilty of an offence under this section and shall be liable on summary conviction thereof to a fine not exceeding ten pounds for every day or part of a day on or during which such place is so used.

11.—(1) Whenever any place in respect of which a public dancing licence is for the time being in force is used for public dancing by a person other than the licensee thereunder or is used for public dancing in contravention of or without due compliance with the conditions and restrictions contained in such licence, the licensee under such licence shall be guilty of an offence under this section and shall be liable on summary conviction thereof to a fine not exceeding five pounds for every day or part of a day on or during which such place is so used.

(2) Whenever any person is convicted of an offence under this section, the Justice of the District Court by whom such person is so convicted may, if he so thinks proper and either in addition to or in lieu of inflicting a fine, revoke the public dancing licence relating to the place in respect of which such offence was committed.

12.—(1) So long as a public dancing licence is in force, the licensee under such licence shall keep or cause to be kept affixed to or inscribed on the place to which such licence relates in a conspicuous position at or near the principal entrance to such place a notice in easily legible letters in the following words, that is to say "Licensed under Act of the Oireachtas for public dancing".

(2) Whenever the licensee under a public dancing licence fails to comply with the foregoing sub-section of this section, such licensee shall be guilty of an offence under this section and shall be liable on summary conviction thereof to a fine not exceeding one pound for every day during which or any part of which such failure occurs.

13.—(1) Any member of the Garda Síochána in uniform may enter any place in respect of which a public dancing licence is for the time being in force at any time while such place is being used for public dancing or at any other reasonable time and there make such inspection, examination, and inquiry as he shall think proper.

(2) Every person who shall prevent or attempt to prevent a member of the Garda Síochána from exercising, or obstruct or attempt to obstruct any such member in the exercise of a power vested in such member by virtue of this section shall be guilty of an offence under this section and shall be liable on summary conviction thereof to a fine not exceeding five pounds.

14.—(1) Immediately upon the passing of this Act, section 51 of the Public Health Acts Amendment Act, 1890, shall cease to apply or have effect in relation to public dancing within the meaning of this Act.

(2) Every licence granted under the said section 51 of the Public Health Acts Amendment Act, 1890, which is in force at the passing of this Act and immediately before such passing had effect as a licence authorising the use of a place for public dancing within the meaning of the Act, shall, in so far as it so had such effect, be deemed as from the passing of this Act to be a public dancing licence granted under this Act and shall have effect under this Act and this Act shall apply thereto accordingly.

(3) Where a public entertainment consists mainly of public dancing as defined by this Act, but includes, as a subsidiary or incidental part thereof, exhibition dancing by special performers, dancing competitions, vocal or instrumental music (in addition to the music provided for the said public dancing), or any similar entertainment, such public entertainment shall be public dancing to which this Act applies and shall not be a public entertainment to which the said section 51 of the Public Health Acts Amendment Act, 1890, applies.

15.—This Act shall not apply in relation to public dancing carried on in any recreation room managed or conducted under the authority **[Deletion: by the Defence Act 1954, s.9, Sched. 1]** of the Commissioner of the Garda Síochána.

16.—This Act may be cited as the Public Dance Halls Act, 1935.

INTOXICATING LIQUOR ACT 1943

No. 7 of 1943

AN ACT TO AMEND AND EXTEND THE LICENSING (IRELAND) ACTS, 1833 TO 1929, IN DIVERS RESPECTS AND, IN PARTICULAR, BY PROVIDING FOR THE LICENSING OF AERODROMES AND PASSENGER AIRCRAFT.

BE IT ENACTED BY THE OIREACHTAS AS FOLLOWS:

PART I

PRELIMINARY

1.—(1) This Act may be cited as the Intoxicating Liquor Act, 1943.

(2) This Act shall be construed as one with the Licensing (Ireland) Acts, 1833 to 1929, and may be cited with those Acts as the Licensing Acts, 1833 to 1943.

PART II

AMENDMENTS OF THE INTOXICATING LIQUOR ACT, 1927

2.—In this Part of this Act the expression "the Act of 1927" means the Intoxicating Liquor Act, 1927 (No. 15 of 1927).

3.—Section 1 of the Act of 1927, is hereby amended by the insertion in sub-section (1) after the word "licence" in each of the definitions of the expressions "licensed premises", "on-licence", and "off-licence" of the following: "(whether granted on production or without production of a certificate of the Circuit Court or the District Court)".

4.—Section 2 of the Act of 1927 is hereby amended—
by the deletion of sub-sections (1), (2), and (3) thereof and the insertion therein of the following two sub-sections in lieu of the said sub-sections so deleted, and the said Act and in particular sub-sections (4) and (5) of the said section 2 shall be construed and have effect accordingly, that is to say:—

"(1) Save as is otherwise provided by this Act, it shall not be lawful for any person in any county borough to sell or expose for sale any intoxicating liquor or to open or keep open any premises for the sale of intoxicating liquor or to permit any intoxicating liquor to be consumed on licensed premises—

(a) on any week day—

(i) during a period of summer time, before the hour of half-past ten o'clock in the morning or after the hour of half-past ten o'clock in the evening, or (subject to the exceptions hereinafter mentioned) between the hours of half-past two o'clock and half-past three o'clock in the afternoon, or

(ii) during any period which is not a period of summer time, before the hour of ten o'clock in the morning or after the hour of ten o'clock in the evening, or (subject to the exceptions hereinafter mentioned) between the hours of half-past two o'clock and half-past three o'clock in the afternoon, or

(b) on any Sunday—

(i) in the case of the county borough of Dublin or the Dublin Metropolitan Area, before the hour of half past one o'clock in the afternoon, or between the hours of three o'clock and five o'clock in the afternoon or after the hour of seven o'clock in the evening, or

(ii) in the case of any other county borough, before the hour of one o'clock in the afternoon or between the hours of three o'clock and five o'clock in the afternoon, or after the hour of seven o'clock in the evening, or

(c) at any time on Christmas Day, Good Friday, or Saint Patrick's Day.

The exceptions referred to in the foregoing paragraph (a) of this sub-section are:

(i) that between the hours of half-past two o'clock and half-past three o'clock in this afternoon on any week-day the holder of an on-licence attached to premises situate in a county borough may receive on such premises orders (accompanied or not accompanied by payment) by post, telegraph, or telephone but not otherwise for intoxicating liquor to be consumed off the premises and to be delivered by such holder at the residence of the person so ordering the same or at a railway station but not otherwise and may so deliver the intoxicating liquor so ordered, but the person so ordering such intoxicating liquor shall not for the purposes of any other section of this Act be a person to whom intoxicating liquor may be lawfully sold or supplied on such premises between the said hours on the said days, and

(ii) that between the hours of half-past two o'clock and half-past three o'clock in the afternoon on any week day the holder of an off-licence attached to premises situate in a county borough may receive verbally or otherwise on such premises orders (accompanied or not accompanied by payment) for intoxicating liquor to be consumed off the premises and to be delivered by such holder at the residence of the person ordering the same or at a railway station but not otherwise and may so deliver the intoxicating liquor so ordered and may open and keep open the said premises for the purpose of receiving such orders and may expose on such premises intoxicating liquor for sale on such orders.

(2) Save as is otherwise provided by this Act, it shall not be lawful for any person in any place not being a county borough to sell or expose for sale or to open or keep open any premises for the sale of intoxicating liquor or to permit any intoxicating liquor to be consumed on licensed premises—

(a) on any week-day—

(i) during a period of summer time, before the hour of half-past ten o'clock in the morning or after the hour of half-past ten o'clock in the evening, or

(ii) during any period which is not a period of summer time, before the hour of ten o'clock in the morning or after the hour of ten o'clock in the evening, or

(b) at any time on any Sunday or on Christmas Day, Good Friday, or Saint Patrick's Day."

5.—Section 3 of the Act of 1927 is hereby amended—

(a) by the deletion from sub-section (1) thereof of all words after the words "save and except", and the insertion in that sub-section of the following words in lieu of the said words so deleted, that is to say, "between the hours of nine o'clock and half-past ten o'clock in the morning on week days during a period of summer time and between the hours of nine o'clock and ten o'clock in the morning on week days during any period which is not a period of summer time",

(b) by the insertion in sub-section (2) thereof, after the words "off-licence is attached", of the words and brackets "(other than premises to which a wine retailer's off-licence within the meaning of the Finance (1909-10) Act, 1910, and no other off-licence is attached)",

(c) by the deletion from sub-section (2) thereof of all words after the words "save and except" and the insertion in that sub-section of the following words in lieu of the said words so deleted, that is to say, "between the hours of nine o'clock and half-past ten o'clock in the morning on week days during a period of summer time and between the hours of nine o'clock and ten o'clock in the morning on week days during any period which is not a period of summer time, and if such premises are situate in a county borough, between the hours of half past two o'clock and half-past three o'clock in the afternoon on week days during any period, whether it is or is not a period of summer time".

6.—Section 5 of the Act of 1927 is hereby amended by the deletion in sub-section (1) of the words "and are situate in a county borough".

7.—Section 11 of the Act of 1927 is hereby amended—

(a) by the deletion in sub-section (1) of the words "licensing area, be entitled to have the seven-day licence transferred at the annual licensing District

Court" and the substitution in lieu thereof of the words "district or adjoining districts, be entitled, on application at any sitting of the justice of the District Court in whose district are situate the premises to which the six-day licence is attached, to have the seven-day licence transferred",

(b) by the deletion in sub-section (2) of the words "licensing area, be entitled to have the ordinary seven-day licence transferred at the annual licensing District Court" and the substitution in lieu thereof of the words "district or adjoining districts, be entitled, on application at any sitting of the justice of the District Court in whose district are situate the premises to which the early-closing licence is attached, to have the ordinary seven-day licence transferred",

(c) by the addition at the end of the section of a new subsection as follows:

"(3) In this section, the word 'district' means a district of the District Court prescribed under section 68 of the Courts of Justice Act, 1924 (No. 10 of 1924)."

8.—Section 12 of the Act of 1927 is hereby amended by the insertion before sub-section (2) of a new sub-section as follows:

"(1A) A person, who is the holder of a wine retailer's on-licence within the meaning of the Finance (1909–10) Act, 1910, may, at any sitting of the justice of the District Court, apply to the Court to certify that the premises to which such licence is attached are a restaurant for the purposes of this Act and the Court, if satisfied after hearing the officer in charge of the Garda Síochána for the licensing area that such premises are structurally adapted for use and *bona fide* and mainly used as a restaurant, refreshment house or other place for supplying substantial meals to the public, shall grant to such person a certificate (in this section also referred to as a restaurant certificate) certifying that such premises are a restaurant for the purposes of this Act."

9.—Section 13 of the Act of 1927, sub-section (1), is hereby amended by the addition, after the words "St. Patrick's Day" of the words "nor on any Christmas Day".

10.—Paragraph (e) of section 14 of the Act of 1927 is hereby amended by the deletion of the words "Christmas Day" and "and St. Patrick's Day".

11.—Section 15 of the Act of 1927 is hereby amended—

(a) by the insertion in paragraph (a) of sub-section (1) before the words "on any week day" of the words "after the hour of six o'clock in the morning",

(b) by the insertion in sub-paragraph (i) of paragraph (b) before the words "on any week day" of the words "after the hour of six o'clock in the morning",

(c) by the deletion of sub-section (2).

12.—Section 16 of the Act of 1927 is hereby amended—

(a) by the insertion in sub-section (1) after the words "(not being or forming part of a county borough)" of the words "or by any holder of an on-licence (not being a six-day licence) attached to premises in such licensing area",

(b) by the deletion of the word "three" where that word occurs in the words "not exceeding in the whole three hours" and the substitution in lieu thereof of the word "four",

(c) by the addition at the end of the section of the following sub-section, that is to say:—

"(4) An area exemption order shall not be granted on the application of the holder of an on-licence unless—

(a) the applicant has, not less than forty-eight hours before making the application, served upon the officer in charge of the Garda Síochána for the licensing area a notice of his intention to make the application, setting out his name and address and the area, day, and period or periods for which the order is required and

(b) the justice of the District Court has heard such officer in relation to the application."

13.—Section 24 of the Act of 1927 is hereby amended by the deletion of the word "drink" and the substitution therefor of the words "intoxicating liquor".

14.—(1) Section 25 of the Act of 1927 is hereby amended by the insertion in sub-section (1) before the words "shall, if the person so convicted" of the words "if the Court in its discretion so thinks proper".

(2) Every conviction which, immediately before the passing this Act, stood recorded under section 25 of the Act of 1927 on a licence then in force, shall, upon the passing of this Act, cease for all purposes to be so recorded.

15.—No order shall be made after the passing of this Act under section 26 of the Act of 1927.

16.—Section 27 of the Act of 1927 is hereby amended by the deletion of the words "if satisfied that by reason of extenuating circumstances (to be stated in the order of the Court) such conviction ought not to be recorded on such licence make", and the substitution of the words "make, if in his discretion he so thinks proper".

17.—(1) In this section the expression "1942 order" means a final apportionment order under section 48 of the Act of 1927 for the year 1942.[1]

(2) Every 1942 order shall, as regards the compensation annuity to which such order relates, be deemed to be the final apportionment order under section 48 of the Act of 1927 for each of the years subsequent to the year 1942.

---

[1] Section 17 no longer applies: see the Intoxicating Liquor Act 1960, s.3, Sched, which repealed s.48 of the Intoxicating Liquor Act 1927

(3) For the purposes of the application of a 1942 order in relation to a year subsequent to 1942, the following provisions shall have effect, that is to say—

(a) the 1942 order shall, as regards the year in question, be deemed to have become final under the Act of 1927 on the 15th day of September in the said year;

(b) where any licence, by reference to which an amount mentioned in the 1942 order is apportioned, has terminated on or after the 2nd day of July in the year preceding the said year and before the 1st day of July in the said year, the mention in the 1942 order of such amount and of the person on whom it is apportioned shall be deemed to be deleted;

(c) subject to the provisions of paragraph (b) of this subsection, every mention in the 1942 order in relation to any particular premises, of a person not the holder, on the 1st day of July in the said year, of the licence in respect of those premises shall be construed as a mention of the person who, on the said 1st day of July, was the holder of such licence, and the latter person shall be regarded for the purposes of section 49 of the Act of 1927 as the person on whom the amount mentioned in the 1942 order in respect of those premises is apportioned for the said year;

(d) the Minister shall not, for the said year, carry out in relation to the compensation annuity to which the 1942 order relates the functions imposed on him by section 48 of the Act of 1927;

(e) no objection shall be capable of being made in the said year in relation to the 1942 order under sub-section (4) of section 48 of the Act of 1927.

(4) A final apportionment order made under section 48 of the Act of 1927 and apportioning a compensation annuity commencing in a year subsequent to the year 1942 may, with the consent of the Minister for Finance, contain a declaration that such order shall, as regards such annuity, be deemed to be the final apportionment order under section 48 of the Act of 1927 for each of the years subsequent to the year in which such order is made.

(5) Where an order contains a declaration under sub-section (4) of this section—

(a) such declaration shall have the force of law in accordance with its terms;

(b) the provisions contained in sub-section (3) of this section shall, in relation to years subsequent to that in which such order was made, have effect as if such order were a 1942 order.

(6) The Minister for Finance, may, by requisition in writing communicated to the Minister before the 1st day of June in any year, require the Minister to make under section 48 of the Act of 1927 an apportionment order in respect of any compensation annuity payable in that year, and, upon any such requisition being so communicated to the Minister, the following provisions shall apply and have effect, that is to say:—

(a) the Minister shall make, under and in accordance with the said section 48, a draft apportionment order in respect of the said compensation annuity for the said year and shall so comply with the said section 48 that such draft apportionment order (with or without amendment) shall in due course become and be final by virtue of sub-section (6) of the said section;

(b) notwithstanding anything contained in the foregoing provisions of this section, the apportionment order so made shall, on becoming final as aforesaid, be the final apportionment order under the said section 48 in respect of the said compensation annuity for the said year and for every succeeding year, until another requisition is made under this section by the Minister for Finance in relation to the said compensation annuity;

(c) the provisions contained in sub-section (3) of this section shall, in relation to years subsequent to the said year (until another requisition is made as aforesaid), have effect as if the apportionment order so made were a 1942 order.

(7) In this section the expression "the Minister" means the Minister for Justice.

18.—Section 62 of the Act of 1927 is hereby amended by the deletion in sub-section (1) of the words "the annual licensing District Court next after the passing of this Act" and the substitution in lieu thereof of the words "any annual licensing District Court".

PART III

Grant of New Licences in Certain Cases

19.—In this Part of this Act—

the expression "the Act of 1833" means the Licensing (Ireland) Act, 1833;

the expression "the Act of 1902" means the Licensing (Ireland) Act, 1902;

the expression "the Act of 1927" means the Intoxicating Liquor Act, 1927 (No. 15 of 1927);

"licence" means a licence for the sale of intoxicating liquor for the grant of which the production of a certificate of the Circuit Court or of the District Court is required.[2]

20.—(1) Where a person (in this section referred to as the applicant) duly gives notice of his intention to apply for a licence in respect of specified premises and, at the proceedings in the Circuit Court in relation to such application, the applicant shows to the satisfaction of the Court–

(a) that the said premises are structurally adapted for use and are *bona fide* and mainly used as a restaurant, refreshment house, or other place for supplying substantial meals to the public, and

(b) that, in respect of the licensing year including the 1st day of January, 1933, a renewal of a licence attached to the said premises or to premises

[2] Inserted by the Intoxicating Liquor Act 1960, s.25(1).

substantially the same as the said premises was in fact issued, and

(c) that, subsequent to the said date, the said licence was not renewed,

the Court shall, notwithstanding anything contained in the Act of 1902, cause such certificate as is mentioned in section 5 of the Act of 1833 to be given to the applicant declaring him to be duly entitled to receive a licence in respect of the said premises, unless the Court, in consequence of an objection made under section 4 of the Act of 1833, prohibits under that section the issuing of such licence on one or more of the following grounds, that is to say, the character, misconduct, or unfitness of the applicant or the unfitness or inconvenience of the said premises.

(2) Where, in a case to which the foregoing sub-section applies, the certificate referred to in that sub-section is given to the applicant, nothing contained in the Act of 1902 shall operate to prevent the grant to the applicant of the licence which the said certificate declares him to be entitled to receive.

(3) This section shall continue in force until the 31st day of December, 1944, and no longer, unless the Oireachtas otherwise determines.

21.—(1) Where a person (in this section referred to as the applicant) duly gives notice of his intention to apply for a licence in respect of premises (in this section referred to as the new premises) to which no licence is attached and, at the proceedings in the Circuit Court in relation to such application, the applicant shows to the satisfaction of the Court—

(a) that the applicant is the holder of a licence attached to premises (in this section referred to as the existing premises) situate in the immediate vicinity of the new premises, and

(b) that the new premises and the existing premises are both situate in the same District Court area prescribed by law for the purposes of the transaction of licensing business, and

(c) that neither the new premises nor the existing premises is situate in a county or other borough, an urban district, or a town, and

(d) that the rateable valuation of the new premises is not less than the rateable valuation of the existing premises, and[3]

(e) that the new premises is more suitable than the existing premises for the business of selling intoxicating liquor,

the Court shall, notwithstanding anything contained in the Act of 1902, cause such certificate as is mentioned in section 5 of the Act of 1833 to be given to the applicant declaring him to be duly entitled to receive a licence in respect of the new premises, unless the Court, in its absolute discretion, prohibits the issuing of such licence either on the ground of the unfitness or inconvenience of the new premises or on the ground that the existence of a licence in respect of the new premises would be unreasonably detrimental to the business then carried on in some licensed premises in the neighbourhood of the new premises.

[3] Substituted by the Intoxicating Liquor Act 1960, s. 33(1)(b).

(2) Where, in a case to which the foregoing sub-section of this section applies, the certificate referred to in that sub-section is given to the applicant, the following provisions shall apply and have effect, that is to say:

(a) the licence (in this sub-section referred to as the new licence) to which the applicant is declared by the said certificate to be entitled and which is granted to him in pursuance of that certificate shall be a licence of the same character in all respects (including conditions inserted therein) as the licence (in this sub-section referred to as the old licence) attached to the existing premises;

(b) nothing contained in the Act of 1902 shall operate to prevent the grant of the new licence to the applicant;

(c) upon the grant of the new licence, the old licence shall be extinguished;

(d) every (if any) conviction which is recorded on the old licence under section 25 of the Act of 1927 at the time of the grant of the new licence shall be deemed to be recorded on the new licence under the said section and to have been so recorded on the date on which it was recorded on the old licence;

(e) if paragraph (1) of section 2 of the Act of 1902 applies in respect of the existing premises, those premises shall upon the old licence being extinguished in pursuance of this sub-section, cease to be premises to which the said paragraph applies, and the Act of 1902 shall thenceforward have effect accordingly in relation to the existing premises.

22.—(1) Where a person (in this section referred to as the applicant) duly gives notice of his intention to apply for a licence in respect of premises (in this section referred to as the substituted premises) to which no licence is attached and, at the proceedings in the Circuit Court in relation to such application, the applicant shows to the satisfaction of the Court—

(a) that premises (in this section referred to as the original premises) in the immediate vicinity of the substituted premises were burnt down, or otherwise destroyed, or rendered uninhabitable by fire or other unavoidable cause or accident not more than **two years**[4] before the date on which the said notice by the applicant was served on the county registrar, and

(b) that a licence was attached to the original premises when they were so burnt down or otherwise destroyed or rendered uninhabitable, and

(c) that at the time of the said hearing before the Circuit Court the applicant is in lawful occupation of the original premises or of the site and remains thereof, **or that he has procured the consent of the lawful occupier of such premises or of the site and remains thereof to the making of the application, and if the licence referred to in paragraph (b) of this subsection is then subsisting, to the extinguishing thereof if and when a licence is granted pursuant to this section,**[5] and

---

[4] Substituted by the Intoxicating Liquor Act 1960, s.26(2)(a).
[5] Inserted by the Intoxicating Liquor Act 1960, s.26(2)(b).

(d) that no certificate under section 5 of the Act of 1833 has already been given by virtue of this section by reference to the original premises having been so burnt down or otherwise destroyed or rendered uninhabitable, and

(e) that no trade or business had been carried on in the original premises since they were so burnt down or otherwise destroyed or rendered uninhabitable,

the Court shall, notwithstanding anything contained in the Act of 1902, cause such certificate as is mentioned in section 5 of the Act of 1833 to be given to the applicant declaring him to be duly entitled to receive a licence in respect of the substituted premises, unless the Court, in consequence of an objection made under section 4 of the Act of 1833, prohibits under that section the issuing of such licence on one or more of the following grounds, that is to say, the character, misconduct, or unfitness of the applicant or the unfitness or inconvenience of the substituted premises.

(2) Where, in a case to which the foregoing sub-section of this section applies, the certificate referred to in that sub-section is given to the applicant, the following provisions shall apply and have effect, that is to say:—

(a) the licence (in this sub-section referred to as the new licence) to which the applicant is declared by the said certificate to be entitled and which is granted to him in pursuance of that certificate shall be a licence of the same character in all respects (including conditions inserted therein) as the licence (in this sub-section referred to as the old licence) which was attached to the original premises when they were burnt down or otherwise destroyed or rendered uninhabitable;

(b) nothing contained in the Act of 1902 shall operate to prevent the grant of the new licence to the applicant;

(c) upon the grant of the new licence, the old licence (if then subsisting) shall be extinguished;

(d) every (if any) conviction which was recorded on the old licence under section 25 of the Act of 1927 and either (as the case may be) would, but for the expiry of that licence, have continued to be so recorded thereon at the time of the grant of the new licence or continues to be so recorded on the old licence immediately before it is extinguished shall be deemed to be recorded on the new licence under the said section and to have been so recorded on the date on which it was recorded on the old licence;

(e) if paragraph (1) of section 2 of the Act of 1902 applies in respect of the original premises, those premises shall, upon the grant of the new licence, cease to be premises to which the said paragraph applies, and the Act of 1902 shall (subject to the provisions of the next following sub-section of this section) thenceforward have effect accordingly in relation to the original premises.

(3) Where, in a case to which the foregoing sub-sections of this section apply, the original premises are reconstructed or new premises are erected on the site of the original premises (or on a site substantially the same as that site) and, at any time thereafter while a licence is attached to the substituted premises, the holder of

that licence duly gives notice of his intention to apply for a licence in respect of the premises so reconstructed or newly erected, the Court shall cause such certificate as is mentioned in section 5 of the Act of 1833 to be given to the said holder declaring him to be duly entitled to receive a licence in respect of the said reconstructed or newly erected premises, unless the Court, in consequence of an objection made under section 4 of the Act of 1833, prohibits under that section the issuing of such licence to the said holder on one or more of the following grounds, that is to say, the character, misconduct, or unfitness of the said holder or the unfitness or inconvenience of the said reconstructed or newly erected premises, and, if the Court causes such certificate to be given to the said holder, the provisions contained in sub-section (2) of this section shall apply and have effect with the necessary modifications and, in particular, with the modifications that the expression "the new licence" shall mean the licence to which such certificate relates and the expression "the old licence" shall mean the said licence then attached to the substituted premises.

(4) Section 11 of the Excise Licences Act, 1825, shall not apply or have effect in relation to a licence.

23.—Section 3 of the Act of 1902 is hereby amended by the insertion after the words "for consumption on" of the words, "or off".

PART IV

Licences in Respect of Aerodromes and Passenger Aircraft

24.—In this Part of this Act—

the expression "the Minister" means the Minister for Industry and Commerce;

the expression "the Act of 1927" means the Intoxicating Liquor Act, 1927 (No. 15 of 1927);

the expression "the Act of 1936" means the Air Navigation and Transport Act, 1936 (No. 40 of 1936);

the word "aircraft" has the same meaning as it has in the Act of 1936;

the expression "approved aerodrome" means an aerodrome (within the meaning of the Act of 1936) which complies with both the following conditions, that is to say:—

(a) it either is licensed by the Minister in pursuance of an order made under Part II of the Act of 1936 or is controlled and operated by the Minister or by the Minister for Defence, and

(b) it is used for the arrival and departure of aircraft operated as part of an authorised air transport service;

the expression "authorised air transport service" means an air service for the transport of passengers, mails, and goods or any of them by air which is either—

(a) an internal air service within the meaning of Part IX of the Act of 1936 the carrying on of which is authorised by or under the said Part IX, or

(b) an international airway or regular international air navigation line established, or created and operated, with the prior authorisation of the Minister under the Air Navigation (International Lines) Order, 1935 (S.R. & O., No. 560 of 1935), or any order for the time being in force amending or replacing that order;

the expression "air transport concern" means a person entitled to operate an authorised air transport service;

the expression "on-licence" means a licence for the sale of intoxicating liquor for consumption either on or off the premises;

the expression "aerodrome premise" means all the buildings for the time being erected in an approved aerodrome irrespective of the purpose for which such premises are used;

the expression "licensed aerodrome premises" means premises in an approved aerodrome in respect of which a licence for the sale of intoxicating liquor granted or renewed by virtue of this Part of this Act is for the time being subsisting, whether such premises are the whole or a part only of the aerodrome premises in such aerodrome.

25.—(1) Whenever the Minister is satisfied that it is expedient that an on-licence should be granted in respect of the whole or a particular part of any particular aerodrome premises, the Minister may issue to a person who appears to him to be a fit and proper person to hold such on-licence a certificate certifying that the aerodrome in which the said aerodrome premises are situate is an approved aerodrome and that the Minister approves of the grant by the Revenue Commissioners to the said person (who shall be named in such certificate) of an on-licence in respect of specified premises which are either the whole or a part of the said aerodrome premises.

(2) On presentation to the Revenue Commissioners of a certificate issued by the Minister under the foregoing sub-section of this section, it shall be lawful for the Revenue Commissioners, notwithstanding anything contained in the Licensing (Ireland) Acts, 1833 to 1929, to grant to the person named in that behalf in the said certificate an on-licence in respect of the premises specified in that behalf in the said certificate.

(3) Whenever an on-licence granted or renewed under this section is subsisting, the Minister may, if he so thinks proper, issue to the holder of such on-licence a certificate certifying that the aerodrome in which the premises thereby licensed are situate continues to be an approved aerodrome and that the Minister approves of the renewal of such on-licence to the said holder thereof in respect of the said premises.

(4) On presentation to the Revenue Commissioners of a certificate issued by the Minister under the next preceding sub-section of this section, it shall be lawful for the Revenue Commissioners, notwithstanding anything contained in the Licensing (Ireland) Acts, 1833 to 1929, to grant a renewal of the said on-licence to the holder thereof.

26.—(1) Whenever it appears to the Minister to be expedient that an on-licence granted or renewed under the next preceding section and for the time being subsisting should, because of the death of the holder thereof or for any other reason, be transferred to a particular person who appears to the Minister to be a fit and proper person to hold such on-licence, the Minister may issue to the said person a certificate certifying that the Minister approves of the transfer of such licence to him.

(2) On presentation to the Revenue Commissioners of a certificate issued by the Minister under the foregoing sub-section of this section, it shall be lawful for the Revenue Commissioners, notwithstanding anything contained in the Licensing (Ireland) Acts, 1833 to 1929, to transfer the on-licence to which such certificate relates to the person specified in that behalf in such certificate.

(3) Whenever it appears to the Minister to be expedient for any reason that the premises to which an on-licence granted or renewed under the next preceding section and for the time being subsisting relates should be varied in any particular respect other than applying such on-licence to premises which are not part of any aerodrome premises, the Minister may issue to the holder of such on-licence a certificate certifying whichever one or more of the following things is appropriate in the circumstances, that is to say:—

(a) that the Minister approves of the extension of the said on-licence to a specified part of the aerodrome premises to another part of which it already applies;

(b) that the Minister approves of the exclusion from the premises to which the said on-licence applies of a specified part of those premises;

(c) that the Minister approves of the transfer of the said on-licence from the premises to which it applies to another part of the same aerodrome premises.

(4) On presentation to the Revenue Commissioners of a certificate issued by the Minister under the next preceding sub-section of this section, it shall be lawful for the Revenue Commissioners, notwithstanding anything contained in the Licensing (Ireland) Acts, 1833 to 1929, to amend the on-licence to which such certificate relates in accordance with the approval of the Minister as stated in such certificate.

27.—Notwithstanding anything contained in the Act of 1927, it shall be lawful to sell intoxicating liquor in licensed aerodrome premises at any time to any of the following persons and to permit intoxicating liquor so sold to be consumed in the said premises by any of the following persons, that is to say:—

(a) persons who have arrived at the aerodrome in which the said licensed premises are situate as passengers in an aircraft engaged in an authorised air transport service and have, immediately before such arrival, travelled in such aircraft for a distance of not less than fifty miles measured by the ordinary flying route of such aircraft to the said aerodrome, and

(b) persons who intend to travel from the said aerodrome as passengers in an aircraft engaged in an authorised air transport service and hold tickets entitling them to travel from the said aerodrome in such aircraft for a distance of not less than fifty miles measured by the ordinary flying route of such aircraft from the said aerodrome.

28.—(1) Section 3 of the Act of 1927 shall be construed and have effect as if, in sub-section (3) thereof, licensed aerodrome premises were enumerated amongst the premises specified in that sub-section as premises to which the said section 3 does not apply.

(2) The holder of an on-licence granted or renewed under this Act may apply under section 5 of the Act of 1927 to a justice of the District Court for a special exemption order (within the meaning of that section) and the provisions of the said section shall apply and have effect in relation to such application as if such holder were the holder of such on-licence as is mentioned in sub-section (1) of the said section.

(3) Section 13 of the Act of 1927 shall apply and have effect in relation to licensed aerodrome premises in like manner as it applies and has effect in relation to premises which are for the time being a hotel or restaurant.

(4) In Part IV of the Act of 1927, the word "licence" shall not include a licence attached to licensed aerodrome premises, and the said Part IV (and in particular sub-section (3) of section 36 thereof) shall be construed and have effect accordingly.

29.—(1) It shall be lawful for the Revenue Commissioners, notwithstanding anything contained in the Licensing (Ireland) Acts, 1833 to 1929, to grant to any air transport concern a licence for the sale of intoxicating liquor to passengers on an aircraft owned or hired by that concern for consumption while such aircraft is in flight.

(2) A licence granted under this section shall be known as a passenger aircraft licence, and shall operate only in respect of such aircraft owned or hired by the air transport concern to whom it is granted as is specified in the licence.

(3) Notwithstanding anything contained in the Act of 1927, a passenger aircraft licence shall operate to authorise the sale, in the aircraft to which such licence relates and at any time while such aircraft is in flight, of intoxicating liquor to passengers in such aircraft for consumption therein.

PART V

MISCELLANEOUS

30.—Nothing in the Licensing (Ireland) Acts, 1833 to 1929, or in this Act, shall be deemed to prohibit any licensed person or his private friends from gaming by way of playing cards for stakes on licensed premises provided that such gaming is carried on in any part of such licensed premises other than the part in which the sale of intoxicating liquor generally takes place and the private friends of the licensed person are being *bona fide* entertained by him at his own expense.

[s.31(1) repealed by the Intoxicating Liquor Act 1960, s.3, Sched.]

32.—(2) A person who is at the one time the holder of a six-day beerhouse licence and the holder of a seven-day beerhouse licence shall, on application at any sitting of the justice of the District Court in whose district are situate the premises to which the six-day beerhouse licence is attached, be entitled to have the seven-day beerhouse licence transferred to the premises to which the six-day beerhouse licence is attached, but subject to the condition that, on such transfer being made, the six-day beerhouse licence shall not be renewed and the premises to which the seven-day beerhouse licence was attached before such transfer shall, for the purposes of the Licensing (Ireland) Act, 1902, be deemed never to have been licensed.

(3) In this section, the expressions "publican's licence" and "beerhouse licence" have the meanings given to them respectively by section 52 of the Finance (1909-10) Act, 1910, for the purposes of Part II of that Act, and the word "district" means a district of the District Court prescribed under section 68 of the Courts of Justice Act 1924 (No. 10 of 1924).

32.—So much of section 1 of the Licensing (Ireland) Act, 1833, as requires the production of a certificate signed by six householders, that is to say, that portion of the said section beginning with the words "upon the production" and ending with the words "the past year" is hereby repealed.

INTOXICATING LIQUOR ACT 1953

No. 30 of 1953

AN ACT TO PROVIDE FOR THE LICENSING, FOR THE SALE OF INTOXICATING LIQUOR, OF THE OMNIBUS STATION OF CÓRAS IOMPAIR ÉIREANN IN ÁRAS MHIC DHIARMADA AT STORE STREET, DUBLIN, AND OF NEW PREMISES ERECTED IN CONSEQUENCE OF THE DEMOLITION BY LOCAL AUTHORITIES OF EXISTING LICENSED PREMISES AND FOR OTHER MATTERS CONNECTED THEREWITH

BE IT ENACTED BY THE OIREACHTAS AS FOLLOWS:—

1.—(1) In this Act—

"the Act of 1902" means the Licensing (Ireland) Act, 1902;

"the Act of 1927" means the Intoxicating Liquor Act, 1927 (No. 15 of 1927);

"the Board" means Córas Iompair Éireann;

"the Court" means, in relation to proceedings in respect of an on-licence, the Circuit Court, and, in relation to proceedings in respect of an off-licence, the District Court;

"the Licensing Acts" means the Licensing Acts, 1833 to 1952;

"licensed premises" means premises licensed for the sale by retail of intoxicating liquor;

"the Minister" means the Minister for Industry and Commerce;

"the omnibus station" means the Board's omnibus station in Áras Mhic Dhiarmada at Store Street, in the city of Dublin.

(2) The Licensing Acts and this Act shall be construed as one.

Omnibus Station

2.—(1) The Minister, if he thinks it proper that an on-licence should be granted to the Board in respect of any particular part of the omnibus station, may issue to the Board a certificate approving of the grant of the licence.

(2) The Revenue Commissioners shall grant the licence on presentation of the certificate to them.

3.—(1) The Minister, if he so thinks proper, may from time to time issue to the Board a certificate approving of the renewal of the licence.

(2) The Revenue Commissioners shall renew the licence on presentation of the certificate to them.

4.—(1) The Minister, if he thinks it proper that the licence should be extended or transferred to another part of the omnibus station or should cease to apply to any part of the station, may issue to the Board a certificate approving of the alteration.

(2) Whenever such a certificate is presented to the Revenue Commissioners, they shall amend the licence accordingly.

5.—(1) Section 3 of the Act of 1927 (which relates to mixed trading) shall not apply to premises licensed under section 2.

(2) Section 5 (which relates to special exemption orders) and section 13 (which relates to the supply of intoxicating liquor with a meal) of the Act of 1927 shall apply in relation to premises licensed under section 2.

(3) Part IV of the Act of 1927 (which relates to the reduction of licences) shall not apply to a licence under section 2.

Premises Demolished by Local Authority

6.—(1) A local authority may, if they think fit, issue to any person a certificate declaring that—

(a) after the passing of this Act particular licensed premises have been or are to be demolished by or by direction of the authority in exercise of any of their functions, and

(b) a particular site acquired by them is approved by them as a site for licensed premises in substitution for the former premises.

(2) The local authority shall not issue a certificate to any person other than the person (or nominee of the person) who holds the lowest estate or tenancy in the premises or, where the premises have been acquired by the local authority, held it immediately before such acquisition unless that person has been offered and has not accepted a certificate.

(3) Where the lowest estate or tenancy is subject to a condition (whether in respect of intoxicating liquor generally or any class of intoxicating liquor) that the holder of such estate or tenancy shall sell only such liquor purchased from or through the immediate lessor, then, for the purpose of subsection (2), the immediate lessor shall be deemed to be the person who holds (or held) the lowest estate or tenancy.

7.—(1) Where the holder of a certificate under section 6, having duly given notice of his intention, applies to the Court for a certificate entitling him to receive a licence in respect of premises on the approved site the Court shall, notwithstanding anything contained in the Act of 1902, cause such certificate to be given to him unless the Court, in its absolute discretion, prohibits the issuing of the licence—

(a) on the ground of the character, misconduct or unfitness of the applicant or the unfitness or inconvenience of the premises, or

(b) subject to subsection (2), on the ground that the existence of a licence for the premises would be unreasonably detrimental to the business then carried on in some licensed premises in the neighbourhood.

(2) The ground of objection mentioned in paragraph (b) of subsection (1) shall not be considered if—

(a) the premises are erected on the site of the previously licensed premises, or

(b) the local authority certify that that site is not available as a site for licensed premises and it appears to the Court that the location of the premises where they are rather than on the former site is unlikely of itself to have a materially adverse effect on the business carried on in the neighbouring premises.

(3)(a) The licence granted in pursuance of this section shall be of the same character and be subject to the same conditions as the licence attached to the former premises.

(b) Nothing in the Act of 1902 shall prevent the grant of the new licence.

(c) Upon the grant of the new licence the former licence (if it has not already lapsed) shall be extinguished.

(d) Any conviction recorded on the former licence under section 25 of the Act of 1927 at the time of the grant of the new licence shall, if the licensee was the holder of the former licence, be deemed to be recorded on the new licence under that section and to have been so recorded on the date when it was recorded on the former licence.

(e) If the former premises were premises to which paragraph (1) of section 2 of the Act of 1902 applied, that paragraph shall, upon the grant of the new licence, cease to apply to them and shall be deemed to apply to the new premises.

(f) If the former premises were premises to which section 6 of the Act of 1902 applied, the new premises shall be deemed to be premises to which the section applies.

8.—(1) Where the holder of a certificate under section 6 proposes to construct premises upon the approved site and to apply to have the premises licensed for the sale of intoxicating liquor, he may apply to the Court for a declaration that the proposed premises would be fit and convenient to be so licensed, and that either—

(a) the premises when constructed will be premises to which subsection (2) of section 7 applies, or

(b) the existence of a licence for the premises would not be unreasonably detrimental to the business being carried on at the date of the application under this section in any licensed premises in the neighbourhood,

and the Court, if it is so satisfied, may grant the application on such terms as the Court may think fit.

(2) Where the local authority propose to construct premises upon a site approved by them as a site for licensed premises in substitution for licensed premises which, after the passing of this Act, have been or are to be demolished by them or by their direction in exercise of any of their functions and to lease the premises for use as licensed premises, the local authority may apply to the Court for a declaration under subsection (1).

(3) The intending applicant shall—

(a) cause to be inserted, at least twenty-one days before the making of the intended application, in a newspaper circulating in the place in which it is proposed to have the premises, notice of intention to make the application,

(b) give to the Superintendent of the Garda Siochana, within whose district it is proposed to have the premises, at least twenty-one days' notice in writing of intention to make the application, and

(c) cause to be deposited with the said Superintendent a copy of the plans of the proposed premises.

(4) The application shall be accompanied by a plan of the proposed premises.

(5) Any person who would be entitled to object to an application for a certificate entitling the applicant to a licence in respect of the premises shall be entitled to object in like manner to the application under this section.

(6) A declaration under this section shall remain in force for three years from the grant of the application or for such longer period as the Court may in any particular case think proper to provide.

9.—If, on the hearing of an application under section 7, it is shown to the satisfaction of the Court that the premises have been constructed in substantial accordance with the terms of a declaration under section 8, the Court shall not receive any objection to the application grounded upon the unfitness or inconvenience of the premises or upon the detriment to any business then being carried on in the neighbourhood.

10.—(1) This Act may be cited as the Intoxicating Liquor Act, 1953.

(2) The Licensing Acts and this Act may be cited together as the Licensing Acts, 1833 to 1953.

INTOXICATING LIQUOR ACT 1960

No. 18 of 1960

AN ACT TO AMEND AND EXTEND THE LICENSING ACTS, 1833 TO 1953, AND THE REGISTRATION OF CLUBS ACTS, 1904 TO 1927, AND TO PROVIDE FOR OTHER MATTERS CONNECTED WITH THE MATTERS AFORESAID

BE IT ENACTED BY THE OIREACHTAS AS FOLLOWS:—

PART I

Preliminary and General

1.—(1) This Act may be cited as the Intoxicating Liquor Act, 1960.

(2) This Act, in so far as it amends and extends the Licensing Acts, 1833 to 1953, shall be construed as one therewith and may be cited together therewith as the Licensing Acts, 1833 to 1960, and, in so far as it amends and extends the Registration of Clubs Acts, 1904 to 1927, shall be construed as one therewith and may be cited together therewith as the Registration of Clubs Acts, 1904 to 1960.

2.—(1) In this Act, save where the context otherwise requires—

"the Act of 1902" means the Licensing (Ireland) Act, 1902;

"the Act of 1910" means the Finance (1909-10) Act, 1910;

"the Act of 1927" means the Intoxicating Liquor Act, 1927;

"the Act of 1943" means the Intoxicating Liquor Act, 1943;

"the Court" means, in relation to proceedings in respect of the grant of an on-licence, the Circuit Court, and in relation to proceedings in respect of an off-licence or the renewal or transfer of an on-licence, the District Court;

"Court area" means a District Court area prescribed by law for the purposes of the transaction of licensing business;

"licence" means a licence for the sale of intoxicating liquor for the grant of which the production of a certificate of the Court is required, and cognate words shall be construed accordingly.

(2) References in this Act to any enactment shall, save where the context otherwise requires, be construed as references to that enactment as amended by any subsequent enactment including this Act.

3.—Each enactment mentioned in the second column of the Schedule to this Act is hereby repealed to the extent mentioned in the third column of that Schedule opposite the mention of that enactment.

PART II

Prohibited Hours

[s.4 amended s.2 of the Intoxicating Liquor Act 1927, which was subsequently substituted by s.25 of the Intoxicating Liquor Act 1988 and amended by s.2 of the Intoxicating Liquor Act 1995]

[s.5 amended s.13 of the Intoxicating Liquor Act 1927, which was subsequently substituted by s.28 of the Intoxicating Liquor Act 1988 and amended by s.4 of the Intoxicating Liquor Act 1995]

[s.6 amended s.56 of the Intoxicating Liquor Act 1927, which was subsequently substituted by s.26 of the Intoxicating Liquor Act 1988 and amended by s.5 of the Intoxicating Liquor Act 1995]

7.—(1) Notwithstanding anything contained in section 53 of the Act of 1952—

(1) Section 2 (which relates to prohibited hours) of the Act of 1927 shall, subject to subsection (2) of this section, apply in relation to premises licensed by virtue of Chapter III (which relates to the licensing of holiday camps) of Part VI of the Act of 1952, and

(b) Section 13 (which relates to exemptions from prohibited hours for licensed hotels and restaurants), other than paragraph (IV) thereof, of the Act of 1927 shall apply in relation to premises licensed by virtue of the said Chapter III in like manner as it applies in relation to premises which are for the time being a hotel or restaurant.

(2) Nothing in section 2 of the Act of 1927 shall operate to prohibit the licensee of a premises licensed by virtue of the said Chapter III from—

(a) supplying intoxicating liquor to be consumed on the premises to a person who for the time being is *bona fide* lodging in the holiday camp which comprises or includes the said premises, or

(b) permitting intoxicating liquor to be consumed on the said premises by such a person—

(i) on Saint Patrick's Day or any Sunday (other than a Sunday which is Christmas Day)—

(I) during the months of June, July, August and September, between the hours of nine o'clock and half-past ten o'clock in the evening, or

(II) during any other month, between the hours of eight o'clock and, during a period of summertime, half-past ten o'clock in the evening, or, during a period which is not a period of summertime, ten o'clock in the evening,

or

(ii) on Christmas Day, between the hours of half-past seven o'clock and ten o'clock in the evening, or

(iii) on Good Friday, between the hours of six o'clock and nine o'clock in the evening, if, in this case, the intoxicating liquor is—

(I) ordered by such a person at the same time as a substantial meal is ordered by him, and

(II) consumed at the same time as and with the meal, and

(III) supplied and consumed in the portion of the said premises usually set apart for the supply of meals.

(3) In this section "the Act of 1952" means the Tourist Traffic Act, 1952.

8.—Section 3 (which relates to mixed trading) of the Act of 1927 is hereby amended by the substitution for subsections (1) and (2) of the following subsection:

"(1) Where—

(a) any business other than the sale of intoxicating liquor (in this section referred to as non-licensed business) is carried on in any premises to which an on-licence or an off-licence is attached (other than premises to which a wine retailer's off-licence within the meaning of the Finance (1909-10) Act, 1910, and no other off-licence is attached), and

(b) the portion of the premises in which the non-licensed business is carried on is not structurally separated from the remainder of the premises,

the opening or keeping open of the premises for the purpose of carrying on the non-licensed business shall for the purposes of this Act be deemed to be an opening or keeping open of the premises for the sale of intoxicating liquor save and except:–

(i) in the case of the premises to which an on-licence is attached, between the hours of half-past seven o'clock and half-past ten o'clock in the morning on weekdays, **and on a Sunday that falls on the 23rd or 24th day of December in any year,** and

(ii) in the case of the premises to which an off-licence is attached, between the hours of nine o'clock and half-past ten o'clock in the morning on weekdays **and on a Sunday that falls on the 23rd and 24th day of December in any year.**"[1]

---

[1] Amended by the Intoxicating Liquor Act 1960, s.8, and the Intoxicating Liquor Act 1962, s.3 as substituted by the Intoxicating Liquor Act 1995, s.3.

9.—The Act of 1927 is hereby amended by the insertion after section 12 of the following section:

"12A. (1) Where on application to a Justice of the District Court in relation to premises to which an on-licence is attached or on the occasion of an application for a new on-licence, the applicant requests the Court to certify that any portion of the premises to which the application relates is a restaurant for the purposes of section 13 of this Act, the Court, if satisfied, in relation to that portion of the premises, after hearing the officer in charge of the Garda Síochána for the licensing area that—

(a) it is structurally adapted for use and *bona fide* and mainly used as a restaurant, refreshment house or other place for supplying substantial meals to the public,

(b) it does not include a public bar or a part of a room in another part of which there is a public bar, and

(c) there is public access to it otherwise than through a public bar,

shall grant to the applicant a certificate (in this section referred to as a limited restaurant certificate) certifying that that portion of the premises is a restaurant for the purposes of section 13 of this Act.

(2) The Court shall not entertain an application for a limited restaurant certificate unless and until satisfied that not less than ten days before the date on which the application is proposed to be made notice in writing of the intention to make the application was given to the officer in charge of the Garda Síochána for the licensing area.

(3) Every limited restaurant certificate shall unless sooner revoked under this section remain in force until the next annual licensing district court for the licensing area.

(4) A Justice of the District Court may, on the application of the officer in charge of the Garda Síochána for the licensing area, at any time revoke a limited restaurant certificate if he is satisfied, after hearing the officer and the holder of the certificate, that the portion of the premises to which the certificate relates has ceased to be structurally adapted for use or to be *bona fide* or mainly used as a restaurant, refreshment house or other place for the supplying of substantial meals to the public or that it includes a public bar or part of a room in another part of which there is a public bar or that there is no public access to it otherwise than through a public bar.

(5) Every holder of a limited restaurant certificate shall cause the certificate to be displayed prominently in the portion of the premises to which the certificate relates.

(6) Where, in relation to any portion of a licensed premises, a limited restaurant certificate is in force—

(a) the portion of the premises to which the certificate relates shall be deemed, for the purposes of section 13 of this Act, but not otherwise, to be premises which are for the time being a restaurant, and

(b) subsection (1) of section 17 of this Act shall be construed and have effect in relation to a person who is found on those premises at a time specified in the said section 13 at which the consumption of intoxicating liquor is permitted with a meal as if references therein (other than the reference in paragraph (b)) to a licensed premises were references to a public bar in licensed premises.

(7) In this section 'public bar' includes any place exclusively or mainly used for the sale and consumption of intoxicating liquor."

10.—Section 4 (which relates to general exemption orders) of the Act of 1927 is hereby amended by the insertion after subsection (9) of the following subsection:

"(10) A general exemption order in respect of premises shall, unless withdrawn under subsection (6) of this section or expressed to expire sooner, remain in force until the annual licensing district court for the licensing area in which the premises are situate next following the granting of the order is held and shall then expire."

11.—Section 5 (which relates to special exemption orders) of the Act of 1927 is hereby amended by the insertion after subsection (4) of the following subsection:

"(5) In this section 'special occasion' means the occasion of a special event in the premises in relation to which the special exemption order is sought."

12.—The Act of 1927 is hereby amended by the deletion of section 17 and the substitution therefor of the following section—

"17.—(1) Subject to subsections (2) and (4) of this section, a person who is found on any licensed premises during any time in which the sale of intoxicating liquor on such premises is prohibited by this Act shall, unless he is either—

(a) the holder of the licence or the owner of the premises, or

(b) resident permanently or temporarily on the premises, or

(c) a person to whom intoxicating liquor may lawfully be sold or supplied on the premises at that time, or

(d) carrying out construction, decorative, repair, replacement or maintenance work in relation to the premises or any of the fittings or equipment thereon,

(e) in the employment of the holder of the licence or of the owner of the premises and is on the premises in the ordinary course of such employment, or

(f) an officer of customs and excise in the course of his duty as an officer,

be guilty of an offence under this subsection and shall be liable on summary conviction thereof to a fine of not less than **£25**[2] and not more than **£50.**[3]

---

[2] Amended by the Intoxicating Liquor Act 1988, s.51, Sched.
[3] Amended by the Intoxicating Liquor Act 1988, s.51, Sched.

(2) Where any business other than the sale of intoxicating liquor (in this subsection referred to as non-licensed business) is carried on in any licensed premises and the portion of the premises in which the non-licensed business is carried on is not structurally separated from the remainder of the premises, subsection (1) of this section shall not apply in relation to the premises during any time in which the premises are lawfully open for the carrying on of the non-licensed business.

(3) Subject to subsection (4) of this section, a person who consumes intoxicating liquor on any licensed premises during any time in which the sale of intoxicating liquor on such premises is prohibited by this Act shall, unless he is a person as respects whom the relevant requirements of this Act for the lawful sale or supply of intoxicating liquor on those premises at that time are satisfied, be guilty of an offence under this subsection and shall be liable on summary conviction to a fine of not less than **£25**[4] and not more than **£50.**[5]

(4) A person shall not be convicted of an offence under both subsection (1) and subsection (3) of this section in respect of the same occasion."

PART III

LICENSING

New Licences

13.—(1) Where a person (in this section referred to as the applicant) duly gives notice of his intention to apply for a licence in respect of premises (in this section referred to as the new premises) to which no licence is attached and, at the proceedings in the Court in relation to such application, the applicant shows to the satisfaction of the Court that—

(a) in respect of each of two premises (in this section referred to as the existing premises) a licence is in force and in respect of each licence either—

(i) the applicant is the holder thereof, or

(ii) if he is not the holder thereof, he has procured the consent of the holder thereof to the extinguishing of the licence if and when a licence in respect of the new premises is granted to the applicant pursuant to this section,

(b) the licences (in this section referred to as the old licences) attached to the existing premises are of the same character,

(c) the rateable valuation of the new premises is not less than ten pounds, and

(d) the new premises are not situate in a county or other borough, an urban district or a town,

---

[4] Amended by the Intoxicating Liquor Act 1988, s.51, Sched.
[5] Amended by the Intoxicating Liquor Act 1988, s.51, Sched.

the Court shall, notwithstanding anything contained in the Act of 1902, cause a certificate to be given to the applicant entitling him to receive a licence in respect of the new premises, unless the Court in its absolute discretion prohibits the issuing of the licence—

(I) on the ground of the character, misconduct or unfitness of the applicant, the unfitness or inconvenience of the new premises or the number of previously licensed premises in the neighbourhood, or

(II) on the ground that the existence of a licence for the new premises would be unreasonably detrimental to the business then carried on in some premises licensed for the sale by retail of intoxicating liquor in the neighbourhood.

(2)(a) The licence granted in pursuance of this section shall be of the same character and be subject to the same conditions as the licences attached to the existing premises.

(b) Nothing in the Act of 1902 shall prevent the grant of the new licence.

(c) Upon the grant of the new licence, the licences attached to the existing premises (in this section referred to as the old licences) shall be extinguished.

(d) Any conviction which became recorded on either of the old licences under section 25 of the Act of 1927 at a time (if any) when the applicant was the holder of the licence and which is still recorded thereon at the time of the grant of the new licence by the Revenue Commissioners shall be deemed to be recorded on the new licence under that section and to have been so recorded on the date when it became recorded on the old licence, provided that if more than two convictions are so recorded on the old licences, only the latest two shall be deemed to be recorded on the new licence.

(e) Upon the grant of the new licence, the existing premises shall, for the purposes of the Act of 1902, be deemed never to have been licensed.

14.—(1) Where a person (in this section referred to as the applicant) duly gives notice of his intention to apply for a licence in respect of premises (in this section referred to as the new premises) to which no licence is attached and at the proceedings in the Court in relation to such application, the applicant shows to the satisfaction of the Court—

(a) that premises (in this section referred to as the original premises) were demolished not more than two years before the date on which the said notice by the applicant was served on the County Registrar or District Court Clerk, as the case may be, and

(b) that a licence was attached to the original premises when they were so demolished, and

(c) that at the time of the said hearing before the Court the new premises are lawfully occupied by the applicant and—

(i) that they are located on the site of the original premises, or

(ii) if they are not so located, that they are located, either, partly on that site or in the immediate vicinity and that the location of the new premises where they are rather than on the site of the original premises is unlikely of itself to have a materially adverse effect on the business carried on in any licensed premises in the neighbourhood, and

(d) that at the time of the said hearing before the Court the applicant is in lawful occupation of the site and any remains of the original premises or that he has procured the consent of the lawful occupier of such site and remains to the making of the application, and if the licence referred to in paragraph (b) of this subsection is then subsisting, to the extinguishing thereof if and when a licence is granted pursuant to this section, and

(e) that the new premises are more suitable than the original premises for the business of selling intoxicating liquor,

the Court shall, notwithstanding anything contained in the Act of 1902, cause such certificate as is mentioned in section 5 of the Licensing (Ireland) Act, 1833, to be given to the applicant declaring him to be duly entitled to receive a licence in respect of the new premises, unless the Court, in consequence of an objection made under section 4 of that Act, prohibits under that section the issuing of such licence on one or more of the following grounds, that is to say, the character, misconduct, or unfitness of the applicant or the unfitness of the new premises.

(2) Where, in a case to which the foregoing subsection of this section applies, the certificate referred to in that subsection is given to the applicant, the following provisions shall apply and have effect, that is to say:—

(a) the licence (in this subsection referred to as the new licence) to which the applicant is declared by the said certificate to be entitled and which is granted to him in pursuance of that certificate shall be a licence of the same character in all respects (including conditions inserted therein) as the licence (in this subsection referred to as the old licence) which was attached to the original premises when they were so demolished;

(b) nothing in the Act of 1902 shall operate to prevent the grant of the new licence to the applicant;

(c) upon the grant of the new licence, the old licence (if then subsisting) shall be extinguished;

(d) any conviction which became recorded on the old licence under section 25 of the Act of 1927 at a time (if any) when the applicant was the holder of the licence and which, either, is still recorded thereon or would, but for the expiry of that licence, be still recorded thereon at the time of the grant of the new licence by the Revenue Commissioners shall be deemed to be recorded on the new licence under that section and to have been so recorded on the date when it became recorded on the old licence;

(e) upon the grant of the new licence, the original premises shall, for the purposes of the Act of 1902, be deemed never to have been licensed.

(3) Where, before the demolition of the original premises, an application in relation to the new premises or (if the new premises have not been constructed) the

proposed new premises is made to the Court under section 15 of this Act, the original premises shall be deemed, for the purposes of that section, but not otherwise, to have been demolished, but an application under section 17 of this Act in respect of the new premises shall not be granted unless the Court (being otherwise satisfied, having regard to the provisions of that section, to grant the application) is satisfied that the original premises have been demolished.

15.—(1) Where a person proposes to acquire, construct or alter premises (not being premises in relation to which an application may be brought under section 8 of the Intoxicating Liquor Act, 1953) and to apply to the Circuit Court or the District Court, as may be appropriate, for the grant of a certificate entitling him to receive a licence in respect of the premises, he may apply to that Court for a declaration that the premises would be fit and convenient to be so licensed, and, if he shows to the satisfaction of the Court—

(a) that, if the acquisition, construction or alteration, as the case may be, of the premises were then completed and the application for the grant of the certificate aforesaid were then made and no objection on the ground of the character, misconduct or unfitness of the applicant were made on the hearing of the application, it would be proper, having regard to the provisions of the Licensing Acts, 1833 to 1960, to grant the application, and

(b) in any case where the applicant proposes to construct premises, that he is the holder of the lowest estate or tenancy in the site on which it is proposed to construct the premises or, if he is not such holder, that the holder thereof has agreed to convey the lowest estate or tenancy in the site to the applicant if and when a declaration under this section is made in relation to the site,

the Court, if it is so satisfied, may grant the application on such terms as the Court may think fit.

(2) Where a club proposes to acquire, construct or alter premises for its occupation and to apply to the Circuit Court or District Court, as may be appropriate, for the grant or renewal of a certificate of registration under the Act of 1904 applicable to those premises, it may apply to that Court for a declaration—

(a) that the premises would be suitable for the grant or renewal, as the case may be, of a certificate of registration under the Act of 1904 applicable thereto, and

(b) if the application is for the grant of such certificate, that the number of clubs registered under the Act of 1904 which are of the character of the club so applying and have premises in the district in which the premises the subject of the application are situate would not be such as to require the refusal of the application,

and the Court, if it is so satisfied, may grant the application on such terms as it may think fit.

(3) The intending applicant under subsection (1) or subsection (2) of this section shall—

(a) cause to be inserted, at least twenty-one days before the making of the intended application, in a newspaper circulating in the place in which it is proposed to have the premises, notice of intention to make the application,

(b) give the Superintendent of the Garda Síochána, within whose district it is proposed to have the premises, at least twenty-one days' notice in writing of intention to make the application, and

(c) cause to be deposited with the said Superintendent a copy of the plans of the premises.

(4) The application shall be accompanied by a plan of the premises.

(5) In relation to premises the subject of an application under subsection (1) of this section, any person who would be entitled to object to an application for the grant of a certificate entitling the applicant to receive a licence in respect of the premises shall be entitled to object in like manner to an application under subsection (1) of this section and, in relation to premises the subject of an application under subsection (2) of this section, any person who would be entitled to object to an application for the grant or renewal of a certificate of registration under the Act of 1904 applicable to the premises shall be entitled to object in like manner to an application under subsection (2) of this section.

(6) A declaration under subsection (1) or subsection (2) of this section shall remain in force for two years from the grant of the application or for such longer period as the Court granting the application may in any particular case think proper to provide.

(7) Where, in respect of any premises, or proposed premises, either a declaration under subsection (1) of this section is in force but a licence has not been granted since the granting of the declaration, or a declaration under subsection (2) of this section is in force but a certificate of registration under the Act of 1904 applicable thereto has not been granted since the granting of the declaration, those premises shall, for the purposes of an objection to an application for the grant of a certificate entitling the applicant to receive a licence or the grant of a certificate of registration under the Act of 1904 applicable thereto, as the case may be, or to an application under subsection (1) or subsection (2), as the case may be, of this section, but for no other purpose, be deemed to be a licensed premises or a club registered under the Act of 1904, as the case may be.

(8) In this section "the Act of 1904" means the Registration of Clubs (Ireland) Act, 1904.

16.—(1) Where a person proposes to acquire, construct or alter premises and to apply for the grant of a restaurant certificate, within the meaning of section 12 of the Act of 1927, in relation to the premises, he may apply to the Court to which it is proposed to apply for the grant of the restaurant certificate for a declaration that the premises would be structurally adapted for use as a restaurant, refreshment house or other place for supplying substantial meals to the public, and the Court, if it is so satisfied, may grant the application on such terms as it may think fit.

(2) Where a person proposes to acquire, construct or alter premises and to apply for the grant of a limited restaurant certificate, within the meaning of section 12A

of the Act of 1927, in relation to any portion of the premises, he may apply to the Court to which it is proposed to apply for the grant of the limited restaurant certificate for a declaration that—

(a) that portion of the premises would be structurally adapted for use as a restaurant, refreshment house or other place for supplying substantial meals to the public,

(b) that portion of the premises would not include a public bar, or part of a room in another part of which there would be a public bar, and

(c) there would be public access to that portion of the premises otherwise than through a public bar,

and the Court, if it is so satisfied, may grant the application on such terms as it may think fit.

(3) The intending applicant under either of the foregoing subsections of this section shall give the Superintendent of the Garda Síochána, within whose district it is proposed to have the premises, at least ten days' notice in writing of intention to make the application and cause to be deposited with the said Superintendent a copy of the plans of the premises.

(4) An application under either subsection (1) or subsection (2) of this section shall be accompanied by a plan of the premises.

(5) A declaration under this section shall remain in force for two years from the grant of the application or for such longer period as the Court granting the application may in any particular case think proper to provide.

(6) In this section "public bar" includes any place exclusively or mainly used for the sale and consumption of intoxicating liquor.

17.—(1) If, on the hearing of an application for the grant of a certificate entitling the applicant to receive a licence in respect of any premises, it is shown to the satisfaction of the Court—

(a) that a declaration has been made by the Court under subsection (1) of section 15 of this Act,

(b) that the premises have been acquired, constructed or altered in substantial accordance with the terms of the declaration, and

(c) where the application is made pursuant to any provision of the Licensing Acts that provides for the extinguishing of one or more existing licences on the grant of the licence—

(i) that the licence or each of the licences in respect of which it was shown to the satisfaction of the Court on the application for the declaration that the applicant was the holder thereof or had secured the consent of the holder to the extinguishing thereof is in force, or

(ii) if such licence or licences or any of them is or are not in force, that the licence or licences not in force has not or have not been

forfeited or extinguished and the premises to which it or they related have not been deemed, by virtue of any provision of the Licensing Acts, never to have been licensed,

it shall not be open to the Court to refuse the application—

(I) in a case where it is made pursuant to section 21 of the Act of 1943, on any ground, and

(II) in any other case, on any ground other than the character, misconduct or unfitness of the applicant,

and where, as respects a licence or licences and the premises to which it or they related, it is shown to the satisfaction of the Court that it or they comply with the provisions of sub-paragraph (ii) of paragraph (c) of this subsection, the licence or licences shall be deemed, for the purposes of the provisions of the Licensing Acts relating to the granting of licences, but not otherwise, to be in force and to relate to the premises to which it or they related and, on the grant of the new licence, shall accordingly be extinguished and the premises to which it or they related shall be deemed never to have been licensed.[6]

(2) If, on the hearing of an application for a grant or renewal of a certificate of registration under the Act of 1904 applicable to any premises, it is shown to the satisfaction of the Court hearing the application that a declaration has been made by the Court under subsection (2) of section 15 of this Act and that the premises have been acquired, constructed or altered in substantial accordance with the terms of the declaration, the Court shall not receive any objection to the application grounded upon the unsuitability of the premises or upon the number of clubs registered under the Act of 1904 which are of the character of the club making the application and have premises situate in the district in which the premises the subject of the application are situate.

(3) A declaration under section 41 of the Tourist Traffic Act, 1952, which is in force at the commencement of this Act, shall, notwithstanding the repeal of that section, remain in force for the period provided for in subsection (5) thereof and shall be deemed for the purposes of subsection (7) of section 15 of this Act and subsection (1) of this section to be a declaration under subsection (1) of section 15 of this Act.

(4) If, on the hearing of an application for the grant of a restaurant certificate, within the meaning of section 12 of the Act of 1927, in relation to any premises it is shown to the satisfaction of the Court that a declaration has been made under subsection (1) of section 16 of this Act and that the premises have been acquired, constructed or altered in substantial accordance with the terms of the declaration, it shall not be open to the Court to refuse the application on any ground other than that the premises are not *bona fide* and mainly used as a restaurant, refreshment house or other place for supplying substantial meals to the public.

(5) If, on the hearing of an application for the grant of a limited restaurant certificate, within the meaning of section 12A of the Act of 1927, in relation to any portion of a premises it is shown to the satisfaction of the Court that a declaration

---

[6] Substituted by the Intoxicating Liquor Act 1962, s.32.

has been made under subsection (2) of section 16 of this Act and that the premises have been acquired, constructed or altered in substantial accordance with the terms of the declaration, it shall not be open to the Court to refuse the application on any ground other than that that portion of the premises is not *bona fide* and mainly used as a restaurant, refreshment house or other place for supplying substantial meals to the public.

(6) In this section references to declarations are references to declarations that are in force.

18.—Premises may be described in a declaration or certificate under any of the preceding sections of this Part of this Act by reference to a map attached thereto.

Hotels

19.—(1) Where a person who holds a licence in respect of a hotel which was granted by virtue of paragraph (2) of section 2 of the Act of 1902 shows to the satisfaction of the District Court, on application thereto at any sitting thereof for the Court area in which the hotel is situate, that, in respect of an ordinary seven-day licence (not being a licence granted by virtue of paragraph (2) of section 2 of the Act of 1902), either—

(a) he is the holder thereof, or

(b) he has procured the consent of the holder to the extinguishing thereof,

the Court may order that the ordinary seven-day licence be extinguished.

(2) When an order under subsection (1) of this section is made—

(a) it shall be lawful, notwithstanding anything contained in the Act of 1902, to have in the hotel a public bar for the sale of intoxicating liquor,

(b) the ordinary seven-day licence shall be extinguished, and

(c) if the premises to which the ordinary seven-day licence was attached immediately before the making of the order were premises to which paragraph (1) of section 2 of the Act of 1902 applied, that paragraph shall cease to apply to them.

(3) Where—

(a) a certificate entitling the holder thereof to receive a licence in respect of a hotel has been granted by virtue of paragraph (2) of section 2 of the Act of 1902, and

(b) on the hearing of the application for the grant of the certificate the holder—

(i) has indicated to the Court that he wishes to have in the hotel a public bar for the sale of intoxicating liquor and has shown, to the satisfaction of the Court, in relation to an ordinary seven-day licence (not being a licence granted by virtue of paragraph (2) of section 2 of the Act of 1902), either—

(I) that he is the holder thereof, or

(II) that he has procured the consent of the holder thereof to the extinguishing of the licence if and when a licence in respect of the hotel is granted, or

(ii) has shown to the satisfaction of the Court that an order has previously been made under this section in relation to the hotel,

then, the Court may by order direct that, upon the grant of the licence in respect of the hotel, the ordinary seven-day licence be extinguished.

(4) When an order under subsection (3) of this section is made, then, upon the grant of the licence in respect of the hotel—

(a) it shall be lawful, notwithstanding anything contained in the Act of 1902, to have in the hotel a public bar for the sale of intoxicating liquor,

(b) the ordinary seven-day licence shall be extinguished, and

(c) if the premises to which the ordinary seven-day licence was attached immediately before the making of the order, were premises to which paragraph (1) of section 2 of the Act of 1902 applied that paragraph shall cease to apply to them.

(5) In this section—

"hotel" means a house containing at least ten, or, if situate in a county borough (which expression shall be deemed for the purposes of this section to include the Dublin Metropolitan District), twenty apartments set apart and used exclusively for the sleeping accommodation of travellers and having no public bar for the sale of intoxicating liquor;

"ordinary seven-day licence" has the meaning assigned to it by subsection (2) of section 11 of the Act of 1927.

[s.20 repealed by the Courts (No. 2) Act 1986, ss.9, 10(5), Sched. 2]

21.—(1) Paragraph (2) (which provides for the licensing of hotels) of section 2 of the Act of 1902 is hereby amended by the substitution for "at least ten apartments" of "at least ten, or, if situate in a county borough (which expression shall be deemed for the purposes of this section, to include the Dublin Metropolitan District), twenty apartments".

(2) The amendment effected by subsection (1) of this section shall not operate to prevent the grant of a certificate entitling the holder to receive a licence by virtue of paragraph (2) of section 2 of the Act of 1902 in respect of a house containing more than nine and less than twenty apartments set apart and used exclusively for the sleeping accommodation of travellers, having no public bar for the sale of intoxicating liquor and situate in a county borough (which expression shall be deemed, for the purposes of this subsection, to include the Dublin Metropolitan District) if it is shown to the satisfaction of the Court hearing the application for the certificate—

(a) that a licence (in this subsection referred to as the former licence) which was granted by virtue of paragraph (2) of section 2 of the Act of 1902 in respect of the house has expired and has not since been renewed, and

(b) if the notice of the application for the certificate required to be given by rules of court to the appropriate County Registrar or the appropriate District Court Clerk, as the case may be, is given more than two years after the passing of this Act, that the day on which the former licence last expired is not more than five years before the day on which the notice aforesaid was given.

PART IV

MISCELLANEOUS

22.—(1) Sections 17 and 18 (which sections relate to search for and seizure of illicit spirits) of the Act of 1831 are hereby extended as follows:—

(a) they shall apply in relation to a house or place irrespective of whether distillation does or does not take place therein, and

(b) they shall apply in relation to a house or place in which it is known or suspected that there are spirits in respect of which an offence under section 22 or section 23 (which sections relate to the possession of illicit spirits) of the Act of 1831 is being committed, and to any such spirits found therein.

(2) Nothing in section 18 of the Act of 1831, or in that section as extended by subsection (1) of this section, shall authorise the search without a warrant of a house used as a dwelling.

(3) A member of the Garda Síochána or an officer of customs and excise:—

(a) if he has reasonable grounds for suspecting that a vehicle is being used in connection with the commission of an offence under section 25 (which relates to the movement of stills and spirits) of the Act of 1831, may require the driver thereof to halt the vehicle and may search the vehicle, and

(b) if he has reasonable grounds for suspecting that a person is engaged in the commission of an offence under the said section 25, may require the production by that person of any bottle or other container carried by him or on his person and may examine and test the contents of the bottle or container.

(4) If any person obstructs, resists or interferes with, or does not comply with a requirement of, a member of the Garda Síochána or an officer of customs and excise in the exercise of the powers conferred on him by subsection (3) of this section, he shall be guilty of an offence under the Act of 1831 and shall be liable on summary conviction thereof to an excise penalty of fifty pounds.

(5) In this section—

"the Act of 1831" means the Illicit Distillation (Ireland) Act, 1831;

"distillation" has the meaning it has in the Act of 1831;

"warrant" has the meaning it has in section 17 of the Act of 1831.

23.—(1) Section 2 (which restricts the grant of new licences) of the Act of 1902 is hereby amended by the substitution for paragraph (1) of the following paragraph:—

> "(1) For premises (not being premises which were licensed by virtue of paragraph (2) of this section) which were licensed at any time during the period of five years immediately before the day on which notice of an application for the grant of a certificate entitling the holder to receive a licence in respect of the premises is given, pursuant to rules of court, to the appropriate County Registrar or to the appropriate District Court Clerk, as the case may be; or".

(2) Subsection (1) of this section shall come into operation on the expiration of the period of two years beginning on the day of the passing of this Act.

24.—Section 6 (which provides for the licensing of premises adjoining premises licensed in 1902) of the Act of 1902 is hereby amended by the substitution for "at the date of the passing of this Act" of "at any time during the period of five years immediately before the day on which notice of an application for the grant of a certificate entitling the holder thereof to receive any such new licence is given, pursuant to rules of court, to the appropriate County Registrar or to the appropriate District Court Clerk, as the case may be".

25.—(1) Section 19 of the Act of 1943 is hereby amended by the deletion of the definitions of "licence", "publican's licence" and "beerhouse licence" and the insertion of the following definition:

"licence" means a licence for the sale of intoxicating liquor for the grant of which the production of a certificate of the Circuit Court or of the District Court is required.

(2) Reference to the Circuit Court in sections 21 and 22 (which relate to the grant of new licences in respect of more convenient premises or premises substituted for destroyed premises) of the Act of 1943 shall, in relation to applications made thereunder by virtue of the amendment effected by subsection (1) of this section for certificates entitling the applicants to the grant of off-licences, be construed as references to the District Court and the reference in the said section 22 to the County Registrar shall, in relation to such applications, be construed as a reference to the District Court Clerk and the sections shall have effect accordingly.

26.—(1) Notwithstanding anything contained in sections 21 or 31 of the Act of 1943 (which sections relate to the grant of licences in respect of more convenient premises and the transfer of beerhouse licences), where the person making an application under either of those sections is not the holder of the licence to be extinguished or transferred under the section but shows to the satisfaction of the Court hearing the application that he has procured the consent of the holder thereof to the extinguishing or transfer thereof, as the case may be, the application shall not be refused on the ground that the person making it was not the holder of the licence to be extinguished or transferred and the said sections shall be construed and have effect accordingly.

(2) Subsection (1) of section 22 (which relates to the grant of new licences in

respect of premises substituted for destroyed premises) of the Act of 1943 is hereby amended by—

(a) the substitution in paragraph (a) of "two years" for "twelve months", and

(b) the insertion in paragraph (c) after "remains thereof" of "or that he has procured the consent of the lawful occupier of such premises or of the site and remains thereof to the making of the application, and if the licence referred to in paragraph (b) of this subsection is then subsisting, to the extinguishing thereof if and when a licence is granted pursuant to this section".

(3)(a) A conviction recorded on a licence transferred under the said section 31 shall, upon such transfer, cease for all purposes to be so recorded and shall be deemed never to have been so recorded.

(b) Where a new licence is granted to any person pursuant to an application under the said section 21 or the said section 22, a conviction recorded on the licence extinguished pursuant to the application (not being a conviction which became so recorded at a time, if any, when that person was the holder thereof) shall, notwithstanding anything contained in the said sections, not be deemed to be recorded on the new licence and the said sections shall be construed and have effect accordingly.

27.—(1) In this section—

"full licence" means a publican's licence within the meaning of Part II of the Act of 1910 which is neither a six-day licence nor an early-closing licence;

"restricted licence" means—

(a) a publican's licence which is not a full licence, or

(b) a beerhouse licence within the meaning of Part II of the Act of 1910.

(2) Where a person who holds a restricted licence in respect of any premises (in this subsection and in subsection (3) of this section referred to as the relevant premises) shows to the satisfaction of the District Court on application thereto at any sitting thereof for the Court area in which the relevant premises are situate that, in relation to—

(a) another restricted licence in respect of premises situate in that Court area, or

(b) each of two other restricted licences in respect of premises both of which are situate elsewhere than in that Court area, or

(c) a full licence,

either—

(i) he is the holder thereof, or

(ii) he has procured the consent of the holder thereof to the extinguishing thereof if and when a full licence in respect of the relevant premises is granted pursuant to this section, the Court shall cause a certificate to be given to that person entitling him to receive a full licence in respect of the relevant premises.

(3) Upon the grant pursuant to an application under subsection (2) of this section of the full licence in respect of the relevant premises—

(a) the restricted licence in respect of the relevant premises shall be extinguished, and

(b) the other licence or licences, as the case may be, to which the application related shall be extinguished and the other premises or each of the other premises, as the case may be, to which the application related shall, for the purposes of the Act of 1902, be deemed never to have been licensed.

(4) Notwithstanding anything contained in the Licensing Acts, 1833 to 1960, the Revenue Commissioners shall, upon application within **three years**[7] after the passing of this Act by a person who holds a restricted licence in respect of any premises and upon payment by that person of the sum of two hundred pounds to the Revenue Commissioners, grant to that person a full licence in respect of the premises.

(5) Upon the grant under subsection (4) of this section of a full licence in respect of any premises, the restricted licence in respect thereof shall be extinguished.

(6) The sum payable under subsection (4) of this section in relation to the grant of a licence shall be in addition to and not in substitution for any sum payable on the licence under section 43 of the Act of 1910.

(7)(a) There shall be established a fund which shall be managed by the Minister for Finance and shall be known as the Restricted Licences Conversion Fund and all sums received by the Revenue Commissioners under subsection (4) of this section shall be paid by them to that Minister for the credit of the Fund.

[s.27(7)(b) repealed by the Restricted Licences Conversion Fund Act 1975, s.2]

(c) An account of the Fund shall be prepared for each financial year by the Minister for Finance and the account shall be audited by the Comptroller and Auditor General and, together with the report of the Comptroller and Auditor General thereon, shall be laid before each House of the Oireachtas.

28.—A licence held by a nominee of a body corporate in respect of premises in which the lowest estate or tenancy is held by the body corporate may, on application by the body corporate to the Court at any sitting thereof for the Court area within which the premises are situate, be transferred, by endorsement made by the Court on the licence or, if the licence is not available, on a copy thereof, to such other person as the body corporate may nominate.

29.—The provisions of section 1 (which relates to the interim transfer of licences by the Court) of the Public House (Ireland) Act, 1855, shall apply in relation to off-licences for the grant of which the production of a certificate of the Court is required.

[7] Substituted by the Intoxicating Liquor Act 1962, s.33.

30.—(1) Where the holder of a licence in respect of any premises (not being a person who holds the licence as a nominee) ceases, for any reason other than death, transfer of the premises or forfeiture of the licence, to carry on the business authorised by the licence, and, if he is ordinarily resident in the State, either ceases to be so resident or cannot be found, the Court may, subject to the provisions of the Licensing Acts, 1833 to 1960, on due application being made to it at any sitting thereof for the Court area within which the premises are situate—

(a) if the licence has not expired, transfer the licence to the applicant, in accordance with the provisions of section 1 of the Public House (Ireland) Act, 1855, and

(b) if the licence has expired and the application is made within one year after such expiry, grant to the applicant the certificate or certificates required to be produced before a renewal of the licence is granted in respect of the premises, and, for the purposes of the application and of the grant of the renewal of the licence by the Revenue Commissioners, the applicant shall be deemed to be the holder of the lowest estate or tenancy in the premises.

(2) An application to the Court under subsection (1) of this section shall not be granted if—

(a) the holder of the licence objects, or

(b) the Court does not consider that the applicant is a suitable person in all the circumstances to be granted the certificate.

(3) Where an application under subsection (1) of this section in respect of a licence is granted by the Court after the licence has expired, the licence shall be deemed to have been renewed immediately after the expiration thereof.

(4) Where the holder of a licence to whom a transfer or renewal thereof was granted by virtue of subsection (1) of this section applies to the Court for the grant of the certificate or certificates required to be produced before a grant of a renewal of the licence is made, he shall be deemed, for the purposes of the application and of the grant of the renewal of the licence by the Revenue Commissioners to be the holder of the lowest estate or tenancy in the premises to which the licence relates.

(5) The holder of the lowest estate or tenancy in any premises in respect of which a licence which is in force, is not held by him and has been transferred or renewed by virtue of the foregoing provisions of this section shall be entitled, on due application being made to the Court—

(a) to have the licence in respect of the premises transferred to him in accordance with the provisions of section 1 of the Public House (Ireland) Act, 1855, and

(b) whether the licence has or has not been transferred to him under paragraph (a) of this subsection, to be granted, subject to the provisions of the Licensing Acts, 1833 to 1960—

(i) in case he is the person referred to in subsection (1) of this section as the holder of the licence, the certificate or certificates required to be produced before a renewal of the licence is granted, and

(ii) in any other case, the certificate or certificates required to be produced before the grant of a licence by way of transfer is made in respect of the premises.

(6) A licence in respect of any premises which has been transferred or renewed by virtue of subsection (1) of this section and is held by a person other than the holder of the lowest estate or tenancy in the premises shall not be capable of being extinguished under or for the purposes of section 4 of the Act of 1902, section 11 of the Act of 1927, section 21 or section 31 of the Act of 1943 or section 13 or section 19 of this Act.

31.—Section 4 (which relates to objections to applications for certificates for licences) of the Licensing (Ireland) Act, 1833, is hereby amended by the insertion after "inhabitant of said parish" of "or the health authority within the meaning of the Health Acts, 1947 to 1958, in whose functional area the house is situate".

32.—(1) Any person may object **to the Court pursuant to section 4(5)(a) of the Courts (No. 2) Act, 1986 against an application to an officer of the Revenue Commissioners for the renewal of a licence**[8] in relation to any premises on the ground of the unfitness of the premises to be licensed and subject to subsection (2) of this section, if the Court is satisfied that the premises are unfit to be licensed, it may refuse to grant the certificate **provided for by section 4(7) or 4(8) (as the case may be) of the Courts (No. 2) Act, 1986.**[9]

(2) An objection under this section shall not be entertained by the Court unless notice in writing of the intention to make the objection together with particulars in writing of the unfitness alleged is given not less than twelve months before the hearing of the application to the person who, at the time of the giving of the notice, holds the licence in respect of which the application is brought.

33.—(1)(a) Section 5 (which provides for minimum valuations of certain licensed premises) of the Act of 1902 is hereby amended by the substitution for "the premises shall be valued under the Irish Valuation Acts at" of "the rateable valuation, as defined in the Interpretation Act, 1937, of the premises shall be".

(b) Section 21 (which provides for the grant of new licences in respect of more convenient premises) of the Act of 1943 is hereby amended by the substitution for paragraph (d) of subsection (1) of the following paragraph:

"(d) that the rateable valuation of the new premises is not less than the rateable valuation of the existing premises, and".

(2) In construing section 5, as amended by this section, of the Act of 1902, section 21, as amended by this section, of the Act of 1943, and section 13 of this Act, "rateable valuation" shall be deemed to include a provisional valuation issued by the Commissioner of Valuation.

---

[8] Substituted by the Courts (No. 2) Act 1986, ss.9, 10(5), Sched.1.

[9] Inserted by the Courts (No. 2) Act 1986, ss.9, 10(5), Sched.1.

34.—Notwithstanding anything to the contrary contained in any other Act, the Revenue Commissioners shall not grant, whether by way of new licence or of transfer or renewal of an existing licence, a cider retailer's off-licence under the Act of 1910 to any person other than a person who is for the time being the holder of a spirit retailer's off-licence under the Act of 1910 or of a wholesale dealer's licence for the sale of spirits, beer or wine under the Act of 1910.

35.—Section 6 (which permits the sale of spirits at specified reduced strengths without giving notice of the reduction) of the Sale of Food and Drugs Act Amendment Act, 1879, is hereby amended by the substitution of "thirty degrees" for "twenty-five degrees".

36.—Section 25 (which relates to the searching of clubs by the Garda Síochána) of the Intoxicating Liquor (General) Act, 1924, is hereby amended by the substitution in subsection (1) of "member" for "officer".

37.—(1) Section 25 (which relates to the recording of convictions on licences) of the Act of 1927 is hereby amended by—

(a) the deletion in subsection (1) of "if the Court in its discretion so thinks proper" (inserted by the Act of 1943) and the substitution therefor of "subject to subsection (4) of this section",

(b) the substitution of "two years" for "five years", "four years" for "seven years" and "six years" for "ten years" in subsection (2), and

(c) the addition to the section of the following subsection:

"(4) Notwithstanding anything contained in subsection (1) of this section, where a person is convicted in relation to any premises in respect of which he holds a licence for the sale of intoxicating liquor by retail of an offence to which this Part of this Act applies and the conviction is the first conviction of that person in relation to those premises of an offence to which this Part of this Act applies, the conviction shall not be recorded on the licence."

(2)(a) Every conviction which, immediately before the passing of this Act, stood recorded under section 25 of the Act of 1927 on a licence then in force, shall, upon the passing of this Act, cease for all purposes to be so recorded and where, before the passing of this Act, the holder of a licence then in force had been convicted of an offence to which Part III of the Act of 1927 applies, such holder shall, for the purposes of subsection (2) and subsection (4) (inserted by this section) of the said section 25, be deemed never to have been so convicted.

(b) Where the holder of a licence is convicted after the passing of this Act of an offence to which Part III of the Act of 1927 applies and which was committed before such passing, the conviction shall not be recorded on the licence under section 25 of the Act of 1927 and such holder shall for the purposes of the said subsection (2) and the said subsection (4) be deemed never to have been so convicted.

38.—(1) A person who consumes, or permits the consumption of, intoxicating liquor during prohibited hours in a refreshment house which is not a licensed premises shall be guilty of an offence under this section and shall be liable on summary conviction thereof to the fine to which he would have been liable if the conviction had been in relation to premises which, at the time of the commission of the offence, were licensed premises.

(2) In this section—

"refreshment house" means premises, or any portion thereof, deemed for the purposes of the Refreshment Houses (Ireland) Act, 1860, to be a refreshment house;

"licensed premises" and "prohibited hours" have the meanings they have in the Act of 1927.

39.—(1) Where an order under section 9 of the Intoxicating Liquor (General) Act, 1924, prescribing the sizes of bottles in which an intoxicating liquor specified in the order may be sold is in force, neither section 28 nor section 29 of the Act of 1878 shall apply in relation to a bottle to which this section applies.

(2) The denomination of a bottle to which this section applies and a line defining its capacity shall be indicated on the bottle by indelible marks.

(3) The Minister for Industry and Commerce may make regulations in relation to bottles to which this section applies—

(a) prescribing the size and position of the line defining the capacity of the bottles,

(b) prescribing the denomination marks for the bottles, their sizes and their positions on the bottles,

(c) prescribing the limits of error to be allowed in relation to the capacity of the bottles as defined by the line aforesaid,

(d) prohibiting any feature in the design of the bottles which appears likely to facilitate the perpetration of fraud.

(4) Where in relation to a bottle to which this section applies there is a contravention of subsection (2) of this section or of regulations made under subsection (3) of this section, the bottle shall be deemed to be an unjust measure for the purposes of section 25 of the Act of 1878.

(5) Every regulation made under this section shall be laid before each House of the Oireachtas as soon as may be after it is made, and if a resolution annulling the regulation is passed by either such House within the next twenty-one days on which that House has sat after the regulation is laid before it, the regulation shall be annulled accordingly, but without prejudice to the validity of anything previously done thereunder.

(6) In this section—

"the Act of 1878" means the Weights and Measures Act, 1878;

"bottle to which this section applies" means a bottle which is required by an order referred to in subsection (1) of this section to be of a size prescribed thereby.

40.—(1) Intoxicating liquor shall not be sold by retail in a sealed container unless the quantity of the contents of the container is indicated on the container.

(2) A person who contravenes or permits a person under his control or in his employment to contravene subsection (1) of this section shall be guilty of an offence under this section and shall on summary conviction thereof be liable, in the case of a first offence, to a fine not exceeding ten pounds and, in the case of a second or any subsequent offence, to a fine not exceeding twenty pounds.

(3) Notwithstanding the provisions of section 8 (which prohibits certain sales of intoxicating liquor otherwise than in marked measures) of the Licensing Act, 1872, a person who sells intoxicating liquor in a sealed container on which the quantity of the contents of the container is indicated shall be deemed not to act in contravention of that section.

(4) In this section, "container" does not include a bottle.

41.—(1) A local authority may, if they think fit and with the consent of the holder thereof, cancel a certificate issued by them under section 6 (which provides for the issue by local authorities of certificates approving of sites for licensed premises in substitution for licensed premises demolished by them) of the Intoxicating Liquor Act, 1953, and may issue under the section another certificate declaring that a site acquired by them, other than the site declared in the cancelled certificate to be approved by them, is approved by them as a site for licensed premises in substitution for the licensed premises which the cancelled certificate declared had been or were to be demolished.

(2) A certificate under the said section 6 may not be cancelled if an application under section 7 or section 8 (which sections provide for the licensing of premises on sites declared by certificates under the said section 6 to be approved by local authorities) of the aforesaid Act grounded on the certificate has been granted.

(3) A certificate under the said section 6 which is cancelled under this section shall be deemed never to have been issued.

SCHEDULE

Enactments Repealed

Chapter and Session or Number and Year	Short Title	Extent of Repeal
6 & 7 Will. 4. c. 38	Licensing (Ireland) Act, 1836	Sections 8 and 9.
23 & 24 Vic. c. 107	Refreshment Houses (Ireland) Act, 1860	Section 24.
No. 15 of 1927	Intoxicating Liquor Act, 1927	Sections 11, 15 and 16; in section 27, the words from "and on the hearing of such appeal" to the end of the section; sections 36 to 54; subsection (2) of section 55; section 57.
No. 3 of 1928	Weights and Measures Act, 1928	Sections 4 to 9.
No. 7 of 1943	Intoxicating Liquor Act, 1943	Subsection (1) of section 31.
No. 15 of 1952	Tourist Traffic Act, 1952	Sections 40 to 42 and 46 to 49.

INTOXICATING LIQUOR ACT 1962

No. 21 of 1962

AN ACT TO AMEND AND EXTEND THE LICENSING ACTS, 1833 TO 1960, AND THE REGISTRATION OF CLUBS ACTS, 1904 TO 1960, AND TO PROVIDE FOR OTHER MATTERS CONNECTED WITH THE MATTERS AFORESAID.

BE IT ENACTED BY THE OIREACHTAS AS FOLLOWS:

1.—(1) In this Act, save where the context otherwise requires—

"the Act of 1833" means the Licensing (Ireland) Act, 1833;

"the Act of 1902" means the Licensing (Ireland) Act, 1902;

"the Act of 1910" means the Finance (1909-10) Act, 1910;

"the Act of 1924" means the Intoxicating Liquor (General) Act, 1924;

"the Act of 1927" means the Intoxicating Liquor Act, 1927;

"the Act of 1943" means the Intoxicating Liquor Act, 1943;

"the Act of 1960" means the Intoxicating Liquor Act, 1960;

"annual licensing district court" means the sitting of the District Court held pursuant to rules of court in a licensing area for the hearing of applications for certificates for renewals of licences for the sale of intoxicating liquor;

"Court area" means a District Court area prescribed by law for the purposes of the transaction of licensing business;

"licence" means a licence for the sale of intoxicating liquor for the grant of which the production of a certificate of the District Court or the Circuit Court, as the case may be, is required, or a licence granted under section 18 of this Act, and cognate words shall be construed accordingly;

"the Licensing Acts" means the Licensing Acts, 1833 to 1960;

"period of summer time" means a period appointed by or under the Summer Time Act, 1925, to be a period of summer time;

"prohibited hours" has the meaning assigned to it by section 2 of the Act of 1927;

"the Registration of Clubs Acts" means the Registration of Clubs Acts 1904 to 1960;

"seven-day licence" means a licence referred to in section 11 of the Act of 1927 as a seven-day licence;

"six-day licence" has the meaning assigned to it by section 8 of the Act of 1927;

"Sunday" does not include a Sunday that is Christmas Day.

(2) References in this Act to any enactment shall, save where the context otherwise requires, be construed as references to that enactment as amended by any subsequent enactment including this Act.

2.—Section 2 (which was inserted by the Act of 1960 and relates to prohibited hours) of the Act of 1927 is hereby amended by—

(a) the substitution of the following paragraph for paragraph (a) of subsection (1):

"(a) on any week-day, before the hour of half-past ten o'clock in the morning or—

(i) during a period of summer time, after the hour of half-past eleven o'clock in the evening, or

(ii) during a period which is not a period of summer-time, after the hour of eleven o'clock in the evening,

or, if the premises are situate in the county borough of Dublin or Cork (subject to the exceptions hereinafter mentioned) between the hours of half-past two o'clock and half-past three o'clock in the afternoon, or",

(b) the substitution of the following paragraph for paragraph (b) of subsection (1):

"(b) on Saint Patrick's Day or any Sunday, before the hour of half-past twelve o'clock in the afternoon, or between the hours of two o'clock and four o'clock in the afternoon or after the hour of ten o'clock in the evening, or"

and

(c) the substitution in both paragraph (a) and paragraph (b) of subsection (2) for "a county borough" of "the county borough of Dublin or Cork"

3.—Subsection (1) (inserted by the Act of 1960) of section 3 (which relates to mixed trading) of the Act of 1927 is hereby amended by—

(a) the substitution in paragraph (i) of "half-past seven o'clock" for "nine o'clock", and

(b) the substitution in paragraph (ii) for "a county borough" of "the county borough of Dublin or Cork".

4.—Section 13 (which was inserted by the Act of 1960 and provides for exemptions from prohibited hours for hotels and restaurants) of the Act of 1927 is hereby amended by the substitution for paragraphs (a) and (b) of the following paragraphs:

"(a) during a period of summer time, between the hours of half-past eleven o'clock in the evening on any week-day and half-past twelve o'clock in the morning on the following day, or

(b) during a period which is not a period of summer time, between the hours of eleven o'clock in the evening on any week-day and half-past twelve o'clock in the morning on the following day, or

(b1) if the premises are situate in the county borough of Dublin or Cork, between the hours of half-past two o'clock and half-past three o'clock in the afternoon, on any week-day, or

(b2) on Saint Patrick's Day or, unless his licence is a six-day licence, any Sunday, between the hours of two o'clock and three o'clock in the afternoon, or between the hours of ten o'clock and eleven o'clock in the evening, or".

5.—Section 14 (which provides for certain exemptions from prohibited hours) of the Act of 1927 is hereby amended by the insertion after paragraph (a) of the following paragraph:

"(aa) the sale at any time at a railway station (being a station to which persons who have recently travelled or are about to travel by ship resort for refreshment) of intoxicating liquor to passengers who have recently travelled or hold tickets entitling them, and are about, to travel by ship for a distance of not less than fifty miles, or".

6.—(1) Section 56 (which was inserted by the Act of 1960 and relates to prohibited hours in clubs) of the Act of 1927 is hereby amended by—

(a) the substitution of the following paragraphs for paragraphs (a) and (b) of subsection (1):

"(a) on any week-day, before the hour of half-past ten o'clock in the morning, or—

(i) during a period of summer time, after the hour of half-past eleven o'clock in the evening, or

(ii) during a period which is not a period of summer time, after the hour of eleven o'clock in the evening,

or, if the club is situate in the county borough of Dublin or Cork, between the hours of half-past two o'clock and half-past three o'clock in the afternoon, or

(b) on Saint Patrick's Day or any Sunday, before the hour of half-past twelve o'clock in the afternoon or between the hours of two o'clock and four o'clock in the afternoon or after the hour of ten o'clock in the evening, or",

(b) the substitution of the following paragraphs for paragraphs (a) and (b) of subsection (2):

"(a) during a period of summer time, between the hours of half-past eleven o'clock in the evening on any week-day and half-past twelve o'clock in the morning on the following day, or

(b) during a period which is not a period of summer time, between the hours of eleven o'clock in the evening on any week-day and half-past twelve o'clock in the morning on the following day, or

(b1) if the premises are situate in the county borough of Dublin or Cork, between the hours of half-past two o'clock and half-past three o'clock in the afternoon, on any week-day, or

(b2) on Saint Patrick's Day or any Sunday, between the hours of two o'clock and three o'clock in the afternoon or between the hours of ten o'clock and eleven o'clock in the evening, or", and

(c) the insertion in subsection (4) after "this section" of " 'period of summer time' ".

(2)(a) For the purposes of the Registration of Clubs Acts, the rules of a club which on the commencement of this Act is registered under those Acts shall, during the transitional period, be deemed to be in conformity with the provisions of section 56, as amended by this section, of the Act of 1927.

(b) In this subsection "transitional period" means the period beginning on the commencement of this Act and ending, either, when the certificate of registration of the club which is in force two months after that date expires, or, if it should sooner happen, when the rules of the club are brought into conformity with the said section 56, as so amended.

7.—(1) (a) Nothing in the Licensing Acts shall operate to prohibit a person from being on, or consuming, or permitting the consumption of, intoxicating liquor on, premises in respect of which an on-licence within the meaning of the Act of 1927 is in force during the period of **thirty**[1] minutes commencing at the beginning of a period during which the sale of intoxicating liquor on licensed premises is prohibited.

(b) For the purposes of paragraph (a) of this subsection a period during which the sale of intoxicating liquor in licensed premises is permitted by or under any provision of the Licensing Acts (other than section 2 of the Act of 1927) shall be deemed to be a period during which such sale is prohibited on such premises.

(2) (a) Nothing in the Registration of Clubs Acts, or contained, by virtue only of subsection (1) of section 56 of the Act of 1927, in the rules of a club registered under those Acts shall operate to prohibit the consumption of excisable liquor on the club premises by any person during the period of **thirty**[2] minutes commencing at the beginning of a period during which the supplying of excisable liquor on such premises is prohibited.

(b) For the purposes of paragraph (a) of this subsection a period during which the supplying of excisable liquor on club premises is permitted by or under

---

[1] Substituted by the Intoxicating Liquor Act 1988, s.27.
[2] Substituted by the Intoxicating Liquor Act 1988, s.27.

any provision of the Registration of Clubs Acts (other than subsection (1) of section 56 of the Act of 1927) shall be deemed to be a period during which such supplying on such premises is prohibited.

8.—Not more than fifteen authorisations shall be granted under section 21 (which relates to the grant of authorisations by the District Court for the supply of excisable liquor in clubs) of the Act of 1924 to any club in any year and subsection (3) of that section shall stand amended accordingly.

9.—(1) For the purposes of the Licensing Acts and the Registration of Clubs Acts a meal served in any premises after the commencement of this Act shall not be deemed to be a substantial meal unless—

(a) the meal is such as might be expected to be served as a main midday or main evening meal or as a main course at either such meal, and

(b) the meal is of a kind for which—

(i) having regard to the prices charged for meals in the premises at times other than prohibited hours, or

(ii) if meals are not normally served in the premises. having regard to all the circumstances,

it would be reasonable to charge a sum that is not less than—

(I) the sum (if any) that for the time being stands fixed under subsection (2) of this section, or

(II) if no sum stands fixed for the time being under the said subsection (2), five shillings.

(2) The Minister for Justice may from time to time, by order, fix such sum, being more than five shillings, as he considers reasonable for the purposes of subsection (1) of this section and may, by order, revoke or amend any order under this subsection.

10.—(1) Subject to the provisions of this section, where, on application to a Justice of the District Court by the holder of a licence in respect of premises situate in any locality not in the county borough of Dublin, it is shown to the satisfaction of the Court that the application has the approval of a majority of the holders of licences in respect of premises so situate and is in respect of a period during which a special event or special events will take place in or near that locality of such kind that, in the opinion of the Court, the period will be one during which a considerable number of persons will be likely to be attracted to that locality, the Court, if it is satisfied that it is desirable to do so for the accommodation of those persons, may, after hearing the officer in charge of the Garda Síochána for that locality, make an order, subject to such conditions as it thinks proper, exempting the holders of licences in respect of premises so situate from the provisions of the Licensing Acts relating to prohibited hours in respect of those premises at such time, and on such days during the period as it thinks fit: provided that where the period aforesaid exceeds nine days, the exemption shall be limited to such times and days as it thinks fit during a period or periods (not exceeding three) comprising in all not more than nine days.

(2) Any person appearing to the District Court to have a *bona fide* interest in the matter may appear and give evidence on the hearing of an application under this section.

(3) The District Court shall not entertain an application under this section unless and until satisfied that the applicant has, not less than seven days before the date on which the application is proposed to be made, served notice in writing of the intention to make the application upon the officer in charge of the Garda Síochána for the locality to which the application relates and published the notice in a newspaper circulating in that locality.

(4) Not more than three orders under this section having effect in any particular year shall be made in respect of any particular locality and, where more orders than one having effect in a particular year in respect of a particular locality are made, the number of days to which the orders relate shall not exceed nine in all and such days shall be either consecutive days or divided into not more than three separate periods of a day or consecutive days.

(5) A person in respect of whom an order has been granted under this section shall, if and so long as he complies with the conditions subject to which the order has been granted, be exempt at the times specified in the order from any penalty for contravention of the provisions of the Licensing Acts relating to prohibited hours in respect of the premises to which the order relates but not from any other penalty under those Acts.

(6) An order under this section shall not exempt the holder of a licence that is a six-day licence from the provisions of the Licensing Acts relating to prohibited hours on Sundays.

(7) Where, on application to a Justice of the District Court, it is shown to the satisfaction of the Court that the application has the approval of a majority of the holders of on-licences in respect of premises situate in a locality in respect of which an order under this section has been made, the Court may, at any time before the commencement of the period to which the order relates, revoke the order and, upon such revocation, the order shall be deemed, for the purposes of this section, never to have been made.

(8) For the purposes of this and the two next following sections a locality that is situate in a county or other borough, a town (whether or not having commissioners under the Towns Improvement (Ireland) Act, 1854) or village, shall include the whole of that borough, town or village, as the case may be, and any surrounding built-up area.

11.—(1) Subject to the provisions of this section, on application to a Justice of the District Court by the holder of an on-licence, the Court may, if it so thinks fit, and is satisfied that a special event is being held at any place to which no licence for the sale of intoxicating liquor is attached grant to the applicant a licence (in this section referred to as an occasional licence) authorising him to sell at that place during such times and on such days (not exceeding **six**[3]), as may be specified in the

[3] Amended by the Intoxicating Liquor Act 1977, s.1.

licence such intoxicating liquor as he is authorised to sell by the on-licence aforesaid.

(2)(a) An occasional licence shall not be granted for a dinner unless it is organised as a special function for the entertainment of the members of a particular association, organisation or other like group.

(b) An occasional licence shall not be granted for a dance unless—

(i) it is held elsewhere than in the open air or in a tent, marquee or other such structure, and

(ii) either—

(I) it is organised as a special function for the entertainment of the members of a particular association, organisation or other like group and a substantial meal (the price (if any) of which is included in the price of admission (if any) to the dance) is served to the persons attending the dance, or

(II) it is held wholly or partly on a day that, in the opinion of the Court, is a day of special festivity generally or in the locality in which the place to which the licence relates is situate.

(3) Occasional licences shall not be granted pursuant to clause (II) of subparagraph (ii) of paragraph (b) of subsection (2) of this section for any premises in respect of more than six different days in a year.

(4) It shall be a condition of an occasional licence granted for a dinner or dance that the sale of intoxicating liquor pursuant to the licence be confined to persons attending the dinner or dance to which the licence relates.

(5) An occasional licence shall not be granted in respect of any Sunday, Christmas Day or Good Friday.

(6) Any person appearing to the District Court to have a *bona fide* interest in the matter may appear and give evidence on the hearing of an application under this section.

(7) The District Court shall not entertain an application under this section unless it is satisfied that the applicant has, not less than forty-eight hours before making the application, served upon the officer in charge of the Garda Síochána for the locality to which the application relates a notice in writing of his intention to make the application, setting out his name and address and the place, occasion and time for which the occasional licence to which the application relates is required.

(8) An occasional licence shall operate to exempt the person to whom it is granted (if and so long as he complies with the conditions subject to which it is granted and the special event for which the licence is granted is held in compliance with the relevant provisions of subsections (2) and (10) of this section) from the provisions of the Licensing Acts relating to the sale and supply of intoxicating liquor at the place and during the time for which the licence is granted.

(9) The provisions of the Licensing Acts requiring an offence to be endorsed on a licence shall not apply to an offence committed in respect of an occasional licence.

(10) An occasional licence shall not be granted for any time after the hour of ten

o'clock in the evening or before the hour of eight o'clock in the morning unless the event to which the licence would relate is a dinner or dance.

(11) (a) Section 13 of the Revenue Act, 1862, section 20 of the Revenue Act, 1863, section 5 of the Revenue (No. 1) Act, 1864, and section 6 of the Act of 1927 are hereby repealed in so far as they relate to licences authorising the sale of intoxicating liquor.

(b) Notwithstanding paragraph (a) of this subsection, a licence for the sale of intoxicating liquor may be granted after the commencement of this Act pursuant to a consent given under subsection (2) of the said section 6 before such commencement and a licence granted (whether before or after such commencement) in respect of an event held after such commencement pursuant to such a consent shall continue in force, but if a licence—

(i) is granted pursuant to a consent under the said subsection (2) for which application was made to the District Court after the 19th day of April, 1962, and

(ii) relates to a dance held more than one month after such commencement,

it shall be deemed to be a condition of the licence that a substantial meal be served to the persons attending the dance.

12.—(1) Section 5 (which relates to special exemption orders) of the Act of 1927 is hereby amended by the substitution for subsection (5) (inserted by the Act of 1960) of the following subsections:

"(5) In this section 'special occasion' means—

(a) (i) the occasion of a special event that is organised for the entertainment of the members of a particular association, organisation, or other like group, or

(ii) the occasion of a private function

in the premises in relation to which the special exemption order is sought and at which a substantial meal (the price (if any) of which is included in the price (if any) of admission to the event) is served to the persons attending the event,

(b) the occasion of a dance that is held in a ballroom licensed under the Public Dance Halls Act, 1935, and forming part of the premises in relation to which the special exemption order is sought being a dance at which a substantial meal (the price (if any) of which is included in the price (if any) of admission to the dance) is served to the persons attending the dance, or

(c) the occasion of a dance that is held in such a ballroom on a day that, in the opinion of the Court, is a day of special festivity generally or in the locality in which the premises are situate.

(6) Special exemption orders shall not be granted pursuant to paragraph

(c) of subsection (5) of this section for any premises in respect of more than six different days in a year.

(7) A special exemption order shall contain as one of the terms thereof a condition that intoxicating liquor shall not be sold at the event to which the order relates during the hours specified in the order to persons other than those attending the event and that members of the public, other than persons attending the event, shall not be admitted to the part of the premises in which intoxicating liquor is being supplied or consumed pursuant to the order.

(8) Notwithstanding the provisions of subsection (3) of this section, a special exemption order may be granted for a Sunday that is New Year's Day, New Year's Eve or St. Patrick's Day.

(9) It shall be a condition of a special exemption order that the special event, private function or dance in relation to which it is granted be held in compliance with the relevant provisions of subsection (5) of this section."

(2) The following provisions shall apply in relation to special exemption orders granted before the commencement of this Act:

(a) an order granted pursuant to an application made before the 19th day of April, 1962, or in respect of an event taking place within one month after the commencement of this Act shall continue in force, and

(b) any other order shall continue in force but it shall be deemed to be a condition of the order that:

(i) intoxicating liquor shall not be sold at the event to which the order relates during the hours specified in the order to persons other than those attending the event, and members of the public, other than persons attending the event, shall not be admitted to the part of the premises to which the order relates in which intoxicating liquor is being supplied or consumed pursuant to the order, and

(ii) a substantial meal is served to the persons attending the event to which the order relates.

13.—(1) Where, on application to it under section 11 of this Act or section 5 of the Act of 1927 the District Court is satisfied that—

(a) a festival consisting wholly or mainly of the presentation of performances of music, dancing or plays or showing of films or of any combination of such performances or showings is being held, and

(b) a *bona fide* club has been formed by the organisers of the festival the members of which are either persons performing at the festival or persons paying a single subscription the payment of which entitles them to attend each event of the festival or each event of a particular class, being a class constituting a significant part of the festival, or one event, at least, on each of five or more consecutive days, and

(c) a social function is being held at a place that is either a place to which no licence for the sale of intoxicating liquor is attached or is a hotel or restaurant by the members of the club, being a function that takes place during the period of the festival or a function that begins on the last day of the festival and ends on that day or on the day following that day,

the Court may, notwithstanding anything contained in section 11 of this Act, or section 5 of the Act of 1927, and irrespective of whether or not a substantial meal is to be served to persons attending the function, grant, upon such conditions as it thinks proper, either an occasional licence or a special exemption order, as may be appropriate, authorising the person making the application (being, in the case of an application for an occasional licence, the holder of an on-licence and, in the case of an application for a special exemption order, the holder of an on-licence for the premises to which the application relates) to sell at the place at which the function is being held, during such times and (subject to subsection (5) of section 11 of this Act or subsection (3) of section 5 of the Act of 1927) on such day or days as may be specified in the licence or order, as the case may be, such intoxicating liquor as he is authorised to sell by the on-licence aforesaid.

(2) It shall be a condition of an occasional licence or special exemption order granted in relation to a social function by virtue of this section that the sale of intoxicating liquor pursuant to the licence or order be confined to members of the club by whom the function is being held and to persons holding an invitation to the function (being a written invitation stating the name of the person invited issued not later than twenty-fours hours before the commencement of the function) from the organisers of the festival during which the function is being held, that a list of the names of the members of the club and the persons invited to the function be kept by the organisers of the festival, that the list be open to inspection by the Garda Síochána and that the function be held in compliance with the relevant provisions of section 11 of this Act and section 5 of the Act of 1927 and of this section.

(3) An occasional licence or special exemption order shall not be granted for a social function by virtue of this section unless it is shown to the satisfaction of the Court that the organisers of the festival during which the function is being held support the application.

(4) An application shall not be granted by virtue of this section in respect of more than one social function on any day in relation to any festival.

(5) In this section "hotel" and "restaurant" have the meanings assigned to them by the Act of 1927.

14.—(1) A Justice of the District Court may, on the application of the secretary of a registered club (within the meaning of the Registration of Clubs Acts) the main object of which is the promotion of any outdoor pastime, sport, game or recreation among its members, authorise, notwithstanding the provisions contained in the rules of the club pursuant to those Acts, the sale or supply by or with the consent of the club to any person for consumption in the buildings or grounds of the club and the consumption in the buildings or grounds of the club by any person, of excisable liquor at such times as may be specified in the authorisation on the occasion of a special event in the club that, in the opinion of the Court, is likely to attract a considerable number of people to the club.

(2) An authorisation shall not be granted under this section in respect of a club in relation to more than one event in a year and the period of the authorisation shall not exceed five consecutive days, but it shall not authorise the supply or consumption of excisable liquor on any day during that period on which the event to which it relates is not taking place.

(3) The sale, supply and consumption of excisable liquors in the buildings or grounds of a club pursuant to an authorisation under this section shall be lawful and shall be deemed not to be a breach of the rules of the club.

15.—(1) A general exemption order for the accommodation of persons attending a public market or fair shall not be granted for any day for any time before the hour of five o'clock in the morning or for any time—

(a) during a period of summer time, after the hour of half past eleven o'clock in the evening, or

(b) during a period, which is not a period of summer time, after the hour of eleven o'clock in the evening.

(2) A general exemption order for the accommodation of persons following any lawful trade or calling (other than fishing in tidal waters) shall not be granted for any day before the hour of seven o'clock in the morning or for any time—

(a) during a period of summer time, after the hour of half past eleven o'clock in the evening, or

(b) during a period which is not a period of summer time, after the hour of eleven o'clock in the evening.

(3) A general exemption order shall not be granted in respect of premises situate in the county borough of Dublin unless a general exemption order was in force in respect of the premises on the 19th day of April, 1962, or at any time during the two years immediately preceding that date.

(4) The preceding provisions of this section shall not affect the validity of general exemption orders granted before the commencement of this Act, but those provisions shall apply in relation to the renewal of such orders.

(5) In this section "general exemption order" means an order granted under section 4 of the Act of 1927.

16.—(1) Subject to the provisions of this section, where, on application to a Justice of the District Court by the holder of a licence (not being a six-day licence) in respect of premises situate in any locality not in a county or other borough, it is shown to the satisfaction of the Court that the application has the approval of a majority of the holders of such licences in respect of premises so situate, the Court may, if it is satisfied that, owing to circumstances in the locality, it is desirable to do so, make an order exempting the holders of all such licences in respect of premises so situate from the provisions of the Licensing Acts relating to prohibited hours in respect of those premises for the period between the hours of twelve o'clock and half-past twelve o'clock in the afternoon on Sundays and Saint Patrick's Day.

(2) The District Court shall not make an order under this section in respect of a period during which or part of which a considerable number of people in the locality to which the order would relate would be likely to be attending Divine Service.

(3) Any person appearing to the District Court to have a *bona fide* interest in the matter may appear and give evidence on the hearing of an application under this section.

(4) An order under this section shall, unless sooner revoked under this section, remain in force until the date (if any) specified in the order on which it is to expire or the date of the next annual licensing district court for the locality to which it relates, whichever is the earlier.

(5) A Justice of the District Court may, on the application of any person appearing to the Court to have a *bona fide* interest in the matter, revoke an order under this section if he is satisfied, after hearing the person on whose application the order was granted and any other person appearing to the Court to have a *bona fide* interest in the matter, that it is desirable to do so.

(6) Whenever an order is in force under this section in relation to any premises, the holder of the licence in relation to those premises shall be exempted on Sundays and on Saint Patrick's Day during the period between the hours of twelve o'clock and half-past twelve o'clock in the afternoon from any penalty for contravention of the provisions of the Licensing Acts relating to prohibited hours in respect of those premises, but not from any other penalty under those Acts.

(7) The District Court shall not entertain an application under subsection (1) or (5) of this section unless and until satisfied that not less than ten days before the date on which the application is proposed to be made notice in writing of the intention to make the application was given to the officer in charge of the Garda Síochána for the locality to which the application relates and that not less than seven days before such date the notice was published in a newspaper circulating in that locality.

17.—(1) Subject to the provisions of this section, where, on application to a Justice of the District Court by the holder of a licence (not being a licence granted by virtue of paragraph (2) of section 2 of the Act of 1902) in respect of premises situate in any locality not in a county or other borough, it is shown to the satisfaction of the Court that the application has the approval of a majority of the holders of such licences in respect of premises so situate, the Court may, if it is satisfied that, owing to circumstances in the locality it is desirable to do so, make an order permitting the holders of all such licences in respect of premises so situate to open or keep open the premises for the purpose of carrying on any business other than the sale or supply of intoxicating liquor during any one period specified in the order and not exceeding forty-five minutes in duration on the mornings of Sundays and Saint Patrick's Day.

(2) The District Court shall not make an order under this section in respect of a period during which or part of which a considerable number of people in the locality to which the order would relate would be likely to be attending Divine Service.

(3) Any person appearing to the District Court to have a *bona fide* interest in the

matter may appear and give evidence on the hearing of an application under this section.

(4) An order under this section shall, unless sooner revoked under this section, remain in force until the date (if any) specified in the order on which it is to expire or the date of the next annual licensing district court for the locality to which it relates, whichever is the earlier.

(5) A Justice of the District Court may, on the application of any person appearing to the Court to have a *bona fide* interest in the matter, revoke or amend an order under this section if he is satisfied after hearing the person on whose application the order was granted and any other person appearing to the Court to have a *bona fide* interest in the matter, that it is desirable to do so.

(6) Notwithstanding anything contained in the Licensing Acts the opening or keeping open of premises pursuant to an order under this section shall not be deemed to be an opening or keeping open of the premises for the sale of intoxicating liquor.

(7) The District Court shall not entertain an application under subsection (1) or (5) of this section unless and until satisfied that not less than ten days before the date on which the application is proposed to be made notice in writing of the intention to make the application was given to the officer in charge of the Garda Síochána for the locality to which the application relates and that not less than seven days before such date the notice was published in a newspaper circulating in that locality.

18.—(1) It shall be lawful for the Revenue Commissioners, notwithstanding anything contained in the Licensing Acts, to grant, on the application of the holder of a greyhound race track licence, to such holder, or a person nominated by him—

(a) a licence for the sale of intoxicating liquor at the race track to which the greyhound race track licence relates for consumption at the race track, and

(b) a renewal of a licence granted to such holder or person pursuant to this section in respect of such race track.

(2) Notwithstanding anything contained in the Act of 1927, a licence granted under this section in respect of a greyhound race track shall operate, during such time as the greyhound race track licence in relation to the track is in force, to authorise the sale and consumption of intoxicating liquor at the track, the keeping open of premises at such track for such sale, and the permitting of such consumption, on the occasion of—

(a) a greyhound race meeting,

(b) a greyhound sale, or

(c) greyhound trials,

at such track during the period—

(i) beginning thirty minutes before the commencement of the race meeting, sale or trials, as the case may be, and

(ii) ending, in the case of a race meeting, **thirty minutes after the time at which the last race of the meeting starts**[4] and, in the case of a sale or trials, at the conclusion of the sale or trials, as the case may be,

but during no other period.

(3) None of the following sections shall apply in relation to premises licensed under this section, namely, sections 4 and 5 of the Act of 1927 and sections 10, 11, 16 and 17 of this Act.

(4)(a) In this section—

"greyhound sales" and "greyhound trials" do not include a sale or trials, as the case may be, held at a greyhound race track on the same day as but after a greyhound race meeting at that track;

"greyhound race track licence" means a licence under section 22 of the Greyhound Industry Act, 1958.

(b) Where a greyhound race meeting, a greyhound sale or greyhound trials lasts or last for more than one day, the part of such race meeting, sale or trials, as the case may be, held on any day shall be deemed, for the purposes of this section, to be a separate meeting or sale or separate trials, as the case may be.

19.—Section 4 (which provides for the grant of new licences in certain cases of increase in population) of the Act of 1902 is hereby amended by the insertion after "part of the parish" of "or for premises situate in a parish in which the increase aforesaid has not taken place if the premises are situate in the city or town and either—

(a) the city or town is within the parish and there is an increase in population in the area comprising the city or town, or

(b) a part only of the city or town is within the parish and there is an increase in population in the area comprising such part,

and the licence is in substitution for an existing licence or licences held in respect of premises situate in the city or town aforesaid and in the parish aforesaid."

20.—(1) An application to the Circuit Court under section 4 of the Act of 1902, section 21 or 22 of the Act of 1943 or section 13, 14 or 27 of the Act of 1960 (which sections relate to the grant of new licences in certain circumstances upon the extinguishment of existing licences) shall not be allowed if the licence, or either of the licences, as the case may be, that would fall to be extinguished if the application were allowed and a licence were granted in pursuance of the section under which the application is made is a licence granted by virtue of paragraph (2) of section 2 of the Act of 1902, or under section 18 of this Act **or a special restaurant licence granted by virtue of the Intoxicating Liquor Act, 1988.**[5]

---

[4] Amended by the Intoxicating Liquor Act 1988, s.49.
[5] Inserted by the Intoxicating Liquor Act 1988, s.23.

(2)(a) An application to the Circuit Court under section 13 of the Act of 1960 shall not be allowed in respect of premises situate less than one mile measured by the shortest public thoroughfare from premises in respect of which there is in force a licence that was first granted on or before the 4th day of July, 1960, and is of the same character as the licence that would fall to be granted if the application were allowed.

(b) For the purposes of this subsection all on-licences shall be deemed to be licences of the same character.

(3) An application under section 19 (which relates to applications to the District Court to allow public bars in certain hotels) of the Act of 1960 shall not be allowed if the licence that would fall to be extinguished if the application were allowed is a licence granted under section 18 of this Act **or a special restaurant licence granted by virtue of the Intoxicating Liquor Act 1988.**[6]

(4) The preceding subsections of this section shall not have effect as respects—

(a) an application notice of which was given, pursuant to rules of court, to the appropriate County Registrar or to the appropriate District Court clerk before the commencement of this Act, or

(b) an application for the grant of a certificate entitling the applicant to receive a licence in respect of any premises on the hearing of which it is shown to the satisfaction of the Court that a declaration was made by the Court in respect of those premises under subsection (1) of section 15 of the Act of 1960 before the commencement of this Act or that notice of an application for such a declaration was given, pursuant to rules of court, to the appropriate County Registrar or to the appropriate District Court Clerk before the commencement of this Act, and that such declaration was made (whether before or after such commencement).

21.—Where a person is convicted (whether before or after the passing of this Act) in relation to any premises in respect of which he holds a licence for the sale of intoxicating liquor by retail and which is situate in the Court area of Swinford of more than one offence (being offences each of which was committed during the period from the 19th day of May, 1961, to the 23rd day of May, 1961) and more than one of the convictions would, but for this section, fall to be recorded under section 25 of the Act of 1927 on the licence, not more than one of the convictions shall be so recorded.

22.—Notwithstanding anything contained in section 17 (which relates to the offence of being on licensed premises during prohibited hours) of the Act of 1927, it shall not be unlawful for a person to be in any yard, stable, outhouse, shed or other like place forming part of premises in respect of which a licence is in force and which are not situate in a county or other borough on a Sunday, Saint Patrick's Day, Christmas Day or Good Friday for the sole purpose of leaving therein, attending to, or removing therefrom, an animal-drawn vehicle.

---

[6] Inserted by the Intoxicating Liquor Act 1988, s.23.

23.—In a prosecution for an offence in relation to prohibited hours in respect of premises—

(a) it shall be presumed, until the contrary is proved, that a licence of the character and subject to the conditions (if any) alleged by the prosecution is in force in respect of the premises, and

(b) if the defendant proves that at the time at which he is alleged to have committed the offence with which he is charged a licence was not in force in respect of the premises, the Court before which the prosecution is heard shall treat the charge as a charge of an offence contrary to section 7 (which prohibits the sale of intoxicating liquor without a licence) of the Act of 1924, and a conviction under the said section 7 shall not be reversed merely on the ground that a licence in respect of the premises is subsequently obtained by the defendant.

24.—Where, after the commencement of this Act—

(a) a person is convicted in respect of premises of an offence under section 7 (which prohibits the sale of intoxicating liquor without a licence) of the Act of 1924,

(b) the person was the holder of a licence in respect of the premises not more than twelve months before the time of the offence, and

(c) the person becomes, after the time of the conviction, the holder of a licence in respect of the premises,

the offence shall be deemed to be an offence to which Part III (which relates to the endorsement of licences) of the Act of 1927 applies and the licence shall, for the purpose of that Part, be deemed to have been in force and to have been held by the person at the time of the conviction, and, accordingly, the conviction shall be recorded on the licence under that Part.

25.—In an application to the District Court under section 10, 16 or 17 of this Act in relation to any Court area a certificate purporting to be signed by the District Court clerk for that area and to certify that a list contained in it is a list of all the holders in respect of premises in that area, or the part thereof to which the application relates (as the case may be), of licences in force at the time when the list is given in evidence shall, without proof of the signature of the person purporting to sign the certificate or that he was the District Court Clerk for that area, be evidence, until the contrary is proved, of the matters certified in and by the certificate.[7]

26.—(1) In this section "unlicensed drinking premises" means premises to which an on-licence is not attached, which are not the premises of a club registered under the Registration of Clubs Acts and which are used or made available for the consumption of intoxicating liquor therein by persons resorting to them other than the *bona fide* occupier of the premises, a member of the family of the occupier, a

[7] Substituted by the Courts (No. 2) Act 1986, ss.9, 10(5), Sched. 1.

person residing or working in the premises (who are referred to in this section as excepted persons) or a *bona fide* private guest of any of those persons.

(2) A person shall not be in or consume intoxicating liquor in unlicensed drinking premises unless he is an excepted person or a *bona fide* private guest of an excepted person.

(3) An occupier of premises that are unlicensed drinking premises shall be guilty of an offence and shall be liable on summary conviction to a fine not exceeding fifty pounds, and, if the premises in respect of which he was so convicted continue, after the conviction, to be unlicensed drinking premises, he shall be guilty of a further offence and liable on summary conviction thereof to a fine not exceeding five pounds for each day on which the contravention was so continued.

(4)(a) A person who supplies intoxicating liquor to premises that he knows to be unlicensed drinking premises for consumption by persons prohibited, by virtue of subsection (2) of this section, from consuming intoxicating liquor in those premises shall be deemed to aid and abet another person in the commission of an offence under subsection (3) of this section.

(b) A person who supplies intoxicating liquor to unlicensed drinking premises pursuant to orders of more than one person (other than an excepted person) within a period of three days shall be presumed, until the contrary is proved, to know that the premises are unlicensed drinking premises.

(5) A person who contravenes subsection (2) of this section shall be guilty of an offence and shall be liable on summary conviction to a fine not exceeding fifty pounds.

(6) Where an offence under subsection (3) of this section, or the offence of aiding and abetting the commission of such an offence, is committed by a person who holds a licence for the sale of intoxicating liquor by retail, the offence shall be deemed, for the purposes of Part III (which relates to the endorsement of licences) of the Act of 1927, to be an offence to which that Part of that Act applies, but where the person holds more than one such licence, a conviction of the offence shall be recorded on such one, only, of the licences as the Court by which the person is convicted considers appropriate.

(7) In a prosecution for an offence under this section in relation to any premises—

(a) it shall be a good defence to show—

(i) that the premises are *bona fide* used as a club (other than a club registered under the Registration of Clubs Acts) established and conducted for purposes not connected with the consumption of intoxicating liquor,

(ii) that the intoxicating liquor (if any) to which the alleged offence relates had been brought to the premises not more than twelve hours before the occasion to which the prosecution relates by or on behalf of members of the club for consumption by members of the club, and

(iii) that intoxicating liquor is not habitually or frequently consumed in the club premises and is not stored therein,

(b) it shall be presumed, until the contrary is proved, that a person found on the premises to which the prosecution relates is not there as the *bona fide* private guest of an excepted person, and

(c) if it is shown to the satisfaction of the Court before which the prosecution is heard that stocks of intoxicating liquor owned by different persons (other than excepted persons) are kept in the premises, it shall be presumed, until the contrary is proved, that the premises are unlicensed drinking premises.

(8) A person found in unlicensed drinking premises on any occasion and charged with the commission of an offence under this section shall not be convicted of the offence—

(a) if, in the absence of evidence that he consumed intoxicating liquor on the premises on the occasion, he states on oath in the Court before which the charge is heard that he did not consume intoxicating liquor on the premises on the occasion and did not intend to do so, or

(b) if he shows to the satisfaction of the Court that he did not know that the premises were unlicensed drinking premises.

(9)(a) Where a Justice of the District Court is satisfied on the information on oath of a member of the Garda Síochána not below the rank of Inspector that there is reasonable ground for supposing that, at any premises, an offence under this section has been, is being or is about to be committed, the Justice may issue a search warrant under this subsection.

(b) The search warrant shall authorise a named member of the Garda Síochána not below the rank of Inspector, accompanied by such other members of the Garda Síochána as that member thinks proper, to enter the premises at any time within forty-eight hours after the issue of the warrant, if need be by force, to inspect the premises and any books and documents found there, and to take the name and address of any person found there.

(c) A member of the Garda Síochána may arrest without warrant any person who, when his name and address are demanded of him under this subsection, fails to give them or gives a name or address which such member has reason to believe to be false or misleading.

(d) Any person who obstructs or impedes a member of the Garda Síochána in the exercise of his powers under this subsection or who, on being asked to give his name and address by such member, fails to give them or gives a name or address which is false or misleading shall be guilty of an offence and shall be liable on summary conviction to a fine not exceeding twenty-five pounds.

(e) If a member of the Garda Síochána is obstructed or impeded in entering any premises or any part thereof in the exercise of his powers under this subsection it shall be presumed until the contrary is proved that that premises were unlicensed drinking premises.

27.—(1) Nothing in the Licensing Acts (other than this section) or in any enactment requiring the authority of an excise licence for the sale or supply of intoxicating liquor shall have effect in relation to intoxicating liquor that is in confectionery if the confectionery—

(a) does not contain intoxicating liquor in a proportion greater than one-fiftieth of a gallon of liquor (computed as proof spirit) per pound of the confectionery, and

(b) either consists of separate pieces each of which weighs not more than one and one-half ounces or is designed to be broken into such pieces for the purposes of consumption.

(2) Intoxicating liquor in confectionery shall not be sold to a person who is under the age of sixteen years.

(3) A person who knowingly contravenes subsection (2) of this section shall be guilty of an offence and shall be liable on summary conviction to a fine not exceeding fifty pounds.

28.—(1) The Revenue Commissioners shall not grant, whether by way of new licence or of transfer or renewal of an existing licence, a wine retailer's off-licence in respect of any premises other than premises where a business of the kind referred to in section 61 of the Act of 1927 is being carried on or in respect of which a spirit retailer's off-licence or a beer retailer's off-licence is in force.

(2) The Revenue Commissioners shall not grant, whether by way of new licence or of transfer or renewal of an existing licence, a cider retailer's off-licence, in respect of any premises other than premises in respect of which a spirit retailer's off-licence or a wholesale dealer's licence for the sale of spirits, beer or wine is in force.

(3) In this section "wine retailer's off-licence", "spirit retailer's off-licence", "beer retailer's off-licence", "cider retailer's off-licence" and "wholesale dealer's licence for the sale of spirits, beer or wine" have the meanings they respectively have in the Act of 1910.

29.—A person who permits a person to be on licensed premises contrary to subsection (1) of section 17 (which was inserted by the Act of 1960 and provides for certain offences in relation to prohibited hours) of the Act of 1927 shall be guilty of an offence and shall be liable on summary conviction, in the case of a first offence, to a fine not exceeding **£300**[8], or, in the case of a second or any subsequent offence, to a fine not exceeding **£600**[9] and the offence shall be deemed, for the purposes of Part III (which relates to the endorsement of licences) of the Act of 1927, to be an offence to which that Part of that Act applies.

30.—(1) In section 8 of the Act of 1902, section 14 of the Act of 1924 and in this section "last census" means the last census of population taken under the Statistics Acts, 1926 and 1946, from which statistics of population, other than statistics which purport to be provisional only, published by the Stationery Office have been derived.

---

[8] Substituted by the Intoxicating Liquor Act 1988, s.51, Sched.
[9] Fines increased by the Intoxicating Liquor Act 1988, s.51, Sched.

(2) In any application to a Court under the Act of 1902—

(a) a document purporting to be published by the Stationery Office and to be compiled by the Central Statistics Office and to contain statistics of population derived from a census of population taken under the Statistics Acts, 1926 and 1946, other than statistics which purport to be provisional only, or to contain statistics derived from the census taken in the year 1901, shall be evidence, until the contrary is proved, of the matters relating to statistics of population stated in the document,

(b) a certificate purporting to be signed by the Director, or other person for the time being in charge, of the Central Statistics Office and to certify that the census referred to in a document of the kind specified in paragraph (a) of this subsection is the last census and, either, that no later census has been taken or that statistics of population derived from a later census, other than statistics that purport to be provisional only, will not be published during the two months immediately following the date on which the certificate is given, shall, without proof of the signature of the person purporting to sign the certificate or that he was the Director, or for the time being in charge, of the Central Statistics Office, be evidence, until the contrary is proved, of the matters certified in and by the certificate,

(c) a certificate purporting to be signed by the Director, or other person for the time being in charge, of the Central Statistics Office and containing statistics of population and purporting to certify that the statistics are derived from the last census and, either that no later census has been taken or that statistics of population derived from a later census will not be published during the two months immediately following the date on which the certificate is given, shall, without proof of the signature of the person purporting to sign the certificate or that he was the Director, or for the time being in charge, of the Central Statistics Office, be evidence, until the contrary is proved, of the matters relating to statistics contained in the certificate and of the matters certified in and by the certificate, and

(d) a certificate purporting to be signed by the Director, or other person for the time being in charge, of the Central Statistics Office and containing statistics of population and purporting to certify that the statistics are derived from the census taken in the year 1901 shall, without proof of the signature of the person purporting to sign the certificate or that he was the Director, or for the time being in charge, of the Central Statistics Office, be evidence, until the contrary is proved, of the matters relating to statistics contained in the certificate and of the matters certified in and by the certificate.

31.—An application under section 15 of the Act of 1960 in respect of any premises may be granted notwithstanding the fact that it is not shown to the satisfaction of the Court that the premises comply with the provisions of section 5 of the Act of 1902, but an application to which both the said section 5 and subsection (1) of section 17 of the Act of 1960 refer in respect of any premises shall not be granted unless it is shown to the satisfaction of the Court that the premises comply with the provisions of the said section 5.

32.—Section 17 (which relates to the licensing or certification of premises the subject of a declaration under section 15 of the Act of 1960) of the Act of 1960 is hereby amended by the substitution of the following subsection for subsection (1):

"(1) If, on the hearing of an application for the grant of a certificate entitling the applicant to receive a licence in respect of any premises, it is shown to the satisfaction of the Court—

(a) that a declaration has been made by the Court under subsection (1) of section 15 of this Act,

(b) that the premises have been acquired, constructed or altered in substantial accordance with the terms of the declaration, and

(c) where the application is made pursuant to any provision of the Licensing Acts that provides for the extinguishing of one or more existing licences on the grant of the licence—

(i) that the licence or each of the licences in respect of which it was shown to the satisfaction of the Court on the application for the declaration that the applicant was the holder thereof or had secured the consent of the holder to the extinguishing thereof is in force, or

(ii) if such licence or licences or any of them is or are not in force, that the licence or licences not in force has not or have not been forfeited or extinguished and the premises to which it or they related have not been deemed, by virtue of any provision of the Licensing Acts, never to have been licensed,

it shall not be open to the Court to refuse the application—

(I) in a case where it is made pursuant to section 21 of the Act of 1943 on any ground, and

(II) in any other case, on any ground other than the character, misconduct or unfitness of the applicant,

and where, as respects a licence or licences and the premises to which it or they related, it is shown to the satisfaction of the Court that it or they comply with the provisions of sub-paragraph (ii) of paragraph (c) of this subsection, the licence or licences shall be deemed, for the purposes of the provisions of the Licensing Acts relating to the granting of licences, but not otherwise, to be in force and to relate to the premises to which it or they related and, on the grant of the new licence, shall accordingly be extinguished and the premises to which it or they related shall be deemed never to have been licensed."

33.—Section 27 (which provides for the grant of a full licence for premises having a restricted licence) of the Act of 1960 is hereby amended by the substitution of "three years" for "two years" in subsection (4).

34.—(1) The power of a Justice of the District Court under the Licensing Acts to transfer temporarily an on-licence or an off-licence upon the death of the holder of the licence shall include power to transfer the licence to any person (being a person approved of by the Court and not disqualified by law) nominated by the executor or administrator of the holder or, if there is no executor or administrator, by any person having an interest in the premises to which the licence relates, and the transfer shall operate to authorise the person to whom the licence is transferred to carry on in the premises to which the licence relates the business authorised by the licence until the date of the sitting of the annual licensing District Court in the Court area in which the premises are situate held next after the expiration of one month from the date of the transfer, or if the Court should then or on any subsequent application to it, think fit to so order, until the sitting of such annual licensing District Court in the year, or in the second year (as the Court may think fit to order) after the sitting aforesaid.

(2) Where a licence has been transferred by virtue of subsection (1) of this section, the licence may, on application by the nominator of the transferee to the Court at any sitting thereof for the District Court District within which the premises are situate, be transferred, by endorsement made by the Court on the licence or, if the licence is not available, on a copy thereof, to such other person (being a person approved of by the Court and not disqualified by law) as the nominator may nominate.

(3) In this section "off-licence" and "on-licence" have the meanings assigned to them by the Act of 1927.

35.—(1) References in the Licensing Acts to the Dublin Metropolitan Area shall be deemed to be references to the Dublin Metropolitan District.

(2) The county borough of Dublin shall be deemed, for the purposes of the Licensing Acts, to include the whole of the Dublin Metropolitan District and such borough and District shall be deemed, for the purposes of those Acts, to be a city.

(3) The preceding subsections of this section shall not have effect as respects

(a) an application under section 13 (which relates to the grant of new licences in rural areas upon the extinguishment of two existing licences) of the Act of 1960 notice of which was given, pursuant to rules of court, to the appropriate County Registrar or to the appropriate District Court clerk before the commencement of this Act, or

(b) an application under the said section 13 for the grant of a certificate entitling the applicant to receive a licence in respect of any premises on the hearing of which it is shown to the satisfaction of the Court that a declaration was made by the court in respect of those premises under subsection (1) of section 15 of the Act of 1960 before the commencement of this Act.

36.—(1) This Act may be cited as the Intoxicating Liquor Act, 1962.

(2) This Act, in so far as it amends and extends the Licensing Acts, shall be construed as one therewith and may be cited together therewith as the Licensing Acts, 1833 to 1962, and, in so far as it amends and extends the Registration of Clubs Acts, shall be construed as one therewith and may be cited together therewith as the Registration of Clubs Acts, 1904 to 1962.

(3) The Act shall come into operation on the second day after the date of its passing.

COURTS (NO. 2) ACT 1986 *(Excerpts)*

No. 26 of 1986

AN ACT TO AMEND AND EXTEND THE COURTS OF JUSTICE ACTS, 1924 TO 1961, AND THE COURTS (SUPPLEMENTAL PROVISIONS) ACTS, 1961 TO 1986, AND TO PROVIDE FOR OTHER MATTERS RELATING TO THE COURTS.

BE IT ENACTED BY THE OIREACHTAS AS FOLLOWS:—

. . .

4.—(1) In this section—

"the Act of 1902" means the Licensing (Ireland) Act, 1902;

"the Act of 1927" means the Intoxicating Liquor Act, 1927;

"the Act of 1952" means the Tourist Traffic Act, 1952;

"the Act of 1960" means the Intoxicating Liquor Act, 1960;

"licence" means a licence for the sale of intoxicating liquor for the grant of which the production of a certificate of the District Court or the Circuit Court (as the case may be) is required **and includes a licence granted under section 13 of the Refreshment Houses (Ireland) Act 1860**.[1]

(2) Subject to subsection (5) of this section, where a renewal is required of a licence for premises which have been licensed in the immediately preceding year, it shall not be necessary to produce a certificate of the District Court to an officer of the Revenue Commissioners empowered to grant a renewal of such a licence.

(3) Where a renewal of a licence is granted by an officer of the Revenue Commissioners and false or misleading information was given to the Commissioners in support of the application for such grant, the applicant shall be guilty of an offence and shall be liable on summary conviction to a fine not exceeding £300.

(4) Where the applicant is convicted of an offence under subsection (3) of this section or where there was a failure to comply with subsection (11) of this section, the District Court may order that the licence be forfeited.

(5) Notwithstanding subsection (2) of this section, a licence shall not be renewable on expiry without the production of a certificate of the District Court for the district court area within which the premises concerned are situate where—

---

[1] Inserted by the Intoxicating Liquor Act 1988, s.50.

(a) a notice of objection to such renewal has been lodged with the Court within the time prescribed in rules of court, or

(b) the licence is one which is renewable by virtue of the provisions of section 30(1)(b) of the Act of 1960, or

(c) it is proposed to insert a condition in the licence in pursuance of section 8 or section 9 of the Act of 1927.

(6) An objection to the renewal of a licence may be made by any person who, but for the passing of this Act, would have been authorised to object to the grant of a certificate required for the renewal of a licence in respect of the premises; and any such objection shall be deemed to be an objection to the grant of the certificate required by subsection (5) of this section.

(7) Subject to subsection (8) of this section the certificate required by subsection (5) of this section shall be as to—

(a) the good character of the licensee,

(b) the peaceable and orderly manner in which the licensed premises were conducted in the year ending on the expiry of the licence, and

(c) in the case of premises licensed by virtue of Chapter III of Part VI of the Act of 1952, the orderly manner in which the holiday camp (within the meaning of that Chapter) in which the premises are situate was conducted in the year ending on the expiry of the licence.

(8) In the case of a renewal of a licence pursuant to the provisions of section 30(1)(b) of the Act of 1960, the certificate required by subsection (5) of this section shall be as to—

(a) the good character of the applicant, and

(b) where business has been conducted in the premises concerned at any time during the year ending on the expiry of the licence, the peaceable and orderly manner in which the premises were conducted.

(9) Notwithstanding subsection (2) of this section, a licence for an hotel, being a licence—

(a) in respect of which effect was given to section 42(1) of the Act of 1952, or

(b) which was granted after the passing of the Act of 1960, by virtue of paragraph (2) of section 2 of the Act of 1902,

shall not be renewable on expiry without the production to the Revenue Commissioners of a certificate that the hotel in respect of which the licence was granted is registered in the register of hotels kept by Bord Fáilte Éireann.

(9A) Notwithstanding subsection (2) of this section, a special restaurant licence shall not be renewable on expiry without the production to the Revenue Commissioners of a Bord Fáilte Certificate (within the meaning of the Intoxicating Liquor Act, 1988).[2]

---

[2] Inserted by the Intoxicating Liquor Act 1988, s.18.

(10) An officer of the Revenue Commissioners empowered to grant a renewal of a licence shall not grant the renewal of a licence to which section 2 of the Beer Licences Regulation (Ireland) Act, 1877, applies without the production of a statutory declaration that the conditions in that section concerning the rateable valuation of the premises which are the subject of the licence have been met, and that such premises have been in the exclusive occupation of the licence-holder for at least three months preceding the date of application for renewal.

(11) In applying for a renewal of a licence, the applicant shall inform the Revenue Commissioners of the following, where applicable:

(a) that section 30 of the Act of 1960 applies;

(b) that he proposes to apply to the District Court for the insertion of a condition in his licence in pursuance of section 8 or section 9 of the Act of 1927;

(c) that the licence is one in respect of which effect was given to section 42(1) of the Act of 1952, or which was granted after the passing of the Act of 1960 by virtue of paragraph (2) of section 2 of the Act of 1902.

(d) that the licence is a special restaurant licence granted pursuant to the Intoxicating Liquor Act, 1988.[3]

. . .

6.—Section 25 of the Intoxicating Liquor Act, 1927, is hereby amended—

(a) by the insertion in subsection (1) before "Whenever" of "Subject to the provisions of subsection (1A) of this section", and

(b) by the insertion after subsection (1) of the following subsection:

"(1A) In the case of a conviction for any offence relating to prohibited hours, the provisions of subsection (1) of this section shall apply only if the Court in its discretion so thinks proper.",

and the said subsection (1), as so amended, is set out in the Table to this section.

TABLE

(1) Subject to the provisions of subsection (1A) of this section, whenever the holder of any licence for the sale of intoxicating liquor by retail is convicted of an offence to which this Part of this Act applies the conviction shall, if the person so convicted is the holder of one such licence only, be recorded on such licence or, if such person is the holder of two or more such licences in respect of the same premises, be recorded on all such licences or, if such person is the holder of two or more such licences which do not all relate to the same premises, be recorded on such one or more of those licences as relate to the premises in respect of which the offence was committed.

---

[3] Inserted by the Intoxicating Liquor Act 1988, s.18.

7.—The Intoxicating Liquor Act, 1927, is hereby amended by the substitution of the following section for section 27:—

> "**27.**—(1) Whenever the holder of any licence for the sale of intoxicating liquor is convicted by a Justice of the District Court of an offence to which this Part of this Act applies, an appeal shall lie from such conviction to the Judge of the Circuit Court within whose circuit the District or any part of the District of such Justice is situate, and the decision of such Judge shall be final and not appealable.
>
> (2) On the hearing of an appeal under subsection (1) of this section from a conviction for an offence relating to prohibited hours, the Judge of the Circuit Court may, although affirming the conviction, make, if in his discretion he so thinks proper, an order declaring that such conviction shall not be recorded on such licence and, whenever such an order is so made, such conviction shall not be so recorded and shall for all purposes be deemed never to have been so recorded and, accordingly, any forfeiture occasioned by the recording of such conviction shall be deemed to be cancelled".

. . .

9.—Each provision mentioned in column (2) of the First Schedule to this Act opposite the mention in column (1) of that Schedule of an enactment is hereby amended in the manner stated in column (3) of that Schedule, and each enactment mentioned in column (2) of the Second Schedule to this Act is hereby repealed to the extent mentioned in column (3) of that Schedule.

10.—(1) This Act may be cited as the Courts (No. 2) Act, 1986.

(2) The collective citation "the Courts (Supplemental Provisions) Acts, 1961 to 1986" shall include this Act (other than sections 4, 6 and 7 and the First Schedule in so far as it relates to the law on intoxicating liquor) and the said Courts (Supplemental Provisions) Acts, 1961 to 1986 (other than the said sections 4, 6 and 7 and the said First Schedule in so far as it relates to the law on intoxicating liquor) shall be construed together as one Act.

(3) Sections 4, 6 and 7 and, in so far as they relate to the law on intoxicating liquor, section 9 of this Act and the First Schedule to this Act, and the Licensing Acts, 1833 to 1983, shall be construed together with those Acts and may be cited together with them as the Licensing Acts, 1833 to 1986.

(4) Section 9 of this Act and the First Schedule of this Act, insofar as they relate to the Registration of Clubs Acts, 1904 to 1981, shall be construed together with those Acts and may be cited together with them as the Registration of Clubs Acts, 1904 to 1986.

(5) This Act, other than sections 2, 3(1), 3(3) to 3(5) and 5 to 8, the repeal of those provisions of the Petty Sessions (Ireland) Act, 1851, and of the Small Penalties (Ireland) Act, 1873, provided for in section 9 and section 10, shall come into operation on such day or days as may be fixed therefor by order or orders of the Minister for Justice, either generally or with reference to a particular purpose or provision, and different days may be so fixed for different purposes and different provisions of this Act.

FIRST SCHEDULE

Miscellaneous Amendments

Enactment (1)	Provision (2)	Nature of Amendment (3)
Licensing (Ireland) Act, 1833	Section 2	The deletion of— (a) ", twenty-one days at least before the first day of the then next general sessions of the peace to be held for the district within which the house for which such person shall desire to be licensed shall be situate," and (b) ", ten days at the least previous to such quarter sessions of the peace,".
Licensing (Ireland) Act, 1855	Section 1	The substitution for "If any person shall apply for and be refused the certificate in the said Act mentioned, to entitle such person" of "If objection be raised to an application". The substitution for "such application" of "the certificate required before the licence can be renewed by an officer of the Revenue Commissioners".
Beerhouses (Ireland) Act, 1864	Section 3	The deletion of— (a) "or to grant a renewal of any such licence as aforesaid to any person applying for such renewal," (b) "or the renewal of a licence for the same house as shall have been licensed in the year last immediately preceding and which licence shall not have been withdrawn or annulled," and (c) "applying for such renewal, or of the person".
Licensing Act, 1872	Section 82	The deletion of— (a) "or to grant to any spirit grocer upon the expiration of his excise license a renewal of such excise license," and (b) ", or, in the case of a renewal, during the past year".

Enactment (1)	Provision (2)	Nature of Amendment (3)
Licensing Act (Ireland), 1874	Section 8	The deletion of— (a) "renewal or" where those words first occur, and (b) "renewal," where that word occurs for the second time.
	Section 9	The deletion of "and of renewals of excise licenses".
	Section 10	The substitution for section 10 of the following section: "10. Every person intending to apply for a new licence or for the transfer of a licence shall, at least 21 days before the intended application is to be heard, cause to be inserted or advertised in a newspaper circulating in the place in which the premises concerned are situate, a notice duly complying with the requirements of section 2 of the Licensing (Ireland) Act, 1833".
	Section 14	The deletion of "not later than seven days before the holding of such session".
	Section 14	The deletion of "The justices may, notwithstanding that no notice of objection has been served, if objection is made in court, adjourn the signing of the certificate to a future day, and require the attendance of the applicant".
Beer Licences Regulation (Ireland) Act, 1877	Section 2	The deletion of ", or to grant a renewal of any such licence as aforesaid".
Registration of Clubs (Ireland) Act, 1904	Section 3 (3)	The substitution for the third sentence of the following sentence: "Such certificate so issued shall, subject to the provisions of this Act, remain in force until the annual licensing district court (within the meaning of the Intoxicating Liquor Act, 1927) held next after the grant of such certificate, and shall then expire.".

Enactment (1)	Provision (2)	Nature of Amendment (3)
Enforcement of Court Orders Act, 1926	Section 16(1)	The deletion of "pursuant to an examination order".
	Section 17	The deletion of "in accordance with an examination order".
Intoxicating Liquor Act, 1927	Section 8	In subsection (3), the deletion of "or renewal" and the insertion after "such certificate" of "and in every such six day licence renewed thereafter".
	Section 9	In subsection (3), the deletion of "or renewal" and the insertion after "such certificate" of "and in every such early closing licence renewed thereafter".
Intoxicating Liquor Act, 1927	Section 62	(a) In subsection (1), the deletion of "a certificate for" where those words first occur. (b) In subsection (2), the deletion of "a certificate for". (c) In subsection (5), the deletion of "a certificate for".
Intoxicating Liquor Act, 1960	Section 32(1)	(a) The substitution for "to an application to the Court for the grant of a certificate under section 11 (which relates to the renewal of licences) of the Spirits (Ireland) Act, 1854," of "to the Court pursuant to section 4(5)(a) of the Courts (No. 2) Act, 1986 against an application to an officer of the Revenue Commissioners for the renewal of a licence". (b) The insertion after "the certificate" of "provided for by section 4(7) or 4(8) (as the case may be) of the Courts (No. 2) Act, 1986".

Enactment (1)	Provision (2)	Nature of Amendment (3)
Intoxicating Liquor Act, 1962	Section 25	The substitution for section 25 of the following section: "In an application to the District Court under section 10, 16 or 17 of this Act in relation to any Court area a certificate purporting to be signed by the District Court Clerk for that area and to certify that a list contained in it is a list of all the holders in respect of premises in that area, or the part thereof to which the application relates (as the case may be), of licences in force at the time when the list is given in evidence shall, without proof of the signature of the person purporting to sign the certificate or that he was the District Court Clerk for that area, be evidence, until the contrary is proved, of the matters certified in and by the certificate.".
Fire Services Act, 1981	Section 24	The insertion of the following subsection: "(2) In any case where a certificate is not required for the renewal of a licence (other than an off-licence) under the Licensing Acts, 1833 to 1986, the applicant for such renewal shall give one month's notice in writing (or such shorter period of notice as the fire authority may in the special circumstances of the case agree to accept) of the application to the fire authority in the functional area of which the premises are situated, and if the fire authority object to such application, such fire authority may appear, be heard and adduce evidence in respect of the application for a certificate provided for by section 4(7) or 4(8) (as the case may be) of the Courts (No. 2) Act, 1986.".

SECOND SCHEDULE

Enactments Repealed

Chapter & Session or Number & Year (1)	Short title (2)	Extent of Repeal (3)
14 & 15 Vic. c. 93	Petty Sessions (Ireland) Act, 1851	Paragraphs 2 to 4 of section 22, in so far as they apply to criminal proceedings. Paragraph 9 of section 22.
17 & 18 Vic. c. 89	Spirits (Ireland) Act, 1854	Section 11.
36 & 37 Vic. c. 82	Small Penalties (Ireland) Act, 1873	The whole Act.
No. 15 of 1952	Tourist Traffic Act, 1952	Section 50.
No. 18 of 1960	Intoxicating Liquor Act, 1960	Section 20.

INTOXICATING LIQUOR ACT 1988

No. 16 of 1988

AN ACT TO AMEND AND EXTEND THE LICENSING ACTS, 1833 TO 1986, TO AMEND THE REGISTRATION OF CLUBS ACTS, 1904 TO 1986, AND TO PROVIDE FOR OTHER MATTERS CONNECTED WITH THE MATTERS AFORESAID.

BE IT ENACTED BY THE OIREACHTAS AS FOLLOWS:

PART I

PRELIMINARY AND GENERAL

1.—This Act may be cited as the Intoxicating Liquor Act, 1988.

2.—(1) In this Act—

"the Act of 1927" means the Intoxicating Liquor Act, 1927;

"the Act of 1960" means the Intoxicating Liquor Act, 1960;

"the Act of 1962" means the Intoxicating Liquor Act, 1962;

"the Acts" means the Licensing Acts, 1833–1986;

"bar" means any open bar or any part of a licensed premises exclusively or mainly used for the sale and consumption of intoxicating liquor and shall include any counter or barrier across which drink is or can be served to the public;

"licence" means a licence for the sale of intoxicating liquor whether granted on production or without production of a certificate of the Circuit Court or the District Court;

"licensed premises" means premises in respect of which a licence has been granted and is in force;

"the Minister" means the Minister for Justice.

(2) References in this Act to any enactment shall, save where the context otherwise requires, be construed as references to that enactment as amended by any subsequent enactment including this Act.

3.—(1) The Acts and this Act, in so far as this Act amends and extends the Acts, may be cited together as the Licensing Acts, 1833 to 1988, and shall be construed together as one.

(2) The Registration of Clubs Acts, 1904 to 1986, and this Act, in so far as this Act amends those Acts, may be cited together as the Registration of Clubs Acts, 1904 to 1988, and shall be construed together as one.

4.—Section 120 of the Children Act, 1908, and sections 10, 11, 12 and 25 of the Intoxicating Liquor (General) Act, 1924, are hereby repealed.

PART II

Special Restaurant Licences

5.—This Part shall come into operation on such day as the Minister may by order appoint.

6.—In this Part:—

"applicant" means an applicant for the grant of a special restaurant licence;

"the Board" means Bord Fáilte Éireann;

"Bord Fáilte Certificate" has the meaning assigned to it by section 8(2) of this Act;

"dining area" means the area set aside in a restaurant for the service and consumption of meals;

"owner" in relation to a restaurant, includes any person having any estate or interest in the restaurant;

"restaurant" means any premises which are structurally adapted and used for the purpose of supplying substantial meals to the public for consumption on the premises and in which any other business carried on is ancillary and subsidiary to the provision of such meals;

"special restaurant licence" has the meaning assigned to it by section 7(1) of this Act;

"waiting area" means an area—

(a) that is set aside as a waiting area in a restaurant for the purposes only of accommodating persons waiting to enter the dining area of the restaurant for the purpose of consuming a meal, and

(b) whose floor area does not exceed 20 per cent of the floor area of the dining area of the restaurant.

7.—(1) In this Act "special restaurant licence" means a licence granted by the Revenue Commissioners pursuant to a certificate of the Circuit Court given under section 8 of this Act to a person in respect of a restaurant of which he is the owner and occupier authorising, subject to the provisions of this Act—

(a) the supply of intoxicating liquor for consumption on those premises, and

(b) the consumption of intoxicating liquor on those premises,

if, in each case, the intoxicating liquor is—

(i) ordered by or on behalf of a person for whom a substantial meal has been ordered,

(ii) supplied in either the waiting area or the dining area of the restaurant,

(iii) consumed in the waiting area of the restaurant before the meal by the person for whom the meal has been ordered, or consumed by that person in the dining area of the restaurant either during the meal or at any time not later than thirty minutes after the meal has ended, and

(iv) paid for at the same time as the meal is paid for:

Provided always that suitable beverages other than intoxicating liquor (including drinking water) are also available for consumption.

(2) Where a special restaurant licence is in force in relation to any premises, the licence shall be deemed for the purposes of the Finance (1909-1910) Act, 1910, to be a retailer's on-licence notwithstanding the fact that it does not authorise the sale of intoxicating liquor for consumption off the premises as provided for in relation to retailers' on-licences generally by that Act.

8.—(1) Where a person (in this section referred to as the applicant) duly gives notice of his intention to apply for a special restaurant licence in respect of a restaurant of which the applicant is the owner and occupier and, at the proceedings in the Circuit Court in relation to such application, the applicant shows to the satisfaction of that Court that there is in force a Bord Fáilte Certificate in respect of the restaurant, that Court shall cause a certificate to be given to the applicant entitling him to receive, on payment to the Revenue Commissioners of the fee specified in section 9 of this Act, a special restaurant licence in respect of the restaurant unless that Court, in consequence of an objection under section 4 of the Licensing (Ireland) Act, 1833, prohibits under that section the issue of the licence on the grounds of the character, misconduct or unfitness of the applicant or of the unfitness or inconvenience of the premises.

(2) Where in relation to a restaurant the Board, having inspected the restaurant, is satisfied that—

(a) in case regulations made by the Minister for Tourism and Transport under section 12 of this Act are in force, the restaurant complies with those regulations, or

(b) in case no such regulations are in force, the restaurant—

(i) is well equipped, well furnished and provides comfortable seating in the dining area and waiting area thereof,

(ii) is operated by a competent management and staff,

(iii) provides a high standard of catering,

(iv) has at least one member of the staff who holds a recognised qualification in cooking or has sufficient experience in cooking to prepare meals of a high standard, and

(v) maintains a high standard of hygiene,

the Board shall, upon application in that behalf by the person who is the owner and occupier of the restaurant, grant to the person a certificate (which shall be known as a Bord Fáilte Certificate) which shall be signed by an officer of the Board authorised in that behalf by the Board stating that the Board is satisfied as aforesaid.

(3) A document purporting to be a Bord Fáilte Certificate signed as aforesaid shall be sufficient evidence in any legal proceedings of the matters certified in the Certificate until the contrary is shown.

(4) A Bord Fáilte Certificate shall, unless it is sooner cancelled pursuant to this Act, continue in force until the date of the next annual licensing district court for the court area in which the restaurant the subject of that Certificate is situated.

(5) If, in any case, the Board refuses to grant a Bord Fáilte Certificate it shall as soon as may be, by notice in writing, inform the person who applied for the Certificate of the refusal and of the reasons therefor.

9.—(1) Notwithstanding anything contained in the Acts, where a person (in this section referred to as the applicant) who is the owner and occupier of a restaurant applies to the Revenue Commissioners in that behalf, the Revenue Commissioners shall, provided that the applicant—

(a) produces to them a certificate of the Circuit Court given to that applicant under section 8 of this Act in respect of the restaurant, and

(b) pays to them a fee of £3,000, or such other amount as may stand specified for the time being in regulations made by the Minister after consultation with the Minister for Tourism and Transport,

grant to the applicant a special restaurant licence in respect of the restaurant.

(2) Upon the grant of a special restaurant licence under this section, any licence, and any existing restaurant certificate, held or granted under the Acts, in respect of the restaurant to which the special restaurant licence relates, shall cease to have effect, and no other licence or restaurant certificate may be granted in respect of those premises while the special restaurant licence is in force.

10.—Where application is made for the renewal of a special restaurant licence, the superintendent of the Garda Síochána for the Garda district in which the restaurant, the subject of the application, is situated or any inhabitant of the parish or health authority within the meaning of the Health Act in whose functional area the restaurant is situated may, without prejudice to any other ground of objection available to him under the Acts, object to the renewal of the licence on the following ground, namely, that the premises concerned have not been *bona fide* and solely used as a restaurant within the meaning of this Act since the grant of the licence or the latest renewal thereof, whichever last occurred, and, if the District Court upholds such objection, the special restaurant licence shall not be renewed by the Revenue Commissioners.

11.—Without prejudice to its powers under the Tourist Traffic Acts, 1939 to 1987, the Board may, for the purposes of this Part, inspect restaurants.

12.—(1) The Minister for Tourism and Transport may, with the consent of the

Minister, make regulations prescribing the standards to be complied with in restaurants for the purposes of the granting or the renewal by the Board of a Bord Fáilte Certificate.

(2) Without prejudice to the generality of subsection (1) of this section, regulations under this section may make provision for all or any of the following matters—

(a) the maximum accommodation in such restaurants,

(b) the maximum accommodation in waiting areas in such restaurants,

(c) the standards to be complied with in such restaurants in relation to—

(i) equipment and furnishing,

(ii) management and staff,

(iii) catering, and

(iv) hygiene

(d) the inspection and certification, of such restaurants by the Board and the fees to be payable in respect of such inspection or certification,

(e) any other matter which the Minister for Tourism and Transport considers to be necessary or desirable.

13.—(1) Where it appears to the Board that a restaurant in respect of which a Bord Fáilte Certificate is in force no longer complies with the standards specified in section 8 or, as the case may be, under section 12, the Board shall give or send by post to the holder thereof a notice—

(a) stating that it appears to the Board as aforesaid,

(b) requiring the holder to take specified steps within a specified period in order to bring the restaurant into compliance with the standards aforesaid, and

(c) informing the holder that, if the requirements in the notice are not complied with, the Board will cancel the Certificate.

(2) If the holder of a Bord Fáilte Certificate fails or refuses to comply with a requirement in a notice under subsection (1), the Board shall cancel the Certificate.

(3) Whenever the Board cancels a Bord Fáilte Certificate, the Board shall give written notice that the Certificate has been cancelled and is no longer in force to—

(a) the holder of the special restaurant licence in relation to which such Certificate was granted,

(b) the district court clerk for the district court area in which the premises to which the Certificate relates are situated,

(c) the Revenue Commissioners, and

(d) the superintendent of the Garda Síochána for the Garda district in which the premises to which the Certificate relates are situated.

14.—(1) It shall not be lawful for any person, in any premises to which a special restaurant licence applies to—

(a) sell or expose for sale, or

(b) open or keep open the premises for the sale of, or

(c) permit the consumption on the premises of,

any intoxicating liquor:—

(i) on any weekday, **or on a Sunday which falls on the 23rd or 24th day of December in any year,**[1] between the hours of half-past twelve o'clock in the morning and half-past twelve o'clock in the afternoon, or

(ii) on any Sunday, **other than a Sunday to which paragraph (i) of this subsection relates**[2] between the hours of half-past twelve o'clock in the morning and half-past twelve o'clock in the afternoon, or between the hours of three o'clock and six o'clock in the afternoon, or between the hours of eleven o'clock in the evening and half-past twelve o'clock in the afternoon of the next following day, or

(iii) on Christmas Day, between the hours of half-past twelve o'clock in the morning and one o'clock in the afternoon or between the hours of three o'clock in the afternoon and seven o'clock in the evening or between the hours of ten o'clock in the evening and half-past twelve o'clock in the afternoon of the next following day, or

(iv) at any time on Good Friday or between the hours of twelve o'clock midnight and half-past twelve o'clock in the morning of the next following Saturday.

(2) The provisions of the Act of 1927 relating to prohibited hours shall apply to any premises to which a special restaurant licence applies as if subsection (1) of this section were substituted for subsection (1) of section 2 (inserted by this Act) of that Act, and as if the reference to a restaurant in section 3 of that Act included a restaurant in respect of which a special restaurant licence has been granted, and the Act of 1927 shall be construed and have effect accordingly.

15.—Any person who contravenes the terms of a special restaurant licence shall be guilty of an offence and shall be liable on summary conviction to a fine not exceeding £500, and the offence shall be deemed, for the purposes of Part III (which relates to the endorsement of licences) of the Act of 1927, to be an offence to which that Part of that Act applies.

16.—(1) A restaurant in respect of which a special restaurant licence has been granted under this Act shall not contain a bar.

(2) Where intoxicating liquor is sold or made available for purchase in a restaurant which does not comply with the provisions of subsection (1) of this section, the holder of the special restaurant licence in respect of that restaurant shall be guilty of an offence and shall be liable on summary conviction to a fine not exceeding—

---

[1] Inserted by the Intoxicating Liquor Act 1995, s.6(1)(a).

[2] Inserted by the Intoxicating Liquor Act 1995, s.6(1)(b).

(a) £150, in the case of a first such offence, or

(b) £350, in the case of a second or any subsequent such offence,

and the offence shall be deemed, for the purposes of Part III (which relates to the endorsement of licences) of the Act of 1927, to be an offence to which that Part of that Act applies.

17.—(1) A holder of a special restaurant licence shall cause the licence to be displayed prominently in the premises to which such licence relates.

(2) A holder of a special restaurant licence shall cause the Bord Fáilte Certificate relating to the premises to be displayed prominently in the premises to which such licence relates.

(3) A person who contravenes subsection (1) of this section shall be guilty of an offence and shall be liable on summary conviction to a fine not exceeding £100.

(4) A person who contravenes subsection (2) of this section or who displays in his premises a Bord Fáilte Certificate which has been cancelled pursuant to section 13 of this Act shall be guilty of an offence and shall be liable on summary conviction to a fine not exceeding £100.

(5) Subsection (1) of this section shall not apply in any case where the holder is required, pursuant to the Acts, to produce the licence.

(6) Subsection (2) of this section shall not apply in any case where the holder is required, pursuant to the Acts, to produce the Bord Fáilte Certificate.

18.—Section 4 of the Courts (No. 2) Act, 1986, is hereby amended by—

(a) the insertion after subsection (9) of the following subsection:

"(9A) Notwithstanding subsection (2) of this section, a special restaurant licence shall not be renewable on expiry without the production to the Revenue Commissioners of a Bord Fáilte Certificate (within the meaning of the Intoxicating Liquor Act, 1988)", and

(b) the insertion in subsection (11) after paragraph (c) of the following paragraph:

"(d) that the licence is a special restaurant licence granted pursuant to the Intoxicating Liquor Act, 1988".

19.—Sections 15 and 17 of the Act of 1960 shall not apply in relation to any application to the Circuit Court for a certificate entitling the applicant to receive a special restaurant licence under this Act.

20.—Section 24 of the Fire Services Act, 1981, shall apply in relation to every application for the grant or renewal of a special restaurant licence.

21.—The holder of a special restaurant licence shall not, for the purposes of obtaining an occasional licence pursuant to section 11 of the Act of 1962, be regarded as the holder of an on-licence.

22.—A special exemption order under section 5 (as amended by section 6 of the Intoxicating Liquor Act, 1943, section 11 of the Act of 1960 and section 12 of the Act of 1962) of the Act of 1927 shall not be granted to the holder of a special restaurant licence in respect of premises to which such licence relates.

23.—Section 20 of the Act of 1962 is hereby amended by:—

(a) the insertion in subsection (1) after "section 18 of this Act" of "or a special restaurant licence granted by virtue of the Intoxicating Liquor Act, 1988", and

(b) the insertion in subsection (3) after "section 18 of this Act" of "or a special restaurant licence granted by virtue of the Intoxicating Liquor Act, 1988".

24.—A draft of every regulation proposed to be made under this Part shall be laid before each House of the Oireachtas and the regulation shall not be made until a resolution approving of the draft has been passed by each such House.

PART III

PROHIBITED HOURS

25.—The Act of 1927 is hereby amended by the substitution for section 2 (as amended by section 4 of the Act of 1960 and section 2 of the Act of 1962) of the following section:

"**2.**—(1) Save as is otherwise provided by this Act, it shall not be lawful for any person to sell or expose for sale any intoxicating liquor, or to open or keep open any premises for the sale of intoxicating liquor, or to permit any intoxicating liquor to be consumed on licensed premises—

(a) on any weekday, before the hour of half-past ten o'clock in the morning, or

(i) during a period of summer time, after the hour of half-past eleven o'clock in the evening, or

(ii) during a period which is not a period of summer time, after the hour of eleven o'clock in the evening, or

(b) on any Sunday, before the hour of half-past twelve o'clock in the afternoon, or between the hours of two o'clock and four o'clock in the afternoon or after the hour of eleven o'clock in the evening, or

(c) on St Patrick's Day, where that day falls on a weekday, before the hour of half-past twelve o'clock in the afternoon or after the hour of eleven o'clock in the evening, or

(d) at any time on Christmas Day or Good Friday.

Provided that where in any year the 23rd or 24th day of December falls on a Sunday, then the provisions of this subsection which relate

to a weekday during a period which is not a period of summer time shall apply to such a Sunday as if it were such a weekday.[3]

(2) Every person who shall sell or expose for sale any intoxicating liquor or open or keep open any premises for the sale of intoxicating liquor or permit any intoxicating liquor to be consumed on licensed premises in contravention of this section shall be guilty of an offence under this section and shall be liable on summary conviction thereof, in the case of a first offence, to a fine not exceeding £400, or, in the case of a second or any subsequent offence, to a fine not exceeding £800.

(3) Every reference in this Act to the provisions of this Act relating to prohibited hours shall be construed and have effect as a reference to the provisions of this section, and all references in this Act to prohibited hours or to times or hours in which the sale of intoxicating liquor is prohibited by this Act shall be construed as references to the hours during which the sale of intoxicating liquor is prohibited by this section".

26.—(1) The Act of 1927 is hereby amended by the substitution for section 56 (inserted by section 6 of the Act of 1960 and amended by section 6 of the Act of 1962) of the following section—

"**56.**—(1) In order that a club may be eligible to be registered under the Registration of Clubs Acts, 1904 to 1986, the rules of the club shall (in addition to the matters mentioned in section 4 of the Registration of Clubs (Ireland) Act, 1904) provide that, subject to the exceptions specified in subsections **(1A),**[4] (2) and (3) of this section, no excisable liquor shall be supplied for consumption on the club premises to any person (other than a member of the club lodging in the club premises) or be consumed on the club premises by any person (other than a member of the club lodging in the club premises)—

(a) on any weekday, before the hour of half-past ten o'clock in the morning, or
  (i) during a period of summer time, after the hour of half-past eleven o'clock in the evening, or
  (ii) during a period which is not a period of summer time, after the hour of eleven o'clock in the evening, or

(b) on any Sunday, before the hour of half-past twelve o'clock in the afternoon or between the hours of two o'clock and four o'clock in the afternoon or after the hour of eleven o'clock in the evening, or

(c) on St Patrick's Day, where that day falls on a weekday, before the hour of half-past twelve o'clock in the afternoon or after the hour of eleven o'clock in the evening, or

(d) at any time on Christmas Day or Good Friday.

---

[3] Inserted by the Intoxicating Liquor Act 1995, s.2.
[4] Inserted by the Intoxicating Liquor Act 1995, s.5(1)(a).

(1A) Where in any year the 23rd or 24th day of December falls on a Sunday, then the provisions of this subsection which relate to a weekday during a period which is not a period of summer time shall apply to such a Sunday as if it were such a weekday.[5]

(2) Nothing contained in the Registration of Clubs Acts, 1904 to 1986, or contained by virtue only of the operation of subsection (1) of this section, in the rules of a club registered under those Acts shall operate to prohibit the supplying for consumption on the club premises of excisable liquor to any person or the consumption of excisable liquor on the club premises by any person—

(a) during a period of summer time, between the hours of half-past eleven o'clock in the evening on any weekday and half-past twelve o'clock in the morning on the following day, or

(b) during a period which is not a period of summer time, between the hours of eleven o'clock in the evening on any weekday and half-past twelve o'clock in the morning on the following day, or

(c) on any Sunday, between the hours of two o'clock and three o'clock in the afternoon, or

(d) on Christmas Day, between the hours of one o'clock and three o'clock in the afternoon or the hours of seven o'clock and ten o'clock in the evening,

if, in each case, the excisable liquor is—

(i) ordered by that person at the same time as a substantial meal is ordered by him,
(ii) consumed at the same time as and with the meal,
(iii) supplied and consumed in the portion of the club premises usually set apart for the supply of meals, and
(iv) paid for at the same time as the meal is paid for.

Provided that where in any year the 23rd or 24th day of December falls on a Sunday, then the provisions of this subsection which relate to a weekday during a period which is not a period of summer time shall apply to such a Sunday as if it were such a weekday.[6]

(3) In this section—

"period of summertime", "weekday" and "Sunday" have the meanings assigned to them by section 1 of this Act.".

(2)(a) For the purposes of the Registration of Clubs Acts, 1904 to 1986, the rules of a club which at the date of the passing of this Act is registered under those Acts, shall, during the transitional period, be deemed to be in conformity with the provisions of section 56, as amended by this section, of the Act of 1927.

---

[5] Inserted by the Intoxicating Liquor Act 1995, s.5.
[6] Inserted by the Intoxicating Liquor Act 1995, s.5(1)(c).

(b) In this subsection, "transitional period" means the period beginning on the date of the passing of this Act and ending, either, when the certificate of registration of the club which is in force two months after that date expires, or, if it should sooner happen, when the rules of the club are brought into conformity with the said section 56, as so amended.

27.—Section 7 of the Act of 1962 is hereby amended by the substitution in paragraph (a) of subsections (1) and (2) for "ten minutes" of "thirty minutes".

28.—The Act of 1927 is hereby amended by the substitution for section 13 (inserted by section 5 of the Act of 1960 and amended by section 4 of the Act of 1962) of the following section:

"**13.**—Nothing in this Act shall operate to prohibit the holder of an on-licence in respect of premises which are for the time being a hotel or restaurant from supplying intoxicating liquor to any person on the premises or from permitting intoxicating liquor to be consumed on the premises—

(a) during a period of summer time, between the hours of half-past eleven o'clock in the evening on any weekday and half-past twelve o'clock in the morning on the following day, or

(b) during a period which is not a period of summer time, between the hours of eleven o'clock in the evening on any weekday and half-past twelve o'clock in the morning on the following day, or

(c) unless his licence is a six-day licence, on any Sunday, between the hours of two o'clock and three o'clock in the afternoon, or

(d) on Christmas Day, between the hours of one o'clock and three o'clock in the afternoon or the hours of seven o'clock and ten o'clock in the evening,

if, in each case, the intoxicating liquor is—

(i) ordered by that person at the same time as a substantial meal is ordered by him,

(ii) consumed at the same time as and with the meal,

(iii) supplied and consumed in the portion of the premises usually set apart for the supply of meals and

(iv) paid for at the same time as the meal is paid for".

Provided that where in any year the 23rd or 24th day of December falls on a Sunday, then, except in the case of a six-day licence, the provisions of this section which relate to a weekday during a period which is not a period of summer time shall apply to such a Sunday as if it were such a weekday.[7]

29.—Section 5 (as amended by section 12 of the Act of 1962) of the Act of 1927 is hereby amended by the substitution for subsection (3) of the following subsection—

---

[7] Inserted by the Intoxicating Liquor Act 1995, s.4.

"(3) No special exemption order shall be granted for any time on a Sunday or for any time between one o'clock and half-past ten o'clock in the morning on a Monday".

PART IV

Provisions Relating to Persons under the Age of 18 Years

30.—In this Part—

"age card" means a card issued under section 40 of this Act;

"child" means a person under the age of 15 years;

"private residence" includes any outhouse, yard, garden or other land appurtenant thereto or usually enjoyed therewith.

31.—(1) The holder of any licence shall not—

(a) sell or deliver or permit any person to sell or deliver intoxicating liquor to a person under the age of 18 years,

(b) sell or deliver or permit any person to sell or deliver intoxicating liquor to any person for consumption on his licensed premises by a person under the age of 18 years,

(c) permit a person under the age of 18 years to consume intoxicating liquor on his licensed premises, or

(d) permit any person to supply a person under the age of 18 years with intoxicating liquor on his licensed premises.

(2) The holder of a licence of any licensed premises shall not sell or deliver or permit any person to sell or deliver intoxicating liquor to any person for consumption off his licensed premises by a person under the age of 18 years in any place other than a private residence.

(3) A person who contravenes subsection (1) or (2) of this section shall be guilty of an offence and shall be liable on summary conviction to a fine not exceeding—

(a) £300, in the case of a first offence, or

(b) £500, in the case of a second or any subsequent offence,

and the offence shall be deemed for the purposes of Part III (which relates to the endorsement of licences) of the Act of 1927 to be an offence to which that Part of that Act applies.

(4) In any proceedings against a person for a contravention of subsection (1) or (2) of this section, it shall be a defence for such person to prove that the person in respect of whom the charge is brought produced to him an age card relating to such person or that he had other reasonable grounds for believing that such person was over the age of 18 years, or, if the person is charged with permitting another person to sell or deliver intoxicating liquor contrary to the said subsection (1) or (2), to

prove that an age card was produced by the person concerned to that other person or that that other person had other reasonable grounds for believing as aforesaid.

32.—(1) A person shall not—

(a) purchase intoxicating liquor for delivery to, or consumption by, a person under the age of 18 years in any place other than a private residence,

(b) deliver intoxicating liquor to a person under the age of 18 years in any place other than a private residence, or

(c) send a person under the age of 18 years to any place where intoxicating liquor is sold, delivered or distributed for the purpose of obtaining intoxicating liquor.

(2) A person who contravenes subsection (1) of this section shall be guilty of an offence and shall be liable on summary conviction to a fine not exceeding—

(a) £300, in the case of a first offence, or

(b) £500, in the case of a second or any subsequent offence.

33.—(1) A person under the age of 18 years shall not—

(a) purchase intoxicating liquor,

(b) consume intoxicating liquor in any place other than a private residence in which he is present either as of right or by permission, or

(c) represent himself for the purpose of obtaining, or being permitted to consume, intoxicating liquor, to be over the age of 18 years.

(2) A person who contravenes subsection (1) of this section shall be guilty of an offence and shall be liable on summary conviction to a fine not exceeding £50.

34.—(1) Subject to subsection (2) of this section, the holder of a licence of any licensed premises shall not allow a child to be at any time in the bar of his licensed premises.

(2) It shall not be unlawful for the holder of a licence of any licensed premises to allow a child to be in the bar of his licensed premises at any time (other than a time during which the sale of intoxicating liquor is prohibited under the Acts) if such child is accompanied by his parent or guardian.

(3) Nothing in subsection (1) of this section shall apply in the case of a child who is—

(a) a child of the licence-holder, or

(b) resident in the licensed premises, or

(c) in the bar of the licensed premises solely for the purpose of passing through in order to gain access to, or egress from, some other part of the premises.

(4) A holder of a licence of any licensed premises shall display in a conspicuous place in the bar of his licensed premises a notice stating that subject to the provisions of section 31 of the Intoxicating Liquor Act, 1988, it is an offence to allow a child

(within the meaning of that Act) to be in a bar at any time during which the sale of intoxicating liquor is permitted unless accompanied by his parent or guardian.

(5) A person who contravenes subsection(1) of this section, or a person who causes or procures or attempts to cause or procure a child to go to or to be in the bar of a licensed premises in contravention of this section, shall be guilty of an offence and shall be liable on summary conviction to a fine not exceeding—

(a) £100, in the case of a first offence, and

(b) £250, in the case of a second or any subsequent offence.

(6) A person who contravenes subsection (4) of this section shall be guilty of an offence and shall be liable on summary conviction to a fine not exceeding—

(a) £20, in the case of a first offence, or

(b) £50, in the case of a second or any subsequent offence.

(7) If a child is found in the bar of a licensed premises unaccompanied by his parent or guardian, the parent or, as the case may be, the guardian, of the child shall unless he establishes that the child was so present—

(i) without his knowledge or consent, or

(ii) in accordance with the circumstances specified in subsection (3) of this section,

be guilty of an offence and shall be liable on summary conviction to a fine not exceeding £50.

(8) In any proceedings against a person for a contravention of subsection (1) of this section, it shall be a defence for such person to prove that he used all due diligence to prevent the child from being admitted to the bar or that he had reasonable grounds for believing that the person in respect of whom he is alleged to have committed the offence was not a child.

35.—(1) Notwithstanding the application of an exemption order under section 4 or 5 of the Act of 1927, or section 10 of the Act of 1962, in respect of the premises, the holder of a licence of any licensed premises shall not allow a person who is under the age of 18 years (other than a person under that age whose employment in the licensed premises is not prohibited under section 38 of this Act) to be on that part of the licensed premises which is used on foot of such exemption order for the sale or consumption of intoxicating liquor at any time during the period in respect of which the exemption was granted.

(2) Notwithstanding the application of an exemption order under section 4 or 5 of the Act of 1927, or section 10 of the Act of 1962, in respect of the premises, a person who is under the age of 18 years (other than a person under that age whose employment in the licensed premises is not prohibited under section 38 of this Act) shall not be on that part of the licensed premises which is used on foot of such exemption order for the sale or consumption of intoxicating liquor at any time during the period in respect of which the exemption was granted.

(3) The holder of a licence of any licensed premises in respect of which an exemption order under section 4 or 5 of the Act of 1927, or section 10 of the Act

of 1962, is in force shall display in a conspicuous place in the part of the licensed premises which is used on foot of such exemption order a notice stating that it is an offence for a person who is under the age of 18 years to be on that part of the premises at any time during the period in respect of which the exemption order was granted.

(4) A person who contravenes subsection (1) of this section shall be guilty of an offence and shall be liable on summary conviction to a fine not exceeding—

(a) £100, in the case of a first offence, or

(b) £250, in the case of a second or any subsequent offence,

and the offence shall be deemed for the purposes of Part III (which relates to the endorsement of licences) of the Act of 1927 to be an offence to which that Part of that Act applies.

(5) A person who contravenes subsection (2) of this section shall be guilty of an offence and shall be liable on summary conviction to a fine not exceeding £50.

(6) A person who contravenes subsection (3) of this section shall be guilty of an offence and shall be liable on summary conviction to a fine not exceeding—

(a) £20, in the case of a first offence, or

(b) £50, in the case of a second or any subsequent offence.

(7) In any proceedings against a person for a contravention of subsection (1) of this section, it shall be a defence for such person to prove that he used all due diligence to prevent the person under the age of 18 years in respect of whom the charge is brought from being admitted to the part of the licensed premises which is used on foot of an exemption order as aforesaid for the sale or consumption of intoxicating liquor during the period in respect of which the exemption was granted or that such person produced to him an age card relating to such person or that he had other reasonable grounds for believing that such person was over the age of 18 years.

36.—(1) Where a licensed premises, or any part of a licensed premises which is structurally separate from the remainder of the premises, is used exclusively or mainly for the sale of intoxicating liquor for consumption off the premises, the holder of the licence of the licensed premises shall not permit a person who is under the age of 18 years and who is not accompanied by his parent or guardian (other than a person under that age whose employment in the licensed premises is not prohibited under section 38 of this Act) to be at any time on such premises or, as the case may be, such part of such premises.

(2) A person who is under the age of 18 years and who is not accompanied by his parent or guardian (other than a person under that age whose employment in the licensed premises is not prohibited under section 38 of this Act) shall not be at any time on a licensed premises, or on any part of a licensed premises which is structurally separate from the remainder of the premises, where such premises or, as the case may be, such part of such premises, is used exclusively or mainly for the sale of intoxicating liquor for consumption off the premises.

(3) Where a licensed premises, or any part of a licensed premises which is

structurally separate from the remainder of the premises, is used exclusively or mainly for the sale of intoxicating liquor for consumption off the premises, the holder of the licence of such licensed premises shall display in a conspicuous place in such premises a notice stating that it is an offence for a person who is under the age of 18 years and who is not accompanied by his parent or guardian to be on such premises or, as the case may be, in such part of such premises.

(4) A person who contravenes subsection (1) of this section shall be guilty of an offence and shall be liable on summary conviction to a fine not exceeding—

(a) £100, in the case of a first offence, or

(b) £250, in the case of a second or any subsequent offence

and the offence shall be deemed for the purposes of Part III (which relates to the endorsement of licences) of the Act of 1927 to be an offence to which that Part of that Act applies.

(5) A person who contravenes subsection (2) of this section shall be guilty of an offence and shall be liable on summary conviction to a fine not exceeding £50.

(6) A person who contravenes subsection (3) of this section shall be guilty of an offence and shall be liable on summary conviction to a fine not exceeding—

(a) £20, in the case of a first offence, or

(b) £50, in the case of a second or any subsequent offence.

(7) In any proceedings against a person for a contravention of subsection (1) of this section, it shall be a defence for such person to prove that he used all due diligence to prevent the person under the age of 18 years in respect of whom the charge is brought from being admitted to the premises or any part of the premises which is used exclusively or mainly for the sale of intoxicating liquor for consumption off the premises or that such person produced to him an age card relating to such person or that he had other reasonable grounds for believing that such person was over the age of 18 years.

37.—(1) Where a member of the Garda Síochána suspects, with reasonable cause, that an offence under section 31, 32 or 33 of this Act is being or has been committed, the member concerned may seize, detain and remove, without warrant, any bottle or container which—

(a) is in the possession, in a place other than a place used as an occupied private residence, of a person by or in respect of whom such member suspects the offence to have been committed and who appears to the member to be under the age of 18 years, and

(b) such member suspects, with reasonable cause, contains intoxicating liquor.

(2) Where a member of the Garda Síochána suspects, with reasonable cause, that an offence under this Part has been committed, the member concerned may—

(a) (i) in the case of an offence under section 34 of this Act, request the person in respect of whom the offence was committed, if such person appears to the member to be a child, to provide the member with his name, address and age, or

(ii) in any other case, request the person by whom, or in respect of whom, such member suspects the offence to have been committed to provide such member with his name, address and age, or

(b) request the parent, or as the case may be, the guardian of the person by or in respect of whom the offence was committed to provide the name, address and age of that person.

(3) Where any person, who is requested by a member of the Garda Síochána, pursuant to subsection (2) of this section, to furnish to him a name, address and age, fails or refuses to furnish to the member the name, address or age, or furnishes a name, address or age that the member has reasonable grounds for believing to be false or misleading, the member may arrest such person without warrant and, if the person fails or refuses to furnish the member the name, address or age requested, or furnishes to the member a name, address or age which is false or misleading, the person shall be guilty of an offence and shall be liable on summary conviction to a fine not exceeding £50.

(4) For the purposes of this section a member of the Garda Síochána may enter without warrant a place that is not a public place.

38.—(1) The holder of a licence of any licensed premises shall not employ—

(a) any person being his sister, step-sister, daughter, step-daughter or sister-in-law who resides with him and is under the age of 16 years, or

(b) any person being his brother, step-brother, son, step- son or brother-in-law who resides with him and is under the age f 16 years, or

(c) any person being a person who is apprenticed to the holder of the licence and is under the age of 16 years, or

(d) any person under the age of 18 years other than a person referred to in paragraph (a), (b) or (c) of this subsection who is over the age of 16 years,

to sell intoxicating liquor for consumption on or off his licensed premises nor shall such holder of a licence permit any such person to engage in any such sale in his licensed premises.

(2) A person who contravenes subsection (1) of this section shall be guilty of an offence and shall be liable on summary conviction to a fine not exceeding—

(a) £50, in the case of a first offence, or

(b) £100, in the case of a second or any subsequent offence,

and the offence shall be deemed for the purposes of Part III (which relates to the endorsement of licences) of the Act of 1927 to be an offence to which that Part of that Act applies.

39.—(1) Where in any prosecution under section 31, 32, 33, 35, 36, 37 or 38 of this Act, it is alleged that the person by whom, or in respect of whom, the offence was committed was a person under the age of 18 years, and such person appears to the Court to have been, at the date of the commission of the offence, a person under that age, that person shall, for the purposes of this Part, be presumed to have been under the age of 18 years at that date, unless the contrary is proved.

(2) Where in a prosecution for an offence under section 34 of this Act, it is alleged that the person in respect of whom the offence was committed was a child, and such person appears to the Court to have been a child at the date of the commission of the offence, that person shall, for the purposes of this Part, be presumed to have been a child at that date, unless the contrary is proved.

40.—(1) The Minister may by regulations provide for the issue to a person of or over the age of 18 years, if so requested by the person and subject to his compliance with the regulations, of a card (in this part referred to as "an age card") specifying the age of the person.

(2) Without prejudice to the generality of subsection (1) of this section, regulations under this section may make provision in relation to all or any of the following matters:

(a) the information as to his age and any other matters specified in the regulations to be furnished by a person (in this subsection referred to as "the applicant") applying for the issue of an age card,

(b) a form of application for an age card,

(c) the charging and payment of fees in respect of the issue or replacement of an age card,

(d) the form of an age card and the particulars (which may include a photograph of the holder thereof) to be specified in an age card,

(e) the period of validity of an age card,

(f) the person by whom an age card shall be issued,

(g) any other matter in relation to which it is, in the opinion of the Minister, necessary or expedient to make provision.

41.—(1) A person shall not forge a document purporting to be an age card, alter an age card, or use such a document or an altered age card, with intent to deceive.

(2) A person who contravenes this section shall be guilty of an offence and shall be liable on summary conviction to a fine not exceeding £1,000 or to imprisonment for a term not exceeding 12 months or to both.

PART V

Registered Clubs

42.—(1) Section 4 of the Registration of Clubs (Ireland) Act, 1904, is hereby amended by the substitution for paragraph (j) of the following paragraphs:

"(j) That no excisable liquors shall be sold or supplied in the club premises to any person under the age of eighteen years:

(k) That no person under the age of eighteen years shall be admitted as a member of the club unless the club is one primarily devoted to some athletic purpose."

(2)(a) For the purposes of the Registration of Clubs Acts, 1904 to 1986, the rules of a club which at the date of the passing of this Act is registered under those Acts shall, during the transitional period, be deemed to be in conformity with the provisions of section 4 (as amended by this section) of the Registration of Clubs Act, 1904.

(b) In this subsection "transitional period" means the period beginning on the date of the passing of this Act and ending, either when the certificate of registration of the club which is in force two months after that date expires, or, if it should sooner happen, when the rules of the club are brought into conformity with the said section 4, as so amended.

43.—(1) If any member of the Garda Síochána is of opinion that there are reasonable grounds for supposing that any club registered under the Registration of Clubs (Ireland) Act, 1904, is so managed or carried on as to constitute a ground of objection to the renewal of its certificate under that Act, or that an offence under that Act has been or is being committed in any such club, or that any excisable liquor is sold or supplied, or kept for sale or supply, on the premises of a club which is not registered under that Act, he may enter and search the premises of such club and take the names and addresses of any persons found therein.

(2) In the event of any person found in such premises refusing to give his name or address when requested by any such member of the Garda Síochána or giving a false name or address, such person so doing shall be liable on summary conviction to a fine not exceeding £50.

(3) Every person who, by himself, or by any person in his employment or acting by his direction or with his consent, refuses or fails to admit any member of the Garda Síochána in the execution of his duty demanding to enter in pursuance of this section, shall be liable on summary conviction to a fine not exceeding—

(a) £200, in the case of a first offence, or

(b) £300, in the case of a second or any subsequent offence.

44.—Section 3 of the Registration of Clubs (Ireland) Act, 1904, is hereby amended by the substitution for subsections (1) and (2) of the following subsections:

"(1) The registrar shall forthwith give notice of such application to the superintendent of the Garda Síochána for the Garda district in which the club, the subject of the application, is situated and, if no objections are taken as hereinafter provided, the court shall, if satisfied that the application has been duly made as aforesaid and that the rules of the club are in conformity with the provisions of this Act, grant the application.

(2) It shall be competent for such superintendent of the Garda Síochána, on receiving such notice, and for any person resident in the parish in which the club premises are situated, to lodge objections to the grant of the certificate on any of the grounds of objection specified in this Act and it shall be competent for any person to lodge objections to the renewal of the certificate on any such grounds. Such objections shall be lodged by the objectors with the registrar within ten days of the receipt or publication of the notice of application, and at the same time a copy of the objections shall be sent by them to the secretary of the club applying for the grant or renewal of a certificate.".

45.—(1) Subject to subsection (2) of this section, a person shall not publish, or cause to be published, any advertisement drawing attention to any function to be held on the premises of a registered club.

(2) Subsection (1) of this section shall not apply to—

(a) the publication of a notice inside the premises of the registered club in which the function is to be held, or

(b) any advertisement in so far as it relates to a function involving any sport, game or physical recreation which does not take place outside the hours during which excisable liquor may be supplied or consumed on the club premises in accordance with the club rules, or

(c) any circular issued by a registered club to its club members.

(3) Where there is a contravention of subsection (1) of this section, then—

(a) the registered club,

(b) every person entered in the register of clubs as an official or member of the committee of management or governing body of the club at the time the advertisement is published and,

(c) any person who published the advertisement or caused it to be published,

shall be guilty of an offence and shall be liable on summary conviction to a fine not exceeding—

(i) £300, in the case of a first offence, or

(ii) £500, in the case of a second or subsequent offence.

(4) In a prosecution for an offence under subsection (1) of this section—

(a) it shall be a defence for a person mentioned in subsection (3)(b) of this section to prove that the advertisement was issued without his consent or connivance or that he exercised all due diligence to prevent the publication of any such advertisement, and

(b) it shall be a defence for a person mentioned in subsection (3)(c) of this section to prove that he is a person whose business it is to publish or arrange for the publication of advertisements and that he received the advertisement in question for publication in the ordinary course of business and did not know and had no reason to suspect that its publication would constitute an offence under the said subsection (1).

(5) For the purposes of this section, an advertisement published by displaying or exhibiting it shall be treated as published on every day on which it is displayed or exhibited.

(6) In this section "advertisement" includes every form of advertising, whether in a publication or by the display of notices or by means of circulars or other documents or by an exhibition of photographs or a cinematograph film, or by way of sound broadcasting or television or by inclusion in a cable programme service, and references to the publishing of an advertisement shall be construed accordingly.

46.—The reference in section 5(d) of the Registration of Clubs (Ireland) Act, 1904, to twenty-five members shall, as respects objections to the grant after the passing of this Act of a certificate of registration under that Act, be construed as a reference to one hundred and fifty members.

PART VI

MISCELLANEOUS

47.—(1) This section shall apply in relation to any premises in which intoxicating liquor is not sold for consumption on the premises, but in which intoxicating liquor is sold for consumption off the premises on foot of an off-licence or a wine on-licence and in which commodities other than intoxicating liquor are sold by retail.

(2) This section shall not apply in relation to any premises where the only business carried on is the sale of intoxicating liquor for consumption off the premises and the sale of commodities ancillary to such business, such as cigarettes, tobacco, cigars, matches, confectionery and beverages other than intoxicating liquor.

(3) In any premises to which this section applies, intoxicating liquor shall not be sold by self-service methods and shall not be sold otherwise than from an intoxicating liquor counter.

(4) If in any premises to which this section applies, there is a contravention of the provisions of this section, the holder of the licence in respect of the premises shall be guilty of an offence and shall be liable on summary conviction to a fine not exceeding £500 and the offence shall be deemed for the purposes of Part III (which relates to the endorsement of licences) of the Act of 1927 to be an offence to which that Part of that Act applies.

(5) In this section—

"self-service methods" means any method of sale allowing a customer to supply himself with the article sold on or before payment therefor;

"intoxicating liquor counter" means a counter, or a separate portion of the licensed premises concerned, from or at which commodities other than intoxicating liquor are not sold or paid for.

(6) This section shall come into operation on such day as the Minister may appoint by order.

48.—Section 12 of the Act of 1927 is hereby amended by the insertion after subsection (1A) (inserted by section 8 of the Intoxicating Liquor Act, 1943) of the following subsection:

> "(1B) Where, following application pursuant to section 4 of the Courts (No. 2) Act, 1986, to an officer of the Revenue Commissioners for the renewal of an on-licence without the production of a certificate of the District Court, the applicant applies to the Court to certify that the premises in respect of which the renewal of the on-licence is sought are a restaurant for the purposes of the Act, the provisions of subsection (1) of this section shall apply and have effect as if that application to the Court were an application, in accordance with that subsection, for a restaurant certificate."

49.—Section 18(2) of the Act of 1962 is hereby amended by the substitution in sub-paragraph (ii) for "at that time at which the last race of the meeting starts" of "thirty minutes after the time at which the last race of the meeting starts".

50.—Section 4 of the Courts (No. 2) Act, 1986, is hereby amended by the insertion after "required" in the definition of "licence" of "and includes a licence granted under section 13 of the Refreshment Houses (Ireland) Act, 1860".

51.—Each provision mentioned in column (2) of the Schedule to this Act of the enactment mentioned in column (1) of that Schedule opposite the mention of the provision in the said column (2) is hereby amended as specified in column (3) of that Schedule opposite the mention of the provision in the said column (2).

SCHEDULE

Increase of Fines

Enactment (1)	Provision (2)	Amendment (3)
Licensing Act, 1872	Section 12 (penalties for drunkenness)	The substitution in the second paragraph for "forty shillings" of "£50".
Licensing Act, 1872	Section 13 (permitting drunkenness or violent conduct on licensed premises and supplying intoxicating liquor to disorderly persons)	The substitution for "for the first offence ten pounds, and not exceeding for the second and any subsequent offence twenty pounds " of "£200".
Licensing Act (Ireland), 1874	Section 23 (powers of constables to enter licensed premises and the penalty for obstructing such entry)	The substitution for "five pounds" of "£200" and the substitution for "ten pounds" of "£300".
Registration of Clubs (Ireland) Act, 1904	Section 8 (penalties for supplying intoxicating liquor for consumption outside registered club)	The substitution for "seven pounds, for a second offence fifteen pounds and for a third or subsequent offence thirty pounds" of "£100 and for a second or a subsequent offence £150".
Registration of Clubs (Ireland) Act, 1904	Section 10 (penalties for offences by officials of registered clubs)	The substitution for "seven pounds, for a second offence, whether in connexion with the same or another club fifteen pounds and for the third or subsequent offence as aforesaid thirty pounds" of "£300 and for a second or a subsequent offence, whether in connection with the same or another club, £500".
Registration of Clubs (Ireland) Act, 1904	Section 12 (penalty for making false application for registration)	The substitution for "fifty pounds" of "£100".
Summary Jurisdiction (Ireland) Act, 1908	Section 10 (penalty for aiding and abetting a drunken person)	The substitution for "forty shillings" of "£50".

Enactment (1)	Provision (2)	Amendment (3)
Intoxicating Liquor Act, 1927	Section 17 (offences in relation to prohibited hours) (inserted by section 12 of the Act of 1960)	The substitution for "one pound" of "£25" and the substitution for "five pounds" of "£50".
Intoxicating Liquor Act, 1927	Section 22 (failure to give name and address to a garda when found on licensed premises during prohibited hours)	The substitution for "five pounds" of "£50".
Intoxicating Liquor Act, 1927	Section 58 (penalty on club where intoxicating liquor is supplied or consumed on the club premises in contravention of the club rules)	The substitution for "twenty pounds" of "£300" and the substitution for "forty pounds" of "£500".
Intoxicating Liquor Act, 1962	Section 29 (permitting persons to be on licensed premises during prohibited hours)	The substitution for "£20" of "£300" and the substitution for "£40" of "£600".

INTOXICATING LIQUOR ACT 1995

No. 33 of 1995

AN ACT TO AMEND AND EXTEND THE LICENSING ACTS, 1833 TO 1994, TO AMEND THE REGISTRATION OF CLUBS ACTS, 1904 TO 1988, AND TO PROVIDE FOR CONNECTED MATTERS.

BE IT ENACTED BY THE OIREACHTAS AS FOLLOWS:

1.—In this Act—

"the Act of 1927" means the Intoxicating Liquor Act, 1927;

"the Act of 1988" means the Intoxicating Liquor Act, 1988.

2.—Section 2 (inserted by section 25 of the Act of 1988) of the Act of 1927 is hereby amended by the insertion of the following proviso to subsection (1):

> "Provided that where in any year the 23rd or 24th day of December falls on a Sunday, then the provisions of this subsection which relate to a weekday during a period which is not a period of summer time shall apply to such a Sunday as if it were such a weekday."

3.—Section 3 (as amended by section 8 of the Intoxicating Liquor Act, 1960, and section 3 of the Intoxicating Liquor Act, 1962) of the Act of 1927 is hereby amended in subsection (1) by the substitution of the following for paragraphs (i) and (ii):

> "(i) in the case of premises to which an on-licence is attached, between the hours of half-past seven o'clock and half-past ten o'clock in the morning on weekdays and on a Sunday that falls on the 23rd or 24th day of December in any year, and
>
> (ii) in the case of premises to which an off-licence is attached, between the hours of nine o'clock and half past ten o'clock in the morning on weekdays and on a Sunday that falls on the 23rd or 24th day of December in any year."

4.—Section 13 (inserted by section 28 of the Act of 1988) of the Act of 1927 is hereby amended by the insertion of the following proviso to that section:

> "Provided that where in any year the 23rd or 24th day of December falls on a Sunday, then, except in the case of a six-day licence, the provisions of this section which relate to a week-day during a period which is not a period of summer time shall apply to such a Sunday as if it were such a weekday."

5.—(1) Section 56 (inserted by section 26 of the Act of 1988) of the Act of 1927 is hereby amended—

(a) by the substitution in subsection (1) of "subsections (1A), (2) and (3)" for "subsections (2) and (3)", and

(b) by the insertion of the following subsection after subsection (1):

> "(1A) Where in any year the 23rd or 24th day of December falls on a Sunday, then the provisions of subsection (1) of this section which relate to a weekday during a period which is not a period of summer time shall apply to such a Sunday as if it were such a weekday."

and

(c) by the insertion of the following proviso to subsection (2):

> "Provided that where in any year the 23rd or 24th day of December falls on a Sunday, then the provisions of this subsection which relate to a weekday during a period which is not a period of summer time shall apply to such a Sunday as if it were such a weekday."

(2) (a) For the purposes of the Registration of Clubs Acts, 1904 to 1988, the rules of a club which at the date of the passing of this Act is registered under those Acts, shall, during the transitional period, be deemed to be in conformity with the provisions of section 56, as amended by this section, of the Act of 1927.

(b) In this subsection "transitional period" means the period beginning on the date of the passing of this Act and ending, either, when the certificate of registration of the club which is in force two months after that date expires, or, if it should sooner happen, when the rules of the club are brought into conformity with section 56, as amended by this section, of the Act of 1927.

6.—Section 14 of the Act of 1988 is hereby amended in subsection (1)—

(a) by the insertion in paragraph (i) after "on any weekday" of "or on a Sunday which falls on the 23rd or 24th day of December in any year", and

(b) by the insertion in paragraph (ii) after "on any Sunday" of "other than a Sunday to which paragraph (i) of this subsection relates".

7.—(1) This Act may be cited as the Intoxicating Liquor Act, 1995.

(2)(a) The Licensing Acts, 1833 to 1994, and this Act, other than section 5(2), may be cited together as the Licensing Acts, 1833 to 1995, and shall be construed together as one.

(b) The Registration of Clubs Acts, 1904 to 1988, and section 5 (2) of this Act may be cited together as the Registration of Clubs Acts, 1904 to 1995, and shall be construed together as one.

APPENDIX C

OFFENCES

Appendix C1

SUMMARY TABLE OF OFFENCES UNDER THE LICENSING ACTS 1833 TO 1995*

1. Offences relating to unlicensed activities
2. Offences relating to prohibited hours
3. Offences relating to underage persons
4. Offences relating to manufacture, storage, possession, processing and offering for sale of intoxicating liquor
5. Other substantive offences: by licensed persons
6. Other substantive offences: general
7. Procedural, enforcement and miscellaneous offences:
    (a) Display of notices
    (b) Obstruction
    (c) Fraud
    (d) Miscellaneous

In this Appendix, Acts are referred to in accordance with the following key:

L(I)A 1833:	Licensing (Ireland) Act 1833
IL(G)A 1924:	Intoxicating Liquor (General) Act 1924
ILA 1927:	Intoxicating Liquor Act 1927
ILA 1960:	Intoxicating Liquor Act 1960
ILA 1962:	Intoxicating Liquor Act 1962
ILA 1988:	Intoxicating Liquor Act 1988

* This summary table is not exhaustive; it merely purports to identify and summarise for the reader the principal categories of offences created under the Licensing Acts 1833 to 1995 and a number of miscellaneous related statutes.

Category of Offence	Offence	Statute	Fine/Penalty	Endorsable Offence	Licence Liable to Forfeiture
1. OFFENCES RELATING TO UNLICENSED ACTIVITIES	Selling, exposing or keeping for retail sale of intoxicating liquor by any person without a licence or by licensed person at unauthorised place	s.7, IL(G)A 1924	(a) up to £50; (b) court may declare liquor to be forfeit; (c) in default of payment of fine, up to six months imprisonment	No	Yes, on second or subsequent conviction for offence under this section, a holder of a licence for sale of intoxicating liquor will forfeit such licence
	Occupying "unlicensed drinking premises" (as defined)	s.26(3), ILA 1962	(a) up to £50; plus (b) £5 per day for post-conviction continuation of offence	Yes, if offence committed by holder of retail liquor licence then Part III, ILA 1927 applies to one such licence held by that person	Yes, if offence committed by holder of licence for retail sale of intoxicating liquor if two current convictions on the licence and a third is directed to be recorded on the licence

Category of Offence	Offence	Statute	Fine/Penalty	Endorsable Offence	Licence Liable to Forfeiture
OFFENCES RELATING TO UNLICENSED ACTIVITIES—*cont.*	(a) Distillation or brewing by unlicensed persons; (b) Possession/use of certain equipment and intoxicating liquors by such persons	s.16, Illicit Distillation (Ireland) Act 1831	(a) £1,000 (judge may mitigate to not less than £500) or in default of payment of fine up to three months imprisonment*; or (b) imprisonment with hard labour for up to six months for a first offence; or (c) imprisonment with hard labour for up to 12 months for any subsequent offence; (d) products and equipment liable to forfeiture	No	No
	Having custody or possession of more than one gallon of spirits without a proper permit or certificate authorising the transportation of such spirits	s.6, Spirits (Ireland) Act 1854	(a) at least £2, up to £10 for first offence; or (b) imprisonment, with or without hard labour for not less than one month, up to three months; (c) at least £4, up to £20 for second or subsequent offence or imprisonment with or without hard labour for not less than two months, up to six months+	No	No

*Fine increased by s.14(1), Customs and Excise (Miscellaneous Provisions) Act 1988.
+Fines doubled by s.30, IL(G)A 1924.

Category of Offence	Offence	Statute	Fine/Penalty	Endorsable Offence	Licence Liable to Forfeiture
OFFENCES RELATING TO UNLICENSED ACTIVITIES—*cont.*	Having in excess of one gallon of illicit spirits or any quantity of spirits on which full duty has not been paid, on one's premises	s.2, Spirits (Ireland) Act 1854	(a) at least £4, up to £10 for first offence; or (b) imprisonment, with or without hard labour for not less than one month, up to three months; (c) at least £10, up to £20 for second; or subsequent offence*; or (d) imprisonment, with or without hard labour for not less than three months, up to six months; (e) spirits and vessels liable to forfeiture	No	No
	Selling beer by retail without licence	s.3, Revenue Act 1863	£20	No	No

*Fines doubled by s.30, IL(G)A 1924

Category of Offence	Offence	Statute	Fine/Penalty	Endorsable Offence	Licence Liable to Forfeiture
OFFENCES RELATING TO UNLICENSED ACTIVITIES—*cont.*	Selling beer for consumption on premises without being duly licensed	s.7, Beerhouses (Ireland) Act 1864	(a) at least five shillings, up to £2 for first offence; or (b) imprisonment, with or without hard labour for not less than one week, up to one month; (c) at least £1, up to £5 for second or subsequent offence; or (d) imprisonment, with or without hard labour for not less than one month, up to three months	No	No
	Illegally dealing in liquor (any person found on premises deemed to be until contrary proved)	s.24, Licensing (Ireland) Act 1874	up to £4*	No	No

*Fine doubled by s.30, IL(G)A 1924.

Category of Offence	Offence	Statute	Fine/Penalty	Endorsable Offence	Licence Liable to Forfeiture
OFFENCES RELATING TO UNLICENSED ACTIVITIES—*cont.*	Hawking, selling or exposing for sale of spirits (other than in premises licensed for the sale thereof)	s.146, Spirits Act 1880	(a) £100 (may be mitigated to not less than £6); (b) liable to forfeiture of spirits; (c) in default of payment of fine, imprisonment with or without hard labour, for at least two months, up to three months	No	No
	Manufacturing intoxicating liquor without required licence	s.50(1), Finance (1909–1910) Act 1910	excise penalty of £500	No	No
	Wholesale dealing in intoxicating liquor without required licence	s.50(2), Finance (1909–1910) Act 1910	excise penalty of £500*	No	No
	Selling intoxicating liquor by retail without required licence	s.50(3), Finance (1909–1910) Act 1910	excise penalty of £1,000 for each offence+	No	No

*Fine increased by s.69, Finance Act 1983.
+Fine increased by s.155, Finance Act 1992.

Category of Offence	Offence	Statute	Fine/Penalty	Endorsable Offence	Licence Liable to Forfeiture
OFFENCES RELATING TO UNLICENSED ACTIVITIES—*cont.*	Soliciting, taking or receiving orders for intoxicating liquor without being duly authorised	s.17, Revenue Act 1867	Same penalty as if convicted of selling without appropriate excise licence	No	No
	Manufacturing or selling methylated spirits without being duly licensed	s.27, Revenue Act 1889	£50	No	No
	Brewing of beer by private brewer other than for his own domestic use or selling/offering such beer for sale	s.51, Finance Act 1989	(a) excise penalty of £1,000; and (b) the beer in respect of which offence was committed and any vessels or brewing equipment in his possession shall be liable to forfeiture	No	No
	Contravention by licence holder of terms of certain licences	s.50(4), Finance (1909–1910) Act 1910	excise penalty of £50	No	No

Category of Offence	Offence	Statute	Fine/Penalty	Endorsable Offence	Licence Liable to Forfeiture
2. OFFENCES RELATING TO PROHIBITED HOURS	Unlawfully selling intoxicating liquor or exposing for sale intoxicating liquor, opening premises, keeping open premises or permitting consumption of intoxicating liquor during prohibited hours	s.2, ILA 1927*	(a) up to £400 for first offence; (b) up to £800 for second or subsequent offence	Part III of ILA 1927 applies	Yes, if two current convictions exist and a third is directed to be recorded on the licence
	Permitting persons to be on licensed premises during prohibited hours	s.29, ILA 1962	(a) up to £300 for first offence; (b) up to £600 for second or subsequent offence+	Part III of ILA 1927 applies	Yes, if two current convictions exist and a third is directed to be recorded on the licence
	Being found on licensed premises, unless exempted person, during prohibited hours	s.17(1), ILA 1927	not less than £25, up to £50*	No	No

*As amended by s.25, ILA 1988. Note that conviction under s.17(1), ILA 1927 precludes conviction under s.17(3), ILA 1927 in respect of the same occasion.
+As amended by s.51 and Schedule ILA 1988.

Category of Offence	Offence	Statute	Fine/Penalty	Endorsable Offence	Licence Liable to Forfeiture
OFFENCES RELATING TO PROHIBITED HOURS—*cont.*	Unlawfully consuming intoxicating liquor on licensed premises during prohibited hours	s.17(3), ILA 1927	not less than £25, up to £50*	No	No
	Falsely representing oneself as a lodger for the purposes of obtaining intoxicating liquor during prohibited hours	s.18, ILA 1927	up to £5	No	No
	Theatre licence holder admitting persons, other than exempted persons to theatre after 9.30 p.m.	s.20, ILA 1927	up to £5	No	No
	Selling or exposing for sale intoxicating liquor in a theatre other than at a permitted time	s.21, ILA 1927	(a) up to £50 for first offence; (b) up to six months imprisonment at discretion of court for second or subsequent offence	No	On second or subsequent offence, forfeiture of theatre licence at discretion of court

*As amended by s.51 and Schedule ILA 1988. Note that conviction under s.17(1), ILA 1927 precludes conviction under s.17(3), ILA 1927 in respect of the same occasion

Category of Offence	Offence	Statute	Fine/Penalty	Endorsable Offence	Licence Liable to Forfeiture
OFFENCES RELATING TO PROHIBITED HOURS—*cont.*	Permitting consumption of intoxicating liquor during prohibited hours in a refreshment house	s.38, ILA 1960	(a) up to £400 for first offence; (b) up to £800 for second or subsequent offence*	No	No
	Consuming intoxicating liquor during prohibited hours in a refreshment house	s.38, ILA 1960	Not less than £25, up to £50+	No	No
	Journeyman, apprentice, servant, artificer, labourer, sailor, seafaringman, or soldier, or any person of the female sex, in Dublin, drinking, tippling or gaming in licensed premises in prohibited hours	s.16, Dublin Justices Act 1824	Not less than five shillings, up to £1; in default of payment of fine up to one month's imprisonment	No	No

*Fines prescribed by s.25, ILA 1988 apply.
+Fines prescribed by s.51 and Schedule ILA 1988 apply.

Category of Offence	Offence	Statute	Fine/Penalty	Endorsable Offence	Licence Liable to Forfeiture
OFFENCES RELATING TO PROHIBITED HOURS—*cont.*	Licence holder in Dublin on whose premises journeymen, etc., found drinking, tippling or gaming during prohibited hours	s.19, Dublin Justices Act 1824	(a) £2 for first offence; (b) £20 for second offence; (c) £50 for third offence; (d) distress may be levied on goods in default; (e) in default of sufficient distress, imprisonment for one month	No	Licence forfeited on third offence
	Licence holder in whose premises persons are found drinking, tippling or gaming during prohibited hours	s.12, Licensing (Ireland) Act 1836	£1*	No	No
	Breach of prohibited hours provisions by holder of special restaurant licence	s.15, ILA 1988	up to £500	Part III of ILA 1927 applies	Yes, if two current convictions exist and a third is directed to be recorded on the licence

*Fine doubled by s.30, IL(G)A 1924.

Category of Offence	Offence	Statute	Fine/Penalty	Endorsable Offence	Licence Liable to Forfeiture
OFFENCES RELATING TO PROHIBITED HOURS—*cont.*	Selling or exposing for sale intoxicating liquor or opening or keeping open a premises to which a special restaurant licence applies or permitting consumption of intoxicating liquor on such premises during prohibited hours	s.14, ILA 1988	(a) up to £400 for first offence; (b) up to £800 for second or subsequent offence	Part III of ILA 1927 applies	Yes, if two convictions exist and a third is directed to be recorded on the licence

Category of Offence	Offence	Statute	Fine/Penalty	Endorsable Offence	Licence Liable to Forfeiture
3. OFFENCES RELATING TO UNDERAGE PERSONS	Selling intoxicating liquor in confectionery to persons under the age of 16	s.27, ILA 1962	up to £50	No	No
	Selling, delivering or permitting the delivery of intoxicating liquor to persons under the age of 18	s.31, ILA 1988	(a) up to £300 for first offence; (b) up to £500 for second or subsequent offence	Part III of ILA 1927 applies	Yes, if offence committed by holder of licence for retail sale of intoxicating liquor if two current convictions exist and a third is directed to be recorded on the licence
	Permitting the consumption of intoxicating liquor by persons under 18 on the premises	s.31, ILA 1988	(a) up to £300 for first offence; (b) up to £500 for second or subsequent offence	Part III of ILA 1927 applies	Yes, if offence committed by holder of licence for retail sale of intoxicating liquor if two current convictions exist and a third is directed to be recorded on the licence
	Supplying a person under 18 with intoxicating liquor on the premises	s.31, ILA 1988	(a) up to £300 for first offence; (b) up to £500 for second or subsequent offence	Part III of ILA 1927 applies	Yes, if offence committed by holder of licence for retail sale of intoxicating liquor if two current convictions exist and a third is directed to be recorded on the licence

Category of Offence	Offence	Statute	Fine/Penalty	Endorsable Offence	Licence Liable to Forfeiture
OFFENCES RELATING TO UNDERAGE PERSONS—*cont.*	Purchasing intoxicating liquor for consumption by persons under the age of 18 other than in a private residence	s.32, ILA 1988	(a) up to £300 for first offence; (b) up to £500 for second or subsequent offence	No	No
	Person under 18 years; (a) purchasing intoxicating liquor; (b) consuming intoxicating liquor other than in private residence; (c) representing himself/herself to be over 18 for the purposes of obtaining intoxicating liquor	s.33, ILA 1988	up to £50	No	No
	Licence holder unlawfully allowing a child to be in the bar of the licensed premises	s.34(1), ILA 1988	(a) up to £100 for first offence; (b) up to £250 for second or subsequent offence	No	No

Category of Offence	Offence	Statute	Fine/Penalty	Endorsable Offence	Licence Liable to Forfeiture
OFFENCES RELATING TO UNDERAGE PERSONS—*cont.*	Licensed person permitting persons under the age of 18 to be on that part of his licensed premises to which a special exemption order, a general exemption order or an area exemption order applies during period that exemption order is in force	s.35(1), ILA 1988	(a) up to £100 for first offence; (b) up to £250 for second or subsequent offence	Part III of ILA 1927 applies	Yes, it two current convictions exist and a third is directed to be recorded on the licence
	Person under the age of 18 being on the premises during period exemption order is in force	s.35(2), ILA 1988	up to £50	No	No
	Child in bar unaccompanied by parent or guardian	s.34(7), ILA 1988 (parent or guardian liable)	up to £50	No	No

Category of Offence	Offence	Statute	Fine/Penalty	Endorsable Offence	Licence Liable to Forfeiture
OFFENCES RELATING TO UNDERAGE PERSONS—*cont.*	Licence holder allowing unaccompanied persons under the age of 18 to be on premises used for sale of intoxicating liquor for consumption off the premises	s.36(1), ILA 1988	(a) up to £100 for first offence (b) up to £250 for second or subsequent offence	Part III of ILA 1927 applies	Yes, if two current convictions exist and a third is directed to be recorded on the licence
	Persons under the age of 18 being on premises used for the sale of intoxicating liquor for consumption off the premises	s.36(2), ILA 1988	up to £50	No	No
	Licence holder employing persons under the age of 18 (or, in certain cases, under the age of 16) to sell intoxicating liquor	s.38, ILA 1988	(a) up to £50 for first offence; (b) up to £100 for second or subsequent offence	Part III of ILA 1927 applies	Yes, if two current convictions exist and a third is directed to be recorded on the licence

Category of Offence	Offence	Statute	Fine/Penalty	Endorsable Offence	Licence Liable to Forfeiture
4. OFFENCES RELATING TO THE MANUFACTURE, STORAGE, POSSESSION, PROCESSING AND OFFERING FOR SALE OF INTOXICATING LIQUOR	Selling intoxicating liquor in sealed container without indication of quantity of contents thereon	s.40, ILA 1960	(a) up to £10 for first offence; (b) up to £20 for subsequent offence	No	No
	Selling or supplying intoxicating liquor in bottles of size other than a prescribed size	s.9, IL(G)A 1924	(a) up to £5 for first offence (b) up to £10 for subsequent offence	No	No
	Keeping or concealing spirits unlawfully distilled, or assisting another to do so	s.22, Illicit Distillation (Ireland) Act 1831*	(a) £1,000 (judge may mitigate to not less than £500; in default of payment of fine up to three months imprisonment); or (b) imprisonment with hard labour for up to six months for a first offence, or 12 months for any subsequent offence (in lieu of forfeiture of licence)	No	Where a licence holder for sale of intoxicating liquor by retail is convicted, the licence shall be forfeited and he shall be disqualified from ever holding a licence again.+

*As amended by s.14, Customs and Excise (Miscellaneous Provisions) Act 1988 and s.27(5), IL(G)A 1924.
+See s.27(5) IL(G)A 1924.

Category of Offence	Offence	Statute	Fine/Penalty	Endorsable Offence	Licence Liable to Forfeiture
OFFENCES RELATING TO THE MANU-FACTURE, STORAGE, POSSESSION, PROCESSING AND OFFERING FOR SALE OF INTOXICATING LIQUOR—*cont.*	Having custody or possession of any quantity of spirits on which duty has not been paid, or having custody or possession in excess of one gallon of spirits without a permit	s.23, Illicit Distillation (Ireland) Act 1831*	(a) £1,000 (judge may mitigate to not less than £500; in default of payment of fine up to three months imprisonment); or (b) imprisonment with hard labour for up to six months for a first offence, or 12 months for any subsequent offence (in lieu of forfeiture of licence)+	No	Where a licence holder for sale of intoxicating liquor by retail is convicted, such licence shall be forfeited and he shall be disqualified from ever holding a licence again.*
	Selling or delivering spirits illegally distilled or on which duty not paid	s.24, Illicit Distillation (Ireland) Act 1831*	(a) £1,000; or (b) imprisonment with hard labour for up to six months for a first offence, or 12 months for any subsequent offence (in lieu of forfeiture of licence)+	No	Where a licence holder for sale of intoxicating liquor by retail is convicted, such licence shall be forfeited and he shall be disqualified from ever holding a licence again.*

*As amended by s.14, Customs and Excise (Miscellaneous Provisions) Act 1988 and s.27(5), IL(G)A 1924.
+See s.27(5) IL(G)A 1924.

Category of Offence	Offence	Statute	Fine/Penalty	Endorsable Offence	Licence Liable to Forfeiture
OFFENCES RELATING TO THE MANU-FACTURE, STORAGE, POSSESSION PROCESSING AND OFFERING FOR SALE OF INTOXICATING LIQUOR—*cont.*	Licensed wine retailer adulterating wine or offering for sale or selling such wine	s.31, Refreshment Houses (Ireland) Act 1860	(a) not less than £10, up to £20 for a first offence; (b) not less than £20, up to £50 for a second offence	Part III of ILA 1927 applies	Yes, if two current convictions exist and a third is directed to be recorded on the licence. Moreover, on a second offence, the court may, in the alternative, disqualify licensed person from selling wine by retail for five years; and if during such five year term, he shall sell wine in defiance of such disqualification, liable to a fine of not less than £25, up to £50
	Person licensed to retail wine under the Refreshment Houses (Ireland) Act 1860, selling such wine other than in standard vessels/measures	s.28, Refreshment Houses (Ireland) Act 1860	(a) £2 per offence; and (b) forfeiture of illegal measures/vessels	No	No

Category of Offence	Offence	Statute	Fine/Penalty	Endorsable Offence	Licence Liable to Forfeiture
OFFENCES RELATING TO THE MANU-FACTURE, STORAGE, POSSESSION, PROCESSING AND OFFERING FOR SALE OF INTOXICATING LIQUOR—*cont.*	Selling intoxicating liquor by retail other than in measures marked according to Imperial Standards	s.8, Licensing Act 1872	(a) up to £20 for first offence; (b) up to £40 for any subsequent offence;* and (c) forfeiture of the illegal measure	No	No
	Licence holder storing unauthorised liquor on his premises	s.10, Licensing Act 1872	(a) up to £20 for a first offence; (b) up to £40 for any subsequent offence;* and (c) forfeiture of the unauthorised liquor	No	No

*Fine doubled by s.30, ILA(G)A 1924

Category of Offence	Offence	Statute	Fine/Penalty	Endorsable Offence	Licence Liable to Forfeiture
OFFENCES RELATING TO THE MANU-FACTURE, STORAGE, POSSESSION, PROCESSING AND OFFERING FOR SALE OF INTOXICATING LIQUOR—*cont.*	Selling adulterated articles of food or drugs to the prejudice of the purchaser	s.6, Sale of Food and Drugs Act 1875	(a) up to £20 for first offence; (b) up to £50 for second offence; (c) up to £100 for any subsequent offence; (d) if fine is more than £50 and convicted person found to be personally negligent, court may sentence him to imprisonment, with or without hard labour, for up to three months.	Part III of ILA 1927 applies	Yes, if offence committed by holder of licence for retail sale of intoxicating liquor if two current convictions exist and a third is directed to be recorded on the licence
	Dealer or retailer receiving, sending out, or possessing any British spirits of strength exceeding that at which a distiller may dispatch spirits of like denomination	s.102, Spirits Act 1880	(a) £50; and (b) forfeiture of the spirits of unlawful strength	No	No

Category of Offence	Offence	Statute	Fine/Penalty	Endorsable Offence	Licence Liable to Forfeiture
OFFENCES RELATING TO THE MANU-FACTURE, STORAGE, POSSESSION, PROCESSING AND OFFERING FOR SALE OF INTOXICATING LIQUOR—*cont.*	Adulteration or dilution of beer by brewer, dealer or retailer of beer	s.8, Customs and Inland Revenue Act 1885	(a) £50; and (b) forfeiture of the beer	Part III of ILA 1927 applies	Yes, if two current convictions exist and a third is directed to be recorded on the licence
	Subjecting a cask to a process to extract spirits absorbed in the wood thereof; or having on one's premises a cask which is being subjected to any such process, or any spirits so extracted	s.4, Finance Act 1898	(a) £50 for each offence; and (b) forfeiture of cask	No	No
	Using trade measure not stamped as prescribed	s.29, Weights and Measures Act 1878	(a) up to £5 for first offence; (b) up to £10 for second offence; (c) liable to forfeiture of measure; (d) any contract/bargain /sale made using such measure shall be void.	No	No

Category of Offence	Offence	Statute	Fine/Penalty	Endorsable Offence	Licence Liable to Forfeiture
OFFENCES RELATING TO THE MANU-FACTURE, STORAGE, POSSESSION, PROCESSING AND OFFERING FOR SALE OF INTOXICATING LIQUOR—*cont.*	Owner or occupier of place where illicit stills, etc, seized	s.17, Illicit Distillation (Ireland) Act 1831*	(a) £1,000 (judge may mitigate to not less than £500; in default of payment of fine up to three months imprisonment); or (b) imprisonment with hard labour for up to six months for a first offence, or 12 months for any subsequent offence	No	No

*As amended by s.14, Customs and Excise (Miscellaneous Provisions) Act 1988 and s.27(5) IL(G)A 1924.

Category of Offence	Offence	Statute	Fine/Penalty	Endorsable Offence	Licence Liable to Forfeiture
5. OTHER SUBSTANTIVE OFFENCES: BY LICENSED PERSONS	Breaching terms of a special restaurant licence	s.15, ILA 1988	up to £500	Part III of ILA 1927 applies	Yes, if two current convictions exist and a third is directed to be recorded on the licence
	Selling intoxicating liquor in a restaurant unlawfully having a bar, *i.e.* a restaurant in respect of which a special restaurant licence has been granted	s.16, ILA 1988	(a) up to £150 for first offence (b) up to £350 for second or subsequent offence	Part III of ILA 1927 applies	Yes, if two current convictions exist and a third is directed to be recorded on the licence
	Selling intoxicating liquor in a theatre in breach of the relevant provisions	s.21, ILA 1927	(a) up to £50 for first offence; or (b) in the case of a second or subsequent offence, at the discretion of the court, imprisonment for up to six months	No	In the case of a second or subsequent offence committed by a holder of a theatre licence, the court may order forfeiture of such licence*

*The courts may impose a prison sentence and order the forfeiture of the licence.

Category of Offence	Offence	Statute	Fine/Penalty	Endorsable Offence	Licence Liable to Forfeiture
OTHER SUBSTANTIVE OFFENCES: BY LICENSED PERSONS—*cont.*	Supplying intoxicating liquor for consumption on licensed premises which is not paid for when supplied	s.8, IL(G)A 1924	(a) up to £5 for first offence; (b) up to £10 for subsequent offence	Part III of ILA 1927 applies	Yes, if offence committed by holder of licence for retail sale of intoxicating liquor if two current convictions exist and a third is directed to be recorded on the licence
	Consuming intoxicating liquor on licensed premises which is not paid for when supplied	s.8, IL(G)A 1924	(a) up to £5 for first offence; (b) up to £10 for any subsequent offence	No	No
	Spirit grocer selling liquor to be consumed in any house, outhouse, or building, hut, tent or place occupied by such grocer	s.2, Licensed Grocers (Ireland) Act 1818	£10	No	No
	Spirit grocer found selling spirits to be consumed on premises	s.2, Spirits (Ireland) Act 1845	£2	No	Licence forfeited on conviction

Category of Offence	Offence	Statute	Fine/Penalty	Endorsable Offence	Licence Liable to Forfeiture
OTHER SUBSTANTIVE OFFENCES: BY LICENSED PERSONS—*cont.*	Person licensed to sell liquor by retail for consumption on premises within a town under the Towns Improvement (Ireland) Act 1854, who harbours on-duty constable	s.74, Towns Improvement (Ireland) Act 1854	up to £1	No	No
	Person in a town (within meaning of the Towns Improvement (Ireland) Act 1854), keeping a place of public resort for sale or consumption of refreshments, knowingly permitting prostitutes or thieves on premises	s.74, Towns Improvement (Ireland) Act 1854	up to £5	No	No
	Licensed person permitting on-duty constable on premises of refreshment house	s.41, Refreshment Houses (Ireland) Act 1860	up to £1	No	No

Category of Offence	Offence	Statute	Fine/Penalty	Endorsable Offence	Licence Liable to Forfeiture
OTHER SUBSTANTIVE OFFENCES: BY LICENSED PERSONS—*cont.*	Person licensed to sell wine permitting drunkenness or disorderly conduct on licensed premises or himself guilty of disorderly conduct	s.31, Refreshment Houses (Ireland) Act 1860	(a) not less than £2, up to £5 for a first offence; (b) not less than £5, up to £10 for a second offence; (c) not less than £20, up to £50 for a third offence	No	On second or third offences, the judge may decide that licensed person should be disqualified from selling wine by retail for up to five years
	Person licensed to retail wine storing spirits in his premises	s.27, Refreshment Houses (Ireland) Act 1860	(a) £50 (which shall be denominated an excise penalty); (b) forfeit all spirits found so stored	No	On conviction licence will become null and void

Category of Offence	Offence	Statute	Fine/Penalty	Endorsable Offence	Licence Liable to Forfeiture
OTHER SUBSTANTIVE OFFENCES: BY LICENSED PERSONS—*cont.*	Licensed person knowingly harbouring thieves, or allowing the deposit of stolen goods on his premises	s.10, Prevention of Crimes Act 1871	(a) up to £10; (b) in default of payment of fine, imprisonment, with or without hard labour for up to four months	Conviction may be recorded, though not an offence to which Part III of ILA 1927 applies	(a) on conviction for first offence, may be forfeited (b) on conviction for second offence, shall be forfeited, and the licence holder shall be disqualified from receiving such licence for two years; (c) where two convictions recorded within a three-year period, in respect of same premises, irrespective of whether persons convicted are the same, no licence shall be granted to any person in respect of those premises for one year
	Licensed person permitting licensed premises to be used as a brothel	s.15, Licensing Act 1872	up to £40*	No	Licence forfeit, and holder is disqualified from ever holding a licence for the sale of intoxicating liquor
	Licensed person permitting drunkeness or violent conduct on licensed premises or supplying intoxicating liquor to drunken persons	s.13, Licensing Act 1872	up to £200+	Part III of ILA 1927 applies	Yes, if two current convictions exist and a third is directed to be recorded on the licence

*Fine doubled by s.30, IL(G)A 1924. +As amended by s.51 and Schedule, ILA 1988.

Category of Offence	Offence	Statute	Fine/Penalty	Endorsable Offence	Licence Liable to Forfeiture
OTHER SUBSTANTIVE OFFENCES: BY LICENSED PERSONS—*cont.*	Harbouring, bribing or supplying liquor to on-duty constables	s.16, Licensing Act 1872	(a) up to £20 for first offence; (b) up to £40 for subsequent offence	Part III of ILA 1927 applies	Yes, if offence committed by holder of licence for retail sale of intoxicating liquor if two current convictions exist and a third is directed to be recorded on the licence
	Licensed person knowingly permitting reputed prostitutes on premises longer than is necessary for obtaining reasonable refreshment	s.14, Licensing Act 1872	(a) up to £20 for first offence; (b) up to £40 for subsequent offence	Part III of ILA 1927 applies	Yes, if offence committed by holder of licence for retail sale of intoxicating liquor if two current convictions exist and a third is directed to be recorded on the licence
	Supplying spirits to a rectifier, dealer, or retailer, or buying or receiving spirits from another retailer without a dealer's licence	s.102, Spirits Act 1880	£50	No	No

Category of Offence	Offence	Statute	Fine/Penalty	Endorsable Offence	Licence Liable to Forfeiture
OTHER SUBSTANTIVE OFFENCES: BY LICENSED PERSONS—*cont.*	Holder of off-licence permitting consumption of intoxicating liquor purchased (a) on the premises; or (b) in a place adjoining the premises	s.13(1), IL(G)A 1924	Up to £100 for first offence	No	Licensed person shall forfeit licence for a subsequent offence
	A merchant removing/delivering spirits without required permit or not in accordance with permit	s. 107 (1) Spirits Act 1880	£500	No	If convicted person is a licence holder, licence is forfeit; no new licence can be granted to him for a year
	Delivering spirits to a purchaser without required permit, or otherwise than in accordance with the terms of the permit	s.10, Excise Permit Act 1832	£200	No	No

Category of Offence	Offence	Statute	Fine/Penalty	Endorsable Offence	Licence Liable to Forfeiture
OTHER SUBSTANTIVE OFFENCES: BY LICENSED PERSONS—*cont.*	Licensed person permitting premises to be used in contravention of the Betting Act 1853	s.17, Licensing Act 1872*	(a) up to £20 for first offence; (b) up to £40 for subsequent offences	Part III of ILA 1927 applies	Yes, if two convictions exist and a third is directed to be recorded on the licence
	Person licensed to sell intoxicating liquor permitting gaming on premises	s.9, Gaming and Lotteries Act 1956	Default provisions of s.44, Gaming and Lotteries Act 1956 may apply⁺	A conviction may, at the discretion of the court, be recorded on the licence	No (Part III of ILA 1927 does not apply)
	Any person holding licence specified in First Schedule to Finance (1909–1910) Act 1910 contravening the terms of that licence	s.50(4), Finance (1909–1910) Act 1910	If penalty is not specified by any Excise or Licensing Acts, then liable to excise penalty of £50	No	No
	Selling intoxicating liquor in National Concert Hall otherwise than as provided	s.2, Intoxicating Liquor (National Concert Hall) Act 1983	up to £500	No	No

*Fine doubled by s.30, IL(G)A 1924.

⁺Gaming and Lotteries Act 1956, s.44 provides that where no specific penalty is prescribed under the Act, a fine/penalty of up to £100 and/or up to three months imprisonment may be imposed.

Category of Offence	Offence	Statute	Fine/Penalty	Endorsable Offence	Licence Liable to Forfeiture
OTHER SUBSTANTIVE OFFENCES: BY LICENSED PERSONS—*cont.*	Using or permitting any internal communication between any licensed premises and any unlicensed premises used for public entertainment and resort, or as a refreshment house	s.9, Licensing Act 1872	up to £20 per day communication is open*	No	If convicted person is the holder of a licence, such licence shall be forfeited
	Making or using any internal communication between the premises of a spirit grocer and any unlicensed premises used for public resort	s.85, Licensing Act 1872	up to £20 per day communication is open*	No	If convicted person is the holder of a licence, such licence shall be forfeited

*Fine doubled by s.30, IL(G)A 1924.

Category of Offence	Offence	Statute	Fine/Penalty	Endorsable Offence	Licence Liable to Forfeiture
6. OTHER SUBSTANTIVE OFFENCES: GENERAL	Being found in any room where illicit distillation is being carried on	s.19, Illicit Distillation (Ireland) Act 1831	(i) £1,000; or (ii) imprisonment with hard labour for up to six months for a first offence, or up to 12 months for any subsequent offence*	No	No
	Employee of holder of off-licence permitting consumption of intoxicating liquor purchased on the premises either (a) on the premises, or (b) in a place adjoining the premises	s.13(2), IL(G)A 1924	(a) up to £50; or (b) in default of payment of fine, up to three months imprisonment	No	No
	Consuming intoxicating liquor purchased in off-licence premises or in adjoining place	s.13(3), IL(G)A 1924	(a) up to £20; or (b) in default of payment of fine up to one month's imprisonment	No	No

*As amended by s.14, Customs and Excise (Miscellaneous Provisions) Act 1988 and s.27(5), IL(G)A 1924.

Category of Offence	Offence	Statute	Fine/Penalty	Endorsable Offence	Licence Liable to Forfeiture
OTHER SUBSTANTIVE OFFENCES: GENERAL—*cont.*	Selling, purchasing or possessing certain materials (related to illicit distillations) without a permit	s.26, IL(G)A 1924	(a) up to £50 for first offence; (b) up to £100 for any subsequent offence; (c) materials may be declared forfeit	No	No
	Selling methylated spirits other than as prescribed	s.28, IL(G)A 1924	not less than £10 up to £100	No	No
	Unlawfully being in or consuming intoxicating liquor on unlicensed drinking premises	s.26(2), ILA 1962	up to £50	No	No
	Keeping or using of a still by an unauthorised person for the carrying on of any trade requiring the use of any still(s)	s.26, Excise Licences Act 1825	£50	No	No
	Removing or carrying illicit stills	s.25, Illicit Distillation (Ireland) Act 1831	(i) £1,000; or (ii) imprisonment with hard labour for up to six months for a first offence, or 12 months for any subsequent offence*	No	No

*As amended by s.14, Customs and Excise (Miscellaneous Provisions) Act 1988 and s.27(5), IL(G)A 1924.

Category of Offence	Offence	Statute	Fine/Penalty	Endorsable Offence	Licence Liable to Forfeiture
OTHER SUBSTANTIVE OFFENCES: GENERAL—*cont.*	Permitting distilling to be carried on in one's house or premises	s.28, Illicit Distillation (Ireland) Act 1831	(a) £1,000; or (b) imprisonment with hard labour for up to six months for a first offence, or 12 months for any subsequent offence*	No	No
	Making signals or giving notice to persons engaged in illicit distilling of approach of officers	s.30, Illicit Distillation (Ireland) Act 1831	(i) £1,000; or (ii) imprisonment with hard labour for up to six months for a first offence, or 12 months for any subsequent offence*	No	No
	Delivering or sending out or receiving commodities without proper permit	s.10, Excise Permit Act 1832	£200 per offence	No	No
	Being found drunk in a public place	s.12, Licensing (Ireland) Act 1836	(a) 10 shillings+; or (b) in default of payment of fine, committal to prison for not less than 12 and not more than 48 hours	No	No

*As amended by s.14, Customs and Excise (Miscellaneous Provisions) Act 1988 and s.27(5), IL(G)A 1924.
+Fine doubled by s.30, IL(G)A 1924.

Category of Offence	Offence	Statute	Fine/Penalty	Endorsable Offence	Licence Liable to Forfeiture
OTHER SUBSTANTIVE OFFENCES: GENERAL—*cont.*	Being drunk in public thoroughfare in Dublin Police District, or being guilty of riotous or indecent behaviour in police station-house while drunk	s.15, Dublin Police Act 1842	(a) up to £2; or, (b) at the justice's discretion, imprisonment for up to seven days	No	No
	Being guilty of riotous or indecent behaviour in any street, police office, or petty sessions court within a town (as defined) while drunk	s.72, Towns Improve-ment (Ireland) Act 1854	(a) up to £2; or, (b) at the justice's discretion, imprisonment for up to seven days	No	No
	Being found drunk, tippling or drinking on premises licensed for the sale, but not consumption of beer on the premises	s.8, Beerhouses (Ireland) Act 1864	(a) up to five shillings for a first offence; (b) not less than five, up to 10 shillings for each subsequent offence	No	No

Category of Offence	Offence	Statute	Fine/Penalty	Endorsable Offence	Licence Liable to Forfeiture
OTHER SUBSTANTIVE OFFENCES: GENERAL—*cont.*	Being found drunk on any highway or other public place, (whether a building or not), or on licensed premises	s.12, Licensing Act 1872	(a) up to £1 for first offence; (b) up to £2 for second offence within 12 month period; (c) up to £4 for third offence within 12 month period; (d) in default of payment of fine, imprisonment, may, in court's discretion, be with hard labour*	No	No
	Being found drunk and disorderly in any public place, or drunk in charge of carriage, etc., or drunk in charge of loaded firearm	s.12, Licensing Act 1872	(a) £50; or (b) in the discretion of the court, imprisonment, with or without hard labour, for up to one month; (c) in default of payment of fine, imprisonment, may, in court's discretion, be with hard labour+	No	No

*Fine doubled by s.30, IL(G)A 1924.
+Fine increased by s.51 and Schedule, ILA 1988.

Category of Offence	Offence	Statute	Fine/Penalty	Endorsable Offence	Licence Liable to Forfeiture
OTHER SUBSTANTIVE OFFENCES: GENERAL—*cont.*	Knowingly selling or delivering spirits to the end that they may be unlawfully retailed or consumed	s.147, Spirits Act 1880	£100	No	No
	Receiving spirits from person unauthorised to sell or deliver same	s.148, Spirits Act 1880	£100	No	No
	Knowingly receiving spirits before the duty payable thereon has been paid or secured, or the spirits have been declared forfeited	s.149, Spirits Act 1880	(a) a fine of treble the value of the spirits; and (b) forfeiture of the spirits	No	No

Category of Offence	Offence	Statute	Fine/Penalty	Endorsable Offence	Licence Liable to Forfeiture
OTHER SUBSTANTIVE OFFENCES: GENERAL—*cont.*	Being in public place under influence of intoxicating liquor so as to be a source of danger to traffic or oneself	s.59, Road Traffic Act 1968	(a) up to £150 on first offence; (b) up to £350 on second offence; (c) on third or subsequent offence within a period of 12 months, up to £350 and/or imprisonment for up to three months	No	No
	Procuring drink for, or aiding and abetting a drunk person on or in vicinity of licensed premises	s.10, Summary Jurisdiction (Ireland) Act 1908	(a) £50*; or (b) imprisonment, with or without hard labour, for up to one month	No	No
	Being found drunk in any public place in charge of child(ren) under seven years	s.9, Summary Jurisdiction (Ireland) Act 1908	(a) up to £2; or (b) imprisonment, with or without hard labour, for up to one month	No	No
	Drinking methylated spirits	s.29, IL(G)A, 1924	Liable on summary conviction to imprisonment for up to six months	No	No

*Fine increased by s.51 and Schedule, ILA 1988.

Category of Offence	Offence	Statute	Fine/Penalty	Endorsable Offence	Licence Liable to Forfeiture
7. PROCEDURAL, ENFORCEMENT AND MISCELLANEOUS OFFENCES: **(a) Display of notices**	Holder of a general exemption order failing to display prescribed notice on the outside of the premises	s.4(4), ILA 1927	up to £5	No	No
	Affixing a notice falsely representing oneself to be the holder of a general exemption order to premises	s.4(5), ILA 1927	up to £10	No	No
	Holder of a special restaurant licence failing to display relevant licence prominently in the premises to which the licence relates	s.17(1), ILA 1988	up to £100	No	No

Category of Offence	Offence	Statute	Fine/Penalty	Endorsable Offence	Licence Liable to Forfeiture
PROCEDURAL, ENFORCEMENT AND MISCELLANEOUS OFFENCES—*cont.* (a) Display of notices	Holder of special restaurant licence failing to display relevant Bord Fáilte certificate prominently in the premises to which the licence relates or who displays a certificate which has been cancelled	s.17(2), ILA 1988	up to £100	No	No
	Licensed person failing to display notice stating that it is an offence for persons under the age of 18 to be on the premises when special exemption order, general exemption order or area exemption order is in force	s.35(3), ILA 1988	(a) up to £20 for a first offence; (b) up to £50 for second or subsequent offence	No	No

Category of Offence	Offence	Statute	Fine/Penalty	Endorsable Offence	Licence Liable to Forfeiture
PROCEDURAL, ENFORCEMENT AND MISCELLANEOUS OFFENCES—*cont.* (a) Display of notices	Licensed person failing to affix notice in specified form to premises	s.25, Excise Licences Act 1825	£20	No	No
	Licensed person failing to affix notice of his name in the specified form to premises	s.11, Licensing Act 1872	(a) up to £20 for first offence; (b) up to £40 for subsequent offence*	No	No
	Unlicensed person having on his premises a notice importing that he carries on licensed trade	s.11, Licensing Act 1872	(a) up to £20 for first offence; (b) up to £40 for subsequent offence*	No	No
	Licensed person failing to display notice stating that it is an offence to allow child to be in bar unless accompanied by parent or guardian	s.34(4), ILA 1988	(a) up to £20 for first offence; (b) up to £50 for second or subsequent offence	No	No

*Fines doubled by s.30, IL(G)A 1924.

Category of Offence	Offence	Statute	Fine/Penalty	Endorsable Offence	Licence Liable to Forfeiture
PROCEDURAL, ENFORCEMENT AND MISCELLANEOUS OFFENCES—*cont.* (a) Display of notices	Licensed persons failing to display notice stating that it is an offence for persons under the age of 18 to be on premises licensed for the sale of intoxicating liquor for consumption off the premises	s.36(3), ILA 1988	(a) up to £20 for a first offence; (b) up to £50 for second or subsequent offence	No	No
	Offences in relation to Retail Prices (Beverage in Licensed Premises) Display Order, 1976 (S.I. No. 146 of 1976)	s.8, Prices (Amendment) Act 1972	(a) on summary conviction: (1) up to £100, plus, in case of continuing offence, further fine of up to £10 per day (capped at £100); and/or (2) imprisonment for up to six months; (b) conviction on indictment: (1) up to £500, plus, in case of continuing offence, further fine of up to £50 per day; and/or (2) imprisonment for up to two years	No	No

Class of Offence	Offence	Statute	Fine/Penalty	Endorsable Offence	Licence Liable to Forfeiture
PROCEDURAL, ENFORCEMENT AND MISCELLANEOUS OFFENCES: **(b) Obstruction**	Licensed person opposing entry of justice or constable searching for illegal assemblies, secret societies, etc.	s.10, Licensing (Ireland) Act 1836	up to £20*	No	No
	Licensed person refusing or delaying to admit justice or constable searching for illegal assemblies, secret societies, etc.	s.11, Licensing (Ireland) Act 1836	up to £4*	No	No
	Persons not quitting licensed premises, or resisting efforts of constables to eject them during prohibited hours, or being found drunk on licensed premises	s.6, Licensing (Ireland) Act 1836	(a) up to £2, not less than 10 shillings; (b) in default of payment of fine, imprisonment for up to one week	No	No

*Fine doubled by s.30, IL(G)A 1924.

Class of Offence	Offence	Statute	Fine/Penalty	Endorsable Offence	Licence Liable to Forfeiture
PROCEDURAL, ENFORCEMENT AND MISCELLANEOUS OFFENCES—*cont.* (b) Obstruction	Spirit grocer opposing or delaying admittance of constables, etc.	s.2, Spirits (Ireland) Act 1845	£2*	No	Licence forfeited on conviction
	Any person occupying any house or place refusing or delaying admission of constable seeking to enter by virtue of a justice's warrant	s.5, Spirits (Ireland) Act 1854	(a) not less than £1, up to £4; or (b) imprisonment for not less than one week, up to two weeks*	No	No
	Obstructing entry of constables to licensed premises	s.23, Licensing Act (Ireland) 1874	(a) £200 for first offence; (b) £300 for second or subsequent offence*	Part III of ILA 1927 applies	Yes, if offence committed by holder of licence for retail sale of intoxicating liquor if two current convictions exist and a third is directed to be recorded on the licence

*Fine doubled by s.30, IL(G)A 1924.

Class of Offence	Offence	Statute	Fine/Penalty	Endorsable Offence	Licence Liable to Forfeiture
PROCEDURAL, ENFORCEMENT AND MISCELLANEOUS OFFENCES—*cont.* (b) Obstruction	Person found on unlicensed premises where liquor has been seized (reasonably assumed for sale) failing to give correct name and address to constable on demand	s.24, Licensing Act (Ireland), 1874	up to £5*	No	No
	Refusing to sell to police officers for purposes of analysis	s.17, Sale of Food and Drugs Act 1875	up to £10	No	No
	Distiller, rectifier, dealer and retailer, failing to assist excise officer in taking account of stock	s.142, Spirits Act 1880	£50	No	No
	Obstructing or attempting to bribe officer in discharge of his duty	s.16, Sale of Food and Drugs Act, 1899	(a) up to £20 for first offence; (b) up to £50 for second offence; (c) up to £100 for any subsequent offence	No	No

*Fine doubled by s.30, IL(G)A 1924.

Class of Offence	Offence	Statute	Fine/Penalty	Endorsable Offence	Licence Liable to Forfeiture
PROCEDURAL, ENFORCEMENT AND MISCELLANEOUS OFFENCES—*cont.* (b) Obstruction	Person found drinking, tippling or gambling in licensed premises during prohibited hours refusing request from appropriate authorities to leave	s.15, L(I)A 1833	(a) not less than 10 shillings, up to £2; or (b) committal to House of Correction for up to one week	No	No
	Licensed person preventing or resisting authorities from entering premises to search for persons drinking, tippling or gaming during prohibited hours	s.17, L(I)A 1833	up to £20*	No	No

*Fine doubled by s.30, IL(G)A 1924.

Class of Offence	Offence	Statute	Fine/Penalty	Endorsable Offence	Licence Liable to Forfeiture
PROCEDURAL, ENFORCEMENT AND MISCELLANEOUS OFFENCES—*cont.* (b) Obstruction	Delaying entry of appropriate authorities onto premises to search for persons drinking, tippling or gaming during prohibited hours by more than 10 minutes	s.18, L(I)A 1833	up to £4*	No	No
	Persons found on licensed premises during prohibited hours failing to provide correct name and address upon demand by Garda	s.22, ILA 1927	up to £50+	No	No
	Person, in relation to suspected underage offences, refusing to furnish Garda with name, address and age of person by or in respect of whom Garda suspects offence to have been committed	s.37, ILA 1988	up to £50	No	No

*Fine doubled by s.30, IL(G)A 1924.

+Fine increased by s.51 and Schedule, ILA 1988.

Class of Offence	Offence	Statute	Fine/Penalty	Endorsable Offence	Licence Liable to Forfeiture
PROCEDURAL, ENFORCEMENT AND MISCELLANEOUS OFFENCES—*cont.* (b) Obstruction	Disregarding order of justice to close in case of riot (an offence against the tenor of the licence)	ss.30, 31, Refreshment Houses (Ireland) Act 1860	(a) up to £5, together with the costs of the conviction, on a first offence; (b) up to £10, together with the costs of the conviction where second offence within 12 months of first offence; (c) up to £50, together with the costs of the conviction, if third offence within 18 months of first two offences	No	Court has option to forfeit licence and to declare premises disqualified for the sale of wine for three-year period upon proof that within two years before third conviction, two convictions have already taken place
	Failure to close licensed premises in event of riot or tumult when ordered by justices	s.21, L(I)A 1833	£4*	No	No
	Failure to close licensed premises temporarily, pursuant to an order of the court, sought and granted in the interest of public peace and order	s.19, ILA 1927+	up to £10	No	No

*Fine doubled by s.30, IL(G)A 1924.

+Section 19 of ILA 1927 confers jurisdiction on a judge of the District Court on the application of the local superintendent of the Garda Síochána to order the immediate clearing of "all premises licensed for the sale of intoxicating liquor" in the interest of "public peace and order" in a town or village "for the remainder of the day or a shorter period". This sweeping provision is surprisingly still on the statute books.

Class of Offence	Offence	Statute	Fine/Penalty	Endorsable Offence	Licence Liable to Forfeiture
PROCEDURAL, ENFORCEMENT AND MISCELLANEOUS OFFENCES—*cont.* (b) Obstruction	Drunk and disorderly persons refusing to leave licensed premises on request	s.42, Refreshment Houses (Ireland) Act 1860	£2	No	No
	Refusal to leave by a drunken, violent, quarrelsome or disorderly person or person whose presence on licensee's premises would subject licensee to penalty	s.18, Licensing Act 1872	(a) up to £10; (b) in default of payment of fine, court may order that committal to prison for non-payment be with hard labour*	No	No
	Persons found drunk in or refusing to leave, or resisting lawful ejection from premises of spirit grocer during prohibited hours	s.87, Licensing Act 1872	(a) not less than 10 shillings, up to £2; (b) in default of payment of fine, imprisonment for up to one week*	No	No

*Fine doubled by s.30, IL(G)A 1924.

Class of Offence	Offence	Statute	Fine/Penalty	Endorsable Offence	Licence Liable to Forfeiture
PROCEDURAL, ENFORCEMENT AND MISCELLANEOUS OFFENCES—*cont.* (b) Obstruction	Preventing or obstructing Garda in investigation of premises suspected of being unlicensed drinking premises, or failing, when demanded, to give his name and address	s.26(9), ILA 1962	up to £25	No	No
	Hindering an officer of Customs and Excise in execution of his duty	s.11, Inland Revenue Regulation Act 1890	excise penalty of £100	No	No

Class of Offence	Offence	Statute	Fine/Penalty	Endorsable Offence	Forfeiture
PROCEDURAL, ENFORCEMENT AND MISCELLANEOUS OFFENCES: **(c) Fraud**	Person forging or altering an age card or using such age card with intent to deceive	s.41, ILA 1988	(a) up to £1,000; and/or (b) up to 12 months imprisonment	No	No
	Applicant for transfer of licence failing to make full disclosure of all relevant facts	s.30(3), ILA 1927	up to £50	If such person is, at the date of such conviction, the holder of such licence, every offence that would have been recorded on the licence (under s.30(2)) had full disclosure been duly made shall be deemed to have been duly recorded	Yes, if offence committed by holder of licence with two current convictions on the licence and a third is directed to be recorded on the licence

Class of Offence	Offence	Statute	Fine/Penalty	Endorsable Offence	Licence Liable to Forfeiture
PROCEDURAL, ENFORCEMENT AND MISCELLANEOUS OFFENCES—*cont.* (c) Fraud	Giving false or misleading information or failing to provide required information on application to Revenue Commissioners for renewal of licence	s.4, Courts (No. 2) Act 1986	up to £300	No	District Court may order licence forfeited

Class of Offence	Offence	Statute	Fine/Penalty	Endorsable Offence	Licence Liable to Forfeiture
PROCEDURAL, ENFORCEMENT AND MISCELLANEOUS OFFENCES: **(d) Miscellaneous**	Failing to produce licence on demand by excise officer	s.28, Excise Licenses Act 1825	£20	No	No
	Witnesses in Excise prosecutions summoned to appear and failing to do so	s.74, Excise Management Act 1827	£50	No	No
	Witness summoned in any prosecution under Refreshment Houses (Ireland) Act 1860 and failing to attend	s.40, Refreshment Houses (Ireland) Act 1860	up to £10	No	No
	Licensed beer retailer failing to produce licence when required on hearing of any offence relating to his licence	s.9, Beerhouses (Ireland) Act 1864	up to £5	No	No

Class of Offence	Offence	Statute	Fine/Penalty	Endorsable Offence	Licence Liable to Forfeiture
PROCEDURAL, ENFORCEMENT AND MISCELLANEOUS OFFENCES—*cont.* (d) Miscellaneous	Failure of license holder to produce licence on hearing of complaint (whether stated in summons or not)	s.33, Licensing Act (Ireland) 1874	up to £20*	No	No
	Various offences in relation to faults in the keeping of retailer, dealer or rectifier's stock book	s.113, Spirits Act 1880	£100	No	No
	Failure by retailer, dealer or rectifier to cancel permits and certificates accompanying spirits received into stock in prescribed manner or to deliver cancelled permit or certificate to customs officer	s. 111, Spirits Act 1880	£50	No	No

*Fine doubled by s.30, IL(G)A 1924.

Class of Offence	Offence	Statute	Fine/Penalty	Endorsable Offence	Licence Liable to Forfeiture
PROCEDURAL, ENFORCEMENT AND MISCELLANEOUS OFFENCES—*cont.* (d) Miscellaneous	Licensed person failing to deliver a note in writing to the clerk of the peace for the area within which the licence has been granted within six days of obtaining the licence	s.10, L(I)A 1833	£20*	No	No
	Failing to comply with provisions relating to notifications to fire authority of licensing applications	s.5, Fire Services Act 1981	Liable, upon summary conviction to: (a) up to £500; and/or (b) imprisonment up to six months	No	No
	Wilful failure of holder of wine licence to produce licence to court when complaint is made against him for any offence against tenor of licence, or against Refreshment Houses (Ireland) Act 1860	s.19, Refreshment Houses (Ireland) Act 1860	up to £5	No	No

*Fine doubled by s.30, IL(G)A 1924.

Class of Offence	Offence	Statute	Fine/Penalty	Endorsable Offence	Licence Liable to Forfeiture
PROCEDURAL, ENFORCEMENT AND MISCELLANEOUS OFFENCES—*cont.* (d) Miscellaneous	Failure of registered proprietor of hotel licensed premises to return registration certificate to the Board, either on expiry of certificate or at the Board's request	s.31, Tourist Traffic Act 1939	(a) up to £50; plus; (b) in the case of a continuing offence, up to £5 per day (capped at £200)	No	No
	Person brought before the court pursuant to s.10 Prevention of Crime Act 1871 failing to produce licence for inspection	s.10, Prevention of Crimes Act 1871	up to £5	No	No
	Judge acting under the Liquor Licensing Acts in relation to premises in which he has a financial or proprietory interest	s.60, Licensing Act 1872	up to £100*	No	If convicted person is a holder of an excise licence, such licence shall be forfeit

*Fine doubled by s.30, IL(G)A 1924.

Class of Offence	Offence	Statute	Fine/Penalty	Endorsable Offence	Licence Liable to Forfeiture
PROCEDURAL, ENFORCEMENT AND MISCELLANEOUS OFFENCES—*cont.* (d) Miscellaneous	Clerk of petty sessions and every other person preventing inspection of register of licences or taking copies or extracts, or demanding unauthorised fee therefor	s.16, Licensing Act (Ireland) 1874	up to £10 per offence*	No	No
	Failure by clerk of peace to deliver a copy of a conviction barring a person from holding a licence to the collector of excise within one week of receipt by the clerk of such conviction	s.22, Excise Licences Act 1825	£10	No	No

*Fine doubled by s.30, IL(G)A 1924.

Class of Offence	Offence	Statute	Fine/Penalty	Endorsable Offence	Licence Liable to Forfeiture
PROCEDURAL, ENFORCEMENT AND MISCELLANEOUS OFFENCES—*cont.* (d) Miscellaneous	Offences against the tenor of the licence	ss.32, 33, Refreshment Houses (Ireland) Act 1860	Penalties (where no specific penalties prescribed elsewhere in the 1860 Act): (a) up to £5, together with the costs of the conviction, for a first offence; (b) up to £10, together with the costs of the conviction where second offence occurs within 12 months of first offence; (c) up to £50, together with the costs of the conviction, if third offence occurs within 18 months of first two offences	No	Court has option to forfeit licence and to declare premises disqualified for the sale of wine for a three-year period upon proof that within two years prior to the third conviction, two convictions have already taken place
	Refusal to give name and address or giving a false name and address to Gardaí on authorised racecourse	s.67(2), Irish Horseracing Industry Act 1994	No penalty	No	No

Appendix C2

SUMMARY TABLE OF OFFENCES UNDER THE REGISTRATION OF CLUBS ACTS 1904 TO 1995*

1. Offences by unregistered club
2. Offences by registered club
   (a) Substantive offences
   (b) Procedural offences
      (i) Obstruction
      (ii) Fraud

In this Appendix, Acts are referred to in accordance with the following key:

RC(I)A 1904:	Registration of Clubs (Ireland) Act 1904
ILA 1927:	Intoxicating Liquor Act 1927
ILA 1988:	Intoxicating Liquor Act 1988

* This summary table is not exhaustive; it merely purports to identify and summarise for the reader the principal categories of offences created under the Registration of Clubs Acts 1904 to 1995.

Category of Offence	Offence	Statute	Fine/Penalty
OFFENCES BY UNREGISTERED CLUB	Sale, supply or purchase of excisable liquor on premises of unregistered club	s.7(1), RC(I)A 1904	(a) up to £50; and/or (b) imprisonment (with or without hard labour) for up to one month
	Keeping excisable liquor for supply or sale on premises of unregistered club (prima facie offence by every officer and member)	s.7(2), RC(I)A 1904	(a) up to £7 for first offence; (b) up to £15 for second offence; (c) up to £30 for third or subsequent offence; (d) and liquor forfeited

Category of Offence	Offence	Statute	Fine/Penalty
OFFENCES BY REGISTERED CLUB (a) Substantive Offences	Consumption or supply of excisable liquor for consumption on premises of registered club in contravention of the rules of the club	s.58, ILA 1927	(a) up to £300 for first offence; (b) up to £500 for second or subsequent offence*
	Adjudication by judge that registered club is being managed/carried on in a manner constituting a ground of objection to renewal of certificate, (prima facie offence by officials of club)	s.10, RC(I)A 1904	(a) up to £300 for first offence; (b) up to £500 for second or subsequent offence, whether in connection with the same or another club*
	Selling, supplying or purchasing liquor in a registered club for consumption outside club premises (by any person)	s.8, RC(I)A 1904	(a) up to £100 for first offence; (b) up to £150 for second or subsequent offence*
	Unlawfully publishing an advertisement for function to be held on the premises of a registered club (offence by club, officials of club, publisher of advertisement)	s.45, ILA 1988	(a) up to £300 for first offence; (b) up to £500 for second or subsequent offence

*Fine increased by s.51 and Schedule, ILA 1988.

Category of Offence	Offence	Statute	Fine/Penalty
OFFENCES BY REGISTERED CLUBS (b) Procedural Offences (i) Obstruction	Persons found in registered club premises being investigated by Garda for suspected breach of the Registration of Clubs (Ireland) Act 1904 failing to give correct name and address on request	s.43(2), ILA 1988	up to £50
	Refusing to admit Gardaí into registered club premises in execution of his duty	s.43(3), ILA 1988	(a) up to £200 for first offence; (b) up to £300 for second or subsequent offence

Category of Offence	Offence	Statute	Fine/Penalty
OFFENCES BY REGISTERED CLUBS (b) Procedural Offences (ii) Fraud	Lodging of application for registration which is false in any material particular	s.12, RC(I)A 1904	up to £100 and/or imprisonment with or without hard labour for up to three months*

*Fine increased by s.51 and Schedule, ILA 1988.

APPENDIX C3

SUMMARY TABLE OF OFFENCES IN DANCE HALLS AND PLACES OF PUBLIC ENTERTAINMENT

In this Appendix, Acts are referred to in accordance with the following key:

PHAAA 1890:	Public Health Acts Amendment Act 1890
PDHA 1935:	Public Dance Halls Act 1935

Offence	Statute	Fine/Penalty	Revocation of Licence
Use of premises for public entertainment without being licensed	s.51(5), PHAAA 1890	£5 per day	No
Breach of terms of licence	s.51(9), PHAAA, 1890	£20 plus daily penalty up to £5 thereafter	Yes, licence liable to be revoked by court of summary jurisdiciton
Use of place for public dancing without licence being in force	s.10, PDHA 1935	Occupier liable to fine up to £10 per day or part of a day	No
Use of place for public dancing by person other than licensee, or in contravention of condition in licence	s.11, PDHA 1935	Licensee liable to fine up to £5 per day or part of a day	Yes, District Court may revoke licence
Failure to put notice in conspicuous place at or near principal entrance	s. 12, PDHA 1935	Licensee liable to fine up to £1 per day or part of a day	Yes, as this statutory requirement is generally contained as a condition in the licence, s.11(2), PDHA 1935 will apply
Any person preventing or obstructing gardaí entering premises in respect of which a public dancing licence is in force	s.13, PDHA 1935	up to £5	No

APPENDIX D

CIRCUMSTANCES IN WHICH NEW LICENCE CAN BE GRANTED

This appendix contains a list of the exceptions to the general prohibition contained in the Licensing (Ireland) Act 1902 against the grant of a new on-licence or off-licence.

1. (a) Application for new licence for premises licensed at any time during previous five years.

   (b) Application to "de-license" portion of a licensed premises:

   section 2(1) of the Licensing (Ireland) Act 1902, as amended by section 23 of the Intoxicating Liquor Act 1960.

2. Application for new licence for suitable premises in immediate vicinity of premises to which licence which became extinguished or surrendered by virtue of the expiration of a lease was attached:

   section 3 of the Licensing (Ireland) Act 1902, as amended by section 23 of the Intoxicating Liquor Act 1943.

3. Application for new licence in city or town where there has been a sufficient increase in population:

   section 4 of the Licensing (Ireland) Act 1902, as amended by section 19 of the Intoxicating Liquor Act 1962.

4. Application for new licence for premises attached to or adjoining licensed premises:

   section 6 of the Licensing (Ireland) Act 1902, as amended by section 24 of the Intoxicating Liquor Act 1960.

5. Application for new licence in respect of more convenient premises:

   section 21 of the Intoxicating Liquor Act 1943, as amended by section 33 of the Intoxicating Liquor Act 1960.

6. Application for new licence in respect of premises substituted for destroyed premises:

section 22 of the Intoxicating Liquor Act 1943, as amended by section 26 of the Intoxicating Liquor Act 1960.

7. Application for new licence in substitution for a licence attached to premises demolished by order of the local authority and in respect of premises erected on a site acquired by the local authority:

   sections 6, 7, 8 and 9 of the Intoxicating Liquor Act 1953.

8. Application for a new licence in a rural area in substitution for two existing licences:

   section 13 of the Intoxicating Liquor Act 1960.

9. Application for new licence in respect of premises substituted for demolished premises:

   section 14 of the Intoxicating Liquor Act 1960.

10. Application for full seven-day publican's licence for premises to which a restricted licence is attached:

    section 27 of the Intoxicating Liquor Act 1960.

11. Application for off-licence in substitution for on-licence in county borough:

    section 62 of the Intoxicating Liquor Act 1927, as amended by section 18 of the Intoxicating Liquor Act 1943, and section 9 of the Courts (No. 2) Act 1986.

INDEX

References are to paragraph number

(Paragraph numbers in **bold** type refer to material which is reproduced in full)